COMPARATIVE GOVERNMENT:

POLITICS OF INDUSTRIALIZED

AND DEVELOPING NATIONS

With chapters contributed by
Edwin O. Reischauer, Roy Hofheinz, Jr., and Van R. Whiting, Jr.
Harvard University

COMPARATIVE GOVERNMENT:

POLITICS OF INDUSTRIALIZED

AND DEVELOPING NATIONS

KARL W. DEUTSCH

JORGE I. DOMINGUEZ

HUGH HECLO

Harvard University

HOUGHTON MIFFLIN COMPANY   BOSTON

DALLAS   GENEVA, ILLINOIS   HOPEWELL, NEW JERSEY   PALO ALTO   LONDON

Library of Congress Catalog Card Number: 80-83433

ISBN: 0-395-29759-1

Printed in the U.S.A.

CONTENTS

PART II: CHINA AND THE THIRD WORLD

PREFACE

This is a book about what governments do, how they work, how they are structured, whom they serve, how well or poorly they do it, and where they seem to be going.

It also is a book about the process of politics in each country—the process on which its government rests—and about the changes in that process and in the society, economy, and culture that influence so much of all that happens in the country.

In this book we seek answers to these questions through making comparisons. Each country is treated as an individual case, but they all are approached via nine major questions.

A FRAMEWORK OF QUESTIONS

Three of these questions are: what is the *nature of politics* in this particular country? What is its historical background, what have been its most prominent tasks throughout its history, and how has the country been perceived by various groups of its people? Second, what are the *stakes of politics* in this country? What difference do the outcomes of politics make and to whom? Third, *who participates in politics* and with what results? Who is trying to get what, when, and how?

A second group of questions deals with the cohesiveness of the particular political system of each country. What are its prevailing *images* of politics, the major political beliefs and doctrines accepted by its people or by politically active parts of it? Is there a major common political ideology, or are there several contending political parties? If so, which political ideas are most intensely believed and supported among which social groups? Another question—our fifth—deals with the *arena* of politics. Within what country and what people are "domestic" politics taking place? Are the boundaries of the national territory well defined, and is there a single integrated nation living within them? Or are there regions and groups longing for secession? In the sixth place, how—and to what extent—do the political institutions and practices in that country form a cohesive political *system*? What are the different levels of that system, how do they cohere, and how do they influence each other?

The last three questions deal with how the system works. How does the political system of that country steer itself? What are the *self-steering capabilities* of the state in this respect, and what are the links between the state and the people? What are the main channels of political communication and control, how do they function, and how are errors corrected in the light of experience? The next question turns to specifics. What are the main features of *the process and machinery of government* in that country? At what points are decisions made, how and by whom, and how are decisions turned into political effects by administration?

Finally, what is the *political performance* of this entire political system? What degree of freedoms and security does it ensure for the people living under it? What social services are provided, and with what results? What prosperity and what standards of living, health, and education do they enjoy?

What about the less tangible aspects of politics? How stable is their political system, their state, and its government, and how legitimate are they in their eyes?

What is the quality of life of the people and of different groups among them— farmers, workers, and managers, men and women, town and country dwellers, old and young, rich and poor, majority and minority peoples, and different religious groups? What kinds of individuals are growing up in that country? And lastly, how well is this political system coping with the ever-present tasks of adaptation and change in the face of new conditions? Is it capable, if need be, of *self-transformation*, without violence and mass destruction and with preservation to some degree of its cultural identity?

A SELECTION OF COUNTRIES

Together these questions form a framework of inquiry, and this framework is then applied to a number of countries, each of which may then be regarded as an individual case. First among these cases are the six largest industrial countries of the world, with a chapter devoted to the politics and government of each: the United States, the Soviet Union, Great Britain, France, the German Federal Republic, and Japan. The chapter on Japan has been written by a leading specialist on that country, Professor Edwin O. Reischauer.

There follows a chapter on the Chinese People's Republic by another specialist, Professor Roy Hofheinz, Jr. A chapter on the world of emerging nations succeeds this, and a separate chapter following introduces case studies from that world in order of their per capita incomes: India, Nigeria, Egypt, and Iran (with a discussion of the Islamic revolution of 1979). The last chapter takes up three cases from Latin America, in the same sequence of per capita incomes: Cuba, Mexico, and Brazil; this study was written by Van R. Whiting, Jr.

This selection of cases places considerable emphasis on the world's six major industrial countries, where most of its power, wealth, and scientific and technological knowledge are still concentrated, but it also tries to take into account eight of the world's major developing countries, which seem destined to have·an increasing influence on the long-range future of humanity. These cases include rich, poor, and economically intermediate countries, democracies and dictatorships, non-Communist and Communist regimes. These fourteen countries, taken together, represent most of the practical political options with which humankind is currently presented.

Collectively, these cases give us some indication of where the world is now headed—what are some of the vast processes of transformation that are under way, and what may be the mainstream of development amid all the national and ideological diversities. They may also suggest what are some of the dangers toward which the world is moving and what may be our chances for action to avert them.

THE CHIEF AIM OF THIS BOOK

The main purpose of this book has been to make the governments of major countries more transparent and the processes of their politics more understandable. Technological developments increasingly empower nation-states to set ever-vaster forces into motion for good or ill. Governments now can do more than ever to oppress and frustrate people and even to destroy the world. But they and their peoples can do more than ever to eliminate extreme poverty and injustice, to bring about more freedom and equality for women and men and among races, creeds, and languages, and to increase the chances for peace and an open future for all humankind.

You too have a stake in this future; and you too can make a difference to it if you add your efforts to those of others. To do this effectively will require insight and commitment, and therefore making choices. If this book can help you to see these choices more clearly and to make them for the things you care for, it will have served its end.

The present book is based on the Third Edition of my larger book, *Politics and Government* (1980), and particularly on its second part. It has also benefited from the advice of the experts who read the drafts of one or another of the revised chapters for that edition: Suzanne Berger, Abram Bergson, Thomas Edsall, Hugh Heclo, Wayne Koonce, and Frieder Naschold.

These chapters were again revised and updated for this 1981 publication by Hugh Heclo for the highly developed countries of the West and by Jorge Dominguez for the developing countries. The chapters on Japan, China, and Latin America were revised by Edwin O. Reischauer, Roy Hofheinz, Jr., and Van R. Whiting, Jr., themselves, respectively; and the chapter on the Soviet Union by Timothy J. Colton.

For updated statistics I remain indebted to Charles Taylor and to Robert Grady,

David Jodice, and Stephen Livingston. I would like to thank the following for their having reviewed and commented on various chapters in manuscript: James Coleman, U.C.L.A.; Don Paretz, SUNY at Binghamton: C. S. Whitaker, Rutgers University; Dmitri Simes, Georgetown University; Kenneth Paul Erickson, Hunter College; Marcus E. Ethridge, University of Wisconsin; Nazli Choucri, M.I.T.; Myron Weiner, M.I.T.; Richard N. Frye, Harvard University. For institutional support, my main debts are to Harvard University and to the International Institute for Comparative Social Research at the Science Center Berlin, and for very valuable secretarial aid to Ina Frieser in Berlin, and to Evelyn Newmark, Robin Shanus, and Erika Peterson at Harvard.

I

Why Study Politics—and Why Do It Through Comparisons?

Politics has many aspects, but at its heart it is the process of making certain kinds of *decisions* that help shape our fate. In our time, these include decisions about the life and death, not only of individuals, but of entire cities, countries, and perhaps all humankind. Some day, such a political decision—perhaps about war or peace—may determine whether you and I, as well as the people we care for most, live or die. We have, therefore, good reason to be interested.

Other political decisions are less dramatic, but they may influence our lives each day. Can you say what you think, or must you look quickly over your shoulder to see whether anybody is listening? The answer may depend on a political decision about democracy. Whether you can expect to be treated fairly, or to be discriminated against because of your color, ancestry, religion, or sex—that too depends in part on politics. Are you confident that you, your family, and your community are safe from polio, tuberculosis, diphtheria, small-pox, malaria, typhoid, and plague? The answer may depend on a political decision about public

health—how it is to be protected and how much public money is to be spent on it. Can you expect to have drinkable water and breathable air? They may depend on political decisions about protecting our environment. The prices you pay at the gas pump and the supermarket, in fact the whole matter of inflation—that is, how much or how little your money will buy—depend at least in part on political action or inaction. The ease or difficulty with which you were admitted to a college, or may later be admitted to a professional or graduate school, or will find a job, also depends to a considerable extent on public policy decisions about education and employment. In these matters, too, we all have good reason to be interested.

Politics, of course, cannot do everything. What it can and cannot do, and under what conditions, and what you and others can do by participating in politics, are among the major topics of political science.

POLITICS AND GOVERNMENT: SOME BASIC DEFINITIONS

When we take a closer look at politics, we discover that it can be defined in more ways than one. Some have called it "the art of getting things done"; others, "the art of the possible." The American theorist Harold Lasswell saw in politics the answer to the question "Who gets what, when, how?" From a similar point of view, David Easton has called it the process of "authoritative allocation," because politics allocates among different claimants many valued things and relationships that are available in a society, and because it often does so not merely by "log-rolling" and "horsetrading," but *authoritatively.* That is, politics allocates in ways that can be enforced and, perhaps more important in the long run, in ways that are considered lawful and right by most people in a given society.

Authority, then, means that people tend to accept a decision, command, or other message because it is "the law of the land" and comes from a *source*—a legislature, government, or court of law—that people accept as *legitimate,* even if they disapprove of that particular law or decision.

Legitimacy is predicated on the compatibility of values. We accept a message, command, or institution as legitimate if we feel it will help us preserve or attain one value for which we care, such as wealth, physical well-being, or personal respect, without inflicting intolerable damage on any other value for which we also care. People do not live by any one value alone ("not by bread alone," as the Bible puts it) but by a configuration of many values. Legitimacy depends on the implied promise and expectation that such a relevant configuration of values will not be destroyed.

Many values of this kind become part of an individual's conscience and thus of his or her thoughts and feelings. Conscience, said an ancient Greek philosopher, is what we are taught before we are six years old. It is the collection of the "do's" and "don't's" that prevail in the society in which we grew up, and that were taught to us by our parents and other people who loved us and cared for us when we were small. We then internalized these rules of moral conduct, making them part of our inner life and our personality—that almost inseparable part that the psychiatrist Sigmund Freud called the *superego*—and for the most part these rules stay within us throughout our lives. Obeying our conscience gives us a feeling of getting approval from the remembered images of our parents and of other people we cared for, and from ourselves. Going against our conscience brings us a feeling of disapproval from all these, which can be a severe form of psychological self-punishment. Governments gain a great deal when their subjects feel bound by conscience to obey and support them, and governments can get in trouble when many of their subjects are moved by conscience to disobey them, perhaps as dissenters, dissidents, or members of resistance movements.

Politics thus deals not with all decisions but with *binding decisions,* as the sociologist Talcott Parsons called them. They are binding in a double sense. First, most people usually comply with such decisions, some for reasons of conscience because they feel the decisions are legitimate, some out of habit and the expectation that most other people will comply. Second, the organized power of the state usually enforces such decisions, directly against the few who are not complying, and indirectly against those who comply only because they expect enforcement against themselves if they do not. In this manner, *compliance* and *enforcement*—grounded in habit, fear, and conscience—reinforce each other in a functioning political system. This interplay constitutes the essence of politics, and makes a given decision distinctively political.

By means of such decisions a country is governed or its population governs itself. To *govern* means "to steer." The word comes from the Greek word *kybernetes,* for "helmsman," the person who governs a ship by means of the rudder. As politics deals with the distribution of values—that is, of valued outcomes—in a society, the process of *government* deals with the distribution of a society's efforts and resources. "The government" is the organized body of persons charged with making these decisions. In this sense, politics is the steering sector of society, and government is society's pilot.

Many political decisions are made outside government. A new generation may rise to political leadership, or voters may become more acutely concerned about tax reduction, inflation, or unemployment, than is the government currently in office. The government then may have to adapt its policy or risk being replaced by another. Conversely, not all government decisions take effect in politics; some may simply stay on paper.

We may think of the whole arrangement as a hierarchy of four steering systems. The biggest and least accurate is society itself; despite its complexity, it steers itself to some degree, just as "life goes on" even after major disturbances. A smaller and somewhat less inaccurate steering system is that of politics, with all its formal and informal processes of allocation and decision. Still smaller and more accurate is the steering of the state with its machinery of administration, laws, courts, police, and military. And on top of it all is the government as an instrument of fine tuning in day-to-day affairs, deliberating on adjustments to new tasks and exercising emergency control in situations of unusual stress on the entire system.

In reality, of course, steering in politics and society works not only from the top down. Rather, the higher level systems must be responsive to changes that occur in the lower ones. In this way, politics becomes a combined process of steering, learning, and evolution, however quick or slow.

POLITICAL SCIENCE:
THE STUDY OF HOW POLITICS
WORKS AND OF HOW IT COULD
BE MADE TO WORK BETTER

Political science as the serious and orderly study of politics is about 2400 years old. Yet to this day there is controversy about whether it is a science in the proper sense of the term.

Is it a science? And what is a science, anyway? The term "political science" comes from the German term *Staatswissenschaft*—the science of, or learning about, the state—of the eighteenth and nineteenth centuries. In German, "science"—*Wissenschaft*—means generally any kind of ordered and organized knowledge. At German universities, law and history are considered to this day sciences, sometimes called "cultural" or "intellectual" sciences. In English-speaking countries, a narrower definition of science has been more popular. Here the term usually refers to the "natural sciences," as if human beings and their activities are somehow outside nature, and as if a zoologist watching monkeys is engaged in science in a sense in which a social scientist observing people is not. By the same rule, a veterinarian, whose patients cannot talk, would seem to be more of a "scientist," that is, closer to the natural sciences, than a physician, whose patients can talk back to him.

The main points of the argument about how narrowly science should be defined are three:

1. Science ought to be based on repeated observation and experiment under controlled conditions. People can be observed, but usually they cannot be experimented with, certainly not under extreme conditions and in large numbers. Neither the French Revolution, nor the Chinese Civil War, nor World War I or II could be repeated for experimental purposes. Even when people have experimented with new laws, constitutions, or other policies, they did so under conditions that were neither completely controlled nor fully repeatable. But the same difficulty applies to many of the "natural" sciences. Meteorologists cannot experiment with hurricanes, nor can a seismologist experiment with earthquakes, or astrophysicists with supernovas. All these scientists can do is compare different examples of such phenomena within their fields and learn as best they can from such comparisons. Just this, however, is what political scientists also do.

2. "Natural" sciences are supposed to be more accurate in their measurements and predictions. But the currently accepted *error margins* of meteorology, seismology, or the geological dating of fossils are much larger than the error margins of election forecasts—although these too are fallible indeed.

3. "Natural" sciences are not supposed to interfere with the events and objects they observe, but political and social scientists may interfere, by the very act of observation, with the processes they are trying to study. This is a serious problem but it has also bedeviled physicists ever since they learned that anything they do to an electron in order to observe it will greatly interfere with the electron, making it impossible to state its position, direction, or velocity at any one time. This embarassing fact, discovered by the physicist Werner Heisenberg, has been called the *uncertainty principle,* but it has not led many people to deny that physics is a science.

Certainly political science suffers from the same special difficulties as other sciences of human culture and behavior: rarity of controlled observations and experiments, considerable margins of error, and occasional interference between observer and observed. But this should be no reason to give up our efforts to understand political processes and institutions as clearly and accurately, and with as much reproducible evidence, as we can. So long as we are trying to do this and are making some modest progress at it, we are still part of the great and common enterprise of science.

Not all human knowledge is scientific, nor will it ever be. The poets and the prophets always will range into ideas that scientists can neither confirm nor deny. Their minds, like those of the great theorists of science, show us the reach of human awareness, which always exceeds the grasp of even provisionally tested scientific knowledge.

Science is but one form of knowledge, and a limited one at that. Its limitations exclude the utterly individual, the unique. But out of these limitations it also derives a certain strength, the strength of shared and tested thinking. This holds true for all sciences, "natural" and "human," and it applies to the study of politics as well.

COMPARING STATES: WHY, WHAT, AND HOW

People learn by making *comparisons.* We think by making comparisons. Consider the way in which we create words and concepts: if several interesting objects or events seem similar enough to us, we put them together into a common class and invent or adapt a word for them. In this manner we call several different structures "houses," and several organizations for ruling different territories "governments." Without comparisons we could neither talk nor think.

Having compared several things or events we have seen, we can extend their comparison by inference and analogy to things we have not seen, but that might exist, or that we might create some day. (The word *analogy* means to lay things side by side, so as to see in what points they are alike. *Inference* means the carrying of information from one place to another, on the chance that it may fit there as well.) All analogies, like all similarities, are imperfect, but according to the mathematician George Polya, there are good analogies and bad ones, depending on how realistic they are and on what we can learn from them. *Good analogies* are based on similarities that are important and durable (like the similarities between apples and pears, both of which are "fruit," are useful additions to our diet, and are perishable in transport). *Bad analogies* are based on similarities that are unimportant, superficial, and fleeting (such as the similarity between a horse and a horse-shaped cloud).

In order to learn about states and governments, and to understand political processes and systems, we must compare them with others of their kind.

When we do this, we learn not only about their similarities but also about the way in which each of them is different from any others. Only by comparing what seems similar can we recognize what is different and what may be unique, and in what specific respects.

In the comparative study of politics, we compare several countries across differences in size, wealth, power, language, culture, level of economic development, and other major aspects. We also compare their political practices: democracies, dictatorships, one-party and multiparty systems, stable and unstable regimes. We compare countries with highly developed welfare services and those with hardly any: countries with lively civic participation and others with widespread public apathy.

Moreover, we must reach back into history for some of our comparisons. If two countries show a fair amount of similarity in culture and religion (as Egypt and Iran do), we ought to find out if one has a long history of popular obedience to government and the other a history of frequent popular resistance. When a particular type of government or regime in one country has perished in a revolution (as several monarchies did in our century), and we then find in another country a current regime that looks very similar, we may well ask how similar the two cases really are, and how long the second specimen of this type of regime will endure.

Finally, we can compare countries across different *social orders,* such as *Communist-ruled* and *non-Communist* ones—or, as the United Nations calls them, *centrally planned economies* and *market economies*—particularly if all the countries are at similar levels of economic and technological development.

A Selection of Cases. In the present volume, fourteen countries will be discussed, seven great or middle powers in detail and seven smaller powers more briefly. They vary greatly in sheer *size.* The United States, the Soviet Union, China, India, and Brazil each extend over a huge part of a continent. Together, these five countries comprise nearly one half of the world's population and income. Cuba,

by contrast, is a relatively small island with only about ten million inhabitants. Other countries are more or less middle-sized, ranging from 115 million inhabitants in Japan to about thirty-five million in Iran.

Six of the countries studied in this book are highly *industrialized;* they have achieved high levels of economic and technological development. Four of them—the United States, Britain, France, and the Federal Republic of Germany—each have a Western *cultural tradition,* a *democratic* and *constitutional* form of government, a market economy, well-developed welfare services, and a *plurality* of interest groups and political parties. A fifth industrial country, Japan, shares all these characteristics except for its profoundly non-Western history and cultural tradition. The sixth industrial country, the Soviet Union, shares many of its cultural traditions with the West but has a centrally planned economy and a nonpluralistic and dictatorial form of government.

The remaining eight countries are all at much lower levels of wealth and industrial development. Six of them are market economies; among these six, three—Nigeria, Mexico, and Iran—have considerable oil exports, and three poorer countries—India, Egypt, and Brazil—do not. The last of our developing countries, China and Cuba, are Communist dictatorships with centrally planned economies. China exports some oil and may export more in the future; Cuba exports none.

The three Latin American countries, Brazil, Mexico, and Cuba, derive most of their cultural traditions from the West, through either Portugal or Spain. Of the four developing countries with non-Western traditions—India, Nigeria, Egypt, and Iran—the first is marked chiefly by Hindu culture, while the last three belong to various branches of Islam.

All the highly industrialized countries studied in this book have well-developed public services for social *welfare,* in areas including education, health, and social security. Among the developing countries, only the Communist regimes of China and

Cuba have done a great deal in this regard. India, Brazil, and Mexico, despite their poverty, also have made considerable advancement in developing their welfare policies. The rest—Nigeria, Egypt, and Iran—are still largely nonwelfare states.

As to polities, among the developing countries only India is a full-fledged *pluralistic democracy*, where elections can lead to a change of the party in power. Nigeria in 1980 had several political parties but had emerged only recently from military dictatorship, and Brazil still has military rule. There is also a good deal of democracy in Mexico, even though this country is in effect governed by a single party, with other parties playing only a marginal role. In Mexico there is a significant degree of freedom for a plurality of interest groups and currents of opinion, and the Mexican people seem free from fear. Egypt, too, is in effect ruled by a single party, but freedom to dissent, and the open play of diverse interests, are much more limited than in Mexico. China and Cuba are, as mentioned, Communist dictatorships, and Iran, after overthrowing a harsh, royal, anti-Communist dictatorship in 1979, is still in the throes of an "Islamic" revolution.

Past revolutions form an indelible part of the history of Britain, the United States, France, Mexico, the Soviet Union, China, Egypt, Cuba, and (with an as yet uncertain outcome) Iran. In the remaining five countries—Germany, Japan, Brazil, India and Nigeria—they have played no such role. Table 1.1 shows the distribution of our fourteen cases with regard to levels of development, prevailing economic institutions, main cultural traditions, and the presence or absence of major welfare service systems. If we wanted to compare each one of our fourteen countries with every other, we would end up with ninety-one comparisons among pairs of states, even without reaching back into history. Not all these comparisons would be equally fruitful, but Table 1.1 may help to identify some of the most interesting ones.

Table 1.1 suggests that some conditions are rare or even nonexistent. There are no highly industrialized countries that lack substantial welfare services. There are no centrally planned countries with pluralistic democratic politics, even though many democratic socialists have aspired for more than a hundred years to establish such a combination and hope yet to succeed. There are no centrally planned countries without major welfare services.

Table 1.1 also suggests some possibilities that are too often overlooked. Democracy can work even in poor and non-Western countries, as it has since 1947 in India and recently in Nigeria. Economic and technological development can also occur against a non-Western cultural background, as it has in Japan. Federal institutions have been functioning in both developing countries and highly industrialized countries, in Western and non-Western cultures, in market economies and centrally planned ones. Welfare services can be provided by countries at different levels of national wealth and economic development, in Western and non-Western cultures, and across different social orders and political regimes. The range of political possibilities may be larger than we sometimes think.

One matter does not appear in Table 1.1 because it applies to all fourteen cases. It is the matter of *political change*. Since 1900, such change has been the slightest in the United States, even with its New Deal and its civil rights legislation; in Britain, even with its successive Labour governments, its National Health Plan, and its *nationalization* of some major industries; and in Brazil, where political change has been limited so far. In these three countries, politics shows a high degree of continuity. In each of the remaining eleven cases, the political changes since 1900 have been dramatic. One way to classify such changes as are dealt with in all fourteen countries is to distinguish among three levels of change: (1) changes in incumbency of governing personnel, the party in power, or some limited administrative institutions or practices; (2) changes in the basic political character of the *regime*—that is, in some major characteristic of the state, such as from a monar-

TABLE 1.1 *Some Comparisons Among Fourteen Countries*

PREDOMINANT ECONOMIC INSTITUTIONS	MARKETS				CENTRAL PLANNING	
MAIN CULTURAL TRADITION	Western		Non-Western		Western	Non-Western
	Wel-fare	Non-wel-fare	Wel-fare	Non-wel-fare		
Highly industrialized	*°US, *°UK, *France, *°FRG		*Japan		°USSR	
Developing, with major oil exports	°Mexico ⟵ ⟶			Iran *°Nigeria		
Developing, without major oil exports	°Brazil ⟵ ⟶		*°India	Egypt	Cuba	China

*Pluralistic democracies
°Federal political institutions

chy to a republic, or from a dictatorship to a democracy; and (3) changes in the basic social order and/or political culture, such as from the predominance of capitalism to that of communism, or from the prevalence of Western cultural patterns to that of non-Western ones, as in the Islamic Revolution of 1979 in Iran. For better or worse, the possibilities for change have become greater in our century than they have ever been, and so has the difficulty of preserving whatever we think worth preserving.

To understand this time of change, what landmarks shall we look for?

Comparing Major Tasks of States. Every state and every government has to perform many tasks at the same time. Some of them matter more than others, but the order of their importance has changed with time and place. Nine of these tasks can be singled out for use in our analysis; most correspond to what Talcott Parsons conceived to be the four basic functions of government.

1. To maintain order, predictability, and the existing distribution of wealth and other privileges among different social groups or classes, against external or domestic threats. This is part of what Parsons has called *pattern maintenance;* and some of it also helps to preserve the *identity* of its memories to its subsequent actions.
2. To acquire *power,* wealth, and higher social standing for its own rulers, personnel, and supporting population, often through conquest.
3. To pursue *wealth* through government regulation, or central planning, of economic production and distribution.

4. To pursue wealth through *laissez-faire,* that is, by protecting the free interplay of market forces with as little government interference as possible. In practice, various compromises between the third and fourth tasks have been put into operation, and the search for workable combinations has not yet been concluded.

5. To provide *welfare* through social, medical, and educational services, as well as through efforts to set minimum wages and maintain full employment.

6. To *coordinate and integrate* all the five tasks above—which often are in tension or conflict with each other—and, generally, all activities and attitudes within the society. This corresponds to Parsons's function of "integration."

7. To promote *adaptive learning* throughout the entire society, through new structures of organization and patterns of behavior, so as to help the society to adapt to major changes in its natural, social, economic, or political environment. Here the initiative stages of learning (see the eighth task below) are eliminated. Adaptive learning must fit the society to a situation that has been given for some time or has recently come into existence, but that in any case cannot greatly be changed. This corresponds to a part of Parsons's function of "adaptation." (The recent energy legislation in the United States and other countries is an example.)

8. To increase the capacities of the society for *initiative learning,* that is, to develop the institutions for, and foster attitudes conducive to, major new undertakings, such as the opening up of new energy sources, or the entry into new places for work (the ocean floors and outer space, for example), or the exploration of new areas of scientific research and technology (for instance, the tiny genetic structures of bacteria, plants, and other living organisms). In such cases, the state helps the society to enter new situations or to create new situations on its own initiative. Thus the state begins something new.

9. To attain some specific new *goal,* such as national independence or a major change in the social order or culture. The new goal may correspond to an old dream or aspiration but it is new in the sense that its attainment is being seriously undertaken here and now, with success expected within one or a few generations.

Tasks 2, 3, 4, and 5, dealing with the goals of power, wealth, and welfare, must be attained time and again and thus correspond to Parsons's more-or-less permanent function of goal attainment. Together with task 1 (pattern maintenance), task 6 (integration), and task 7 (adaptation), these first seven tasks correspond to Parsons's four basic functions. The last two of these tasks—initiative learning and new goal attainment—may go further. They may create a major *change in the goals* of society, and to its considerable *self-transformation,* while still preserving its essential identity.

Usually, one or a very few of these tasks command most of the public's attention and efforts, and most of the resources of the state, while other tasks recede into the background without wholly disappearing. Thus the nineteenth century conservative governments of Benjamin Disraeli in Britain and Otto Prince Bismarck in Germany stressed pattern maintenance, combined with some government intervention in economic life and the pursuit of large empire-building goals in foreign policy. The contemporary conservative government of Prime Minister Margaret Thatcher in Britain seeks to maintain the social pattern, and to promote economic growth through reducing government intervention in business and restoring considerable *laissez-faire* competition in the marketplace. France, West Germany, and Mexico seek economic progress through various combinations of market competition, government regulation, and welfare policies. Russia, China, and Cuba each made the victory of the revolution, and subsequent national consolidation, its paramount goal, followed by major efforts at development through central economic planning. We can similarly compare and analyze other governments according to how they set priorities among their tasks.

A Second Checklist: Values People Seek to Gain Through Politics. When we turn from governments to people, we note that they seek to gain many values—that is, valued outcomes—for themselves or the people they care for, and that they seek to gain them through the processes of politics. Such values are for them the "what" in Harold Lasswell's definition of politics in terms of "who gets what," and Lasswell has set up a concise scheme for classifying all kinds of values under just eight headings. These eight values are:

1. *Deference,* or high status, that is, receiving access and attention before others ("Is our government sufficiently respected in the world?");
2. *Power,* that is, chiefly, the capacity to change the probability of outcomes ("Are we the strongest military power in the world?" "And can we control unemployment and inflation?");
3. *Rectitude,* that is, the capacity to act according to one's own moral beliefs and to make them prevail over those of others ("Abraham Lincoln said, 'I am concerned to know, not whether the Lord is on my side but whether I am on the Lord's side'.");
4. *Affection,* that is, being liked or loved by others ("Do other peoples like us—or don't we care?");
5. *Wealth* ("How high is our per capita income? What does it buy? And who doesn't get it?");
6. *Skill* ("How good is our technology?");
7. *Well-being,* from the health of the body to its various pleasures ("What is the state of our public health?" "And are there playgrounds for children?");
8. *Enlightenment,* including both rational and emotional knowledge, and the experience of beauty ("Are educational standards rising or falling?" "And how well can we make sense of what we learn?").

Each of these values is of course more inclusive than the example given next to it. There is more to well-being than health and more to enlightenment than education.

But can any government or political system get all these values for all people living under it? To what extent can each of these values be shared,

and to what extent must they be competed for? A recently developed branch of social science called game-theory distinguishes two basic types of games, each of them with many parallels in political and social institutions. One type is called a *fixed-sum* or *zero-sum game,* such as chess or poker. In games of this kind, what one player wins, another player must lose; any outcome good for one competitor cannot be good for his or her rival. The other type of game is called *variable-sum game,* where the sum of everyone's winnings can go up or down; the players may be able to win jointly by cooperation, or one player may try to beat the others by competing. Such situations are sometimes called *mixed-motive games,* since the players may have something to gain from competing, but also something to gain from cooperating and something to lose from not cooperating. Many situations in politics resemble mixed-motive games. Game theory was developed by mathematicians by analyzing social games we play for fun, but the insights apply to many game-like situations in politics and economics, where people "play" in deadly earnest.

Laswell's eight values have been listed in the order of both their essential scarcity and the intensity with which people must compete in order to get them. *Deference* ordinarily is a stake in a fixed-sum or *zero-sum game.* Usually, only one person can go through a door first. The same holds for *power over people;* if one person is to become stronger than others, the others must become weaker, at least by comparison.

Power over nature, however, is different. Pursuing this power, one person could gain at the expense of another, perhaps by grabbing scarce equipment. But both can also win or lose together. Their situation resembles that of players in a variable-sum game, or a mixed-motive game, since people may choose cooperation or competition, and some of them may profit either way.

In pursuing their values of *rectitude,* such as seeking to establish righteous conditions in society, people's motives also may be mixed between conflict and cooperation. Anybody's view of rectitude, if it is not linked to humanity and tolerance, must be made to prevail over other people's views of rectitude. Even *affection* cannot always be easily shared; anyone's capacity to give affection is at least as limited as time, and jealousy is known to exist among siblings as well as among lovers.

The other four values can be shared more easily. *Wealth,* in its tangible form of course, usually is subject to the laws of scarcity: if we give an object away we no longer have it. But we can make some things abundant, as clean drinking water is in most cities in highly developed countries; we can all try to produce more wealth, so long as energy, raw materials, and equipment for production are easily available; and insofar as wealth consists in information, we can duplicate and share it without losing it at all.

For the last three values, the possibilities for cooperation may be still greater. *Skill* may have to be taught by teachers and equipment that are both expensive and scarce. If so, its acquisition must be competed for. But many skills can be self-taught, or gained mainly through practice, often in cooperation with other people; to that extent we can gain skills without denying them to others.

Something similar holds true for physical *well-being.* Some health or sports facilities are scarce and expensive, so people must compete for them. But we can do much for our well-being through our own efforts, and also by our common efforts to build and maintain playing fields, hospitals, and public health clinics.

Finally, *enlightenment* most often can be gained by personal effort and passed on freely to others, and still more of it, as in science, can be gained by cooperation. Whatever knowledge I transmit to others through speaking, writing, or artistic creation does not leave me more ignorant. To be sure, enlightenment also needs some scarce material facilities, such as paper, books, printing equipment, laboratories, instruments, schools, and universities, but the proportions between what is

scarce and competitive on the one hand, and what can be shared freely or gained cooperatively on the other hand, are still very different from the proportions that prevail in regard to deference and power.

Lasswell's scheme of eight substantive values should be supplemented by four major modes in which we usually want to enjoy any one value. There are other modes of enjoyment, but these four chief ones are:

9. *Security.* How long and how reliably can we enjoy our well-being, our health, our power, or the affection of another?

10. *Liberty.* How free from external restraints shall we be in our enjoyment?

11. *Freedom.* How wide a *range of choices* shall we have among our values and our ways of enjoying them?

12. *Spontaneity.* To what extent shall we be able to act in accordance with our habits and impulses, and to what degree shall we have to hold ourselves back?

All these values, including the four major modes of enjoyment, often may be in conflict. *Trade-offs* may be necessary. How much wealth should we spend, personally or publicly, for better health or more enlightenment? How much physical pleasure or well-being shall we forego for the sake of rectitude? How much spontaneity shall we sacrifice for the sake of security? How much deference—to be won, perhaps, through the single-minded pursuit of a career—shall we give up for the sake of affection?

Politics in every country must deal with such trade-offs among different values. These include not only values held by different groups but also those held within one group or even by the same persons. Politics, then, must seek solutions that make the pursuit of several goals more compatible with each other and hence more legitimate. In the mixed-motive game between competition and cooperation, politics is thus not limited to the "authoritative allocation" of values among competing claimants; it also includes the search for more people through better patterns of cooperation.

Time and again, not only individuals but entire peoples and their governments must make such choices, and their politics will show it. In addition to the bases of comparison we have already discussed, we can also compare different governments and nations in terms of the values they profess, the specific choices among values they must make, and the solutions they have found to these problems.

A Third Checklist: Some Operating Aspects of Politics. So far we have singled out two rather abstract topics: the different tasks that governments are expected to perform, and the values that politics is expected to help distribute. What people expect, however, is not always what they get. Between intentions and outcomes stand the ways in which things really work. Just how do politics and governments actually operate in each country? And which operating aspects of politics in each country seem most comparable and most worth comparing to those in other countries, so as to reveal the most important similarities and differences?

What follows is a list of nine major operating aspects of politics. (In another book of mine, *Politics and Government: How People Decide Their Fate,* each of these aspects has a whole chapter to itself.) An attempt has been made to pay attention to each of these aspects in the course of discussing each country, so this list functions as an organizing principle in each chapter, or section of a chapter, devoted to the analysis of a particular case. In this manner, the case studies presented here contain an implicit theory of politics. Once they recognize this theory, students and other readers may criticize it, or replace it with some other theory or scheme of interpretation. This book should include enough factual material to permit them to do so by reorganizing this theory in line with checklists 1 and 2, given earlier, or with any other plan of their choice—so long as they keep paying sufficient attention to the operating aspects of politics to keep their analysis realistic.

The nine major operating aspects in each country are:

1. *The Meaning of Politics.* Meaning is context. When we ask what something "means"—a word, a thing, or an event—we are asking what environment or context it belongs in and what difference it could make there. What then does politics *mean* in the context of a country's time and space—of its historical background, its geography and economy, its educational and social structure, its language and culture (or languages and cultures), and of its international problems, as history, geography, and the scarcity or abundance of particular economic resources may have shaped them? One country might copy the constitution of another, but that constitution, and most of politics as well, may mean something very different from anything they ever meant in the first place. Politics means something different in Western and non-Western cultures, in a long-established nation and in a recently independent one, in rich countries and poor ones, in agrarian societies and industrialized, information-rich ones, in countries with a majority of illiterates and those with a majority of high school graduates, in nations that remember a successful major revolution and those whose history followed other patterns.

2. *The Stakes of Politics.* What outcomes in each country can the political process decide, and what values can it allocate? How large a part of the *gross national product* (GNP)—the total of goods and services produced in the country—is passing through the *public sector,* that is, through the revenues or expenditures of the national, state, and local governments, together with the turnover of government-owned agencies and corporations, such as, in the United States, the Post Office and the Social Security Administration? Or is the entire political and social order at stake, as it has been in some major revolutions? By contrast, which matters in each country are not subject to current political decisions? What is already fixed by custom and culture, by the rigidity of economic and social institutions, by sheer poverty and lack of resources, or by international constraints? What is

at stake in politics in each country may vary from time to time, but the importance of politics is always likely to depend on it.

3. *The Participants in Politics.* Who actually takes part in politics—in voting; in meetings, demonstrations and campaigns; in lobbying and informal attempts to exercise influence over governments or other public agencies? Who shares in the organization and activities of political parties, labor unions, employers' associations, farmers' organizations, and other interest groups? And who is excluded from politics by distance, age, ignorance, apathy, law, or administrative regulations? Who, though living and working in a country, is excluded from politics as a foreigner (perhaps, an "undocumented alien"), or is not legally eligible to vote because of lack of property or education, or for reasons of race or sex? (Each of these cases exists in the world today.) Who, though eligible to vote, is excluded from voting because he or she has not been registered to vote? Among those who do participate in politics, who are the most active and who the most influential? And has the circle of participants in the country's politics been narrowing or widening in recent years?

4. *The Images of Politics.* What images of politics prevail in the country? What do the participants in politics there imagine they are doing, and what does the mass of the population think of them. Which images of politics are currently being accepted and which debated? Here we are asking about political ideas and *ideologies,* that is, about more or less standard ways of thinking that are designed to make the world look simpler than it is. Liberalism and conservatism are prominent among the political ideas debated in the United States, as they are, together with socialism, in Britain. Marxism-Leninism is the ruling ideology in the Soviet Union and, in different varieties, in Yugoslavia and China. Gandhi's ideas still play a role in the political heritage of India, and an

Islamic ideology may be developing in Iran. The ideas of fascism dominated Italy and Germany on the eve of World War II. They receded with the defeat of these powers, but many people are concerned that they might again become powerful in some country in the future.

5. *The Arena of Politics.* Just what is a country? Where are its economic and political boundaries? A *country* is an area of multiple economic and social interdependence, where what happens in any one region has substantial effects on what happens in others. A country could be inhabited by two or several peoples, speaking different languages, as is the case in India; or these peoples may be separated by different cultures, even though they speak the same language, as the English, Scots, and Irish do. A *people,* then, is a group of persons who for reasons of language or culture can communicate more easily, quickly, and accurately among each other than with outsiders. Better able to understand each other, they find it easier to predict each other's behavior and to trust each other. Members of a people often wish to gain control over the political system of enforcement and compliance under which they live. If they strive actively to do so, we call such a people a *nationality,* and there are many such groups trying to assert themselves, from the Breton nationalists in France to the Kurdish minority in Iran, or from the Jewish people in Palestine before 1948 to the Palestinian Arabs on the West Bank today. If members of such a people succeed in gaining control of the state machinery of an entire country, we call them a *nation* or a *nation-state.* France, Italy, Israel, and Egypt are among today's nation-states. Nowadays such nation-states have replaced most of the former empires as *arenas* of politics, that is, as areas within which most political activities, contests, and decisions occur.

6. *The Political System.* Just as people within a country are interdependent in terms of economics and social development, so they are interdependent within a *political system* in terms of political events. Such events in any one part of the system

have significant effects on all or most other parts. Political systems exist at different *levels,* such that a higher-level system includes some lower-level ones. Thus, individuals are included in families and small groups, small groups in villages or cities, cities in districts, states, or provinces, and these in turn in nation-states. Beyond the nation-state, there exist regional political systems, such as the European Economic Community (EEC), the Organization of African Unity (OAU), and the Organization of American States (OAS). Beyond all these extends the political system of world politics and its corresponding organizations; the United Nations covers, in principle, the world.

7. *The Self-Steering Capacities of Political Systems and Governments.* Are governments and political systems condemned to drift along with the flow of events and accidents, or can they set their own goals and their own course, and steer themselves around obstacles and dangers? Most governments are trying to do so, but some are succeeding better than others. Steering depends on a country's *intake* of information through its "receptors" (such as embassies abroad or statistical offices at home) from the outside world, the recall of other information from *memory* (including memories about where one wants to go), the transmission of commands for action to "effectors," and the *feedback* of information from the outside world about the results of the action just taken. It is by responding to this feedback information that errors can be rectified and the entire course corrected. The same process occurs in politics. Governments must receive "intelligence" about their foreign environment, but also information about domestic affairs, the electorate, and the general population on whose support and compliance they depend. They also must recall from written records and the memories of officials some information about their former policies and goals, as well as about past experiences, and in the combined light of newly incoming information and recalled memories they must decide what to do. Then the government must issue orders of some kind to its effectors—usually administrative officials, policemen, and soldiers—who are to carry

them out. And finally the government must get feedback information about the actual results of what it did—which may be very different from what it expected—and must try to correct its actions accordingly.

8. *The Process and Machinery of Government.* These determine to a large extent how successfully a government can steer itself. Here we are concerned with the setting of *public policy* and with *public administration,* the functioning of the courts and of other public agencies. To what extent do these agencies succeed or fail in the *implementation* of the laws and orders of the political system? How are the servants of the government educated, recruited, and motivated? Is there a *civil service* with fixed rules of employment and promotion, or a *spoils system* in which public jobs are controlled by the political patronage of the party or faction currently in power? How much corruption is there and in what areas? On the whole, is the country governed by a *"soft state,"* where government orders and decisions are most often poorly carried out, or by a *"hard state,"* where supposedly binding decisions are really binding? And with what results and for whom is this whole governmental machinery working?

9. *The Performance of the Political System.* This last item represents the "bottom line" of the political process. People are not here for politics, politics is here for people. What is politics doing for them and to them in this particular country? "Life, liberty and the pursuit of happiness" were listed by the authors of the U.S. Declaration of Independence among the "unalienable rights" of human beings. The set of indicators these three terms suggest may not look political, but the information it provides is in part a result of politics. What is happening to people's *life expectancy,* particularly that of small children, in different states and under different governments? How much liberty is there, in what respects, and with what security? What about well-being and public health, enlightenment and education? What about the degree of economic and social equality or inequality, and

how do people feel about the degree of rectitude and social justice about them?

Another set of performance indicators deals with large-scale processes. How stable is the government? How much room does it offer for political and cultural choice? How prosperous is the country and what gains is it making in scientific, technical, and economic development? And what is the *quality of life,* and for whom, in that country?

A last indicator deals with individuals. It was proposed long ago by the British political philosopher John Stuart Mill. What kind of individuals grow up under this or that political system? Do they dare to walk upright and think straight? Or do they bear the mark of fear? Are their minds creative or sterile? Do they expect truth or lies from their public authorities? These, too, are signs of how governments are performing.

SUMMING UP

This chapter has offered three checklists of possible questions for comparing governments. With their aid we can ask about the currently prevailing tasks of each state, about the values that are produced and distributed under its control, and about the chief ways in which it operates. Answering all these questions for all of our fourteen countries would take a long time. Students and other readers will have to choose where, if anywhere, they wish to pursue their inquiries in greater depth. But this book was not written to finish inquiries. It was written to help get them started.

KEY TERMS AND CONCEPTS

politics, political
allocation
authority, authoritative

legitimacy, legitimate
conscience
superego
compliance
enforcement
to govern, government
kybernetes (helmsman)
political science
science, natural vs. social
error margins
uncertainty principle
comparisons
analogy
inference
good vs. bad analogies
social order
Communism, Communist
centrally planned economies
market economies
size (of nations, population)
industrialization, industrialized
cultural tradition (Western or non-Western)
democracy, democratic
constitution, constitutional
plurality, pluralistic
dictatorship, dictatorial
oil exporting vs. non-oil-exporting countries
Hindu culture
Islam, Islamic
welfare vs. nonwelfare states
revolution, revolutionary
political change
changes in incumbency
changes in regime
changes in social order/political culture
nationalization, to nationalize
tasks or functions of government
pattern maintenance
identity
power
wealth
laissez-faire
coordination

integration
adaptive learning
initiative learning
goal, goal attainment
goal change
self-transformation
value, values
deference
rectitude
affection
skill
well-being
enlightenment
zero-sum game
variable-sum game or mixed-motive game
security
liberty
freedom (range of choices)
spontaneity
operating aspects of government
meaning (context and background of politics)
stakes of politics
gross national product (GNP)
public sector
participants, participation in politics
images of politics
ideology, ideologies
arena of politics
country
people
nationality
nation
nation-state
political system
system levels
European Economic Community (EEC)
self-steering capacities
intake of information
"intelligence"
receptors
memory
effectors
feedback
process and machinery of government
public policy
public administration

civil service vs. spoils system
patronage
corruption
performance of the political system
life expectancy
quality of life

FOR FURTHER STUDY

Almond, G. A., and G. B. Powell, Jr. *Comparative Politics: System, Process and Policy,* 2nd ed. Boston: Little, Brown, 1978. PB

——. *The Civic Culture Reconsidered.*

Aristotle. *Politics.* Trans. Sir Ernest Barker. New York: Oxford University Press, 1958.

Bachrach, P. *The Theory of Democratic Elitism.* Boston: Little, Brown, 1967.

Beer, S. H., et al. *Patterns of Government,* 2nd ed. New York: Random House, 1962.

Blondel, J. *Comparing Political Systems.* New York: Praeger, 1972. PB

Dahl, R. A. *Modern Political Analysis.* Englewood Cliffs, N.J.: Prentice-Hall, 1967. PB

——. *Polyarchy: Participation and Opposition.* New Haven: Yale University Press, 1972.

Deutsch, K. W. *Politics and Government,* 3rd ed. Boston: Houghton Mifflin, 1980.

——. *The Analysis of International Relations,* 2nd ed. Englewood Cliffs, N.J.: Prentice-Hall, 1978. PB

——. *The Nerves of Government,* 2nd ed. New York: Free Press, 1966.

——. *Nationalism and Social Communication,* 3rd ed. Cambridge, Mass.: MIT Press, 1981.

Easton, D. *Framework for Political Analysis.* Englewood Cliffs, N.J.: Prentice-Hall, 1965.

Friedrich, C. J. *Man and His Government.* New York: McGraw-Hill, 1963.

Gurr, R. T. *Why Men Rebel.* Princeton: Princeton University Press, 1970. PB

Habermas, J. *The Legitimation Crisis.* Boston: Beacon Press, 1975.

Jain, S. *Size Distribution of Income.* Washington, D.C.: World Bank, 1976.

Lane, R. E. *Political Man.* New York: Free Press, 1972. PB

Lasswell, H. D. *Politics: Who Gets What, When, How?* Cleveland: World Publishing, 1968. PB

———, and A. Kaplan. *Power and Society: A Framework for Political Inquiry.* New Haven: Yale University Press, 1980. PB

Lindblom, C. E. *Politics and Markets.* New York: Basic Books, 1977. PB

Lipset, S. M. *Political Man: The Social Basis of Politics.* New York: Macmillan, 1959.

Macridis, R. C., et al. *Modern Political Systems: Europe,* 4th ed. Englewood Cliffs, N.J.: Prentice-Hall, 1979.

Mannheim, K. *Man and Society in the Age of Reconstruction.* New York: Harcourt, Brace, 1967. PB

Merritt, R. L. *Systematic Approaches to Comparative Politics.* Chicago: Rand McNally, 1970.

———, and S. Rokkan, eds. *Comparing Nations.* New Haven: Yale University Press, 1966.

Moore, B., Jr. *Injustice: The Social Bases of Obedience and Revolt.* New York: Pantheon, 1978.

Parsons, T. *Societies: Evolutionary and Comparative Perspectives.* Englewood Cliffs, N.J.: Prentice-Hall, 1966.

Plato, *The Republic.*

Prewitt, K., and A. Stone. *The Ruling Elites.* New York: Harper & Row, 1973.

Rapoport, A. *Fights, Games, Debates.* Ann Arbor: University of Michigan Press, 1960. PB

Rawls, J. *A Theory of Justice.* Cambridge, Mass.: Harvard University Press, 1971.

Schelling, T. C. *Strategy of Conflict.* Cambridge, Mass: Harvard University Press, 1960. PB

Thurow, L. *The Zero-Sum Society.* New York: Basic Books, 1980.

Verba, S., et al. *Participation and Political Equality.* Cambridge: Cambridge University Press, 1978.

PB = *available in paperback*

PART I

SIX MODERN COUNTRIES

II

The United States

Nobody really understands the United States—neither foreigners nor its own people. Winston Churchill once spoke of the Soviet Union as "a riddle wrapped in a mystery inside an enigma." Much the same might be said about the United States by any harassed Kremlin specialist in American research. If American "Kremlinologists" find it hard to forecast the Soviet Union's moves, Soviet "Pentagonologists" or "Washingtonologists" find it equally difficult to forecast United States behavior.

We can make at least some progress toward understanding American politics by asking first about the particular nature of politics in the United States, as it has developed in the course of the history of the American people. We shall inquire what "government" and "governing" have meant to Americans at different times in the past and what they mean now. We shall ask what values have arisen here; how and to what extent expectations of legitimacy and habits of compliance have developed; what priorities in the political decision process have tended to prevail; and how far and in what ways the American political system has shown capacities for learning and self-transformation.

After this excursion into history, we shall look more closely at present-day American politics. What are its stakes, and who are its participants? What major images and theories or ideologies have people formed about its working? And what is now the arena of American politics, both domestic and worldwide? These questions will have been answered in good part by our historical discussion, so briefer remarks should suffice.

After these concerns, we shall take a closer look at the structure of the American political system. What holds it together, at which levels do the main political processes occur, and which institutions have been most important and enduring? How does the system steer itself? What channels and processes of communication, corrective feedback, and decision making are most effective? To what extent does the political system of the United

States—or, put differently, of the American people, Union, and nation—show processes similar to memory, consciousness, and will? Who or what—which persons, groups, institutions, or organizations—most often or most effectively remember, are aware, harden or change their will and that of the nation? What particular political processes and pieces of machinery seem to be most relevant for the outcome? What is the outcome of American politics, and what are its costs—when, where, for whom, in what respects? What, in short, is the performance of the American political system in regard to which tastes, which values, and which groups of people?

Most of these questions can be answered only with difficulty, in part, and with ever-present risks of error. Even if we could answer all of them, we should only have begun to understand the politics and policies of the United States. But even a start will be well worth undertaking.

THE NATURE OF AMERICAN POLITICS:
THE ROLE OF HISTORY

The political system of the United States has been marked by a large land area, a short history, a young and mobile people, a succession of moving frontiers, and vast resources in wealth and opportunity. It also has been marked by competing individuals and interest groups; uneven and uncertain images of legitimacy and habits of compliance; great influence and power conceded to money; conflicting ideas and values, often held by the same people; tolerance of a wide variety of surface fads and fashions; serious readiness to learn and change quickly and boldly in particular sectors; and widespread insistence on visible overall continuity of the nation's basic morality and culture.

Political moods in America often swing back and forth between optimism and pessimism; trust in education and distrust of the educated; a confi-

dent faith in the improvement of human beings through knowledge and kindness and a hardheaded claim that most people can be moved only by wealth or force. In such a system and such a political culture it is often hard to agree on priorities and to set a consistent course of action, yet in major crises in the past this usually has been done. Despite its diversities and inner conflicts, the political system has preserved its unity; despite tragedies and errors—some past, some still continuing—it has often been a force for good in the world; and there is reason to think that it retains the capacity to renew itself and develop into something still better.

SOME WAYS IN WHICH AMERICA
IS DIFFERENT

The United States has much in common with other modern industrial nations. The whole point of this book is comparative political analysis; if the United States were incomparable, it could not be included here, and Americans and people from other countries would have little or nothing to learn from each other in regard to politics. But many aspects of American politics, both assets and handicaps, are indeed peculiar to this country, and we must look to history for help in understanding them.

In American history a few background characteristics stand out. The United States is the first of the world's new nations. Emerging in the 1760s and early 1770s and taking shape in an anticolonial revolution, the American people faced many of the problems of nation building that the world's emerging nations are encountering today. But since 1791 the United States also has been the oldest steadily functioning constitutional political system in the world. In contrast to the United States, every other political system has undergone more radical changes in recent times. This includes Sweden, Norway, Denmark, and Switzerland, whose written constitutions all date from the first half of the nineteenth century; and it is certainly true of all other large countries. Compared with the rest of the world, then, the changes in the American political system have been moderate, and the continuity of its tradition has been remarkable. This has not always been a blessing; the United States was the last modern country in the world to abolish slavery. But for good or ill, the historic facts of early anticolonialism and political traditionalism very likely have contributed to the traits of impatience and conservatism so evident in American politics.[1]

Second, in terms of economic capability the United States is the largest political system in the world. For a brief time after the end of World War II, it had more than one-half of the world's income and productive machinery. After the war the United States continued to grow, but as other countries recovered from the war and often grew faster, the relative share of the United States declined. In 1978 the United States still had nearly 25 percent of the gross national product of the world, together with nearly as large a share of the world's capital equipment. The United States also has on a per capita basis one of the highest average living standards in the world. In population and in area the United States is the world's fourth largest political system. Only three countries—the Soviet Union, Canada, and China—are bigger in area, and only three countries—China, India, and the Soviet Union—are larger in population.

In less than two centuries the American political

---

[1]For two fascinating books, each exploring a different aspect of this paradox, see Seymour Martin Lipset, *The First New Nation* (New York: Basic Books, 1963); and Daniel Boorstin, *The Genius of American Politics* (Chicago: University of Chicago Press, 1953). For the emergence of the American people, see the quantitative evidence from the colonial newspapers, presented by Richard L. Meritt, *Symbols of American Community, 1735–1775* (New Haven: Yale University Press, 1966).

system has succeeded in organizing a country on the scale of a continent. Only religious ideologies have done comparable jobs of organization on such a vast scale, and they did so much earlier in history. The religion of Lao-tse, together with the Confucian philosophy, helped unite Chinese culture; Hindu religion kept India together; and Byzantine Christianity was the basis of the Russian state. The United States is the child of the eighteenth-century Enlightenment, the only secular ideology that has *created* a huge country and kept it intact. Varieties of communism have taken over large existing countries, such as Russia and China, but the United States started off with a bundle of colonies with 3 million people and parlayed this population into a country of over 200 million—close to what Benjamin Franklin predicted at its start.

At present the United States is perhaps the largest country in the world in capabilities for good and evil, insights and errors. It did more than any other country in relieving famines after World Wars I and II and again in the 1950s and 1960s. Its economic aid under the Marshall Plan in 1948–52 was crucial in the reconstruction of Western Europe. Its technological contributions—from Edison's electric light and the Wright brothers' airplane to nuclear energy and the landings on the moon—have changed the world. But its errors can be more devastating, shattering, and damaging than those of any other country because they have had more power behind them. Only slowly are some other countries drawing closer to the United States in their national power and their capacity to do vast damage to themselves and others by their errors.

Government by Design. To be sure, the United States was intended not to commit errors, but to be the world's first truly rational government. Its political system was shaped by the ideas of applied social scientists who were familiar with the most advanced theory of their time. Franklin, Jefferson, Hamilton, James Wilson, and especially Madison—all were men who had studied carefully what was then called "the science of government."[2] These founders of the Republic were deliberately trying to set up the United States as a government founded on reason—today we might say as a piece of social engineering. They *designed* the American political system with several tasks in mind. It was designed for expansion across a continent and, in some minds, at least, for further expansion across the oceans. It was also designed to attract capital from abroad and from within the country and to promote its investment in advanced technologies. And it was meant to give its inhabitants a better opportunity for spontaneity, freedom, and self-expression than could be found anywhere else.

People by Development. Unlike its political institutions, the American people, of course, was not produced by anyone's design. It was formed by history and by the decisions of millions of immigrants. The American colonists were molded into a new people by their common experience in the New World, the growing communication among the colonies, the distance from Europe, and finally, their growing revolutionary movement. They learned to think of themselves as Americans, and of the colonies as one country, before the first shots were fired at Lexington and Concord.[3] The experience of the American Revolution deepened this sense of a common identity and made it more widespread, but it had been clearly established before 1776 in the press, in the flow of many transactions of everyday life, and in the minds of such leaders as Benjamin Franklin.

Americans became recognizable as a people as they became more and more associated with certain distinctive traits. One of the persistent characteristics of the American people has been its great geographic mobility. About one-third of Americans live outside the state of their birth, and there is reason to believe the proportion has been this high since the Revolution. This figure is much higher than the exchange of population among the states of Western Europe. Even within Germany, as late as 1870 only 5 percent of the inhabitants of Bavaria came from outside Bavaria. Benjamin Franklin commented on the ability of Americans, thanks to a plentiful supply of land, to move freely in order to take up farming or other work in new locations. Traveling in America a half century later in the 1830s, Alexis de Tocqueville contrasted the scarcity of workers and abundance of land with the opposite situation prevailing in Europe and recognized this as a fundamental factor in promoting individual equality and liberty.

The resulting capacity for mobility put a limit on what anyone could do to people. If local government or conditions of work became oppressive, they could pick up their possessions—which for most of them were sparse enough to be mobile—and move on. Mobility dispersed them, first along the eastern seaboard and then across the continent, but this constant flow of migrants kept Americans uniform in culture. In the late eighteenth century, British travelers reported that the speech of the American people was almost identical over a thousand miles' distance, in contrast to the speech of the English rural population, which differed by dialect every hundred miles.

Another shared characteristic of the American people was a relatively high degree of literacy, which was uncommon in eighteenth-century Europe and is yet to be reached by many developing countries. A third was the high degree of political participation, in rural areas as well as in towns. A fourth trait was the habit of self-government and the widespread ability to form and maintain self-governing groups for a variety of political, economic, and social purposes.

[2]The reading lists of these men have become available. See Douglas Adair and Walton Hale Hamilton, *The Power to Govern: The Constitution, Then and Now* (New York: Norton, 1937); and Douglas Adair, " 'That Politics May Be Reduced to a Science': David Hume, James Madison, and the Tenth Federalist," *Huntington Library Quarterly,* 20 (1957), 343–60.

[3]For the growing use of the words "American" and "Americans" in the colonial press, see Merritt, *Symbols of American Community.*

Two final common conditions, in part underlying the others, were the facts that most farmers owned their land and that they did not feel bound by tradition in choosing their methods of tillage. As a result, American farmers were more independent, innovative, and prosperous. Unlike their European counterparts, they owned guns and horses; they wore felt hats and leather boots; they were free to hunt and fish; and most of them never had been subject to large landowners or nobles. In short, they were not *peasants.* Their mobility and their resources gave them far greater capabilities to escape oppression or frustration or to resist them successfully. Thus the Constitution did not *give* freedom to the American people. Rather, it helped them to make more effective use of the freedom that was already woven into the fabric of their lives. This point is often forgotten by those who would transplant political institutions and constitutions from one society to another.

If American farmers were far more free than the peasants of Europe, the black people in America were slaves, having neither freedom nor mobility. But the model of free farmers and free workers was set for everybody; and once the slaves were liberated, their descendants sooner or later would insist on claiming the same freedom in full measure.

Above all, most Americans discovered that much in their lives was not irrevocably fixed by past tradition, long-entrenched institutions, or immemorial usage. Within the limits of practicality and of their own resources, they could choose their place of residence, their line of work or line of business, their religious denomination, their patterns of family life and community relations; and they often could change any or all of these by simply moving on or by combining with their neighbors to make some changes where they lived.

In many places they could get land, claiming it formally or informally for settlement or buying it cheaply from some owner, since land was abundant. There was no one to deny it to them; no king, no aristocracy, no powerful state church monopolized much of the land, as so often had been the case in the Old World. Neither were

mineral rights a royal or state monopoly; mining claims often were not difficult to stake. Established class barriers rarely seemed insurmountable. Nor was there a stifling weight of well-nigh unchangeable cultural tradition, for too many Americans had come from too many different countries and backgrounds.

More than people in most other countries, Americans felt free to innovate, unhampered by tradition. It was an attitude well expressed by Mark Twain in *A Connecticut Yankee in King Arthur's Court,* and it has found more recent expression in government-financed American footprints and car tracks on the moon.

The Underlying Premise: Economic Abundance. American politics has been based on a belief in optimism, spontaneity, harmony of interests, readiness to experiment, and willingness to compromise. For over two hundred years, these traits have stood out more strongly and continuously in American politics than in those of, say, Germany, France, or Russia. Why did these beliefs prevail and why did the political system succeed? Perhaps most important, the American political system was superimposed from the beginning on a highly prosperous economy with plentiful resources. For a long time operation of this economy was nearly automatic. At the start of the republic there was no dogmatic taboo against government's acting in economic matters, but most of the expansion of the frontier was done by individuals, not government. Most of the nation's farming, manufacturing, mining, and transporting was undertaken spontaneously by individuals seeking profit and was guided automatically by the market mechanism.

In most markets people vote not with ballots, but with dollar bills or their equivalent. In the United States the distribution of income is such that the top 10 percent of individual income receivers hold about 28 percent of the income, the second 10 percent hold about 15 percent, and the third 10 percent have at least 10 percent or more

TABLE 2.1 *Income Distribution in the United States,*
1977 and 1971 (in 1977 Dollars)

| CLASS | YEAR | | | | CHANGE | |
| | 1971 | | 1977 | | 1971–77 | |
	All families	Black families	All families	Black families	All families	Black families
Poor (under $5,000)	9.9	23.5	9.4	23.8	−0.5	+0.3
Unskilled labor ($5,000–7,500)	8.6	15.1	9.0	15.6	+0.4	+0.5
Skilled labor and lower middle class ($7,500–15,000)	29.7	33.3	27.5	31.7	−2.2	−1.6
Middle class ($15,000–25,000)	29.6	18.6	31.7	20.9	+2.1	+2.3
Upper middle and top class (over $25,000)	22.2	9.5	22.4	9.1	+0.2	−0.4

Sources for Figures 10.1(a) and 10.1(b) and Table 10.1, above:
U.S. Department of Commerce, Bureau of the Census, *Current Population Reports,* ser. P-60, no. 116 (July 1978); ser. P-60, no. 85 (1972).
For conversion of 1971 incomes to 1977 incomes: U.S. Department of Labor, Bureau of Labor Statistics, *The Consumer Price Index for January 1972* (April 1972).
Ibid., *CPI Detailed Report–November 1977* (Washington D.C.: U.S. Government Printing Office, 1978).

(see Table 2.1). That is, 30 percent of the American people have more than 50 percent of the dollar votes in the market. One must never forget that in voting with dollars there is a differential franchise that makes a permanent minority of over two-thirds of the American people. But in voting with ballots these two-thirds have a better chance of making their needs known and their voices heard, provided that they use their ballots effectively and combine them with other forms of political participation.

The American economy worked as well as it did because the energy and diligence of its people were further supported by a number of visible and invisible subsidies—in other words, advantages conferred outside the range of market exchanges and rewards for individual effort.

The first of these subsidies was land. It was abundant, much of it being of good quality, well watered and timbered, and had a favorable climate and excellent natural facilities for communication, such as lakes, rivers, harbors, and a long coastline. It was virtually free for the taking. Dispossessing the British Crown and a few Indians was relatively cheap. Ground rents were lower, and the ratios of land to labor—and hence the potential economic rewards available for labor and capital—were higher than in any other advanced

FIGURE 2.1 *Income Distribution in the United States:*
(a) For 1977; (b) Recent Changes (Between 1971 and 1977)

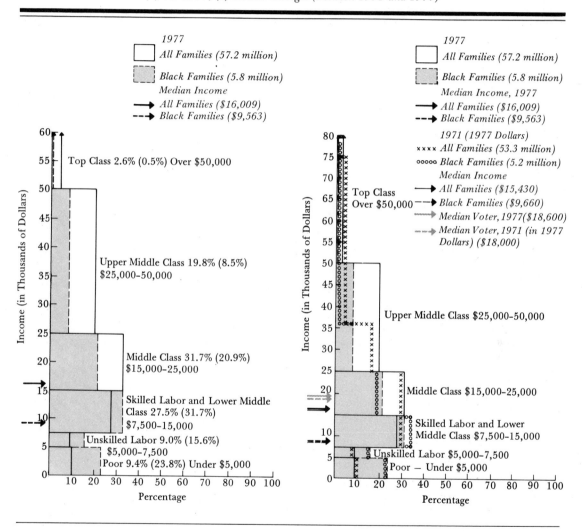

Source: See Table 2.1

country. Accordingly, more labor and more capita streamed into the United States for many decades.

The country also was unusually well supplied with highly skilled personnel. From the beginning, American settlers had many more skilled crafts-people among them than did Latin American settlers from Spain or settlers in Canada or Australia.

Second, immigrants to the United States between 1775 and 1875 came with more capital. The average covered wagon with which pioneers—many of them foreign born—crossed the prairies in the mid-nineteenth century contained in current prices about $5,000 worth of axes, rifles, blankets, ammunition, and other things. New capital was found and new labor kept arriving through immigration from Europe. Most of the new arrivals were of prime working age, whereas the babies and the aged stayed in the Old World. The cost of raising babies until they were husky twenty-year-olds was borne by the European economies. The *dependency burden* stayed in Europe, and the working personnel came to America. In this sense, throughout the nineteenth century the rest of the world subsidized the United States—perhaps to a larger degree than the United States has subsidized the rest of the world in the twentieth.

Added to this voluntary subsidy by adult immigration was a grim involuntary subsidy. The import of black slaves until 1808 transported net labor power from Africa to the United States. It left the terrible cost of this traffic mainly in Africa and took some of the economic growth of the country out of the bones of the slaves.

Additional capital, too, was accumulated in the outside world and then imported here. Alexander Hamilton's policies specifically aimed at making capital import attractive to foreign investors. But the United States not only attracted more capital than other countries; it squandered less. Both American and foreign observers in the nineteenth century often commented on American wastefulness and corruption. They overlooked the fact that the proportionate cost of all such scandals was much less than the regular cost of maintaining monarchies, aristocracies, and large standing armies, as the European powers did. The large amounts European nations spent on the splendor of monarchs and on cannons and barracks were spent in America on factories, fields, and mines. The United States had the smallest standing military force among nineteenth-century powers and the highest rate of economic growth—something that might remind us of Japan's small military expenditures and spectacular economic growth between 1948 and 1980.

The result of this uniquely productive, uniquely prosperous, and invisibly subsidized economy with its vast resources of land, labor, and capital was a steady growth of living standards. At the time of the American Revolution the American people used more iron per capita than any other country in the world. They were using more tonnage of shipping than any other country in the world as well. On the average, and for most people, the American living standard was ahead of the European as early as the 1840s and 1850s. It has never lagged.

This prosperity—fostered by the presence of the frontier until 1890, by business growth until 1929, and by the revival of business growth in the years following the prosperity of World War II—produced a popular belief in private enterprise. The American economy was characterized by what the economist Gunnar Myrdal has called a *spread effect*. Since there was so much capital and so much managerial talent available, these factors of production often spread into the less-developed regions. In this manner, capital and managerial talent in the 1970s also flowed in increased measure into the "sunbelt states" of the Southwest and the South. This effect is the opposite of the *backwash effect* in areas where skilled personnel, management, and capital are rare and where economic growth elsewhere leads to a draining of these resources out of the poorer regions and into richer ones. Appalachia, Mississippi, West Virginia, and South and North Dakota long were examples of regions and states where wealth flowed out rather than in. But in most other states the American economy pumped wealth in rather than out, and the exceptions—the poor regions, neighborhoods, and strata—were frequently forgotten.

Although most Americans enjoyed the fruits of their economic practices, they had a hard time finding a precise name for them. Since economic activities within a country are interdependent in many ways, it seemed natural to think of them as forming an economic system. An economic system, however, is far more complex than the simple labels—"capitalism" and "socialism"—that nineteenth-century economic thought made current. *Capitalism* is the name for a system in which factories and land are privately owned and economic development is directed by the automatic working of supply and demand in the market. *Socialism,* by contrast, is a system in which land and factories are owned publicly, either by the state or by large cooperatives, and economic development is directed by plan.

The American economy from the beginnings of the republic has been mixed. It was clearly much more capitalist than socialist; but from the Erie Canal to the Panama Canal and from the original land grants (to railroads) to the current vast public activities in education and research, the government's share has never been negligible.

Since capitalist elements clearly predominated, however, and since most Americans approved of the results, businesspeople were proud until 1929 to call themselves capitalists and the United States a capitalist system. In 1929 the national treasurer of the Democratic Party, John J. Raskob, listed his occupation in *Who's Who* as "capitalist." The Great Depression, with its mass unemployment, then made capitalism unpopular. Whether or not businesspeople privately thought of themselves as "capitalists," their public relations advisers preferred the words "business" or "private enterprise" or "management" to the term "capitalism." Radicals enthusiastically used the words "capitalist" and "capitalism" for persons and practices they did not

like. Many moderates began to shun these words as potentially misleading or divisive. Only in the 1960s did use of the terms revive. Conservative leaders like Barry Goldwater and a few writers praised capitalism at the same time as the same term became more widely criticized by the left half of the political spectrum. By 1980, with many people in a generally conservative mood, the term "supply side economics" had gained prominence in highlighting traditionally "capitalist" ideas—increasing profits, savings incentives, and reduced taxes as means to overall prosperity.

At present, both conservatives and their critics think of capitalism not only in terms of an economic system, but also in terms of a social class and of the power that it is supposed to have, or ought to have, within the political system. Some political scientists have taken part in this debate, but others have preferred the use of the term "elite" as permitting a more discriminating and precise analysis. By "elite" they have understood a group that gets on the average substantially more of the good things in a country—such as wealth, power, status, and the like—than do most other people living there. Moreover, usually members of this group tend to transmit most of their privileges to their children. Many political scientists agree, however, that at the heart of the debate stand two important questions: Which groups in the United States have the most power? And how is the unequal distribution of power related to the economic system?

THE STAKES OF POLITICS IN A MOBILE SOCIETY

Just because human behavior in the United States was less rigidly controlled than in other countries by long-standing sociological and cultural mechanisms, a greater burden of social control fell on the economic mechanisms of money and the marketplace and, since these often did not suffice, on the political process. Politics had to produce the laws that determined land grants to railroad companies, homestead farmers, and universities; that regulated municipal zoning for land use in cities, suburbs, and towns; that first backed and later abolished slavery; that regulated industries, public utilities, the rights of workers, and the activities of labor unions. Indeed, politics in alliance with religion produced laws that for a time permitted a man to have more than one wife, as it did in nineteenth-century Utah, and later politics denied this permission even to the most sincere of Mormon believers. Politics decided at one time that no Americans should be permitted to drink alcohol and that a beer brewer who continued business in the United States would be a criminal; later politics reversed all this. At one time, politics forbade Americans in several states to practice birth control or even to give or receive information about it. At another time, politics provided public money to make such information more widely available. In some other countries people have tried to change many matters through new laws or decrees, but they have done so usually only during a few years or decades of revolutions. In some respects, such as labor-management relations, government control of industry, and the provision of medical services, the United States has tended to leave more to the market than most other industrial countries have done. In such matters, the United States government has less control over the private sector. But in many other regards, it is doubtful that any other country in the world has used its political system—its legislatures, laws, and courts, as well as the administrative agencies of government—so continuously and extensively to control and change its own life and that of other nations as the United States has done.

Some political decisions are invisible. Often they are *nondecisions,* that is, decisions *not* to discuss a problem or *not* to put a project on the agenda of the council, committee, or administrative agency that has the legal power to deal with it. For many years the problems of inferior and segregated schools for black children were not discussed by many local school boards. Projects of publicly owned hydroelectric power stations faded from the national agenda after the 1930s. For many years projects for a national health insurance plan, such as have long existed in many modern countries, got little effective attention from Congress and the White House. Such selective inattention often is convenient for those groups whose interests it suits to keep these matters outside the arena of practical politics, but it works to the detriment of the persons and groups who might be helped by government attention and action, but who are not strong enough to obtain them.

Other concealed decisions may consist in scheduling for an early part of a meeting a question one favors, so that it is likely to be discussed and passed, and putting some other item one dislikes so far back on the agenda that it is likely to fail for lack of time to consider it or for lack of funds not yet committed to other purposes. Such techniques of deferring political intervention or making it selective tend to benefit those groups who have the power and organizational skills to use them, and they hurt those groups who have not.

Almost every political decision or nondecision makes someone richer or poorer, more or less free to follow his or her desires, more powerful or less so. Highway construction, zoning laws, building permits, and land values; government subsidies and grants; tariffs and import quotas; interest rates and monetary policy; government purchases and contracts at federal, state, and local levels; minimum wage laws or exemptions from them; bans on or permissions for the use of chemicals and pharmaceuticals; welfare payments and rules of eligibility; regulation of the rates charged by railroads, airlines, telephone, gas, and power companies—all can make someone's fortune in the marketplace or ruin someone else. When politics has worked to raise the postal rates for magazines, some periodicals have ceased publication, as *Life* magazine did when faced with the prospect of a sharp rate increase in 1972; a change in postal and tax policies might have saved many of these magazines and, with them, a valuable source of free and diversified information and opinion.

In a similar manner, American politics decides about the level of our defense expenditures, although this is accomplished partly in interplay with the arms decisions and actions of other major powers. In 1979 President Carter's agreements on partial arms limitations with the Soviet Union seemed to portend a continuing decline in defense spending, but the Iranian crisis and the Soviet invasion of Afghanistan quickly reversed the national mood, which resulted in a much larger defense budget. American politics decides to a large extent about the intervention or nonintervention of the United States in the affairs of weaker nations; and it decides about the risks of a larger war that are to be accepted or avoided.

Political power also includes the power to be noticed, for politics also decides which problems are to be neglected or ignored, which ideas can be expressed with a chance of getting serious attention, which questions are not to be discussed, and which groups of people are to be forgotten or persistently overlooked, as if they were invisible— often for years or decades. Occasionally, when politics changes at some later time, these formerly invisible groups and unmentionable questions then move into the focus of attention, and the public suddenly becomes aware of some flagrant facts about race discrimination, or discrimination against women, or the neglect of the social, cultural, and economic needs of the *Chicanos*— Americans mainly of Mexican origin—even though these conditions had long existed. Likewise, once Americans encountered the energy crisis of the 1970s, they became much more willing to debate a series of what previously were nondecisions regarding oil company policies and profits.

In all these ways, American politics decides about much more than the spending of the more than one-third of American gross national product that passes through our public sector. It decides about the fortunes and careers of millions of private individuals, about their social and economic status, about the physical quality of our environment, and about the cultural and moral quality of our lives. Short on traditions and long on geographic and social mobility, the United States perhaps has made the stakes of day-to-day politics higher than have most other countries.

These stakes, to be sure, are not equally high for everyone, nor are they equally visible to everybody. These considerations lead us directly to the problem of political participation.

POLITICAL PARTICIPATION, INFLUENCE, AND POWER

In Western democracies such as Canada, Britain, France, and West Germany, turnout in national elections regularly exceeds 70 or 80 percent of the eligible voters. In the U.S. presidential election of 1976, almost one-half of adult American citizens did not cast a vote. Nearly one-third had not been registered voters, and of those registered, about one-fifth, or about 13 percent of all adults, had not cared to vote. Mr. Indecision and Ms. Apathy, it seemed, represented more Americans in this bicentennial year election than did the candidates of either of the major parties.

The actual voting turnout in 1976 was about 54 percent of the population of voting age of eighteen and above; and it remained at 53 percent in 1980. These levels were lower than had been customary during most of the past 120 years. (The only exceptions were the years 1920–24, which gave the presidencies of Warren G. Harding and Calvin Coolidge to the Republic, and the elections of FDR in 1932 and Harry Truman in 1948). The turnout figures are shown in Table 2.2, and they suggest that American voting in the twentieth century has tended to be substantially lower than it was in the second half of the nineteenth.

Part of the explanation for this trend may consist in the greater extent of fraudulent voting in the nineteenth century, in the enfranchisement

TABLE 2.2 *Voter Participation in Presidential Elections, 1860–1980*

Period (presidential) years	Percentage of voting-age population voting
1860–1876	77
1880–1896	78
1900–1916	65
1920–1936	52
1940–1956	57
1960	64
1964	63
1968	62
1972	55
1976	54
1980	53

Sources: U.S. Bureau of the Census, *Historic Statistics of the United States,* Part 2, p. 1071, and *Statistical Abstract of the United States* (Washington, D.C.: U.S. Government Printing Office, 1978), p. 520; *The Economist,* Nov. 8–14, 1980, p. 24.

of women from 1920 onward, and in the temporary increase of eligible voters of relatively recent immigrant stock after 1900. But these conditions do not suffice to account for the magnitude of the observed changes. According to Walter D. Burnham, the figures rather suggest a considerable degree of alienation of part of our adult population from the existing political system. These men and women, it is suggested, have found casting their ballots unrewarding, and they expect from further voting little, if any, improvement in their lot.

Participation Through Money. The relative decline in the *participation by voters* has been paralleled by an increase in the political role of money. Even though popular participation in the 1972 campaign was low, the *participation by money* was conspicuous. Total campaign expenses, raised by the need to use expensive television time, were estimated at $400 to $500 million, or roughly $6 for each of the approximately 74 million votes cast. In the 1976 campaign the Federal Election Campaign Act of 1971, with its amendments of 1974 and 1976, had some effect in limiting spending, at least for the presidential contest, for which $72 million was paid out from public funds to all major party candidates and national committees.[4] In the congressional elections of 1978, however, money again was talking, loud and clear. In the future the need for campaign money is likely to increase, for a larger share of voters will be scattered in the suburbs, where they can best be reached by costly television advertising, supplemented by radio and print.

Interest groups expect a return on such financial investments, particularly from an incumbent candidate or from one very likely to win. In 1972 the dairy industry was reported to have contributed more than $400,000 to President Nixon's campaign for re-election, beginning with a visit by dairy industry representatives to Nixon on March 23, 1971, and a $25,000 contribution on March 24. The next day the Nixon administration reversed its earlier policy and permitted a 30-cent increase per hundredweight in the federal government's support price of milk. In 1971 as a whole, wholesale milk prices per hundredweight were 16 cents higher than in 1970. With United States consumption per year totaling about 500 million hundredweight, this price rise increased the annual gross income of the dairy industry by more than $30 million or, on an annual basis, by about 200 times the amount of its total reported contributions to Nixon's campaign.[5]

Such practices are not restricted to national

[4]See Herbert E. Alexander, *Financing Politics: Money, Elections and Political Reform* (Washington, D.C.: Congressional Quarterly Press, 1976).

politics, nor are they the monopoly of any one political party. In state and local politics, perhaps four-fifths or more of the larger campaign contributions come from individuals, firms, or interest groups who have business pending or planned with the government office that is being contested in that campaign. Such contributions are paid either directly to the candidate or to one of the organizations and committees working on the candidate's behalf; and the amount of each contribution often tends to be roughly 1 percent of the sum or value of the contract, permit, or other favor in which the donor has a direct financial interest.[6] When very large amounts of money are at stake, those willing to pay for political favors may get something like a quantity discount; in such cases, one-half of 1 percent or less of the sums at stake may suffice to purchase the candidate's favor. Since such contributions may pay at a rate of 100:1 or more, the donor may find it to his or her interest to give some money to a candidate who is not certain to win, or even to make campaign contributions (discreetly if possible) to two or more of the contending candidates.

Some large contributions, of course, come from wealthy individuals who agree with the candidate on ideals or issues, or are related to the candidate by family ties, or would like to have closer ties and easier access to the government after "their" candidate has won. Candidates have generally found the *"fat cats"*—the large contributors—

indispensable to winning and have felt obliged to pay some current or future price for their support.

The 1974 law on campaign finance reform moved to reduce somewhat the role of very large contributors in American elections. Individuals may not contribute more than $1,000 to any candidate in a federal election, and the names of all persons giving more than $100 must be publicly disclosed. The Supreme Court ruled, however, that it was a violation of the right of free speech to restrict how much a candidate or any family member could spend on his or her own campaign, or on "independent" advertising to support another candidate. A reform intended to restrict the political power of big money in favor of smaller contributors has also had the effect of spurring the growth of new forms of organized financial power. Corporations, labor unions, and special interest groups were allowed to establish political action committees (PACs), which could contribute up to $5,000 to any candidate in a federal election so long as the PAC raised money from at least fifty donors and gave funds to at least five different candidates in a federal election. In 1980 there were well over two thousand PACs supporting individual candidates, adding further impetus to the pluralistic rather than party-based nature of American politics. The 1974 law also provided federal matching funds to candidates in presidential primaries, but only if the candidate had already raised $5,000 in each of twenty states in contributions of $250 or less. Once nominated, presidential candidates (but not Congressmen) receive full federal funding for their campaign costs. Since the funds go directly to the candidate and his or her own campaign organization, the effect may be to further weaken party organizations.

Since money can be invested in this manner to buy influence, it increases the political power of those who have it. As long as a substantial part of campaign expenditures is still financed from private funds, the need for money in campaigning will tend to distort the political market, which in a

[5]Some of these campaign contributions by the dairy industry were publicly reported only after the election. See "Dairy Industry Gifts to Nixon Campaign Disclosed," *New York Times,* December 29, 1972, p. 23. The calculation of price changes and the sales volume of the dairy industry are based on U.S. Department of Agriculture data, reported in *The 1973 World Almanac and Book of Facts* (New York: Doubleday and Newspaper Enterprise Association, 1972), pp. 975–81.

[6]For data for a single state that may well be representative of others, see Thomas B. Edsall, "The Governor Raiseth," *Washington Monthly,* February 1972.

democracy counts all ballots as equal, and to move it appreciably closer to the commercial market, which allots purchasing power to individuals and groups in proportion to their wealth.

Participation Through Activity. Luckily, money is not the only way of exercising influence in American politics, nor is it always the decisive one. Since 1930 the presidential candidates with more money behind them have been defeated seven times: in 1932, 1936, 1940, 1944, 1948, 1960, and 1964. In at least some of the years in which the better-financed candidates won—1952, 1956, 1968, and 1972—they won primarily for other reasons than merely the advantage of more money and more television time. What often weighed more heavily in deciding the outcome were major events and the experiences that citizens derived from them, such as depressions, wars, inflation, race conflicts, and the like; the autonomous interests, attitudes, beliefs, and convictions of voters in matters of economic policy, but also of religion, culture, and morality; and the political activities of men and women in trying to make the casting of their own votes effective and in working to influence the political decisions and actions of others.

Political activities, however, are also distributed unequally, including considerable inequalities by class. A large and careful survey, made in 1967 by Sidney Verba and Norman Nie and published in 1972, showed consistently higher-than-average activity levels among those Americans who were in the top one-third of income and *socioeconomic* status and consistently lower-than-average activity among the socioeconomically lowest third of citizens. Within each third on the socioeconomic status scale, political activity likewise increases in the direction of the higher status levels. (The findings of Verba and Nie are summarized in Figure 2.2.) Altogether, their results, as well as those of another major study by Almond and Verba, show that "social status has a closer relationship to political participation in the United States than in all but one of nine other countries"

for which comparable data could be found. As Table 2.3 shows, in India, caste-ridden in the past and still partly so, the correlation between social status and political activity is only slightly higher.

Who Is the Median Voter? The effect of income and status—that is, roughly, of class—on voting is considerable. During the period 1952–79 in the United States these effects seem to have increased.

FIGURE 2.2 *Who Puts Effort into Politics: Status Composition at Varying Levels of Participation*

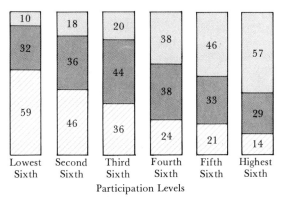

☐ *Upper Status (Upper Third of Whole Population on SES Index)*

■ *Middle Status (Middle Third of Whole Population on SES Index)*

☐ *Lower Status (Lower Third of Whole Population on SES Index)*

Numbers on bars refer to the percentage of each participation group coming from a particular socioeconomic status group. All figures have been rounded to the nearest significant digit. Percentages may not add up to 100 for this reason.

Source: S. Verba and N.H. Nie, *Participation in America: Political Democracy and Social Equality* (New York: Harper & Row, 1972), p. 131.

TABLE 2.3 *Correlation of Social Status and Participation in Ten Countries*

Civic culture data		Cross-national program data	
United States	.43	India	.36
United Kingdom	.30	Yugoslavia	.36
Italy	.28	United States	.35
Mexico	.24	Netherlands	.23
Germany	.18	Nigeria	.22
		Austria	.12
		Japan	.12

Note: Verba and Nie say: "We present two separate sets of correlation because the data come from two different studies. In each column the measures are comparable, but not across the columns, because different measures are used. This explains the two different figures for the U.S."

The data in the left column . . . are discussed in Norman H. Nie, G. Bingham Powell, and Kenneth Prewitt, "Social Structure and Political Participation," *American Political Science Review,* vol. 63 (June and September, 1969), pp. 361–378. Those in the right column in S. Verba, N. H. Nie, and J. Kim, *Participation and Political Equality* (Cambridge: Cambridge University Press, 1978), p. 64.

Back in 1952, studies showed that among given income classes of potential voters only about 53 percent of those receiving less than $2,000 a year had voted, as against 76 percent in the middle group, receiving between $3,000 and $4,000, and 85 percent in the highest income category, receiving $5,000 or more. In the two decades since 1952, both average incomes and the value of the dollar have changed, so that roughly, the bottom third now gets less than $5,000 annually, the middle third about $5,000 to $9,000, and the top third above $9,000. But the voting frequencies are

still highly unequal among socioeconomic status groups. For the top one-third in the presidential election of 1968, 90 percent of eligible voters cast ballots; for the middle group, 77 percent; and for the bottom third, 61 percent; the average for all three groups was 76 percent. In 1972 the average probability of voting for all income levels was 55 percent; estimates for the probability of voting at each level are given in Table 2.4.

This unequal frequency of voting has a significant effect on American politics. If one wants to win an election, one must gain the vote of, say, 51 percent of the voters actually voting. If all adults voted, and if the issue was one in which they might line up according to their relative wealth or poverty or, more generally, their socioeconomic status, then the voters around the fiftieth income percentile, say, from the forty-seventh to the fifty-third percentile, would constitute the pivotal middle group with the *swing vote* to decide elections between the "big money" and the "little people" parties or factions above and below them. Success in politics would depend on pleasing and persuading this midway group, and political and economic compromises would have to be tailored to suit it. The *median income voter* would be the kingpin of the system.

In fact this is not so, even though some people have imagined that it is. If, for example, only 60 percent of the voters in the bottom third of the income scale are actually voting, while 76 percent in the middle third and 85 percent in the top third do so, then the voting turnout will be 73 percent of adults, and 37 percent will suffice for a majority. Since 28 percent out of the 33 percent of top income receivers will still vote, they will need the votes of only another 9 percent to win. If, as we are supposing, the issue is an economic or otherwise class-related one, these votes may well be found among the top percentiles of the middle third of income receivers, say, those between the forty-first and the forty-ninth percentile of income. Since at least 76 percent of these upper-middle-level individuals are likely to vote, the small group between

TABLE 2.4 *Some Schematic Models of Voting Participation at Different Income Levels in the United States: The Location of the Pivotal Middle Group of Voters: 1952, 1967, 1968, 1972, and 1976*

Percentile of income receivers		Expected votes cast if everybody votes	Midpoint	1952			1967 poll ("regular voters")		
				Probability of voting (%)	Expected votes cast (%)	Midpoint	Probability of voting	Expected votes cast (%)	Midpoint
Top	1-33	33		85	28		60	20	
	34-41	8			*6*			*4*	*24*
	42-49	8		76	*6*	*36*	47	4	
Middle	50-57	*8*	*50*		*6*			4	
	58-65	8			*6*			4	
Bottom	66-100	34		53	18		38	13	
Total		100			71			49	
Average probability of voting		100		71			48		

Note: All percentages are rounded. All percentages refer to the total of citizens of voting age. All midpercentiles and midpoints are italicized.
[1]In 1972 the bottom third of families received less than $6,600, the top third of families, more than $12,400.
[2]In 1976 the bottom third of families received less than $10,800; the top third of families, more than $19,300.

Sources: For voting behavior: U.S. Department of Commerce, Bureau of the Census, *Current Population Reports: Population Characteristics*, "Voting and Registration in the Election of 1972," ser. P–20, no. 253 (October 1973); U.S. Department of Commerce, Bureau of the Census, *Current Population Reports: Population Characteristics*, "Voting and Registration in the Election of 1976," ser. P–20, no. 322 (March

the thirty-third and the forty-sixth percentile will suffice to produce the additional 9 percent of votes that the top income receivers need to prevail. The new swing group with the power to decide the election, and hence the group to be accommodated in the policies proposed, will now be the voters around the forty-fifth income percentile, counting from the top downward. The middle-middle-level voters between the forty-eighth and fifty-second percentile will have lost much of their former power, since they no longer can form a majority by siding with the voters who are poorer than themselves.

Something like this may have been the situation in 1952, if the survey data in our sources are to be trusted. (They may actually overstate *voting frequencies* for 1952, either because survey respondents tend to overreport their having voted or because voting ratios may have been reported on the basis of registered voters only, rather than on

TABLE 2.4 (Continued)

1968			1972[1]			1976[2]		
Probability of voting	Expected votes cast (%)	Midpoint	Probability of voting	Expected votes cast (%)	Midpoint	Probability of voting	Expected votes cast (%)	Midpoint
90	30		85	22		67	22	
	6			5			5	27
77	6	38	45	5	28	54	5	
	6			5			4	
	6			4			4	
61	21		35	14		44	14	
	75			55			54	
76			55			55		

1978). For income levels: U.S. Department of Commerce, Bureau of the Census, *Current Population Reports: Consumer Income*, "Money, Income and Poverty Status of Families and Persons in the United States: 1972," ser. P–60, no. 89 (July 1973); U.S. Department of Commerce, Bureau of the Census, *Current Population Reports: Population Characteristics*, "Money, Income and Poverty Status of Families in the United States: 1976," ser. P–60, no. 114 (July 1978). For 1952: Robert E. Lane, *Political Life* (New York–Glencoe, Ill.: Free Press, 1959), p. 49. For 1968: computed from University of Michigan Survey Research Center, 1968 Presidential Election Data. For 1972: *New York Times*, November 12, 1972, p. 40. For the frequencies of voting at different income or status levels, see Lane, *Political Life*; Verba and Nie, *Participation in America*, pp. 31-37, 132; and *Time*, November 6, 1972, p. 47.

the basis of all citizens of voting age; but our sources are not clear on this.) For the 1960 election, we do have a figure for the percentage of voting for the entire adult population. In that year, 64 percent of adult Americans voted; so if we allow for differential frequency of voting at different income levels, as shown in Table 2.4, we find that the pivotal midgroup may have moved up to the thirty-seventh percentile.

Finally, we recall that in the 1972 presidential election only about 55 percent of adult Americans voted. The midgroup needed to win might have been up at the twenty-eighth percentile, at the edge of the top one-third of income receivers, if the election had been closely contested. In fact, of course, Nixon received 61 percent of the votes cast, corresponding to nearly 34 percent of all adult Americans. But even this landslide majority could have been produced largely within the more affluent half of the American people. From these examples it seems that in practical American politics the "middle" is above the middle: the key group to be convinced, the typical or "middle" voter in the United States, is somewhere between the twenty-fifth and thirtieth income percentiles, with a 1978 income of nearly $18,000 per year. As long as many millions of Americans do not change their political habits, it will be these solid citizens who must be won over by anyone who wishes to win a national election.

Other Forms of Political Participation. Americans are more active in politics than many people think. Only about 22 percent seem to do practically nothing. Another 21 percent are *voting specialists;* they limit their activities to voting. For at least one-half of the American people, however, there are three other major ways in which they participate in politics. They can take part in political campaigns; in the 1967 Verba and Nie survey, 15 percent were classified as being such *campaigners.* Other people form groups that cooperate in regard to some local community problem. These *communalists*—about 20 percent of all respondents—vote and work at community affairs but shun partisan campaigning. People can also initiate direct contacts with public officials at the local or national level in regard to a specific problem or grievance; this seems to require the most effort, and only 4 percent appeared to specialize in actions of this kind. Verba and Nie call them "parochial participants," but *contact specialists* seems a better name for them. While one-fifth of the people engage in none of these forms of participation, about 11 percent all-around *activists* engage strongly in all, except in initiating contacts on specific matters with particular officials.[7] As Table 2.5 shows, these four types of political participation are distinct in practice.

[7]Another 7 percent of the sample could not be classified. The types of participators were computed by scoring each survey respondent on several reported acts for every activity type. Thus, talking to people to influence their vote, attending meetings, giving money, working for a candidate, being a member of a political party, and working actively in it all turn out to be highly correlated

These data already suggest that political participation in the United States is not narrowly concentrated in the hands of a few. Only 53 percent of the American people in the sample were inactive in regard to the six activities studied in the model (though many were politically active in easier ways, such as voting). In practice, in other words, although no one of these six rarer types of political activity was reported by more than one-fifth of the respondents, they were so well dispersed that nearly one-half of the respondents had been engaged in at least one; but they still were so well concentrated that almost 6 percent reported having engaged in more than four of these activities, ten times more than the sixth-tenths of 1 percent who should have done so if the distribution had been random.[8]

Participation in American politics thus shows a good deal of openness but also a considerable amount of structure. Almost any number can play, but if they do, what are their chances of winning?

The Effects of Participation—and Who Benefits from Them. The various modes of political participation have their greatest effect when they are applied in combination. Voting applies pressure to the holders of elective offices and to all those who aspire to leadership in a democracy. But in most instances voting conveys no precise information about which problems and issues are most impor-

with each other, and this is confirmed by factor analysis. They are counted, therefore, as elements of a single overall *compaign activity,* for which a score is computed. These scores are then standardized in order to show the extent to which each respondent is above or below the average of all others in the survey. Finally, each respondent is grouped into a type or "cluster" with all other respondents who are most like him or her in having high or low scores on all four major ways or "modes" of political partcipation. See Verba and Nie, *Participation in America,* pp. 79–81, 127–33, and 350–57 for the survey data on particular activities. The latter seem to tally well with the earlier data reported in Lane, *Political Life,* pp. 45–56.

[8]See data and analysis in Verba and Nie, *Participation in America,* pp. 35–40.

TABLE 2.5 *Participatory Profiles of the American Citizenry*

Groups produced by cluster analysis	Voting	Campaign activity	Communal activity	Particularized contacting	Percentage of sample in type
1. Complete activists	98	93	92	15	11
2. Campaigners	95	70	16	13	15
3. Communalists	92	16	69	12	20
4. Parochial participants	73	13	3	100	4
5. Voting specialists	94	5	3	0	21
6. Inactive	37	9	3	0	22

Source: From data in Verba and Nie, *Participation in America,* p. 79. Italics supplied.

tant to which groups of voters, what their priorities are, and just what each group wants done. High on power, but low on information, voting by itself is a blunt instrument indeed.

It is the other modes of participation that convey more specific information about who wants what. Political activists can influence the nature of candidates nominated, the promises they make and the policies they pursue. This combination of voting power with other forms of political participation in the nomination and campaign processes consistently demonstrates its power, as, for example, in the defeat of leading liberal senators by highly mobilized conservative forces in 1980. Likewise, active groups in a local community can help to translate general policies and budget categories into specific decisions about particular school construction, police and welfare procedures, zoning laws, municipal wages, health and safety standards, interracial employment policies, and much else. And the initiating of particular direct contacts with elected officials and administrative officers at each level of government— national, state, or local—can pinpoint the interest of individual groups in obtaining some specific decision in a particular case. Together, these three modes of participation at their best can convey much of the precise target information about public policy decisions that voting fails to give.

Without the present or potential pressure of voting, however, such information and the mode of participation conveying it would remain powerless. This is, in fact, the case in communities where voting turnout is low or where no effective voting power is available to those concerned. Hearings are useful for letting all interested groups and persons have their say and for making legislators or administrators listen to them for awhile, but mere hearings lack the power to compel responsiveness. That can be done only by the pressure of some negative or positive *sanction:* electoral, administrative, judicial, or financial. Examples of negative sanctions are the flight of industry and high-income families from a city or town where the crime rate or the taxes are too high or where the amenities of life have declined below the level that they find tolerable. Positive sanctions are getting re-elected or gaining increases in the local tax base through the inflow of capital, industry, service establishments, or high-income residents. When information about voter and group interests is working together with some known likelihood of sanctions, the responsiveness of government is likely to be higher—but it will remain unevenly distributed.

How can we measure the responsiveness of political leaders and public officials and agencies? *Responsiveness* in general can be defined for any person, organization, or technical device as its average probability of producing a response of acceptable content and quality within an acceptable time limit in answer to some input or request for service. Thus, a telephone system that gives us a 90 percent chance to reach a called station within one minute is more responsive than one that would take an average of two minutes to do so or would offer us only an 80 percent chance of success. Such a measure also could be developed for public service systems and political administrations. What is the average delay time and likelihood of success for some particular type of request directed to each of them?

This procedure, however, would give us only specific measures for particular organizations and types of service. How could we get a more general indicator of responsiveness that could be applied over a variety of issues or types of service and over a large number of different communities or agencies? Verba and Nie proposed an ingenious answer for their analysis of politics in sixty-four local communities chosen to be representative of American politics in general. They compared the order of priorities in public policy, as expressed by different groups of voters, with the priorities expressed by the political leaders and decision makers in the community. Every instance in which

a leader concurred with the order of priorities expressed by a group of voters was then counted by Verba and Nie as a *concurrence statement* obtained by that group; and they found that the more closely the priorities of the leaders agreed with those of a particular group of citizens, and hence the larger the proportion of concurrence statements, the more responsive were the local leaders to the desires of that group. Thus if a group of poor voters put housing and welfare first on their agenda and the leaders also put these items first, then the leaders were counted as responsive to the demands of that group. But if the leaders had put law and order first, they would have been counted as unresponsive to that group and as more responsive to the views of some other group of voters. Furthermore, at the local level at least, the citizens' activities seem to be much more powerful in influencing the leaders' priorities than the other way around; indeed, the effect of the leaders' activities on citizens' political priorities was so small that it did not rise significantly above the chance level. And once the leaders have accepted the agenda and priorities set by some interest group, the substantive content of the leaders' or officials' decisions is also likely to fit in with the desires of that group. Accordingly, the statistical measure of the extent to which the policy agenda of leaders corresponded to that of some particular group of citizens was regarded by Verba and Nie as a good indicator of what this group would actually get from government in terms of the decisions and services it wanted.[9]

Who Gets the Day-to-Day Rewards? In these terms, who, then, gets what out of the American political process? The first answer is those who put in most by way of participation and who have the resources or allies. A second answer tells us who these people—the most actively participating and most likely to succeed—are: they are the members of the upper income groups.

[9]Verba and Nie, *Participation in America*, pp. 328, 332.

The members of the top one-third of the people by status and income furnish about three-fifths of the activists at the top level of participation; and as Figure 2.3 shows, they get 38 percent of the total of concurrence statements—that is, responsiveness—from community leaders that go to that most active group. The middle-status one-third of citizens furnish about 30 percent of the top activists and get 30 percent of responsiveness; but the bottom one-third by status furnish only 10 percent of the most intensive participation and get about 20 percent of responsiveness. In short, the top one-third of citizens, by status and

income, participate six times as much at the top level of activity as does the bottom one-third, and they get nearly twice as much responsiveness from government.

By contrast, the few lower-status citizens who participate most actively get less concurrence—and presumably less responsiveness—than do less active lower-status citizens.[10]

Other conditions have minor effects. Catholics and older people rank higher on voting, but lower on other modes of political activity. Local participation is higher in relatively isolated or well-bounded communities than in small suburbs, especially those of the "dormitory" type, in which most residents commute to work elsewhere. Some political belief systems increase participation beyond the effects of status and income: strong Republican convictions—that is, conservative beliefs—seem to double steadily the rate of activity; recently, black militancy has had a similar effect, but its long-term steadiness and strength remain to be seen. Despite these modifications, the inequalities of income, education, and status remain the most important influences on the extent of political participation and on the distribution of its rewards. Small numbers of highly active lower-status citizens, about 2 percent of the population, together with a few upper-status converts to their views, may use highly visible and dramatic tactics; but, as Verba and Nie report, "they are counterpoised against the almost glacial pressure of a much larger number of conservative activists. The latter group may not speak as dramatically, but as our data . . . make clear, they speak very effectively."[11]

If this is the case in day-to-day politics at the local level, who holds most power in regard to the larger political decisions in the states and the nation?

FIGURE 2.3 *Who Gets Influence out of Politics: Participation and Concurrence for Three Socioeconomic Groups: Individual-Level Data*

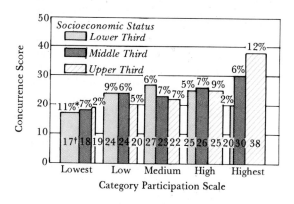

*These percentages are the proportion that the particular group is of the population as a whole.
†The circled figures are the average concurrence scores of that group, indicating roughly the influence it is likely to exercise.

Source: Verba and Nie, *Participation in America*, p. 337.

[10]See Figure 2.3 and Verba and Nie, *Participation in America*, p. 337.
[11]Ibid., p. 339.

LOCATIONS OF POWER OVER LARGER ISSUES

Where does the power lie in the United States? Some people think that it is concentrated in the hands of a small group, perhaps even an anonymous one. Others think that power is widely dispersed among the people or that in a democracy it ought to be. Our concern is with the actual *distribution of power* in the United States, which lies somewhere between. Though this distribution is highly unequal, it is by no means fully concentrated in any one group—and it is subject to continuing change.

In order to study this distribution more closely, one might make a distinction between *general purpose elites* and *special elites*. The former have influence in regard to many matters; the latter have influence in some narrower field.

The Core of the American Establishment. Probably the greatest single concentration of influence and power for general purposes in the United States comprises the credit, banking, and investment communities. Since money is needed for many purposes, those who control its flow will have power in many matters, if they choose to exercise it. The sociologist Robert Lamb proposed that one could find the leading families of any small American town by looking up the names of the board of the local bank twenty-five years earlier. Insofar as these families had not left town, they would be the leading families today.

It is safe to say that the banking-financial community—which is fairly broad, reaching from the small-town banker all the way to the president of the Chase Manhattan Bank—has the greatest amount of influence. Studies of congressional mail show that a letter from a small-town banker weighs more with a representative in Congress than a letter from most other people.

Also at the core of the establishment is the top political leadership of the country. This includes the leaders of both major parties, in or out of office. The political scientist Ralph Huitt recounts

how an ambitious graduate of Yale and the Harvard Business School went to work for the Wall Street firm of Morgan Guaranty Trust. After a time he concluded that the decisions were no longer made by financiers, but by politicians. Accordingly, he moved to the Midwest and in due course became Senator William O. Proxmire of Wisconsin.

The interchange between bankers and the government is extensive. Andrew Mellon as Secretary of the Treasury under Hoover, Douglas Dillon in the Kennedy and Johnson years, and the executives of Dillon, Read and Company and other investment houses in New York as major officers in the Defense and State departments after World War II all reflect the close ties between the investment interests and the federal government. After Carter's election in 1976, however, bankers became rare in the administration, and the press commented on a decline of business confidence.

A second large group influential in government is manufacturing. A list of the ten biggest industrial corporations in the United States ranked in order of their advertising budget was published some years ago. Included in this list were General Motors in first place, Procter and Gamble, and the Ford Motor Company. In the late 1950s and early 1960s, when these firms were among the ten top advertisers in the United States, the American secretaries of defense were Charles Wilson of General Motors, Neal McElroy of Procter and Gamble, and Robert S. McNamara of Ford. More recently, advertising methods played a major part in the presidential campaigns of 1968 and 1972.[12] Ties of this kind were much less prominent in the administration of President Carter, but both his first and second secretaries of the treasury, Michael Blumenthal, founder of the Bendix Corpo-

[12]See, for example, Joe McGinniss, *The Selling of the President* (New York: Simon and Schuster, 1968); and E. R. May and J. Fraser, eds., *Campaign '72: The Managers Speak* (Cambridge: Harvard University Press, 1973).

ration, and William Miller, formerly of Litton Industries, continued the practice on a diminished scale. Since then the power of the oil and energy interest groups in Congress has been growing.

The law firms are another major link in connecting the financial community, the industrial community, and the government. Such firms as Sullivan and Cromwell, in which the late Secretary of State John Foster Dulles was a partner, is a good example. President Nixon's law firm is another; his law partner, John Mitchell, ran his presidential campaign in 1968, became his attorney general, then was active again in President Nixon's 1972 campaign. Such influence, however, has its limits. By early September 1973, Mitchell was out of office, had pleaded guilty to a charge of perjury, and had served some time in a federal prison.

An important development in American law is the rapid growth of law practice in Washington, D.C., and particularly the founding and expansion of Washington branches of law firms based in such cities as New York, Chicago, and Houston. This recent change reflects the increasing importance of the national government in the daily lives of American citizens and corporations, as well as the awareness by clients that federal legislation and bureaucratic regulation are today the major determinants of their well-being. Resort to litigation in the courts remains a key element in American economic life, but increasingly pervasive federal regulation and control have enhanced Washington's status as a center of influence in the high-stakes game of economic activity. Whereas businesses previously were content to allow their regional law firms in New York or Texas to contract with Washington firms specializing in administrative law in order to handle affairs relating to the federal government, these same clients today are urging such regional firms to open their own branches in the capital, staffed by lawyers with expertise in dealing with bureaucratic agencies, regulatory commissions, and Congress.

Since 1942 the military establishment has become a major force in the economic community. A United States senator recently pointed out that two thousand high-ranking former military officers now occupy high-level executive posts in American industry, usually in firms that have had and continue to have contracts with the Defense Department. The late General Douglas MacArthur was board chairman of Remington Rand, and General Omar Bradley was on the board of Bulova Watch Company. The list of eminent military alumni is long. It should be remembered that good generals are competent executives, that business firms are perfectly willing to hire good executives whenever they can get them, and that generals know very well what kind of goods the armed forces are likely to buy.

There has also been an interchange of military and financial decision making. For instance, in World War II an investment banker, Robert Lovett, was undersecretary of defense in charge of bombing strategy. The selection of targets for investment and the selection of targets for strategic bombing are intellectually analogous processes. In each case, one is trying to find key facilities—in one, to buy; in the other, to destroy—but in both the same type of judgment is involved.

Then there are the information and communication services: the advertising and public relations complexes on Madison Avenue and the mass media empires, such as the Henry Luce magazines and the Scripps-Howard and Hearst chains. In recent years the major television and radio networks—NBC, CBS, and ABC—have outgrown the newspaper chains in importance. Still more important are the great news agencies, Associated Press (AP) and United Press International (UPI), which supply news to newspapers and news magazines, as well as to radio and television. Some great newspapers, however, such as the *New York Times* and the *Washington Post,* sometimes can exercise great influence, aided by a powerful tradition of investigative reporting.

Putting these five groups together—banking, large industry, the military complex, law firms, and fringe services such as advertising and mass media—we get the core of *the establishment*. Somewhat more dependent at the fringes are the large foundations and major private and public universities.

Conflicts Within the Establishment. Though the members of the establishment often have been united by interest, lifestyle, intermarriage, and social life, there have been some substantial conflicts among its components. Big-city financial and real estate interests stand to lose from prolonged situations of intense threat of nuclear war, which might induce industries and people to migrate to the hinterland. Consumer industries and department stores stand to lose, rather than gain, from protracted large-scale United States wars in Asia, which divert customers and friends from their sectors. Rentiers and persons on fixed incomes stand to lose from war-induced levels of inflation and taxation. All these are readers of or advertisers in the metropolitan press; and in becoming more critical of the Vietnam War, the major newspapers were also speaking to their concerns. Though most of the press and the electronic media supported President Nixon against his rivals in the presidential campaigns of 1968 and 1972, Nixon continued to believe that the media were against him; and a minority of them did indeed take the lead in drawing attention to difficulties and scandals in his administration, such as the Watergate affair, and persisted in reporting such matters in detail. Public attacks by President Nixon, Vice President Spiro T. Agnew, and other administration spokespeople—speaking for a government with some power over broadcasting licenses, newsprint imports, postal rates, and the like—sometimes tended to depress in the stock market the value of shares of those newspapers and of radio and television networks that had incurred the government's displeasure.

An even broader split in the establishment was indicated in 1973 by the list of "enemies" of the Nixon administration, drawn up in 1972 by President Nixon's White House assistant, John Dean, and revealed in the course of the Watergate investigation by a Senate committee. The list included well-known journalists, writers, scholars, former officials of the Johnson administration, and the presidents of Harvard, Yale, and the Massachusetts Institute of Technology. A memorandum accompanying the list suggested that these persons could be punished informally through extensive examination of their income tax returns, through changes in "grant availability" to themselves and to their institutions, and in other ways. Much of this plan remained a paper project, but some persons listed were in fact subjected to harassing income tax audits and had to establish their innocence at considerable cost in time and legal assistance. Whether such divisions within the establishment—and particularly between its older East Coast-oriented elements and the more recent oil and defense interests of such states as Texas, Florida, Arizona, and California—will prove to be a passing episode or whether they indicate a deeper and more lasting split remains to be seen. Yet, united or divided by conflict, the five major establishment groups—banking, big industry, the defense complex, top law firms, and advertising and mass media—carry more general influence than any other group.

The Power of Special Interests. The establishment interests must be distinguished from special interests; the five groups named above are so diversified that they are interested in many things, not only a few. General Motors and Du Pont are involved in dozens of products in dozens of lines. Rarely will they exert all-out pressure on one particular law because their interests are so diversified. One division of General Motors or of Du Pont may want a protective tariff for its specialty, but another division, making a product for export, may want free trade.

Special interests have much clearer configurations. First, there are the aircraft and electronics industries. The military effectiveness of strategic bombing was discredited after World War II by the strategic bombing survey, after the Korean War by the failure of the air force to stop the flow of ammunitions to the Korean front, and again in Vietnam. But the belief in air power does not stop, since the aircraft industry continues to sustain it. Just as smoking does not disappear with a report from the surgeon general, but is more related to the persistence of popular habits and to the advertising budget of the tobacco industry, so the belief in air power is related in part to the persistence of military traditions and popular habits of thought, as well as to the public relations budgets, organized *lobbies,* and *lobbyists* of the aircraft and electronics industries. Their large social and economic interests will continue to have an input into the political and communication systems of the United States.

The oil companies form another obvious major interest group. The old oil interests of Standard Oil have now merged with the general financial community, through such institutions as the Rockefeller interests and the Chase Manhattan Bank. More recent, special oil interests, such as those formed by some Texas oil drillers, are on the fringes. They are more inclined to express their grievances against the eastern establishment through support of raucous, superpatriotic groups and to suspect all of Wall Street as "unpatriotic."

The mineral interests in the southeastern states and the copper and tin interests in overseas operations are also special interest groups, having strong views on Latin American affairs. Cotton, tobacco, and sugar interests are located mainly in the southern states. Large-scale farming is more prominent in the Midwest and in California. Control of the import of bananas from Central America and of sugar from the Caribbean, together with the plantations producing these commodities, long has been concentrated in Boston and New York. There are declining interest groups, such as the railroads, and rising interest groups, such as road building, heavy construction, and urban redevelopment—all of which have very close ties to local political parties and to state and local governments. Building and road contractors are usually involved in politics. The electronics industry is growing, and so is the research industry; they have many common ties and form a rising interest group.

Labor unions also form a powerful complex of interest groups. On some issues they are united. Unions of all types tend to support a federal minimum wage and higher wages in general. On other issues, such as the maintenance of a restrictive apprentice system that can almost close a trade to newcomers and thus tends to work to the disadvantage of black people and other minorities, only some highly skilled craft unions will commit their efforts. In contrast, proposed laws against race discrimination are more likely to be supported by industrial unions, comprising both skilled and unskilled workers, such as the United Automobile Workers of America.

Special interest groups tend to use their power only in regard to matters of specific concern to them. On these matters they may form shifting coalitions; and for their particular objectives they usually get fairly good service from the political system.

Interest groups are highly unequal in their ability to mobilize their members for political action, to arouse larger constituencies to their support, and to coordinate their activities in an effective manner. Some interest groups have strong permanent organizations with professional staffs; quick access to relevant information; large financial resources; well-defined channels of communication to their membership; well-established habits of political participation, activity, and discipline; and a tradition of rapid, large-scale, and coordinated action. Intensity of need or size of reward is thus only one, and not always the decisive, factor in the power of an interest group. Often its capabilities to organize and act will count for more.

Usually, members of the middle and upper strata of society have greater capabilities along these lines. They have more time and money, better education and information, greater skills of communication and organization, and stronger self-confidence and expectations of success. Often they do not choose to invest these capabilities in political action, since they often are not too dissatisfied with their lot and since most of them usually have more rewarding uses for their time; but when their fears are aroused or some major interest of theirs is touched, their political power can be formidable. Their old interest organizations will gain new strength from their increased support, and new committees and organizations may spring up spontaneously to supplement or surpass these.

Poorer people, by contrast, may have intense needs and potential interests, but they are often less aware of them, less united, less active, and less organized, and they generally have lower capabilities for long-sustained effective action. Hence, the poorer groups most often lose out in the competition among a plurality of interest groups; and those better-organized interests who have greater capacities for taking an effective part in the pluralistic contest will get and keep more of its spoils. Here, too, as an old saying puts it, "To those that have is given."

There is, however, one large exception. The capabilities of interest groups are not unchangeable. The unaware can gain awareness, the inexperienced and unskilled can learn to become steadfast, and the weak can become strong. When these things happen to a group, its position in politics changes. When they happen to several groups that comprise large numbers of people, they will change the distribution of political influence and power. And if these changes are large enough, they may change the operation—and even the structure—of the political system. This large-scale mobilization of once-passive groups is what is meant by the term *macropolitical intervention*. The rise of the consumer, environmental, and women's movements in the 1970s are good examples. Before that, the civil rights movement vividly demonstrated how a once-forgotten group, by becoming conscious of its interests, can change the distribution of power.

Such changes often take time, but sometimes new coalitions form quickly, cutting across classes and strata. Property taxes, assessed on all or part of the market value of real estate, long had been the mainstay of local finances, paying for schools and a growing array of municipal services. By 1978, however, rising land prices and municipal budgets were pushing up these taxes, threatening to drive many older or poorer people out of their homes, for their incomes were rising at a much slower rate or even not at all. Together with wealthier voters who always had disliked paying high taxes on their larger houses, many of these distressed voters joined in a *"tax revolt"* that swept much of the United States during that year. In California, Proposition 13 was passed by referendum, putting a legal limit on the level of local property taxation. Similar referenda passed elsewhere, and still further measures of this kind were introduced for future action. It seemed that state and local services would have to be cut back or else municipal finances would have to be based less on property taxes and more on a combination of other sources, including new service charges for garbage removal and other municipal services, sales taxes, and state income taxes, in order not to hurt any large group of voters quite so badly. The tax revolt of 1978 contributed to an ongoing, general mood of budget cutting and economy at all levels of government. Beyond this, it offered another example of macropolitical intervention, checking and sometimes changing the normal power of the "establishment" composed of the usually active and influential groups. The problem, of course, is one of sustaining this kind of power. Studies two years after the passage of Proposition 13 showed the major beneficiaries had been not small homeowners but big businesses, and in 1980 California voters decisively rejected another tax-cut proposition sought by the founders of the tax revolt movement.

Social Strata and Their Power. Below the interest groups are the social strata. The middle class, or what can be called the middle class in the United States, has been steadily growing. Today the

United States probably has the broadest middle class in the world. Depending on how one defines it (and whether one includes what is called the *lower* middle class, to which nobody wants to belong, but which always turns up in the statistics), the American middle class goes down from the ninety-fifth to at least the sixtieth percentile of income and possibly to the fortieth percentile. This group overlaps in part with the clerical and service occupations, the white-collar occupations that also have grown. Most mass media cater to the tastes and views of the middle class, and so does much of the advertising they carry. Politicians bow to middle-class mores and values; those who do not rarely are elected to national office. Almost the only ones who sometimes purposely offend it are its children—but often with the opposite political results from those intended.

Though the middle class is generally respected in matters of form, it may fail to get its way on some large matters of substance, such as ending an unpopular war or keeping America's central cities habitable. Nevertheless, although most of the political coalitions among interest groups change from issue to issue, they remain within a general middle-class setting. Civil rights legislation in the 1960s was put through by a coalition of liberals, conservatives, labor groups, businesspeople, intellectuals, and others who felt an injustice was being done. Last, but not least, was the pressure of the black Americans themselves. This pressure, too, was motivated in no small part by the desire of blacks to win access to middle-class living standards on equal terms.

Labor as a social stratum is less powerful. As a rule, it can prevail politically only in coalition with other groups. Production-line labor has not grown for twenty-five years. The skilled workers, insofar as they are union members, are now in the middle third of the income distribution in the United States. Unskilled and nonunion labor are well below this level. Farmers have been reduced to 5 percent of the work force; less than 2 percent produce major surpluses of food; the remaining 3

percent are subsistence farmers. Then come the forgotten Americans, the 20 percent who are poor and the 10 percent who are very poor.

This inequality in income, status, and power is greater in the United States than in any other highly advanced industrial country. Some of the poor are urban blacks, but at present at least half and possibly more than half of the very poor are not black. There is poverty in Appalachia, and there is poverty in the neighborhoods of Chicago as well. A second group is less poor, but still forgotten: the hard-working whites at the fringe of poverty and at the edge of respectability. These are tense and worried people who resent the increase in attention given to the poor. A third forgotten group is the mobile disfranchised. These are the professional people, the students, and in part the young—all those who for one reason or another do not make it into the ranks of stable, organized interest groups and registered voters. They number many millions. Together, these three groups get far less political influence and consideration than their needs and their numbers should entitle them to.

This unequal distribution of power—from the core establishment to the most disadvantaged—will not change quickly, but it *is* changing, and larger changes are on their way. Later in this chapter we shall ask whether these changes can add up in time to a transformation of the American political system. First, however, we must look at some other aspects of that system, beginning with one that in the past has been a force for both stability and change: the major images of the American political community that have developed in this country.

SOME IMAGES OF THE AMERICAN POLITICAL COMMUNITY

"Who is this new man, the American?" asked an eighteenth-century Frenchman, J. Hector St. John (Jean de Crèvecoeur), who had been farming in America at the time of the American Revolution.

His question has not been fully answered to this day. Many Americans agree that they somehow belong together and that they have some important things in common. They often find it harder to agree on what these things are and what their felt *community* consists in.

It is not blood and descent. No nation on earth has had a wider variety of ancestors. It is not the land as such. There is little in common between the geographies of Maine and Hawaii, Iowa and Florida, Nevada and Maryland, or Texas and Vermont. It is not even will. The nineteenth-century southerners who wanted to secede from the United States in the Civil War were still Americans, whatever they might have become if they had succeeded. Perhaps, more than anything else, it is the common culture and communication habits of the people, the ability of each to foretell much of what his or her compatriots will do, and their knack of joining quickly into teams or crews that can cooperate effectively at any time or place, on wagon trains or airlines, whaling ships or spaceships.

Political Culture: Standardization, Novelty, and Pragmatism.

Americans are a people of survivors from the frustrations and shipwrecks of the Old World, from which their ancestors came. Ours is a *culture* of simplification, like the household goods of people who had to move on often by sea or land and who could take only the essentials with them, sifting and repacking them often. But it is also a culture of practical boldness and innovation; its simplified components have been made more uniform, but also more suitable to being disassembled and put together again, probably in new configurations. It is a culture of ever-present tension and potential conflict between conservative standardization and combinational novelty and change; and the contest between these two cannot be won by either, since each depends on the other for effectiveness.

A third element in the culture is its stress on performance, on efficiency, and on practicality. "American gadgets have one peculiarity," a Euro-

pean writer once observed; "they work." So did the floating American harbors brought to the coast of Normandy in World War II, and later the American vaccines against polio, and the American landing vehicle on the surface of the moon. The early American settlers had to be practical in order to survive on their new continent, and those who came in later generations had to be practical in order to survive among the descendants of the earlier settlers. Out of this necessity came *pragmatism*—at the popular level, roughly the notion that "true is what works"—and a readiness to accept whatever seemed to be the realities of the American environment.[13] This practicality, however, is often culture-bound, and it causes difficulties in foreseeing the long-run consequences of actions. Popular pragmatic attitudes also often include a propensity to ignore or override the realities of foreign countries or of minorities in the United States if they do not seem to fit the general pattern.

Some Basic Value Orientations: Mastery, Equality, and Performance.

There are other themes that hold American culture together. Americans expect to master their environment, natural or political; failing that mastery, they tend to ignore it or to withdraw from it. They will refuse to submit to it or even to work *with* it on a basis of genuine understanding and mutual give-and-take. Many of us are descendants of people who were so impatient with the frustrations of the Old World that they left it and moved to the New. Later Americans would leave the stony acres of New England for the fertile plains of Iowa and Kansas and the sunnier sky of California. When topsoil and timber were exhausted, when lakes or rivers became polluted—a condition that was rare in the early years when there was much clean water and few people—it was often possible to move on or to tap

---

[13]For the far more subtle and flexible views of the original American pragmatic philosophers, see John E. Smith, *The Spirit of American Philosophy* (New York: Oxford University Press, 1963); and for some legal and political applications, see Max Lerner, ed., *The Mind and Faith of Justice Holmes* (New York: Halcyon House, 1948).

a new source of supply. But now, with about 225 million Americans and an economy using vast amounts of water and other natural resources, American practicality will increasingly demand a more responsible treatment of the ecology and the environment, even against the opposition of some short-range interest groups.[14]

Similar problems arise in politics proper. Many Americans leave the centers of their big cities when too many black or poor people arrive, and they prefer to ignore in the temporary safety of the more affluent suburbs the mounting problems of their central cities. And in international politics we tend as a nation to reduce our interest and participation in the United Nations if the other 150 countries will not see things our way. (But what place could we use as a suburb of retreat from the problems of this planet? Does this desire to move away from unmasterable problems underlie some of our fascination with space and science fiction?)

One major theme in American culture suggests that the alien environment is to be mastered rather than listened to; another theme insists that people, if they are at all real to us, must be treated as equals. When this theme predominates, American human relations are *collateral,* like those among peers or brothers and sisters, and not *lineal,* like those between superior and subordinate, officer and soldier, or father and son in a patriarchal (that is, father-dominated) family. But though the theme of equality is a general demand of American culture and most Americans feel uncomfortable if they must act contrary to it, some major institutions in the United States require them to do just that. Not only the armed forces, now much

[14]*Ecology* refers to the mutually supporting and/or balancing network of physical processes and life forms in an area, such as water, wind, moss, grass, trees, fish, insects, birds, animals, and often also human beings. In a broader sense, ecology then refers to the knowledge or study of such interdependent life systems, often linked to a concern for their conservation.

larger than they were before World War II, but also the civil service and most of the middle-sized and large business organizations are *command systems,* in which orders flow down and mainly reports of obedience are expected to move up. The promise, often implied in American culture, that anyone can work to the top, does not work often enough or fast enough in practice to overcome this command character. Many educational institutions also resemble command systems: school boards and superintendents give orders to grade school and high school principals, principals give orders to teachers, and teachers give orders to students. Even at some colleges and universities, the high school pattern is repeated; and even when there is no intent to have this happen, the necessary difference between the level of knowledge of the faculty and the relative ignorance of the students puts special difficulties in the way of creating and maintaining a more collateral educational relationship.

There is some built-in conflict and tension between the themes of equality, or collaterality, on the one hand, and of efficiency and performance on the other. Often competitive and supposedly equal opportunity is expected to resolve the conflict. "Never mind his color—can he pitch?" asked a small white boy on a World War II poster about a black youngster at the forming of a sandlot baseball team. It was the same question, in essence, that was asked by the whalers in Herman Melville's novel *Moby Dick* when the copper-colored and richly tattooed Maori Queequeg was hired as a harpooner. But in present-day politics, economics, and social relations, competition and opportunities are still in significant part unequal and limited. This is a growing problem in American life, as a larger proportion of young people reach out for higher education and for freer and more meaningful jobs and career chances thereafter; and it seems likely to play a larger part in the politics of the 1980s.

Doing and the Future. The themes of performance and achievement in American culture are also linked to the theme of action, of *doing,* in contrast to mere *being,* or *being-in-becoming,* which is an anthropologist's term, roughly, for development. Americans usually esteem other people and themselves according to what they do, or have done just recently, or are likely to do in the near future. They might well agree with Goethe's *Faust:* "In the beginning was the Deed." Doing, for most Americans, is a value in itself.

Past deeds and achievements count for little, however, if those who accomplished them do not seem likely to do as well or better in the future. "What have you done for me lately?" is the proverbial answer to an American politician's appeal for gratitude; and to call a person a has-been in politics is to dismiss him or her from serious consideration.

At this point, the American orientations toward *action* and toward the *future* meet. "I do not know who my grandfather was," Abraham Lincoln is supposed to have said; "I am much more concerned to know what his grandson will be." On the stock exchange, in publishers' contracts, in university appointments, almost everywhere are present decisions guided by expectations of future performance. In contrast, protecting the works of the past—such as landmarks of earlier styles of architecture in American cities—is perennially difficult and requires much effort.

Human Nature: Good and Partly Manageable. A final theme in American culture—and one that apparently every culture must define for itself—concerns the view of human nature. Are human beings predominantly good, bad, or mixed? And is human nature basically capable of improvement, or is it fundamentally unalterable? The mainstream of American culture treats human beings as basically good and as capable of further improvement. A conservative minority view asserts that "human nature can't be changed." Here again is a tension between two partly conflicting assumptions. Belief in the goodness of people leads to the corollary that they should not be too closely controlled and directed by government. At the same time, belief that people can be improved has

often been interpreted to mean that they can be changed in quite specific ways, in a very short time and without fundamental disturbance, if only the government or some other controlling agency will push them hard enough and skillfully enough. This view leads to a belief in manipulating people to make them do what we want them to, because we think it moral, or advantageous to ourselves, or both. In their time, American public and private agencies have tried through intensive programs to Americanize European immigrants; alter the sex-and-family behavior of Asian peasant populations; improve the future school performance of black preschool children; teach college students and others how to read and comprehend a thousand words per minute; abolish poverty; end race discrimination; wipe out alcoholism, prostitution, and drug abuse; train corporation executives to greater sensitivity; and free people from loneliness—in short, to channel human behavior into directions that these agencies held to be desirable, usually with good reason.

The methods used often showed a common pattern. A mechanical or chemical device or a special psychological or social procedure was applied to a narrow aspect of the life of the target population or group, in order to change that particular aspect, but otherwise to leave essentially undisturbed their personalities, lifestyles, culture, housing, and other social and economic circumstances.

Sometimes these methods were successful. But more often, success proved transitory or did not materialize at all, particularly when the behavior to be changed was embedded in a larger structure of interlocking, mutually reinforcing, and self-restoring conditions. Thus, unemployed adults or adolescents from broken families, when moved from slums into public housing, often stayed unemployed; their home environment stayed damaged; and the concentration of similarly disadvantaged neighbors in the same low-income housing projects often created an even greater resentment and despair than had prevailed in the slums from which they had been moved. To gain and consolidate major improvements would have required a sustained attack on a whole cluster of conditions, but such an attack would have required more resources, more personnel, more help toward self-rule and self-development, and last, but not least, more political support and power than usually were available. Yet, though the widespread American confidence in simple, quick solutions often led to conflicts and disappointments, perhaps at least it kept alive the efforts at improvement until better methods, larger resources, and broader and more steadfast political support could be mobilized. Perhaps even the failed attempts made it less likely that the bad conditions would be accepted indefinitely under the cloak of a philosophy of resignation.

Conflict and Unity Among American Values: A Sense of Direction? In each of the major orientations and themes of American political culture we have found not only much that is admirable, but also profound inner tensions and contradictions, many of which are likely to persist for a long time and to generate recurrent conflicts. But they also keep the political culture of the United States alive, changing, and developing. Together with the effects of mobility, transport, communication, and continuing economic prosperity—of relative plenty for most Americans, compared to most other peoples in the world—the common culture orientations and themes have kept the American political community together. Any political creed or idea that could win a substantial following in the United States would have to stay somewhere within these basic orientations of American political culture.

This need to stay within the mainstream of its political culture is probably essential to the identity and unity of the American people. The French, English, and Germans have remained distinctive peoples under a wide variety of political regimes. Americans, except for a scant dozen years before 1776, have lived under the same set of basic political principles and orientations ever since they emerged as a distinctive people. If these principles

were abandoned or destroyed—if, as we might imagine, the "self-evident" truths of the Declaration of Independence and the principles of the Bill of Rights should ever be explicitly rejected, perhaps under some fascist or authoritarian regime—then the American people as we now know them might well disintegrate. In abandoning their own basic political principles and value orientations, the American people might have more to lose, therefore, than other nations. Even if we should not perish in a nuclear war that a genuinely fascist regime would be likely to bring about, we should still be apt to lose our cohesion and existence as a nation.

Luckily, such dangers do not seem close at hand. What is more likely to happen, and has happened often in the past, is that we should retain the American principles and value orientations, but visibly fail to live up to them. In that case, however, our political culture and its aspirations would continue to live in our memories, and they would be apt to become salient time and again in periods of crisis and decision.

More than a hundred years ago, Senator Stephen Douglas taunted his opponent in debate, Congressman Abraham Lincoln, by saying that a statement in the Declaration of Independence, "all men are created equal," was not a self-evident truth, as the Declaration had asserted, but by now (1858) was a "self-evident lie," since slavery had been and was being practiced in the United States. Lincoln answered that the Declaration did not describe past or current practice, but stated the direction in which the American people wanted to go; and he suggested that that direction would prevail. He was right; slavery was abolished five years later, in 1863. Aided by an array of cumulative changes in the political, social, and economic fabric of the American people, the basic ideas of its political culture triumphed eventually over the practices that had so long denied them.

Much later, in the 1930s, the Swedish social scientist *Gunnar Myrdal* made a similar prediction about the future of racial discrimination in the

United States, which then was far more pervasive and brutal than today and seemed solidly entrenched. The main thrust of American ideals and values was against racial discrimination, he suggested, and together with the large ongoing social changes in the lives of black and white Americans, they would eventually defeat racial oppression and its defenders. He may well have been right, for the following decades brought a succession of legal, administrative, and judicial changes in racial politics and practices and, not least among them, a broader political awakening of black Americans and a change in attitudes among many of the young of all races. But these struggles and changes still are going on; and all of us in the United States are still writing by our actions and behavior the current chapter of the story related to Gunnar Myrdal's prediction.

SOME PATTERNS OF RESPONSE

In response to the tensions and conflicts in American political culture and to the different experiences and interests of various groups, at least four major types of political outlook have emerged. They can be found in every region of the country, in almost any town, large place of employment, university, or other large community, albeit in different proportions. Which configuration each individual will pick deliberately—or grow into without noticing, or conform to in deference to friends, family, and neighbors—will depend not only on that person's social and economic circumstances, experiences, and interests, but also on his or her family and personal associates, and not least on his or her own personality. We can predict reasonably well, therefore, which views will be more widespread among which social groups and classes. But we shall do much less well in predicting which smaller groups will hold what images of politics, and we can predict very little about which particular individuals will end up holding what

beliefs. Moreover, each of these outlooks has been presented by major philosophic spokespeople in highly differentiated and subtle terms, although the bulk of its present-day adherents are likely to hold their particular view of politics in a much simplified form. It is with these popular political outlooks that we shall be concerned here.

American Liberalism. The first popular image of American politics is a kind of traditional *liberalism* that goes back in its roots to the Declaration of Independence, the Bill of Rights, and the works and presidency of Thomas Jefferson. It continues in the writings of Ralph Waldo Emerson, later in the abolitionists and Abraham Lincoln, and then in the philosopher William James, Justice Oliver Wendell Holmes, Franklin D. Roosevelt and Wendell Willkie, in such poets as Carl Sandburg and Archibald MacLeish, and in the liberal Democratic and Republican spokespeople of our time. In this view, America is mainly a country of self-employed small businesspeople, farmers, lawyers, physicians, and other professional people; and those Americans who are employed by others and work for wages or salaries ought to model themselves on the self-employed group.

Opinions, works of art, forms of entertainment, and people should be—like commodities—free to compete in the marketplace. Education should offer students choices and aid their self-development. Economic competition is to be encouraged; public utilities should be supervised and regulated to prevent any misuse of "national" monopolies; and antitrust laws should be enforced, or one should threaten to enforce them, in order to curb the formation of new monopolies and limit all restrictive arrangements "in restraint of trade."

Legal race discrimination must be abolished, but the private preferences of people in their personal and social arrangements should be left undisturbed as much as possible. Unions have their place in helping those wage earners who join them freely; they should not acquire too much power, but their internal arrangements and membership policies should not be disturbed by any uprisings of a majority of the current members. Welfare legislation and institutions should help the needy who cannot provide for their own needs, and experts should tell the clients of these welfare institutions what to do in order to become self-supporting. Taxes should be kept low, but may be raised if essential welfare needs or national security demands it. Simultaneously, government spending should be closely watched for any signs of graft, inefficiency, or waste.

Above all, the American political system is rational, despite some local or temporary distortions; and most voters are rational, too. They know their true interests, and in the long run they will vote accordingly. They will support reasonable new experiments, but they will want their leaders to be practical, not doctrinaire. One must have patience. Perfection can never be expected. Politics is the art of the possible, and in the long run it will produce a reasonable approximation to the good.

American liberals believe in human dignity and equality, as well as in mobility, initiative, and self-control as means to master nature and one's own fate. They put human rights above property rights, but see the two as normally compatible. They trust human nature as good and have faith in our ability to build a better future, but in any case they see the meaning of life in doing the best one can here and now. If years of efforts should dim their confidence, the best among them still may say what William the Silent said centuries ago in the long Dutch War of Independence: "It is not necessary to hope in order to persevere."

The American Conservative Tradition. *Conservatism* in the United States goes almost as far back as liberalism does: to Jefferson's great contemporary, Alexander Hamilton. If the spirit of the Declaration of Independence of 1776 was primarily liberal, parts of the federal Constitution, drafted in 1787 and ratified in 1791 (albeit together with the liberal Bill of Rights), express a more conservative mood. Later notable conservative thinkers and writers include, between 1830 and 1860, John C. Calhoun and George Fitzhugh in the South; around 1900, the sociologist William Graham Sumner; at mid-century, Senator Robert Taft; in the 1960s, Senator Barry M. Goldwater and the writer William F. Buckley, Jr.; and in the 1970s, Ronald Reagan, while he was governor of California and campaigning for the presidency.

American conservatives used to be more inclined toward abstract principles than their British counterparts. Only in the early 1970s did some of President Nixon's advisers publicly recall the very flexible methods of Britain's nineteenth-century Conservative prime minister, Benjamin Disraeli, and did President Nixon himself show a comparable tactical flexibility in changing his own earlier positions. Thus he moved to improve relations with China and the Soviet Union, effectively devalued the dollar twice by an aggregate of about 20 percent in foreign trade and international finance; instituted temporary wage and price controls in the domestic economy; suspended military conscription; and withdrew most American ground troops from South Vietnam. Despite these striking changes in tactics and methods, however, President Nixon gave no indication that he had changed in any way his commitment to the general principles of American conservatism in economic life. Many of these policies and principles were then continued in 1975–76 by President Ford, to some extent, in 1977–79 by the administration of President Carter, and in much stronger terms by President Reagan.

What are these principles? The first principle deals with the relation of politics to economics. Government should not interfere with the activities of individuals and the rights of property, particularly the latter. In most conflicts between government and some existing business interest, American conservatives tend to oppose the government—the tax authorities, the regulatory agencies, and the like—and to side with the individual or corporation, if these represent interests of substance. However, in many conflicts between some individual and the police, American conservatives are inclined to side with the police, particularly if the individual happens to be non-white, poor, or young. And whenever government activities and power are likely to benefit property interests, conservatives, from Alexander Hamilton onward, have tended to favor them.

American conservative thought is often relatively theoretical and explicit. It tends to accept Locke's view of property as an inalienable natural right of individuals; and it extends this notion of natural rights to large private business corporations, which other schools of thought might view as highly artificial organizations, created by the laws under which they are chartered. American conservatives also often share Adam Smith's trust in the benefits of economic laissez faire and Herbert Spencer's belief in the "survival of the fittest" in society and nature. Sometimes this latter theme is developed along the lines of social Darwinism; that is, human nature is seen as fundamentally bad, or at least aggressive, and a highly simplified image of the process of natural selection in the jungle is turned into an image of human relations in society. The members of the richer and more powerful social strata and classes, together with their families, are then said to be biologically superior and likely to transmit their superior genetic traits by heredity to their off-spring. By the same logic, the weak and poor are seen as inferior; the ethic of the New Testament (and of many religions other than Christianity), which commands that they should be loved, helped, and respected, is often suspected as bad biology and unsound economics. Once this view is accepted, it seems unreasonable to give voting rights and civil liberties to the socially and biologically inferior majority, instead of keeping them firmly under the rule of "the rich, the well-born, and the wise." Accordingly, many conservatives have traditionally viewed democracy with a good deal of suspicion; and some of them have continued to insist that the United States ought to be called not a "democracy"—which it should not be—but a "republic," in which unequal political rights should be preserved in perpetuity.

The basic appeal of conservatism, in America as elsewhere, goes deeper than mere attachment to habits, family, social position, and possessions. While all these play an important part as sources of reinforcement and support, conservatism at bottom is also a strategy for defending one's identity and self-respect. To be proud of what one is and has can be a source of emotional security. To hope that family, position, property, and reputation will survive beyond one's own life is a way of seeking reassurance against death—even though some major religions have been skeptical about it. And if some form of traditional religious assurance and credible ritual can be added to the conservative system of beliefs, the combination may be powerful indeed.

In foreign relations, conservatives usually stress power politics, ideological anticommunism, the pursuit of national security through large armaments, and the vigorous defense of the property rights and creditor interests of American corporations in foreign countries.

At the same time, the American conservative tradition has its generous and imaginative aspects. Herbert Hoover in the late 1920s was the first American president to speak of the abolition of poverty within the United States as a national goal. Under Hoover's administration, too, Secretary of State Frank B. Kellogg negotiated the Kellogg-Briand Pact of 1927, which formally renounced war as an instrument of policy—a principle that many nations, including our own, still have to live up to in their actions. Senator Robert Taft was a champion of public housing; and the principle of a guaranteed minimum income for every American family was first proposed officially under President Nixon's administration. In international affairs many conservatives supported American economic aid to war-devastated Europe under the Marshall Plan and later, within more stringent limits, some economic aid to developing countries. Many conservatives also have supported or accepted United States membership in the United Nations, and some have favored a federal world government (though often on the assumption that such a world authority would be primarily influenced by the United States and would limit itself mainly to the protection of law, order, and property along conservative lines).

Despite many differences there usually has been enough overlap between conservative and liberal values and interests in American politics to preserve a dialogue between the two traditions in the realm of ideas and values and to permit agreement on the forming of coalitions and support for specific common policies, regardless of the philosophic cleavage between the two systems of belief. The result has been an intermittent and limited consensus between conservatives and liberals that often has provoked radicals to bitter criticisms against both.

The Classic Radical Tradition. Like the preceding two traditions, American *radicalism* is as old as the United States. It is a tradition that has included such early patriots as Samuel Adams, Patrick Henry, and Tom Paine; the abolitionists and the radical Republicans before and during the Civil War, such as John Brown and Thaddeus Stevens; some populists and muckrakers of the 1890s and 1900s, as different from each other as William Jennings Bryan, Lincoln Steffens, and Upton Sinclair; the Socialists such as Eugene V. Debs and Norman Thomas; the leaders of the farmer and labor movements of the 1920s and 1930s, such as father and son La Follette in Wisconsin, and later Henry Wallace and Wayne Morse; and in the 1960s such writers as Michael Harrington and religious spokespeople such as the brothers Daniel and Philip Berrigan. For a time in the mid-1930s the small number of American Communists seemed part of this varied and contradictory current of opinion, but their attempts to direct and control it, their rigid defense of Joseph Stalin, and their complete commitment to the changing foreign policies of the Soviet Union eventually made them unpopular even in radical circles. Most of the individuals of radical temper who had joined them in the 1930s sooner or later left the Commu-

nist Party, some because of the hostile pressure of public opinion, congressional and other investigatory committees, employers, and the like, but perhaps more often because of genuine disappointment with a party and an ideology that seemed so manifestly ill fitted to the moral and political concerns of most Americans. The trials of the dissidents in the Soviet Union during 1978, essentially for what Americans in the United States would have considered as expressions of political opinion, once more highlighted the contrast between the political values of the two countries.

Radicalism in the classic and American patterns stresses the work ethic, performance, competence, and practical results. But it also insists on the rights and dignity of all working people, not only of an elite of competence or merit. Radicals often favor far-reaching social and political changes, including changes in economic structure and property relations. They distrust people in positions of power and prestige. They attack oppression, fraud, hypocrisy; they are quick to raise such accusations, even on incomplete evidence. Even then the classic radicals are sincere, not cynical; most of them would reject the use of deliberate political deception. They tend to be puritans and to take themselves rather seriously. When they resort to laughter, it is apt to be closer to satire than to clowning. Most of them have rejected drunkenness, drugs, and sexual promiscuity. They live for the future; they work to do good as they see it and to change the world. In the experience of solidarity with the men and women of their time, in taking part in the transformation of the world, and in making their own lives a part of the emerging future, radicals, too, can feel that death cannot really touch them because it cannot stop this larger movement of humanity or the movement—as many radicals believe or feel—of the entire universe of which humankind is just one part.

All three classic American traditions, then—liberalism, conservatism, and radicalism—offer not only an image of politics, but also an implicit philosophy of life, hidden but discoverable. What new elements, if any, have the "new politics" and the counterculture of the late 1960s and 1970s brought into the contest among these American images of politics and human nature?

A New Kind of Radicalism. During the 1960s a new pattern of political and social beliefs and values seemed to be emerging among some groups in the United States, and similar views found adherents in several other highly developed countries. Most of the ideas involved had been put forward earlier, most often by older people, but by the late 1960s they had found their strongest echo among the young, particularly the fifteen- to twenty-four-year-olds. The new attitudes went by many names, ranging in the late 1960s and 1970s from *"the new politics"* and "the new left" to *"the counterculture"* and, less formally, to *"being with it"* or "tuning in, turning on, and dropping out," but in any case to "doing one's own thing." Doubtless the slogans and the names would change, but the underlying moods and images might last a good deal longer. What are some of these feelings and images?

Perhaps most visible is the longing for sincerity and authenticity, for the undistorted expression of one's needs and feelings, for the freedom to express one's impulses as spontaneously and directly as possible. Most young people have to inhibit their impulses, from their childhood onward, in homes, schools, universities, offices, and factories and in the society dominated by their elders. This society, as the new radicalism sees it, is both manipulative and repressive. It prescribes and forbids endlessly what people may or may not do. Its pervasive commands and prohibitions thwart and frustrate everything—sex, love, music, art, one's very speech, body, dress, and hair style, the arrangement of one's room, one's time, one's plans, and one's desires. Why not use any "unprintable" word whenever and wherever one feels an impulse to do so? Moreover, what this repression cannot command it tries to govern through manipulation and suggestion, which come from everywhere—from parents, teachers, advertisements, and television sets. For the new radicals this whole system of repression and manipulation is the main enemy; it must be resisted and dismantled whenever possible.

To get rid of manipulation, this same ideology suggests, one must get rid of the notion of linking differences in rewards to differences in effort, competence, and performance; one should break or weaken the links between achievement and rewards. The pursuit of achievement leads to inequality, to elitism, to envy and unhappiness. Those who reject achievement can be equal, fraternal, and serene. Not only the achievement of money, careers, or academic grades should be rejected. Even the achievement of beauty is sometimes suspect. "We cannot all be beautiful," said a student in all seriousness, "but we can all be ugly."

People should be rewarded, not for what they do, but for being what they are—human. In the language of some social scientists, achievement is replaced here by ascription; specific rewards, by diffuse good will; and preferences for particular nations, races, or classes, by universal solidarity.

People should not only avoid competing for rewards, but they should not even strive for them. To disdain consumer goods, money, and economic security will make one happier through living simply, close to nature, and devoting oneself to human relations, art, and contemplation. If work must be done to earn one's sustenance, let it be simple work, such as carpentry, in preference to a career in science, business, medicine, or law; in the 1970s one could find quite a few former brilliant undergraduates who were trying to live in accordance with this prescription.

This new lifestyle can become practical for all, many of the new radicals believe, because we are now living in a "postindustrial" age, in which the production of wealth is no longer important for society. The machines are already now producing most of this wealth automatically. Hence, production is no longer a major task or problem; only distribution and enjoyment are.

In addition, this belief system has room for exploration and experiment, provided that these are not conducted in a too controlled, precise, and "uptight" manner. People should strive less to add to the stock of accurate and verified knowledge (which is already vast and unimportant) and rather seek more vivid and intense ways of enjoyment and experience, without any confining commitments for the future. In this lifestyle, people do not study subjects deeply, but rather say that they are currently "into" some subject—be it astrology, extrasensory perception, organic gardening, or Zen philosophy—until their changing interests get them "into" something else. And if these half-playful explorations should not lead to enough intellectual and emotional excitement, there is still the chance to borrow some sense of ersatz excitement from drugs, much as some people in earlier generations borrowed it from alcohol (often ending up, however, not in a new freedom, but in a new dependency).

What do these feelings and beliefs add up to? They often imply serious concerns with human frustration, a sincere desire for human sympathy and warmth, genuine indignation at the lies, oppression, injustice, cruelty, and inclination toward war found in many of the political and social practices of many countries. Like the classic liberals and radicals, the adherents of these new protest movements want to change the world. But they often want to do it here and now, when their mood moves them, and not through the long commitment to the hard work of a lifetime. If they are more skeptical of the status quo and of the views of their elders, they are often touchingly willing to believe the things they want to. Many of them will believe in the effectiveness of whatever tools they are currently using—whether flowers, bombs, or votes—until they get around to trying something else. They will even try sustained political activity, provided that the experiment does not last too long and does not require them to adjust too many of their current habits or to trouble too much about the risks and costs of their own errors.

Despite its occasional bizarre language and trappings, the new radical ferment is still connected with many elements of American political culture. The belief in the essential goodness of people and the desire for equality and friendliness are characteristic of the mainstream of the American tradition. Henry David Thoreau would have understood the new radicals' interest in living with nature rather than conquering it and their interest in nonviolent and noncoercive forms of politics.

The weakest points in this new radical set of beliefs were perhaps its distance from reality, its partially built-in resistance to reality correction, its underestimation of the feelings of other groups in the population, and its underestimation of world poverty and of the consequent need for more, not less, widespread productivity and competence. By 1978, more than a decade after its rise, the movement seemed to have declined throughout most of the United States, but it had caused some changes in the political landscape.

On the surface the college generation of "the movement" was replaced by "the *me generation*," as journalist Tom Wolfe called it. Jobs, careers, grades, and personal advancement seemed to be the center of its members' attention. Some of this change was genuine and necessary in a time of declining employment opportunities for young people. But many attitudes had changed for good. Racists and haters of minorities had themselves become a minority in the country, particularly among the young. Lifestyles had become more informal. Women's needs and rights had gained political weight and had to be taken into serious consideration. Many of the young activists of the 1960s had re-entered mainstream political life, and some of them had won important public office by election or appointment.

One small fringe sect that had started amid the counterculture went on to bizarre extremes that ended in horror. This was the People's Temple of the Reverend Jim Jones, who in November 1978 led over nine hundred of his tightly controlled followers to mass murder and suicide in his settlement at Jonestown, Guyana. But most of the recent small religious movements in the United States eventually found an accepted place for themselves and their members. As long as a religious movement did not strive to control totally the minds of its converts, nor try to cut them off from all contacts with their families, friends, and people with different beliefs, and as long as its members retained the chance to leave freely, they seemed likely to remain in the future within the larger community of the American people and humankind.

A Neoconservative Challenge to the Liberals.

In the 1970s, a new kind of conservatism began to emerge, less rigid than the traditional ideas of such Republican leaders as senators Robert Taft or Barry Goldwater. The new version appealed to both Republicans and Democrats, with such leaders as Democratic Senator Henry Jackson and former California Governor Ronald Reagan as its vague symbols, and with a range of academic advisers as its increasingly explicit spokespersons. Not all members of this school of thought agree with each other on all points. Yet many of their ideas overlap. They are in debate among themselves; they are beginning to be seen as a group; and though their views doubtless will undergo further development and change, the 1980 landslide election of Ronald Reagan and a Republican Senate showed that neoconservatism will be one of the trends of the 1980s that will have to be reckoned with.

The following are some of the propositions that can be found in neoconservative thought or are implied in it.

Stability and institutions are more important than activity and participation.

Legitimacy should be a major goal of government, loyalty and duties a major concern of citizens. These are more important than any quick increase in the demands and rights of citizens and minorities.

The economic and social matters, the habits, liberties, and property rights of individuals and corporations should be strengthened against the state, but in matters regarding crime, subversion, and foreign influence, the power of the state, as well as its liberty of action, should be increased against individuals. Courts and police forces should be given more power and discretion to supervise, search, and arrest potential suspects, and more discretion to sentence them to varying lengths of imprisonment.

The United States should remain "Number One"—paramount in military strength with both conventional and nuclear weapons. It should be ready and able to intervene anywhere in the world to protect its national interests and those of its allies. Proposals for arms limitations and arms control should be viewed with great skepticism, and considered only within the limits of preserving or restoring the preponderance of United States power in the world. Nuclear wars need not be avoided at any price. If necessary, the United States should seek to win them by "first strike" tactics or, in any case, to prevail in them.

The main external enemy of the United States is and remains the Soviet Union, with China and the claims of the Third World as a lesser threat. All these countries must be watched with tense alertness. Any mood of *détente* or relaxation of tensions in regard to these threats would be a dangerous illusion.

The main internal threat to America, the neoconservatives believe, is government itself. High taxes and excessive regulation are crippling the productive power of the economy. Government intervention should be reduced in favor of increased reliance on market mechanisms: tax cuts, balanced budgets, deregulation, and incentives for saving and investment should have top priority.

Welfare policies, social reforms, and improvements in the lot of minorities do not have a high priority as ends in themselves, but they should be advanced mainly as instruments to the extent that they help stabilize the present American political and economic system.

Similarly, economic aid to poorer countries and the promotion of human rights abroad should be used to the extent that these programs realistically serve as instruments of United States foreign policy, strategy, and power.

Some of the policies may be unrealistic. Long-term imprisonment as a way to control may be more expensive and less effective than its neoconservative advocates believe. More freedom for market forces may not suffice to reduce unemployment and inflation. Greater military force and an unrestrained arms control competition may reduce, not increase, the security of the United States.

Nonetheless, all these proposed policies have deep psychological roots in the feelings of substantial parts of the American people. Even traditionally liberal voters from some previously disadvantaged groups that now have become well established, such as many Americans of Irish, Italian, or Jewish background, may now find these ideas more appealing. Inflation and fear of crime affect almost everyone. If an American consensus on public policy is to emerge in the 1980s, the neoconservative views and the feelings to which they appeal cannot be wholly disregarded.

Liberals and Radicals in Search of a Response. Neoconservatism posed a serious challenge to liberals and radicals for two reasons. For one, it had taken over some of their own appeals to freedom, spontaneity, and security. Some neoconservatives called themselves "libertarians" in attacking bureaucracy and the welfare state in the United States and other countries; but neoconservatives also promised more law and order, stability and security, for individuals, property, and familiar patterns of morality.

Second, some of the liberal trust in progress had proved disappointing; and some of the radical experiments had failed in practice. "Progress" sometimes had meant bulldozers, superhighways, crowding, and a decline in the perceived quality of life. Radical school experiments sometimes had not lived up to the hopes of their proponents; many communes had broken up, with members staying only an average of perhaps eighteen months and then drifting away; dropping out often had ended in poverty and boredom; the counterculture had produced few impressive works, if any.

Above all, the old evils—poverty, unemployment, inflation, and the risk of war—had not been abolished, although liberals had set the tone in the decades of effort to that end, from President Franklin D. Roosevelt in the 1930s to President Jimmy Carter in the late 1970s. When inflation climbed toward 20 percent and the Soviet threat seemed greater in 1980, political leaders of both parties jointly embraced many parts of the neoconservative agenda for lower taxes, balanced budgets, and more defense spending. Liberals who worried about unemployment and social needs and radicals who worried about vested privilege seemed to have few persuasive alternatives to contribute. Would their silence in the political debate continue in the 1980s?

Perhaps liberals would have to regain some of the spirit of experimentation of the early 1930s without losing some of the more sophisticated understanding gained from almost fifty years' additional experience. Perhaps radicals may have to become more interested in the realistic and the practicable, in developing consistent policies, coherent coalitions, and habits of patience, tenacity, responsibility, and competence, while widening and deepening their compassion and imagination. In any process of that kind, the boundaries between liberalism and radicalism would become blurred. Liberalism, one recalls, has long meant faith in people and in the goal of freedom, but it often has changed in its views of particular institutions and instruments to promote these values. Perhaps in the 1980s liberal thought will have to reach further and cut deeper than before if it is to survive as a major intellectual and moral force.

Thus far, adherents of all of the five major political belief systems—liberalism, conservatism, classic radicalism, the new radicalism, and neoconservatism—in the United States—in contrast to, say, Germany in the 1930s—have remained on speaking terms with one another. Indeed, most persons are not pure representatives of any single one of these configurations. Rather, most individuals are drawing on all four as resources in the development of their thoughts and feelings about politics and life, even though each may draw most heavily on the view he or she finds most congenial. In their interplay and overlap, these four systems of political images, together with the American political culture in which they are embedded, go far to determine the arena of American politics.

THE ARENA OF AMERICAN POLITICS

The images of American politics and the inputs and outputs of the American political system are all part of the arena of American politics. Most immediately they touch those people who live in the United States. But these images reach out much further, into foreign countries and international relations.

An arena is to politics what a market is to business. Two businesspeople are in the same *market* if they receive to a large extent the same information about prices and offers to buy and sell and if they take this information into account in making their own decisions—or, differently put, if this information then makes an observable difference in their economic behavior. Two political actors are in the same *arena* if they are members of the same domain, subject to the same power holders, and if they receive to a large extent the same information about who is demanding power over whom and in regard to what activities.

In the modern world the arena of politics is, first, the national state. During the history of the United States its political arena has changed with its geographic expansion: beginning with a strip of states along the Atlantic coast in the late eighteenth century, spreading over the Midwest and adding Texas and California during the nineteenth century, and reaching out across land and sea to add Alaska and Hawaii as full-fledged states

and Puerto Rico as an associated commonwealth in the twentieth century. Correspondingly, the nonself-governing possessions of the United States have dwindled to a few islands in the Pacific and the Caribbean.

In another sense, however, the American political arena is much larger. It comprises many areas not directly governed by the United States, but in many ways clearly subject to its overwhelming political, economic, and military power. In effect they are part of the domain of the United States, but they have relatively little influence on American political decisions. In 1980 these areas included such countries as the Dominican Republic, Haiti, and other Central American republics; South Korea and Taiwan; and Singapore, Israel, Jordan, and Liberia. Other countries under lesser, but still considerable, United States influence were Turkey, Greece, Pakistan, Bolivia, Paraguay, and Spain. By 1980, United States influence seemed lost in five minor countries: Vietnam, Laos, Cambodia, Ethiopia, and Afghanistan, as well as in the more important oil-producing Iran. It had somewhat weakened in America's old friend, Israel, and in its quarreling allies, Greece and Turkey. But American influence had increased in Egypt, Somalia, and Bangladesh, to some extent in India, and perhaps slightly in China. On balance, the reach of American influence had not been diminished. It was striking to note, however, that United States influence usually fell short of effective control; that after decades of American involvement most of these countries remained poor; and that the governments of many of them remained authoritarian, military, and dictatorial.

Some critics concluded from this state of affairs that such announced United States policy goals as independence, prosperity, and democracy for all countries should be viewed with skepticism. Others felt that American purposes were more divided and that American capabilities to achieve national policy goals in foreign countries were far more limited than had been expected. Still others suggested that some American voters might be willing to support a limited effort to defend some or all of these countries against what they perceived as the threat of communism, but that most voters were unwilling to do much else for them. Yet a sudden crisis in any one of these countries might bring the United States to the brink of war; and any such war might escalate to a world war with thermonuclear weapons, endangering the survival of the American people.

Other countries, though allied with the United States, were much less subject to direct American political influence. These included France, Britain, the German Federal Republic and the other members of the European Economic Community, Japan, Canada, Australia, and New Zealand. In most of these countries, United States influence had been very high in the early 1950s. By early 1973, however, it had dropped dramatically. When President Nixon, shortly before Christmas 1972, ordered the massive bombing of the city of Hanoi in order to influence the peace negotiations with North Vietnam, his use of large-scale bombing as an instrument of diplomacy was condemned by political leaders and public opinion in most of these countries. The moral prestige of the United States improved again after 1975, with the end of the Vietnam War, and even more in 1977 and 1978, with President Carter's international campaign for human rights. Even so, the United States had a very hard time convincing its European allies to support the boycott of the 1980 Olympics in Moscow, in response to the Soviet invasion of Afghanistan.

Finally, the United States political arena in the middle and late 1970s included two countries, the Soviet Union and China, whose actions, demands, and probable responses had to be taken into account in the making of major American policy decisions.

The American political arena thus consisted of a central portion, the United States itself; a periphery of about two dozen less developed countries, subject to much influence from the United States but exercising little in return; and more than a dozen democratic countries—many in Western Europe, but also Canada, Australia, and Japan— that in earlier years had often been treated as partners of the United States, but whose views had come to be increasingly disregarded and whose political ties to the United States in many ways were weakening. The vision of an Atlantic community of North America and Western Europe, so confidently proclaimed in the 1940s, now was dimmer than it had ever been.

Yet the fates of all these countries remained tied together and, to a considerable degree, dependent on the political processes and decisions of the United States. Perhaps never before in history has there been such widespread political interdependence combined with such limited capabilities for common consultation, decision, and control. By the early 1980s, some common institutions had been created for these tasks, such as annual economic summit meetings among the heads of chief industrial "Western" countries, including Japan. Whether these meetings would lead to common actions, however, only the legislators and voters of these countries could decide. Alternatively, the arena of political interdependence and the domain of American political influence might well start shrinking again, reaching the level of the large, but limited, capabilities of the American political system.

THE AMERICAN POLITICAL SYSTEM: THE MACHINERY AND PROCESSES OF GOVERNMENT

In our look at the American political system, we shall ask first what holds the system together. Then we shall look at the specific machinery and processes of government and then ask how, and how well, this large and complex system manages to steer itself. Finally we shall focus on two key dimensions of political performance: how much freedom and self-development the system permits individuals living under it, and what capabilities the system has developed for its own growth and self-transformation.

The Roots of Its Cohesion. The American political system is being held together, perhaps first of all, by the high mobility of the population. As people move from place to place and job to job, they keep much of their character, memories, loyalties, and habits of communication, so that they then still have ties to the people they have left behind and to the people among whom they have come to live now. If they keep moving often, and often back and forth, they weave a web of common memories and habits that make them more coherent, that is, more apt to understand each other and more reluctant to be separated. This seems true of many people but even more so of Americans. About every third American lives in some state of the Union other than the one in which he or she was born. Along with this geographic mobility has gone also a remarkable degree of mobility among occupations and even among roles and positions in society.

Second, the American political system is held together by the experience and expectation of *joint rewards* from the high national income, living standards, and educational and social opportunities that have been shared in some form and to some extent by perhaps 85 to 90 percent of the population.

And third, the political system of the United States is held together by the *social and cultural cohesiveness* of the American people—by the interlocking of social roles, the similarity of expectations and experiences, and the community of habits, values, character, and culture. The legal rules and the political and administrative arrangements that provide for the formal and institutional unity of the system derive most of their strength from these underlying social, economic, and psychological conditions.

All three of these basic conditions are somewhat older than the Constitution of the United States, as

it was ratified in 1791. However, the Constitution was designed to fit these conditions and the needs and resources of the American people that went with them; and once the Constitution was in force, its design influenced the further development of the nation.

Federalism and the Separation of Powers. One of the primary characteristics of this design for the government of the United States was its basic pattern of *federalism,* which was then a radically new idea in its application on a continental scale. (Prior to the establishment of the United States, the only successful large republic had been that of ancient Rome, which was not federal. Since Rome's collapse, only small republics like Venice, small confederations like Switzerland, and the small-scale federal institutions of the Dutch had flourished.)

This federal design combined a legislative congress, representing the diversity of the states, and a single chief executive—an "elective monarch," as this individual has been called—to direct the power of the nation. In such a federal union, every person is subject at one and the same time to two governments that are partly independent of each other. The federal government and the government in each state are separated in scope—in *what* they are supposed to govern—but united in domain—in *whom* they are governing. In the United States the federal government and the state governments each operate directly on the individual, within their respective spheres of powers. Those *residual powers* not explicitly given by the Constitution either to the Union or to the states are now held to belong to the federal government. This usage has been confirmed by several decisions of the U.S. Supreme Court, despite the long-lasting opposition of states' righters who would have preferred the opposite outcome.

Here federalism in Canada differs from that in the United States. In Canada the residual powers—those not explicitly allocated to provinces—were left by the British North America Act to the federal government. However, that act also included an "illustrative" list of central government powers and a vaguely defined power of the provinces in regard to "property and civil rights." Later court decisions have tended to expand this power of the provinces into a "sort of residuary competence . . . and to treat the Centre's residuary power as confined to the listed matters, matters similar to them, and national emergencies."[15] Under this arrangement, in Canada or the United States, no small region or group nor any individual has been able to dictate to the rest.

Some theorists have claimed that government is based on two monopolies: the monopoly of violence and the monopoly of legitimacy. The American experience casts doubt on this view. During its formative decades the United States was relatively decentralized. For many decades after the ratification of the Constitution there was no federal monopoly of violence and, indeed, no federal monopoly of legitmacy. In part, this was due to a physical fact: the army of the United States federal government in the 1790s had fifteen hundred soldiers strung out over almost as many miles along the Indian frontier. The state militia of a single state such as New York, on the other hand, had twenty thousand men. Therefore, the federal government in the early years of the republic had no way of coercing the states. Only if the states backed the federal government could the federal government make its will prevail.

The American system also offers remarkable freedom of opposition. Americans traditionally have refused to believe that anything was right merely because the government said so. Some Americans even held that rebellion was legitimate. Jefferson said of Shays's Rebellion (1786) that it might be necessary for the United States to have such an uprising every twenty-five years. These views did not prevent him from being later elected president of the United States.

[15]Geoffrey Sawyer, *Modern Federalism* (London: Watts, 1969), p. 31.

In its essence, then, the American federal system has always tended to permit searching criticism of basic practices and institutions by the people, as well as by their elected representatives. Again it was Jefferson, this time after his tenure of office, who said of slavery, "I tremble for my country when I reflect that God is just." Serious criticism of one's own country is as old as the republic. Through freedom of criticism the United States has remained cohesive and its federal system has remained strong, and both have become more so in the course of time. The argument that criticism is divisive, or that dissent weakens national unity, runs counter to the mainstream of American experience.

America's federalist scheme has been imitated widely, but not always with the same degree of success as in America. Federalism worked as a political system in the United States for a combination of two basic reasons. First, as we noted, Americans early became a single people and identified themselves as such. Being highly mobile, they perceived of their needs and interests as shared, more often than not, and thus were willing to commit themselves to supporting a national government. Second, and equally important, America had a long tradition of independent and self-governing states. If either of these factors had existed alone, federalism might not have succeeded. The existence of both of them in combination helped provide the workable balance between local and national government that is the essence of federalism.

A System of Checks and Balances. Another characteristic of American government is that it is based on a *separation of powers,* that is, a sharp separation of legislative power from executive power and of judicial power—the power of judges and courts—from both. This concept was advanced by eighteenth-century theorists like Montesquieu, but the United States was unique in the thoroughness with which it put it into practice. To ensure the independence of all three branches of government, and at the same time to ensure that these three branches made up one coherent government, a system of *checks and balances* was developed (see Figure 2.4).

For nearly two centuries, separation of powers among the legislative, executive, and judicial branches has worked remarkably well. For the stronger and better organized groups, at least, it has provided a framework within which their different interests could be expressed and brought together into acceptable programs for action.

Pluralism Versus Populism. American government is also characterized by an informal separation of powers, which some political scientists call *pluralism:* a plurality of competing interest groups and a diversity of rival interests—regional, social, economic, religious, and psychological. As James Madison pointed out in the "Tenth Federalist Letter," no special interest commands a majority in the United States: no one religion, no one economic interest, and no one region. Madison

FIGURE 2.4 *The Separation of Powers: A Simplified Sketch*

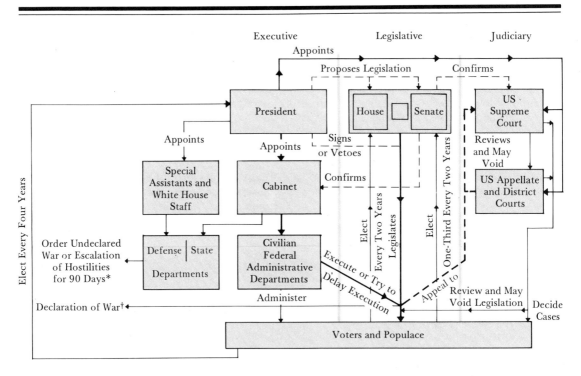

*If Congress directs by concurrent resolution, such forces shall be removed by the president before the 90 days are up.
†Note that there are two separate war powers: the power to declare war, which the Constitution reserves to Congress, and the power to wage undeclared war, which has been claimed by the president.

was confident that this fact would prevent the rise of tyrannical popular majorities for a long time. In the short run, he thought, there could be a tyrannical popular majority, but even that would be difficult to achieve and it would soon vanish. The view that the will of a popular majority should prevail in all matters, including science, art, and morals, and that neither experts nor minorities ought to have any valid claims against it became known in nineteenth-century American politics as *populism*. The quick decline of populism in the 1890s and McCarthyism in the 1950s (the demagogic and intolerant kind named after Senator Joseph McCarthy of Wisconsin) can be taken as examples of Madison's wisdom.

Populism can, at least, produce a consistent political will for limited populations, regions, periods of time, and small sets of issues. Here the popular *initiative* to move matters toward legislation and the *referendum* to decide on a new law by popular vote can be highly effective. The passing of Proposition 13 by referendum in California is a recent example. If populations become large, areas more diversified, time perspectives longer, and issues more varied, then populist majorities risk falling apart. After the success of Proposition 13, populist reformers tried to move on to a national referendum or even a constitutional convention to override the normal course of pluralistic politics. All such efforts failed against the resistance of established groups, *including* public interest groups, whose lobbying power could be undercut by such forms of direct democracy.

The Carter presidency was an excellent example of how populism can produce sudden political phenomena but how quickly such power can evaporate. In 1976, President Carter was elected on a quasi-populist platform. He appealed to the resentment of many voters against the distant bureaucracies and elites in far-off Washington, against costly foreign policy adventures in remote countries, against the long-standing neglect of some of the economic and medical needs of

ordinary people, and against injustices between races, sexes, and age groups, and he represented a revival of a fundamental morality in public life that was based on more than mere expectations of pragmatic success.

By 1980 the Carter administration had made some major advances in all these respects, but its supporters had returned to their old quarrels among themselves. Whereas many younger voters demanded more permissiveness, many older voters called for a reaffirmation of traditional morality. *Feminists* asserted each woman's right to maintain control over her own body, including the right to have her own pregnancy terminated on demand, but other voters, including many women, asserted a *"right to life"* for an embryo in the first weeks and months after conception, even against the mother's will. A practical *trimester solution* was handed down by the Supreme Court. It treated the embryo as a part of the mother's body during the first three months and as a person to be protected in his or her own right thereafter; but even this decision did not still the controversy.

On these and other issues the populist origins of the Carter presidency were soon overlaid with pluralistic politics. Political appointments emphasized representatives from minority, consumer, environmental, and other groups. Much of the White House staff was organized around such pluralistic constituencies. As Jimmy Carter fought for renomination against Senator Edward Kennedy and the left wing of the Democratic party, the president and his aides worked through interest group endorsements, telephone calls to thousands of local leaders, and appeals to "the people" that were prepared through meetings with small elite groups of publishers, editors, and other media executives. In his first months in office President Carter annoyed many members of Congress by attacking their use of *porkbarrel politics*, that is, the granting of federal money for local projects as a means of trading favors. In contrast, by 1980 there was a remarkable coincidence in the Carter administration's announcement of big federal projects and the timing of primary elections in key states. In short, President Carter depended on a semi-populist coalition to gain office, but it was a pluralistic coalition on which he depended, unsuccessfully, to keep office. Indeed, by 1980 American politics seemed more pluralistic than ever.

Does Pluralism Give an Equal Chance to Everybody? Pluralism, however, is not an unmixed blessing. In its early stages, half the interest groups of a political system may be unorganized and the other half may run the show. In that case, pluralism helps the strong, but can be merciless against the weak. Later, when everybody is organized, the political system may become immobile, as seemed to be the case during the long debate about a national energy policy during the Carter administration. Unless political leaders play a brilliant role in discovering workable policies and organizing broad coalitions to carry them out, this immobility may lead to weak compromises that fail to meet the larger issue at stake or it may persist. But such diplomacy and leadership happen rarely. If they do not happen, then the immobility-emergency syndrome will set in, and some leaders may start looking for emergencies—foreign, military, or other—to force quick action.

Pluralism and the Distributions of Political Opinion. The danger of immobility may be compounded by the dangers of *polarization,* the risk that many voters may desert the middle ground on several important issues and move to one or the other extreme pole—far left or far right—in regard to all of them. But if voters shift attitude to the left on one issue and to the right on another, the two shifts might balance or cancel each other out and the voters might still vote for a candidate in the political middle. This is what advocates of pluralism usually hope for, but it does not always happen. When it exerts its full power, political polarization implies that voters move to more extreme attitudes on several issues consistently; that is, some voters move on several issues to the left, and others move on several issues to the right. The plurality of opinions then is reduced to two, directly opposed to one another.

Just this has happened in the United States from the 1950s to the 1970s. In 1956 only 25 percent of American voters had such consistent attitudes: 12 percent leftists and 13 percent rightists in their views. A vast majority, 75 percent, were in the middle: 41 percent were centrists, and the remaining 34 percent were divided between the moderate left and the moderate right. The whole profile of voters' attitudes resembled the capital letter *A,* or a curve of normal statistical distribution. But by 1973 this profile had changed to one resembling a *W.* The centrist group had shrunk greatly, to 27 percent; the moderate left had declined from 19 to 12 percent, and the moderate right had grown slightly, from 15 to 17 percent, so that the three middle groups together now totaled only 56 percent. But at the extreme ends of the political spectrum, consistent leftists had risen from 12 to 21 percent and consistent rightists from 13 to 23 percent.

The changes from 1956 to 1963 are shown in Figure 2.5, and the 1973 situation still seems to be reflected by the results of the 1978 congressional elections. The 1980 election suggested that the right side of the *W* may be enlarging but throughout his campaign candidate Reagan moved steadily toward the center. The three center groups still constitute a majority, but there is no certain majority either to the right or to the left of center. The difficulties for any president or other national leader are now larger than they would have been twenty years ago.

Two-Track Legislation for the Nation. An important political invention reflecting American pluralism has given the national legislature its distinctive cast. This invention deals with the relations of large and small states and their representation in Congress. The legislature was organized into two chambers. In the House of Representatives, equal representation was given to the people. In the Senate, equal representation was given to the states. England had long had a two-chamber legislature comprising its House of Lords and House of Commons, but the use of the two-chamber system to accommodate the interests of large and small states in a federal union of continental dimensions was an American invention.

Representing the People by Numbers: The House. In the House of Representatives the people are represented by one representative for every equal number of inhabitants as fixed by law—originally one for every 30,000, now one for almost every 500,000.[16] The representatives are chosen directly by the people for two-year terms. They are elected from congressional districts, all intended to be equal in population. To ensure this equality, congressional districts are supposed to be readjusted, both among and within states, after each decennial census. The manner of adjustment within each state, like the qualifications for voting, is left to the state's legislature, and allocation of districts among states is entrusted to Congress. All these provisions were intended to ensure equal representation of the people in the House of Representatives.

In practice the representation in the House has turned out to be much less equal. Although congressional districts are supposed to be readjusted every ten years, at the start of the 1960s there were some state legislatures that had neglected this duty for as long as half a century. Many legislators from rural districts were benefiting from this neglect because they did not have to share power with representatives of the faster-growing urban areas. In the eighteenth and nineteenth centuries a similar neglect to provide adequate representation for the rapidly growing cities of Britain led there to the evils of the *"rotten boroughs"*—thinly populated rural districts overrepresented in Parliament. These were abolished by Britain's Reform Bill of 1832, although Britain today is still far from achieving absolutely equal representation for all its people. In the United States, major efforts to provide just apportionment of congressional districts gained momentum only in the 1960s, and

FIGURE 2.5 *Distribution of Population by Political Beliefs, 1956 and 1973*

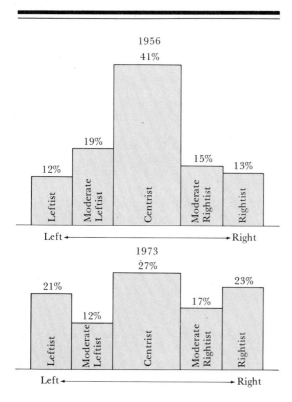

[16]Until the abolition of slavery in 1865, only free persons were counted fully: according to Article 1, Section 2, Paragraph 3 of the Commission, each slave, though without vote, was to be counted as three-fifths of a person, for the benefit of the state in which he or she was held in bondage. Nowadays representation is by the number of people who live in a state, even if they are not registered to vote. Southern states have increased their seats in the House by counting many blacks to whom, nevertheless, they denied the right to vote.

Source: Norman H. Nie, Sidney Verba and John R. Petrocik, *The Changing American Voter* (Cambridge: Harvard University Press, 1976), p. 143.

then with the aid of the courts. By that time it was charged that rural voters in some sparsely settled Illinois districts had nine times the voting power of citizens in some of Chicago's crowded precincts. Moreover, the new suburbs on the edge of many big cities had long remained underrepresented in Congress.

By the end of the 1960s, the doctrine of *"one man one vote"* had been established by decision of the United States Supreme Court, and the courts were beginning to demand that redistricting plans, in order to be constitutional, had to provide for districts that would vary by no more than 10 percent in their number of voters. This principle was also applied by the courts to state legislatures, with far-reaching implications for the distribution of political power within the states and, indirectly, throughout much of the country. These developments promised to wipe out the last elements of representation by wealth or ownership of land.[17] During the 1970s the effects of redistricting—or *legislative reapportionment*—in accordance with the "one man one vote" principle facilitated substantial changes in the congressional system of seniority and in the structure and operations of congressional committees, reducing the power and length of tenure of committee chairs. Similarly, it facilitated changes in the structure of the executive, reducing the secrecy of its operations and extending the areas of congressional oversight. Beyond this, however, reapportionment mainly strengthened the power of suburban voters whose districts had grown most rapidly in population. Although the overrepresentation of rural districts had helped to make the House more conservative than

the Senate—contrary to what the nation's founders had expected—the suburban voters and their representatives in Congress favored reforms in some areas, such as openness of government, protection of the environment, and a low-risk foreign policy, while also developing more conservative attitudes in regard to taxation, affirmative action, and federal pressure for racial integration of local public schools. On these issues the voting records of newly elected surburban representatives after 1976 furnished striking evidence.

The two-year term for representatives may have had a similar effect. Intended to keep representatives close to their constituents, this provision has involved many legislators in contested districts in expensive and almost permanent campaigns for re-election, giving them little time for what was to have been their first responsibility, legislating for the people. This same provision, of course, gives disproportionate influence to those of their colleagues who are virtually unopposed in their rural districts or in urban districts dominated by a single ethnic group or political machine. Legislators from such safe one-party districts get re-elected time after time; and through the congressional custom of *seniority* (which allocates committee chairs to legislators with the longest continuous term of service) they have traditionally dominated the important committees of the House and thereby much of the legislative business (see Table 2.6). These conditions have condemned many urban voters in contested districts to a feeling of powerlessness. Even if they succeed in electing a representative of their choice, he or she rarely seems to get anywhere in Congress.

By the end of the 1970s, internal changes in the House had weakened the grip of seniority and party loyalty, promoting greater pluralism in representation. Election by secret ballot in the party caucus made the position of committee chairperson less secure. The arbitrary power of such leaders was reduced, committee sessions were opened to the public, and every House member

[17]Conservative opponents of thoroughgoing equality among voters have backed a constitutional amendment proposed by the late Senator Everett Dirksen of Illinois that would explicitly permit the allocating of districts and, in effect, the weighting of votes by standards other than the equality of voters. In 1972 the Supreme Court refused to review the decision of an appellate court that permitted the departure from the "one man one vote" principle in a case involving the election of local judges. In fact, however, the principle prevailed.

TABLE 2.6 *Democratic Representatives, January 1964 (in percentages)*

	NORTH		SOUTH	
	Rural	Urban	Rural	Urban
All Democratic representatives (255)	21	42	29	9
Major committee chairs held by Democrats	18	29	53	0
Safe seats occupied by Democrats	7	30	52	11

Source: R. E. Wolfinger and J. Heifetz, "Safe Seats, Seniority, and Power in Congress," *American Political Science Review* 59 (1965), pp. 337–49.

was guaranteed at least one major committee assignment. By 1980 there were approximately two hundred committees and subcommittees in the House—almost enough to assure every member a position as chairperson or ranking minority member of some specialized subgroup of the House of Representatives.

Representing the People by States: The Senate. If one branch of Congress was intended to represent the people in all regions of the country more or less equally as individuals, the other branch was designed to represent them unequally as individuals, but equally as states. For this reason the small states of the Union, inferior to the large ones in population and effective political power, have the same representation in the Senate as their large neighbors: two senators for each state.

Those small states that are virtually one-party states, such as Mississippi, Arkansas, and, until recently, Maine and Vermont, can gain disproportionate influence in the Senate through the seniority system that in time tends to put their senators at the head of major Senate committees. The effects of the seniority system, still accepted by many senators from industrial or urban states, make it harder for a senator from New York or California to head a key committee. However, this power of seniority is declining. As two-party competition spreads to formerly one-party states, senators from two-party states may be gaining in influence.

The framers of the Constitution expected the Senate to serve as a counterweight to the House. They believed that senators would be older, more conservative, and more representative of the established elites of their states—those whom an eighteenth-century writer called "the rich, the well-born, and the wise." As we shall see, this is not quite what eventually happened.

Senators are elected for a term of six years, in order to have a greater measure of stability and independence for their term of service. At every congressional election, every two years, only one-third of the Senate faces re-election, in contrast to all the members of the House. This is to protect the composition of the senate from quick changes in the mood of the voters.

Originally, the senators were elected indirectly by the legislatures of their states. But in 1912 the *Seventeenth Amendment* to the Constitution changed this to direct election by majority vote of those voters who "have the qualifications requisite for electors of the most numerous branch of the state legislatures." The effect of this change has varied somewhat by region. In most northern and western states the registered voters make up a large part of the adult population, though by no means all of them. In some southern states, owing to various discriminatory practices against blacks and the poor, less than half of the adult population have been registered to vote and less than one-fourth have actually voted. Yet the sharp increase in the registration of blacks in the South after the Voting Rights Act of 1965 suggests the beginnings of a change.

Since the Senate is supposed to represent the states equally, regardless of population, it has been

particularly sensitive to regional or sectional differences and more distrustful of simple national
majorities. The still continuing practice of the
filibuster—or its threat—and the long struggle for
workable rules of *cloture* confirm this built-in bias.

Despite the conservative role intended for it by
the nation's founders, the Senate in many matters
has become more liberal than the House. Senators
must be elected by the voters of an entire state, so
the unequal apportionment of voting districts has
no effect on them. Voters from urban and industrial areas within each state have their full share of
influence on the election of their senators. It is also
much more difficult for any political machine,
ethnic group, or special interest group to dominate an entire state, compared with the relative
ease with which such groups can hold sway over a
congressional district. There are, to be sure, a few
senators with well-known concerns for the interests of cotton or tobacco growers, dairy farmers,
aircraft manufacturers, or defense contractors,
but they make up a relatively limited part of the
Senate, and even seniority cannot put them in
charge of *all* Senate committees.

To get re-elected, therefore, most senators must
be responsive to both rural and urban interests in
their states, to many different ethnic groups and
economic interests, and to the independent voters
who may hold the balance in many two-party
states. The smaller size of the Senate makes
individual senators more highly visible. The mass
media, particularly television, have reinforced
these opportunities and have made it easier for
many senators to entertain ambitions for higher
office—at the Cabinet level, on the Supreme
Court, or for the presidency—all of which, at one
time or another, have been attained by former
senators. These conditions often favor the selection of more statesmanlike candidates, and the
six-year term gives them a better opportunity to
build a record of accomplishment. Although many
legislators in the House as well as in the Senate
have done their best to serve the public good as
they saw it, the prestige of senators has usually
been higher, perhaps with good reason.

Beyond the prestige of its members, the Senate
as a whole and its committees have certain powers:
to direct national attention to particular problems,
to put new issues before the public, and to become
a potentially important source for new legislation
and political initiatives. To what extent these
opportunities are used may depend in part on the
political situation and the public mood, but also on
the individual senators, on their staff assistants,
and on the particular Senate committees, staffs,
and philosophy under which they operate.

During the 1970s the Senate implemented many
of the same "democratizing" (or "pluralizing")
reforms already in effect in the House of Representatives. By 1980 there were 121 Senate committees and subcommittees, more than enough to
guarantee each senator his or her own decentralized "piece of the action" in pluralistic representation at the national level.

Latent Tensions: Congress and the Chief Executive.
A brilliant conservative theorist of American politics, Willmoore Kendall, once remarked that many
American voters, when stepping into the polling
booth, develop a split personality. First, they think
of themselves as far-sighted and generous. They
consider the problems of the nation as a whole,
both in domestic matters and in world affairs, and
like to think about world leadership by the United
States. Willing to accept some American responsibilities toward humankind, they then cast their
votes for the presidential candidate most likely to
represent these aspirations. As soon as they have
done this, says Kendall, our voters turn around
and ask themselves this question: what about *my*
district, *my* locality, *my* special economic interest,
and *my* ethnic group? All the grand, costly national
and international policies go out the window. Now
they seek the most distrustful, tightfisted, narrow-
minded, intensely parochial candidates they can
find—and in this mood they pick their representatives to Congress. Once their president and representatives reach Washington, they must try to work

out the conflicts that the voters failed to resolve in their own minds.[18]

Kendall's sketch may be overdrawn, but there is some truth in it. Congressional and presidential candidates of the same party rarely receive the same number of votes from a particular district. In districts where one party is strong enough to win at least 65 percent of the vote for a congressional seat, the victorious legislator tends to run ahead of the presidential candidate of the same party. In all other districts, on the average, the opposite tendency prevails; the representative, more often than not running behind the presidential ticket, tends to benefit from the pulling power of the leader's coattails. Once elected, however, the entire Congress is likely to approve less than one-half of the president's proposals, whatever the party of the president.

The Making of a Crisis: A Critical Congress and a Single-Minded President. After 1968, and especially after 1972, this situation began to change. Both times, President Nixon was elected, although the voters at the same time refused his party a majority in either house of Congress. As a result, the latent tension between the presidency and the legislature become increasingly manifest, since each of these two branches could claim to have received a mandate from the voters.

The crisis had been long in the making. The exclusive *right of Congress* to declare war in full legal form had gradually fallen into disuse during the decades of the Cold War after 1945; and the president's power to order units of the armed forces into battle had correspondingly increased. President Jefferson early in the nineteenth century had ordered a small force of Marines into action

against the Algerian pirates. But by the 1960s this executive power was being exercised on a grand scale: President Kennedy sent 16,000 "advisers" into South Vietnam, and President Johnson raised this force to over 500,000. By early 1973, President Nixon had reduced the American ground troops in that country to less than 30,000 but kept more than 100,000 in the area, on ships, and on bases in neighboring Thailand, while ordering unprecedentedly heavy bombing raids on North Vietnamese cities and neighboring Cambodia. All these actions were taken without any explicit vote of Congress—some of them in the face of explicit congressional opposition. Only later in 1973 were all American ground troops evacuated from Vietnam, and on August 15, 1973, all American bombardment of Indochina officially ceased. In April 1975 the last American troops and personnel were evacuated from South Vietnam, which later was merged with North Vietnam under Communist rule. As such, Vietnam is now a member of the United Nations, recognized by the United States.

At the same time, President Nixon began to "impound" moneys specifically authorized and appropriated by laws passed by Congress. He refused to let his administration execute these laws and spend these moneys, claiming as his reason that these expenditures—some of them quite moderate—would contribute to inflation. At the same time he continued to spend public funds for the military, naval, and air activities that he had ordered on his own authority. In this manner the priorities of spending preferred by the chief executive were made to prevail over the duly enacted decisions of the legislative branch—a practice very different from that which the Constitution had ordained; and it became explicitly illegal in 1975 under a new law passed by Congress and signed by President Ford.

In late 1972, President Nixon requested Congress to delegate to him the right to suspend, at his discretion, the execution of specific items in any

---

[18]In recent years, the opposite of Kendall's surmise sometimes was true. Repeatedly, voters have elected liberal representatives and senators from their districts and states, while electing at the same time a strongly conservative president, as happened in the 1972 election. But the split in the inner attitudes of many voters remained, giving both Congress and the president an equal, but incomplete mandate.

law that Congress henceforth might pass. Congress, however, refused to vote in favor of this request on the grounds that such a general authorization would take away the power of the purse from Congress and shift it to the president, thus destroying the constitutional separation of powers and the balance among the three main branches of government. Thereupon, some spokespeople from the White House told the press that the requested congressional. authorization really had not been needed: the president, they said, already had these powers. Had he not already impounded sums that Congress had appropriated to be spent, and was not this in effect the same kind of item veto over money bills that the president had requested? (According to Article I, Section 7, of the Constitution the president may refuse to sign a bill passed by Congress. This refusal—usually called a *veto*—will prevent this entire bill from becoming law, unless it is passed once more by a two-thirds majority in each house of Congress. But the Constitution does not give the president the power of an *item veto,* that is, the power to strike out just one part of a bill, while letting the rest of it become law, perhaps with a drastically altered balance.)

By early September 1973 it seemed that neither the president nor Congress wanted the conflict to reach extremes, and several bills had been permitted to pass in a spirit of compromise. However, the basic conflict of views remained unresolved. It still seemed that a constitutional crisis was in the making if the president and Congress should continue on their collision course. In the end, the Supreme Court, with four Nixon-appointed and Senate-confirmed justices among its nine members, voted against Nixon in deciding that he had to turn over to a judge the tapes he had made of White House conversations, which he had wished to define as executive secrets.

Throughout his term Nixon had insisted that any action whatsoever was lawful if the president ordered it to be taken "in the national interest" and that he alone had the right to make such

decisions. For a long time top members of his staff had shared this view. One of his aides was asked by a congressional committee whether he thought that a presidential order would justify his committing murder; he replied that a line would have to be drawn somewhere, but he did not wish to be the one to draw it. In essence, this view would have meant that the president could be above the law.

Defenders of President Nixon pointed out, truthfully, that similar cases could be found during the preceding two centuries of American history for almost all the abuses of which President Nixon and his staff were accused. But it seems also true that never before had so many abuses been committed on so large a scale within so short a time. Many American voters felt a "critical mass," or body of violations large enough to threaten an explosion in one direction or another, had been reached.

At last, in August 1974 a congressional committee voted to impeach President Nixon for his crimes and misdemeanors, and the president resigned rather than risk a vote on the House floor or a trial in the Senate. This outcome was ratified by the voters in the elections of 1974 and 1976.

Earlier, Vice President Agnew had resigned in disgrace on charges of tax evasion, and President Nixon had appointed Gerald Ford as his successor in the vice presidency. After Nixon's resignation President Ford pardoned him for all offenses committed during his term of office, left him his presidential pension, and then proceeded to rescind or modify many of Nixon's policies. Many of Nixon's highest associates, however, were sentenced to jail terms by the courts.

The 48.9 percent of the popular votes cast for major-party candidates received by President Ford in 1976 (as opposed to President Carter's 51.1 percent) showed that after years of intense conflict the candidate of the Republican party had retained the confidence of only slightly fewer electors than his Democratic rival, President Carter, had won. The social and economic underpinnings of both major parties in the United States seemed to have remained more solid than observers might have expected.

If President Nixon had prevailed in the final conflict, the political system of the United States might have become very different indeed. But in a major collision between the Constitution and the president, the American people had decided to keep the Constitution, and they had done so without fatally tearing the country apart. Ex-President Nixon immediately ceased to be a significant figure in American politics.

Another Kind of President—But the Same Kind of Congress? In Jimmy Carter the American people elected a president who was no less individualistic than some of his recent predecessors, but markedly less assertive. He had won his office as the builder of a popular coalition (see p. 63, above), but he never forgot the wide differences among its components, and he was frequently reminded of them. But in his first year in office he underestimated the power of Congress and its peculiarities. When he proposed to veto the pet projects of many of the members of Congress; when he sometimes failed to consult congressional leaders before making important decisions; and when he appointed many people from his native state of Georgia to important positions in the White House and elsewhere, by-passing possible candidates whom some representatives and senators had suggested to him for these posts; then by all these measures he laid a solid foundation for conflict. During the same first year President Carter had proposed to by-pass or override important interest groups, such as big industry and banking, the oil interests, the armaments and aircraft industry, the leaders of George Meany's AFL-CIO, the backers of local water projects, and others. These interest groups soon transferred additional lobbying efforts and political support to Congress, where they found willing allies for their views. Carter's proposal to increase and improve provisions for registration and disclosure of lobbying activity never cleared the Senate Governmental Operations Subcommittee, and soon a considerable number of his

legislative proposals were delayed or defeated, including his important program on energy, which finally passed in a weakened version in 1978. In the public mind these many instances of congressional resistance seemed to outweigh the president's legislative successes, (such as the Senate's ratification of the Panama Canal Treaty) and contributed significantly during the 1980 elections to President Carter's reputation for ineffective leadership.

How Legislators Vote and Work. Once in Congress, legislators try to represent their constituencies as well as their own convictions. The votes cast by representatives are shaped by what their constituencies are like and by what they themselves are like; by what the voters in their constituencies think and by what they think their voters think; by the events that impinge on both the voters and their representatives; by the legislative system, which offers them specific choices; and by their perceptions of these options. These seven conditions and the way in which they shape the votes cast by legislators are shown in Figure 2.6.

An eighth consideration is not represented in this diagram. Many legislative decisions have a technical or economic dimension and are likely to have consequences that cannot be estimated without expert knowledge. In the days of George Washington, such expert knowledge was perhaps equally scarce in Congress and in the executive and perhaps even scarcer in the rest of the country. But from the 1930s through the 1950s, the executive branch of the American government grew vastly in personnel and also in the number and quality of its experts. Presidents and Cabinet members could present their legislative proposals, backed by an impressive array of arguments and data compiled by the specialists on their staffs, which neither representatives nor senators nor even congressional committees could match. During these decades a knowledge gap was beginning to open between the executive and legislative branches of government. Though lobbyists for special interest groups were eager to supply data to both bureaucrats and legislators, their evidence was often biased and at best was of limited help.

From the 1960s onward, however, this situation began to improve. Representatives and senators acquired their own professional staffs, usually between eight and twelve persons, at salary levels permitting the employment of adequately trained and competent individuals. Gifted young lawyers, economists, political scientists, and others found rewarding positions on these staffs. In addition, Congress greatly strengthened important governmental accounting and supervisory institutions, such as the *General Accounting Office (GAO)*, endowing some of them with important additional research functions. It even created new research and

analysis bodies, such as the *Congressional Budget Office (CBO)*, through which Congress could seriously analyze the president's budget proposals.

The House and Senate work in strikingly different ways. Having 435 members, the House is larger, more impersonal and formal in its proceedings, and more hierarchically organized. It is governed by more rigid rules, but is geared to quicker action. Power in the House is more unevenly distributed, and apprentice periods for first-year legislators are longer. With shorter terms and smaller and less important constituencies, House members carry less prestige. Because they more often represent local and small-town interests, their politics tend to be more conservative.

FIGURE 2.6 *Why Representatives Vote as They Do*

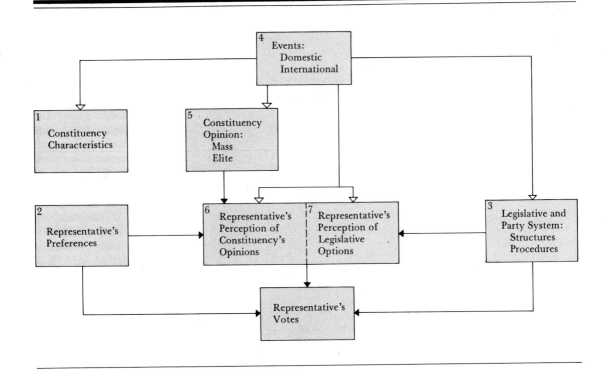

The 100 members of the Senate run their smaller chamber in a less formal manner. The Senate is less hierarchical, its rules more flexible, its actions slower, and its politics more personal. Power in the senate is more evenly distributed, and apprentice periods for new members are shorter. Often the Senate has been called a "club." With longer terms and larger and more important constituencies—entire states—senators carry more prestige. Representing statewide interests, they are often politically more liberal.

The Work of Congress: Passing Legislation. For both branches of Congress the workload has grown. The First Congress (in 1790–92) passed one law for every five of the few days it was in session. In the 1970s, Congress met much longer and worked much faster: it passed over nine times as many laws, or more than two laws per day. In such a crowded calendar, a bill's chances of becoming law are uncertain. (In today's Congress about twenty thousand bills are introduced, but usually no more than two hundred are passed.) A bill's hopes of passage depend first on its substance—the interests at stake. It is more likely to pass if more members support it, if their support is more intense, if its supporters are influential, and particularly if support comes from congressional leaders and the president. Its chances further improve if its supporters are strategically located, such as on the committee or subcommittee to which the bill is assigned or on the Rules Committee, which determines which committee will be assigned the bill. Finally, the bill is more likely to succeed if its opponents are few, lukewarm, lacking in influence, and poorly located.

Most bills are neither so popular in Congress as to be certain to breeze through nor so unpopular as to be hopeless. Proponents of such uncertain bills must win additional support for their proposals, and they do so by bargaining. Some of this bargaining may occur without overt negotiation. Legislators seem to go ahead and act, but in fact they take into account what they anticipate will be the reaction of their colleagues. In other cases there is more direct negotiation, explicit or implied.

The simplest technique is *logrolling*. Legislator A votes for legislator B's project, expecting or arranging that B will reciprocate. Legislator A expects B to be an "honest politician," that is, one who never fails to repay favors. Sometimes logrolling may extend over time. A legislator will vote for a colleague's project in return for an invisible legislative IOU to be cashed in at some future date. A raft of well-rolled logs is found in the omnibus rivers and harbors bills, which comprise a large number of separate and independent projects, each one dear to a particular legislator, but all of them as a package appealing to a sufficient number to ensure the support of a majority of legislators.

Sometimes logrolling involves large interest groups. In 1964, when the House passed a cotton bill, the Senate tacked on a wheat section. When this cotton-wheat bill was returned to the House and still needed additional support for passage, the rural Democrats supporting it made a deal with urban Democrats who wanted a food stamp plan. As part of the bargain, the Food Stamp Bill had to be reported to the floor of the House first, but eventually both bills became law.

Another form of bargaining is the making of *compromises*. The proponents of a bill settle for less than they had originally demanded and then modify the bill to meet their opponents halfway. Compromises may end up exactly halfway between different positions or at some other highly visible or prominent solution that is acceptable to both sides; or else a compromise may give much to one side and little to the other, reflecting perhaps their unequal power or bargaining skills.

Finally, bargaining may involve *side payments*—advantages distinct from the content of the bill. Positive side payments to legislators may consist of federal judgeships, postmasterships, or other patronage appointments being placed under their control in exchange for their support of legislation important to the president. Other side payments may come from within Congress, such as desirable committee assignments or subcommittee chairs. Still other side payments may come from outside the government—from the national party or from special interest groups—and may include campaign contributions, well-paid speaking engagements, and the like. Influential legislators have reported annual income from such sources in excess of $100,000.

Outside pressures on Congress—such as from voters, interest groups, or the executive branch—clash or mesh in a changing balance with *inside influences* from congressional leaders or ordinary members. Inside influences tend to prevail and inside strategies are more likely to succeed, according to Nelson Polsby, when (1) the pending decision can be made a matter of procedure rather than substance; (2) one side has much greater inside strength, while both are evenly matched outside; and (3) the members are shielded from surveillance by outsiders. When these conditions are reversed, outside forces and the strategies designed to marshal them are likely to predominate.

Miniature Legislatures: The Congressional Committees.

The Ninety-sixth Congress, including the House and Senate, meeting between 1979 and 1981, worked through 53 committees and 263 subcommittees. Congressional committees resemble small cross sections of Congress. They often are selected in a biased manner, favoring some groups in Congress at the expense of others. Nonetheless, their contribution is indispensable. They permit bargaining, compromising, and logrolling with a minimum of publicity, until a workable majority coalition emerges. After a bill is reported out of committee, other members of Congress know more readily how to vote on it; they can pick up cues from committee members who are familiar with the measure and who have outlooks and interests similar to their own. A bill that passes in committee has a good chance to pass on the floor. Without the work of the committees a larger percentage of legislation would be defeated. In addition to making legislation more acceptable to their fellow legislators, the committees also tend

to make it less ideological, as abstract and sweeping provisions are whittled down and specific points are changed or added. Finally, by involving diverse interest groups outside Congress through formal hearings or informal communications, committee work makes tbe ultimate legislation more acceptable to the country.

The House Committee on Appropriations performs a particularly important task: it deals with money. Its decisions shape the federal budget and over the course of time much of the national government. Most of the increases or other budgetary changes it makes when voting on the budgets of federal agencies are marginal; and the overall pattern of its decisions is balanced and conservative. Within this pattern, says Richard Fenno, most increases go to those agencies that have much support in the House outside the committee and in the country at large or that have won the confidence of the committee in the course of time. A very few agencies, such as the Federal Bureau of Investigation, meet all three tests. The Appropriations Committee is greatly trusted by the House; from 1947 to 1962, by Fenno's count, 90 percent of its recommendations were accepted.

Representation in the committees is heavily weighted on the rural and conservative side. Rural representatives made up half of the House Democrats in 1964, but held nearly three-quarters of the House's major committee chairs; and rural representatives from the South contributed less than 30 percent of the House strength, but had more than one-half the chairs. Significantly, southern representation among major committee chairs corresponded almost exactly to the proportion of southern safe seats in the House (see Table 2.6). On the important House Rules Committee, the giving of half the Democratic seats to southerners had become traditional.

In 1972 a somewhat more liberal House and Senate were elected by the same voters who refused to vote for Senator George McGovern for president and voted for President Nixon without sharing his entire political outlook. The new House of Representatives included about fifty younger and more liberal members, and about a half-dozen of the most senior—and often conservative—committee chairmen did not return. The election of 1974 reinforced this trend, which was not reversed until the 1980 election. However, the new members of Congress from suburban districts depended less on their national party organizations or on favors from the executive. They were more responsive to local opinion from their constituencies and to the pressure of local interest groups, ranging from environmentalists and pacifists to local bankers and business-people, alarmed patriots and members of ethnic groups of European descent—despite the slowly declining influence of the latter. Neither a liberal president nor the traditional conservative coalition of Republicans and southern Democrats could take their support for granted. The new members' impulse, as indicated by the democratizing reforms mentioned earlier (see p. 68), were for greater decentralization and pluralism. The actions of Congress therefore became harder to predict and more difficult to manage than they had been for many years.

In *roll-call votes* (when each legislator present publicly records his or her vote by name), a Democratic president could count within House committees on an average support of 73 percent from the Democrats and 37 percent from Republican committee members. The same held true for Senate committees. For a Republican president in a Congress dominated by Democrats, the proportions might be reversed if the presidential program were not shaped to attract more bipartisan support. Conversely, a Republican president might choose to try to by-pass Congress and to enhance the powers of that office. President Nixon's choice of the latter course ended in disaster. President Carter, facing an unruly majority from his own party in Congress, struggled vainly to find a viable strategy of compromise.

The Favored Elements in Congress. In matters of procedure Congress is dominated by two parties. Democrats and Republicans compete to organize Congress to determine its majority and minority, its committee chairs, and, within each party, the committee assignments. But on matters of substance many writers have seen four parties at work in Congress: northern Democrats, mostly urban and liberal; southern Democrats, mostly rural and conservative; liberal Republicans, mostly from northeastern cities, suburbs, and rural areas; and conservative Republicans, mostly from the rural Midwest, suburban California, and parts of the urban South. None of these four has a majority in Congress. On many issues an informal coalition of conservative Republicans and southern Democrats has commanded a majority. (No such coalition was able to control the 1965–66 Congress; much of the program of social legislation that it passed had been held up for decades.) A still more detailed division would add two more groups to the four listed: middle-of-the-road Democrats and middle-of-the-road Republicans. These two are minorities, but they are likely to be needed in helping majorities to form, and thus their influence is often great.

All told, Congress has come a long way from the days when Ralph Waldo Emerson called it "a standing insurrection." In its operations it is slow, conservative, and compromising in domestic matters. It is replete with lawyers, farmers, and businesspeople. Of some of its members it must be said that their prejudices seem more rigid than their ethics. In foreign affairs after World War II, Congress drifted into the habit of backing a vast expansion of foreign involvement and military expenditure with little supervision or criticism, reserving its distrust mainly for the foreign economic aid programs that are now allocated about $2 billion (less than one-quarter of 1 percent of the GNP), or about one-tenth the share that foreign aid had in 1949. Nevertheless, domestic expenditures for health, education, welfare, housing, and urban development had become almost three times as large as defense spending by 1979. And these expenditures, rather than defense spending, had become the target of protests by middle-class taxpayers. By the beginning of the 1980s, however, foreign threats became more prominent. Real increases in defense spending seemed to be acceptable once again to Congress, public opinion, and the press even if that meant holding down growth in spending for social policy.

Despite its continuing problems, Congress has enacted a vast program of legislation since 1933—one that has in many ways transformed the country—and it is likely to go on doing so in the decades ahead. Congress remains one of the broadest and most essential channels of communication between the American people and their government; it is a necessary instrument for translating communication into agreement and agreement into action.

Legislative Representation and State Politics. On the state level, as on the national level, bicameral legislatures are the rule. (Only Nebraska still has a single-chamber legislature.) In the states, too, the twentieth-century trend has been toward direct election of both chambers.

Unlike politics on the national level, state politics has been characterized more often by unequal districts or districts of bizarre shape, deliberately drawn to favor one party at the expense of the other. The first such district was drawn in the early years of the republic with the advice of Elbridge Gerry of Massachusetts; because it was elongated like a salamander, Gerry's opponents called it a new monster, the *gerrymander,* thus adding both a noun and a verb to the language of politics. Together with restrictive residence requirements and other voter registration laws and practices, these conditions have favored the domination of many states by political machines well entrenched at the state, county, and municipal levels. In recent years, industrialization, mass migration, and the growing participation of large numbers of people in politics have put mounting pressure on these ancient practices. Struggles over voter registration, equal representation, legislative reapportion-

ment, and the breaking or limiting of the power of state political machines now loom large in American politics and may continue to do so for some time.

The struggle for political control on the state level has been a persistent factor in American government, for state politics is critical to the working of the federal system. There are four basic ways by which it affects the federal system. First, it indirectly controls the nomination and election of all United States senators and, thus, the composition of one branch of the federal legislature. Second, the major political parties in the nation are actually little more than federations of state party organizations. The state organizations of each party control more personnel and resources than each party's national committee. Both national parties, therefore, depend heavily on influence and patronage within the states. Control of national parties is often won or lost at the state level. Without control of jobs and favors at the state level a party cannot hold together much of its organization. With such control a party can survive for many years out of national office.

Third, the party organization in each state often plays a decisive part in the nomination and election of candidates for the United States House of Representatives. And finally, state politics, state parties, and sometimes state *primaries*—"first-round" elections in which the candidates to be nominated by a party for a public office are chosen by members of that party—often determine the nomination of major party candidates for president of the United States. In this respect, the party machine in each state sometimes has been more important than the party voters. In 1968 both Republicans and Democrats nominated presidential candidates who seemed to be more popular with the regular party organizations than with the mass of voters, but in 1976 the opposite happened after primaries had become more open in both major parties. Still, in 1980 state politics continued to exercise a direct influence on the composition of Congress and an indirect, but powerful, influence on the selection of the chief executive of the United States. This influence, however, has its limits. When conservative Republicans in 1964 captured the party machine and the presidential nomination for Senator Barry Goldwater, and in 1972 when well-left-of-center Democrats, young activists, and some adherents of new lifestyles captured the Democratic national convention and the presidential nomination for Senator George McGovern, both these candidates were badly defeated at the polls. On the average, voters are more moderate in their views than party activists, despite some increase in political polarization (p. 64 above), and the activists and machine controllers forget it at their peril. Remembering this fact of life enabled the Republicans in 1980 to nominate a candidate with strong right wing credentials who could also appeal to basic concerns of the broad middle mass of Americans.

The Presidency and Executive Power. The most demanding job in federal government is the presidency of the United States. It is always wearing, often thankless, and sometimes deadly. Abraham Lincoln once remarked that his position reminded him of a comment by a man being ridden out of town on a rail: "If it were not for the honor of the thing, I would rather walk." For more than a century there has been a bitter reality behind Lincoln's quip. The presidency has killed many of its incumbents, four by assassination—Lincoln, Garfield, McKinley, Kennedy—and others, such as Wilson and Franklin D. Roosevelt, by strain and overwork (see Figure 2.7). When it has not killed them, the presidency has certainly worn them down (see Figure 2.8).

Yet the office has never wanted for occupants; there has never been a need to put a For Rent sign on the White House lawn. The presidency has always been the most powerful office in the United States, and with the coming of nuclear weapons it has become one of the most powerful on a planet that no single country, office, or officeholder can

control. Today the president of the United States can be both the nation's chief executive and its executioner: the president shares with the rulers of the Soviet Union the power to destroy civilization and to kill most of humankind. At the same time, with the coming of the welfare state and of international economic aid, the United States presidency has become crucially involved with a growing range of human needs. Its potentialities for good, too, are vast and still growing. But while the powers of the office have grown vastly, the mental and moral capacities of its incumbents have not. Inevitably, they have remained ordinary human beings, each of whom, as one politician put it, "has to put on his trousers one leg at a time."

In the past some American presidents have chosen not to use their full powers; they have been passive in office. When the writer Dorothy Parker was told that President Calvin Coolidge had died, she asked: "How could they tell?" But just as the passive presidents of the 1850s—Fillmore, Pierce, and Buchanan—were followed by the Civil War, the passive presidents of the 1920s—Harding, Coolidge, and Hoover—were followed by the Great Depression. Again, during the 1950s many voters wanted President Eisenhower to preside over a relaxed nation and a passive government, and some of the things left undone in those years may have borne bitter fruit in the unemployed young, the neglected minorities, and the urban riots and crises of the 1960s. The presidency is the primary place from which unified leadership can be offered to the American people. The costs to the country are high when presidents neglect their opportunities—but also when they underestimate the limits of their power.

The President's Election. The American president and vice president are elected for a four-year term, and the president is limited to two terms in office. Both are elected by all the people, and in their election the people's votes have more nearly equal weight than in the election of any other branch of government.

Even here, however, the weighting of votes is

not completely equal. As a matter of form, the president is elected indirectly by an *Electoral College*. Each state has a number of electors equal to the sum of its senators and representatives; and its state legislature may provide for the appointment or election of these electors in any manner it sees fit. This arrangement favors somewhat the smaller states, since even the smallest ones must have at least two senators and one representative in Congress and thus cannot have fewer than three votes in the Electoral College. Nonetheless, in 1980 the massive electoral votes of the seven most populous states—California, New York, Pennsylvania, Illinois, Ohio, Texas, and Michigan—accounted for 211 of a total of 538 electors. These states have been decisive in past elections, and they are likely to continue to be decisive in the future.

Despite the intentions of the framers of the

Constitution, the election of the president has, in effect, become the result of a popular vote, and most voters so perceive it. Electors are usually *pledged* to vote for a particular candidate; most voters neither know nor care who the electors are, but vote for a slate of electors because these electors promise to cast their ballots for the candidate whom the voters favor. In some states, however, it is legally possible for a slate of electors to present itself *unpledged* to the voters, perhaps with the promise to strike the best bargain in the Electoral College in regard to some issue of particular importance to the voters of that state. Electors pledged to the candidate of a minority party might play a similar role if no major party candidate were able to command a majority of electoral votes. It is also legally possible for an elector to break his or her pledge to his or her

FIGURE 2.7 *Woodrow Wilson*

Source: Bettman Archive.

voters and cast a ballot for another candidate. The Constitution provides no remedy against such a breach of party discipline or of faith to the voters.

As the only officer of the United States government elected from a nationwide constituency, the president is expected, therefore, to act as president of all the people. And in practice the presidency often has been the branch of government that is most responsive to urban and industrial voters and to the needs of ethnic, religious, or racial minorities. The mechanism ensuring this responsiveness rests in the present composition of the Electoral College and the crucial role of the seven largest states within it. These seven are highly urban and industrial; each includes a high concentration of minorities; and the votes of each state must be cast as a unit. A presidential candidate therefore must win or lose each state as a whole; and for winning, that candidate depends heavily on the urban, industrial, and minority group voters within it. In 1980, Jimmy Carter

counted on this base of support, but his personality, associates, record, and changing style and tactics did not represent the feelings of many traditional urban Democrats, blue-collar workers, and ethnic groups. Accordingly, he lost many big cities or carried them by small margins, while Ronald Reagan, who was widely perceived as a safe change, attracted the substantial support of voters in the countryside, suburbs, and South, and added the votes of some of the disaffected Democrats.

This winner-take-all provision for the electoral votes of each state represents in one sense an injustice against the voters of the losing party. Their votes are not counted, and they might well prefer some scheme of proportional representation among the electors of their state. But in another sense the winner-take-all arrangement is a countervailing injustice. Often it balances the overweighting of the small states and of the rural areas and old-stock elements in the population; as

FIGURE 2.8 *Jimmy Carter*

Source: Wide World Photos

we have seen, this overweighting has long characterized the way in which the House of Representatives and, to a lesser extent, the Senate are elected.

In the late 1960s, various proposals for reforming the procedure for presidential elections were discussed. There seemed to be widespread agreement that the Electoral College should be replaced by the direct vote of the people, but there was disagreement whether to retain majority rule within each state or whether to replace it by some scheme of proportional representation. If the latter device were adopted, voters from urban and industrial areas and from minority groups might find their influence drastically reduced. Lacking any compensating change in other aspects of political representation, such voters might then feel permanently underrepresented in the American political system and become alienated from it. Under the present arrangement, voters disappointed with their representation in Congress often still look to the presidency for redress. Conversely, of course, voters dissatisfied with the policies of a president may find some help for their concerns in Congress. A constitutional amendment to abolish the Electoral College was proposed by Senator Birch Bayh, but interest in the matter declined during the 1970s when the prospects of a strong third party faded and Governor George Wallace in 1978 announced his withdrawal from political life.

Since the president is an essential part of the system, he or she must be promptly replaced in case of death or disability. Detailed rules for the succession to the presidency have been worked out to guarantee a rapid and peaceful transfer of power. If the president dies in office, he or she is succeeded by the vice president. After the assassination of President Kennedy, the transfer of his office to Vice President Lyndon B. Johnson was accomplished within an hour. If both the president and the vice president should die, the speaker of the House would become president; after that individual the office would go to the president pro tempore of the Senate, and then to the secretary of state, the secretary of the treasury, and the rest of

the Cabinet. There are also specific provisions for succession in case of the president's illness or incapacity. These seem unique, and they contrast strikingly with the practice of dictatorships. They also appear as reasonably safe as can be expected. Even in the age of nuclear weapons, when one large hydrogen bomb could wipe out Washington, D.C., it seems unlikely that all these persons could be killed at once. Some continuity in the office of chief executive thus seems to be as well assured as anything else in the American political system under conditions of modern weaponry.

The President's Many Roles. Once elected, the president must fulfill many different roles that may be only partly compatible with one another. In military matters he or she is *commander in chief* of a peacetime defense force of 2.5 million people in uniform (not counting another 1.1 million civilian Defense Department employees)[19] and of the entire nation in times of war. In recent years the increasing power of modern weapons systems has made this individual responsible for more destructive power than any human being should have. The same modern technology has made the president potentially more helpless. On the eve of an all-out war the president would have to depend on radar echoes and other types of electronic information, hard to interpret and subject to error. The president would have to make decisions under extreme constraints of time and would then have to live on the bull's eye of a target, with Washington and the White House exposed to the thermonuclear weapons of an enemy. There might be only a few minutes to decide, and the president might have to use much of this short time just to move to some presumably safer shelter; and any orders given to American aircraft and missiles might soon prove impossible to recall. The military technology that has so vastly in-

---

[19]Data from *Statistical Abstract of the United States, 1972,* p. 259.

creased the president's power also has tended to make him or her its prisoner.

In regard to conventional weapons and troop commitments, the president has a wider range of discretion. According to the Constitution, only Congress can declare war. But tradition has long permitted American presidents to commit troops and ships—and more recently aircraft—to smaller "police actions" on their own authority. Such precedents reach from Jefferson's sending a few ships against Algerian pirates to numerous skirmishes on the Indian frontier of the United States and to various interventions by the American Marines in the Caribbean and Mexico during the first two decades of the twentieth century. In recent years these police actions have tended to become much bigger in such places as Korea, Lebanon, the Dominican Republic, and Vietnam. They have involved not only professional soldiers and volunteers, as in earlier police actions, but also large numbers of drafted citizen soldiers, including many reluctant or unwilling ones; and the size and duration of some of these undertakings have proved increasingly difficult to control. These powers of the president were reduced, however, in the 1970s by new legal restrictions voted by Congress. The key example was the War Powers Resolution of 1973, passed by Congress over President Nixon's veto. The result was to formalize what had historically been left to informal understandings and trust between the president and Congress.[20]

Although the president's role as commander in chief was intended primarily to provide powers against foreign threats, the law has long been vague about what the president could order the armed forces to do if he or she chose to perceive the danger of a domestic insurrection. The power of the president to have the governor of a state removed by federal force was made subject to judicial review in the famous judgment *ex parte Milligan,* when the Supreme Court reversed such a decision made by President Abraham Lincoln at the time of the Civil War. But what would have happened if the president had ordered the soldiers to arrest not a governor, but the Supreme Court, perhaps stating that he perceived the justices as constituting a danger to national security? Or if a president someday should order the armed forces to disperse or arrest the members of Congress?

Luckily, the problem has not arisen in the more than two-hundred-year history of the United States. But when President Nixon was about to resign in August 1974, Secretary of Defense James M. Schlesinger issued an order to all armed forces of the United States not to carry out any order from their commander in chief without Schlesinger's countersignature. The formal legal basis for this order seems unclear, but its basis in common prudence seems self-evident. By the late 1970s, however, no formal legal procedure for dealing with such problems had been established.

At home the president is the country's bureaucrat in chief. As head of the executive branch of government, he is in charge of more than 2 million civilian employees. Many of these are now protected by civil service regulations designed to prevent their hiring and firing on political grounds. About 2,000 top-level government jobs are defined in various ways as *policy-making appointments* and are in the president's gift, and so are another 1,800 high-level jobs somewhat further down the line.[21] The president also appoints the *White House staff,* which has grown substantially in recent years, both in numbers and in the scope and importance of affairs entrusted to it. This growth continued under President Carter despite his earlier campaign declarations to the contrary. The president

[20]Under this resolution the president must "consult" with Congress before sending U.S. soldiers into hostile areas and report within forty-eight hours that he has dispatched such troops. After that, the president has sixty days to engage the troops but must then withdraw them unless Congress has acted to the contrary (or is unable to meet because the nation is under attack).

[21]From data in Hugh Heclo, *A Government of Strangers: Executive Politics in Washington* (Washington, D.C.: Brookings Institution, 1977).

also appoints members of *presidential commissions* to report on matters of fact or policy, and a variety of informal advisers and associates can be selected. For the appointment of ambassadors, federal judges, and the members of the official Cabinet, which comprises the heads of the major departments of the government, the *advice and consent* of the Senate is required. Such consent is only rarely refused to Cabinet nominees. Generally, the president anticipates the probable response of the Senate in nominating such persons for appointment or else, if possible, entrusts the task to a member of the White House staff who is not subject to Senate confirmation.

The president is also the party leader, and dispenser in chief of federal patronage and favors. Through these powers the president can exercise not only moral, but also material, influence on the votes of representatives and senators. The more responsive they are to the wishes of the president the more receptive the executive may prove to the needs of their districts, states, party organizations, and personal acquaintances. Some presidents have been more vigorous than others in reminding members of Congress of their presidential powers. Franklin D. Roosevelt was a master of such methods; and so, more bluntly, was Lyndon B. Johnson.

A major source of presidential power is the role as the symbol of national unity and as media manipulator in chief. Anything the president does makes news if he or she so chooses and sometimes even if he or she does not. The president often can define a situation and thus can predetermine much of the response of American opinion. After taking over the presidency in 1963 Lyndon Johnson chose to define the fighting in South Vietnam as a case of simple foreign aggression by the North Vietnamese, and in August 1964 he defined an ambiguous incident in the Gulf of Tonkin as an attack on the United States Navy. These definitions went far to prepare Congress and the voters to accept the escalation of the American commitment in South Vietnam from 16,000 "advisers" in late 1963 to over 540,000 troops in late 1968. By

contrast, the Johnson decision *not* to define the capture of the American electronic intelligence ship *Pueblo* by the North Koreans in 1968 as an act of war kept public opinion relatively quiet and permitted the government to obtain the return of the ship and its crew through negotiation. From 1972 on, President Nixon calmed public feelings by his visits to China and the Soviet Union and his conduct of peace negotiations with North Vietnam, and later he stressed the relaxation of tensions when he received the Soviet leader, Leonid Brezhnev, in Washington and when he completed the official withdrawal of United States troops from South Vietnam. On the whole, this presidential policy of détente was endorsed—though not always under this name—by Presidents Ford, Carter, and Reagan. Even in situations beyond the control of a president, his central position as symbol of national unity makes him the natural rallying point for public support. There has been no better example of this than the dramatic upsurge of public support for President Carter that occurred early in the Iranian hostage crisis of 1979–80.

Beginning in 1970, President Nixon and Vice President Agnew stressed heavily what they considered to be the obligation of the mass media to support the policies of the administration, particularly in all matters of foreign and military policy. By early 1973, radio and television stations had been reminded of their dependence on federal licenses, publishers of newspapers and periodicals had been made aware of the difference that postal rates and regulations could make to their revenues, and prosecutors and judges had been encouraged to cooperate in sending journalists and scholars to jail for refusing to name the sources of their information, as the latter had often been permitted informally to do in the past. In the short run, at least, this tactic of heavier administrative pressure produced more opposition, rather than more conformity. In mid-1973 the major mass media did not fail to report in detail the revelations of administration scandals and of the Watergate affair; and members of Congress seemed well aware that the destruction of the independence of the press and the electronic media would also wipe out much of the power of Congress itself. Congressional investigations would lose much of their effect if the press, radio, and television were no longer free to report their results. The mass media are an essential link to the American people for Congress, as well as for the president, and they are an essential link for the people to their elected representatives. The mass media must balance their freedom and their responsibility; but if in doubt, it is perhaps best for the country if they take their chances on the side of truth. The issue is not simple, however, and it is likely to play a role in American politics throughout the 1980s.

The president's power to define issues and direct public attention is scarcely less in domestic affairs. Presidential support and leadership, or their lack, have decided the success or failure of many a civil rights or social welfare program.

Despite all these assets, the president's powers are severely limited. He or she cannot allocate a large amount of money without congressional support. Even some of the major official appointments depend on senatorial good will. Beyond Congress, the president depends on the courts, which may declare his or her acts unconstitutional—even though they usually are reluctant to do so. Yet the Supreme Court did exactly this when it threw out some of the early acts of Franklin D. Roosevelt's New Deal. Major executive acts, such as President Harry S. Truman's seizure of the strike-bound steel industry in 1952, likewise may be subject to court scrutiny. Beyond the courts, the president depends on the voluntary cooperation of government officials and the people. Only if the great majority of them comply can presidential decisions be enforced on the rest.

In regard to these many elements, the president often must act as a political broker, striving to put together a coalition that is like-minded enough to agree and strong enough to act. As a rule, a chief executive can be no stronger than the coalition behind him or her. But even if backed by all elements of the American political system, the president is not all-powerful in world politics. The actions of many foreign nations cannot be controlled. Nor is power over nature and technology unlimited. Inescapably, the president is human and fallible—and so are the American people. One test of greatness for both consists in the ability to recognize these limitations.

Finally, the president also is supposed to be something of a human model for the nation. Ideally, he or she should unite the moral virtues of goodness, honesty, and truthfulness with the worldly skills of shrewdness, energy, and competence. Even a well-publicized divorce is a liability for a presidential candidate. If all these virtues cannot be found in equal excellence in a single candidate, American voters have more than once elected presidents whose moral virtues had been open to criticism. Grover Cleveland was the admitted father of an illegitimate child; some of Warren G. Harding's close associates were deeply involved in corruption; yet both were elected. But American voters have always insisted on an image of competence in chief executives. Like passengers of a ship at sea, they want their captain to be virtuous, but they insist on competence in navigation. But if the American people, for one reason or another, should want to get rid of an unsatisfactory president, how under the Constitution could they go about it?

Emergency Exit in Slow Motion: The Procedure of Impeachment. By mid-1973, President Richard M. Nixon had become the target of twofold pressure. The Watergate scandal had thrown grave doubts on the integrity of some of the highest and closest associates of the president; and it had led many voters to doubt the veracity of the president himself. (Only 11 percent in a Gallup poll in August 1973 said they believed President Nixon's claim that he had not known for a long time either of his associates' involvement in the Watergate burglary and other illegal actions or of their later attempts to cover up the whole matter.) Simultaneously, the president's competence in halting inflation and managing the American economy came under attack as prices continued to rise.

At the same time, however, Nixon reminded the American people that he was the only president they had. Indeed, the Constitution provides no means for removing a president from office except through the cumbersome and divisive procedure of *impeachment*. A president of the United States can be impeached—that is, formally accused and put on trial—only for "treason, bribery, or other high crimes and misdemeanors" (U.S. Constitution, Article III, Section 4); and such impeachment must be voted by the House of Representatives. If the House so votes, the president then must be tried by the Senate with the chief justice of the United States presiding; and conviction is possible only "with the concurrence [the vote] of two-thirds of the Members [the senators] present" (Article I, Section 3). If convicted, the president would be removed from office, which then would devolve upon the vice president. If both president and vice president should be removed or otherwise incapacitated, the speaker of the House of Representatives would succeed to the presidency, followed by the president pro tempore of the Senate and the members of the Cabinet in order of seniority of their departments, beginning with the State Department. Further details are regulated by the Twenty-fifth Amendment to the U.S. Constitution, passed in 1967.

In the history of the United States only one president, Andrew Johnson, has been impeached, and his conviction in the Senate failed, being one vote short of the required two-thirds majority. In 1974, however, the removal of a president again came close to fulfillment when a congressional committee voted to impeach President Nixon. He then resigned and later was pardoned by his successor (see page 70, above).

Federal Powers and the Judiciary. Federal powers, characteristic of the American system, are very great over credit, commerce, and contracts. These powers were crucial for the integration of the United States into one country. The first large step in the development of federal power was taken by the states under the Articles of Confederation with

the *full faith and credit clause*. Under this clause each state had to give full faith and credit to the public acts, records, and judicial proceedings of every other state. The Constitution now embodies this principle, but it shifts the main integrative task to federal institutions.

A major channel of federal influence is the institution of *judicial review:* the right and duty of the courts to decide whether any law or act is valid under the Constitution. It does not appear in the Constitution, but grew up as an interpretation of it. In no other country in the world does a court have as much power and as much respect as the United States Supreme Court. The Court has functioned in a very important way, beginning in 1800 with Chief Justice John Marshall's opinion in the famous case of *Marbury* v. *Madison*. Ever since, the courts have had the right to review the executive acts of the federal and state governments and the laws of the national and state legislatures.

The power of the judiciary to determine the constitutionality of legislation and executive acts has five major consequences. First, the courts settle many serious political conflicts peaceably. Second, they are one of the chief instruments of balance in the American political system, by limiting the power of the other branches of government and by protecting individuals and minorities. Third, they often slow down change until it becomes acceptable to a larger proportion of the people. Fourth, they sometimes accelerate change, or they bring about immediate changes that the other branches of government have failed to produce. Fifth, the courts offer in all these respects an additional channel of communication between the people and their government and a long-term feedback circuit by which the American political system can steer itself.

The courts contribute an important check and balance by their practice of judging acts of the legislative and executive branches of government in the light of the judges' understanding of the

Constitution. As Charles Evans Hughes said before he became chief justice, "The Constitution is what the judges say it is." Though the Constitution looks like a simple document, it is often not at all clear how it should be applied to the many complex problems that have arisen since its enactment. The judges' latitude in interpreting it is great indeed, and their decisions, in particular those of the Supreme Court, have become an important part of *"judge-made" law*. Because most Americans habitually respect and obey their courts and because the lower courts accept the overriding decisions of the higher courts, the entire judiciary system has important powers over what happens in government and throughout the country.

The courts have thrown out important acts of Congress, such as the National Recovery Act in the 1930s. They also have declared illegal some major acts of the president, including some taken in the name of national security. Thus the Supreme Court in the decision *ex parte Milligan* held illegal certain emergency powers assumed by the Lincoln administration during the Civil War. A later Supreme Court took a very critical view of the compulsory internment of Americans of Japanese descent during World War II. In both cases the Court acted, however, only after the emergency had passed; and the compensation finally paid to the illegally and unjustly interned Japanese-Americans for their lost properties amounted to about ten cents on the dollar.[22]

The courts cannot act quickly. In times of emergency they are reluctant to stop the other two branches of government from acting; and even later they cannot always ensure full redress to victims of injustice. Nevertheless, they can provide at least partial redress. They can free individuals from prison; they can restore rights that were denied; they can clear people's names; and they can make clear what individuals and agencies of government cannot do within the law. In serving these functions, the courts protect individuals as

well as the soundness of the American political process.

"The brain is an organ of inhibition," said an Austrian labor leader many years ago; the Supreme Court has long been a vital part of the mind and conscience of the American republic and its people. As an agency of inhibition, the Supreme Court has often acted as a brake on change. On the average, Supreme Court justices in the twentieth century have held that position for twelve years; ordinarily they cannot be removed against their will. No president has been able during a single four-year term to appoint a majority of Supreme Court justices. So the justices often represent the memories and standards of a somewhat earlier day and, at least intermittently, the view of an older generation.

For this they have often been chided. Justice Oliver Wendell Holmes criticized his colleagues for clinging too closely to nineteenth-century doctrines of government nonintervention in the labor market when they held that sweatshops and night work for women should not be interfered with by state governments. The Constitution, said Holmes, did not enact the prejudices of Herbert Spencer, the nineteenth-century British laissez-faire writer. (Later, Justice Holmes's views on this point were accepted by the Court's majority.) In the 1930s, President Franklin Roosevelt complained of the "nine old men" of the Supreme Court who in his view were going too far in defending property rights and thwarting the will of the voters.

At their best, however, the courts also represent some of the more enduring values and long-term points of view. During the decades since 1945 the Supreme Court has particularly stressed the rights of individuals. It has often opposed or limited the new controls over individuals introduced by the government in the name of national security. In the face of congressional legislation and administrative practices the Court has limited the requirements for security clearances, and it has tended to favor the traditional rights of Americans to keep

[22]See Morton Grodzins, *Americans Betrayed* (Chicago: University of Chicago Press, 1949).

their jobs, to travel abroad freely, to face their accusers, and to be held innocent until proved guilty by due process of law.

Sometimes the courts have been important instruments of change. They have struck down laws that no longer had the backing of the majority of voters, but were so intensely defended by influential minorities that no legislative majority could be found for their repeal. Since these laws no longer corresponded to the convictions of the majority, they threatened penalties for what Burke might have called "artificial crimes"; yet there seemed to be no practical legislative remedy. This was the case with the legal ban on birth control information that in the early 1960s was still on the books in Connecticut and Massachusetts and made almost all local doctors and druggists into lawbreakers. When the courts finally struck down these laws as unconstitutional, no politician made any serious effort to resurrect them, and doctors and druggists could breathe more freely.

Finally, the courts function as a major communication channel both to the memories and traditions of the past and to the perceived needs of the present and future. The Supreme Court, said Finley Peter Dunne's Mr. Dooley, follows the election returns, In one sense this is true, but the Court often follows these returns with a time delay of one or two decades, during which it becomes clear whether these earlier returns reflected a passing mood or a genuine trend of development.

In this manner many Supreme Court justices have followed the advice of Roscoe Pound to view law as an instrument of social control and to use it as such. Some justices have been eminent lawyers, whereas others have been highly skilled in practical affairs, often having served as governors of states, Cabinet members, United States presidents (Taft), or presidential candidates (Hughes and Warren). Whatever their background, many of them have had a refreshing sense of the practical. In the early 1920s a Court majority confirmed a lower court decision that barred an immigrant grandmother, Rosika Schwimmer, from citizen-

ship on the grounds that as an avowed pacifist she would not "bear arms" in defense of the Constitution. Justice Holmes dissented. For three centuries, he wrote, the Quakers had been pacifists, refusing to bear arms, yet they had done well by their country. Besides, he added dryly, the United States would be in a perilous position indeed if it needed the armed service of a grandmother to defend it. In later years this dissent of Justice Holmes, too, became the Court's majority doctrine. Pacifism is not a bar to United States citizenship any longer; and the 1969 verdict of an appeals court, throwing out a lower court's conviction of Dr. Benjamin Spock (for allegedly having "conspired" to thwart the draft for the Vietnam War), was in the Holmes tradition.

Another problem of reconciling legal, moral, and practical considerations occurred at the time of the sit-down strikes in the late 1930s, when striking auto workers occupied the factories of several major auto manufacturers. Some business and conservative interests called on the governor of Michigan, Frank Murphy, to use military force to defend property rights and evict the strikers, regardless of the bloodshed that could be expected. Governor Murphy refused to do this. His refusal compelled both sides to negotiate. In time the strikes were settled; the union was recognized; the strikers returned to work; and Governor Murphy was appointed to the Supreme Court. Some lawyers said that the Court henceforth would offer "justice tempered with Murphy," but the balance between property rights and human rights, between strict law and the politically practical, has remained among the Court's significant concerns—as such cases as *Baker* v. *Carr,* favoring legislative reapportionment, have demonstrated.

In one respect the role of the judiciary is unique. Both legislation and administration are processes designed primarily to deal with human beings in large numbers. Inevitably, they are most often concerned with mass legislation and mass administration. The courts alone are primarily designed to deal with individuals and with specific cases. It is this ability that we have in mind when we say that every person ought to have a right to "a day in court"—the day when the legal and political system is focused on that person's problems as an individual. This function of the courts has often been obscured in practice by the enormous costs and delays of court procedures. Carrying a case through the trial court, the higher courts, and the Supreme Court by now usually costs upward of $50,000. "A poor man has a chanst in coort, . . ." said Mr. Dooley more than half a century ago. "He has the same chanst there that he has outside. He has a splendid poor man's chanst."

In recent years the Supreme Court has handed down several decisions that are beginning to make a difference to a poor person's chances. Indigent defendants in federal felony trials have won the right to a free lawyer, and in *Gideon* v. *Wainwright* the Court extended this right to the state courts, where most of the actual felony trials are held. A suspect in police custody has long had the right to ask for a lawyer if the suspect can pay for one or can get one free. In *Escobedo* v. *Illinois* the Court ruled that the police must honor such a request for consultation; and in *Miranda* v. *Arizona* it said that before being questioned in police custody individuals must be told of their right to keep silent and to have a lawyer (free, if they are poor) and they must be warned that anything they say may be used against them—a warning customary in federal practice and long-standing in Britain. Together these decisions give the same protection of legal rights to the innocent suspect and the ignorant lawbreaker as the professional criminal and the large-scale operator of crime have had for many years. The effects on actual police practice have thus far been moderate. Nonetheless, these decisions have been charged with hampering the work of the police and endangering the victims of future crimes. Recent decisions by a somewhat more conservative Supreme Court have once again tended to increase slightly the powers of the police. Despite such back-and-forth shifts of opinion, a basic problem has remained: what risks would people rather run—those from unchecked

crime or those from an uncontrolled police? In making its rulings, the Court has had to decide between these conflicting viewpoints and values—the rights of individual citizens as opposed to the convenience of administration and the fears of the community—and during the last thirty years it has decided more often in favor of the individual.

In the long run such Court decisions require the backing of the people if they are to be effective. But these decisions show that the Court may sometimes try to lead opinion rather than merely follow it. This is the important question of *judicial activism:* how far should the courts go in leading opinion and deciding on public policy? In the days of Chief Justice Marshall between 1800 and 1820, and again during the last thirty years, the courts have been more active in deciding matters with large political implications than they were during most of the decades in between. Although the courts may still be deciding individual cases, the implications of their decisions and the remedies they impose can affect huge numbers of people. In recent years, for example, the courts have handed down decisions determining how a state's prison system will be administered; where schoolchildren will be bused; what language they will be taught in (Spanish if they are Hispanic); how school budgets will be allocated to buildings, books, and teachers' salaries; and where state mental patients will be housed and treated. Therefore, how the courts act can make an immense difference to politics and public policy. Leading or following, the judiciary helps to decide where the American people and their government will go next. The size and importance of its contribution to this self-steering process make the American political system different from all others in the world.

HOW DOES THE AMERICAN POLITICAL SYSTEM STEER ITSELF?

In its domestic politics the American system has more effective channels for the intake of information than does the political system of any other large industrial country. American political culture, too, places high value on listening to people and on paying attention to the views at the grassroots. At the same time, intake channels for information from abroad are poorer: far less well coordinated, more handicapped by inattention and secrecy, and often overridden by the streams of messages from major domestic interest groups that command a higher priority in the attention of political decision makers.

Domestic Intake Channels. There are more than a half-dozen groups of major intake channels bringing to the various levels and agencies of government a wide variety of information about domestic conditions, popular feelings, specific needs and demands of large interest groups, and the problems of numerous small groups and individuals. Every senator and member of Congress, every state legislator, every member of a municipal council is a potential listening device: people approach or write to him or her to present their problems and requests for legislative or administrative help or, in the case of less than 3 percent of the population, simply to express their views on some political issue; moreover, the members of the staffs of legislators and committees can search out information and bring it to bear on the legislative work.

Administrative officers and agencies—from the president and the governors of the fifty states to the various specialized administrative agencies, federal, state, and municipal—receive a similar stream of information. Some of this information may be aggregated in regional conferences, such as those of the governors or legislators from the resource-rich western states or of the governors of depression-sensitive New England; or they may aggregate information from the nation's urban areas, such as the U.S. Conference of Mayors.

A third system of intake channels is the court system, through which complaints about alleged violations of legal and constitutional rights of individuals and groups can be raised and often brought to a decision. And a fourth ensemble of information-carrying agencies and individuals consists of the lobbying organizations and lobbyists representing large corporate enterprise, industry, agriculture, and various labor unions and public interest groups.

In all four of these systems of channels—legislative, administrative, judicial, and lobbying—messages can be and often are initiated by parties at interest, that is, by individuals and groups outside the government. They can also be initiated, however, by some part of the government that is in search of information. Congressional committees can use their staff members to look into a variety of matters, and they can initiate formal investigations, using—and sometimes abusing—their powers to compel witnesses to testify before them. Administrative agencies, such as the Federal Trade Commission and the Civil Aeronautics Board, can initiate their inquiries. Lobbyists are legally required to register and reveal the names of their employers or clients, but so far little information has been obtained and made public about their activities. Courts and grand juries can investigate and compel testimony; and in the early 1970s this long-existing power of judges and grand juries was being used more vigorously than had been the long-established practice, as prosecutors and other government authorities put pressure on journalists and scholars to reveal sources of information to whom they had promised anonymity in return for cooperation.

Three other systems of intake channels bring information into the political system and up to the higher levels of government. These are the press, television, and other mass media; the universities, foundations, and research organizations, such as the Ford Foundation, the Carnegie Corporation, the Brookings Institution, the Rand Corporation, and the Battelle Institute; and, finally, the churches and religious organizations. All these can raise questions, gather information, stimulate attention, and at times suggest possible answers or solutions.

This wide variety of potential information-intake sources is one of the essential strengths of democracy and government in the United States. Any attempts to cut down the range and freedom of these flows of information; to intimidate the universities, the foundations, the television networks, and the press; to make the government listen less and talk more loudly—all such efforts, if successful, cut down both the intrinsic values and the long-run operational effectiveness of the American political system.

Information Intake from Abroad. If the facilities for the intake of domestic information are relatively good, the facilities for getting information about the rest of the world are less so. Today only a few American newspapers and periodicals maintain news-gathering staffs abroad. Universities and research organizations do more than they did a quarter of a century ago, but the scholarly books, articles, and research reports they produce are not read widely, nor usually at high levels of government. Diplomatic reporting has long been constrained by nonrecognition policies: in 1979 there still were no United States embassies in, and hence no continuous diplomatic reporting from, such countries as Cuba, North Korea, and Vietnam, all of which were important to the security and other interests of the United States. A United States mission was established in China only in 1973 (and this was raised to embassy status in March 1979), after a lapse of twenty-four years, but it would take time to overcome the results of such a long period of mutual ignorance. From countries where United States diplomats were stationed, reporting often had been constrained by pressures within the government to report only or mainly facts confirming the wisdom of the official policies of the day and to play down or omit all facts that might have suggested their revision.

The reports from abroad by the large intelligence organizations, such as the CIA, suffered in part from similar pressures toward conformity with current policy and perhaps still more from the secrecy that usually protected such reports from comparison with information known to the press or the scholarly community, which might have led to re-evaluation or correction. Secret information is often better than none, but is usually inferior to information that can be publicly discussed and tested. During the last two decades, crises in Cuba, Angola, Zaire, and Iran revealed that the CIA knew little about the real state of affairs in these nations and that it had passed on even less than that to Congress and the president.

Many American or multinational business organizations, of course, have a distinct interest in getting realistic information from abroad; but this information often is limited to their special fields of activities or distorted by some specific conflict of interest with a foreign government, as in the conflict between the International Telephone and Telegraph Company and the Allende government in Chile. Moreover, much of the limited information obtained by a business corporation is held confidential in order to deny its use to potential competitors.

In general, the information coming from the rest of the world into the American political system is inferior to the domestic information arriving there, in quantity and in quality, and the attention that it receives is less widespread and knowledgeable. Consequently, domestic maladjustments and errors have a better chance to be detected earlier and mitigated or corrected than errors in foreign policy and military matters. This disproportion has had its heavy costs in blood and treasure from the intelligence failure at Pearl Harbor in 1941 until the present day, and it involves even more serious risks of error in a nuclear crisis or confrontation in the future.

The Distribution of Memories. The imbalance in information intake is reinforced by an imbalance in the distribution of memories. Many Americans, inside and outside government, remember a great deal about domestic conditions. With the aid of these memories they can evaluate relatively quickly and effectively much of the new information about domestic political, social, and economic problems; but their memories about the rest of the world usually are far more unrealistic, inaccurate, and incomplete.

In addition, many of the memories of individual Americans, as well as of public or private agencies and organizations, are specialized and limited. Some persons or groups may know how to manage the economy in good times in order to produce an unemployment rate of 5 to 6 percent, and they may know what effect this measure, more or less by itself, may have on the rate of inflation. But they may not know how to keep the economy working within these limits when an economic depression deepens, or when events abroad push up radically the price of imported oil, and then indirectly the price of domestic fuels and everything else in the economy. And even in times of relative prosperity, they may remember little, nor care much, about the differential impact of unemployment on young people, blacks, and other minorities. Nor would they necessarily remember or care much about connections between unemployment among young people and the frequency of crimes, violence, political alienation, and divisiveness in the political system.

Rich and diversified as the memory facilities of that political system are, they often suffer seriously from the lack of cross-connections and coherence among the different specialists and special agencies. A few agencies, such as the president and the Cabinet, then are supposed to put and keep all these memories and information streams together—an overwhelming task for anyone to assume. In fact, of course, those charged with this responsibility are human, and they react to their overloads by coping as best they can with whatever decisions are most immediately pressing, putting off the rest. The result is once again the immobility-emergency cycle.

Decision Points and Institutions. In this matter of memories, the American political system—like that of other countries—is also vulnerable in another way. Memories held today are potential premises for decisions made tomorrow. They come to be regarded as the "lessons of history." These memories may seem unimportant now, but the future decisions swayed by them may be fateful. Relatively small rewards or penalties prevailing at one time may influence what is remembered—the articles and books that are published, the ideas and symbols that are accepted as normal and sound; the persons who are employed in government or promoted therein to higher office; the problems that are investigated and the questions that are asked. But this seemingly harmless manipulation of the accepted doctrines and assumptions today is in effect a process of *cognitive corruption*. It is a manipulation of the future memories of the population and of the political community, which may go far in controlling some major decisions in a subsequent crisis.

Compared to these weaknesses of American political memories in regard to international affairs, the *decision points* in the government of the United States are relatively clearly defined. The presidency, the governors of the fifty states, the United States Congress and the state legislatures, the federal and state courts—all have relatively well-defined tasks. In widely recognized emergencies they can decide relatively fast; and if any one agency or decision point should become incapacitated, others quickly can take over its functions. In recognized emergencies this system is more prone to overreact or react in the wrong direction than to delay acting at all. Widely perceived emergencies in the 1960s, such as Vietnam, illustrated this design. In situations that are not regarded as emergencies the reverse danger is more likely—delay in actions that could have prevented a bad situation from becoming worse. The "slow-motion crises" such as inflation and energy shortages, which crept up on Americans in the 1970s, are examples of the risks of delay.

Effectors and Outputs of the System. The effectors of the American political system are varied and powerful, and some of them are formidable. Among them must be counted the armed forces and their weaponry, having vast forces of destruction, but only limited capabilities for control of foreign areas with unwilling populations, and having even more limited capabilities for protecting American cities against thermonuclear missiles in the event of all-out war against a major power. Other effectors of the political system are United States diplomats, information services, and economic aid agencies abroad and the entire array of government agencies and employees at home. Most of these function well in discharging their special tasks, but the unified direction and coordination of their efforts are more likely to be relatively weak or intermittent.

The Problem of Consciousness and Coherence. It is difficult to find in the political system of the United States a single center of comprehensive awareness or *consciousness*—a point at which abridged and summarized information about all significant political, social, and economic processes in the United States and in the world at large is assembled for simultaneous inspection, comparison, and decision. There are "situation rooms" and "big boards" for strategic information at various high-level command posts of the armed forces and in the White House, but all these deal primarily with foreign countries, forces, and events, and with the deployment of American and allied forces in relation to them. Though American intake channels of information from abroad are relatively weak, serious efforts are made to coordinate the information they do yield.

The situation seems to be reversed in regard to domestic politics. The strong and rich information streams from domestic affairs are not well coordinated, except in the head of a very busy president or through the competing efforts of a few assistants. There does not seem to be a comparable situation room in the White House, or in any other high-level government agency, currently showing the interacting amounts and effects of poverty, malnutrition, unemployment, labor conflicts or settlements, race conflicts, drug addiction, crime,

campus unrest, protest activities, environmental improvement or deterioration, and the like. It seems that we have made more progress in the United States in coordinating our poor knowledge of foreign affairs than our rich knowledge in domestic matters.

Awareness of many of these problems and of their possible joint effects seems to be low or intermittent at the top of the political pyramid. Special agencies seem to be knowledgeable about some of these problems and events but not about others. Some awareness of the overall picture is embodied in certain nongovernmental organizations, such as the major political parties, the National Industrial Conference Board, the universities and the major foundations, and some of the better newspapers, periodicals, and television programs; but it is often less deep and accurate than necessary because of the pressures of time, special interests, and limited staffs and equipment. Despite these handicaps, a network of such organizations and facilities, intercommunicating more or less freely, may supplement the very incomplete consciousness of political and social reality available at the top of the pyramidal structure of formal government, whenever cognition and awareness within this pyramidal structure should fall short or fail. Any successful attempt to reduce the intake and free communication and evaluation of information within this informal nongovernmental network would have its very real cost in reducing the capabilities of cognition and awareness for the entire political system.

The Maintenance of Will. The situation is quite different in regard to the political *will*, its formation, and its maintenance.

Once established, popular images and political, economic, or strategic doctrines are likely to be defended tenaciously by interest groups who benefit from them and by officials who associate them with a rise in their careers. Persons and groups with dissenting views usually are less united and less motivated to bring about a change in policy. This may help us understand why the United

States, which tends to innovate more quickly in some sectors of technology and business methods than many other countries, often is conspicuously slower in changing some of its policies.

In domestic affairs, legislation for social security and for medical care for the elderly was adopted much later than in most of Western Europe; and a national health service or health insurance scheme—long established in Western Europe, Canada, and other countries—has yet to be adopted in the United States. In international affairs the United States took ten years longer to recognize the Soviet Union than did the anti-Communist governments of France and Britain and more than twenty years longer to recognize the government of Communist China. In 1972, President Nixon impressed Americans and world opinion by his official visit to China, which changed a nonrecognition policy of more than two decades, and by 1980 Chinese-American relations had become relatively friendly, even though characterized by some continuing ups and downs.

There are some advantages in this capacity of the American political system to hold fast for a long time to a policy once it has been adopted. The powers of the United States, both at home and in world affairs, are very great, though not unlimited; fickle, erratic behavior in a giant might be even more dangerous than relatively rigid resistance to any major change of course. But both drifting and rigid persisting are deficiencies in the process of steering. If the United States is to live safely with its own large resources and powers, its capabilities for steering itself will still need major improvements.

Creativity and Innovation. There are many points in the American system at which different items of information can be separated from each other, then selected and recombined into patterns that did not exist before, at least not at that particular time and place. These twin operations of breaking down old patterns of information into smaller components and of recombining them in new ways are at the heart of the process that we call *creativity*.

In politics, creativity involves perceiving the needs and demands of individuals and groups; the known material resources and technical possbilities for meeting them; the legal, technical, and administrative requirements for making each of these possible arrangements work in practice; and the political conditions for obtaining acceptance and support for any one of them, as well as the interests and groups likely to be arrayed in opposition in each case. Analyzing this information into its elements and trying out new combinations of these elements may then lead to proposals of new solutions, perhaps in the form of new legislation, such as the Social Security Act of 1935, or the G.I. Bill of Rights after World War II, or Medicare in the 1960s. Often it also may produce proposals for new administrative agencies, such as the Tennessee Valley Authority in the 1930s, the National Aeronautics and Space Administration in the 1950s, the National Science Foundation and the National Endowment for the Humanities in the 1960s, or the Family Assistance Plan or "negative income tax"—not yet enacted—of the 1970s.

The places in the political system where such new proposals are worked out are those where different streams of information meet and where the people at work there—be they legislators, legislative staff members, federal, state, or local bureaucrats, or persons working for nongovernmental research organizations, such as the Brookings Institution—have the time, the motivation, and the resources to engage in this work of analysis and recombination of information into tentative "candidate solutions" and then to critically re-examine and reshape these tentative projects or political inventions into more fully developed versions that can be proposed for action to major elements in the political system.

Turning an invention into large-scale practice is the essence of the process of *innovation*. It often involves the changing of existing habits and arrangements among relatively large numbers of people, the overcoming of the resistance that usually goes with change, and the mobilizing and arraying of positive expectations and support, broad enough and strong enough to help the innovation to prevail in the political decision process and eventually in the daily practice of the society. The more far-reaching and fundamental the innovation is, the more habits and institutions it requires to be changed, and the more likely it is to affect noticeably the structure of the political and social system. The more flexible the larger system is, the more likely it will be to succeed in accepting and accommodating even major innovations without losing its own cohesion and the sense of continuity and identity of its populations.

Judged in these terms and compared with other nations, the political system of the United States in the last sixty-plus years has not done badly. During that period it accepted first the eight-hour working day and then the forty-hour week; industrial labor unions, grievance committees, and collective bargaining in the factories; votes for women and, more recently, significant pressures for their equal pay and promotion; a federal minimum wage; widespread unemployment compensation and a large array of welfare services; nearly universal old-age pensions through social security; publicly financed medical care for persons aged sixty-five and older; publicly supported education for nearly one-half of all young people of college age; public legal assistance for needy defendants; and the large—though still inadequate—reduction of racial discrimination and oppression. Many of these changes were long and bitterly resisted, evoking dire predictions that each of them would ruin the nation or destroy its cherished way of life—predictions that so far have not come true. Rather, most often a majority of Americans has agreed that *not* to have made these changes would have threatened greater damage to the country.

But what if the United States should confront even greater problems, both foreign and domestic, and if it should face the need for even more surprising political and social inventions and for even greater and more rapid innovations and reforms? What if such needed changes should seem to require more serious transformations of

the present American political and economic structure? How would the American republic and its democracy respond to such a challenge?

A Key Test of Performance: Capabilities for Change and Self-Transformation. Such improvements in the American political system may require major structural reforms that may add up to a process of more or less far-reaching self-transformation. In the end, these capacities for survival through adaptation and self-transformation, more than current wealth and power, will constitute the most important test of the performance of the American political system. But what are the resources, forces, and capabilities of American politics for such a process of continuing change?

The Elements of Change. To discover something about the future of American politics, we must study the processes of both change and resistance to change at work. Many of these processes occur on a large scale, beyond the power of any individual or small group to speed or slow them. Nonetheless, these processes are important for the limits and opportunities they pose for the actions of individuals and groups. A man who wants to sail a boat may not be able to create the wind and the currents; but if he knows how to navigate, he can make use of them, and if he has an engine in the boat, he can do even more. But he still must know the speed and direction of the current and the wind.

Currents of Change in American Society. Two major elements of change in America are the continuing shifts in occupation and residence. In 1940, 20 percent of the American people were in agriculture; today there are less than 5 percent. Yet more than 40 percent of the members of Congress still list rural or small-town addresses, and a majority of the heads of important congressional committees, such as the Appropriations Committee in the House, come from small towns and rural neighborhoods. The nation, therefore, stands at the threshold of a structural change in its representative system. A nonagricultural majority of more than 95 percent is still partly represented—or misrepresented—by a heavily agriculturally oriented and overweighted Congress.

The second shift is from rural residence to urban. Only about 20 percent of the American people still live in rural areas; four-fifths live in cities, towns, and suburbs. Indeed, more than half the American people live in cities over 50,000 in population. These metropolises would be the most endangered targets in a nuclear war. Yet their representatives have little influence on foreign policy. In the meantime the majority of small-town legislators believe in "deterrence" and legislate accordingly.

Another population shift now in progress is that from the central city into the suburbs. Currently this is favored by the tax system, which still puts part of the national welfare burden for migrants and other needy groups on the taxpayers in the central cities.

A fourth shift in process is from the rural South into southern cities. This has had a definite effect on southern politics. Observers in the North and West tend to believe that American youth is moving in a liberal, humanitarian direction. They do not see the movement, like that in South Africa or Zimbabwe (formerly Rhodesia), of rural and young ex-rural southern whites into the cities, a shift that may be producing a more militant racial conservatism in southern cities. This trend resulted in 1968 in a vote for George Wallace in southern cities amounting to 20 percent—and over 30 percent among the South's young people. In 1972 in many southern areas, as in the nation, President Nixon ran ahead of the combined shares of votes that had been cast for him and Governor Wallace in 1968. Other southern whites have remained in the countryside, but have shifted to greater political participation and greater use of mass media. During the 1970s many southerners became more tolerant, and fewer remained racist or stayed indifferent. In time the *"white backlash"*

and the Wallace movement faded, and with the campaign of Jimmy Carter a more liberal southern tradition came to the fore, resulting in the election of the first president from the Deep South since the Civil War.

In addition, there was a large movement from the rural black South to the central cities of the North. The mechanization of cotton picking and other changes have driven black people from the countryside, and low southern relief rates have driven them north. Gradually, this shift slowed down as the pool of black rural southerners declined and as more jobs opened in southern cities and industries. In the North, however, this slowdown was balanced by the rise in black births in its cities and the entry into the adult job market by black youths. Together these changes are causing a revolution in northern city politics.

While poor blacks long have been moving to the North, white skilled and professional personnel and other members of the white middle class (and, in the late 1970s, even some poor or black people), working or retired, have been moving to the South, settling particularly in the Sun Belt states, which stretch from Florida to Arizona and southern California. As a result, these states have become less typically southern or western. They have become more tolerant with regard to race relations, but perhaps somewhat more conservative with regard to taxes and inflation.

There are four further shifts. From grade school to high school and college, a radical change is under way in the educational level of the American people. Women have entered the work force in much greater numbers than before, and in many cases their attitudes have changed. They demand access to a wider range of jobs. They want to be not only hired, but also paid equally and promoted on the strength of their performance. They are taking a new look at many of the traditional roles of women and are beginning to change some of them, sometimes with good results, sometimes at considerable human cost—and with many of the results not yet apparent.

In the highly filtered news media there is a great shift from newspapers, which simply do not print what they think is not fit to print, to television, in which the pictures on the camera let through a great deal of information that was not intended to be seen. Television is more difficult to censor, and it entails more total involvement and immersion by its audience. This creates new opportunities for criticism and independent thought. Perhaps this explains why people seem to resent discovery of a lie on television more than an untruth in print. Newspapers, on the other hand, can offer depth, follow-up, summary, and coherence if their editors and publishers choose to do so; and a number of newspapers and periodicals are continuing to perform this essential service.

Finally, a new kind of lobby has appeared. These *public interest lobbies* speak, or claim to speak, not for business, farmers, or labor, but for nonprofit causes, among which are consumer protection (such as Ralph Nader's "Raiders"), conservation of the natural environment (such as the Sierra Club), and improvement in government (such as Common Cause). Not all of their causes are compatible, nor do they often agree on the priorities among them. But on the whole they make a start toward counterbalancing the older pressure groups and to assist at least some processes of change in political and social values and practices.

The Resistances to Change. Resistances to change come from many sources. Some are habitual, for the habits of millions of people are hard to change. Other resistances are based on age groups. In the United States there are nearly three registered voters over fifty years of age for every two registered voters under thirty, and older voters are more reluctant to accept change. At the end of the 1960s, on many issues American voters over fifty years of age were more conservative—by 20 percent—than voters under thirty. In 1972, in particular, many voters over forty and fifty were repelled by much of the new lifestyle associations and images surrounding the McGovern nomination and campaign. President Nixon's victory in

that election represented in part a cultural backlash more than an economic or political one.

Resistance also comes from special interest groups. In the late 1960s there was a food stamp scandal. Food stamps, it was reported, were being manipulated in the interests of the farmers who wanted to sell their produce and not in the interests of the hungry children who needed adequate food. Reformers urged transfer of the program from the Department of Agriculture, which serves only the producers, to the Department of Health, Education, and Welfare, which presumably has a greater interest in children. Many changes of this kind are technically possible, but they require the substantial weakening or removing of certain conservative bulwarks. The overrepresentation of rural areas, small towns, and voters who never move is such a bulwark, as is the electoral underrepresentation of the young, the educated, and the mobile. Still other obstacles survive in the congressional systems of committees and seniority, despite recent reforms. When the powers of the presidency and of the Supreme Court majority are added, at least temporarily, to these conservative influences, the array of forces against change may look formidable indeed— perhaps as formidable as it looked half a century ago, in the days of Presidents Harding, Coolidge, and Hoover. But as experience has shown, the power of such coalitions against change does not last forever. Some groups opposing change eventually decline in strength or lose popular backing. Other groups find that some kinds of change may be in their own interest. Although it never was transferred from the Agriculture Department, the food stamp program has changed substantially, and it has been one of the more successful public programs significantly to reduce hunger.

Opportunities for Change. To some extent the mass media are sensitive to needs for change and to communications from individuals. Partisans of change can help to increase the popularity of those persons (such as Ralph Nader) and programs (such as the nuclear protest movement) that promote newer attitudes. Any individual can write to newspapers and broadcasting stations, although the person who always writes is often discounted, whereas the many who occasionally write are much needed. Individuals can gain even more influence by founding groups that have cohesion, political know-how, and capacity to form coalitions. Coalitions get more results than does mere rhetoric.

But can the American political system change far enough and fast enough to cope with the mounting problems that confront it? At a slower pace it has always been changing since the first days of the republic. In some periods and in some sectors it has changed very rapidly. The entire population has become more politicized, and this process is continuing. Today Americans of southern and eastern European ancestry are just as active in politics and as insistent on their rights as old-stock Americans have ever been. Millions of black Americans, too, have become aroused to political concern and participation and so have many of the poor of all races. Large professions whose members used to think themselves too genteel to join a labor union—such as teachers, journalists, actors, and radio and television personnel—are all becoming unionized in many cities. So are the poorest and most often forgotten groups of workers, such as the hospital orderlies and garbage collectors. Also awakened to political participation are large parts of another previously passive group—the young.

As more Americcans have become politically active, the political system has accepted a wider range of responsibilities. Medical care for those over age sixty-five is no longer disputed in principle. It is now law, and the discussion turns on the best ways to make it work. Public aid to low-rent housing and scholarships or loans to students seeking higher education have become accepted principles. Broader voter registration and fairer apportionment of legislative districts are now under way. The abolition of race segregation in public schools has become national policy and the law of the land, and beginnings have been made to

put these into practice. In some of the big cities a search has started for methods of decentralization that will give different ethnic groups and neighborhoods a greater share in the decisions affecting their lives and the education of their children. City politics may be rediscovering in some respects the principle of "concurrent majorities" that John C. Calhoun proposed more than a century ago for the politics of the nation. If accepted, this principle would mean that decisions directly affecting a black urban region, such as Harlem in New York City, would require majority support in Harlem as well as in New York City as a whole. There have been many political inventions and innovations in the American past; there may be more in the future.

The American political system has the capacities for change if its people have the will to use them. There is a gap between the interests that are already organized and the potential ones that are not. The great majority of American society has nothing to gain from perpetuating poverty or war. It is passionately interested in its own survival and that of its children. But these majority interests have yet to be organized. There is a vast opportunity for discovering and developing strategies of *coalition building* and action to this end. If reformers can recover the commitment, the dedication, and the intellectual and political skill to keep people of good will working with each other instead of against each other, then the most powerful country in the world can turn itself around and move in the direction selected by its founders. Such an outcome would require more openness from moderate conservatives and liberals, more self-control and willingness to compromise from radicals and adherents to new lifestyles, and more patience and perspective from perfectionists. But the possible results might well be worth the effort.

One part of such a reorientation and renewal of American politics would be a rethinking of United States foreign policy. In the last twenty years, America's position of dominance in the world has declined dramatically. This is not because the United States has failed to expand but because other nations have grown so much faster. Between 1960 and 1970 other peoples were able to claim far more of the world's cars and telephones, produce more of its steel and oil, and—most ominously— spend more of the world's resources on the means of war. The result is that America must deal in an international setting where it holds fewer of the cards in its own hands. Its foreign policy will have to steer a careful course, neither resigning from duties of leadership in the free world nor trying, from some mistaken sense of nostalgia, to dominate that world.

No nation could go on indefinitely thinking itself omnipotent and invincible, least of all in today's world. When its people were told their country "never lost a war," they increasingly suspected that some historical evidence had been stretched a little. Or else they thought that earlier administrations had been wise enough not to involve the nation in wars that could not be won or were not worth winning. History knows no nation that was never defeated, but it knows the vital difference between those nations that survived their defeats and learned from them and those that failed to do so.

As every nation must learn to survive its setbacks in world politics, it also must learn to cooperate effectively with allies. The United States did so with spectacular success in two world wars and in the great reconstruction of Western Europe after World War II under the Marshall Plan. Since that time, however, the sheer size of the population and economy of the United States has often tended to dwarf the interests of America's allies, unless these allies were able to find strong American domestic interest groups to speak for them. During the first decade after World War II, the impoverished nations of Western Europe were glad to follow American policies, particularly as long as these coincided with their own needs for European reconstruction. In the 1960s, however, such newly more prosperous nations as France, West Germany, and Britain demanded more independence for themselves, more consideration for their views. They wanted less Western involvement in Asian wars and more American attention to European needs.

The Western alliance was further tested in 1973, when the Organization of Petroleum Exporting Countries (OPEC) imposed drastically increased oil prices on the world, despite American protests. When the United States let the international value of the dollar decline between 1971 and 1979, regardless of the objections of its foreign allies and its trade partners, the OPEC countries threatened to refuse to accept dollars alone in payment for their oil. The European powers announced efforts aimed at creating a European currency that might replace the dollar in much of international trading; and the private bankers and traders of the world lowered the value of the dollar against the yen, the Swiss franc, the Deutsche mark, and the price of gold. Only time will tell whether the United States government and electorate will be able to preserve international economic stability and renew a meaningful Western alliance through the 1980s.

In the meantime, the domestic experience of the United States has much to offer the rest of the world. The American social and political habits that emphasize equality and mobility, respect for all kinds of work, including manual labor, and interest in discovery and practical solutions could be of real help to many societies whose politics have remained bound by more rigid barriers of class and status, tradition, or ideology. And other nations may secretly admire the American optimism that undertakes impossible technical tasks, such as a series of voyages to the moon, and completes them not only with great success, but on schedule.

Foreign nations may be less enthusiastic about the American unconcern—in practice, if not in theory—for the conservation of natural and human resources. They watch the wasteful American use of energy and the extraordinary difficulties of the American political system in attempting to control it. They know that Americans easily discard old things rather than mend them, that they like to use throwaway packages and contain-

ers. They fear that this habit may carry over into
an American inclination to have throwaway cities
and perhaps even throwaway people. They note
that Americans are quick to use things and people
and, sometimes, foreign countries, without knowing them well. And they are worried by the
occasional American propensity to see foreign
people as so many dominoes blindly falling with
each push of power. Foreigners watching pictures
of American race riots or urban blight on their
television screens may feel in no particular hurry
to imitate American politics or institutions. In
times such as these, the United States perhaps
needs more constructive innovators working at
home and fewer political propagandists traveling
abroad. It needs to advance its ideas in the world
arena more by example than by attempts at
persuasion. If the example is good enough, other
nations will find their own ways to respond to it.

KEY TERMS AND CONCEPTS

government by design
dependency burden
spread effect
backwash effect
capitalism
socialism
nondecisions
Chicanos
political participation (participation by voters)
campaign financing (participation by money)
"fat cats"
socioeconomic status
swing vote
median income voter
voting frequencies
contact specialists
activists
sanctions
responsiveness
concurrence statement
distribution of power
general purpose elites

special elites
the establishment
lobbyists
"tax revolt"
political community
political culture
pragmatism
basic value orientations
ecology
collateral
lineal
command systems
action orientation
future orientation
Gunnar Myrdal's prediction
liberalism
conservatism
radicalism
the new politics and the counterculture
the me generation
market
arena
mobility
joint rewards
social and cultural cohesiveness
federalism
residual powers
separation of powers
checks and balances
pluralism
populism
feminism
"right to life"
trimester solution
porkbarrel politics
polarization
"rotten boroughs"
"one man one vote"
legislative reapportionment
seniority
Seventeenth Amendment
cloture
rights of Congress versus rights of the president
veto

item veto
General Accounting Office (GAO)
Congressional Budget Office (CBO)
caucus
logrolling
side payments
roll-call votes
gerrymander
primaries
Electoral College
pledged electors
commander in chief
policy-making appointments
White House staff
advice and consent
détente
impeachment
full faith and credit clause
judicial review
Marbury v. *Madison*
"judge-made" law
ex parte Milligan
Baker v. *Carr*
Gideon v. *Wainwright*
Escobedo v. *Illinois*
Miranda v. *Arizona*
judicial activism
cognitive corruption
decision points
consciousness
will
creativity
innovation
"white backlash"
coalition building

ADDITIONAL READINGS

American Politics: General

Barber, J. D. *Citizen Politics*. 2nd ed. Chicago: Rand McNally, 1972. PB

Barone, M., et al. *The Almanac of American Politics 1980*. New York: Dutton, 1979.

Dahl, R. A. *Democracy in the United States*. 3rd ed. Chicago: Rand McNally, 1976, PB

Lockard, D. *The Perverted Priorities of American Politics*. 2nd ed. New York: Macmillan, 1976, PB

Mitchell, J. M. and W. C. *Political Analysis and Public Policy: An Introduction to Political Science*. Chicago: Rand McNally, 1969.

Historical Background

Adair, D. " 'That Politics May be Reduced to a Science': David Hume, James Madison, and the Tenth Federalist." *Huntington Library Quarterly* 20 (1957), 343–60.

Boorstin, D. *The Genius of American Politics*. Chicago: University of Chicago Press, 1953. PB

Elkins, S., and E. McKittrick. "The Founding Fathers: Young Men of the Revolution." *Political Science Quarterly* 76 (June 1961), 181–216.

Genovese, E. *Roll, Jordon, Roll: The World the Slaves Made*. New York: Random House, 1976.

Hofstadter, R. *The American Political Tradition*. New York: Knopf, 1973.

Lipset, S. M. *The First New Nation: The United States in Historical and Comparative Perspective*. New York: Basic Books, 1963. PB

Potter, D. M. *People of Plenty: Economic Abundance and the American Character*. Chicago: University of Chicago Press, 1954. PB

Woodward, C. V. *The Strange Career of Jim Crow*. 3rd rev. ed. Oxford: Oxford University Press, 1974. PB

————. *Tom Watson: Agrarian Rebel*. London and New York: Oxford University Press, 1973.

Participation and Power

Agger, R., D. Goldrich, and B. Swanson. *The Rulers and the Ruled: Political Power and Impotence ·in American Communities*. Rev. ed. North Scituate, Mass.: Duxbury Press, 1972. PB

Alexander, H. A. *Financing Politics: Money, Elections and Political Reform*. Washington, D.C.: Congressional Quarterly Press, 1976.

Bachrach, P. *The Theory of Democratic Elitism*. Boston: Little, Brown, 1967. PB

————, and M. S. Baratz. "Two Faces of Power." *American Political Science Review* 56 (December 1962), 947–53.

Dahl, R. A. *Who Governs? Democracy and Power in an American City.* New Haven: Yale University Press, 1962. PB

Heard, A. *The Costs of Democracy.* Chapel Hill: University of North Carolina Press, 1960.

McGinniss, J. *The Selling of the President.* New York: Trident, 1969. PB

Prewitt, K., and A. Stone. *The Ruling Elites: Elite Theory and American Democracy.* New York: Harper & Row, 1973. PB

Verba, S., and N. H. Nie. *Participation in America: Political Democracy and Social Equality.* New York: Harper & Row, 1972. PB

Wilson, J. Q. *Varieties of Police Behavior.* New York: Atheneum, 1970. PB

Images and Ideologies

The Conservative Papers. With introduction by Melvin R. Laird. Garden City, N.Y.: Doubleday Anchor, 1964. PB

Harrington, M. *Socialism.* New York: Bantam Books, 1973. PB

Hartz, L. *The Liberal Tradition in America.* New York: Harcourt, 1962. PB

Hofstadter, R. *Anti-Intellectualism in American Life.* New York: Random House, 1966. PB

Lasch, C. *New Radicalism in America.* New York: Random House, 1967. PB

Lipset, S. M., and E. Raab. *The Politics of Unreason: Right-Wing Extremism in America, 1790–1970.* 2nd ed. Chicago: University of Chicago Press, 1978. PB

Lowi, T. *The End of Liberalism: Ideology, Policy, and the Crisis of Public Authority.* New York: Norton, 1969. PB

Roosevelt, J., ed. *The Liberal Papers.* Chicago: Quandrangle Books, 1962.

Steinfels, P. *Neoconservatism.* New York: Simon and Schuster, 1979.

Wise, D. *The Politics of Lying: Government Deception, Secrecy, and Power.* New York: Random House, 1973. PB

Political Machinery and Processes: *Congress and Voting*

Campbell, A., et al. *The American Voter: An Abridgement.* New York: Wiley, 1964. PB

Fenno, R. *Congressmen in Committees.* Boston: Little, Brown, 1973. PB

———. *The Power of the Purse: Appropriations Politics in Congress.* Boston: Little, Brown, 1966.

Froman, L. A., Jr. *The Congressional Process: Strategies, Rules and Procedures.* Boston: Little, Brown, 1967. PB

Matthews, D. *U.S. Senators and their World.* New ed. New York: Norton, 1973. PB

Nie, N. H., S. Verba, and J. R. Petrocik. *The Changing American Voter.* Cambridge: Harvard University Press, 1976. PB

Polsby, N. "Policy Analysis and Congress." *Public Policy* 18 (Fall 1969), 61–74.

Price, E. *Who Makes the Laws? Creativity and Power in Senate Committees.* Cambridge: Schenkman, 1972. PB

Redman, E. *The Dance of Legislation.* New York: Simon and Schuster, 1973.

Rieselbach, L. N. *Congressional Politics.* New York: McGraw-Hill, 1973.

Truman, D., ed. *The Congress and America's Future.* 2nd ed. Englewood Cliffs, N.J.: Prentice-Hall, 1973. PB

Political Machinery and Processes: *The Presidency*

Barber, J. D. *The Presidential Character.* Englewood Cliffs, N. J.: Prentice-Hall, 1973. PB

Berger, R. *Impeachment: The Constitutional Problems.* Cambridge: Harvard University Press, 1973.

Bernstein, C., and B. Woodward, *All the President's Men.* New York: Warner Books, 1976. PB

———. *The Final Days.* New York: Simon and Schuster, 1976. PB

Burns, J. M. *Roosevelt: The Lion and the Fox.* 2 vols. New York: Harcourt Brace Jovanovich, 1970.

Carter, J. *Why Not the Best?* New York: Bantam, 1976. PB

Eisenhower, D. D. *The White House Years.* 2 vols. New York: Doubleday, 1963–65.

Johnson, L. B. *The Vantage Point.* New York: Popular Library, 1972. PB

Kearns, D. *Lyndon Johnson and the American Dream.* New York: New American Library, 1977. PB

Miller, M. *Plain Speaking: An Oral Biography of Harry S. Truman.* New York: Putnam, 1974.

Neustadt, R. *Presidential Power: The Politics of Leadership.* New York: Wiley, 1976. PB

Nixon, R. M. *Memoirs.* New York: Grosset and Dunlap, 1978.

———. *Six Crises.* Garden City, N.Y.: Doubleday, 1962.

Schlesinger, A., Jr. *The Imperial Presidency.* Boston: Houghton Mifflin, 1973.

———. *A Thousand Days: John F. Kennedy in the White House.* Boston: Houghton Mifflin, 1965.

Sorensen, T. *Kennedy.* New York: Harper & Row, 1965.

White, T. H. *The Making of the President, 1972.* New York: Ateneum, 1973. PB

———. *The Making of the President, 1968.* New York: Ateneum, 1969. PB

Witcover, J. *Marathon: The Pursuit of the Presidency, 1972–1976.* New York: Viking Press, 1977.

American Performance and Prospects

Arlen, M. J. *An American Verdict.* Garden City, N.Y.: Doubleday, 1973.

Barnet, R. J. *Roots of War: The Men and Institutions Behind U.S. Foreign Policy.* Baltimore: Penguin Books, 1973. PB

Beer, S. H., and R. E. Barringer, eds. *The State and the Poor.* Cambridge: Winthrop, 1970. PB

Galbraith, J. K. *Economics and the Public Purpose.* Boston: Houghton Mifflin, 1973.

Harrington, M. *The Other America.* Rev. ed. New York: Macmillan, 1970.

Hoopes, T. *The Limits of Intervention.* 2nd ed. New York: Longman, 1974. PB

Jencks, C., et al. *Inequality.* New York: Basic Books, 1972.

Kail, F. M. *What Washington Said: Administration Rhetoric and the Vietnam War, 1949–1969.* New York: Harper Torchbooks, 1974. PB

King, M. L., Jr. *Why We Can't Wait.* New York: Harper Torchbooks, 1964. PB

Kitagawa, E. M., and P. M. Hauser, *Differential Mortality in the United States.* Cambridge: Harvard University Press, 1973.

Malcolm X (with Alex Haley). *The Autobiography of Malcolm X.* New York: Grove Press, 1965. PB

Miller, S. M., and P. Roby. *The Future of Inequality.* New York: Basic Books, 1970. PB

Moynihan, D. P. *The Politics of a Guaranteed Income: The Nixon Administration and the Family Assistance Plan.* New York: Vintage Books, 1973. PB

The Pentagon Papers: As Published by The New York Times. New York: Bantam Books, 1971. PB

Perloff, H., ed. *The Future of the United States Government: Toward the Year 2000.* New York: Braziller, 1971.

Pressman, J. L., and A. B. Wildavsky. *Implementation.* Berkeley and Los Angeles: University of California Press, 1973. PB

Russett, B. M. *What Price Vigilance? The Burdens of National Defense.* New Haven: Yale University Press, 1970. PB

Sampson, A. *The Sovereign State of ITT.* New York: Stein and Day, 1973.

PB = *available in paperback*

III

The Soviet Union

Revised by **TIMOTHY J. COLTON**

Perhaps the best way of getting a sense of the nature of the Soviet political system is to take a look at its similarities to and differences from the political system of the United States. In this way we can get a first impression of what these two huge countries have in common, in what ways each is unique, and in what direction each is going. Such a comparison is not easy to make; and some of our preconceptions make it harder. Most studies of the Soviet Union available to Western readers resemble descriptions of hell written by fair-minded theologians. It is particularly hard for Westerners to understand that most members of the Soviet population are loyal to their government and will fight to defend it against foreign attack. Soviet citizens have a similar difficulty in understanding political loyalties in the West. But anyone who thinks that either Americans or Russians would not defend their government against any direct attack has been deceived. The Japanese military discovered this when they attacked the United

States at Pearl Harbor. So did Hitler when he attacked the Soviet Union. In the 1980s it would be madness for either Russian or American leaders ever to forget that fact.

TWO EXPANDING PEOPLES—
TWO IDEAS OF GOVERNMENT

Like the United States, the Soviet Union has been shaped by a unique combination of vast historical development and deliberate political design. The United States is the product of an outpouring of largely English-speaking (followed by non-English-speaking) people westward across rivers and mountains and then across a continent and onward to Hawaii and Alaska. This has made Scottish and Irish Americans, Pennsylvania Dutch, Louisiana French, Minnesota Swedes, Slavic and Italian Americans, Spanish and Indian Americans, Jews, Puerto Ricans, and black Americans all members of the American people. The Soviet

Union, now a continental society with a population of about 262 million, is the product of an eastward outpouring of Slavic-speaking people, mainly Russians and Ukrainians, across the land mass of Eurasia all the way to Vladivostok and Sakhalin Island. To a far greater extent than the United States, the Soviet Union emerged from its expansion as a *multiethnic* and *multilingual* country. The 138 million ethnic Russians accounted in 1979 for only 52 percent of the Soviet population. Twenty-two major non-Russian nationalities (each numbering more than 1 million) composed another 44 percent, and more than a hundred ethnic splinter groups made up the rest.[1]

Apart from the realities of territorial expansion and linguistic diversity, it is important to realize that both of these huge countries, the United States and the Soviet Union, grew out of revolution and out of a deliberate political design at a decisive stage in its history.

A Common Dream. Out of each revolution came a political system engineered by theorists who had tried to master what they held to be the social science of their day. These theorists were desperately determined to make their blueprints practi-

cal. The purpose of each design was no less than the liberation of the people and the creation of the political conditions for their happiness. Now, over two hundred years after the event, we can see the good and bad that have come out of the vision of the American revolutionary theorists: the triumphs, the disappointments, and the hopes deferred, but perhaps not quite forsaken. It is difficult to realize that the Soviet system was also created by theorists with no less idealistic a vision—even though Lenin and his Bolshevik comrades would have bridled with indignation at the very word "idealism," which they considered bourgeois.

The word *idealism* has many meanings, among which three stand out. In common speech "idealism" means, first, a selfless aspiration to make things better, particularly for others; here it is opposed to the common meaning of "materialism"—a preoccupation with tangible rewards, often with overtones of selfishness. Second, also in common speech, "idealism" sometimes means an inclination to see things as better than they actually are; here it is opposed to the ordinary meaning of "realism." A third meaning pertains to the philosophy of knowledge. Here "idealism" means the doctrine that thoughts, abstract forms, or ideas are more real and enduring than tangible things and events and that individuals' inner lives are more real than the world around them. It was this third, philosophic meaning of "idealism" that Marx and Lenin opposed. They contrasted it with philosophic *materialism,* which taught that the outside world was real, independent of the wishes of observers. To put ideas first, they believed, was to stand knowledge on its head. Only by putting its feet on the ground and seeing the world as it was, they argued, could the world be changed for the better.

Philosophic materialists, of course, may be quite capable of unselfish—or idealistic—behavior. Lenin, the revolutionary, and Krasin, the economic planner, Stalin and Trotsky, Radek and Bukharin, even perhaps Khrushchev and Kosygin—all had their vision of a better social order. Each

---

[1]Census data for 1979 taken from *Vestnik statistiki*, 2 (February 1980), pp. 11–30. It should be noted that in the Soviet Union nationality *(natsionalnost)* is defined in terms of psychic identification with a distinct ethnic group. Although nationality inevitably has a strong historical connection with language, in the Soviet Union national or ethnic groups are not coterminous with language groups. In 1979 more than 16 million non-Russians reported that Russian was their first language and another 61 million were fluent in Russian as a second language. These two subgroups accounted for 62 percent of the entire non-Russian population, leaving 38 percent (48 million people, about the size of the population of England) without fluency in the country's principal language. One wonders how many English-speaking Americans would know how to deal with such a situation in their country, somewhat similar to what might have happened if the United States and Mexico had formed a single federal union.

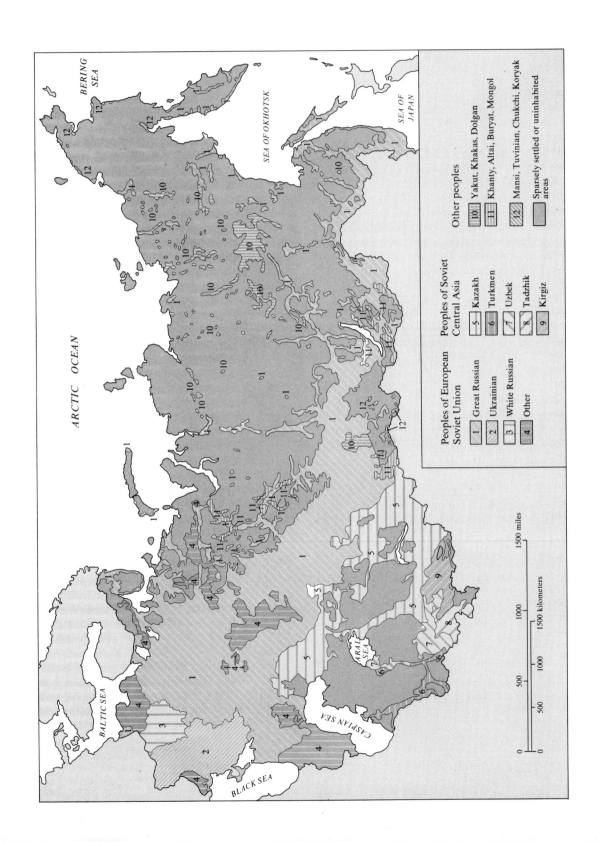

ARCTIC OCEAN

BERING SEA

SEA OF OKHOTSK

SEA OF JAPAN

BALTIC SEA

BLACK SEA

CASPIAN SEA

ARAL SEA

Peoples of European Soviet Union
1 Great Russian
2 Ukrainian
3 White Russian
4 Other

Peoples of Soviet Central Asia
5 Kazakh
6 Turkmen
7 Uzbek
8 Tadzhik
9 Kirgiz

Other peoples
10 Yakut, Khakas, Dolgan
11 Khanty, Altai, Buryat, Mongol
12 Mansi, Tuvinian, Chukchi, Koryak
Sparsely settled or uninhabited areas

0   500   1000   1500 miles
0   500   1000   1500 kilometers

attempted to transform his vision of the good society into reality for a vast, poor, and backward country in order to implement human happiness there.

If the underlying visions and aspirations were in some way similar in the Soviet Union and in the United States, there were nevertheless profound differences between these nations' attempts to realize their dreams and between the outcomes each attempt produced.

Two Revolutions and Their Differences. The American Revolution had five characteristics that distinguished it from the Russian. It began with a vision of *plenty.* Not only were the 3 million colonists of the 1770s and 1780s at the edge of a rich continent; on a per capita basis they also had the richest capital equipment in the world. Thus, in that sense, the Americans were already, at the time of their Revolution, the most advanced people in the world.

Second, the American people at the time of the Revolution had had a long tradition of local *self-government,* of spontaneous organizations in small, self-governing groups, such as church congregations, town meetings, and committees of correspondence. By the end of the eighteenth century the English-speaking world had had at least a century-old tradition of local self-government and of voluntary agreements.

Third, the American revolutionaries envisioned the possibility of harmony or at least of a workable *compatibility of interests* within the country. Divergent interests would be accommodated not through factionalism or violence, but through accepted and legal channels of government. These ideas later found expression in James Madison's "Tenth Federalist Paper." On the whole they also felt that if America stayed out of international

entanglements after winning its independence and remained reasonably well defended, no foreign countries would have a major motive to harm the United States. Such thinking pervades George Washington's farewell address.

A fourth basic characteristic was the American trust in the *spontaneity* of individuals. Setting people free to pursue their happiness, as the Declaration of Independence put it, implies having automatic trust in their knowing what will be good for themselves. Both before and since the Revolution the mainstream of American culture has trusted the spontaneity of men and women.

Finally, from the American Revolution onward, there has been an American tradition of *moderation.* This might now be called into question by some, but there seems to be a fair chance that it will endure. Extremist episodes always have been short-lived. In major emergencies the American people have tended to move toward the middle, whereas some of the European populations, such as those of Russia and Germany, have tended to move toward the extremes. Comparing the extreme German responses to the Great Depression of the 1930s with the American responses shows the American tradition of moderation, which is sometimes frustrating and irritating, but which has stood the country in good stead.

In contrast to the American experience, the Russian tradition began with *scarcity,* in a poor country with many people and little capital. At the time of the Russian Revolution the peasants of Russia had long been among the poorest of all the poor peasantries of Europe. The 1917 revolution occurred at the end of a bloody world war that had exhausted the country and ruined its economy. Food was scarce in the big cities before the first shots of the revolution were fired. And scarcity remained a critical factor even after the end of the revolution. A Soviet teamster at the building of the Dnieper River dam in the late 1920s exhorted his helper to take good care of the horses: "You can always make a man," he said, "but just try to make

(Left) MAP 3.1 *Major Ethnic Groups in the Soviet Union*

a horse." Twenty years and two five-year plans after the Russian Revolution, only one pair of shoes was being made each year for every member of the population. This was seen by many Russians as an improvement; in the days of the czar the normal winter footwear of 100 million peasants was burlap rags tied around their feet.[2]

Second, for many centuries, self-government was very limited at the village level and almost nonexistent at any other. *Violent conflict,* like scarcity, had long been a basic assumption of Russian politics, and the Russian Revolution merely reinforced it. Revolutionary Russia saw itself in the position of a besieged fortress. And, indeed, from its start in 1917 the new Soviet government faced foreign conflict. Fourteen foreign countries made war on the Soviet government in the first four years of its existence. They did so ineffectively and halfheartedly, but they still killed many people, and the intervention helped prolong the Russian civil war to 1921. The situation of the Bolsheviks resembled that of the embattled Jacobins in the French Revolution of 1793, who were besieged by more than a half-dozen European monarchies and who resorted to a terrorist dictatorship to save the republic. A similar mood of desperate determination was characteristic of the Russian Revolution. In contrast, the American Revolution had strong foreign allies: France, Spain, and the Netherlands.

Whereas the leaders of the American Revolution believed in spontaneity, the experiences of the Russian revolutionaries led them to a different conclusion. Prior to the revolution, Lenin and the members of his conspiratorial Bolshevik party had had an almost full-time job dodging the czarist secret police. The leaders who emerged from these struggles believed in *discipline,* direction, and organization. The Soviet leaders distrusted spontaneity and do so to this day.

Finally, whereas the American tradition stressed moderation, the Russian tradition stressed desperate *ruthlessness.* In order to get things done, any

[2]In 1978 the U.S.S.R. produced 740 million pairs of leather shoes, or 2.8 pairs per person.

means were acceptable. Lenin said he would make an alliance "with the devil and his grandmother" if it would help the revolution. It is tempting for Westerners to sit back and criticize the tactics of the Russian revolutionaries. Living where and when the Soviet leaders did, they regarded ruthlessness as the only realistic way of completing their revolution. But we should not forget that even when a price seems inevitable, it still has to be paid. Bertolt Brecht, the pro-Communist German poet, said that even righteous indignation will make one's voice hoarse. And the Soviet people and their government have paid with more than hoarseness of voice.

THE BASIC THEORY: MARX

Not unlike the United States, the Soviet Union is the child of an encounter between a developing nation and an international idea. In each country the images and values accepted by its governments and people had a significant influence on what they did in politics and on what they thought they were doing. And if the two nations and their histories were different, the crucial ideas adopted by each differed still more. The American Revolution had adopted the international ideas of the eighteenth-century Enlightenment, stemming largely from John Locke, and supplemented them to a lesser extent with notions of populism, resembling some of the ideas of Jean Jacques Rousseau. The ideas that became dominant in the Russian Revolution and in the Soviet Union that emerged from it came from another age and setting. They are the ideas of nineteenth- and early twentieth-century Marxism and Leninism.

Essentials of Marxism. The originator of the theory that was taken over by Lenin and the Bolsheviks in Russia was Karl Marx. Marx's theory was rooted in a profoundly pessimistic evaluation of the nineteenth-century private enterprise system, based mainly on the experience of England (where Marx spent much of his adult life) in the first half of that century. Marx assumed that the conditions that he had seen were not unique characteristics of a particular society at a specific time, but general tendencies of an entire economic system. Among these tendencies, as he saw them, were increasingly frequent wars and depressions, increasing oppression, increasing misery of working people, and increasing alienation of people who were being treated more and more like things or commodities. Marx assumed that the only response to this experience would be a struggle among economic classes, out of which the industrial wage earners would eventually emerge as the most numerous—and eventually the dominant—class. Indeed, the middle classes would disappear; the children and grandchildren of the peasants and artisans would overwhelmingly end up as factory workers or unemployed wage earners, only a tiny minority becoming property owners. These workers would become increasingly dissatisfied and radicalized. Factory work would teach them organization and discipline. They would learn to form unions and fight for higher wages. Communists would teach them class consciousness and the need for revolution. The resulting class struggle, Marx asserted, would determine the future course of history.

Marx believed in stages of historical development. After the stages of primitive communism and of feudalism, there would be a stage of private enterprise in which middle-class capitalist rule would replace the power of the nobles and the landowners. Only after this stage had reached its height would social revolution and socialism follow. Marx believed that socialism would be an outgrowth of capitalism: socialism would grow under the surface, within the husk of the private enterprise society, so that one would have only to remove the shell and the full-blown industrialized socialist economy would emerge, nearly completed.

At this point the working class would be united, Marx believed. Workers would, on the whole,

accept the Marxist ideology; and since they would be united and enlightened and would constitute the vast majority, they would exercise a dictatorship over the remaining few former members of the owning classes. This new regime somehow would not be a dictatorship over the workers themselves, because there would be so many of them and they would all know what they wanted. They would be able to be dictators and yet act spontaneously. It would be the rule of the many over the few.

Socialism: How Long a Period of Scarcity and Inequality?
Two economic stages would follow capitalism. The first, which Lenin later called *socialism* (Marx just called it a lower stage of communism), would be an *economy of scarcity*, in which land, machines, and means of production would be owned collectively, but the society would still be poor. In this society people would work according to their ability and be paid according to their performance. Those who worked more or did more complicated or more urgently needed work would be paid better regardless of their needs or those of their families. The society of socialism, therefore, would be unjust, and the state machinery would still have to be used to defend the higher incomes of what we now would call the *meritocracy*, the more productive or more skilled workers, technicians, and managers.

Marx's logic vis-à-vis this question could be extended to the relationship between highly productive and less productive regions of any large country at this still-poor stage of economic development. Each region might be expected to contribute according to its economic capacities and to receive from the exchange of goods and services no more than corresponds to its limited capacities; the power of the socialist state will regulate and limit the migration of the poorer population to the richer and more advanced cities and regions. Transfers of resources from these more advanced regions to the poorer ones will be limited, despite genuine beliefs in solidarity. Only slowly will

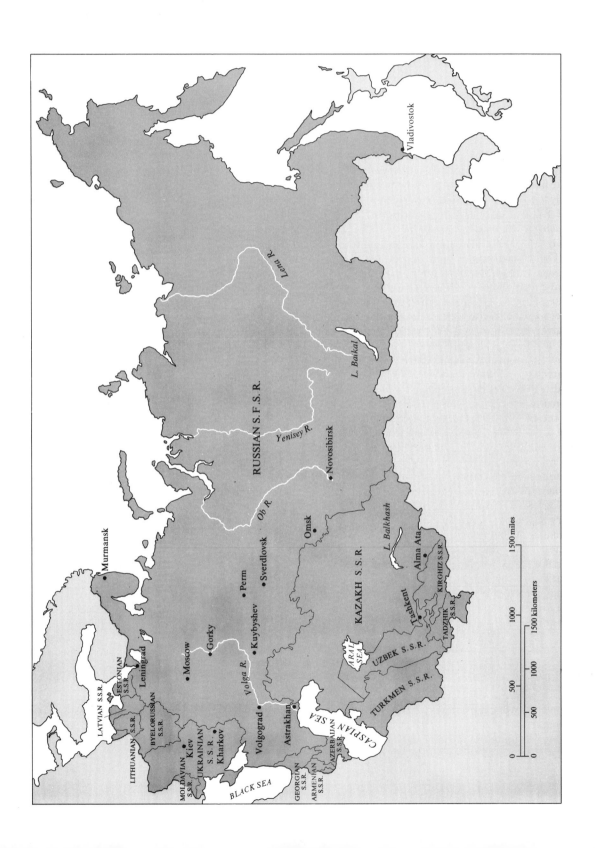

Vladivostok

Lena R.

L. Baikal

RUSSIAN S.F.S.R.

Yenisey R.

Novosibirsk

Ob R.

Omsk

L. Balkhash

Murmansk

Sverdlovsk

Perm

Alma Ata

KIRGHIZ S.S.R.

KAZAKH S.S.R.

Tashkent

TADZHIK
S.S.R.

Gorky

Kuybyshev

Moscow

Leningrad

ARAL
SEA

UZBEK S.S.R.

ESTONIAN
S.S.R.

Volga R.

LATVIAN S.S.R.

TURKMEN S.S.R.

LITHUANIAN S.S.R.

BYELORUSSIAN
S.S.R.

Kiev

Volgograd

Astrakhan

UKRAINIAN
S. S. R.

Kharkov

CASPIAN SEA

AZERBAIJAN
S.S.R.

MOLDAVIAN
S.S.R.

GEORGIAN
S.S.R.

ARMENIAN
S.S.R.

BLACK SEA

0   500   1000   1500 miles

0   500   1000   1500 kilometers

greater skills be learned by the unskilled or their children, will capital be invested at an increased rate in the less developed regions, will the economic inequalities decline or become less important. But during this time of transition the socialist state will continue to defend the basic injustices and inequalities of its present condition, offering only the hope and promise of overcoming them in the future. And that future has turned out to be much more distant than Marx's followers originally expected.

The same inherent logic of Marx's thought can be applied on the international level to the exchange of goods and services among socialist states. Here again, highly developed socialist countries would tend to export high-priced products of high technology, skilled labor, and intensive capital investments, whereas less developed countries would be more likely to export farm goods, raw materials, and goods produced with less capital and cheaper, less skilled labor. Thus, the international market among socialist countries, according to the implications of Marx's logic, will continue for a long time to show many of the inequalities and inequities that critics have pointed out in today's capitalist world markets. And each socialist state is likely to defend its national advantages in capital, natural resources, skilled labor, and technology against other socialist states, making only very limited modifications in the name of international solidarity. The possibility of economic disputes, military threats, and even warfare among socialist states should have been predictable from Marx's own theory, as he wrote it down in 1875,[3] long before some of these possibilities became realities a century later in the bloody clashes between the troops of different Communist states,

[3]See Marx's *Critique of the Gotha Program* (of the Social Democratic Party).

———

(Left) MAP 3.2 *The Union of Soviet Socialist Republics*

at the borders of Russia and China in 1969, and at those of China and Vietnam in 1979.

Marx tried to be a genuine scientist, to see reality whether or not it would please him or his adherents. If the first stage of socialism still was to include much poverty, scarcity, and injustice and if a repressive socialist state was to exist during this stage, he did not shrink from making this fact clear in his writing. But most of his followers, and most of the adherents of socialism in general, expected something very different. They expected socialism to be the fairly prompt fulfillment of all their hopes for universal freedom, friendship, and plenty—in short, all their moral, political, and economic aspirations for humankind. Once the socialist revolution had triumphed and large estates and factories had become collective property, they expected workers, peasants, and intellectuals to rule together in freedom. At most they might be willing to work and wait for ten or twenty years, but then surely the "vast productive forces" of modern industry would bring about that economic abundance on which a free, rich, and nonrepressive socialist society would be based. They would have been appalled to learn that the transition to this hoped-for state would take not merely years or decades, but several generations and perhaps one or two centuries.

The Soviet leaders may have shared some of these impatient illusions. (Estimates of time always have been a weak point in Marxist theory.) In any case, they did not dare to disillusion their followers. Rather, they used the Soviet state, its mass media, and the Communist Party to assert that much of this freedom and fellowship already had arrived in their country and that the Soviet government was not repressing anyone except the members of the former enemy classes, the landlords and capitalists. In short, they claimed that Soviet society was much richer and freer than it actually was. They still are caught in this pretense today: they still must claim that much of what Marx hoped for in the future is existing in their country here and now.

Measured against this claim, even their real successes must fall short. Many people must notice that things are not as good as the government says they are. Some persons go on working, defer their hopes, and are reinforced by limited, but visible, improvements; others become disillusioned and respond by opportunism and cynicism; still others focus their attention on their private lives; and a few respond by some degree of opposition to the regime, try to emigrate, or become *dissidents*. Such dissidents seek to spread their critical dissenting views within the country by means of "self-published" writings, called *samizdat*, and also with the help of foreign newspapers, radio stations, and personal contacts. Often they are targets of official efforts at repression. They risk jobs, careers, and prison terms, but from the early 1960s onward they have persistently turned up in Soviet life. Though many ordinary Soviet citizens may think of them as "foreign agents," they are a product of Soviet society and perhaps of the clash between the hopes and realities of the unexpectedly long Marxist path to which the Soviet Union remains committed.

This path still is expected to lead to Marx's vision of the more distant future, regardless of whether it should turn out to be decades, generations, or centuries away.

Marx's Vision of the Long-Range Future. However long it might take, this early stage—socialism— would have only one purpose: to put itself out of business. It would amass ever more wealth, capital, and machines until finally production would become efficient and goods plentiful. The symptoms of the transition to the age of plenty would be clear to see, Marx thought: the differences between worker and intellectual and between town and countryside would disappear. He held similar hopes for the economic differences between regions and nations. Ultimately, economic abundance would make these differences unimportant, too.

Marx expected a society of plenty to emerge, first within a few highly advanced countries and eventually as a worldwide phenomenon. Within such a society the government of people would be replaced by the administration of things. Marx's notion was that a great deal of the productive equipment of humankind would eventually become semiautomatic or automatic. It would have to be maintained, but the business of government would be replaced by the business of maintenance. Thus, sitting in the library of the British Museum behind his bristling beard, Marx envisioned a society of freedom and generosity for all people. In the middle of a long economic discussion in the third volume of *Das Kapital* there is a revealing throwaway sentence in which he speaks of "that full development of all human capacities and powers which is an end in itself." This is what Marx wanted to live for: the full realization of human capabilities, the end of the subordination of human beings to the division of labor, a new age of the all-sided development of individuals. After the revolution, all this would depend on economic growth. Only after people had made the transition from poverty to plenty would they move "out of the realm of necessity into the realm of freedom." Only then would the prehistory of humankind end and the real history of human beings, the interesting history, begin.

Some of Marx's Predictions—and the Facts. Marx assumed the existence of a high degree of technological determinism: a hand mill meant a society of landlords and serfs; a steam mill meant capitalists and wage workers. His assumption has turned out to be partly false, for modern machines have served a variety of social systems. Henry Ford's tractors have worked on Soviet collective farms as well as on American private enterprise farms.

Second, Marx foresaw automatic growth of all the elements for a socialist economy under the capitalist surface. This has not materialized. Countries that have wanted public planning agencies and skills have had to create them by deliberate political effort.

Third, he thought that the advanced countries, and particularly their urban and industrial sectors, would be the most likely areas for Communist success. He had blistering phrases of contempt for peasants and for what he called "the idiocy of rural life." The best thing Marx might have said about peasants was that their children or grandchildren might someday become honest, upstanding proletarians. Here reality has differed from this prediction in a crucial way. Indigenous Communist revolutions have triumphed thus far only in semideveloped or underdeveloped countries, such as Russia, Yugoslavia, China, Cuba, and Vietnam, and then only with the help of peasant uprisings.

Fourth, Marx predicted that the proletariat—the wage-earning factory workers—would become the vast majority. This has not been the case. In the United States, for instance, production-line jobs have not increased in numbers since the end of World War II. The main increase in the work force has been in services and clerical work, not in manual labor. The same is true of all other highly industrialized countries, including those ruled by Communists. Some dissident Communist writers, such as the Yugoslav Milovan Djilas, have attacked this growth of bureaucracy and management as heralding the rise of a "new class." Some Communist regimes have tried to slow the trend or at least play it down in their published statistics, or they may define as a "proletarian element" any government or Party official who was once a worker, even many years ago. More recently they have begun to define office workers as proletarians. None of this necessarily proves the rise of a new hereditary class of privileged persons in these countries but rather indicates the pressure of modern technology, which requires fewer people in performing manual work and more in handling information.

Finally, Marx expected the workers in the highly industrialized countries to move spontaneously toward revolution and proletarian dictatorship. All efforts at reform and real wage increases would fail in the end, he thought; history would drum revolution into the heads of most workers. This, too, has not happened. The majority of factory workers in the advanced Western countries have benefited from reforms and higher living standards; and most often they have become attached to labor unions committed to further reforms, further wage increases, and constitutional government.

THE MODIFIED THEORY: LENIN

When Marx died, his most important follower in Russia was only twelve years old. His name at birth was Vladimir Ilyich Ulyanov. He came from a family of professionals that included some petty nobles. He earned a law degree and might have become a civil servant. But in 1887 his older brother was hanged by the czarist authorities for conspiracy against the monarch. This act of deterrence proved counterproductive for the czar. Young Ulyanov, at seventeen, became a revolutionist and within a decade turned to Marxism, seeking in the social conditions of his country an explosive more powerful than dynamite. By the end of the century he had been banished by the czarist government to Siberia, and soon after 1900 he went into exile in western Europe. After his Siberian banishment he called himself Lenin, or "the man from the Lena River." Years later, in 1912, a large strike in the gold fields at the Lena River was smashed by czarist forces, who killed about two hundred workers. From then on, Ulyanov's chosen name had a more ominous ring: the man from the Lena River, like a ghost of the slain, would come back to claim the czar and the entire social order that he stood for.

Lenin's Theoretical Contributions. Marx's assumptions were partly modified and changed in several ways by Lenin. First, Lenin believed in *uneven development* among the countries of the world. Some countries would become highly industrialized, but others would stay far behind for the indefinite future. Modern technology would increase the political choices open to a society rather than completely determining the outcome through economic influence alone.

Second, like Marx, Lenin thought there was an automatic tendency in most societies toward weakening the power of landowners and replacing it by the power of industrialists and businesspeople. This is what he called the *bourgeois revolution.* Unlike Marx, however, he expected far less support for this revolution from the bourgeois proper—the big and middling businesspeople—except in colonial and semicolonial countries, where a native business class might struggle against foreign rulers or competitors. Major support for a bourgeois revolution would come from the peasants, Lenin believed, particularly from tenants and landless laborers who would revolt to make themselves owners of the land they tilled. Also unlike Marx, Lenin no longer maintained that the tendency toward socialism would be automatic.

Third, Lenin felt that the countries particularly well suited for a revolution were those that formed the *weakest links* in the chain of capitalist countries. They had to be backward enough to keep the workers poor and disgruntled, but advanced enough to keep them numerous and concentrated at strategic centers. In these countries, Lenin predicted, bourgeois revolutions would break out, but they would remain weak and incomplete; out of them, however, proletarian revolutions would emerge and finish the job. The best bets for such combined revolutions were Russia, China, and Spain.

Lenin saw two alternatives. Once revolution had triumphed in one country, it either would spread quickly throughout the whole world, in which case Lenin would preside over a *world revolution,* or else one or a few countries would have to set up their own Communist regimes and try to establish *socialism in one country* (as Stalin later called it). These regimes, Lenin came to believe by 1920, would hold out as long as needed, even for decades or for generations, until the rest of the

world would accept the new doctrine. Sooner or later, revolutions in colonial countries would destroy imperialism and much of the capitalist world market, making capitalism in western Europe unworkable. This is the thought behind Lenin's reported remark that the way to Paris might lead through Peking. Such expectations were behind Lenin's "new economic policy" in 1921, in which he made major concessions to private enterprise among the peasants. At the same time he tightened authoritarian control over the Russian Communist Party at the Tenth Congress, which forbade the forming of groups or factions within the Party and prohibited any criticism of a policy after the Party had adopted it.

Fourth, Lenin assumed that *peasant-worker alliances* would be extremely important, whereas Marx had relegated the peasants to the fringes of his intellectual universe. Lenin believed there would be peasant revolutions against the landowners in all developing countries and that the art of Communist revolution would consist in synchronizing the strikes and uprisings of disgruntled urban workers with the uprisings of disgruntled peasants. (Later Mao Tse-tung in China went one step further by putting the major weight of revolution on the peasantry.) Lenin assumed that the peasant revolution would result in the minority rule of workers, who would be allied with the peasants but exercise power over them. The Communist Party in each country, in turn, would lead the working class. It was to be the *vanguard* of the workers, thinking and acting today in the way most workers would act tomorrow. (In theory, it would *not* become, therefore, a permanent *elite,* different from the workers. Maintaining this principle to any extent in practice has been one of the continuing and acknowledged problems of the Soviet regime, as we shall see later.) In Lenin's view the resulting "proletarian dictatorship" would no longer be spontaneous; it would deliberately direct further economic development. In effect, it would be a dictatorship of the Communist Party, but it would have to be skillful enough to retain enough popular support among the peasants and workers to stay in power.

Finally, Lenin made a more radical psychological break with the existing order than had his ideological forerunners. Lenin was thoroughly alienated both from his government's bureaucracy and from western Europe. Both Marx and Engels were the most radical revolutionists of their day, but they felt very much at home in western Europe. In contrast, Lenin—who spent many years in the West—in many ways remained a stranger in the Western world. Yet Lenin put great stress on maintaining close contacts with workers everywhere; and it is recorded that, unlike many other radicals, he spent considerable time listening to peasants and plain people when in Russia.

This psychological distance from the mainstream of Western tradition had something to do with Lenin's fifth basic contribution to Communist theory, his *distrust of spontaneity*. When left to their own initiative, Lenin thought, workers would always try to behave like the American Federation of Labor: getting higher wages but not really questioning who was running the economy or whether their wages came from a war contract. It was the intellectuals, the Bolsheviks, the revolutionaries, who had to supply the sense of historical mission. But only individuals fully committed to this mission could do so, and they had to devote their lives to it. Such intense commitment had occurred also in the West, briefly and exceptionally, during the revolutionary period of Cromwell in England and of Robespierre in France. In Russia, however, this style of leadership proved more lasting and significant.

Lenin's distrust of spontaneity had a practical side as well. A spontaneous, loose, liberal organization, such as a Western-type political party, he felt, would be a sitting duck for the police forces of the czar, the most elaborate secret police organization of the time. Dodging the police would be a full-time job; and, being a revolutionary, a profession.

As a result of these ideas, Lenin developed a concept of a tightly disciplined, small party of full-time *professional revolutionists*. The czarist regime, like other anti-Communist dictatorships, unwittingly aided this development. By denying alternative employment to intellectuals who opposed it, it turned additional numbers of them into such professional revolutionists. Leninist Party members were much less likely to express themselves spontaneously, but might develop a sense of common pride and dedication. In the long run, however, these professional revolutionists could turn into a kind of underground bureaucracy, which was dedicated to the revolution and later to the regime that its victory created, but which in time often became rigid and one-sided in its thinking.

Lenin's Tactical Contributions. The quarrel between the two concepts of a party—the loose and the tight—came to a head in 1903 at a congress of Russia's Social Democratic (SD) Party held in Brussels and London. Lenin's followers were defeated on this issue, but the withdrawal of some members of the SD Party during the congress enabled Lenin's minority to become a majority at the end of the congress, when elections were held for the central committee. From the Russian word for majority, they were henceforth called *Bolsheviks;* and the "minority," their more Western-minded opponents, became known for a similar reason as *Mensheviks.* From 1919 until 1952 the full name of the ruling party of the Soviet Union was Communist Party of the Soviet Union (Bolsheviks)—CPSU(B).

In order to keep his small party disciplined, doctrinally pure, and uncontaminated by the capitalist environment, Lenin insisted on authoritarianism both in matters of party strategy and in terms of doctrine. At the same time he exhibited a mastery of coalition tactics and tactical retreats and topped it all off with a ceaseless demand for what he called "Bolshevik tenacity." In some ways one might compare the social organization that Lenin built with an organization developed for entirely different purposes by Saint Ignatius of Loyola in the sixteenth century. Jesuit fathers were taught to be masters of compromise, adjustment, and practicality, and yet to have the utmost devotion to both the general teachings of the church and the specific authority of the head of the Jesuit order. This combination of external flexibility and intense internal commitment was something that the Jesuits had successfully incorporated into their religious organization. Lenin tried to do something similar in the name of a secular doctrine.

Lenin died in 1924. He lived long enough to see that his plans for world revolution would have to be put off and that for some time his followers would have to hold out in a single country. But should they concentrate on internal development or on foreign revolutions? And through what means should they pursue these goals? These unresolved questions in Lenin's thought surfaced in a set of fateful quarrels among his successors.

THE STALINIST YEARS

With the death of Lenin, a fierce struggle for the control of the Communist Party and of the future of the Soviet Union began. Although a number of able politicians and theoreticians were involved, the most important focus for the struggle was the contest between two men; Leon Trotsky and Joseph Stalin. Trotsky was a revolutionist who, far more than Lenin, saw revolution as attractive for its own sake. A brilliant writer and orator, he was better at commanding than at listening. He was not a member of Lenin's party from 1903 until 1917, but in that year of revolution he offered his services to Lenin, and Lenin accepted him. Soon Trotsky appeared as an arch-Bolshevik to most people, although not to all insiders from the old party organization. Trotsky made his mark as the main tactician of the 1917 seizure of power and as the highly effective organizer of the Red Army during the period of civil war. As people's commissar of war (an office he retained until 1925), he was often inclined toward highly authoritarian solutions to social as well as military problems.

This streak in his character was most in evidence in 1920, when he advocated organizing all of Soviet industry on the Red Army model.

Trotsky Versus Stalin. Trotsky was much more cosmopolitan than either Lenin or Stalin. He was more at home in the West both emotionally and intellectually than in Russia. Before 1917, he had spent most of his politically active years abroad. He distrusted the Russian base of the revolution; Russia, to him, was uncouth and backward. Like Marx, he regarded Germany in particular, and France and England to a lesser degree, as the predestined countries for revolution. He strove, therefore, to push revolution in the West as fast as possible. Short of revolution in the West, he argued, economic development must be pursued in the Soviet Union only as part of an "international division of labor" with the capitalist West. Neither revolution at all costs nor cooperation with external enemies was a policy likely to appeal to most Russian Communists or to most of the Russian people. They contributed much to Trotsky's political defeats, first in 1920 and then in the mid-1920s, to his exile in 1929 (which eventually was followed by his assassination in Mexico in 1940), and to Stalin's ultimate victory.

Stalin's career took a different course. Born in Georgia in the Caucasus as the son of a shoemaker and a washerwoman, educated for a time on a scholarship in a seminary for Orthodox priests, he joined the Marxists at the age of nineteen and soon became a professional revolutionary. He was an early member of Lenin's faction and became an insider in its organization, in contrast to the individualist Trotsky, whom the old-line Bolsheviks distrusted. Stalin spent almost all his prerevolution career inside Russia, much of it in Siberian exile. His personality remained a riddle, even to his close associates and, it would appear, to his family. In many ways he was the epitome of the *apparatchik*—the man of the apparatus. A member of the Bolshevik Central Committee since 1912, he was appointed the Party's first *general secretary* in 1922, two years before Lenin's death, in large part because of his unassuming style and his taste for bureaucratic detail.

Both Stalin and Trotsky sought power. Stalin got it, partly because of his old Party connections, partly because of his control over Party patronage as general secretary, and partly because he chose policies that suited his nation. Stalin's most important decision, and probably the primary reason for his success, was his commitment to the possibilities of Russian-based socialism. He insisted from late 1924 onward that a collectivistic economy could be built in Russia, with Russian workers (few as they were), Russian industry (backward as it was), and Russian peasants (numerous as they were). After years of political maneuvering, Stalin came out strongly in support of socialism in one country and repudiated both the notion of expecting an immediate world revolution (which, of course, did not take place) and Trotsky's idea of linking Soviet development to the capitalist-dominated world economy.

In addition, Stalin wished to make a much greater attempt to industrialize the country than any of his opponents espoused. In the mid-1920s he criticized Trotsky as a "leftist" for his plan to tax the peasants heavily and his proposals for immediate industrialization. However, having defeated Trotsky and his allies, Stalin then condemned his own allies as "rightist" and, between 1927 and 1929, unveiled a program for radical development before which even Trotsky's schemes paled. More than any of his colleagues, Stalin demanded decisive action to curb the economic and political independence of the peasantry and to commence the rapid buildup of the industrial and urban sector of the economy. And more than anyone else, Stalin believed in a type of centralized planning that would require new machinery and a new style.

Planning: The Second Russian Revolution.
Once firmly in power, Stalin began to reorganize every facet of Soviet life. Central to his vision was the new apparatus for planning and administering the economy on a massive scale. He decided to transform Russia's peasant society, and this transformation was in fact undertaken in two five-year plans, from 1927 to 1937.

First, he began the *mechanization of agriculture,* largely with the help of American tractors. Second, he pushed the peasants into *collective farms.* These were farms in which the home, the household, the kitchen, and, in practice, the garden plot remained in private hands, but the fields were held in common and the tractors were owned by the government. Third, he *industrialized* the country by moving a large portion of the work force from the fields into the factories. Progress was slow: when Stalin started, 80 percent of the work force was in agriculture, but by the time he died it was down to approximately 50 percent. Thus, about one-third of the Russian work force was transferred from agriculture into the industrial sector, but at fantastic cost.

In effect, the first two five-year plans marked a second Russian revolution, hardly less desperate and costly than the first. As collectivization proceeded, the peasants slaughtered much of their livestock; it took over twenty-five years to get back to pre-1927 levels. Indeed, about 1 percent of the peasants, or approximately 1 million people, including the wealthier, or more tradition-minded, or more independent, resisted to the bitter end. Their defiance was ultimately broken by brutality and by deportations to Siberia. But the graves of collective farm leaders who were killed by the peasants in model collective farms tell a harsh story. It was a second civil war in the countryside.

Stalin insisted on squeezing every last bit of the available grain from the collective farms. If somebody had to starve, it was not going to be the cities and the workers on whom the Soviet regime depended. There followed in 1932–33 a manmade famine that cost the lives of several million peasants in the Ukraine and elsewhere in the Soviet Union. The next spring, the regime provided additional incentives for the surviving peasants to work harder, which they did, to produce a bumper

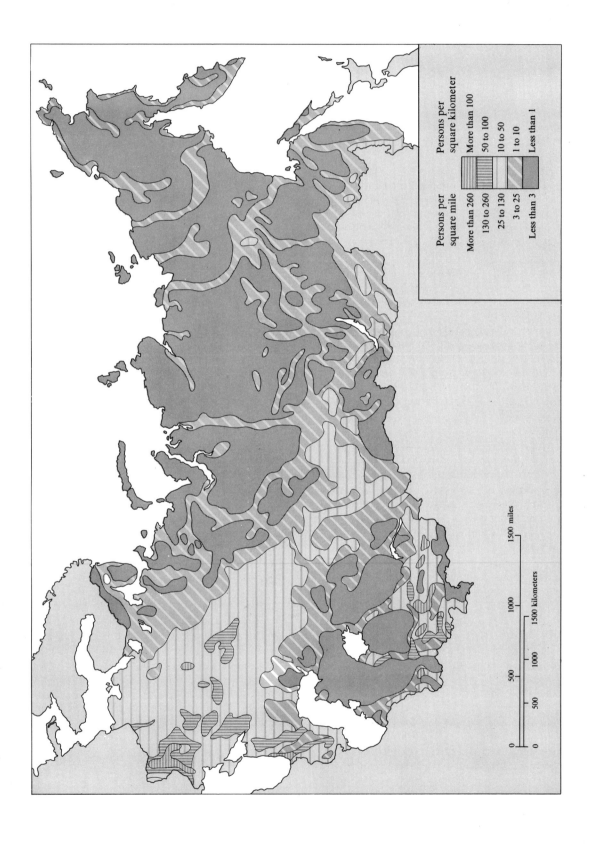

Persons per
square mile

More than 260

130 to 260

25 to 130

3 to 25

Less than 3

Persons per
square kilometer

More than 100

50 to 100

10 to 50

1 to 10

Less than 1

0   500   1000   1500 miles

0   500   1000   1500 kilometers

crop. But a price had been paid. The famine had hit women and children, producing unimaginable suffering. It had produced a death toll estimated at 5 million, comparable to the toll of the civil war.

The Stalinist defense was that until that time there had been frequent natural famines in Russia; that everybody had said they were catastrophes about which nothing could be done; and that Stalin's ruthless policies had ended them. The fact is that although crop failures have recurred, in no peacetime year since the mid-1930s has there been a famine. Stalin's reforms eventually left agriculture sufficiently productive to yield food and industry for export in order to buy additional food abroad when needed.

Costs and Achievements. The achievement of the Stalin era was, on the whole, an unprecedented success in rapid industrialization. Never before was so agrarian a country transformed into so industrial a state in so few years. Agriculture became capable of feeding the entire country even though there were many fewer people in the rural work force, and the youngest, most energetic, most able people had left the villages. In no other large country did literacy spread so fast or science and technology grow so rapidly and extensively. The nearest parallel in the non-Communist world is the industrialization of Japan in the the late nineteenth and early twentieth centuries, which took longer and was also accompanied by dictatorship—and, incidentally, by very warlike, military regimes for a large part of the time. The last test of Stalin's regime was perhaps the most grueling—World War II. On the whole, when that test came, most of the Soviet population, with its many different languages, fought for the Soviet regime, often displaying great heroism.

The cost of Stalin's ruthlessness was high. A balance sheet might suggest that in the long run

Stalin's ruthlessness saved more lives from famine and foreign intervention than it cost. But such a method of rationalistic analysis may be shallow. We must also ask what this brutality, this willingness to sacrifice millions for some future good, does to the minds of the people who practice it, wherever and for whatever reason. When Stalin and his followers actively accepted ruthlessness and dictatorship, they agreed to go to almost any lengths to reach their goals. They also learned to expect hostility everywhere. As a result, they learned to fear each other. Indeed, one of the most dangerous security risks to the Soviet government has been the secret police, and a police chief's lot in Russia has not been a happy one. Three of Stalin's police chiefs, Yagoda, Yezhov, and Beria, were shot by the government. At other times the accusations by such men sent others to their doom. Thus, in the end the dictatorship of Stalin became a dictatorship of suspicion and paranoia.

The hidden costs of his paranoia—the inability to tell friends from enemies, reality from fantasy, and an honest difference of opinion from an attempt at sabotage and subversion—were, perhaps, even more serious. The memoirs of Stalin's daughter, Svetlana Alliluyeva, are a poignant illustration. There were losses of life and liberties far beyond the costs inherent in the policies themselves. Most of the original Bolsheviks who preached ruthlessness in the name of revolution ultimately perished at the hands of other Communists who had been reared in the same creed. Stalin's purges, which began in earnest in 1934, went into high gear from 1936 to 1938, and, as the Soviet governments has publicly stated since 1956, a large number of those purged were completely innocent. They were the victims of frameups, manufactured evidence, forced confessions.

One can see near the motion picture theater Udarnik, located on one of the main streets of Moscow, a plaque in memory of Marshal Mikhail N. Tukhachevsky, who was tried and executed for treason in 1937. After Stalin's death it was revealed that Tukhachevsky had been completely

---

(*Left*) MAP 3.3 *Population Distribution of the Soviet Union*

innocent, and laudatory biographies of him were published. None of this could bring him back to life, but it may have helped his family and perhaps some of his surviving fellow officers, and the plaque continues to remind Russians of the bloody errors a powerful government can commit.

Others suffered more slowly. Alexander Solzhenitsyn's book entitled *One Day in the Life of Ivan Denisovich,* published in the Soviet Union in 1962, is a former inmate's description of one day in a labor camp in Stalin's era. These camps, at their peak in 1950, had 10 million people in them; and since many died there and others were released, probably over 20 million Russians were in these camps at one time or another. Nearly every second family in the Soviet Union had somebody who was touched, brushed, or hit by the Stalin terror in the years between 1934 and 1953. In the years after Stalin's death in 1953 the number of political prisoners has declined to less than 20,000, but the memory of those terrible years remains vivid among the present generation of Soviet citizens.

A MEASURE OF PROSPERITY—AND THE NEW STAKES OF POLITICS

The Stalin era laid the basis for the second largest concentration of economic power in the world. The Soviet Union, with 6 percent of the world's population, has 12 percent of the world's income. It ranks behind only the United States, which has 25 percent of the income (with 5 percent of the world's population). The Soviet Union ranks first in the world in the production of a number of basic industrial commodities, including coal and steel. American per capita income in 1978 was about $9,640; Soviet per capita income was $4,004, if the Soviet output of goods and services is valued in 1978 dollars. This corresponds to about 42 percent of the United States figure. According to the 1978 estimate, this Soviet level was well below that of West Germany, Japan, and France, but only slightly behind Britain and Italy.

To place the Soviet figures in perspective, bear in mind that around 1920 United States per capita income already was close to $1,000, while Soviet per capita income—after years of foreign and civil wars—was below $100. Even in 1928, Soviet per capita income was only one-fifth of that in the United States. The American-Soviet income gap, therefore, has shrunk from 10:1 to 5:1 to 2.4:1. Gross national product—not per capita income—is arguably more important for assessment of potential power in world affairs. Here a 1980 estimate puts total Soviet GNP at 60 percent of that of the United States, as against only 40 percent in 1955.[4]

[4]Such rankings may vary, depending on the source of data. The 1978 figures here are drawn from Herbert Block, "Soviet Economic Performance in a Global Context," in Joint Economic Committee, U.S. Congress, *Soviet Economy in a Time of Change* (Washington, D.C.: U.S. Government Printing Office, 1979), vol. 1, pp. 114–17. The 60 percent figure was given by *Time* Magazine in its special issue *Inside the USSR,* June 23, 1980 (European edition), p. 57, col. 1.

There are several pitfalls in comparing Soviet data on gross national product (GNP) and national income with those for the United States.

First, the Soviet Union has 262 million inhabitants, compared with 221 million in the United States. Hence, even if one accepts the 1980 figure of 60 percent for the ratio of the total Soviet GNP to that of the United States, the Soviet *per capita* GNP still would be only 50 percent of the American per capita figure.

Second, the gross national product figures in each country include replacement for worn-out machines and other capital equipment. "National income" is the *net* national product (NNP) of a country and excludes these replacement costs, so that NNP in most countries is on average between 10 and 20 percent smaller than GNP. If capital goods are more expensive in the Soviet Union than in the United States—and there is reason to think they are—then their replacement costs also should be higher, and the difference between GNP and NNP should be greater in the Soviet Union. If so, Soviet national income, i.e., NNP, should lag farther behind the United States national income than the gap between the GNP figures of the two countries.

Third, Soviet and American GNP can be valued in Soviet prices or in American prices. The first method makes Soviet GNP appear smaller, because it contains a larger share of foodstuffs and other basic goods, which

A per capita income of $4,004 does not mean that the Russians live or eat as well as the British. Part of the Soviet per capita income is circling the globe in the form of sputniks and assorted space hardware. Other parts of their income are buried in intercontinental missile sites in the Ural Mountains. Thus, a fair degree of Soviet income does not get to consumers. Russian consumer standards are much lower than those of the Western European and North American countries. Back in 1955, when Soviet total per capita income was only 38 percent of the United States level, Soviet *consumption* spending per capita totaled only 37 percent of the corresponding United States amount, but

the total for *nonconsumption* items, such as capital investments and defense, already then amounted to 63 percent of the American level. By the 1970s, when total Soviet per capita income had reached nearly one-half of the United States amount, Soviet consumption levels were still well below— and Soviet defense and investment expenditures were well above—that overall Soviet average.[5]

These high and sustained rates of growth and this consistent favoring of investments and defense spending, as opposed to consumption, have been among the large stakes of Soviet politics. How much to spend how fast on what is never a purely technical question in any country or under any system. What people want and value, what messages they respond to, how they perceive or misperceive reality, and which persons or groups have the power to make their current values and perceptions prevail over those of everybody else— all these are political questions, albeit within the limits of given economic and technological constraints.

The political aspects of what might look like purely economic decisions are highlighted by the Soviet tendency to concentrate efforts on *decisive sectors,* as the Russians call them. This now means space technology; earlier it was intercontinental rockets and nuclear energy; during World War II it was the tank program and earlier still the tractor program. Coming decisive sectors may well be automation, agricultural biology, and the chemistry of fertilizers. Even if the leaders should misjudge the next decisive sector, however, Soviet industry now has a productive capacity that can survive a great deal of error and difficulties.

Nevertheless, certain critical economic problems remain as yet unsolved. First, Soviet planners have

---

are cheaper in the Soviet Union, and fewer consumer durables, such as automobiles, which are expensive there. The United States GNP includes much machinery and consumer durables, high-priced in Russia, so that the American GNP will be higher if calculated in Soviet prices, and so the gap between the Soviet and American figures will be larger. Calculating both figures in American prices has the opposite effect: Russian bread, potatoes, and housing are more expensive at American prices, and American machinery and consumer durables are cheaper in the United States than in the Soviet Union; hence the Soviet GNP will appear somewhat closer to the United States level. (The same holds for comparisons of Soviet and American military spending: valuing the feeding, clothing, and other maintenance of each Soviet soldier at American prices makes the Soviet military budget appear particularly high, since the Soviet Union uses relatively high amounts of manpower.)

Moreover, GNP data for the United States include services; official Soviet data do not, being limited to national material product (NMP), so that the value of services in the Soviet economy must be estimated.

Finally, the relatively closed nature of Soviet society, the treatment of some economic data as state secrets, and the official insistence on a single approved interpretation—or, in Western eyes, propaganda line—make it difficult, although not impossible, to get a realistic overview of Soviet economic performance. The Western observer is strongly tempted to pick from the many possible figures just those that support his or her preconceived view. Seeking a more balanced picture is harder but more worth while.

For valuable information on these matters I am indebted to Professor Abram Bergson of Harvard University.

[5]See Abram Bergson. "Comparative National Income of the USSR and the States," in D. J. Daly, ed., *International Comparison and Output* (New York: National Bureau of Economic Research and Columbia University Press, 1972), p. 178.

not resolved the problem of recurrent *disproportions in investment.* They invest heavily in industry, which often gives *increasing returns to scale:* the more you make, the cheaper you can manufacture each additional product. Agriculture and mining, in contrast, tend to produce *diminishing returns:* the more crops or minerals you need, the poorer the soils or deposits you must go to and, ultimately, the more expensive it becomes to produce each additional item. To some extent the force-feeding of capital into industry and the underinvesting in agriculture occasionally have led to bad years in which economic growth has slowed down or sometimes has even stopped. These are not cyclical depressions, as in the West, but they look like depressions and can be as serious, if not more serious. After five decades, Communist planning is still neither perfect nor smooth.

The second disproportion is between investment goods and *incentive goods,* that is, goods for which people are willing to work harder, such as better clothes, washing machines, and television sets. Historically, Communist ideology has thought of consumer goods as luxuries; at times the Communists have been almost like the Puritans of the seventeenth century and Adam Smith in the eighteenth. They have been slow to realize that many consumer goods are also incentive goods. A color television set is not merely a luxury, but an incentive good that makes a plumber show up on the job the next day in order to meet the installment payments on his television set. The Russians have not yet fully discovered the tremendous power of consumer goods as incentives to further productive effort.

Moreover, the Communists have not avoided the problem of the tension between *equalitarianism* (making wages relatively equal) and *performance payments* (paying more to people who do important or good work than to people who work less, who do less important work, or who work less well). Much of the emotional appeal of socialist or Communist ideas comes from their implied promise of greater equality. Much of the motivation to work in the Soviet Union, as elsewhere, comes from material incentives, such as better pay, that are unequal for unequal work.

Reliable data on Soviet income differences are not easy to come by. The most careful calculations done to date, by the British economist Martin McAuley, show the general distribution of income as it existed in the late 1960s. McAuley's findings are presented in Table 3.1. Basic incomes for selected occupations in the early 1970s are shown in Table 3.2. And data from the period 1960–1978, aggregated by economic sector, can be found in Table 3.3.

A glance at these tables shows that there are indeed substantial differences in income in the Soviet Union. To be sure, these are not as great as the disparities found in most Western countries, including the United States. Even allowing for secondary benefits like vouchers for luxury goods, special medical benefits, and holiday facilities—which generally are not reflected in official statistics—it is virtually impossible for members of even the most elite sectors of Soviet society to aspire to the income and wealth realized by businesspeople, celebrities, and others in the West.[6] Moreover, there is evidence that income inequality in the Soviet Union has been on the decline for at least twenty-five years. Table 3.3 gives some idea of changes by economic sector. Apart from the general equalizing trend (albeit with some backsliding since 1970), the most striking change is the greatly improved position of the agricultural work force. Another measure of improvement is the ratio of the earnings of workers and employees in the top 10 percent of the income scale to those in the bottom 10 percent. In 1956 this ratio was 4.4:1. It declined to 3.7:1 in 1964

[6]On this much vexed problem, see Mervyn Matthews, *Privilege in the Soviet Union* (London: George Allen and Unwin, 1978); and Alastair McAuley, *Economic Welfare in the Soviet Union* (Madison: University of Wisconsin Press, 1979), especially chapters 3–4, 9.

TABLE 3.1 *Distribution of the Soviet Population by Per Capita Income, 1967 and 1968 (by Percent)*

Monthly income (rubles)	Collective farmers, 1967	Nonagricultural workers and employees, 1968
–20	6.2	—
20–30	16.3	5.1
30–40	20.4	10.6
40–50	17.6	16.6
50–60	13.1	18.2
60–70	10.7	16.9
70–90	11.1	16.4
90–110	3.3	7.6
110–130	0.6	3.3
130–	0.5	5.1

Source: From data in Alastair McAuley, *Economic Welfare in the Soviet Union* (Madison: University of Wisconsin Press, 1979), p. 65.

and 3.2:1 in 1970, and a ratio of 2.9:1 was planned for 1975.[7]

However one qualifies the picture, these inequalities are still large. In Russia, as in the United States, they create a lasting tension between what may be a good incentive for production and what is apt to be accepted by the public as legitimate and just. In the Soviet Union this tension is enhanced by the promise of social justice that is inherent in so much of Soviet thought and in the broader socialist tradition from which it is in part derived. The extent, distribution, and future increase or decrease of these income inequalities are among the continuing stakes of Soviet politics.

[7]Jerry F. Hough and Merle Fainsod, *How the Soviet Union Is Governed* (Cambridge: Harvard University Press, 1979), pp. 265–66, relying on calculations by Peter Wiles and G. S. Sarkisyan.

TABLE 3.2 *Average Monthly Earnings (Wages and Salaries) for Selected Soviet Occupations, Early 1970s (Rubles)**

Occupation or rank	Monthly earnings
General secretary of Party	900
First secretary of Union of Composers	800
Secretary of Party Central Committee	700–800
Army major general	600
Director of research institute	500–700
Well-known ballet dancer	500
Director of large coal mine	480
Director of large metallurgy plant	390
Junior official of Party Central Committee	300
Editor of national newspaper	240
Scientific researcher	200–250
Construction engineer	200
Industrial worker	140
Worker on state farm	109
Trade clerk	99

*Includes official income only (excludes noncash benefits, bonuses, and other secondary benefits).

Source: First eleven lines are estimates from Mervyn Matthews, *Privilege in the Soviet Union* (London: George Allen and Unwin, 1978), pp. 23–27; last four are from *Narodnoye khozyaistvo SSSR v 1972 g.* (Moscow: Statistika, 1973).

With inequalities of income often go inequalities in education, lifestyle, chances of success in primary and secondary schools, and, hence, opportunities for higher education, other advanced training, and subsequent careers—all of which contribute once more to the inequalities in the income structure of the next generation. A comparison of the educational aspirations of secondary school graduates from different social strata

TABLE 3.3 *Average Monthly Earnings (Wages and Salaries) of Soviet Workers and Employees, by Economic Sector, 1960–1978 (Current Rubles)* *

Rank, 1978	Sector	Number employed, 1978 (millions)	Average monthly earnings			% change, 1960–1978
			1960	1970	1978	
1	Construction	11.03	92	150	191	108
2	Transportation	9.86	87	137	190	118
3	Industry	36.01	91	133	177	95
4	Science	4.07	105	140	170	62
5	Credit and insurance	.60	71	111	148	108
6	Administration	2.35	87	123	145	67
7	Agriculture	11.26	54	101	143	165
8	Communications	1.60	63	97	139	121
9	Education and culture	9.92	70	105	125	79
10	Trade	9.36	59	95	124	110
11	Housing and local services	4.21	58	95	123	112
12	Art	.45	64	95	121	89
13	Health	6.03	59	92	116	97
Average			81	122	160	98
Highest as percentage of lowest			194	163	165	

*Includes official money income only. Does not include collective farmers and several other small categories of agricultural workers (15.14 million persons in 1978) or 1.85 million persons (1978) in miscellaneous occupations.

Source: From data in handbook *Narodnoye khozyaistvo SSSR v 1978 g.* (Moscow: Statistika, 1979).

in one Soviet region with their successes in continuing their education is presented in Table 3.4.

Since the different occupational and educational strata are not evenly distributed over all the regions and ethnic groups of the Soviet Union, there are also observable inequalities in the levels of income and education among its different regions and the peoples that live in them. According to Soviet statistics, income per capita in the Russian Republic, the territory inhabited mainly by ethnic Russians, was 10 percent above the Soviet average in 1978. In the three small Baltic republics (Estonia, Latvia, and Lithuania) and in Belorussia, income was also above average (by 27, 18, 10, and 1 percent, respectively). In each of the ten remaining union republics—the Ukraine and Moldavia in the west, the three Caucasus republics in the south, and the five Central Asian republics—per capita income was below the national average, and by amounts ranging from 6 percent for the Ukraine to 33 percent for Tadzhikistan. These regional inequalities were nar-

TABLE 3.4 *Personal Plans of Secondary School Graduates. Their Successes, and the Social Status of Their Families (Novosibirsk Oblast, 1965)*

Occupational status of family	Percentage of graduates who said they wanted to continue studies	Percentage of graduates who succeeded in continuing studies	
		Those desiring further study	All graduates
Urban nonmanual	93	88	82
Manual, industry and construction	83	73	61
Average of all students	83	73	61
Manual, services	76	78	59
Rural nonmanual	76	76	58
Manual, transport and communications	82	55	45
Manual, agriculture	76	13	10
Others	38	66	25

Source: From data in V. Aspaturian, "The Soviet Union," in R. C. Macridis and R. E. Ward, eds., *Modern Political Systems: Europe,* 3rd ed. (1972), p. 553, with reference to V. N. Shubkin, "Youth Starts Out," *Voprosy filosofii,* no. 5 (May 1965). Adapted by permission of Prentice-Hall, Inc., Englewood Cliffs, N.J.

rowed somewhat in the 1960s, but have tended to widen since 1970.[8]

The uneven incidence of new investments could either reduce or increase these inequalities. Since many investments have in fact been channeled into the more prosperous areas, including the Russian Republic (which takes in the vast and underdeveloped Siberian region), the net effect since 1960 has been to enhance slightly the relative advantages of the Russian heartland and of other "have" regions. The arguments about where to

[8]Martin C. Spechler, "Regional Developments in the U.S.S.R., 1958–78," in Joint Economic Committee, p. 151.

direct large investments most often were couched in terms of economic or technological rationality, but this made their social and political implications no less real; and Soviet decision makers and ordinary citizens often are well aware of them. The professed overall aims of Soviet policy remain, of course, the full and equal development of all Soviet regions and peoples, but the lag of equality behind development has persisted. Its extent is illustrated by the estimated per capita income ratio of almost 2:1 between the most highly developed union republic, Estonia, and the least developed one, the Tadzhik Republic. This is comparable to the current 2:1 ratio between the richest state and the poorest state in the United States—Connecticut and Mississippi.

In the long run there are still bigger things at

stake in Soviet politics. For in the Soviet Union, even more than in many other countries, political decisions can influence the entire direction of its economy and culture and the course of the continuing transformation of its society.

Such political decisions also shaped the responses of the Soviet regime to such external challenges as the foreign anti-Soviet interventions of 1917–21; the Nazi threat of 1933–45; the all-out onslaught of the Cold War, particularly in 1946–55, and its continuation, though less intense, since then; and since the early 1960s, a certain pressure from China after the Mao government's resurrection of disagreements over Soviet border territory. The challenge from China increased with the establishment of more friendly relations between China and the United States and the brief war between China and the Soviets' ally, Vietnam, in 1979. Finally, the stakes of Soviet politics also include the degree of attention and support, if any, that will continue to be given to the ideological, missionary, and geopolitical ambitions and aspirations of those Soviet interest groups and leaders who are concerned about international affairs beyond a mere general interest in national security. The extent of aid given to such countries as Cuba or Vietnam and the risks accepted for their protection also will be determined largely by the political processes within the Soviet system.

PARTICIPATION IN POLITICS AND THE MACHINERY OF GOVERNMENT

A Persisting Element: Government by Pyramid. In politics, as well as in economics, the Soviet system depends on the guidance of a *pyramid* of political authorities and on the intense efforts of millions of activists—about one adult out of every five—organized in the Communist Party or its youth organization, the Young Communist League (*Komsomol*). All these organizations call for civic efforts and try to channel and control these actions

closely. The scope for public articulation of differences of opinion in politics in the Soviet Union has always been narrower than in the Western democracies. It is now, however, much broader than it was in Stalin's lifetime, and much broader than it is commonly thought in the West. Under Stalin's successors, Nikita S. Khrushchev from 1953 to 1964 and Leonid I. Brezhnev since October 1964, there has been some oscillation in the degree of toleration of heterodox political views, from inside and outside the political establishment. Still, the boundaries on expression put into place after Stalin's death and partial disgrace have not been seriously questioned. Nor have shifts in the balance of liberality and conformity in the official line changed the basic structure of the Soviet regime.

All modern countries, in a sense, are governed by pyramids of administration and decision making. The Soviet system is more pyramidal than most. It consists, in fact, of a multiplicity of pyramids. There is the pyramid of lawmaking governments—called "soviets" after the Russian word for council—from villages, towns, and districts all the way up to the Supreme Soviet in Moscow. There is the pyramid of the Communist Party, from the primary organizations to the Politburo and Secretariat of the Central Committee in the capital. There are military and security-police pyramids, and another pyramid of economic planning and management. Finally, there are several lesser pyramids of mass organizations, such as trade unions, civil defense organizations, consumer cooperatives, youth and sports leagues, and the like.

In the Soviet Union all these pyramids interlock and interact at every level. Directly or indirectly, the Soviet one-party state reaches into every nook and cranny of social life. At the same time the system offers many opportunities for participation; it has many ties to the life of the population and many opportunities to win popular support.

Last, but not least, despite its multiplicity, complexity, and popular connections, it is well suited to centralized direction from above.

The National Government. The Soviet Union as a whole is formally governed by a *Supreme Soviet* of 1,500 delegates. This parliamentary body is so large, and meets for such a limited time each year, that its main tasks consist of confirming and ratifying legislation produced by smaller groups. Under the current (1977) constitution of the U.S.S.R., the Supreme Soviet is elected every five years and is divided into two chambers of equal numbers of delegates. The *Soviet of the Union* consists of deputies elected from districts with equal populations (about 300,000 people); the *Soviet of Nationalities* includes deputies representing Soviet republics and other territorial units based on nationality. In the former, voters are represented in proportion to their numbers; in the latter, akin to the United States Senate, the smaller republics, areas, and nationalities are deliberately overrepresented.

The Supreme Soviet has many of the trappings of a Western legislature, including a set of standing committees (fifteen in each house). It elects a *Presidium,* which we shall abbreviate PSS, to function as the collective chief of state of the Soviet Union. The chairman of this Presidium, Leonid Brezhnev since 1977, fulfills on ceremonial occasions a role analogous to that of president of the Soviet Union. Besides the chairman, the PSS has 38 members including a first deputy chairman (who often stands in for Brezhnev), a secretary, 15 deputy chairmen (one for each union republic), and 21 other members. Between sessions of the Supreme Soviet, the Presidium "functions as the highest organ of state authority," under the constitution. For most of the time, the PSS formally exercises all the state powers of the Supreme Soviet, including the passage of legislation, as well as far-reaching executive powers.

The PSS, however, is not the government of the Soviet Union. It directly controls neither the execution and administration of policy nor the Soviet bureaucracy. These tasks fall to the *Council of Ministers,* which the constitution calls "the highest executive and administrative organ of state power." In 1979 the Council of Ministers had 109 members, including a chairman, one first deputy chairman, twelve deputy chairmen, and the heads of sixty-two ministries, seventeen state committees (three of these men are also deputy chairmen of the council), and four specialized agencies, as well as the premiers of all fifteen union republics *(ex officio).* The decrees and orders of the council are binding and form the great mass of Soviet legislation. Since the Council of Ministers is much too large for efficient deliberation, it rarely meets in full session. Its principal decision-making powers are entrusted to the much smaller *Presidium of the Council of Ministers* (PCM), which includes the council chairman and his deputies. The chairman of the Council of Ministers (and of the PCM) has always been a top-ranking member of the Communist Party, ranging from such early leaders as Lenin, Molotov, and Stalin to such more recent incumbents as Khrushchev, Kosygin, and Tikhonov. The office of *chairman of the Council of Ministers* somewhat resembles that of prime minister in Britain or France.

Directly subordinate to the Council of Ministers is the enormous bureaucratic apparatus of the national government, most of it organized in ministries. Some of the national ministries—the Ministry of Defense, for example, or the Ministry of Communications (which runs the post office and telegraph network)—have direct analogues in the governments of almost any Western country. But many of the others are economic production agencies, the prime instruments for administering the state-owned Soviet economy. They control plants and mills scattered across the Soviet Union and provide many housing and social services normally provided by other means in the West.

Territorial Units and Ethnic Groups. Below the all-union level there are fifteen *union republics,* the constituent units of the Soviet federation, each with its own constitution, supreme soviet, council of ministers, prime minister, and bureaucracy. By far the largest union republic is the Russian Socialist Federated Soviet Republic (RSFSR)—itself a federation—which includes the majority of the population and land area of the Soviet Union. Each union republic is defined as the political homeland of one of the country's major nationali-ties, and each (except for the RSFSR) has two official languages—Russian and the tongue of the major ethnic community in the republic.

Within the union republics (see Figure 3.1) are units of regional government of great complexity. The three most important regional units are the *autonomous republics, oblasts,* and *krays.* The twenty autonomous republics (sixteen of them in the

FIGURE 3.1 *The Hierarchy of Governments in the Soviet Union, 1979*

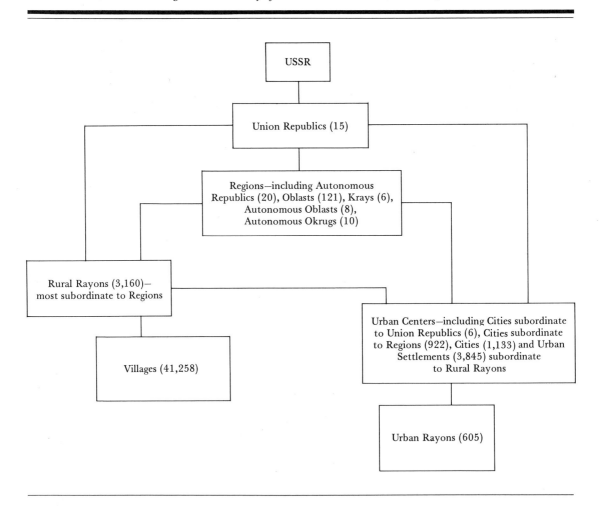

RSFSR) are all defined on an ethnic basis and have certain special rights related to language and education. As of 1979, there were 121 *oblasts* and 6 of the larger *krays* (found only in the RSFSR), none of them set up along nationality lines.

The regional units (and the small union republics, which do not have regional tiers) are in turn subdivided into rural districts called *rayons*, which roughly correspond to counties in American states. Each *rayon* has its own soviet and executive. It is only beneath this level that one finds truly local institutions. Thousands of village and town soviets function on the local level. As for full-fledged cities (with populations of 50,000 and up), they are generally self-governing units reporting directly to the regional authorities and exempt from the control of the *rayons*. Many Soviet cities are themselves subdivided into internal boroughs or districts, which are also known as *rayons*.

The local, regional, and republic soviets are best seen as administrative vehicles. Each has a limited amount of legal authority (subject always to the check of soviets at higher levels), an administrative staff, and powers of taxation. Most of their day-to-day work is delegated to bureaucrats, to the executive committee *(ispolkom)* of the soviet, and to a large network of standing and ad hoc committees.

The pyramid of soviets also serves as an instrument for public participation. At all levels, deputies to the soviets are elected directly. The nomination of candidates at every level is closely controlled by the Party, and there are no competing candidates. Even so, the elections and the work of the soviets serve to solidify the connections between the people and their government. They help the government present its policies to the people; and, as in other countries, the experience of local and regional government provides many opportunities for the training of political talent and its recruitment for higher office. Unlike the process in many other countries, all this happens in the Soviet Union under the initiative and surveillance of the Communist Party.

The Party Pyramid. The Communist Party of the Soviet Union (CPSU) in its organization and ideology, is itself one of the major political inventions of the twentieth century. As we saw earlier in the chapter, it grew out of a tightly knit body of professional revolutionists. These were organized into small conspiratorial groups that were well suited to escape the persecutions of the Okhrana, the czarist secret police. Each group was so self-contained that its discovery by the police was unlikely to expose other groups. These groups—at first called *cells,* but called *primary party organizations* since the 1930s—were organized as a rule where the people worked. Most often they were formed in factories, offices, institutions, or military units or mass organizations; sometimes they were organized in villages or urban neighborhoods.

The extent to which the Party now penetrates the different Soviet social and occupational groups is shown in Table 3.5. Though no longer secret, primary organizations still exist largely in the compact form, centered in the workplace, that was pioneered by the early Bolsheviks. Every Communist Party member is expected to work actively under the control of the primary unit and to report his or her activities to it. This basic organizational design seeks to combine the personal commitment of each individual with the motivating and sustaining power of small groups in which members know each other personally. An American psychiatrist, Stanley Elkes, has called the small group "the engine of society"; the Communist Party, by its design, seeks to harness this engine to its purposes.

Since Lenin's time the number of primary units has grown enormously and so has Party membership. In 1979 there were about 16.7 million Party members in the Soviet Union—over 6 percent of the total population, or 9 percent of those of the voting age of eighteen years and over. Yet Party membership remains selective. Party members must first serve for a time as *candidates* under the supervision of a primary organization, and each candidate must be sponsored by three Party members for admission. Members are dropped for

TABLE 3.5 *Social Composition of the Communist Party of the Soviet Union, 1905–1979*

	1905	1917	1920*	1932	1956	1961	1967	1971	1979
Workers	61.7%	60.2%	33.2%	64.5%	32.0%	34.5%	38.1%	40.1%	42.7%
Peasants	4.7	7.6	36.9	27.8	17.1	17.5	16.0	15.1	13.2
Intelligentsia	33.6	32.2	22.1	7.7	50.9	48.0	45.9	44.8	44.1
N =	8,400	23,600	612,000	3,172,215	7,173,521	9,176,005	12,684,133	14,455,321	16,721,322

*The 1920 column adds up to only 92.9 percent. In that year, the last of the civil war, a large number of individuals from other groups may still have been in the Red Army.

Source: For 1905–1976, data in V. Aspaturian, "The Soviet Union," in R. C. Macridis, ed., *Modern Political Systems: Europe,* 4th ed. (1978), p. 394 (adapted by permission of Prentice-Hall, Inc., Englewood Cliffs, N.J.). For 1979, *Yezhegodnik Bolshoy Sovetskoy Entsiklopedii* (Moscow, 1979), p. 13.

failing to pay dues for three consecutive months; they may be reprimanded or expelled for inactivity or deviation from Party policy. In 1951–56 an annual average of about 100,000 members were expelled. In the more permissive Khrushchev period of 1956–64 this dropped to about 50,000, or less than 0.5 percent of the total membership per year. In 1971–76, in the Brezhnev era, expulsions numbered about 70,000 a year, again about 0.5 percent.

Communist Party members are closely supervised and are supposed to be unceasingly active—often at some cost to their families' and their own peace of mind. They gain improved chances of promotion and careers and sometimes of power and prestige. Less tangibly, they may gain a sense of belonging to a "vocation of leadership," to a band of persons committed to a historic mission, which may give added meaning to their lives. Such commitment exacts a price. The more intensely members respond to motives of this latter kind, the more bitter will be their disputes in case of disagreement, and the more painful will it be for them to be reprimanded or expelled for disagreeing with the party line or to support it silently against their personal convictions.

The interplay of Party practices and individual motivations has produced a Party membership that is markedly more intellectual, or at least more oriented to white-collar work, more urban, better educated, more managerial, and more predominantly Russian than the general Soviet population (see Table 3.6).

Party members were organized in 1979 into 403,000 primary units, averaging forty-one members per unit. The primary Party organizations in each locality report to local Party committees, of which there were 4,322 in 1979. Local Party committees are found in about 40 percent of Soviet towns and cities, in about 90 percent of rural *rayons,* and in all urban *rayons.* None exists at the village level. Each local Party committee has one or several secretaries and, depending on the size of the locality, additional staff resources as well. All Party executives (members of committees and of their internal leaderships, usually called "bureaus") are formally elected at local Party conferences. As in the machinery of state, there are also elections, political executives, and an administrative apparatus at the regional and union republic levels. Generally speaking, the larger the region or republic, the larger the executive and the larger the apparatus. The exception here is the RSFSR, the largest union

TABLE 3.6 *The Communist Party and the Soviet People, 1932 and 1976*
(in percentages)

	Stalin Era, 1932			Brezhnev Era (1976 data)		
	Share in population	Party members	Overrepresentation or under-representation	Share in population	Party members	Overrepresentation or under-representation
	A	B	B/A	C	D	D/C
Intelligentsia	4	8	2.0	27	45	1.7
Urban dwellers	n.a.	n.a.	n.a.	61	80	1.3
Russians	n.a.	n.a.	n.a.	52	61	1.2
Workers	14	64	4.5	51	42	0.8
Peasants	78	28	0.3	22	14	0.6
Women	52*	15†	0.3	54	24	0.4

*1939 data
†1937 data

Sources: V. Aspaturian, "The Soviet Union," in R. C. Macridis and R. E. Ward, eds., *Modern Political Systems: Europe,* 3rd ed. (1972). Adapted by permission of Prentice-Hall, Inc., Englewood Cliffs, N.J. *The USSR in Figures for 1975* (Moscow: Statistika, 1976). This latter source includes some 1976 figures.

republic, which does not have independent Party machinery. Regional Party organs in the RSFSR report directly to the central CPSU leadership.

At the top of the pyramid is the set of central Party authorities (see Figure 3.2). At five-year intervals, an *All-Union Party Congress* meets in Moscow to ratify basic policy decisions. Of the several bodies the congress elects, the most important by far is the *Central Committee,* whose mandate is to direct Party affairs between congresses. The Central Committee, which in Lenin's day was a small body, has now grown into a group of several hundred. The Central Committee in turn elects its own compact political executive, the *Politburo.* The Politburo, which is the point of ultimate decision making for most important questions in Soviet

politics, contained as of late 1980 fifteen full members and eight candidate, or non-voting, members. The Central Committee also selects a *Secretariat* (with ten members in 1980), which oversees intra-Party administration and in doing so accumulates enormous power over political decisions of all kinds. Since Stalin's time, the most powerful individual in the entire Soviet system has been the man who parlays primacy in the Secretariat, with its control over Party patronage, into primacy in the Politburo. Currently that man, General Secretary Brezhnev, is one of five secretaries who sit as full members of the Politburo. The other full Politburo members include five members of the Council of Ministers (among them its chairman, Nikolay Tikhonov, Defense Minister Dmitry Ustinov, and Foreign Minister Andrey

FIGURE 3.2 *The Central Organs of the Communist Party, 1980*

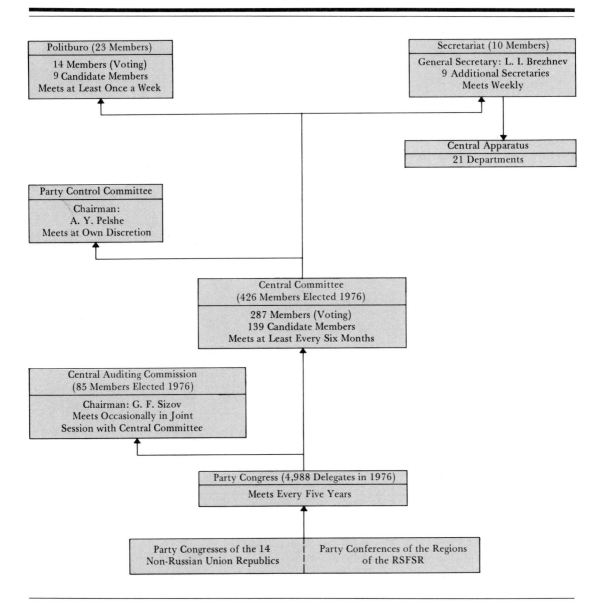

Sources: Adapted from V. Aspaturian, "The Soviet Union," in R. C. Macridis ed., *Modern Political Systems: Europe,* 4th ed. (1978), by permission of Prentice-Hall, Englewood Cliffs, N.J. and from T. J. Colton, University of Toronto, 1980.

Gromyko),* the head of the Party Control Commission (the final authority on admission and expulsion questions), and four republic and regional Party bosses.

In theory, the constituent body of Party members or delegates should be the highest authority at each level. In fact the most important function of the periodic assemblies of members and delegates is to create and legitimate the Party committees that act as the Party's governing bodies between sessions. These committees meet more frequently and, in turn, elect bureaus to act for them between their sessions. Together, the committees and bureaus at each level supervise the secretarial apparatus. At the same time, the committees and bureaus are responsible to the Party conference or congress at the next higher level, and each Party secretary or secretariat is responsible to the next higher secretariat.

In theory, too, this design is meant to balance a democratic control from below by Party members and their elected delegates with centralized supervision and direction from above in a pattern called *democratic centralism*. This pattern supposedly permits Party members to discuss political issues freely—though usually within the Party—before a Party decision is reached, but obliges them to execute and defend both outside and within the Party any decision that has been reached, even if they had opposed it earlier. Moreover, no Communist may deviate from a decision once made or from the *party line* once laid down, nor—since the Tenth Party Congress in 1921—may a member reopen an issue for reconsideration. Finally, neither before nor after a decision may Communists organize in separate groups or factions to promote their views within the Party. These last two provisions may have been meant as emergency measures in 1921, but they still remain in force.

Practice differs from theory, however. Party secretaries alone are full-time Party officials. Their

influence prevails in the bureaus, whose other members have other responsibilities and cannot devote their full energies to bureau work. The secretaries also prevail in committees and the constituent bodies, which meet only infrequently. In theory the members of the constituent body elect the members of the committees and the committees elect the members of the bureaus. But in practice the secretaries pick the candidates who are then duly elected to these bodies. Party secretaries are not freely elected, but are chosen by the next higher secretary; this is the hierarchy to which they tend to look for guidance and instruction, which they then transmit to their own committees. As permanent links between higher and lower organizations, the secretaries form a chain of power that in effect controls the Party. An old Soviet joke distinguishes three epochs of human history: the matriarchate, the patriarchate, and the secretariat. Since the days of Stalin, the dictatorship of the proletariat has turned, in many ways, into the dictatorship of the secretariat.

Despite its bureaucratization, the Communist Party continues to be the heart and soul of the Soviet system. The Party is the chief source of legitimacy. It is the chief formulator of political and social goals and of the policies by which they are to be pursued. In all these ways it is the Communist Party that makes the Soviet system work. In the Soviet Union as in all countries, the bureaucrats, the police, and the military apply power in the execution of policy, but in no country have they shown themselves capable of formulating policy over long periods of time. They cannot create fundamental goals. In non-Communist countries, such as the United States, they depend on interest groups and on competing political parties to set these goals, whereas in the Soviet Union they depend to a crucial degree on the Communist Party alone. Not surprisingly, in every major clash between military leaders, police chiefs, or state bureaucrats, on the one hand, and Party secretaries, on the other hand, the Party secretaries thus far have always won.

*The five representatives of the Council of Ministers include Kosygin, who actually resigned as chairman of the council in October 1980 after sixteen years in that office. His request to leave the Politburo was not acted upon immediately.

Party and State: The Interlocking Pyramids. The Communist Party penetrates the government at every level (see Figure 3.3). The government in turn runs the economy, of which nearly 90 percent is government-owned and much of the rest is owned by state-controlled cooperatives. The government also runs the armed forces and police, as well as the educational system, the mass media, and almost all means of support for artistic and literary life. These enormous powers of the government enhance the power of the Communist Party and, particularly, the power of the Party leaders over their own members as well as over the rest of the people; this, in turn, enhances the Party's control of the state.

At the top the Party Secretariat and the Politburo interlock closely not only with each other, but also with the Presidium of the Supreme Soviet and the Council of Ministers. As we have seen, Leonid Brezhnev, the general secretary of the Communist Party and leading member of its Politburo, is also chairman of the Presidium of the Supreme Soviet. The chairman of the Council of Ministers, Tikhonov, is a Politburo member, along with several of his ministerial colleagues. The names of the incumbents change—although hitherto more slowly than top officeholders do in many other countries—but the tight interlocking of Party and government jobs persists.

Something similar holds true down the line. At the all-union level, the Party Central Committee interlocks in terms of personnel and decision making with the Supreme Soviet. In the union republics, the bureaus of the Party interlock with the ministers and presidia of the supreme soviets, and the party central committees interlock with the supreme soviets. There are similar interlockings at all lower levels.

THE PERFORMANCE OF THE SOVIET UNION

After the preceding discussion, it should be unnecessary to summarize the performance of the political system of the Soviet Union in any great detail. On the positive side, the Soviet regime has done things that had been thought impossible. Within fifty years it transformed a less-developed country into a highly developed one, despite the intervening devastations of World War II. It has demonstrated that a highly developed industrial economy can be run by a decision system of politics and planning without any major influence of private enterprise or a Western-style market system. It has transformed the educational and cultural levels of what now are over 262 million people. And it has done all this with a considerable—though not complete—amount of social solidarity and popular support, tested in the crucible of World War II.

On the negative side, the persistence of dictatorship or government-decreed uniformity in many fields of opinion, culture, and expression are manifest for all to see. But a wide variety of communications and of new recombinations of information are not just a luxury or a consumer good. Like freedom, they are in the long run conditions for the production of new knowledge. Consequently, after more than a half-century of existence the Soviet Union still must import—mainly from capitalist countries—much more knowledge in science, technology, styling, and design, as well as in culture, films, and other arts, than it creates and exports to the outside world.

Finally, the Soviet system has paid for its achievements with vast human costs. The memory of the terror of the Stalin years remains to testify to its vulnerability to many degrees of potential deformation and distortion away from its own goals and standards. In the past this deformation was brought about by the behavior of some of its own rulers. The Soviet system then had no adequate counterweights or correctives against this trend. It is not clear to what extent, if any, it is now better protected against a possible repetition of the domestic crimes and tragedies of the Stalin era.

Perhaps more important than striking an exact balance for the past is assessing the prospects of the Soviet system for the future. Here we turn to

Mass Organizations	First Party Secretaries of Union Republics and Regional Organs	Premiers of Republics	Presidium of the Supreme Soviet	Council of Ministers	Communist Party Politburo	Communist Party Secretariat
			Brezhnev (Chairman)		Brezhnev	Brezhnev (General Secretary)
				Tikhonov (Chairman)	Tikhonov	
					Suslov	Suslov
					Kirilenko	Kirilenko
					Chernenko	Chernenko
				Kosygin (Former Chairman)	Kosygin	
					Gorbachev	Gorbachev
				Gromyko (Foreign Affairs)	Gromyko	
				Ustinov (Defense)	Ustinov	
Shibayev (Trade Unions)			Shibayev	Andropov (State Security)	Andropov	
					Pelshe	
	Romanov (Leningrad)				Romanov	
	Grishin (Moscow)				Grishin	
	Kunayev (Kazakh)				Kunayev	
	Shcherbitsky (Ukraine)				Shcherbitsky	
	Rashidov (Uzbek)		Rashidov		Rashidov	
				Demichev (Culture)	Demichev	
		Solomentsev (RSFSR)			Solomentsev	
	Kiselev		Kiselev		Kiselev	
					Ponomarev	Ponomarev
	Aliyev (Azerbaidzhan)				Aliyev	
			Kuznetsov (First Deputy)		Kuznetsov	
						Kapitonov
						Dolgikh
						Zimyanin
						Rusakov
	Shevardnadze (Georgia)				Shevardnadze	

Note: Those Party leaders who hold important positions in the all-union government, in mass organizations, or in the union republics are indicated by shaded backgrounds.

Source: Vernon V. Aspaturian, "Soviet Politics", in MODERN POLITICAL SYSTEMS:Europe, 4th ed., by Roy C. Macridis, c. 1978, p. 414. Adapted by permission of Prentice-Hall, Inc., Englewood Cliffs, NJ.

its unfinished business: its unresolved problems and its potentialities for future growth, self-transformation, and preservation of identity.

SOME UNRESOLVED POLITICAL PROBLEMS

International Polycentrism. To the Soviet Communist leaders the interlocking of party and state has been a great source of strength within their own country. In international politics, however, the close linkage between a supposedly internationalist party and a national state has threatened to create almost as many liabilities as assets.

In the international arena of Communist parties and regimes the Russians now face a continuing problem of pluralism, or *polycentrism,* as it is called by writers on the Communist world. The Russians no longer form the only Communist country. There are now at least sixteen of them, depending on one's definition, and the big ones like China cannot be dictated to.[9] Indeed, neither can some of the smaller ones, like Yugoslavia, Albania, or Vietnam. Nor do non-ruling Communist parties always follow Russian policies, as they did in earlier days. In Czechoslovakia in 1968 the will of the Russian Communist leadership could be made to prevail over that of the Czech and Slovak

Communists only by the physical invasion of the country by Soviet and Soviet-bloc troops. Overall, then, the Russian Communist government has lost absolute control of the international Communist world.

Though less powerful outside their country than formerly, the Soviet leaders have not become much more tolerant. There is growing national diversity in the Communist world. Yet inside each country Communists tend to claim that they are infallible and that anybody who is not with them is against them. When two Communist regimes differ in opinion, their discussion resembles that of two medieval would-be popes. It is a discussion between two sides in which both insist on being right. For the last five hundred years the Catholic church has been most careful to avoid schismatic elections. Communism, on the other hand, has built-in schisms. Although these rifts have become increasingly evident, the Communists have not yet discovered that tolerance is not a luxury, but a necessity.

A Gap in Communist Ideology. Another unresolved problem faced by all Communist countries involves the question of the property of nations. Communists agree that, in regard to means of production, individuals may not retain private property against the claims of the nation-state. But they are not clear whether a nation-state may legitimately retain the capital and land within its borders as its collective quasi-private property against the claims of poorer nations or of any international community. Most Communists have not thought through the question of whether a Communist state owns property collectively and has the right to deny its use to poorer Communist nations. If the Russians own some empty real estate in Siberia and the Chinese are overcrowded in China, is the Russian government right in closing off all its land as its own property, or is the Chinese government correct in thinking that this is a bourgeois way of behaving? The quarrels be-

[9]The U.S.S.R., Mongolia, Bulgaria, Czechoslovakia, German Democratic Republic, Hungary, Romania, and Poland are linked in the Pact for Mutual Economic Assistance (sometimes called COMECON in the West); Cuba and Vietnam are associated with this pact, and Laos and Cambodia are currently (1980) linked to Vietnam. China, Albania, and Yugoslavia each are independent, as is North Korea, which is trying to stay on good terms both with the U.S.S.R. and China. Several other countries, such as South Yemen, Iraq, Syria, Ethiopia, Angola, and Mozambique, were seen in Moscow as countries "aspiring to socialism." Whether Afghanistan would become included in that category depended in mid-1980 on the outcome of the civil war and massive Soviet military intervention as well as on the consequences of the widespread international protest against this act.

tween the haves and have-nots of the Communist world may pose as serious a problem as whether the rich free-world countries owe anything to the poor free-world countries.

Relating to the Capitalist World. One of the major commitments of the post-Stalin leadership has been to improving the country's relations with the Western countries, above all the United States. At the same time, the regime has sought to expand Soviet influence abroad, both in the developed nations and in the Third World. In the early 1970s, Brezhnev and his colleagues put more emphasis on the first line of policy than on the second. The highly publicized summit meetings and agreements on European security, arms control, trade, and scientific and cultural exchanges were the result. Since about 1975, the latter strain in Soviet thinking has come to the fore, though the policy of *détente* has by no means been repudiated. Capitalizing on the buildup of its own military forces, on hesitation in the West, and on the opportunities presented to it in the field, the Soviet Union has taken a number of initiatives to enlarge its system of friends and clients—most important the December 1979 invasion of Afghanistan, one of only three countries along its frontiers that is neither a Soviet ally nor clearly aligned against it. These actions have produced a marked stiffening of attitude by the United States and its allies; and by mid-1980 the worsening climate was threatening to poison the fruits of earlier peacemaking.

It is premature to write the obituary of Soviet-American détente. As many Americans see it, the Russians must now make a more explicit choice than before between better relations with the West and an expanded sphere of foreign influence. In making that choice in the early 1980s, traditional nationalism and Communist ideology can serve as no better than ambiguous guides. Both Nationalism and ideology push Soviet leaders to compete with the United States as an equal and to seize opportunities for empire building. Yet national

feelings and ideals also draw the regime's attention to domestic social and economic needs, particularly if, as is likely, these needs become more acute as time goes on. The choice is theirs to make. The most the West can hope for is to define its own interests clearly and to affect the climate within which Soviet decisions are made.

The problem may be more complicated. Deadly collisions between states cannot be avoided by the moral superiority of one side, no matter how clearly and profoundly most Westerners—and not only Westerners—prefer the degree of democracy, individual freedom, and opportunity for openness and truthfulness in the United States and other Western countries. To avoid a war, it is also necessary to consider how their adversaries think. In the view of many Soviet leaders, the United States and other Western countries also have a choice. They, too, have serious economic problems at home, such as inflation and other matters, yet they continue to carry on worldwide policies and commitments. To choose their policies in accordance with Western wishes might seem to these Soviet leaders like an act of capitulation; they would like to put the burden of choice on the United States and its allies.

Developments in the "Third World" may well make matters worse. Many developing countries are seeking the "Western," market-oriented way to economic modernity under democratic or dictatorial political regimes; others may seek some kind of "Eastern," collectivist course of one-party dictatorship and central planning. Revolutions and civil wars, arising from this issue, are likely to tempt foreign powers to intervene. In the view of some Soviet leaders, the United States also will have to choose how far to go in supporting those countries and factions whose policies it prefers.

Such conflicts between today's two superpowers may well continue for years to come, even though both are exercising only a declining influence over a growing and unruly world population. In the Soviet Union, perhaps even more critically than in the West, the outcome may depend on the domestic political and economic conditions under which the Soviet government will decide its future policies.

The Soviet Military-Industrial Complex. The Soviet Union shares a problem with the Western world as it makes decisions about its domestic and foreign priorities. It, too, has a *military-industrial complex* of its own, comparable in absolute size to (and in some ways bigger than) the much-discussed military-industrial complex of the United States. A Soviet general or admiral, as a professional soldier, is as keen on getting the best modern hardware in the largest possible amounts as is any professional officer anywhere. This individual is apt to be as skillful in lobbying and forging connections to the political decision system as his counterpart anywhere in the world. A Soviet officer will find allies among the enormous agencies that produce armaments and military goods. Eight Soviet ministries manufacture basically for military use. Representatives and veterans of these organizations, and of the armed forces themselves, are found in many crucial institutions, including the Party Central Committee and Politburo.

But the Soviet system is not a monolith. Within the limitations set by the political system, groups vie for influence and power and their share of the system's resources. The manager of a tank plant may want priorities in investment money for his factory and the plants that supply him, yet there is sure to be a department store manager clamoring for more consumer goods or an official in the agricultural bureaucracy pushing for more irrigation. In other words, there is a political process in the Soviet Union behind the facade of unanimity and common will—partially hidden, but real.

Where will this political process lead? Will escalation in the conflict between East and West make Russian society more and more rigid, its military-industrial sectors more powerful, its ideology more intolerant, and intra-Communist quarrels—as well as quarrels between Communists and non-Communists—more tense and more likely to lead toward war? Or will a de-escalation of

international tensions lead toward more discovery, more experimentation, and more freedom in the Soviet Union? Whether world affairs grow more tense or more relaxed depends on the actions of the West as well as those of the Eastern European powers.

New Economic Difficulties. A serious constraint on Soviet actions, abroad and at home, is bound to be the state of the country's economy. The economic formula that produced such dividends under Stalin and in the several decades after his death—with its stress on centralized planning, rapid growth of the labor force, and high rates of investment—is now yielding diminishing returns. Annual economic growth of more than 10 percent a year was the rule in the 1930s. This index of performance has declined more or less steadily—to 6 or 7 percent in the 1950s, about 5 percent by the late 1960s, and about 3 percent by the late 1970s.

What is worse, there are factors at work that are almost sure to depress Soviet growth rates even further. The first of these is an impending and very serious labor shortage. The Soviet population of working age increased by an average of 2.5 million a year during the early 1970s. By 1980 the increment was down to 1.6 million. By the mid-1980s it will be less than 0.5 million, and in many parts of the country (including the RSFSR) there will be an absolute decline in the labor force. The second critical factor is the growing pressure on Soviet energy supplies. Soviet oil production may already have peaked. The U.S.S.R. has huge oil and gas reserves, great hydroelectric potential, and ambitious plans for building nuclear reactors. But to pursue any of these options will be costly and uncertain. The first Soviet experiments with solar energy were reported only in 1980.

Again, the system's leaders must make choices. Forces beyond their control will not permit them to continue with business as usual. Without large-scale technological and economic innovation, and without planning and administrative and other reforms, the Soviet economy may experience zero growth by the middle or end of this decade. Such a state of affairs might force political changes on the regime that are far more drastic than it is willing to contemplate now. Can reforms take place? This will hinge on the flexibility of the Soviet system, on its ability to accept criticism and change.

The Limited Responsiveness to Criticism. Often one hears this question: "How do individuals or small groups make their views felt in the Soviet system?" To find the answer, one must distinguish the channels provided by official theory and doctrine from the way things actually work.

A look at Soviet ideology shows important differences from the ideas underlying the defunct dictatorships of Nazi Germany and Fascist Italy. The word *totalitarian,* applied to all three of these regimes, stresses only what they have in common (single-party control, concentration of leadership, and mobilization of all efforts of the population toward a single goal, with no tolerance for opposition). But it is seriously misleading, because it fails to show their differences in goals (forced economic growth in the Soviet Union versus a rapid and unceasing military conquest for the Fascists and Nazis) as well as in some of their methods. The Nazi and Fascist regimes were based on the *leadership principle:* authority flowed only from the top down. The leaders were supposed to be always right and did all the talking; the people only had to listen and, as Mussolini put it, to "believe, obey and fight." In Soviet ideology, greater stress is put on flexibility, tactical retreats, self-correction of mistakes, collective authority, and listening to the people. Soviet tradition pictures Lenin not only addressing revolutinary crowds from the top of an armored car, but also patiently sitting down for hours and listening to peasants. In practice, however, Soviet listening has been highly selective.

In theory, there are at least four channels through which individuals can make their views known. First, they can write letters to the press, and the Soviet press has been quite diligent in printing such letters; however, in practice, these letters are screened. The decision to print the letter is itself treated as a political decision. A letter that is compatible with current policy or that offers only minor modifications has a fair chance of being printed. A letter that says "Reverse basic policy" does not.

A similar channel is what used to be called *Bolshevist self-criticism.* Such criticism is encouraged and permitted by doctrine; the people at Party meetings are supposed to speak up and criticize the practices of their own unit, their own group, the management of their factory or farm, the local government of their village or town. They may criticize themselves, the local Party secretaries, and others. In practice, such criticism is used to prepare and mobilize opinion for changes in policy, to loosen bureaucratic rigidity, and to provide a safety valve for accumulated tensions. In general, however, criticism suggesting how basic policy can be better carried through is more acceptable than criticism attacking basic policy.

The Soviet Union is run to this day by people who think in the style of emergency politics, the style in which its political system was founded. They will not permit opposition to basic policies that, rightly or wrongly, they consider necessary. As a result, most criticism is muzzled and limited to details of policy, to personalities, and to methods of carrying out programs. Sometimes initiatives from below are encouraged, but only if they fit into the general plan. Thus, an initiative movement among Central Asian farmers to dig more irrigation canals was picked up by the mass media and greatly amplified, increased, and backed. Similarly, in the 1930s the Stakhanovite movement of people who proposed improvements in production was widely publicized. This is somewhat like the kind of freedom of speech that employees have when they are permitted to drop suggestions to management into specially designated suggestion boxes. Bolshevist self-criticism is a relatively limited kind of freedom, to put it mildly.

A third channel is the particular units of the Party in which candidates are picked. For a time after Stalin's death there was talk of permitting more candidates to run than there were offices so that the voters would have some degree of selection. Yet this latitude has in fact been limited to some trade union elections and does not seem to have been applied in elections to the soviets or to Party posts. The right to nominate has not been given to the people, and there is no right to organize interest groups, factions, or opinion groups within the ruling Communist Party. Nor is there any other party that has the right to contest an election. To some extent, then, a major link of control of the society inheres in the control over the nomination process and the control of personnel policy, or *cadre policy,* as the Communists call it—that is, in deciding who gets promoted, appointed, or moved around. Here, too, there is only a very limited degree of freedom for the individual.

Poetry and literature provide a fourth, although indirect channel. Because free political discussion is not possible and a free political vote does not exist, some of the people's desire to express its views has shown up in aesthetic judgment. If it is not permissible to say that the policy of the Party secretary is stupid, it is permissible to say that a play praising that policy is boring. Similarly, it is possible to find that certain poetry is beautiful and exciting even if it happens to stress emotions not completely accepted in the Party program. The Russian poet Yevgeny Yevtushenko pointed out that in the Russian language the words for "poet" and "fighter" are phonetically very similar; from this notion he developed the idea that it was the task of poets and writers in Russia to take upon themselves the role of fighting for a better expression of popular moods.

Poetry has become a substitute for other forms of expression that are banned. A similar attitude exists toward movies and plays. Again, there is political control, but when the party line changes or weakens or when there is a period of freer discussion, a good deal of material gets through that otherwise would be prohibited. For example, in the mid-1950s the Russian film entitled *The Rumyantsev Case* showed a truck driver whose load

of textiles was highjacked, thereby conceding that there are highjackers and robbers in the Soviet Union after forty years of Soviet government. Railroaded by the police through a trial, the man is promptly clapped into jail, whereupon his fellow workers in the factory hold a meeting, march on the police station, and protest against what has happened to their comrade. This was a film made at the height of the *de-Stalinization* campaign. This is the kind of loosening up that sometimes occurs, but since 1965, and especially since the intervention in Czechoslovakia in 1968, Soviet cultural policy has again become rather more restrictive. A nationwide exhibition at Moscow of young Soviet painters in the fall of 1972 showed less of the varieties of art than the uniformity of bureaucracy; these young painters had aged before their time. In 1978, harsh sentences against dissidents in the Soviet Union once again aroused worldwide attention. No one can tell how long this stifling climate in many sectors of Soviet life will continue.

Yet the real picture is more complex. There is a fifth channel toward greater autonomy and variety in present-day Soviet culture. This is the rediscovery of the works of the past and the increase in direct access to them. The great writers of the world and of Russia are being published and read again—not only Leo Tolstoy and Maxim Gorky, but also Fyodor Dostoyevsky and Anna Akhmatova, of whose political views the Bolsheviks had not approved. Similarly published and read in translation are such writers as Shakespeare, Dickens, Hemingway, and many others. Each of these writers conveys to his or her readers a world of images, ideas, human characters, feelings, and actions far richer than any single group of ideologues or censors could control. Many Russian high school graduates have a more thorough grounding in this wider literary tradition than have some of their counterparts in the United States; and with this knowledge they have major potential resources for independent thought.

A similar process is occurring in the world of

art. Many Russians in the 1970s were engaged in the rediscovery of the great artistic and architectural traditions of their country. They can be seen standing in long lines in the Kremlin to view the beautiful sixteenth-century images of saints, called *ikons,* by such great masters as Andrei Ryublev, or touring the eighteenth-century palaces of the czars at Peterhof and Pavlovsk near Leningrad, destroyed by the Nazis in World War II and now restored again by the painstaking efforts of Soviet scholars and craftspeople (whose pictures sometimes are on exhibit next to explanations of their difficult labors).

These are not trivial matters. After decades of struggle, large numbers of Soviet citizens are discovering beauty; and with it they discover a deeper pride in the achievements and capabilities of their peoples, even decades and centuries before the revolution. Clearly, this revolution and its results are here to stay. But like every great revolution, it must reach a stage at which it will reincorporate the longer past of its country and its people, giving them added resources for richer and more varied responses to the problems of the future. Some time after the French Revolution, the French became proud of the royal palace at Versailles and of the castles of the nobles in the valley of the Loire River, without having to remind themselves constantly that the kings and the nobles had been oppressors of the people. Russia, it seems, is now approaching this stage. The old social order will not come back, even though a gifted writer in exile like Alexander Solzhenitsyn remembers it with nostalgia; but its heritage of artistic and literary achievement is now being shared more widely and deeply than before.

There is one other element that may make for more independent thoughts and feelings: the universal experience of the tragedies and sufferings of World War II, together with the profound desire for peace that is found on all levels of society. In Piskarevsky cemetery at Leningrad, which President Nixon visited in 1972, lie nearly half a million Leningraders, victims of bombardment and starvation during Hitler's siege of the city in World War II. "We cannot list your names here," says the inscription on a granite slab, "but nothing is forgotten and nothing is forgiven." It goes on to recall their proud saying during the great siege: "Let death become afraid of us, rather than that we should be afraid of death." But the cost is fully remembered. There is the scrawled diary of a small girl, Tanya, who recorded the deaths by illness and starvation of every member of her family during the siege, ending with the entry "Now I am all alone"—written just before her own death. Today the cemetery has become a place of commemoration to the people of the city and the nation. Crowds come out to visit it; brides on their wedding day lay their bouquets on the graves.

SOME RESOURCES FOR CHANGE

In Czechoslovakia in 1968, Communist Party members in high standing argued that intra-Party factions should be legalized, discussions should be free, and groups defeated in one Party congress should have the right to ask for a reopening of the issue at the next Party congress. (Of course, they argued, such groups would have to offer new information or new experiences relevant to the issue and have majority support for getting it back onto the agenda.) After the Russian tanks rolled into Prague in the summer of 1968, these proposals were silenced and some of those who had made them, or supported them, were demoted.

Nevertheless, the Czech experience shows that such lines of thought can arise under the crust of a totalitarian system and that nothing but a foreign occupation may be able to stop them—at least for a time. Hannah Arendt's theory of totalitarianism argued in the early 1950s that Communist dictatorship was like death: permanent and irreversible. Her view of this matter has been proved false. Politics, human beings, aspirations, and efforts at self-expression all exist even under Communist dictatorship. Thus, there is a degree of uncertainty and potential openness about the future even in Communist-ruled countries.

Yet, as far as anyone can judge, the bulk of the Soviet people continues to be loyal to a collectivistic economy. There is no mass support of any kind for giving the country back either to a czar or to private corporations. People have grown used to the way that basic industries are being developed, and they seem to like it. Despite the devastations of World War II they have seen the steel output of their country rise from less than 10 percent after World War I to more than 100 percent of that produced in the United States today. At such rates of growth, sooner or later appreciable improvements trickle down to consumers, first in the cities and eventually in the countryside. This has already happened in the fields of basic nutrition and public health. By lengthening life expectancies and lowering infant death rates, the Soviet Union has now reached the level of the United States. In the meantime, many young people continue to find careers in the expanding industrial and technological sectors of their society. Still larger numbers can derive a sense of pride from the visible accomplishments of their country, ranging from the spectacular growth of its cities (62 percent of the population lived in cities in 1979, compared to 18 percent in 1913) to its continuing share in the exploration of the moon and the planets.

The very successes of Soviet industrialization in the past are now creating new kinds of problems for the future. As consumers become more affluent, they will insist on a wider range of choice. They will demand a better combination of planning and a market in which choices can be made.

Other problems will arise on the production side, through the growing need for innovation. Until recently, the Soviets could apply inventions and innovations developed and tested abroad at the expense of other countries. Henceforth they will need not only to apply new inventions and innovations, but also to produce them by their own

efforts. However, bureaucracy, dictatorship, and rigid official ideology are not conducive to the creation of new knowledge that fosters invention or to the repeated breaking of old habits that is essential to innovation. In many ways the Soviet Union and its people were more inventive and innovative between 1917 and the mid-1930s than they have been since. Some of this intellectual slowdown may be attributable to the effects of Stalin's purges, but it has long survived his death. To an increasing extent, bureaucracy, conformity, and dictatorship are hampering the future economic, scientific, and technological development of the country. They do not impede the production of more pig iron, but they will curtail the introduction of new ideas and practices. Soviet leaders now speak of the new *scientific-technical revolution*—that is, the transformation of economic life through the development and large-scale application of new methods of science and technology—that their country must undergo in order to cope with its vast future economic tasks. But without more room for experiment, criticism, nonconformity, innovation, and freedom it seems unlikely that this new peaceful revolution will be able to develop its full potential. Eminent Soviet scientists like Peter Kapitsa and Andrey D. Sakharov have repeatedly pointed to these problems.

Similar problems are arising in the work force, in human relations, and in Soviet culture. One cannot tell people for thirty years to admire only one officially approved style in painting and poetry and also expect them to remain resourceful and eager for change in industry and science. There will be other ideological difficulties. The ideological image of the Soviet Union as a country of workers is clashing increasingly with the fact that, as in all industrial countries, manual labor is being replaced by automation, and the clerical and professional occupations—the so-called white-collar personnel—are expanding. These groups are peripheral in Marxist theory and Soviet ideology, but they are becoming central in Soviet life.

Industrialization requires mass education as well as a large expansion of higher education. The success of the Soviet government in promoting both will eventually create another set of political problems. A good deal of research shows that, in general, people with little education prefer to be told only one side of a problem. When presented with two conflicting views, they tend to become confused and angry. This fact has contributed to the observed tendency toward an "authoritarianism of the poor" in many countries. It has also contributed to the success of the one-sided indoctrination methods of the Soviet government during the decades when a large part of its people were illiterate or had only a primary school education. Now the Soviet people are becoming a nation of high school or college graduates, particularly in the younger generation. Such better-educated people tend in most countries to feel angry and insulted when presented only one side of an issue. They want to hear all sides and make their own decisions. In the years to come, a growing proportion of the Soviet people may press for far-reaching changes in the cultural and information policies of their government.

The change in generations may well bring these pressures to a head in the 1980s. Many people form their basic political ideas around the age of twenty—more broadly, between fifteen and twenty-five—but these people tend to attain most power around the age of fifty-five, when they become heads of departments or organizations. The present Soviet leaders formed their political ideas at the height of Stalin's power. They experienced his purges, but also the successes of his economic development and military preparedness policies. More and more, the Soviet leaders of the 1980s will be of the generation of the poet Yevtushenko, who was born in 1933. They will have been in their early twenties when de-Stalinization was at its height and Stalin's crimes were revealed to the Soviet people. When this generation comes into control, it may be more willing to cooperate with popular demands for change and liberalization.

All these considerations suggest that the Soviet Union will need, first, leaders who will seek to improve their own society and government. Beyond that, they will have to improve their ability to accept other nations—both Communist and non-Communist—as neighbors deserving genuine cooperation and equality. The Soviet Union will have less need for missionaries to press or persuade other nations to copy current Soviet policies and institutions. To be able to say that a few more nations have adopted some type of Communist government might be a convenience for the Soviet rulers of the 1980s. To develop their own society, and to improve it thoroughly, will be a necessity.

KEY TERMS AND CONCEPTS

multiethnic
multilingual
idealism
materialism
socialism
economy of scarcity
meritocracy
dissidents
samizdat
uneven development
bourgeois revolution
"weakest link" theory
world revolution
socialism in one country
peasant-worker alliances
vanguard versus elite
distrust of spontaneity
professional revolutionist
Bolsheviks
Mensheviks
apparatchik
general secretary of the Communist Party
collective farms
decisive sectors
disproportions in investment
increasing returns to scale

diminishing returns
incentive goods
equalitarianism
performance payments
government by pyramid
Komsomol
Supreme Soviet
Soviet of the Union
Soviet of Nationalities
Presidium of the Supreme Soviet (PSS)
Council of Ministers
Presidium of the Council of Ministers (PCM)
chairman of the Council of Ministers
union republic
autonomous republic
oblast
kray
rayon
ispolkom
Party cells (primary organizations)
Party candidate
All-Union Party Congress
Central Committee
Politburo
Secretariat
democratic centralism
party line
polycentrism
détente
military-industrial complex
totalitarian
leadership principle
Bolshevist self-criticism
cadre policy
de-Stalinization
scientific-technical revolution

ADDITIONAL READINGS

Alliluyeva, S. *Twenty Letters to a Friend*. Trans. P. McMillan. New York: Harper & Row, 1967. PB

Aspaturian, V. "The Soviet Union." In R. C. Macridis, ed., *Modern Political Systems: Europe.*

4th ed. Englewood Cliffs, N.J.: Prentice-Hall, 1978.

Brzezinski, Z. *The Soviet Bloc*. Rev. ed. Cambridge: Harvard University Press, 1967. PB

———, and S. P. Huntington. *Political Power: USA/USSR*. New York: Penguin Books, 1977. PB

Carrère, d'Encansse, H. *Decline of an Empire: The Soviet Socialist Republics in Revolt*. New York: Newsweek Books, 1979.

Colton, T. J. *Commissars, Commanders, and Civilian Authority: The Structure of Soviet Military Politics*. Cambridge: Harvard University Press, 1979.

Fleron, F. J., ed. *Communist Studies and the Social Sciences*. Chicago: Rand McNally, 1969. PB

Friedrich, C. J., ed. *Totalitarianism*. 2nd ed. New York: Grosset and Dunlap, 1964. PB

Hough, J. *The Soviet Prefects: The Local Party Organs in Industrial Decision-Making*. Cambridge: Harvard University Press, 1969.

———, and M. Fainsod. *How the Soviet Union Is Governed*. Cambridge: Harvard University Press, 1979.

Inkeles, A. *Social Change in Soviet Russia*. Cambridge: Harvard University Press, 1968.

———, and R. Bauer. *Soviet Citizen: Daily Life in a Totalitarian Society*. New York: Atheneum, 1968. PB

Kassof, A., ed. *Prospects for Soviet Society*. New York: Praeger, 1968. PB

Lenin, V. I. *State and Revolution*. San Francisco: China Books, 1965. PB

Lipset, S. M., and R. B. Dobson. "Social Stratification and Sociology in the Soviet Union." *Survey* 388 (Summer 1973).

McAuley, Alastair. *Economic Welfare in the Soviet Union*. Madison: University of Wisconsin Press, 1979.

Medvedev, R. *Let History Judge*. New York: Random House, 1973. PB

Mickiewicz, E. *Handbook of Soviet Social Science Data*. New York: Free Press, 1973.

Reed, J. *Ten Days that Shook the World*. New York: International Publishing Company, 1967. PB

Sakharov, A. D. *Progress, Coexistence and Intellectual Freedom*. Trans. The New York Times. New York: Norton, 1968.

Schapiro, L. *The Government and Politics of the Soviet Union*. Rev. ed. New York: Vintage Books, 1978. PB

Skilling, H. G., and F. Griffiths, eds. *Interest Groups in Soviet Politics*. Princeton N.J.: Princeton University Press, 1971. PB

Solzhenitsyn, A. *One Day in the Life of Ivan Denisovich*. Trans. M. Hayward and R. Hingley. New York: Praeger, 1963. PB

Ulam, A. *The Rivals: America and Russia Since World War II*. New York: Penguin Books, 1972. PB

———. *The Unfinished Revolution*. New York: Random House, 1960. PB

Yevtushenko, Y. *Bratsk Station and Other New Poems*. Garden City, N.Y.: Doubleday Anchor, 1967. PB

———. *A Precocious Autobiography*. Trans. A. R. MacAndrew. New York: Dutton, 1962. PB

PB = *available in paperback*

IV

The United Kingdom

Some years ago, a popular book by a Frenchman bore the title *The English—Are They Human?* Many foreign observers long have wondered just what the English—and, since the eighteenth century, the British—people are like. Some, like Hitler's air force in World War II, found out the hard way. Now once again, when Britain has entered the European Common Market and is coping with the different and new world of the 1980s, people are asking this question: what makes the people of England—and of Britain—act in politics the way they do?

THE BACKGROUND OF BRITISH POLITICS AND THE CONTINUING DEVELOPMENT OF POLITICAL INSTITUTIONS

Two conditions, perhaps more than any others, have long influenced English politics and the behavior of the English people. These two major influences are their class structure and their histo-

ry. Class distinctions in Britain—and particularly in England—are more marked and pervasive than in almost any other highly industrial nation. Some English people like it that way, and they are found not only among those who are personally favored by the class system. Such persons think that the different social classes complement each other, providing greater security and strength for all. They seek progress within and through the traditional class system, which they consider, broadly speaking, just and fair; and they tend to support one of Britain's two major parties, the Conservatives, who since 1979 once again have been entrusted by a majority of voters with the government of the country. Another group of people feel that the traditional British class system is unjust, frustrating, and oppressive; that it is bad for the development of individuals and the progress of the nation; and that its barriers and distinctions should be reduced and, whenever possible, abolished. Persons holding these views are more likely to support Britain's other major party, the Labour Party, which was the governing party in 1945–51, 1964–70, and 1974–79. In the last period, however, it was dependent on the support of smaller parties, the Liberals and the Scottish National Party. These Nationalists, too, represented a protest vote, but their defection in 1979 from the informal coalition with Labour forced a new election, resulting in a Conservative victory and a virtual elimination of the Scottish Nationalists from Parliament.

One thing most British voters will not do is to ignore class. The Liberal Party, whose leaders tried to do just that since World War II, has averaged about one-tenth of the national vote (reaching a postwar peak of 19 percent in 1974).

Later in this chapter we shall look at these matters in more detail. Here let us cast only a quick glance at the British class system and at the long history that has produced it.

Such a glance at English society shows that at least four strata have long existed, like the layers of a cake. At the top there has long been a very thin layer—really a glaze on the cake—composed of an aristocratic group with inherited wealth supplemented by a group with new wealth whose secure position allows them to rise above the normal cares of workaday life. This *upper class* has for many years constituted less than 1 percent of the population. Many of its members are self-assured and relaxed about their pleasures, much as their ancestors were in the unblushing days of Fielding's *Tom Jones.* Beneath this upper layer is the *higher middle class,* which includes military officers, professional people, employers and managers in large industrial or business enterprises, high civil servants, and other well-educated white-collar workers. Frequently these people have received their education and their typically British manners in *public schools,* which are privately run and similar in many ways to exclusive clubs. Many continue to accept the morals of Victorian responsibility, which is an extension of the middle-class Protestant ethic of self-control.

Taken together, the upper class and top of the higher middle classes are often referred to as *the establishment* in British society. Like other shorthand phrases this term overlooks many real distinctions, but it does contain an important core of truth. More than any other country, Britain has evolved a class system in which the privileges of those at the top have been widely accepted, and therefore established. Their power has been regarded as legitimate. Their conduct and taste have been admired as superior even though—and especially because—they are not in the reach of most people. Thus, the British establishment and traditional British *deference* are two sides of the same coin.

Below the two top elite groups comes the third layer: the owners and managers of small firms, shops, and farms, some of whom are sometimes called *tradespeople,* and—often linked to them by family ties—the intermediate and junior managerial personnel and nonmanual workers in semiprofessional sales and clerical occupations. Together, all these individuals make up the *lower middle classes,* totaling with their families about 30 percent of the population. Many own property and employ or supervise labor, but they lack the full education and manners of the higher middle class. Here we also find the more simply educated white-collar employees. Some of these adhere to tighter standards of hard work and success; others try to imitate the gentility of their "betters"; but still others have grown impatient and angry with upper-middle-class manners and respectability, which seem stuffy and pretentious to them. Whatever the attitude, most of them are likely to stay trapped in this middle stratum. In the eyes of many English people the abyss between the establishment and tradespeople has remained: an engineer is a kind of plumber, and a plumber is not a gentleman.

The fourth layer is a working class consisting mainly of *manual workers.* They include both skilled and semiskilled personnel and make up roughly half of the total population. At the bottom of this stratum are the very poor, consisting of the least skilled and lowest paid workers, as well as other severely disadvantaged persons.

From this society the English have produced a *four-layer culture:* at the top a libertarian culture of the avant-garde in the style of Virginia Woolf and the Bloomsbury set of artists and writers; next the Victorian respectability of the upper middle class; then a tight lower-middle-class respectability; and at the bottom an irrepressible working-class hedonism that is reflected in the writings of Alan Sillitoe and many others. All these are stereotypes but clearly there is no single English character.

For more than a century this class structure has changed with only glacierlike slowness. But it has changed, and as Table 4.1 shows, since the late 1950s the rate of change has accelerated. Early in this century over three-quarters of the employed population were engaged in manual work, compared to two-thirds in 1951 and only about one-half in 1971. In general the shape of the British class structure has changed during this period, resembling less a large-based, sharp-pointed pyramid and more an electric light bulb with a bulging middle. At the same time the traditional gross distinctions between higher middle class, lower middle class, and working class have weakened as sharper group identifications within each class have grown.

Thus, although material living standards have greatly improved for much of the population (see pp. 171 and 183) many in the working class have felt disadvantaged by gains made not only by the middle class, but also by other workers of their class. The result has been more militancy and strikes—often *wildcat strikes* without union authorization—in which train engineers try to keep up with miners, garbage collectors with dock workers, and so on.

Similarly, many people in the growing middle classes have come to feel that they, too, are wage earners, but that their salaries have risen very little in real purchasing power. Here they see a contrast to the limited, but real, gains that most manual workers have made, often aided by their unions (see pp. 163–65 below). The result is a narrowing of the traditional gap in material welfare between middle and working classes.[1] These clerical and service employees have begun to demonstrate a new militancy, going out on large strikes in hospitals and government offices, two work places in which their salaries have not kept pace with inflation or the rise of wages in industry. Some members of these groups may come to identify with the cause of labor and the working class. But others among them may see themselves as part of the "general public," may feel annoyed by the inconvenience caused by the strikes, and may shift their support at least temporarily to the Conservative Party—as they did in the 1979 election. Still others may feel disenchanted with unions as well as with management and with both big parties, Labour and Conservative, that represent them; their response may be to retreat into nonvoting or to support minor parties as a gesture of protest.

All of this adds up to greater fragmentation and difficulty of governing in what has traditionally been a very tightly integrated social and governmental structure. It means an establishment that is less sure of steering the country either on its own terms or in combination with the less deferential, more divided middle and working classes.

The actions and reactions to pocketbook economic issues explain much of the ebb and flow of current British politics. But behind it may be an even bigger change: the search of almost one-third of the British population—the salary earners and service employees—for their social identity. If they choose to identify themselves with Labour or some third party, then British society and politics may become different in the 1980s.

The variety of possible nonclass and third-party options and identities is enhanced by the ethnic and cultural diversities among the British, for the peoples of Scotland and Wales, who together with the English and the Northern Irish form the United Kingdom and the British nation, have their own distinct characteristics. They are less class-ridden within, but more disadvantaged as a group

[1]Between 1968 and 1975 the ratio of nonmanual to manual workers' earnings narrowed from 1.24 to 1.16.

TABLE 4.1 *Distribution of Economically Active British Population by Occupational Category, Sex, and Class, 1911, 1951, 1971*

	1911		1951		1971	
	(Percentage by column)					
	M	F	M	F	M	F
UPPER CLASS	< 1%		< 1%		< 1%	
Self-employed and higher professionals	1.5	1.0	2.8	1.0	6.1	1.4
Employers and owners	7.7	4.3	5.7	3.2	5.2	2.9
Administrators and managers	3.9	2.3	6.8	2.7	9.9	3.3
HIGHER MIDDLE CLASS	11.5%		12.7%		16.3%	
Technicians and lower grade professionals	1.4	5.8	3.0	7.9	5.5	10.8
Supervisors and foremen	1.8	0.2	3.3	1.1	4.5	1.2
Sales and clerical workers	10.1	9.7	10.0	29.9	10.0	37.4
LOWER MIDDLE CLASS	14.0%		23.3%		30.0%	
Skilled manual	33.0	24.6	30.3	12.7	29.4	9.3
Semiskilled manual	29.1	47.0	24.3	33.6	21.2	27.3
Unskilled manual	11.5	5.1	13.8	7.9	8.2	6.4
WORKING CLASS	74.5%		64.0%		53.1%	

Source: Calculated from A. H. Halsey, *Change in British Society* (Oxford: Oxford University Press, 1978), p. 26.

and more likely to engage in social or national protest. In 1974 some of their voters backed nationalist parties, but in 1979 most of them returned to the Labour Party and thus reduced the Conservative majority in the new Parliament. All these peoples somehow have remained cohesive around the English core; and the different kinds and strata of British citizens have remained a single people of remarkable energy, endurance, and political resourcefulness.

A UNIQUE POLITICAL ARENA: THE ISLANDS THAT SHAPED A STATE

In Britain more than in any other country, politics can be understood only against a background of

NORTH SEA

ATLANTIC OCEAN

SCOTLAND

• Edinburgh

Glasgow

Tyne R. • Newcastle

NORTHERN

N. IRELAND

NORTHERN YORKSHIRE
AND HUMBERSIDE

IRISH SEA

• York

NORTH WEST

Leeds/
Bradford

Manchester •

Humber R.

Dublin •

Liverpool •

• Sheffield

IRELAND

EAST MIDLANDS

ENGLAND

WEST
MIDLANDS

• Norwich

EAST ANGLIA

WALES

• Birmingham

Severn R.

Avon R.

Thames R.

• London

• Bristol

BRISTOL CHANNEL

SOUTH EAST

SOUTHWEST

• Southampton

ENGLISH CHANNEL

0   50   100 miles

0   50   100 kilometers

history. It is the history of a state that changed its major tasks five times in nine hundred years—and of a people that became stronger with each change.

Openness and Isolation. The English state is a unique combination of a response to given conditions and a political inventiveness. The British state derived its flexibility from its geography, rich in its variety of coastlines, plains, and mountains. Geography permitted options of basic policy: the British could choose whether they wanted the state to be strong or weak, centralized or decentralized.

The *Celtic* culture of England and Ireland was native. Later it fused with Christianity brought by Roman missionaries. Between 500 and 800 A.D., Ireland was the most learned country in Europe. More Irishmen knew Greek at that time than did Frenchmen; and it was the Irish who sent out missionaries to civilize the Swiss. After the Celtic and Roman influence in Britain came the *Saxon* tribes and, still later, the Scandinavian or Viking culture. The civilization and knowledge that the seafaring Vikings brought from Byzantium and the Arab countries also found their way to England. In the Middle Ages, England was at one and the same time the end of the road and the crossroads of Europe, where many cultural influences met. With its long coastline and high hills and mountains, the country was suited both to receive and to shelter people and ideas. Many habits could persist unchanged for centuries in mountainous seclusion, yet all the world could come by boat.

The whole tradition of the moving frontier and the savage Old Testament practice of meeting other cultures with the edge of the sword are built into British history. There were four frontiers in the British Isles—the Cornish, the Welsh, the Scottish, and the Irish. England also had a continental frontier in Europe. From the thirteenth

century on, it held territories on the European continent. Bordeaux was under British rule for two hundred years. Calais may have been to Mary, the Catholic queen who died in 1558, what Saigon became to some American policy makers in the 1960s: a beachhead and guarantee of long-standing involvement and aspiration on a continent that was increasingly ungrateful and inhospitable.

From 1497 onward, starting in the days of Henry VII, England turned to sea power. In the middle of the sixteenth century, the turn was completed: on ascending to the throne, Queen Elizabeth I gave up Calais, thereby liquidating the commitment on the Continent. Beginning with a modest business partnership between the queen of England and the pirate Sir Francis Drake, this new policy led to four centuries of dominion of the seven seas.

Before England could extend its frontiers, however, it first had to become united at home. At a crucial time, much of this unity was imposed by outsiders.

The Conquest That Lasted. In the eleventh century Saxon England was economically advanced, having many towns and widespread use of money. But it was a politically weak and internally divided country, and was conquered by recently Frenchified Scandinavian roughnecks. In 955 a Scandinavian with the expressive name of Hrolf the Ganger (fairly close in meaning to the modern word "gangster") had settled with his followers in Normandy. He soon became Rollo, le Duc de Normandie. In 1066 a descendant, William the Conqueror (since he was of illegitimate birth, the Saxon appellation of William "the Bastard" is technically not inaccurate), invaded England with the blessings of the pope. The conquest was shattering and thorough, though precarious. There were a million Saxons and not very many Norsemen in the country. The result was a high

(*Left*) MAP 4.1 *The United Kingdom*

degree of solidarity among the *Norman* rulers. They had to stand together to defend their lives and to control their Saxon subjects.

POLITICAL INSTITUTIONS AND INVENTIONS: THE CREATION OF CHARACTERISTIC ELEMENTS OF BRITISH GOVERNMENT

The First Modern State. To strengthen their solidarity and control, the Norman conquerors built a highly centralized state with the aid of the latest administrative techniques provided by the church. For its day their state was very modern. In the twelfth century the Normans established a sophisticated administration of royal taxes and spending, called the *exchequer*. This was the first modern office of the treasury in Europe outside of Italy. Out of the old Roman roads the Normans developed a network of king's highways; the king's law applied everywhere within arrowshot of both sides of the highways. Another statute of the time specified that contracts everywhere in England could be enforced in the king's courts. This action shifted the attention of everyone interested in merchandising, trade, and money away from the local powers and toward the king and the central state. Thus, by the thirteenth century there were king's courts, king's highways, and the king's law (which soon became the *common law*, because the king's law largely adopted customary law). In this manner the English genius combined bold innovation with deeply rooted elements of tradition. The king's courts and king's highways were new. The use of customary law linked old law to a new political system.

Centralization and solidarity were the unique gifts of Norman administration, and they became two of the key aspects of British government. In the thirteenth century French nobles paid an average of 3 percent of their income as taxes to the Crown. English nobles paid 6 percent to their king. As a result, the English monarchy, though ruling a less populous country, had more money

than the French, and the Hundred Years' War eventually was fought on French soil. Without this superior political and financial performance England's sea power and island position would not have kept the war from its shores, any more than they had been able to prevent the Norman conquest. From the days of the tax assessments of the thirteenth century to the rationing system of World War II, the English have made a point of obeying their laws and paying their taxes. Thanks in part to the greater cohesiveness of its elites and the compliant habits of its common people, England was able to achieve more power than many larger states or kingdoms.

Soon after the Norman conquerors set up their state, they began making peace with the different elements of English society. At the time of the conquest William depended completely on his Normans. Thereafter he and his successors worked with several diverse groups, often playing them against one another. When some of William the Conqueror's Norman barons rose against him in 1086, he promptly called out the Saxon territorial militia against them. Step by step, the Saxons were brought into the English system; and by the fourteenth century their language had come back into respectable use in the courts and in public administration.

The story of England is the story of the refusal of a people to adapt its ways to the conquerors'. Rather, things worked the other way around. The conquerors were assimilated by the people. For three hundred years England was governed in French, but eventually the beer brewers and then other guilds in London brought the use of English back into the courts after 1362. By the time of Chaucer a common language had been restored, albeit one with 48 percent of its vocabulary taken from Latin and French.

A Legacy of Institutions. Perhaps most important, the interplay of Normans and Saxons created in England a set of political institutions that continued to grow and function long after the differences between Normans and Saxons had faded. An *institution* is a pattern of interlocking habits and expectations of behavior—and hence a configuration of social roles—such that these roles, habits and expectations tend mutually to preserve and reinforce one another and to produce a more or less consistent and systematic effect on the society.

Such an institution may be limited at any time to a unique set of persons: the Roman Catholic church is an institution, but it is unique, and there is only one legitimate pope at a time. Similarly, there is only one British monarchy with one legitimate monarch. But the word "institution" also may refer to a class of such institutions. If we call Christian churches "institutions," we find that there are many different denominations. So, too, with the institution of monarchy, or of marriage, or of private property, or of central planning—each exists in many countries and in many specific circumstances.

English institutions of this kind included from an early time the centralized monarchy, the exchequer, and the common law. Others, as we shall see presently, were the tradition of enquiry and eventually of commissions of enquiry; inquests; Parliament; and the new tradition of the gentleman. Later stages of English, and later British, history were to add still other institutions of their own. More than those of many other countries, English institutions, once established, tended to be preserved and carried on for centuries, but they also tended to be modified and developed with greater boldness and flexibility, making them at one and the same time carriers of continuity and instruments of innovation.

The Tradition of Enquiry. Another key aspect of English politics from early times onward—in addition to centralization and solidarity—has been the *tradition of enquiry,* that is, the systematic asking of questions, listening to evidence, and searching for facts. William the Conqueror, foreshadowing the best modern practice in government and social science, began his reign with a statistical survey. The results were recorded in his *Domesday Book,*

which counted every piece of real estate and every potential taxpayer as well as the population as a whole. It was an inventory of the national resources of England at the end of the twelfth century, a report that surely could have gone to a national resources planning board, had one existed at the time.

The notion of enquiry lies at the heart of British political and administrative tradition. Among its major points the *Magna Carta* in 1215 required that when a dead body was found anywhere in England, a board of enquiry had to be set up and an *inquest* held by a coroner. This was not an inevitable position. The conquering Norman elite might have said that when a dead Norman body was found, the next Saxon village would be burned. They could have introduced hostage systems, massacres, or other reprisals, leading to escalating hatred. Instead they chose to start specific inquests, which turned out to be a more civilized and durable way of coping with murder. The Magna Carta marked the rise of the secular tradition that every individual's life and death matters. The English poet W. H. Auden said that it is not wholly accidental that there is a detective story tradition in English-speaking countries. If a person dies in most parts of the English-speaking world, it is not something one takes for granted, as part of an Oriental fatalism or as the result of mute historic forces; it is considered a matter of human importance and thus gives rise to searching curiosity.

Parliament, too, developed from a tradition of enquiry. Arising out of the king's great council around 1240, it was based on the principle that "what touches all should be approved by all." This is still a reasonable principle of government. Hearings, consultations, and eventually the grant to people of a widening share in decision making are characteristic of the English tradition of government and have had a profound effect on British society. *Royal Commissions* of Enquiry in the nineteenth century produced the facts and recommendations that led to the legislation abolishing chattel slavery, child labor, and exploitation of women in mines and factories. Similar commissions laid the foundations for Britain's present-day "cradle-to-grave" social security system and for the humanizing reform of British penal law. The principle of enquiry spread to other English-speaking countries. In Canada, a Royal Commission on Bilingualism and Biculturalism has opened the way for improving relations between French-speaking and English-speaking Canadians. The essential contribution of all such commissions is not advocacy, but discovery. They see their task not primarily as bargaining between parties for some compromise, nor as a public relations job to arouse support for some preconceived policy, but as a probe of the facts of the problem before them in order to discover new and genuine solutions.

A Link Across Two Classes: The Gentleman. Another part of the English tradition has been the building of human and communication bridges between groups. One of the forces helping to break the barriers between the nobles and commoners was the concept of the *gentleman*—the person who carried his gentle breeding wherever he went. Gentlemen sending their younger sons into towns to become guildsmen were typical of fifteenth-century England. Most other European nobles would rather have been found dead than have had their children join guilds of artisans or merchants. Only in England did one-third of the apprentices in the tailors' and skinners' guilds in 1485 turn out to be the sons of gentlemen. In Berne and Zurich there was a touch of social equality, but in most of Europe an abyss separated commoners from nobles. In England, in contrast, the upper middle class and the lesser nobles merged in the new elite of gentlemen.

The English *law of primogeniture* aided this development. It reserved the noble title and the family estate to the oldest son of the family. It made all other sons commoners, and the latter then were free to intermarry with commoners, to engage in business ventures, and to profit from the wool trade or from shipping—all of which they did.

The social, cultural, and psychological unity between the upper middle classes and the nobility took more than four centuries to develop fully. In the nineteenth century, great public schools were founded to mold the sons of aristocrats, successful businessmen, and some professional men into a single class of gentlemen. This class was expected to rule every major aspect of British life by its example, charm, upper-class manners and accent, and the social, political, and economic power of the "old-boy" network, through which the graduates of public schools find jobs for each other.

This far-reaching consolidation of the nobility and the upper middle class was paid for by a wider gap between gentlemen and tradesmen (or the lower middle class) than is found in many other countries. England long has been more democratic on top, but more class-ridden in the middle and bottom layers of society. There one finds more deference and more resentment than in the United States. Whereas some English voters are more responsive to the snob appeal of voting for their betters, others have long responded to the class appeal of the Labour Party and its promise to change the social system. The basis for the power of both appeals is rooted deeply in English society and history. Polite British taxi drivers still may call high-tipping passengers "governor" and "sir" and then vote for the Labour Party with its program to nationalize the coal, steel, and transport industries.

Links Across Localities and Classes: Members of Parliament. During the reign of Queen Elizabeth I, in the mid-sixteenth century, England abandoned the tradition of completely local representation, which is still the formal law and usual practice in the United States. Any constituency, borough, or shire in England became free to elect anyone as its *members of Parliament,* whether or not he was a local resident. In the words of Edmund Burke, Parliament was no longer "a congress of ambassadors from different and hostile interests

. . . but . . . a deliberative assembly of one nation, with one interest, that of the whole. . . ."

By the middle of the sixteenth century about one-fifth of Parliament was made up of country districts represented by rural nobles, called knights of the shire. Another fifth consisted of *burghers*—local citizens—from the boroughs, and three-fifths came from communities that were represented by noblemen elected by middle-class voters. This was the political tradition that later pervaded George Washington's Virginia. A political elite of noblemen by birth, upbringing, and education had enough leisure time in which to master the art of politics; and such an elite won and retained the confidence of the English burghers—and later of the Virginia frontiersmen. This was the tradition of building *cross-class coalitions.*

THE FIRST GREAT MODERN POLITICAL REVOLUTION, 1640–90

From Person to Institution: The Differentiation Between King and Crown. The Crown function, as well as the parliamentary function, was firmly established quite apart from the existence of a given monarch by the end of the fifteenth century. During the century before Elizabeth, in the civil wars between the houses of Lancaster and York, the English learned to keep the institution of the Crown functioning even without knowing who was king. The *Crown* became the symbol of a continuing impersonal organization: the public administration and bureaucracy and the property, treasury, and machinery of the state. All these somehow kept working, usually in cooperation with Parliament, no matter what happened to the person of the monarch. When strong absolute monarchs, like Henry VIII and Elizabeth I, increased their power against the great nobles, these powers soon shifted to the Crown. But inevitably,

the separation of the Crown from the monarchy weakened the power of the British king. In reaction, as the government became increasingly able to function without one, a monarch might be tempted to assert his or her power more, trying to balance the loss of real power by an effort of his or her political will.

King James I, successor to Queen Elizabeth, succumbed to this temptation. James, perhaps a genius, was a man of tremendously high intelligence, but of such bad political judgment that his contemporaries called him, "the wisest fool in Christendom." A strong proponent of the *divine right theory,* according to which a monarch ruled by the will of God and was answerable to no one else for his or her actions, James tried hard to block or reverse the spread of power to Parliament and the growing independence of the courts. And for twenty to thirty years he succeeded in halting the increase of Parliament's power.

James also carried out constructive reforms, some with lasting effects. He introduced the name "Great Britain" for England and Scotland, and he persuaded the English Parliament to vote citizenship for all Scotsmen born after 1603 and the Scots Parliament to do as much for Englishmen. Thus he laid the foundations for the British political system and people.

James's son, Charles I, was less bad as a ruler than his father, but it was Charles who paid the price for both. His fate reminds one of a principle mentioned by Saint Thomas Aquinas in the thirteenth century. Aquinas said that if a country has an unusually bad prince, one should not overthrow him; in the nature of things he will die sooner or later, and a less bad one is likely to succeed him and make the system work. But if the ruler is of average or better quality (as Charles proved to be), and if life is nevertheless intolerable under him, then there is something wrong with the system of government itself; in that case the government must be overthrown, because an improvement in the incumbent will not cure a bad system. Four centuries later, the English revolution seemed to corroborate Aquinas's view.

Charles was conscientious, good-looking, and almost charismatic. He tried to govern England as it once had been governed, but could no longer be, and set off a revolution in the process. The revolution against him was led by a cross-class coalition. Country gentlemen, mainly from the shire of Cambridge and the east of England, were at first the main sources of the armies fighting him, but Parliament raised armies, too. The issue was decided by the actions of the mass of the people. A painting in the House of Commons still shows the shuttered shops in London when the City of London voted to close them all so that apprentices and journeymen could go out and take up weapons "until the city of Gloucester be relieved." Commanded by Oliver Cromwell, the armies of country gentlemen from Cambridgeshire and of Parliament—the *roundheads,* or "ironsides," as they were known—swept away the royalist *cavaliers.* The king was tried and beheaded, for as Cromwell's secretary, the poet John Milton, noted in *The Tenure of Kings and Magistrates,* kings had their office only as long as they kept their agreements with the community; otherwise they became public enemies and had to be treated as such.

Milton's doctrine was grim and perhaps more extreme than most English people were completely willing to accept at the time. After Cromwell's death his generals, the "military complex" of the time, brought back a Stuart king, Charles II; Cromwell's bones were disinterred and scattered. England, having had twenty years of Puritan dictatorship and publicly enforced morality, went to the other extreme. After the Battle of Naseby in 1645, Cromwell's soldiers had slashed the faces of women camp followers of the Royalist Army so that they should not endanger the virtue of Puritans in the future. Twenty years after that inhuman outbreak of instant righteousness, Restoration comedies became popular, plays that to this day cannot be advertised in a family newspaper without changing their titles.

In 1688 the Stuarts were thrown out once more, and England settled down in 1690 to an Act of Toleration and parliamentary supremacy. In the military sphere, standing armies, which were considered a threat to liberty, were abolished. The British began to concentrate on building up the navy, though keeping the army relatively small. A strong navy could dominate the seas, but not the English people. In 1707, England and Scotland were formally united under a single Parliament, and the country formed was henceforth to be called Great Britain—the name that James I had introduced a century earlier.

The English revolution took more than half a century to run its full course. It was a real *revolution,* for it did not merely replace some rulers with others, but it also changed the habits and political culture of the people, the structure of many political and social institutions, and the structure of the relationships among them. It made England the first great modern nation. Its first phase—the war of Parliament against the king—and the days of Cromwell are often called in England "the Great Rebellion"; its second period, the almost bloodless expulsion of the last Stuart king in 1688, is called "the Glorious Revolution." The relative importance of these events in the minds of the British seems clear: it is Oliver Cromwell's statue that now stands in front of the House of Commons to commemorate his role as protector of parliamentary power. The two waves of revolution also left their invisible but real monuments in the world of ideas. The political theories of Thomas Hobbes and of John Locke are responses to the experiences of the times, but they have influenced political thought and action, directly and indirectly, at many times and places ever since.

In 150 years the reforms of absolute monarchs and two waves of revolution had merged England into Britain and made it the most modern country of the world. In the course of these events, kings lost power to the Crown, and the Crown lost most of it to Parliament (see Figure 4.1).

A LASTING RESULT: GOVERNMENT BY PARLIAMENT

There is not a thing between heaven and earth that Parliament cannot do, said English jurist John Austin. This is largely true. Under the British system there are no legal limits on the power of Parliament. Nor has Britain a written constitution. Nor is there a separation of powers as in the United States. Indeed, Britain has no such thing as judicial review of the acts of Parliament.

The Emerging Power of the House of Commons. For a time, power in Britain was divided among three parties: the Lords, the Commons, and the Crown. The *House of Lords* and the *House of Commons* were the two chambers of Parliament. The House of Lords represented and was composed of the high nobility, the peers of England, as they were called. These were the barons, viscounts, earls, marquises, and dukes, each of whom took his seat by heredity as soon as he inherited his title. By contrast, the members of the House of Commons were elected,

FIGURE 4.1 *Parliamentary Government, ca. 1600*

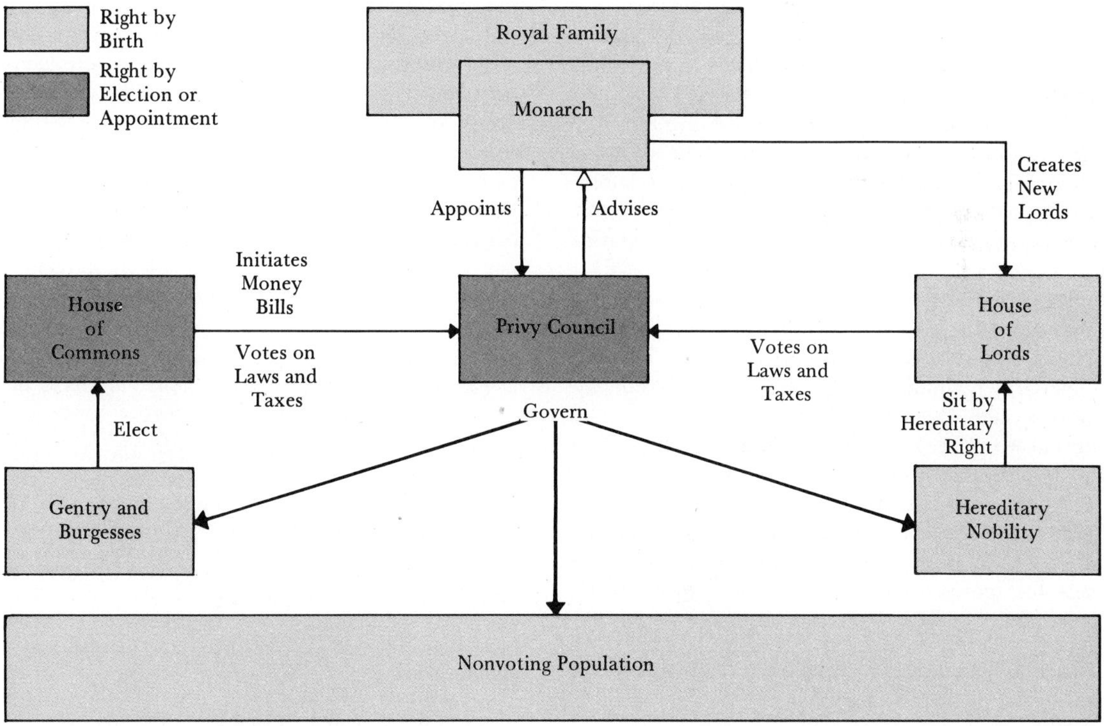

each representing one of the boroughs or shires of the kingdom (much as they now represent the 600-odd parliamentary constituencies—that is, electoral districts—of the country).[2]

In the course of time, power shifted increasingly to the House of Commons. The revolutions in the seventeenth century accelerated this process, which was completed by the middle of the twentieth. The seventeenth-century revolutions destroyed many of the old families of peers. Their places were taken by new peerage created by James II and his successors from courtiers and successful speculators. As the monarch became increasingly obliged to choose ministers only with the advice of the House of Commons and then to follow the advice of these Parliament-controlled ministers in his or her own political actions, the House of Commons—or, more exactly, the prime minister and the Cabinet—gradually acquired the powers of the Crown. In consequence, the House of Commons became ever more likely to prevail in any conflict with the House of Lords.

Other circumstances strengthened the hand of the Commons. Governments always need more money, and from early days the Commons alone could introduce money bills. In the nineteenth century it gained exclusive control over appropriations; this was formally recognized by law in 1911. Other types of legislation had to be passed by majorities in both houses, so the Lords had, in effect, a right of veto. This right gradually eroded. The Crown could create new peers by bestowing appropriate titles on whomever it chose. The threat to create many new peers often was used to make a recalcitrant majority in the House of Lords temper its resistance to the monarch and to the Commons majority and Cabinet advising him or her. Finally, in 1911 the House of Lords lost its absolute power of veto over legislation, retaining

only the right to delay legislation by one year.[3] A final reason for the increase in power of the Commons was the consent of the governed. Ordinary people became less inclined to obey the Lords, but remained willing to support the Commons.

The Cabinet and the Party System. The primary result of these shifts in power has been the transformation of the *Cabinet* from a council of advisers to the king or queen, chosen by and responsible to the monarch, into an instrument of the House of Commons. Today the Cabinet, the chief executive power headed by the prime minister, is a committee of Parliament. In theory, it is Parliament's creature. Parliament can make it or unmake it; if Parliament votes "no confidence" in the Cabinet, the Cabinet must resign. This has remained settled policy in England for several centuries. This power is taken for granted so unquestioningly that Parliament has rarely exercised its prerogative. In March 1979, when the House of Commons voted out of office Prime Minister James Callaghan's Labour Cabinet, it was the first time a Cabinet had been overthrown by Parliament since 1924. A prime minister who discovers that he or she is about to lose a majority may choose instead to step down in advance. Neville Chamberlain did so in 1940, in favor of

---

[2]Until 1963 no peer of England could renounce his title in order to represent a constituency in the House of Commons. For this reason Winston Churchill refused a peerage after World War II: he wanted to remain in the House of Commons.

[3]To compensate somewhat for this final loss of power, the Conservative government after 1945 introduced the practice of having the monarch make distinguished persons peers for their own lifetime, but without any hereditary title for their descendants. It was hoped that these lifetime peers would increase the quality and prestige of the House of Lords. In addition, the monarch has continued to create hereditary lords from among meritorious commoners, including nowadays deserving trade union leaders as well as business executives. In 1971 there were 838 hereditary peers and 19 hereditary peeresses, together with 157 life peers and 23 life peeresses. Since 1964 no new hereditary peerages have been created.

The ordinary rank of knight, with its title "Sir," is still bestowed by the monarch as a governmental honor on British subjects in many walks of life. It implies no peerage, is not hereditary, and does not bar its bearer from membership in the House of Commons.

Winston Churchill, whom all parties trusted. Over time, however, the prime minister's power vis-à-vis Parliament has grown.

In practice, the prime minister and the Cabinet depend on the support of their party. To function well, the British system requires political parties and *party discipline*. Parties began to emerge among the still narrow political elites in the late seventeenth century. The *Whigs* (who took their name from Scottish lowland opponents of the monarchy) favored increasing the power of Parliament and reducing that of the monarch. They drew their support from urban and mercantile interests and a minority of the great landed families. The *Tories* (named after bands of outlaws favoring Catholicism and the traditional monarchy) formed the court party. They stressed the claims of the hereditary nobility and the divine right of kings. Their supporters were a majority of the landed nobles and a minority of urban and commercial groups interested in monopolies and court favors. The Whigs were more inclined than the Tories to favor freer competition and more permissive goverment, at least for the educated and the well-to-do. Neither party advocated revolution.

In the eighteenth century both parties were deeply entangled in the inefficiency and corruption that characterized British politics at the time, and for a while the Tories were practically defunct. In the course of the nineteenth century the revived Tories became the modern *Conservative Party,* and the Whigs became the *Liberals.* In the twentieth century the *Labour Party* was founded, and after World War I it became one of the main pillars of the two-party system, relegating the Liberals to a minor role.

As time went on, candidates for the Commons came to depend on party support for election and re-election. They had reason, therefore, to follow the orders of their party while in Parliament. Each party organized its members in the House into a disciplined group called the *parliamentary party,* in contrast to the *national party* outside Parliament. The parliamentary party elects floor leaders, called party *whips,* to instruct members how to

vote. *Free votes,* left to the discretion of each member, are rare.

The majority party designates the *prime minister,* who is then formally entrusted by the monarch with the task of forming a government. Specifically, the prime minister chooses the members of the Cabinet and assigns them their tasks. He or she may change their assignments or drop them from the Cabinet and replace them by others. In all this, the prime minister needs the support of Parliament and, above all, the support of his or her own parliamentary party. Parliament can overthrow this official by an adverse vote if a majority strongly opposes his or her Cabinet choices or policies, but, as we have seen, this is rare. (The prime minister may even draw some Cabinet members from the House of Lords, provided that the Commons continues to back this government.)

Thus, Britain is governed by a double feedback process. Parliament can give instructions to the government that exercises leadership in the House of Commons, and the leaders can be overthrown by the House of Commons. But the Cabinet can also dissolve the House of Commons and can appeal over its head to the voters in a general election. The voters then elect a new Parliament, and a new Cabinet may emerge as a result (see Figures 4.2 and 4.3).

The same double feedback process includes the parties. A prime minister ordinarily is the leader of his party both within and outside Parliament. But a parliamentary party may revolt against a prime minister, or a national party may induce the members of the parliamentary party to do so. When Parliament is dissolved by the prime minister, perhaps because no new majority can be formed, elections must be called, and the former majority is very likely to lose. Members of the House of Commons do not like to risk their seats and, hence, do not overthrow governments lightly.

The British system, thus, has two feedback cycles: a short one between Cabinet and Parliament during normal times and a long one from the Cabinet to the voters via the new House of Commons to the new Cabinet. What the United States would call the "executive branch" is one part of the process. What it calls the "legislative branch" is the other part of the process. In Britain the two are on the same feedback cycle. Both systems, British and American, most often have worked well in providing constitutional and democratic government.

This comparison of the British and American governments shows that background conditions limit the range of political choices, but that within these limits such choices do exist. Having chosen different types of political machinery, Britain and the United States have continued to face common problems: the struggle between conservatism and change and between the power of elites and broader political participation.

FIGURE 4.2 *Parliamentary Government, ca. 1980: The Slow Feedback Cycle*

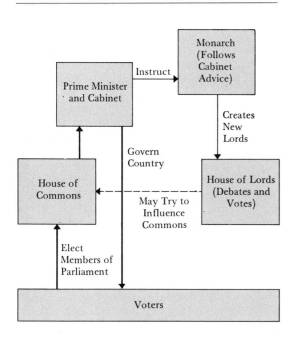

THE FROZEN DECADES, 1790–1832

A nation that has its own great revolution in relatively recent memory is unlikely to feel much need for another. Grandchildren and great-grandchildren of revolutionaries tend to be somewhat conservative. In the second half of the eighteenth century, British politics was just that, in contrast to the incipient revolutionary changes going on in British industry and science.

The British system failed to respond to the needs of the American colonists, although the colonists might have seceded anyway. When the French Revolution broke out so much nearer to their island nation, the British for a moment faced the possibility of a broader middle-class and lower-class revolution of their own. But within two years, as the revolution become more radical and violent, English public opinion switched toward opposition to the French Revolution, and democratic agitation was silenced at home. This change in the public mood was accomplished in part by the deliberate political strategy of the British elites.

One of the intellectual architects of this strategy of counterrevolution was Edmund Burke. Burke emphasized that the French Revolution was godless. By exaggerating the case, he built a bridge between the privileged and established Church of England and the underprivileged Protestant sects. The latter included the Presbyterians, Methodists, and other small Protestant groups whose members had been treated as citizens of lesser right and prestige. In the name of religion, but really in the interests of a more general conservatism, differences among Protestant denominations were played down.[4]

---

[4]In Ireland this strategy was carried even further, perhaps far beyond Burke's intentions. The English royal house made a deliberate alliance with the Presbyterians of Ulster. The first Irish patriotic and revolutionary leaders had all been Protestants. Now, in the late 1790s, the *Orange Order* was founded in order to woo away the Protestants from the cause of Irish independence. Deliberately, members of Protestant sects were given privileges and special ties to the British establishment to divide them from the poorer Catholic Irish in

THE GREAT REFORMS, 1832–1918

From 1790 to 1825 the British economy and technology changed quickly, but the British political system remained almost frozen. After 1825,

conservatism began to wane. The first trade unions were legalized, and the first political organizations began to function in opposition to the government.

Within a relatively few years, in 1832, the *Reform Bill* was pushed through the Parliament. It had been opposed to the last moment by Napoleon's nemesis, the Duke of Wellington, who, like many military heroes, had become a conservative political leader after his victory. By 1832 the "Iron Duke" was out of a job and England was getting a

the south of the island. The price of this successful, but diverse, strategy is still being felt nearly two hundred years later in the still unresolved bloodshed and intermittent civil war in British-ruled and Protestant-dominated Northern Ireland.

FIGURE 4.3 *Parliamentary Government, ca. 1980: The Fast Feedback Cycle*

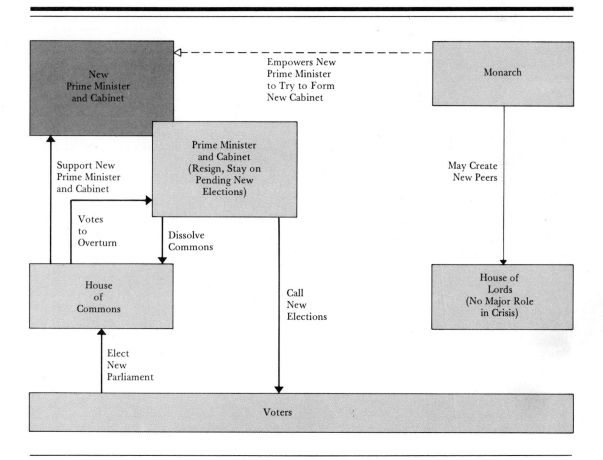

new constitutional settlement through the enfranchisement of the middle class, the abolition of urban "rotten boroughs" and "pocket boroughs," and the enfranchisement of new cities such as Liverpool and Birmingham. The English working class in the towns got the vote a generation later, in 1867. The writer Thomas Carlyle compared the enfranchisement of laborers to "shooting Niagara," because he felt it was so dangerous to give working men the vote. In 1885 the rural laborers were enfranchised. In 1918, by a somewhat unchivalrous piece of legislation, women over thirty got the vote; in 1928 the British decided to entrust the ballot also to women between twenty-one and thirty.

Changes in the right to vote went hand in hand with social change. After 1832 the first wave of labor unrest, known as the Chartist movement, went through England, leaving in its wake the first factory inspection acts. With Tory help a labor-conservative coalition was formed at the time against liberal factory owners of the laissez-faire school of thought. This resulted in 1851 in the first limitation of working time, the ten-hour law. After 1889 the first great dock workers' strike and the second wave of labor unrest followed, bringing with them the rise of the unskilled workers and the mass trade unions. The Independent Labour Party was founded in 1893 and the Labour Party in 1900. The first avowedly socialist government took office as a minority in 1924; the first absolute Labour majority was won in 1945, the second in 1964, the third in 1966.

THE NEW REFORMS, 1945–80

During the decades 1870–1920, Britain's overseas empire had been greatly enlarged. There had been much agitation for *imperialism,* the policy aimed at making the empire even bigger. Conservatives and radicals agreed that such an empire was indispensable to private enterprise at home. From this, Conservatives concluded that empire was good, and radicals decided that private enterprise should be curbed or abolished.

The Exit from Empire. "I have not become His Majesty's First Minister to preside over the dissolution of the British Empire," growled Sir Winston Churchill during World War II. His successors, the Labour government, did just that—and turned their policy into a success. Said Prime Minister Clement Attlee in 1947 to a crowded Albert Hall audience celebrating the beginning of Indian independence, "this is the proudest day in British history."

During its history the English state has performed a succession of changing tasks. Its first task was to consolidate the Norman conquest; its second, to unify the British Isles into a single political and economic system. Its third task, lasting from the sixteenth to the eighteenth century, was the conquest of the seven seas and the acquisition of beachheads from Bombay and Calcutta to Gibraltar and Halifax. The fourth task, continuing from the mid-eighteenth through the nineteenth century, was the conquest of vast inland areas and populations in Asia and Africa and the establishment of the largest empire the world had ever seen. In 1911, when King George V of England was crowned king-emperor of India, the sun did not set on his dominions, and more than 500 million people lived under the British flag. Britain's victory in World War I added new countries and peoples in the oil-rich Near East to the lands under British control. "Wider yet and wider may thy bounds be set," ran a popular hymn of those years; "God who made thee mighty, make thee mightier yet." But during the heyday of imperial expansion, domestic economic growth was neglected. British capital was sent overseas, and equipment in many industries at home was allowed to become obsolete.

After World War II, Britain faced a radically new task. The days of empires were ending, but not all imperial nations were aware of this fact.

Britain's government and people met this new challenge with the same courage with which they met the Battle of Britain. They cooperated with local nationalists to organize in rapid succession the independence of India, Pakistan, Burma, and Egypt. In the next two decades there followed the independence of most of British Africa, Cyprus, Malaya, and the islands of the Caribbean.

At certain times and places the British resisted political independence, and fighting broke out between local nationalists, on the one hand, and British troops and sometimes British settlers, on the other. Malaya, Kenya, and Cyprus, the British opposition to the establishment of Israel in 1948, and the short-lived Suez War in alliance with Israel and France against Egypt in 1956 are all examples of such conflicts. But if one adds up all such fighting, one still must conclude that never before in human history had so many people received their independence with so little resistance from their former rulers. Britain moved faster into the postimperial age than did France, Belgium, the Netherlands, Portugal, and a large part of American public opinion.

In 1980 the last British colony in Africa gained its independence when Rhodesia became the new nation of Zimbabwe. For almost fifteen years Britain had resisted the independence claims of white Rhodesians so long as the black majority in the country was denied equal political representation. Finally, in a remarkable display of British persistence and diplomatic skill, the new nation gained both independence and black majority rule without being plunged into a deep civil war. Few nations have matched the British in their practical concern for human rights all around the world.

The British adjustment to the loss of its colonies was smoothed by the *commonwealth* concept. The term harks back to the government of England in Cromwell's day, but the word was applied widely to Britain's relations with its former colonies only from the 1920s onward. The substance of the new arrangements was developed from the nineteenth century on, at first under other names. In 1867, Britain granted to Canada the status of a dominion, which implied far-reaching rights of internal self-government. Between the 1890s and the 1920s, Canada's rights of dominion were extended to include control over foreign trade, immigration, military matters, and eventually external affairs. During the same period *dominion status* was extended to Australia, New Zealand, and the Union of South Africa. From the 1920s on, it became increasingly clear that nonwhite territories would also become self-governing and that the Commonwealth would become an organization of equals. After World War II, this happened in the sense that the former dominions became sovereign and the old notion of dominion status disappeared. The newly sovereign countries, such as India and Pakistan, chose to accept Commonwealth membership, side by side with the former dominions. At the end of the 1970s the Commonwealth of Nations included thirty-six sovereign states and their dependencies, comprising close to 1 billion people.

Today Commonwealth membership implies mainly arrangements for political consultation, financial cooperation, and somewhat freer mobility of persons. There are also sentimental ties: some Commonwealth members have retained the British monarch as their symbolic head, although others like India and Ghana, have become republics.

As the Commonwealth loosened and the empire was dissolved, they became less important issues for British politics at home. The majority of British voters recognized that the empire was impracticable to maintain at any tolerable cost. Their aspirations shifted toward building, as William Blake's popular hymn put it, a new "Jerusalem in England's green and pleasant land."

A New Start at Home. After 1945 the new Jerusalem of the Labour government began with years of stiff austerity. Many of the former sources of income from the old empire were gone, as were many British foreign assets that had been spent during the war. British industry had to be reconverted to peacetime production. Maintenance of equipment deferred for six war years had to be made up, and so, too, did the neglect of several preceding decades in mining and other industries. War damage had to be repaired in London, Coventry, Birmingham, and other cities and new housing constructed for returning soldiers and their families.

The Labour government attacked these tasks by a great expansion of governmental powers. Mining, gas and electricity, railways and other inland transport, and the iron and steel industry were *nationalized* and partly re-equipped. Public control over land use was strengthened by new planning legislation that eventually led to the building of twenty-five new towns. Finally, a comprehensive *National Health Service* was created, giving every person present in the British Isles—including visiting American businesspeople and students—a claim to free medical care whenever needed. Together, these measures did much to modernize the British economy and social structure.

The Two-Party Pendulum. By the early 1950s voters had grown tired of austerity, with its prolonged rationing and holding back of consumer goods. In this mood they returned Conservative governments until the mid-1960s. These governments made greater concessions to middle-class consumers and to the private business sector. To some extent, they permitted the entire population to consume more, even at the risk of hurting Britian's competitive position in the world market. At the same time they accepted the nationalization of coal, railroads, and health services as part of their own policies and created a series of new universities. These actions made British conservatism very different from what goes by that name in the United States.

After thirteen years of Conservative relaxation (Conservative election victories were sometimes referred to as "the lull before the lull") the voters once again became anxious for change. Many Britons—particularly the younger ones—became concerned about inequality and immobil-

ity in the country's social and economic life. In their view, members of the old establishment still had too many privileges and contributed too little to the modernization and welfare of the nation. Accordingly, they elected a Labour government in 1964 and increased its majority in 1966. Behind these and subsequent swings of the political pendulum lay a preoccupation with British economic policy.

During much of the 1950s the British could console themselves with the idea expressed in the Conservatives' 1956 campaign slogan; economically speaking, Britons "had never had it so good." But by the 1960s it was impossible to overlook the fact that other Western countries, once devastated in World War II, were pulling ahead of Britain. An economic growth rate of 2 or 3 percent annually between 1950 and 1964 was good by historic British standards, but it was alarmingly low compared with the 5 to 9 percent growth rate being regularly registered by countries such as France, West Germany, Italy, and Japan during the same years. At this growth level Great Britain would soon be a second- or even third-rate economic power. Added to this was an unusually high inflation rate in Britain, a persisting balance of payments problem (that is, an excess in the value of imports over the value of exports), and periodic crises of confidence from foreign holders of the nation's currency.

Thus, from the early 1960s to the present day, the political debate in Britain had tended to concentrate on which party could best cope with the nation's economic problems. The reform promises on which Labour won the 1964 and 1966 elections called for more government planning, technological modernization in industry, and throwing over the outworn inequalities and lack of mobility in British life (much as the Beatles from Liverpool were, at the same time, overhauling popular music, and Carnaby Street was breaking through traditionalism in clothing fashions).

Unfortunately, the traditional lethargy of the nation's economic system could not be so easily or quickly changed as its popular fashions, and the Labour government soon abandoned most of its plans in favor of short-term crisis management in order to maintain the international value of the currency. In November 1967 this battle was lost and the pound was devalued. The government, with much resistance from the left wing of the labor movement (see p. 164, below) then embarked on a policy to restrain private consumption and public spending in order to shift resources into investment and exports. In effect, this meant that after the 1967 devaluation, the Labour government found itself trying to regulate price and wage increases (an *incomes policy*) as well as to control strike activity and collective bargaining in key sectors of employment (an *industrial relations policy*).

By the time of the 1970 general election there were signs of economic improvement, even though economic growth was well below the 4 percent rate the Labour government had promised when it arrived in office in 1964.[5] But now the political pendulum took another swing. Going into the parliamentary opposition after 1964, the Conservatives had chosen Edward Heath as their new leader and developed a new program that was philosophically similar to what became known in the United States a decade later as neoconservatism (see Chapter 2). In the 1970 election campaign the Conservatives promised to stop government intervention in incomes policy and to leave wages and prices to be set by the free market. Control over unions and strikes would be instituted to assure a freer working of the labor market. Likewise government spending and taxes would be cut to spur economic competition and growth. The 1970 election gave the Conservatives a sur-

[5]By 1970 exports were growing much faster than imports, leaving the balance of payments and the international value of the currency in a strong position. As Table 4.2 shows, Labour was also holding down public spending and increasing investment at the expense of consumer spending. These latter restraints and the failure to achieve the promised growth were powerful factors working against Labour in the 1970 election.

prise victory, in large part because many traditional Labour supporters were upset at the Labour government's economic restraints and did not vote (at 72 percent, turnout was the lowest in thirty-five years).

Unfortunately, electoral changes did little to solve fundamental problems and, by adding to a spirit of confrontation, seemed to make them worse. The Heath government's hands-off policy toward industry faltered when several major companies, including Rolls Royce, edged toward bankruptcy and required government subsidies. The government's attempt to impose legal controls on unions and strike activity eventually succumbed to widespread worker resistance and harsh criticism from the Labour Party (which suppressed the memory that the Labour government at the end of the 1960s had advocated a similar industrial relations policy). After two years the Heath government also had to abandon its promise to shun government intervention in the market through an incomes policy. Wage increases had shot up after the return to "free collective bargaining," and late in 1972 the government—which had already angered workers with its proposed union legislation—set its face against further large wage increases.

The inevitable confrontation came in the coal mining industry, which had been under government ownership since 1945. Coal miners felt they had fallen behind wage increases achieved by other workers, and in late 1973 they went on strike. The Heath government agreed to treat miners as a special case and allow a wage increase of 13 percent, but stated at the outset that this was a final offer. Union leaders, who had originally claimed to deserve increases of 20 to 47 percent, refused to participate in negotiations that began with a final offer, and the strike was on. The Heath government tried to break the strike, actually closing down much of British industry to operate on a three-day week, in the hope that this would turn the public mood against the strikers. As luck would have it, the oil-exporting Arab nations began the first of their many dramatic oil price increases. The British economy was clearly in an emergency, and Prime Minister Heath went to the nation for a vote of confidence. The election, he claimed, was to decide whether the government or the unions governed Britain.

The result was close. Labour lost a close popular vote (polling 300,000 votes less than the Conservatives, with a total of 30 million people casting ballots), but gained a plurality of five seats in Parliament over the Conservatives. A second 1974 election, in October, increased Labour's lead to a paper-thin majority. In fact, the elections of 1974 revolved around the issue of not so much *who* (government or unionists) would govern but *how* Britain would be governed—through confrontation or accommodation and cooperation with the country's powerful unionists.

The answer was cooperation. But it took time and a national crisis to produce a workable compromise between union demands and the national interest. On going into opposition against the Conservatives during 1970–74, Labour abandoned its earlier (1967–69) support for government wage controls and spending restraints as a way of making Britain pay its way in the world. The result of the Labour government's "hands off" approach is evident in Table 4.2. In an economy that was stagnant and even shrinking, public spending increased, workers' earnings soared, and inflation rose to 24 percent. Meanwhile, the Labour government hung on to a thin majority in Parliament.

Not surprisingly, 1974–76 was a crisis period, when the collapse of Britain's economy, and possibly of its political system, was widely discussed. But this did not happen. Staring into the abyss of national bankruptcy (and under pressure from the International Monetary Fund, which could provide international loans to stave off bankruptcy) the Labour government and union leaders finally came to a working agreement—a *social contract*—by which annual wage increases generally were kept to 4½ percent and government taxes on those wages somewhat reduced. At the same time, tight controls were put on public spending against the

wishes of many in the left wing of the Labour Party, and the government embarked on a program to encourage investment in several of the most profitable sectors of the economy. By the end of 1978, inflation had fallen from over 20 percent to under 10 percent, earnings were rising at more than the government's preferred 6 to 7 percent guidelines but still not at the more than 20 percent rate of two years earlier, and public spending had risen very little since 1976.

The real difficulty here was one of sustaining a consensus on economic policy that had—temporarily—been created by crisis. In the winter of 1978–79 many unions, white-collar no less than manual workers', breached the social contract with large wage demands and very disruptive strikes (for example, truck drivers, hospital workers, and other public employees). In the spring of 1979 there was another classic confrontation between the parties and another swing in the electoral pendulum. Prime Minister James Callaghan, who had taken over as Labour leader from Harold Wilson in 1976, claimed a success in reducing inflation and a demonstrated capacity to work out compromises with the unions. On the other side, Margaret Thatcher, who had taken over as Conservative leader from Edward Heath in 1975, hammered away on the themes of excessive government taxation and the threat to law and order posed by disruptive strikers. The result was the largest victory margin the Conservatives had achieved since before World War II (see Figure 4.4). Although the Thatcher government promised many of the same neoconservative policies that Heath had in 1970, the actual application of these principles was a good deal more flexible. Tax levels were reduced, but only very moderate restraints were imposed on public spending. The government took a firm stand with the unions, but in practice was generally willing to compromise on wage demands and refrained from proposing any strong legal controls on strikes or union organization. Not least important was the fact that by the

TABLE 4.2 *Key Indicators of British Economic Performance**
(percentage change over previous year)

	Gross domestic product	Consumer spending	Manufacturing investment	Public spending[1]	Wages and salaries[2]	prices[3]
1961	2.6	2.2	18.8	3.6	5.0	3.4
1962	1.2	2.2	−7.7	3.1	3.0	4.3
1963	3.8	4.3	−12.2	1.6	4.0	2.0
1964	5.8	3.3	13.0	1.5	7.3	3.2
1965	2.9	1.5	10.6	2.7	7.3	4.8
1966	1.7	1.9	2.7	2.8	6.7	3.9
1967	2.1	1.9	−2.0	5.6	3.6	2.5
1968	4.0	2.5	6.5	0.3	7.8	4.7
1969	1.8	0.4	6.8	−1.6	8.0	5.4
1970	1.8	2.5	7.7	1.5	12.1	6.4
1971	1.7	3.0	−6.6	3.0	11.3	9.4
1972	2.2	5.9	−12.7	3.7	13.0	7.1
1973	5.3	4.5	7.2	4.1	13.4	9.2
1974	0.0	−1.0	12.0	3.0	17.5	16.1
1975	−1.7	−0.3	−13.5	3.3	26.7	24.2

*All indicators adjusted for inflation at 1970 market prices
[1]Current expenditures of all public authorities
[2]Earnings in all industries and services; 1961–63 figures are estimates based on average manual workers' wages
[3]Annual movement in retail price index

Source: Calculated from statistical appendix in Michael Stewart, *The Jekyll and Hyde Years: Politics and Economic Policy since 1964* (London: J. M. Dent and Sons, 1977), pp. 261–62.

end of the 1970s, North Sea oil was finally beginning to flow into the British economy, reducing the need for expensive oil imports from the Middle East and offering prospects in the 1980s for Britain to become a net oil exporter to its neighbors in the European Economic Community. For a little while, Britain had achieved a breathing space amid the normal routines of economic crisis.

Yet as the decade of the 1980s got under way, it was clear that none of the many reforms and political promises of the last twenty years had reassured Britons that they had the political means for dealing with their economic problems. Reviewing Table 4.2, all the high hopes of the early 1960s for increasing the nation's rate of economic growth had been disappointed by both Labour and Conservative governments. A Conservative government pledged to cutting government spending and increasing investment had tended to produce just the reverse effects, and Labour governments, with their alternate bursts and brakes on public expenditure, had done little better. Both parties had first denounced and then in the press of circumstances had resorted to wage and price controls.

These policy failures, in combination with deeper changes in the once-orderly British social structure (see p. 146, above), have tended to produce more volatility in the British political scene. Nevertheless, the elections of the 1970s showed that the gross class contours of British voting and party support remained familiar. There were defections from each side, but the

FIGURE 4.4 *Party shares of Popular Vote and "Swing"* in the Electoral Pendulum*

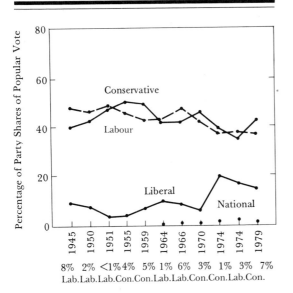

8% 2% <1% 4% 5% 1% 6% 3% 1% 3% 7%
Lab. Lab. Lab. Con. Con. Lab. Lab. Con. Con. Lab. Con.

"Swing" in the Electoral Pendulum

*Swing is defined as the difference between a winner's gain over the last election less the loser's loss over the last election. Thus if Conservatives gained 8 percent over their previous vote share and Labour lost 2 percent in their share of the vote, the swing would be 6 percent.

Source: William Schneider, "The Mistress of Downing Street," *Public Opinion*, June/July, 1979, p. 51.

majority of working-class voters still voted Labour and the majority of middle-class voters still supported the Conservative Party. But as Figure 4.4 shows, the swings of the electoral pendulum have been fairly small. This gives particular importance to those who are willing to switch their voting allegiances, and those who are so inclined have become increasingly prominent in British politics in recent years. This volatility was reflected in several ways. During the 1960s and 1970s, more Britons were willing to give their votes to Liberal and Nationalist parties. Likewise, although 90 percent of adults still identify themselves with one of the two major parties, fewer and fewer claim very strong partisan preferences for Labour or Conservative parties.

In short, Britain's two main parties can no longer feel assured that they have a body of stalwart supporters who are loyal to one party from one election to another. As Table 4.3 shows, the 1979 Conservative victory was very much in line with this trend. The Conservatives made considerable gains among workers generally, and skilled manual workers in particular. Labour continued to make inroads in the professional and managerial groups, and suffered a smaller Conservative swing among office workers than it did among working-class voters. It would be going too far to say that the economic turmoil of the last twenty years has produced a major realignment in the social bases of British politics. What has happened, gradually and quietly, is a growing *dealignment*—in other words, more tentativeness and changeability in the partisan support Britons are willing to give to either of the two major parties.[6]

Swings Within Each Party. In addition to the electoral swings between each party, there has

[6]For further details, see Ivor Crewe, Bo Särlvik, and James Alt, "Partisan Dealignment in Britain, 1964–74," *British Journal of Political Science*, vol. 7, (1976); and Richard Rose, *Politics in England*, 3rd ed. (Boston: Little, Brown, 1980), chapter 9.

TABLE 4.3 *Percentage of Vote Going to Three British Parties, by Job Group*

GROUP	CONSERVATIVE		LABOUR		LIBERAL		Swing to Conservatives
	Oct. 1974	May 1979	Oct. 1974	May 1979	Oct. 1974	May 1979	
Professional and managerial	63	65	12	17	22	15	−1.5%
Office and clerical	51	57	24	21	21	20	4.5%
Skilled manual	26	44	49	45	20	10	11.0%
Semiskilled and unskilled manual	22	31	57	53	16	12	6.5%
Trade unionists	22	30	57	51	17	15	7.0%

Source: Ivor Crewe, "BBC/Gallup Survey Prepared for *The Economist,*" SSRC Archive, University of Essex.

been a second and more extreme pendulum movement within each major party. We have already seen how, during the last twenty years, the Conservative Party and the Labour Party would successively denounce and then enact an incomes policy, depending on whether the party was in power or had moved into the opposition. But the intraparty swings go much deeper than that particular policy issue.

At present there are two kinds of Conservatives. One kind is highly traditional, nationalistic, nostalgic for empire, hostile to nonwhites and, indeed, to most foreigners, and sympathetic to the government of South Africa and to the white minority in Zimbabwe. Such Conservatives are strong in rural party organizations, among retired officers, and also among small businesspeople and lower-middle-class enclaves in urban industrial areas. This right wing of the party supported the Suez War in 1956 and the racist policies of the former Cabinet minister Enoch Powell, who was disavowed by the leadership of his party. In 1979 he was a member of Parliament for the Unionist Party of Northern Ireland, a militantly Protestant group at the geographic and political periphery of the

Conservative Party. The other, more moderate wing of the Conservative Party favors modernization, reform, economic integration with Europe, cooperation with the nonwhite countries of the Commonwealth, and a continuation of the more moderate policies of the welfare state. The Conservative Party leadership has to maneuver between both wings and try to keep them together, a task facilitated by the British tradition of strong party discipline in Parliament and the country. For a short time the current party leader, Margaret Thatcher, tried to do this by incorporating some of Powell's attacks on nonwhite immigration into her own rhetoric, but then muted this theme in her successful 1979 campaign.

The Labour Party has its own internal divisions. Its left wing is concerned with the ideology of socialism and advocates further nationalization of industry. It stresses class interests and the working-class character of the party. It favors planning and distrusts the play of forces in the market. It opposes increased defense spending and the remnants of empire, demands sharp measures against the white minorities of Zimbabwe and South Africa, rejects the concept of the Cold War, and is uneasy about Britain's alliance with the United States. This wing draws much of its support from the disadvantaged regions of Britain, such as Wales and Scotland, as well as from a minority of intellectuals. The right wing of the Labour Party is stronger in London and in southern England and among many of the better-paid groups of labor and public employees as well as among a majority of intellectuals. Right-wing leaders stress evolution and pragmatism, more reliance on market forces and consumer interests, greater cooperation with the United States and Western Europe, greater caution toward nationalization of industries, and further expansion of the public sector. They stress common interests among the classes and urge restraint in the further wage demands of the trade unions.

The Labour Party leadership, like its Conservative counterpart, must manage to work with both wings of its party and, for this purpose, makes heavy use of party discipline. As an added complication, the big trade unions, which for a long time cared little about ideology, insist on free collective bargaining without government interference (the one sphere where they do not want to see planning of the socialist type). This can mean, as it has in the past, frequent, large wage increases that have upset Labour governments' economic plans. These unions command large blocs of votes at the party conference, and the Labour leadership cannot afford to quarrel too seriously with the Trade Union Congress, any more than the Conservative leadership can afford to quarrel too seriously with the financial interests in the City of London and industrial interests throughout the country.

The record of the last twenty years shows that each party, when it loses office and goes into opposition, tends to swing away from its moderate, pragmatic center and give increased prominence to the program of its more extreme wing (the right for the Conservative Party, the left for the Labour Party). Why? There are basically two reasons. First, each party, when in power, is constrained by political realities and by the need to maintain a national consensus to act in such a way that it cannot fulfill the wishes of its more extreme wing. When the government loses an election, that wing claims that defeat came from the temporizing nature of the ousted government's policies. Second, in the British parliamentary system, a party goes into opposition to do just that: to oppose whatever it is the new government is doing. Often this means rejecting the very things (incomes or industrial relations policies, for example) the opposition party itself had done when in power. Thus the need to frequently oppose the ruling party amounts to an implicit endorsement of approaches taken by the more extreme wing of each respective party.

These two pendulum swings—within and between the two major parties—seem to be built into the underlying dynamics of British government. The question is whether this sort of movement will suffice to cope with the basic problems of choice posed by the stakes of British politics. In the continuing contest between the major parties and their interest group allies, these stakes include basic choices about the distribution of economic wealth, political power, social status, educational opportunity, and the future directions of British society and culture.

THE STAKES OF BRITISH POLITICS

The leverage of government on the British body politic has become powerful indeed. In the 1970s, 30 percent of the British labor force was working for government in one or another of its forms. This is over six times as many as before 1940.[7] In

---

[7]Total public employment is broken down as follows: 4 percent are in the armed forces; 16 percent work for the National Health Service; 11 percent for the central government; 28 percent for nationalized industries (including public corporations and the Post Office); and the largest share, 41 percent, work for local government units. See "Employment Analyzed by Sector and Industry," *Economic Trends*, January 1979, pp. 132, 136.

1979, taxes at all levels of government, together with national insurance contributions, had risen to 40 percent of the GNP, but public expenditure, already at 51 percent of national income in 1969, was officially reported at 62 percent in 1976.[8] Some of these fluctuations have been due to inflation, but the public sector in Britain now hovers around one-half of the GNP—no matter which party is governing.

Conservative governments in the mid-1950s and early 1960s and the government of Prime Minister Edward Heath from 1970 to 1974 have made little headway in reversing this long-term trend. Indeed, the acceptance after 1945 by the Conservatives of the bulk of the Labour Party's welfare-state program with its greatly expanded scope of services—and of much of the public employment entailed by them—has been an essential element in the British political consensus of the last four decades. Together with the budgetary powers wielded by the Treasury—heir to the exchequer of olden days—and with the available legal powers over land use and employment policies, the size and scope of this public sector offer to any British government an array of powerful instruments to influence the social, economic, and political course of the nation.

But for what aims and policies are these powers to be used?

What National Role for Britain? In the early 1980s, two generations after their "finest hour" in World War II, the British people have not yet decided where they want to go. They have given

up most of their empire, but they are reluctant to let go of their role as a world power even though it is becoming largely imaginary in comparison to the much greater resources of the United States and the Soviet Union.

Britain under Conservative leadership entered the *European Common Market* in 1973, and in a unique referendum in 1975, two-thirds of the votes cast supported this policy (which is still more popular among a large part of the elites).

Another possible direction would be to concentrate primarily on domestic modernization, technological development, and economic growth. A strong body of public opinion in Britain would appear to favor this view.[9] But it is difficult for a country with Britain's large and continuing roles as a world banker and investor, side by side with its continuing dependence on a vigorous export sector, to pay for its needed imports of food and other goods. In these matters Britain's future self-definition and world role are at stake—its choice between the dangers of underachievement and overcommitment. Eventually, by commission or omission, British politics within the next decade or two will have to settle the problem identified twenty years ago by a former American secretary of state. "Britain," said Dean Acheson, "has lost an empire and has not yet found a role."

How Much Economic Growth? Some parts of these larger decisions are already at stake here and now. How much economic growth do the British people want, how fast, in what direction, and by what means? Their nation has grown less than most other major industrial countries. Their absolute gross national product has been overtaken by those of Japan, West Germany, France, the Soviet Union, and China. Their per capita GNP, too, has lagged and is now below French, West German, and Soviet levels.

The fact is that Britain has always been a

[8]Samuel H. Beer, "The British Political System," in S. H. Beer and A. B. Ulam, eds., *Patterns of Government: The Major Political Systems of Europe*, 3rd ed. (New York: Random House, 1974), p. 293; Central Statistical Office *Annual Abstract of Statistics, 1977* (London: HMSO, 1977), pp. 341, 344. For a discussion of the politics surrounding these figures, see Hugh Heclo and Aaron Wildarsky, *The Private Government of Public Money*, 2nd ed. (London: Macmillan & Co., 1980).

[9]In 1978 one-half of Britons polled said they would rather their nation become like Sweden or Switzerland, and only 31 percent wanted Britain to be a leading world power (*Gallup Political Index*, no. 216, July 1979).

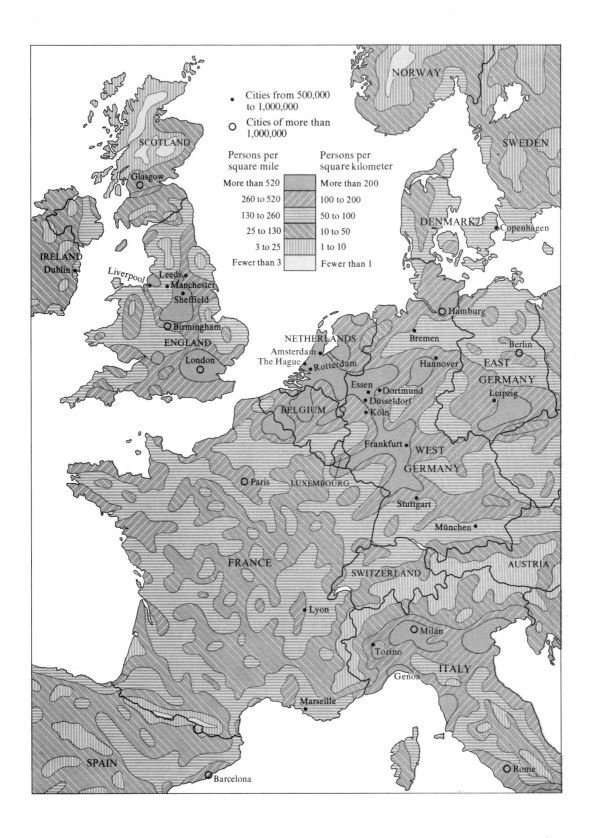

- • Cities from 500,000 to 1,000,000
- ○ Cities of more than 1,000,000

Persons per square mile	Persons per square kilometer
More than 520	More than 200
260 to 520	100 to 200
130 to 260	50 to 100
25 to 130	10 to 50
3 to 25	1 to 10
Fewer than 3	Fewer than 1

NORWAY

SWEDEN

SCOTLAND

Glasgow

IRELAND

Dublin

Liverpool

Leeds

Manchester

Sheffield

Birmingham

ENGLAND

London

DENMARK

Copenhagen

Hamburg

Bremen

Berlin

NETHERLANDS

Amsterdam

The Hague

Rotterdam

Hannover

EAST GERMANY

Essen

Dortmund

Düsseldorf

Köln

Leipzig

BELGIUM

Frankfurt

WEST GERMANY

Paris

LUXEMBOURG

Stuttgart

München

FRANCE

SWITZERLAND

AUSTRIA

Lyon

Milan

Torino

Genoa

ITALY

Marseille

SPAIN

Barcelona

Rome

slow-growing nation, at least when compared with the 5 to 7 percent annual growth rates achieved by nations such as West Germany, France, and Italy between 1950 and 1970. During the nineteenth century, when Britain's industrial revolution gave it a preeminent position in the world, the nation's growth in GNP per capita averaged an annual rate of only 1 to 2 percent in one decade after another. In the past thirty years that overall rate has not changed very much (with annual growth averaging 2.7 percent from 1951 to 1970 and 1.8 percent from 1971 to 1978) despite, as we have seen, the competing promises of each party to push Britain forward economically. Trends in growth seem to depend on very deep-seated cultural and other factors that are not easily reached by short-term political competition.[10]

One obstacle to growth has been the British workers' choice of strikes and wage increases for their own trades at the expense of growth of the national economy as a whole, because they fear that they might not get a fair share of the latter. Moreover, British workers and British managers seem to prefer to work at their own pace, with time out for tea and without stressful adjustments to new technologies. This may have improved their health, but not the outmoded equipment in some of their plants or the average per capita income in their country.

The British press, in large part identified with the business community's point of view, has heavily publicized the British workers' technological conservatism and their propensity to strike. (The

[10]See Edward F. Denison, *Why Growth Rates Differ* (Washington, D.C. Brookings Institution, 1967). Historic trends are discussed in Phyllis Deane and W. A. Cole, *British Economic Growth, 1688–1959,* (Cambridge: Cambridge University Press, 1962).

(Left) MAP 4.2 *Population Distribution of the United Kingdom, France, and the German Federal Republic*

latter, in fact, is no higher than the average in other countries; see Table 4.7.) What has been less often noted is the silent strike of British financiers and investors that began in the 1960s, if not earlier. They have been reluctant to invest in many branches of industry, fearing that these might be nationalized without adequate compensation or made unprofitable by too high wages and too low *productivity* (market value of output per employee). As a result, British industries often have less modern equipment, and the remarkable ingenuity of British scientists and engineers often fails to be applied and to bear fruit in production. These failures, in turn, tend to restrict Britain's exports and foreign exchange earnings, to promote inflation, and to keep real wages low in comparison with those in other countries.

Although these troubles are visible to many, each side tends to blame the other for them. Whenever the Conservatives rule, Labour complains of social injustice; whenever Labour holds office, Conservatives complain of lack of economic motivation. Economic growth seems to the Conservatives to require more inequality, but social peace and justice seem to Labour to demand more equality, both in meeting human needs and in enjoying the better things in life. At heart this problem is common to all modern industrial societies, but in Britain it has been posed particularly clearly. Perhaps the British people will find a better answer to it in the future; they need it urgently.

Thus far, they are just wrestling with the questions. Should Britain shift its energies toward an all-out effort at economic growth in order to regain its lost lead? Or should the people accept the economic slowdown as part of the price for continuing far-flung military and political commitments? Or should they take a more skeptical view of international power and military reputation and concentrate, somewhat like the Scandinavians, on the quality of their lives—on health, leisure, culture, and greater political and social equality and harmony—even without trying to catch up with, say, Sweden's high per capita income figures?

More Equality or Less? In any case, do the British people want more equality at home? Most authorities agree that during this century there has been a slow trend, especially evident during war years, toward greater equality in the distribution of income and wealth. Before World War I, the wealthiest 1 percent of Britons held 70 percent of all personal wealth. As the bottom half of Table 4.4 shows, Britain is no longer *that* kind of unequal society. But it is also true that Britain retains a considerable degree of inequality. Even after the redistributive impact of taxes, the share of income received by the bottom 80 percent has increased only marginally since the end of the 1950s. The inequality in wealth stands out even more strongly in the second part of Table 4.4. The wealthiest one-fifth of the adult population still held four-fifths of all personal wealth. The main redistribution appears to have been from the top 1 percent to others in the next-richest groups, not to the bottom of the distribution. Again we can think of the same light bulb–shaped distribution suggested earlier in this chapter regarding social structure. Many Conservatives argue that redistribution has already gone so far that the incentives needed for a vigorous economy have been eroded. Many labor leaders see these figures as a sign that more determined efforts are needed to change the enduring structure of economic inequality.

This unresolved problem of inequality has arisen even more sharply in regard to many health and welfare services. Here the adherents of equality, and the Labour Party, have generally favored a principle of *universalism*, a flat rate of benefits or service being offered equally to all, in order to avoid the stigma of charity or poverty, the humiliation of the applicants' being subjected to means tests (tests to prove their poverty), and also to avoid the bureaucratic costs of administering such a system of controls. But such flat rates of service for all will be very expensive, if they are to meet middle-class standards, or else they will be rejected by many middle-class persons as inadequate to

their own needs and expectations. Accordingly, Conservatives have steadily urged services according to a principle of *selectivity:* offered free only to the needy, they are offered for pay to everybody else, preferably through private agencies operating in the market.

A third proposal has come from an academic expert, the late Professor Richard M. Titmuss, and has been publicized by the Fabian Society. He advocated a two-tier system of flat-rate universalist service standards for all as a base, supplemented by additional amounts and kinds of services for those whose *needs* are greatest, without a test for the means that they may or may not have. This, Titmuss argued, will free the recipients and their children from the social stigma of poverty and failure and from the feelings of personal inadequacy and inferiority in their own minds. In American terms, this proposal would amount to replacing the question of whose "fault" it is that a case of medical or other need arises—the fault of the individual, of society, or of the physical and technological environment—by the principle of "no fault" insurance against such needs, paid for by all members of society through taxes and, hence, in accordance with their ability to pay. The proposal leaves unanswered many questions of detail, and it raises, of course, major questions of ideology or principle—above all, who will decide whose needs are greatest. On the technical side it probably can be worked out; but in regard to values and a general sense of political and cultural direction, political decisions will have to be made by voters, elites, and the political parties through which their political efforts are channeled.[11]

So far, none of the three competing approaches to welfare policy has fully prevailed, neither flat-rate universalism, nor means-test selectivity, nor Titmuss's two-tier system of "positive discrimination" in favor of needs, not lack of means. Some

[11]Richard M. Titmuss, *Commitment to Welfare* (London: Allen and Unwin, 1968), pp. 113–37, especially pp. 122–23, 134–35.

TABLE 4.4 *Distribution of After-Tax Income and Personal Wealth, 1960–75**

	1959/60	1964	1968	1972	1975
INCOME AFTER TAXES	%	%	%	%	%
Top 1 percent[1]	5.3	5.3	4.6	4.6	4.0
Top 5 percent	15.8	16.0	14.4	14.6	13.7
Top 10 percent	25.2	25.9	23.6	24.1	23.2
Top 20 percent	40.9	42.0	39.1	40.0	39.0
Bottom 80 percent	59.1	58.0	60.9	60.0	61.0
PERSONAL WEALTH					
Top 1 percent[2]	38.2	34.4	32.7	29.9	23.2
Top 5 percent	64.3	59.3	59.0	56.3	46.5
Top 10 percent	76.7	73.5	73.8	71.9	62.4
Top 20 percent	89.8	88.4	89.4	89.2	81.8
Bottom 20 percent	10.2	11.6	10.6	10.8	18.2

*The table should be read: the highest 1 percent of all income earners received 5.3 percent of all after-tax income; the top 5 percent of all wealth holders owned 64.3 percent of total personal wealth; and so on.
[1]Top 1 percent of all income tax units
[2]Top 1 percent of persons aged 18 or older

Source: Royal Commission on the Distribution of Income and Wealth, *Report No. 5,* Her Majesty's Stationery Office, London, CMND. 6999, tables 4 and 33.

compromises have been reached, but every vote for the Labour Party promotes some efforts toward greater equality, whereas every electoral victory of the Conservatives, such as that in 1979, will move welfare policies somewhat in the opposite direction. Whether old people will get their eyeglasses and false teeth from the National Health Service without charge, as they did for a time, or whether they will have to pay for them or else prove their poverty will thus hinge on a series of political decisions.

The need for such decisions might be eliminated, however, if both major parties should come to agree that Britain's economic position is so strained that payments from old people for many health and welfare services are indispensable, as both parties were beginning to agree during the late 1960s in the last years of the Labour government of Prime Minister Harold Wilson. In that case the stakes of politics seemed to contract. Voters, at least in the short run, were left without a real choice in regard to this range of issues; and the motivation of some of them to take part in politics was apt to be reduced. By 1974 this trend was reversed, and the Labour program stressed again its socialist beliefs. But some ebb and flow of opinion within and between the major parties seems likely to continue.

One Work Force or Two? Underpaid Service Jobs and Immigrant Labor. Another question at stake in British politics, as in those of several other highly developed industrial countries, is whether there is to be one work force or two. As real wages rise, the low-paid and often unpleasant jobs in many *service occupations*—garbage collectors, street cleaners, dishwashers, hospital orderlies, laundry workers, and the like—will tend to be deserted by the next generation of workers, who are finding more attractive opportunities in other occupations.

This exodus of local labor creates a problem and an option among ways to meet it. Either local service labor is to be lured back by means of higher pay and better working conditions, at a substantial increase in average service cost; or these service jobs are to be mechanized in large part, by means of substantial capital investments in new machinery, also at the price of higher service costs; or the service is to be cut back and partly neglected, through lack of personnel and equipment, at the cost that such neglect entails.

Finally, the service may henceforth be performed by cheap foreign labor, specially recruited from some of the poorest and least developed countries and regions in the world, such as *nonwhite immigrants* from Pakistan and the West Indies in the case of Britain. This keeps the service relatively cheap, except for some costs resulting from the lack of skill and cultural familiarity on the part of the newcomers. But it piles up other social costs: housing; schooling; the necessity perhaps of coping with major differences of culture and sometimes of language; the risks and costs of ethnic and racial conflicts; and, in short, the whole range of costs of acculturation. Thus far, British working-class and lower-middle-class voters have tended to oppose such immigration, whereas some other sectors of opinion have favored it. In early 1979, large strikes of hospital workers for higher wages alarmed the British public, and substantial wage increases had to be conceded. Cheap foreign labor in such service occupations might seem to some observers to offer one way of keeping costs down, but there is a social and political price.

Here, as in the case of equal versus unequal health and welfare services, technical specialists may eventually discover more attractive options.

Cultural changes may produce shifts in popular values and priorities and perhaps also in the values of a part of the elite, therefore changing the probabilities of acceptance or rejection of this or that proposed solution. In the end, however, it will be the political process by which the decisions will be produced.

What Kind of Morality and Culture? Last, but not least, the stakes of British politics now include a good deal of the future cultural orientation of the country. Whether children will be lawfully beaten in government-supported schools—traditionalists approve, reformers protest—may in time make a difference to British culture. So may the new tolerance for homosexual behavior under a law passed in the late 1960s, which permits it in private and among "consenting adults." The abolition of the death penalty for all crimes except treason, piracy, and certain military offenses is another portent of cultural and ethical change, and so are the changes in the legal and actual treatment of conscientious objectors. The abolishing or lessening of censorship of plays and films and the weakening of obscenity laws may be seen as an increase in human freedom or else as a step toward the moral and cultural pollution of unwilling cities and neighborhoods where people wish to raise their children in a less sex-oriented environment. Some voters tend to react to all these changes with intense fear and resentment, seeing in them the downfall of order, morals, and authority; others hail all such changes as improvements; still others try to discriminate among them; but all must use politics to get the changes they desire, once they can agree on what they want.

Which Package of Policies? The six stakes just named—extent of public services and size of public sector, overall policy goals, rate of economic growth with levels of prices and employment, degrees of social and economic inequality, integrated or segregated recruitment of unskilled service workers, traditional or change-oriented culture patterns—are all interdependent; and most of them depend heavily on the level of available means and capabilities. A backward, stagnant, or declining economy can support neither an ambitious world role, nor a high and rising level of real wages, nor a vigorous program of domestic services. An inadequate level of real wages and welfare services cannot be distributed justly, on either equal or unequal terms, and the resulting inadequacies and injustices will be resented. An embittered and disgruntled work force, ever ready to engage in spontaneous slowdowns or to take bribes, is unlikely to contribute much to economic growth or to encourage the private or public investment indispensable to growth. A culture oriented toward mass consumption, self-expression, permissiveness, and quick pleasures—rather than toward thrift, hard work, and the steadfast striving for more distant goals—is less likely to favor the accumulation of savings, capital, and skills and, hence, less likely to permit much economic growth. But a stagnant or inadequate level of real wages and social services, in turn, juxtaposed with the continuous demonstration of high living and consumption standards on television and in the other mass media, is likely to engender more frequent frustrations, and social conflicts between labor and the middle classes, among different groups of workers, and between native labor and recent immigrants, particularly those from nonwhite countries. Yet a country that becomes known for treating nonwhites badly—or for treating them conspicuously less well than in the past—cannot maintain in the long run a commercial or political world role that also depends inevitably on the trust and good will of the nonwhite peoples and countries, which make up more than two-thirds of humankind.

These facts of multiple interdependence limit severely the choices among policies that are likely to be practicable, for one cannot choose policies one by one and hope realistically for their success. British voters would have to choose whole packages—viable configurations—of several such policies, all at once and in proportion and timed sequence to each other. Such viable configurations are relatively rare and hard to find. They must be discovered or invented, and much of this job has yet to be done.

The result is a seeming paradox. For a long time the size and importance of the stakes of British politics have tended to move a larger part of the British people toward political participation. But in recent years the ineffectiveness of many isolated policies, the lack of effective choice on some issues, the lack of plausible and workable overall patterns of policy, and the resulting apparent unresponsiveness and intractability of the British political and social system have left much of the British population frustrated and less inclined to participate in politics than they were earlier.

THE CHANGES IN POLITICAL PARTICIPATION

The broadening of political participation in Britain during the nineteenth and twentieth centuries has been a model case of its kind. The widening of the franchise is shown in Table 4.5.

As the right to vote widened, so did the numbers and proportions of those who actually voted. In 1874, actual voters numbered 1.6 million, or 53 percent of those who had the right to vote. A century later, in May 1979, actual voters totaled 40.1 million, or 76 percent of registered voters.

This change in the scale of participation brought with it a change in the scale of politics. In 1874 almost 30 percent of all constituencies (that is, electoral districts) for the House of Commons were uncontested. Some of these were multimember constituencies, with up to four elected. In the contested constituencies the average vote per constituency was about 8,000, regardless of the number of members to be elected from it.[12] In

[12]Beer, "The British Political System," p. 243.

TABLE 4.5 *Enfranchised Voters as a Percentage of the Population over Twenty Years of Age*

Year	Percentage
1831	5
After 1832 (first Reform Act)	7
After 1867 (second Reform Act)	16
After 1884 (third Reform Act)	29
After 1918 (vote for women over thirty)	74
After 1928 (Equal Franchise Act)	97

Source: Judith Ryder and Harold Silver, *Modern English Society: History and Structure, 1850–1970* (London: Methuen, 1970), p. 74, with reference to S. Gordon, *Our Parliament* (London: Cassell, 1964).

1979 all constituencies were contested, and the average vote in each was about 49,170.

The state of political participation in Britain during the last decade is presented in Table 4.6.

The long-term increase in political participation has not continued during the last quarter century. Turnout of voters at general elections has been tending downward since 1959 and stood at 76 percent in 1979. As we have seen, this decline in turnout has been paralleled by a decline in party identification and increased volatility and dealignment in partisan support. The main message of Table 4.6 is that, apart from voting, the great mass of British adults stay on the political sidelines, whereas minorities of activists in parties, voluntary groups, and local government involve themselves directly in the political contests of government.

In recent years it is not so much political party structures but economic interests that have mobilized larger numbers of ordinary Britons. Trade union membership as a proportion of the work force had risen from 11 percent of the total employed population in 1892 to 42 percent in

1953; but it declined progressively to 38 percent by the late 1960s. Union membership edged upward during the 1970s, largely through new growth in unions for white-collar workers. By the end of that decade it stood at about 50 percent of the work force, or more than twice the level of 22 percent union participation in the United States.[13]

At the same time, strikes increased. The total strike days per five-year period averaged 2.2 million in 1947–56, rising slightly to 3.6 million in 1957–66, then shooting up to 23.8 million for 1967–70 and to 55 million in 1972–76. Even so, in 1967–76, there were fewer strikes in Britain than in the United States, Italy, and Canada[14] (see Table 4.7).

One proposed explanation of the strike waves has been the increased affluence of many workers, which allows them to go on strike more often, but weakens their identification with any more ideological working-class appeal and, hence, with the Labour Party. Another explanation has pointed to a general weakening of organizational discipline, particularly among younger workers, vis-à-vis both management and unions; most of the strikes after 1966 were not authorized, but arose spontaneously. Power, it was said, had moved from central union headquarters all the way down to the shop floor, where shop stewards were elected and strike votes taken. A third consideration might be that British labor has tended at some times in the past to alternate political and industrial action. If the government or the political system proved unresponsive to the workers' demands, they would resort to strikes; if strikes were unsuccessful, they would shift their effort back into politics.

If elements of all three explanations should contain some truth, then labor-based political and social conflicts and activities may well continue for

[13]Robert Price and George S. Bain, "Union Growth Revisited," *British Journal of Industrial Relations*, vol. 14, no. 3, 1976; and U.S. Department of Labor, Bureau of Labor Statistics, *Handbook of Labor Statistics: 1977* (Washington, D.C.: U.S. Government Printing Office, 1977).
[14]Beer, "The British Political System," p. 286; interview of British Foreign Minister David Owen, *Der Spiegel* (Hamburg), February 12, 1979, p. 118.

TABLE 4.6 *Interest and Participation in British Politics in the 1970s*

	Estimated percentage of adult population
Eligible electorate	98
Voters in national election (1979)	76
Voters in local government elections	42
Member of at least one voluntary organization	61
Member of an "issue organization"[1]	19
Officer in voluntary organization	14
Identifies self as a supporter of a political party	90
Claims to take a great deal of interest in politics	19
Takes part in multiple political activities beyond voting[2]	7
Individual, dues-paying members of a political party	5
Ever contacted local elected official	17
Ever attended meeting of local government body	10
Ever participated in a street demonstration	6
MPs, senior civil servants, locally elected officials	0.15

[1]For example, a union, employers' organization, or some other group working on questions or public policy.
[2]These are generally identified as political activists inasmuch as they not only vote but also help with fund raising, urge others to participate, contact their MPs, and so on.

Source: Compiled from Richard Rose, *Politics in England,* 3rd ed. (Boston: Little, Brown, 1980), pp. 170–77.

a longer time than was expected in the prosperity-oriented climate of the 1950s. In that case, British politics might continue to show the marks of a cycle in which periods of convergence between the two major parties would be accompanied by some decline in voting turnout, but this eventually would be followed by the rise of new issues or the revival of old ones, the renewal of political conflicts, and a new increase in political participation. Each turn of this cycle would then put its own strains and stresses on the processes and machinery of government.

THE POLITICAL SYSTEM: ITS SELF-STEERING PROCESS AND MACHINERY

A considerable part of the British political system and its major institutions in the context of their historical development have been described in earlier sections of this chapter. There we encountered the Crown; Parliament with its two houses, the Lords and the Commons; the prime minister and the Cabinet; and the major political parties, Conservative (or Tory) and Labour, and the formerly major and now minor party, the Liberals, the successors to the Whigs. Here it should suffice to state some of the main characteristics of the system as it works today.

TABLE 4.7 *Strikes: Days Lost per 1,000 Employees, 1967–76*

Canada	1,906
Italy	1,824
U.S.A.	1,349
Britain	788
Federal Republic of Germany	56

Source: Interview of British Foreign Minister David Owen, *Der Spiegel* (Hamburg), February 12, 1979, p. 118.

The Location of Power: The Prime Minister and the Cabinet. The main power, so far as short-range or crisis decisions are concerned, is in the hands of the prime minister and the Cabinet. Since the prime minister has the power to appoint and dismiss Cabinet members or to change their assignments, it is his or her will that counts far more than any other. The prime minister is also the leader of his or her party in Parliament and in the nation. If rebellious members of that party in Parliament should break discipline by voting against his or her policy on some important issue, they would be unlikely to be renominated by the local party organization and re-elected by the voters unless backed by very strong popular feeling and/or local interests. Most often, their political careers would be finished. Ordinarily, therefore, the prime minister in office is likely to prevail over Parliament and over any opposition within his or her own party or in the country. Parliamentary acts and decisions, in turn, are likely to be executed by the civil service and the armed forces and obeyed by the vast majority of the population.

When Compliance Fails: The Civil War in Ulster. The most notable exception to this state of affairs was the refusal in 1912 of the Protestant population in Northern Ireland—or *Ulster*—to accept "home rule" for Ireland as a whole, which would have subordinated them to the Roman Catholic majority in the rest of that island. Their defiance, entailing the threat of civil war, was backed by a large part of the Conservative Party and unofficially by some members of the armed forces, which had numerous officers from the Protestant parts of Ulster. At that time the government retreated from home rule; British and Protestant power remained paramount until the Civil War of 1918–21 brought independence to the twenty-six counties of the south, which eventually became today's Ireland. However, the tight rule of the Protestant two-thirds majority was maintained through an autonomous regime in the remaining six counties of Northern Ireland. In the late 1960s the Roman Catholic minority there had become as intransigent and defiant as their Protestant neighbors. A new guerrilla-type civil war ensued. By the late 1970s over 1,200 persons had been killed; British troops were occupying Ulster; British direct rule had been restored; but neither troops nor government found much voluntary obedience and support from either Protestants or Catholics in that strife-torn section. The tragedy of Ulster reveals how much of the domestic power of the British government depends not merely on the procedures, but also on the substance of its decisions.

More peaceful—but no less clear-cut—examples of these limits on popular compliance come from the field of industrial relations. The general strike of 1926, called by the unions, had been forbidden by the Conservative government of the day, but the workers went on strike anyway. For nine days much of British business and industrial activity was paralyzed until the workers went back. They had failed to win their goals, but had succeeded in demonstrating their freedom of action. Lesser strikes in the 1960s and 1970s, against explicit prohibitions of the Labour government of prime ministers Harold Wilson and James C. Callaghan, taught the same lesson—that government, without strong popular backing, could not compel reliable compliance with its commands against large, concentrated, and highly motivated opposition groups.

Power as the Consonance of Many Actors. Power in the British political system, therefore, is not the exclusive property of any one of its components even the most influential. Rather, power in Britain is a result of a consonant and mutually supportive relationship among the major actors. That prime minister is powerful indeed who is backed by the Cabinet, by a strong majority in Parliament, and by his or her party's organization, members, and voters throughout the country; accepted by the main interest groups; criticized—although not sabotaged—by the other major party acting as "loyal opposition" or even supported by it under a coalition agreement; and overwhelmingly supported by public opinion. Such was Prime Minister Winston Churchill's power from June 1940 to July 1945. By contrast, a prime minister is much weaker in a crisis if two of the Cabinet ministers resign, if an appreciable part of the parliamentary party is in revolt, if the opposition party is mounting a major attack, if public opinion in the country is split down the middle, if important member nations of the Commonwealth threaten to secede, and if the major foreign powers oppose his or her policy. This remarkable combination of handicaps confronted Prime Minister Sir Anthony Eden (later Lord Avon) in the Suez crisis of 1956. It was followed by his resignation and by the abandonment of the policy of military intervention that he had espoused.

Information Channels to the Government. Many aspects of the British political system seem designed to make sure that the government will propose only laws and policies that will in fact be widely supported and overwhelmingly obeyed. This is made more likely by the elaborate procedures of public hearings, commissions of enquiry, and confidential consultations with interest groups before any important legislation is introduced and enacted.

One major system of channels of information is composed of the large and well-organized interest groups. On the manufacturing employers' side these comprise the *Confederation of British Industry* (CBI), formed in 1965 through the merger of three small bodies. The CBI now includes 180 trade associations, 12,500 firms, and a highly professional staff of about 300 officials. Merchants, insurance houses, truckers, and the like are organized locally in about 100 chambers of commerce and nationally in the *Association of British Chambers of Commerce* (ABCC), representing about 60,000 firms. Both the CBI and the ABCC are very influential in the shaping of pending legislation and administrative practices. Farmers are organized in the still influential *National Farmers Union* (NFU) with about 200,000 members. A "bosses' trade union," the *Institute of Directors,* has over 40,000 members and looks after the interests of business executives in regard to legislation about corporate taxes, death duties, and the like. Not surprisingly, all these organizations are closest to the Conservatives.

On the side of labor, and allied with the Labour Party, there is the *Trade Union Congress* (TUC) with 10.4 million members, about 39 percent of the work force, and about 95 percent of all union members. Also allied with the Labour Party is the *Cooperative Party,* which is the political arm of over 1,200 cooperative societies and includes about 90 percent of the membership of the *Cooperative Union.* The latter, through its 565 affiliated retail distributive societies, has a total membership of over 12 million and accounts for about 9 percent of national retail sales. The TUC is a major force in the Labour Party, where each member union has a bloc vote corresponding to the size of its membership. Accordingly, the union vote accounts for a large majority of votes at the party's annual convention; and many Labour members of Parliament are sponsored by unions. Compared to the TUC, the Cooperative Party's representation and influence within the Labour Party are considerably smaller.

Professional organizations are less closely linked to either of the major parties. The British Medical Association (BMA) with 84 percent of general practitioners, the National Union of Teachers (NUT) with 85 percent of teachers in state schools, and the National and Local Government Officers' Association negotiate with and put pressure on each party and government in accordance with their understanding of the interests of their members.

Much of the influence of interest groups is exercised through the day-to-day contact with legislators and administrators, the furnishing of detailed information, the representation of viewpoints and of likely responses from the membership and from the general public, and the probable practical response to this or that proposed wording of a law. As a result, most of the legislation introduced by a government has been cleared with all major interest groups before it reaches Parliament; and additional amendments or deletions may be made there in accordance with the desires of some interest groups. Thus, the final act of Parliament is likely to be the result of negotiations and compromises with all major groups.

As in other countries, the power of large, well-financed, and permanently organized groups threatens to overshadow the needs or desires of weaker or less well organized groups. In Britain, however, there has been in recent years a notable increase in the numbers, strength, and activity of *voluntary associations,* founded more or less spontaneously by groups of citizens in order to deal with particular policy issues. Combining the methods of publicity, legislative lobby, endorsement of parties or candidates, and sometimes dramatic, semilegal direct action in the streets, such organizations have had a number of successes. At the start of the 1960s the Campaign for Nuclear Disarmament (CND), advocating unilateral renunciation of nuclear weapons, came close to capturing the Labour Party. In 1970 the Fair Cricket Campaign (FCC) and the Stop-The-Seventies-Tour (STST) brought about the cancellation of a proposed tour by the white South African cricket team, as a protest against the conspicuously discriminatory race policies of that country. The Howard League for Penal Reform was effective in bringing about the abolition of the dealth penalty. The Homosexual

Law Reform Society played a part in the repeal of most of the laws penalizing homosexuality. An organization called SHELTER drew attention to the plight of homeless persons and families. Founded in 1966, it had raised by 1969 about £2 million (about $5 million) and had provided homes for three thousand persons. "In 1960, the first Association for the Advancement of State Education was set up; by 1966 there were 120. . . . In the early sixties, membership in the [long-established] National Union of Students . . . grew rapidly from 150,000 to nearly 400,000." By 1977 they had grown to 700,000 members.[15]

Although, this new activity in an array of voluntary organizations brought a new element into politics, perhaps a counterweight to the bureaucratization of the old established major parties and interest groups.

Local self-assertion merged with a new ethnic self-assertion in a rise of Celtic nationalism. The Scottish National Party had polled less than 1 percent of the vote in Scotland in 1959, but in October 1974 its share of the Scottish vote there rose to almost 31 percent, and it won eleven seats in Parliament. However, it lost almost all of them in 1979 when many of its voters shifted back to Labour. The Welsh Nationalist Party also grew rapidly during the 1960s. In 1974, with 35,000 members, it received 11.1 percent of the vote in Wales and three seats in Parliament. Depending on the votes of these parties, the Labour government proposed schemes of administrative *devolution* for Scotland and Wales, in order to shift an array of powers to assemblies elected by the voters of each country.[16] In 1979 these arrange-

---

[15]Beer, "The British Political System," pp. 320–21; *Directory of British Associations, 1977–78* (Kent, England: C.B.D. Research Ltd., 1977).

[16]Scotland and Wales are called "countries," and athletic events between their teams and England's are called "international" in Britain.

ments were tested by referendum votes in each country. They were rejected by the voters of Wales (only 20 percent of those voting—or just 11 percent of the total electorate—favored devolution), whereas the voters of Scotland evinced no clear preference for or against the proposed scheme (52 percent voted yes, constituting only 34 percent of the electorate). This was followed by significant losses of support for both nationalist parties in the 1979 general election. The Scottish National Party lost nine of its eleven seats, as its share of the Scottish vote dropped by half (to 16 percent); and the Welsh Nationalist Party lost one of its three seats, taking only 8.1 percent of the vote in Wales. Whether these results signal the ebbing of ethnic self-assertion in Great Britain or merely a temporary downswing remains to be seen.

Another system of information channels is offered by Parliament itself. Members of Parliament come from over six hundred constituencies, each small enough to permit them to remain in touch with local opinion. Within each constituency there is, as a rule, at least one local organization of each of the two major parties, and in many constituencies there are local party agents on an honorary or professional basis. These parties and agents transmit local views and concerns not only to the sitting member of Parliament, but also to the national headquarters of their party. Each MP, in turn, has the right to direct *questions in Parliament* to the government and to particular ministers in it; and the government is obligated to furnish an answer in the House of Commons, before an audience of MPs who do not take kindly to evasions. In this manner, specific cases of alleged wrong done to some individual can be raised, as well as larger questions of administrative practice and public policy. The weekly question period in the Commons gets wide attention from the public and the press, and political reputations have been made or broken through the manner in which ministers answered the questions put to them in Parliament.

The practices about which the ministers are

likely to be questioned in this manner are most often those of the civil service; and it is the civil servants in the minister's department who are responsible for briefing their minister on the answers.

A Continuing Support: The Civil Service. The cohesion and effectiveness of the British government are provided by the civil service. Relatively new in British history, the civil service is a child of the great liberal reforms of the nineteenth century. Earlier, many offices, including commissions in the army, were sold for cash. Private companies, such as the East India Company until 1857, governed large territories through their employees.

When the inefficiencies of the old system became intolerable at home as well as in the colonies, the civil service system took its place. Its members were recruited by open competitive examinations and were to be promoted strictly on the grounds of merit, in contrast to the old practices of patronage and bribery. The civil service thus became a channel for the rise of many of the brightest sons of the British middle classes—even though civil servants with an upper-class background tended to have a better chance to reach its highest levels. For nearly a century British civil servants ran the empire; after 1945 they superintended its replacement by new independent nations.

In the British system, civil servants are expected to remain politically neutral. With equal efficiency they are to serve Conservative ministers in encouraging private enterprise and Labour ministers in nationalizing it. In exchange for such political self-denial they enjoy permanence of tenure. Ministers come and go, but the permanent undersecretaries in their ministries remain. In practice this often means that the policy of the ministries also remains constant, and only the minister's signature changes. From their long experience, civil servants in each department of the government develop "the departmental view," which no minister will override lightly. To this extent the civil servants—most notably those of the

Treasury—actually govern the country.[17] (This practice, as we recall, contrasts with the arrangements in the United States under which a large number of top-level federal jobs are defined as policy making, to be staffed and restaffed at the discretion of each president.)

Though civil servants are influential and respected, their real income has declined. In 1975 their salaries bought only about three-quarters of what they had bought in 1938 when the Great Depression had kept goods and services cheap. These workers, too, in increasing numbers are choosing the path of militant unionism and the weapon of the strike. In late February 1979 a strike by 1,300 civil servants, including code clerks, computer operators, court clerks, and airport customs officials, provoked the conservative *Daily Telegraph* to the sensational statement that civil servants "have declared war on the government"; this remark then was duly headlined in the American press.[18] The civil servants may have a just grievance, and so may the public for being deprived of their services. In the end, both sides probably will succeed in keeping their tempers, and Britain will muddle through to another tolerable compromise solution.

New Institutions: Mixed Boards and Public Corporations.

Civil servants in Britain work well not only with politicans and fellow bureaucrats, but also with businesspeople, trade union leaders, scientists, and technicans. They do so on numerous *mixed boards*, of which the London Passenger Transport Board is an early and successful example. Set up in 1933 by a Conservative government, this board, now called the London Transport Executive, brings together representatives of the government, the county of London, and the former private subway, bus, and streetcar companies that were merged into a single transport system for greater London. The system is managed by the board, which plans new lines, construction, and investments and sets the rates and conditions for service. It also acts as a board of directors, appointing managers and supervising their work.

Boards of this type straddle the line between public and private enterprise. They are expected to look out for the interests of stockholders and bondholders, thousands of employees, and millions of passengers or other consumers and also for the interests of the cities and of national development. Similar boards function in other countries, such as the Port Authority of New York and New Jersey in the United States and the Northeast Swiss Power Stations in Switzerland. Britain, however, has gone furthest in developing this type of organization. Judging from the quality of London transport, which is clean, fast, dependable, and very pleasant to ride, the system has been a success.

Another successful type of mixed authority, linking a plurality of public bodies, is the *University Grants Committee*. This body brings civil servants together with representatives of the universities for the purpose of distributing government subsidies among the universities in a way that protects both the institutions and their scholars from political pressures.

Finally, Britain has created a whole series of *public corporations* to manage various publicly owned services. These, too, provide for the representation of several public organizations and interests. They range from the British Broadcasting Corporation (BBC) and British Airways Corporation (BA), both set up by Conservative governments before World War II, to such creations of Labour governments as the National Coal Board, the Electricity Generating Board, and the Electricity Council. In 1967 the Labour government set up an Industrial Reorganization Corporation with

[17]Many of them are trained at Oxford or Cambridge. Loyal members of the latter university are fond of saying, "Oxford may speak for England, but Cambridge runs it."
[18]"Civil Servants 'Declare War' in Britain," *Boston Globe*, February 26, 1979, p. 4.

$360 million capital to stimulate mergers in private industry; and the Land Commission was created to buy land for public purposes. Like the civil service, these various organizational devices contribute an array of stable machinery to aid the government in meeting its growing responsibilities, and this general trend is likely to continue under either major party.

ACCOMPLISHMENTS AND UNFINISHED BUSINESS: AN INTERIM SCORE

In the generation in which 500 million people have become independent from British rule, the average Englishman has grown one inch taller than his father. The British people also have become better educated, better nourished, better housed, and longer lived.[19] Polls show the greater popularity of the National Health Service, and both major parties vie in promising to improve it further. With less than half of the per capita income of the United States, British life expectancy is higher.

Today Americans read in their newspapers mostly of the things that Britain has not done or that are difficult for it—much as the British are informed mainly about America's worst foibles, follies, and sometimes tragedies. Americans do not read of the things that Britain has accomplished. The jet engine is a British invention. The decisive tube that made radar possible was brought from Britain to the United States by Sir Henry Tizard in World War II. Penicillin is a British contribution. In the mid-1960s eighteen Nobel Prize winners

were teaching at Cambridge University alone. Britain, as we saw, is ahead of the United States in new towns and town planning, in national health services, and in the large-scale use of nuclear energy for peaceful purposes. The British have doubled enrollment in their universities, as have the Americans. They have kept a good deal of their high quality work still going, better than in the United States, and they have struggled with many of their problems more successfully. Although they have their problems with racial differences, they are developing legal instruments to fight discrimination. After a long period of rigidity, they now have more humane laws about drugs and homosexuality than in the United States and yet have a much lower crime rate. Their streets are cleaner and safer. What they often lack in science and technology is large-scale application. Very often an invention is developed in England and applied in the United States.

This slowness in applying innovations on a large scale seems due at least as much to the attitude of managers and investors as to labor's distrust of innovations that might eliminate some existing jobs. There is a general reluctance to make large investments in new equipment and facilities, both in the private and in the public sectors. The main circular road around London, the airport at Heathrow, the construction of a large number of modern office buildings and apartment houses— all these projects seem well behind in London, compared with their counterparts that have been completed or are under construction in Paris. Statistics confirm this picture. The British per capita income is lagging well behind that of France or West Germany and shows no signs of catching up. The traditional movements of British politics—the pendulum swings between and within parties—have not worked well in coping with the nation's economic problems. It seems as if the British government has found it easier to develop constructive working relationships with foreign colonial peoples than with the powerful economic interests in its own island.

[19]Deaths of infants under one year old, per 1,000 live births in the United Kingdom, numbered 150 in 1870–72; 110 in 1910–12; and 67 in 1930–32. In 1942 the death rate was 53, but in 1952 it had been reduced to 29 and in 1968 to 19. In less than one century, it had thus been cut by seven-eights. About 800,000 children were born each year in 1870–72 and again in 1968. But in the latter year, more than 100,000 children's lives were saved in comparison to the earlier period (Ryder and Silver, pp. 143, 311, 314).

The Search for Partnership Abroad. After the 1890s a British-American alliance began to grow, and in World War II it reached its peak. As late as 1949, American and British pilots flew their planes side by side to break Stalin's blockade of Berlin, and still later, a British brigade fought alongside United States troops in the Korean War. But although the two countries remained allied (with fourteen others) in the North Atlantic Treaty Organization (NATO), the "special relationship" of Britain and the United States faded in the 1950s.

By the 1960s United States leaders were paying little attention to their British allies, who were told of completed American policy decisions rather than being consulted about them in advance. Since the decisions involved matters of life and death for both countries, as in the Cuban crisis of 1962, the British were unenthusiastic about their new state of dependence. "Annihilation without representation," as the British historian Arnold Toynbee said earlier, "is unfair." At present, Britain still needs the alliance with the United States, but it also needs to regain a greater sense of equality and independence—a greater measure of control over its own fate.

The ties to the Commonwealth cannot give Britain this power. The Commonwealth countries that are predominantly white—Canada, Australia, and New Zealand—continue to accept British exports, immigrants, and capital on favorable terms and to supply Britain with cheaper food and raw materials to the extent that the transitional arrangements after Britain's entry into the Common Market in 1973 permit them to do so. The nonwhite Commonwealth nations, from Bangladesh to Jamaica, furnish Britain with cheap labor and an increase in racial and housing problems within the limits of Britain's tightening legislative and administrative curbs on immigration. South Africa furnishes some gold transactions, useful to the ailing British currency, at the price of grave political conflict over South African racial discrimination. But all these ties are no longer adequate.

On balance, Commonwealth relations are becoming, to most of the British, a matter of the past more than of the future.

Yet Britain cannot see any promise in a policy of isolation. It has sought, therefore, to tie its economy, and perhaps in time its politics, to those of Western Europe. Such a policy of *European integration* may sound fine in general, but has become awkward in specifics. Joining the European Common Market may mean higher food prices for British consumers, sharper competition for British industry and labor, and less freedom of decision for British voters and their government. Even though Britain has belonged to the Common Market since 1973, many of these problems are nowhere near solution. Britain's new role in European and world affairs still has to be defined.

Some Enduring Assets. Britain's agenda for change seems impressive, but so are the nation's resources. The economic growth rate, the balance between exports and imports, inflation and the value of the pound, the process of planning for rapid technological progress, the removal of class or caste lines, the balanced growth of science and the humanities and the integration of these "two cultures"—all are weak points in Britain. Yet in a very important way, Britain has managed to be innovative and still remain cohesive. It can function under tremendous strains, as it did in the Battle of Britain in 1940, and it can come up with new and sometimes very surprising ideas. New ideas and new dreams still are being generated in British universities. On the level of recent popular culture, young Britons gave the world much of the early hippie movement, the Beatles' contribution to rock and roll, and the miniskirt.

The British people's strange and happy combination of tremendous persistence and unceasing inventiveness—their insistence on being both innovative and coherent—suggests that their social and political system may repay deeper study. The British are trying to build a new social order while keeping much of their old culture and habits. This may seem impossible to do, but the British are not likely to stop trying. Though they will be harder to imitate than most other nations, the world can still learn from them.

KEY TERMS AND CONCEPTS

public schools
establishment
deference
four-layer culture
wildcat strikes
Celts
Saxons
Normans
exchequer
common law
institution
tradition of enquiry
Domesday Book
Magna Carta
Royal Commission
gentleman
law of primogeniture
member of Parliament
burgher
cross-class coalition
the Crown
divine right theory
roundheads
cavaliers
revolution
parliamentary government
House of Lords
House of Commons
Cabinet
party discipline
Whigs
Tories
Conservative Party
Liberals
Labour Party
parliamentary party

national party
whips
free votes
prime minister
Orange Order
Reform Bill of 1832
imperialism
Commonwealth
dominion status
nationalization of industries
National Health Service
the two-party pendulum
incomes policy
industrial relations policy
social contract
swing
dealignment
European Common Market
productivity
universalism versus selectivity in social services
service occupations and nonwhite immigrants
Ulster
Trade Union Congress
voluntary associations
devolution
questions in Parliament
mixed boards
University Grants Committee
public corporations
European integration

ADDITIONAL READINGS

Beer, S. H. "The British Political System." In S. H. Beer and A. Ulam, eds. *Patterns of Government: The Major Political Systems of Europe.* 3rd ed. New York: Random House, 1974. PB
————. *British Politics in a Collectivist Age.* Rev. ed. New York: Random House (Vintage), 1980. Note especially last chapter. PB
Blondel, J. *Voters, Parties and Leaders.* Harmondsworth, England: Penguin Books, 1963. PB
Butler, D., and D. Kavanagh, *The British General*

Election of October 1974. London: Macmillan & Co., 1975.

Butler, D., and J. Freeman, *British Political Facts, 1900–1968.* 3rd ed. New York: St. Martin's, 1968.

Butler, D., and M. Pinto-Duschinsky. *The British General Election of 1970.* London: Macmillan & Co., 1971.

Butler, D., and D. Stokes. *Political Change in Britain: Forces Shaping Electoral Choice.* 2nd ed. New York: St. Martin's, 1976. PB

Cole, G. D. H., and R. Postgate. *British Common People, 1745–1945.* London: Methuen, 1965. PB

Finer, S. *Anonymous Empire,* 2nd ed. London: Pall Mall Press, 1966. PB

———, and M. Steed. "Politics in Britain." In R. C. Macridis, ed., *Modern Political Systems: Europe.* 4th ed. Englewood Cliffs, N.J.: Prentice-Hall, 1978.

Halsey, A. H. *Change in British Society.* Oxford: Oxford University Press, 1978.

Heclo, H., and A. Wildavsky, *The Private Government of Public Money.* 2nd ed. London: Macmillan & Co., 1980.

MacInnis, C. *Cry of Spades.* London: MacGibbon and Kee, 1958. PB

Mackenzie, R. T. *British Political Parties.* 2nd ed. New York: Praeger, 1964.

Osborne, J. *Look Back in Anger.* New York: Bantam, 1967. PB

Rose, R. *Governing Without Consensus: An Irish Perspective.* Boston: Beacon Press, 1971. PB

———. *Politics in England.* 3rd ed. Boston: Little, Brown, 1980. PB

Russell, B. *Autobiography.* 2 vols. Boston: Atlantic–Little, Brown, 1967 and 1968. PB

Ryder, J., and H. Silver. *Modern English Society: History and Structure, 1850–1970.* New York: Barnes and Noble, 1977. PB

Sampson, A. *The New Anatomy of Britain.* New York: Stein and Day, 1973. PB

Sillitoe, A. *Saturday Night and Sunday Morning.* New York: New American Library, 1973. PB

Stewart, M. *The Jekyll and Hyde Years: Politics and Economic Policy Since 1964.* Totwa, N.J.: Rowman and Littlefield, 1977.

Titmuss, R. M. *Commitment to Welfare.* Winchester, Mass.: Allen and Unwin, 1976.

Verney, D. V. *British Government and Politics: Life Without a Declaration of Independence.* New York: Harper & Row, 1976. PB

Wilson, H. *The Labour Government, 1964–1970.* London: Penguin, 1974. PB

PB = *available in paperback*

V

France

For centuries the French people have dazzled and baffled their neighbors. They have acquired so many reputations that almost everyone has an image of the French, but the different images do not easily fit together.

THE MANY IMAGES OF FRANCE

Perhaps the best-known image of the French between 1789 and 1960 has been one of individualism, unrest, ceaseless change, and infinite variety. "Two Frenchmen are a political party," goes an old saying, "and three Frenchmen are a constitutional crisis." Even the French have wondered about themselves. Asked President de Gaulle, "How can you govern a country that has 247 kinds of cheese?"

Time and again in the last two centuries French governments have fallen by revolution. Even in periods of constitutional government, change has been the rule, not the exception. During the period from 1945 to 1961 the average tenure of a French chief executive was eight months. Some foreign observers were tempted to think that if one did not like a particular French government, one had only to wait a while, but a French proverb seemed even more accurate: the more it changes, the more it stays the same. Yet this first picture may now be out of date. After 1958 French politics seemed to become remarkably stable. President de Gaulle stayed in office for eleven years; and his successor, Georges Pompidou, held office for almost five years, until his death in April 1974. Pompidou's successor, Valéry Giscard d'Estaing, by 1980 had completed the first six years of his seven-year term, still representing the same majority coalition of moderate-to-conservative parties.

An entirely different image is that of the orderly French. This image sees the French as precise, logical, and bureaucratic. Indeed, their public gardens appear to have been designed with ruler and compass, as long, straight vistas emerge between shrubs and trees that have been neatly clipped into shape. Their scholars are famous for close "explications of texts," their thinkers for bold Cartesian logic,[1] their writers for lucidity. Their provincial middle classes are known for their conservatism and the housewives and *rentiers*— people who live on fixed incomes from pensions or investments—for their thrift.

A third image focuses on the segmentation of French life. The French put many things into compartments, including themselves. Individuals tend to join mostly those voluntary associations that fit their own social group, in contrast to Americans, whose associations tend to cut across such boundaries. The "typical" French landscape, observes Geoffrey Gorer, "is divided into contrasting segments . . . modified by human handiwork. The world of ideas is similarly compartmentalized. . . ." In such compartments, lives can be led in lonely privacy, and distrust of one's fellow citizens flourishes. "In no other country," says André Siegfried, "can one feel so utterly alone as in France where people barricade themselves in their homes as if they were fortresses." Neither the charms of French conversation in salons and cafés nor the eloquence of French orators and writers can overcome the divisions separating individuals from individuals and groups from groups.

A fourth image pictures the French as a nation of doubters. A medieval French monk, Peter Abelard, invented the scholastic method of reasoning, which lines up contradictory authorities on both sides of every question. Centuries later,

Descartes introduced the Cartesian technique: to doubt everything as deeply as possible, so that only the simplest and most self-evident propositions will survive. And the skeptical smile on the death mask of Voltaire, the great satirist who made such merciless fun of tyrannies, follies, and dogmas of his time, was called "the smile of France" by the writer Victor Hugo.

A fifth image dwells on French elegance and taste, imagination and creativity. France has long furnished the models for both designer clothing and ideas. In the arts, from modern painting to motion pictures, France has given the world the word and concept of *avant-garde*—the vanguard that does today what slower folk will do tomorrow. French technological pioneering since 1945 is reflected in such well-known jet aircraft as the Caravelle, the supersonic fighter plane Mirage, and the supersonic intercontinental passenger plane Concorde, which was developed jointly with Britain. Other examples are the innovative automobile Citröen DS 21 and the exploration of the underwater world by Jacques Cousteau. French thinkers have excelled not only in their logic, but also in what the mathematician Pascal called the *esprit de finesse,* the spirit of subtlety that lives on among French scientists and existentialist philosophers.

A related image portrays France as the country of the good life. "To live like God in France" is a wistful German phrase for the utmost in well-being. The French gourmet is a renowned expert on good food and wine, and French has long been the language of love, even for some English and German writers.

A final image of the French is one of courage, loyalty and pride. From the Crusades and Joan of Arc to the Battle of Verdun in World War I and the underground Resistance in World War II, this tradition has stayed alive.

Each of these images is one-sided and somewhat overdrawn, yet each contains some truth. Taken together, they tell us something of France's com-

[1]The term is derived from the name of the French philosopher René Descartes (1596–1650), who has been widely considered the chief representative of the French intellectual tradition. Similarly, Georg Wilhelm Hegel (1770–1831) has been seen as typical of German thought, Giambattista Vico (1668–1744) of Italian ideas, Jeremy Bentham (1748–1832) of the British empirical tradition, and Thomas Jefferson (1743–1826) of the wide-ranging thought of the United States. However, no one person can completely represent the style of thought of an entire country.

plexity and of its capacity to produce surprises. How has one people acquired so many reputations, and how do all these traits work together in a single political system?

The French themselves have sometimes wondered which is the real France. Some of their writers have stressed the distinction between *le pays légal*, the legal France, divided by disputes about politics and laws, and *le pays réel*, the real country, held together by a profound unity of tradition and culture. If we are to find this real country, then, history must help us seek the answer.

The Heritage of Central Monarchy.

The French were the first people on the Continent—and, after England, the second in Europe—to achieve a modern absolute monarchy for a large territorial state. Their centralized government was a work of art, will, and ruthless power. The English got their unified monarchy a little earlier, but as late as the fifteenth century, two kings were fighting each other for England's one crown. England was not yet well centralized in the 1470s when Louis XI and his equally absolutist successors were putting France together. The first task of the English state was to consolidate a foreign conquest—that of England by the Normans. The first task of the French state was to prevent a foreign conquest—that of France by the English. A period of unscrupulousness was necessary for the successful completion of this task, but its rulers' politics of organized murder and cruelty eventually gave France a higher degree of civic peace, unity, and power than other countries in Europe had at that time.

The Weakness of Self-Government in the Cities.

One decisive choice was made by the French, perhaps unconsciously. The French cities, feeling too weak to balance the power of the nobles and the countryside, backed the king and central monarchy. They did so to the point of yielding much of their powers of self-government to the royal administration. As a result, France has had less of a tradition of decentralized, urban self-government than has Germany or England. For backing the king, the bourgeois of the French cities won much of what they had hoped to receive from him: security, order, and protection for their businesses.[2]

By 1630 the French monarchy had obtained wide support. In many other countries, such as Germany, the church opposed a strong central government. But in France and Spain it backed central government that, in turn, supported Roman Catholicism as the national religion. After the Reformation many of the more independent-minded cities and nobles became Protestant. When they were defeated by the Catholics in alliance with the monarchy, local and provincial self-government was defeated, too.

Continuing Centralization.

The church in the France of the seventeenth century was led by a political genius, Cardinal de Richelieu, one of the great practitioners of power politics of all time. It was Richelieu who conceived the idea that the main interest of Catholic France was to destroy the power of Catholic Spain. This could be done best, he felt, through intervening in the war between Protestants and Catholics in Germany, where the Hapsburgs were uniting the resources of Austria and Spain on the Catholic side. If the French Catholic king would back the Protestant king of

---

[2]In exceptional situations when the burghers of a city tried to cling to self-government, they were mercilessly suppressed. In the sixteenth century the city of Bordeaux (which had been English for a time and had less of a tradition of submission to the French crown) rose in defense of its ancient liberties. A royal army besieged the city and forced its capitulation. When the burghers killed a representative of the king, the royal army beheaded the civil consul in retaliation. The consul, who was executed for vindicating the rights of the citizens against the king, had an interesting name: Guillotin. He was beheaded by hand. More than two centuries later, another man named Guillotin, a doctor of medicine, developed a machine for beheading people that would make the process faster, more reliable, and, he thought, more humanitarian; in the French Revolution his invention was applied to the king and many nobles.

MAP 5.1 *France*

Sweden with money and persuade him to intervene on the Protestant side in Germany, these actions would weaken the Hapsburgs. Richelieu's maneuver succeeded brilliantly. The Swedes invaded Germany, and the Protestants and Catholics fought each other to a standstill. By 1648 two-fifths of the German people—8 million out of 20 million—had perished.

For Germany and central Europe the hundred-year period after 1620 was a century of devastation and decline. In French history books, however, this period is called *Le Grand Siècle*—The Great Century. During these years France became the leading power of Europe, and the fruits of Richelieu's work were reaped by Louis XIV—the king who so simply said, "The state—that is I." From about 1680 to 1780, France was the most brilliant, the richest, and the leading country of Europe, losing to England on the high seas but outshining all nations in most other respects. Throughout this period it remained predominant both as a power and as a model of official culture and elite behavior on the Continent.

Within France, Louis XIV broke the last resistance of the provincial nobles and at the same time laid the foundations of French leadership in taste and fashion. He built the most splendid palace of his time at Versailles and made the nobles reside there. He thus turned noblemen into courtiers. Far from their estates in the provinces, they had less power and were more dependent on the favor of the king. At court they were amost constantly in each other's company, and they were encouraged to compete not only in court intrigues and love affairs, but also in luxury and elegance. Court taste and court speech became the single standard for the nation. The results of this centralization have never been reversed. Isolated at Versailles, the nobles became assimilated in a common style of life and thought, but estranged from most of the rest of France. The legacy of this class division has lingered, too.

Even today, after the French monarchy has been swept away by a chain of revolutions, its heritage lives on. French administration has remained highly centralized, as authority flows from the top down. So has French culture. Paris is still the center of almost everything that is important in France—the arts, sciences, mass media, education, business, finance, and politics. Messages and ideas from the provinces count for little, unless their proponents move to Paris first.

In France a relatively modern centralized state was established before the Industrial Revolution and before any political middle-class revolution like those in England and the United States. Later, the effects of the French Revolution and the Napoleonic age further strengthened the power of the state and its machinery, modernizing it somewhat by increasing its claims to legitimacy and popular support. The result was a strong bureaucratic state that remained somewhat authoritarian in its dealings with its people and somewhat remote from them.

The Distance Between Government and People.

Communications also move most often from the top down. They flow from government to the bureaucracy; from bureaucrats and party leaders to the people; from professors to students; and from Parisian designers and avant-garde artists to consumers. Little information, if any, flows upward in return.

The little people—workers, peasants, shopkeepers, taxpayers, soldiers, and voters—may resent this situation, but they are unlikely to be heard or heeded. The best they can do is to build defenses for themselves. They defend their individuality and their privacy. They distrust all government. If government is far away, they prefer to keep it there. They limit its power legally whenever they can; and they evade it at every opportunity. Voltaire expressed the attitude of many French citizens in classic form when, in the face of the powerful central monarchy, he quietly announced that he was going home to "cultivate his garden," that is, withdraw to private life.

Millions of French people are still doing so, at least in a figurative sense. They keep out of the political debate in ordinary times and, thus, make the moderate center of political opinion seem weaker than it is. But they return to political activity when stirred by unusual events, making politics in France—as shown in Figure 5.1—often more exciting and less predictable than anywhere else.

The Heritage of Revolution. It is hard to imagine just how rigid the French monarch and social system had become by the 1780s and how long it took to gather the forces that were to transform France and, in due time, the world. In 1789, France finally exploded in revolution. The French did not revolt against Louis XV, a bad ruler, but rose against Louis XVI, who was no worse than eighteenth-century monarchs generally were. If France could not be governed under a ruler of Louis XVI's quality, then something was fundamentally wrong with the system and it would have to be changed. In this sense the revolts against Charles I of England and Louis XVI of France involved the same need: to change a system, not a ruler.

From the king on down, the French people then showed another trait that has endured—their resistance to compromise. After the English revolution and the return of the monarchy, even Charles II accepted a bill of rights voted by Parliament. James II was driven out when he refused to compromise further; and two years later England got another monarch, William of Orange, whose reign led to the Act of Toleration. In the end the English monarchy gave in gracefully to the need for making concessions to the demands for constitutional government. The Bourbon kings of France were different. Of them it was said then and later that they never forgot and they never learned.

The French tried to establish a constitutional monarchy in 1791 with Louis XVI as monarch. But Louis refused to accept any constitutional limits to his power. He secretly corresponded with other absolute rulers of Europe (some of whom were his relatives) to persuade them to make war against France and restore full power to him. The correspondence was discovered and the king put on trial as a traitor before the National Assembly. Maximilien de Robespierre, the radical leader of the Jacobin Party,[3] displaying brilliant French logic, made the decisive point for the prosecution. If the king were innocent, he pointed out, then he was by the grace of God the absolute king of France; he had rightfully tried to organize the subjection of his rebellious subjects; and those sitting in the assembly were themselves rebels and traitors who ought to be beheaded. If, on the other hand, the assembly were truly representative of the French nation, then the king was a traitor to his country and it was he who had to be beheaded. Accepting this logic, the members of the assembly voted predictably. The king was beheaded and the *First Republic* established.

In this case logic was used to prevent compromise rather than permit it. This tactic revealed its greatness and strength as well as its long-run one-sidedness in the events that followed. Six European countries invaded France after the king's execution in 1793. But the war had already been started by the moderate Girondist government of France, which had come to power under the First Republic in 1792.[4] It had started the war in the hope that a foreign war would increase national unity. The Girondists turned out to be grievously mistaken and perished for their folly. They started a war that they could not conduct successfully, yet that became vital to the French people once it had begun. The Jacobins, the most radical middle-class leaders, took power under

---

[3]The *Jacobins* were the main radical party of the French Revolution. Centered in Paris, they got their name from one of their early meeting places, a former monastery of Saint James, whom the French called Saint Jacques (i.e., Saint Jacob). Their ranks included members of the prosperous middle class as well as professional people and poor artisans.

[4]The *Girondists* became the main moderate party of the revolution by 1792. Strongest in the provinces, they were named after the Gironde, a fertile plain in southern France. Their members included the well-to-do of the smaller towns.

FIGURE 5·1 *Twelve French Political Regimes, 1788–1978*

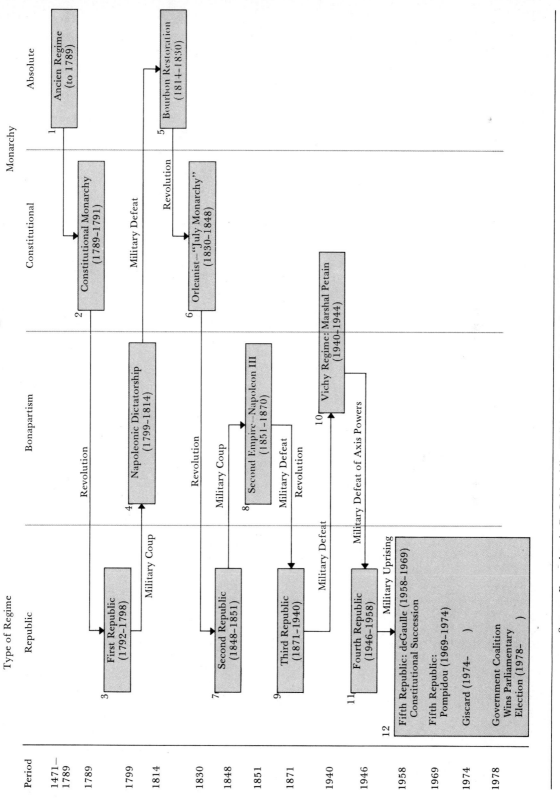

Source: From data in R. C. Macridis, "Politics of France," in *Modern Political Systems: Europe*, 4th ed., by Roy C. Macridis, c. 1978, p. 99. Adapted by permission of Prentice-Hall, Inc., Englewood Cliffs, N.J.

Robespierre in 1793 and mobilized the entire French nation.

The Nation in Arms. In one year France brought 1.3 million men under arms in fourteen armies and thereby changed the scale of warfare in Europe. This could not possibly have been done by an unpopular draft. The only way of getting 5 percent of the French people into uniform was through the voluntary support of large numbers of the French people. This support made possible the enforcement of the laws of the Republic. It seemed as if Rousseau's "general will" had taken armed shape. Robespierre and the Jacobins seemed to be executing his ideas. Backed by a large part of the people, they were forcing the French populace to be "free." They did so with relentless logic and frequent cruelty. The city of Lyon rose against the central government and was destroyed by a republican army. The general in charge reported back to Paris, "Lyon rose against the Republic. Lyon is no more."

Revolutionary France was marked by extremism of all sorts. The conservatives thought the republicans mad. The republicans, in turn, thought the conservatives to be walking corpses, people of the dead past. Each side felt that its opponents had no right to live. For a time there was a law that made it a crime to fall under suspicion.

If divisiveness and intolerance were extreme, so too were the heroism and efforts of the people. The Parisians descended to the cellars of Paris to scrape saltpeter deposits from the walls to get enough ammunition to blast the armies of the European monarchs out of France. In Paris alone, there were 243 open-air forges to make cast-iron cannon. The revolution produced the first massed artillery that would later make Napoleon's military reputation.

The French soldiers fought with high morale; they did not run away in the field or in battle. Unlike the involuntary soldiers of the European monarchs, they did not need to fight in conspicuous uniforms and to march in close order into enemy fire so that their sergeants could keep an eye on them. The French soldiers fought against the royal armies in open skirmish lines, firing from whatever cover they found, and then attacked in massed columns. They won, and in the process they changed the art of war in their epoch.

The Politics of Revolution. But though they won foreign battles, they could not agree on how to run France. Not all the French favored the revolution. Not only aristocrats but also many of their servants, friends, or more loyal peasant subjects bitterly opposed the republican regime. The republican government tried to crush all resistance by public execution in a deliberate campaign of *terror*—much as the Bourbon kings had publicly executed those who resisted them or defied their laws. But soon the revolutionists turned against one another with the same ruthlessness that they had used against their enemies.

The Republic introduced rigid price controls to help the poor, which then turned the middle class (which had been part of the original Jacobin movement) against the more radical Jacobins. The very radical Jacobins—"the enraged," as they were called—also rose against the more moderate radicals, as the very conservative Jacobins had.

Robespierre thus had to fight enemies on both flanks. At first he used the radicals to behead the moderates. Then he used the surviving moderates to destroy the radicals. Danton on his right and Hébert on his left both died under the guillotine. But soon Robespierre himself was attacked and put to death by those who feared that their own gains from the revolution might now be in danger.

Robespierre had not been an extreme terrorist. In fact, he had cut down the executions in the provinces, brought all the trials to Paris, and reduced the indiscriminate killing. But when he was sentenced and executed, the whole responsibility for the terror was put on him even by those who themselves had led executions. When one provincial leader of the terror, who had voted against Robespierre, was reminded in the French assembly of his own share in the killings, he looked straight at his colleagues and answered, "Robespierre's grave is big enough to bury our differences in."

There followed a period of domestic relaxation and corruption, called *Thermidor,* and a period of government by five directors. Under this regime, called the *Directory,* the call rose for more freedom for speculators and for more law and order against the poor. The foreign wars continued. Quietly, the nation was getting ready to hand over its problems to a general.

The General Who Set a Precedent. The French in times of crisis have tended to turn to a general as their savior—Cavaignac in 1848; MacMahon in 1875; Foch in 1914; Pétain in 1940; de Gaulle in 1940, 1944, and 1958. But more than once they lived to regret it. The general who began this precedent was a young Corsican, Napoleon Bonaparte. As a Corsican, he understood revolutions well because Corsica had had its own revolution against Genoa, which had ended only when the island became French in 1768. By 1798, Napoleon's mastery of French was rapidly improving, though he still spoke it with an Italian accent. Earlier, he had helped the Directory come to power by beating down the last radical flare-up in Paris. He had then won a victorious campaign in Italy that had made him a popular hero. Now in 1798, he made himself master of the Republic. It was an inside job, done with the help of some members of the government; two of the five directors helped bring about Napoleon's seizure of power. This occurred on the famous *eighteenth of Brumaire,* as the date was called in the French revolutionary calendar.

By 1800, Napoleon had made himself consul and the dictatorship had been formalized. In 1804 he had himself crowned emperor of the *First Empire.* At his coronation Napoleon took the crown out of the pope's hands and put it on his own head. Napoleon's vast self-confidence kept growing, while his judgment worsened. Like other rulers of great power, he lost critics and gained "yes men."

He led France into an unending series of wars—and ultimate disaster. After his fall there was a revulsion against war in France and much of Europe. This made it possible to restore many of the old dynasties throughout Europe, including the Bourbons in France. People wanted quiet. There followed a period of withdrawal to family life and of distrust of politics.

More Revolutions, More Generals. The next generation rose again in revolution in 1830. France became a liberal monarchy. The subversive colors of red, white, and blue became official once again and replaced the lily of the Bourbons. The new constitutional monarchy advised the middle classes: "Enrich yourselves, gentlemen!" And they did, abundantly.

The next wave of revolution swept through France in 1848. It included the poor, the lower middle class, and the working class, many of whom felt that they were becoming not richer, but poorer. The *Second Republic* was set up, but the 1848 uprisings promptly produced a split between labor and the middle classes. The middle classes rallied to a new general, Cavaignac, who led the bloody suppression of the labor revolt in Paris. In 1851 the conservative, military republic was replaced by a new monarchy—the *Second Empire* under Napoleon III, the first Napoleon's nephew.

The Second Empire lasted twenty years. It was marked by speculative prosperity, demagogy, minor foreign wars, and domination of the legislature by an imperial executive. Ultimately, the Second Empire led France into a big war that ended disastrously with a total Prussian victory. Once again Paris rose, this time with the first labor government, the communist-anarchist–oriented *Paris Commune,* which established itself for a few weeks in 1870 before being beaten down by soldiers from the rest of France, most of them peasant sons in uniform. More than ten thousand workers were killed on the barricades and in the Paris streets they blocked; the Paris Commune, like the year 1848, entered the collective memory of the political left as a symbol of working-class heroism and government repression. The other France, the conservative France, had asserted its power. All subsequent French regimes show marks of its influence and the distrust between the political left and right in the nation.

The France That Resists Change. France has produced many revolutions and many conservative reactions. Its revolutions flare up in Paris and a few other big cities and industrial areas. Its conservatism is supported by wealthy minorities in these centers, but draws its main strength from the small towns and the countryside.

More Proprietors, Fewer Babies. After 1800, French peasants became patriotic and conservative. It is this France that used to change slowly, that still furnishes many officers and soldiers, and that has given the nation its reputation for conservatism. The French Revolution, by making the peasants proprietors, had given them something to conserve. The revolution was followed by a long slowdown in the growth of population. It may be that the new property laws had an effect on the number of new babies. The revolutionary laws of the Jacobins abolished feudalism and gave the peasants land. These laws, later organized into a systematic legal code by Napoleon, also declared that all brothers in a family had the same right to their father's land, and therefore a farm had to be divided among all sons. But the more sons, the smaller piece of land would remain for each and the poorer each would be. If a peasant did not want his land to be divided and his sons impoverished, he had to limit their number. Many peasants took to marrying later in life; those who already knew methods of birth control now had a stronger motive to practice it; and those who did not know now had a motive to learn.

Throughout much of the next 140 years the population of France grew more slowly than that of any other major country. The practice of birth control had begun in the last years of the Bour-

bons, but the population slowdown proceeded under all forms of French government in the nineteenth century, and there was a further slowdown after 1870. In 1789, the French population, at 26 million, had been the largest in Europe (excepting Russia). By 1913 it had climbed to only 40 million and stood at 53 million in 1978, a figure that had long ago been exceeded by Britain, Germany, and Italy. Limiting the growth of population proved conservative in its effects; it preserved more of the status quo.

France is still one of the more slowly growing countries in the world, but it is now one of the faster growing countries of Europe. More recent laws subsidize babies through family allowances. Also, fewer people live on farms or have an inheritance of land to conserve. Now, as in the past, legislation must come together with a change in human motives if the habits of millions of people are to be changed. In France customs changed slowly until the mid-1960s; but since then, changes in many aspects of life have accelerated. By 1980 these changes had not yet found any major expression in the political system; but as they continue to accumulate, the pressures on the political system will be growing also, and political adjustments are quite likely to occur within the next decade.

Conservative Social and Economic Practices. Throughout the nineteenth and early twentieth centuries the French social structure underwent little change. With more peasant proprietors, more people stayed in the country than streamed into the cities. Fewer people moved into industry. To this day, the proportions of industrial workers, of city dwellers, and of wage and salary earners all are lower in France than in West Germany or Britain (see Table 5.1).

Thus, the proclivities of French peasants to stay where their parents had been, and where they liked it, went together with the proclivities of the French middle class to slow down the growth of industry and labor in order to minimize the likelihood of further social revolutions.

For the same reasons, French governmental

TABLE 5.1 *Some Conservative Aspects of the French Social Structure, 1975*

	A Percentage of resident population in cities above 100,000	B Percentage of resident population in localities under 100,000	C Percentage of self-employed and family members among work force	D Percentage of labor force employed in agriculture
United Kingdom	72	28	7	3
United States	65	35	9	4
Japan	56	44	28	12
German Federal Republic	52	48	9	6
France	41	59	18	11
Soviet Union	33	67	0	22
China	11*	89	0	85†

Sources: Columns A and B are from C. L. Taylor and M. C. Hudson, *World Handbook of Political and Social Indicators,* 2nd. ed. (New Haven: Yale University Press, 1972), p. 219; and *United Nations Demographic Yearbook, 1976,* figures calculated from table 8. Note: The Taylor and Hudson figures are 1960 data and are for metropolitan areas above 100,000. *The Demographic Yearbook,* on the other hand, lists only cities over 100,000 (except for the U.S., for which metropolitan data is given). Because the population of metropolitan areas is a better guide of urbanization, in those instances in which the 1960 metropolitan area population exceeds the 1975 city population (the case for the U.K. and China), the 1960 Taylor and Hudson data are used (see discussion in Taylor and Hudson, p. 201).

Columns C and D are from *Yearbook of Labour Statistics, 1977* (Geneva: International Labour Organization), table 2B, with two exceptions: column C, United Kingdom: *Annual Abstract of Statistics, 1977* (London: Central Statistical Office of the United Kingdom), p. 151; column D, China: *National Basic Factbook, July 1, 1978* (Central Intelligence Agency, p. 38).

*Data for China are for cities and metropolitan areas taken from census returns in 1953, 1957, and 1970.
†Data for China are for 1966.

policies were aimed at preserving a high proportion of small entrepreneurs in industry and commerce, as well as of independent artisans, in both towns and countryside. As late as 1975, the self-employed made up as much as 18 percent of the French work force, a higher proportion than in most industrial countries. The power and influence of the self-employed middle class were multiplied by several conditions. In the countryside its members became assimilated to the rural viewpoint, and in turn its small businesspeople, notaries, and lawyers furnished leadership not only to agriculturists, but also to a large part of the entire rural population. This included, in 1976, the 30 percent of the population who lived in communities of less than 2,000 inhabitants and, presumably, a part of the small-town population as well. In addition, this rural population is strongly overrepresented in the French political system. Finally, the self-employed middle class, through family ties and social life, has assimilated many of the middle-level salaried employees and technicians to its own outlook in social relations, economic policies, politics, and culture. Small businesspeople, though often backward in terms of economics and technology, thus have exercised a greater influence in France than in most other major countries.

A Strong Middle Class, a Weak Political Center.
The proagricultural bias of the French has left its mark on modern-day France. In the mid-1970s manual workers in France still were only 37 percent of the work force, compared with 47 percent in Germany and about 56 percent in England. Although workers can be highly militant in France and about half of them tend to vote for the Communist Party, all workers are a permanent minority. Marx's prediction that the proletariat would become the great majority of society has been contradicted by the development of France, the country where the theory of class politics and the class struggle was invented.

The French class structure, in fact, has remained remarkably rigid. Within the work force, in the 1970s, the 37 percent of workers—even with another 6 percent added by service personnel—were outnumbered: the large middle class, both salaried and self-employed, included government officials and officers in the armed forces and constituted 45 percent; and the farmers and farm workers formed another 10 percent. Within the middle class, small businesspeople, artisans, and petty investors predominated until the 1950s and marked its political style. Since many of these middle-class people, like peasants, are keenly interested in keeping what they have, this slow-changing French social structure has not lent itself to sweeping restructuring or basic reform.

Only in the 1950s and 1960s did the pace of economic and political change begin to quicken. Until then, the France that resisted change prevailed over all internal challenges.

The Third Republic: A Paradise for Legislators.
The *Third Republic,* which lasted from 1875 to 1940, bore the marks of this change-resisting social structure. Incredibly enough, this longest lived of all French regimes was actually created as a "temporary" measure. With the Second Empire discredited, Frenchmen rushed to elect a National Assembly in 1871 that could negotiate peace with Bismarck and the victorious Prussians. The new legislators clearly would have preferred a restored monarchy, but they could not agree among themselves which of the three "royal" families had the legitimate claim to rule (Bourbon, Orleans, or Bonaparte). After years of wrangling, the Assembly finally adopted, in 1875, by a margin of one vote, a provisional arrangement for a republic in which the president would be elected by a joint meeting of the two houses of the legislature. The result was a regime that espoused much of the radical rhetoric of republicanism but in fact was too weak to do much more than reaffirm the established conservative interests in France.

The government of the Third Republic, like that of the United States, was divided into three branches. Its president, however, was much weaker and its legislature, the National Assembly, much stronger than their American counterparts. The legislature consisted of two chambers, of which the lower, called the Chamber of Deputies, was the more important; but the upper chamber, the Senate, also had a significant share of power, which it often exercised in defense of property rights. The president of the republic was elected by the legislature, not by the people. Like the king of England, the president was to reign ceremonially but not to rule. The actual head of the executive branch of government was the premier, or prime minister, who, as in Britain, could remain in office only with the backing of a majority in the Chamber of Deputies. Unlike the British counterpart, however, the French premier did not have the power to dissolve the legislature and call for new elections. Moreover, the system of proportional representation in voting (by which any party was allowed a number of legislators based on its share of votes) helped guarantee that each French premier faced an undisciplined plurality of parties rather than just a single opposition party.

The legislators, thus, had most of the power. They could at any time overthrow any premier by a vote of "no confidence," but they did not have to answer for their actions to the voters by calling for new elections. For the length of the legislative term of four years, members of the legislative majority were virtually irremovable as long as they themselves did not vote for new elections. In effect, though the premier and the Cabinet were responsible to the legislators, the legislators between elections were responsible to no one.

This arrangement not only ensured a weak president and a succession of weak premiers, but also a multiplicity of weak political parties and temporary political factions. A legislator who voted to bring down the government had little to fear from his or her party as long as the next election was some years away. The rural and local character of much of French politics combined with the individualism of many French voters and politicians to make the weakness of nationwide political parties and government into a tradition. Following this tradition, members of the French middle class often did not scruple to evade direct taxes by filling out false tax returns, nor did they hesitate to take their money out of France and speculate against the currency of their own country whenever it seemed profitable or they happened to dislike the policies of the government. As a rule the Assembly refused to pass effective legislation that would have ensured full collection of direct taxes or a real control of French currency. Under such conditions a government could not control the world of finance, but a financial panic could easily bring down a government.

An Administrative Elite: The Residual Center.
Though French political leadership was often unstable, French administration remained the mainstay of the state. While legislators played political games, civil servants ran the country. The French civil service, even more than the British,

has a great tradition and commands high prestige to this day. Its top administrators, such as the inspectors of finance, are still drawn from the *"great schools"*—the École Normale Supérieure, the École Polytechnique, and the École Nationale d'Administration—which are more selective and more highly respected than even the country's greatest universities.[5] Throughout all governmental crises the French civil service has kept the country going.

Like all bureaucrats and technocrats, the French civil servants cannot create policies. They can only administer the policies of others. In the 1930s the Third Republic failed to produce policies adequate for the times. The depression divided labor from the upper middle class: workers demanded more welfare; proprietors, less public spending. Soon members of the French right began to mutter that they would prefer the rule of the German government under Hitler to any native left-of-center government in France. French Communists, in turn, in September 1939 refused to support the French middle-class government. At both ends of the political spectrum the French

[5]The recruitment into these great schools was based on achievement, particularly on the student's record in the system of French academic high schools, the *lycées*. In practice, the *lycées* were open to the children of the upper bourgeoisie and of the middle class, whose home background equipped them with the skills, habits, and motivations to succeed in schools of this type and whose families could afford to support them during the last years of their secondary education and often thereafter. But this track through the academic high schools to the universities and elite institutions remained much less open to children of peasants and was nearly closed to children of working-class background. For all these children a second, parallel system of education had developed, stressing practical skills, but making a higher-level career quite unlikely. More definitely than in other advanced countries, with the possible exception of Britain, the career opportunities of many people were already set, on the day they entered their first job, by the type of secondary and higher education they had received or missed.

people disliked domestic opponents more than they disliked foreign enemies.

The Third Republic collapsed after brief and ineffective resistance against the Nazi invasion of France in 1940 and was succeeded by a conservative and authoritarian regime under the aged Marshal Pétain, a pathetic figurehead, and the unscrupulous Premier Pierre Laval, a willing collaborator of the Nazis. Calling itself the "French state" and located at the resort of *Vichy,* this regime was a puppet of the German occupying power. It was swept away by the invasion of the Allies in 1944, when a new republic was formed.

Promptly, most of the old political parties reappeared. Members of several of them had been active in the underground *Resistance* movement against the Nazi occupiers, which boasted a record of suffering and heroism; and some of these now emerged as candidates for leadership. But some who had avoided taking any risks during the occupation or had prudently waited to join the winners after the liberation also retained their influence or even increased it, and so did some outright Nazi collaborators, after having benefited by amnesty in the 1950s. Even more important, the party system, the social structure, and the tradition of an administrative elite persisted.

The Fourth Republic: Fast Economic Growth with Small Political Changes.

The *Fourth Republic,* which lasted from 1946 to 1958, in many ways resembled the Third: there were the same irresponsible legislature, weak parties, weak presidents, and quick-changing premiers. There had been over one hundred different cabinets in the sixty-five years of the Third Republic. The Fourth Republic did not improve on this average of more than one new government a year, producing twenty cabinets with seventeen premiers in its twelve years of existence. The same game of musical chairs was being played by nearly the same small group of *ministrables*—politicians eligible for Cabinet seats.

General de Gaulle, who was elected the Fourth Republic's first president, tried to be strong, but

failed and withdrew to private life. Politics-as-usual followed, but some of its content changed.

The leaders of the Republic placed more emphasis on planning for economic growth and social welfare legislation. Several industries were nationalized, including mining, aircraft, and part of the automobile industry. (When overtaken on the road by a new Renault car, made in a state-owned factory, one might reconsider the timeworn notion of "creeping socialism.") There also were marked improvements in health and welfare benefits, in access to higher education, and in special assistance to families with children. But in economic life the high degree of economic inequality persisted, among regions as well as among social strata, and reform of the tax system proved politically impossible.

The Fourth Republic accepted as general and distant goals the Atlantic community and the unification of Europe. It joined a number of important European organizations, including NATO, the European Coal and Steel Community (ECSC), Euratom (which promotes nuclear energy development), and, most important, the European *Common Market*—the developing customs union of West Germany, Great Britain, Italy, the Netherlands, Belgium, Luxembourg, Denmark, and Ireland. During these same years, however, France rejected membership in the proposed European Defense Community (EDC) and the European Political Community (EPC). In other matters the Fourth Republic moved further away from its European partners. It continued to send its soldiers to fight for the preservation of an empire that could not be preserved. Embittered officers and soldiers returned from Indochina, and soon even larger numbers found themselves in a war in Algeria that the Fourth Republic could neither win nor end.

Overcommitment Abroad and Reorganization at Home.

In foreign policy between 1880 and 1920, France had been successful to the point at which it had taken up commitments beyond its strength. By the 1920s France was the ruler of North Africa, the ruler of a part of the Middle East (both Syria and Lebanon), the ruler of Indochina, and the ruler of a substantial part of sub-Saharan Africa. From then on, as these countries and populations became politically active, France was involved in one bloody war after another. In 1920, to subjugate the Syrians, the French killed twenty thousand people in the bombardment of Damascus. From 1925 to 1927 they fought in Morocco. After 1945 they killed thousands of people in Morocco and Madagascar while trying to restore French rule. And they fought nine years in Indochina, from 1945 to their defeat at Dien Bien Phu in 1954.

The End of Empire. The force requirements for maintaining the empire became increasingly larger than the capabilities of metropolitan France. Yet the ties of the French elites, the French business community, and the French middle class to the empire were stronger in those days than the present ties of America's industrial and business groups overseas. The French middle class got more jobs out of the empire, French industry and commerce more sales, and the French military establishment more command posts than do comparable interests in the United States today. Thus, the eventual rejection of empire by the French set a significant precedent for all large nations.

Algeria: A Choice and a Decision. Blind acceptance of the theory of *economic determinism*—the simple view that economic facts and interests determine everything—would expect to find France still in Algeria. But what happened in France in the 1950s and early 1960s is a case study of how a large, modern country broke with its tradition of empire by refusing to carry on endlessly a frustrating military campaign. The country also broke economically from imperial policy, by shifting many of its economic efforts from policing the Casbah[6] to modernizing France. Finally, the country also broke morally with colonialism. The war in Algeria had led to massacres, torture, and a decline of exactly those moral values that the defense of France was supposed to maintain. As these atrocities became known, French intellectuals, students, and some members of the armed forces spoke out in protest, often at considerable risk to themselves. France could not remain civilized, cultured, and humane, they insisted, and still continue the Algerian War in the way it was being waged in the mid-1950s.

Reorganization at Home. In late 1957 and early 1958, French public opinion turned against the Algerian War. Individuals had protested earlier in increasing numbers, but by now public opinion poll returns had to be treated as state secrets "so as not to give comfort to the enemy."

By the spring of 1958, the French army was openly declaring its hostility to the Fourth Republic, which it accused of supplying inadequate backing for the war. Units of the French military in Algeria were in revolt. In May aircraft and paratroopers moved from Algeria and Corsica against the mainland of France, and they received indications of support from the police and from the conservative parties. Moderates and members of the left called for mass demonstrations in defense of the Republic. Intense negotiations led to a quick compromise, once again disguised as strong-man rule.[7] The government of the day legally handed over power to a former president of the Fourth Republic and hero of the Resistance, Charles de Gaulle. De Gaulle had the confidence of the military and was acceptable to the left, who remembered that during his presidency Communists had sat in the French Cabinet. The right expected him to keep Algeria French; the left and an increasing number of persons in the center expected him to take France out of Algeria.

Often before in French history, factions of the right and left had balanced each other with

---

[6]The Casbah was the native quarter of the city of Algiers.

[7]For details, see James Meisel, *The Fall of the Republic* (Ann Arbor: University of Michigan Press, 1962).

incompatible desires and approximately equal strengths, with the richer classes calling for order and the poorer ones for change, and all demanding a stronger government to give them what they wanted. Out of such conditions *Bonapartism* had been born, exhibiting a skillful blend of military force and sweeping promises of social betterment. Under both Napoleons more and more force and less and less betterment had followed. Would Charles de Gaulle prove to be just another Bonapartist general?

This time the outcome was different. Appointed premier on May 31, 1958, de Gaulle soon obtained full powers to govern absolutely for six months. Changing the imperial policies of nearly a century also involved changing the French domestic political system that had produced them. Therefore, during the six-month interval of absolute rule de Gaulle had a constitution drafted. When it was submitted to a direct popular vote, a referendum of the French people, they overwhelmingly endorsed it. De Gaulle reassured the military by well-chosen ambiguities that he would hold Algeria, while quietly preparing to concede its independence to its Arab majority.

At the same time he announced an accelerated program of nuclear weapons development for the purpose of making France a nuclear power independent of all others. This program for an independent French *force de frappe*—a nuclear striking force—split the French military. Technology-minded officers now parted company with their still-empire-minded colleagues. To many new-style military professionals, nuclear weapons were more important than Algeria. They continued to support de Gaulle, even after his new policy in Algeria became visible. During this critical period some of the colonialist military faction tried to assassinate de Gaulle (they succeeded in assassinating several minor opponents of the war); and they conspired in a secret army organization, *OAS*, to overthrow the de Gaulle government.

The matter was ultimately decided in part by the response of the French enlisted troops in Algeria, who acted much as their relatives in France had

acted when they voted in the referendum on de Gaulle's constitution. They had obeyed their commanders in the Algerian War, but now they refused to move against the government. In 1962 the Algerian War was formally ended. Thereafter nearly a million French were evacuated from Algeria, primarily to France, where in the 1960s most of them became integrated with the mainland French. Also in 1962 a national referendum overwhelmingly approved (62 percent of all votes cast) a constitutional amendment providing for direct popular election of the president. The machinery of de Gaulle's Fifth Republic had begun to work—as it would continue working in the 1970s after his departure. It is this machinery that we must now briefly survey.

THE PROCESS AND MACHINERY OF POLITICS: THE SELF-STEERING OF THE FRENCH POLITICAL SYSTEM

The Fifth Republic: All Power to the Executive. The *Fifth Republic* was designed to avoid the weaknesses of its predecessors. Major executive powers were given to the president, not to the premier. Its president is strong and is elected directly by the people. Like the president of the United States, he is fully independent of the legislature. Under the constitution, as it finally emerged in the early 1960s, his legal powers are much greater than those of the American counterpart. The French president has the legal right to dissolve the assembly at will; the only limit is that it can be done only once each year. The president nominates the premier and thus can control this official and the Cabinet. The president may call a referendum, issue decrees having the force of law, or declare a state of emergency and "take the measures commanded by . . . circumstances" (Article XVI of the French constitution). At no time is this individual responsible to the Assembly.

The constitution describes the president as the "arbiter," charged with making the ultimate decision among conflicting interests and policies. During de Gaulle's term in office he also took on the role of "guide" to the nation. As de Gaulle stated flatly in 1964, "The President elected by the nation is the source and holder of the power of the state."

De Gaulle was clearly not an absolute monarch, but his statement was a powerful affirmation of a deeply embedded French tradition of strong exec-

utive leadership, carrying the echo of Louis XIV's declaration, "The state—that is I." Backed by a large and growing staff, the office of the presidency in the Fifth Republic has become the center of policy making in both foreign and domestic matters (see Figure 5.2).

In 1973, Prime Minister Pierre Messmer, himself a retired general, stated bluntly that if the alliance of the left should win a majority of seats in the National Assembly, President Pompidou

FIGURE 5.2 *Modern Constitutional Structure in France*

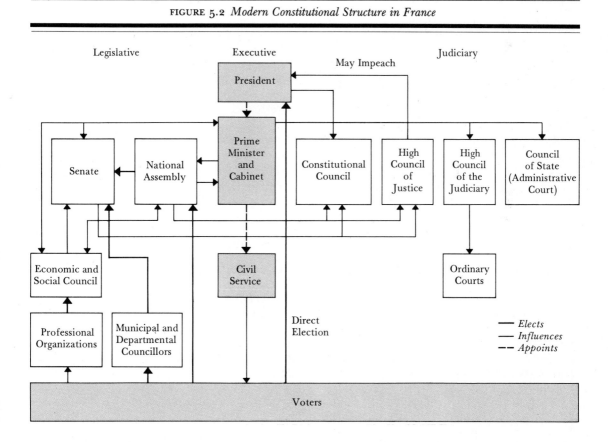

Source: R. C. Macridis, "France," in *Modern Political Systems: Europe*, 4th ed., by Roy C. Macridis, c. 1978, p. 114. Adapted by permission of Prentice-Hall, Inc., Englewood Cliffs, N.J.

would use the full constitutional powers of his office to prevent a Socialist-Communist government from taking charge. Similar predictions were made, less explicitly, for President Giscard's policy in case of a leftist majority emerging from the 1978 elections. In both years the voters did not take the risk. The majority was still preserved, and the old Gaullist coalition and regime seemed likely to endure (see Figure 5.4).

The structure of the Fifth Republic looks much like that of the Third and Fourth, but the relative powers of its various organs have changed. There still are a two-chamber legislature, a premier and Cabinet, a president, and a system of courts. A few details have been added, but the real power has shifted.

The role of the premier and the Cabinet is weaker vis-à-vis the president, but stronger vis-à-vis the National Assembly. The premier and Cabinet members are appointed by the president, whom no legislature vote can overthrow. The legislature technically may force the Cabinet's resignation, but its powers are much less than they were under the Third and Fourth Republics. Usually a Cabinet can be toppled only through a motion of censure, which requires an absolute majority of the members, so that blank ballots and abstentions count *for* the administration. In actuality, the Cabinet is an instrument of the president, carrying out the policies he or she determines. Some of the key ministers, such as those of foreign affairs and defense, often work with the president without much intervention from the premier. All Cabinet decrees require the signature of the president for their validity.

A Shackled Legislature. The legislature consists of two chambers, the more important one being the *National Assembly* of 491 members (1978) who are elected directly by the people for five-year terms. A change in electoral law after 1958 away from proportional representation has given the strongest party a disproportionately large share of seats, which works to the great advantage of the Gaullist

Party. But legislative seats mean less than they used to.

The Assembly legislates on all matters of law, but these are enumerated restrictively by the constitution, which leaves all other matters to the *rule-making power*—the power to issue binding regulations—of the executive branch. Even the enumerated lawmaking powers may be delegated to the executive branch by an *organic law*—that is, a law that affects the constitution and is passed by a majority of the members of both houses. The Assembly's order of business is determined by the administration. The Assembly may have no more than six committees and may not meet for more than six months each year. Most important, the French legislature has lost the power of the purse; it no longer controls money. The executive alone draws up the budget and puts it before the Assembly. Any motion in the Assembly to reduce taxes or other government receipts or to increase government spending for any purpose is automatically out of order. If the Assembly fails to approve the government's budget within seventy days, it may be made public by executive decree, which makes it law.

All of the above limits on the National Assembly suggest that whereas the legislative forms have been retained, and thus meet the formal requirements of French republicanism, the reality of legislative power depends very much on what the executive will allow to occur in the decision process. This shackling of the Assembly, and the legislature as a whole, becomes understandable only when seen against the backdrop of Assembly dominance over the executive during the Third and Fourth Republics. It is one of many examples we have seen in these chapters of constitution makers trying to steer a course that corrects for the perceived mistakes generated by the last round of political experiences. In the case of the Fifth Republic, cutting the powers of the legislature was seen as a way of correcting for the instability of previous governments.

The *Senate*'s 283 members are indirectly elected for nine-year terms by local and departmental councilors and representatives of the cities. The

Senate overwhelmingly represents rural and small-town France, but it has even fewer powers than the National Assembly.

Though a bill can become law only if passed in identical form by both houses, the real decision in the case of disagreement lies in the hands of the premier, who is primarily an instrument of the president. If the premier wishes a bill to pass he or she convenes a conference committee, which represents both the Assembly and the Senate, to seek agreement on its contents. Should they fail to agree and the premier likes the Assembly's version of the bill, he or she may simply resubmit it to the Assembly. A bill passed twice by the Assembly can override a senatorial veto and become law. Thus, in such cases, the Senate has merely the power to delay. If the premier, however, does not like the Assembly version, he or she can refuse to convene the conference committee. The bill then dies, and the Senate has exercised an absolute veto—thanks to the premier.

The Senate was intended to serve as a source of advice and mild delay and as a potential ally of the government against a recalcitrant Assembly. Actually, it has worked the other way: after the 1962 elections the new Assembly threw its support behind the Gaullist government and the Senate turned against it. The adherents of de Gaulle did well among the mass electorate and, with their allies, soon captured a majority of the Assembly (see Table 5.5). Owing to weak local organization, however, they failed to take the Senate.

The Senate has continued to represent the entrenched power structures of local governments, which have remained strongholds of the traditional political parties. It has rejected a large number of government bills that then have had to be repassed over its veto by the Assembly. By the late 1960s the weakness of the Senate was evident; ministers stopped attending its debates and answering written or oral questions from its members.

A Sidelined Judiciary. Other divisions of the government have still less political power. The Constitutional Council supervises elections and referenda and decides disputes about them. It passes on the constitutionality of any bill or treaty before promulgation, but only at the request of the president, premier, president of the National Assembly, or president of the Senate. Once a bill has become law, the council can judge its constitutionality only in restricted cases and on request of the government. Judicial review in France is, thus, radically weaker and narrower than in the United States. The courts in general are independent, but lack power to nullify or modify laws or administrative actions.

Successes and Surprises. The entire constitution of the Fifth Republic seemed custom-tailored to fit the imposing figure of President de Gaulle, and from 1958 to 1969 he wore his responsibilities well. During these years France acquired a great deal of prosperity, many new buildings and much productive equipment, a temporary surplus in its foreign trade, and a good deal of prestige. French technology moved forward. Acquiring a significant striking force, France became one of the world's nuclear powers. Through the development of its civilian jet plane, the Caravelle; its high-speed fighter plane, the Mirage; and the British-French supersonic plane, the Concorde, France joined the leaders of world aviation. French planning organizations were well staffed, forward-looking, and often effective. French scientists won Nobel Prizes, and the government took steps to safeguard the development of a national computer industry. The enrollment in French universities grew by leaps and bounds—from about 142,000 in 1952–53 to about 706,000 in 1975—and new universities were added.

Suddenly, some of the new policies backfired. In the years prior to 1968, thousands of students had grown resentful at the overcrowded universities. Even where new buildings had been built, old authoritarian methods of instruction had remained; and the more numerous the students became, the dimmer seemed their chances for future employment. Even where jobs did promise to be available, they appeared dull and unattractive in a country whose trappings of grandeur and reforms hid so much that was still stodgy and traditional.

When students struck and occupied the universities in May 1968, workers soon joined them for reasons of their own. Inflation had eaten into their wages, which both private employers and public authorities had been reluctant to increase. "The pennies, Charlie, the pennies!" workers in the streets had cried out at President de Gaulle, but to no avail. A wave of strikes soon closed factories. Some intellectuals were delighted. "You have created new possibilities," the best-known French philosopher, Jean-Paul Sartre, told a student leader. But the solid majority of the French was shocked.

After a wage increase was granted, the workers went back to their jobs. Their unions and the Communist Party showed no interest in revolution and condemned the radical students as adventurers. In the "election of fear" of June 1968, French voters gave de Gaulle an increased majority. Only 6 percent of the vote shifted from the left and center to the right, but under the French electoral system this was enough to produce a landslide in the Assembly (see Figure 5.3).

Politically, de Gaulle had won (see Table 5.5). In terms of control over economic policy, however, de Gaulle had lost. In response to the pressure of rebellious workers, there were major wage increases and a jump in private consumption. Once again French speculators and investors took their money out of the country. The surplus in international payments turned into a deficit. The national currency, the franc, became shaky. Inflation continued and increasingly hurt the *rentiers,* salaried employees, civil servants, and large parts of the middle class. These more conservative groups joined with labor and the intellectuals in a common resentment against de Gaulle's high-handed personal leadership, which each group now blamed for its troubles.

The situation came to a head in the spring of 1969, when de Gaulle added to these resentments by antagonizing the localist party interests represented in the Senate. The Senate, although limited in power, has always been closely identified with the local and regional politicians who elect it and has consistently voiced opposition to Gaullist policies. President de Gaulle decided to bypass both chambers of the legislature and submit a constitutional amendment to a direct popular referendum. A vote in favor of the president's proposal would have meant dismembering the existing Senate, with a compensating promise of greater autonomy for regional governments. This time de Gaulle—opposed not only by the left but also by center parties, local notables, and their followers who would have seen their national position diminished—lost the popular referendum. A majority of voters, 53 percent, rejected not only his plan but in effect his method of pre-emptory leadership and personal regime.

The president resigned and returned for the last time to his home in a small village. The Fifth Republic, however, survived its creator.

THE PARTICIPANTS IN POLITICS

Political participation for a large part of the French people is more intermittent than it is in some other highly developed countries, such as Britain or the German Federal Republic. Though the local prefects concentrate a good deal of power in their hands, they are appointed from Paris, and they depend somewhat less on the political decisions of the local voters and somewhat more on the plans, orders, and regulations of the central government. The French state and its administrative machinery were created in the days of the Bourbon kings and to an even greater extent during the empire of the first Napoleon, before industrialism, autonomous interest-group representation, and sustained civic participation in politics had become major aspects of public life. The national administration in France keeps functioning, therefore, whether or not most citizens take the trouble to be active in politics. Indeed, it is public unrest and activity, such as the student revolt and industrial strikes of May 1968, that is more disturbing to the quiet work of the civil service, which can continue unhampered in the face of public apathy or inactivity.

Voting Habits. French voters turn out fairly regularly. About 18 to 20 percent stay at home in most elections or referenda, as they did again in 1978. In rare moments of crisis, the portion of abstainers may decline to about 15 percent, and in equally

rare times of unusual apathy it may rise to 25 percent. Another 2 percent, more or less, spoil their ballots or cast blank ones. Compared to the first years of the Fifth Republic, voter participation has increased somewhat, to a high of 82 percent in the second round of the 1978 election (see Table 5.2).

Nonvoters are more frequent among women, particularly among women living alone, such as the unmarried, the widowed, or the divorced; among French citizens of foreign origin, such as Muslim Algerians; and among members of religious minorities, such as Protestants (and nonpracticing Catholics), in contrast to practicing

FIGURE 5.3 *French National Assembly, 1968*

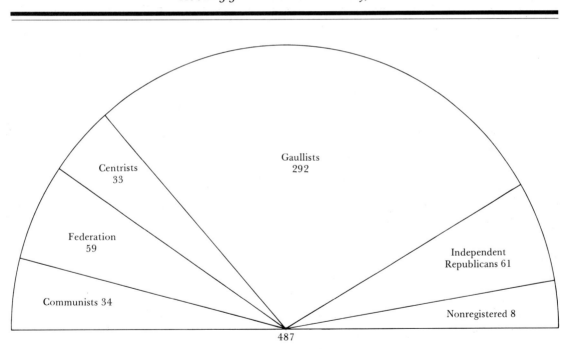

Source: R. C. Macridis, "France," in *Modern Political Systems: Europe,* 2nd ed., by Roy C. Macridis, Robert E. Ward, c. 1968, p. 228. Adapted by permission of Prentice-Hall, Inc., Englewood Cliffs, N.J.

TABLE 5.2 *Participation Rates and Abstentionism in French Voting*

A. LEGISLATIVE ELECTIONS, 1946–78

Year	Total registered voters (millions) (%)		Valid votes cast (%)	Abst. & void (%)*
1946	25.1	100	76.5	23.5
1951	24.5	100	78.0	22.0
1956	26.8	100	79.5	20.5
1958	27.7	100	75.8	22.4
1962	27.5	100	68.7	33.4
1967	28.3	100	78.5	21.3
1968	28.3	100	78.5	21.4
1973	29.7	100	79.0	21.0
1978 (Round 1)	35.2	100	81.1	18.9
1978 (Round 2)	31.0	100	82.2	17.8

B. PRESIDENTIAL ELECTIONS, 1965–74

Year	Total registered voters (millions) (%)		Valid votes cast (%)	Abst. & void (%)*
1965 (second ballot)	28.2	100	82.2	17.8
1969 (first ballot)	28.8	100	77.2	22.8
1969 (second ballot)	28.7	100	64.6	35.4
1974 (first ballot)	30.6	100	84.1	15.9
1974 (second ballot)	30.6	100	86.1	13.9

*The slight discrepancies reflect the lack of uniform treatment of void ballots in French voting statistics. Such errors are always smaller than 0.7 million votes.

Sources: Data for 1946–73 from R. C. Macridis, "France," in R. C. Macridis and R. E. Ward, eds., *Modern Political Systems: Europe,* 2nd ed., 1968. Also from *Le Monde,* June 17, 1969, and March 6, 1973. For Assembly elections 1978: *Keesing's Contemporary Archives,* November 24, 1978, pp. 29322-23. Data for 1974–78 from R. C. Macridis, "Politics of France," in R. C. Macridis, ed., *Modern Political Systems: Europe,* 4th ed., 1978. Adapted by permission of Prentice-Hall, Inc., Englewood Cliffs, N.J.

Catholics, who traditionally have tended to identify more closely with the nation. Abstention from voting—*abstentionism*—is also high among groups relatively isolated from the outside world, perhaps by geography or by language, as in the Breton-speaking parts of Brittany, and among individuals poorly integrated in their social environment, such as the ill, the handicapped, the old, and the politically alienated. The latter included the Poujadists in 1958 on the right and the adherents of extreme leftist or anarchist groups on the left.[8]

In the case of a referendum on a topic remote from the immediate concerns of French voters, the proportions of abstentions and blank or spoiled ballots may become very high. The referendum of April 1972 on the enlargement of the European Economic Community had been planned by President Pompidou as a nationwide vote in favor of European integration, as well as of his own cautious policy moves in that direction. Almost 40 percent of the voters did not trouble to vote, and the favorable two-thirds majority among the valid votes cast represented about 40 percent of the registered voters, while a little more than 20 percent voted in opposition.[9]

Campaign Activity and Party Work: Notables and Militants. A second form of participation—sustained activity in political parties and election campaigns—is relatively rare. Compared to their counterparts in other Western European nations, French parties have few members. The French seem to resist the idea of becoming regular dues-paying members of political or any other organizations. Nor is this likely to change in the next generation. A 1973 survey revealed that less than 100,000 younger persons were associated with any

party in 1973, or a party membership rate of 1 out of every 150 persons aged fifteen to twenty-nine.[10]

This lack of activism does not mean that participation in parties is unimportant for the French political system. The fact that the parties are home to fairly small numbers of strong-minded activists helps ensure that the French passion for theoretical distinctions will be vigorously reflected in organized political life. In every country one finds ideological components within parties (for example, neoconservatism or radicalism in the United States, left and right wings of British parties). In France, however, every political party seems to be regarded by its active loyalists as a device for staking out a distinctive ideological position and defending it against all comers.

On the political right and center, the permanent party *cadres*—in other words, core personnel—are typically small in number and consist mainly of local notables; dues-paying party members are nonexisting or unimportant; and the wider circle of habitual or potential adherents of the party is mobilized only at election time. French political parties of this type can grow very quickly across a few elections and then decline again. This was the case of the Catholic-centrist MRP between 1946 and 1962 and the short-lived Poujadist Party, whose demagogic and militantly pro-small-business appeal in the mid-1950s was followed by its collapse in 1958 and its loss of political significance thereafter. The Gaullist Party has reflected similar tendencies, although in this case it was obviously a question of not only local notables with their core followers but also a single great national notable and his followers (those whose faithful support dated back to June 1940 have been called "Gaullists from the first hour"). Since the passing of de Gaulle and this older cohort of followers the party has been changing, and in 1976 it acquired a new name (RPR, or Rassemblement pour la

[8]Philippe Braud, *Le Comportement électoral en France* (Paris: Presses Universitaires de France, 1973), p. 42, with reference to Alain Lancelot, *L'Abstentionnisme électoral en France* (Paris: Colin, 1968), pp. 171 et seq., 184, 205 et seq., 213, 217 et seq.
[9]Jean Stoetzel and Alain Girard, *Les Sondages d'opinion publique* (Paris: Presses Universitaires de France, 1973), pp. 92–93.

[10]Colette Ysmal, "L'attitude des jeunes," *Le Monde,* February 20, 1973.

République), a new dynamic leader (Jacques Chirac), and a new drive for the expanded membership. When in 1977 Chirac won a dramatic victory as the new mayor of Paris, party membership jumped over the one-quarter-million mark. (By comparison, the old Gaullist Party in 1975 had claimed 255,000 members, but only 145,000 of these were paid up in their party dues. Whether this marks a new era of greater mass membership for the political right remains to be seen.)

On the political left, membership parties with larger bodies of regularly organized members are the Communists and, to a lesser extent, the Socialist Party and a much smaller Party of Socialist Unity (PSU).

In the Socialist Party, members are organized in local sections that elect delegates—one for every twenty-five—to the Party Congress. This is the highest authority of the party in all matters. In practice, party secretaries, local government functionaries, and parliamentarians have a larger share of influence, but the scope for discussion and participation in decision making by the membership is not inconsiderable.

A drawback of this broader participation is that the faithful and long-established members, to say nothing of many party functionaries, do not welcome newcomers to the party if the latter are looking for a chance to make a political career. When in 1944 and 1945 many younger people, including former members of the Resistance, tried to join the Socialist Party for their political career, they were rebuffed; and by 1951 the party had the oldest parliamentary delegation in the National Assembly. In the late 1960s and 1970s, under the leadership of François Mitterand, this pattern changed; and in the 1973 and 1978 elections a number of young and conspicuously able Socialist legislators were elected. Dues-paying membership, which had been at 80,000 under the old, unrevived party of the 1960s, had doubled to 160,000 by 1976. Still, this left the French Socialist Party as one of the smallest in Western Europe. By 1978 its vote total had grown to about 6.5 million—or roughly forty-two votes for each party member.

The French Communist Party has a larger membership and expects more activity from it, but keeps most of the real decision-making power within a narrower circle of persons. It had the support of nearly 6 million voters in 1978, compared to 5 million in 1946, 1951, 1967, and 1973. In other elections between these dates Communist votes rose as high as 5.5 million in 1956 and declined as low as 3.9 million in 1958. On the whole its voting strength and its share of the electorate—about one-fifth of valid votes cast in 1978—have remained remarkably stable since 1958.

Behind the nearly 6 million Communist voters stands the second largest Communist Party membership in Western Europe (after Italy). Although the party's vote has not changed very much, party membership has apparently grown during the Fifth Republic. It is difficult to be sure because the party's own claims consistently overstate the membership (a reported 600,000 at the end of the 1970s) and the government's official figures consistently underestimate the Communist strength (at 100,000 party members). A reasonable estimate seems to be 500,000 members, or about 1 for every 12 Communist voters. Among these members there are perhaps about 30,000 *militants,* roughly 7 percent of the total membership. Militants engage in more sustained and active work for the party; and many may strive to rise eventually through the party hierarchy. Among the militants, in turn, there are about 10,000 cadres, or skeleton staff, who work full-time for the party as secretaries and as members of higher-level bureaus or else as leaders of trade unions and similar mass organizations. At the center of the cadres and of the French party, then, is the leadership of about 100 persons, including the members of its politburo, secretariat, and central committee.

It has been pointed out that the influence of the Soviet Union on the policies of the French Communist Party adds an element of unreality to the notion that its members participate in any meaningful sense in the making of important policy decisions. "The Communists," the French Socialist leader Guy Mollet remarked some years ago, "are not Left but East"—a tune that he later was to change.

For times, indeed, have somewhat changed. The Communists protested in the 1960s against Soviet prison sentences for the dissident writers Sinyavsky and Daniel, and copies of the French Communist daily, *L'Humanité*, were confiscated in Moscow. Later, the French party criticized the Soviet invasion of Czechoslovakia in 1968; and it has generally moved away from too close conformity with the Soviet views and nearer to the views and feelings of its French members and voters. Unlike the Italian Communist Party, however, the French Communist Party by early 1979 had not yet changed its inner structure. It was still being run from the top down, with rank-and-file members having little influence on major policy decisions. Nonetheless, by 1973 the Socialist Party had accepted the Communists, who had qualified their emphasis on the class struggle, as allies for a *Common Program* that favored free elections to decide on future governments. For the Communists this seemed a major departure from earlier doctrines, which had rejected "bourgeois democracy" and extolled the "dictatorship of the proletariat." Some observers saw in it an example of the cumulative influence of the French political environment on the Communist Party, moving it toward its eventual political transformation.[11] Even so, the uneasy alliance of Socialists and Communists was distrusted and rejected by enough French voters to narrowly fail in its bid for a majority of seats in the 1978 elections to the National Assembly.

[11]For a somewhat overstated account, see André Laurens and Thierry Pfister, *Les Nouveaux Communistes* (Paris: Stock, 1973); but see also François Borella, *Les Partis politiques dans la France d'aujourd'hui* (Paris: Seuil, 1973), pp. 169–202; and Maurice Duverger, *Le Cinquième République*, 4th ed. (Paris: Presses Universitaires de France, 1968), pp. 197–203. See also *Programme commun de Gouvernement du Parti communiste francaise et du Parti socialiste (27 juin 1972)* (Paris: Editions Sociales, 1972).

To the extent that such a transformation of the Communist Party should actually materialize, it would bring back about one-fifth of the French into a more genuine communication with the rest of the country. At the same time, it would make their political potential available for coalitions in favor of continued modernization and far-reaching social reforms. The French, through their participation or abstentionism, are involved in a process of deciding whether the Communist Party's newfound commitment to moderation is sincere—in other words, their determination to support free democratic methods to achieve and transfer power, their independence from Moscow, and their adherence to a Western alliance. Only the future will reveal the answer.

If moderation on the left is to make political participation more meaningful across the entire spectrum of parties and ideological tendencies in France, it will have to start within the framework of the institutions of the Fifth Republic as they have developed under presidents de Gaulle, Pompidou, and Valéry Giscard d'Estaing. But can it end there? The question is whether that framework of French government can accommodate the changes that may be involved. The elections and politics of the 1960s proved that the Fifth Republic could be established. The 1970s showed that it could work without Charles de Gaulle. The 1980s will determine whether this political structure can be sustained amid the rigidities and changes in French society.

A POLITICS OF COUNTERVAILING TRENDS

We can now begin to see the basic paradox of France's political system. Its *political center,* as represented by the party system, is extremely weak. This has produced instability and unpredictable change. Yet the *government center,* as represented by the central administrative bureaucracy and other cohesive French elites, is remarkably

TABLE 5.3 *Approximate Annual Averages*
of French Industrial Production, 1909–76

	1909–38 (during the Third Republic)			
	A	B	C	D Increase, ca. 1911–36
	1909–13	1925–29	1934–38	100 (C–A)/A
Aluminum (thousand tons)	14	29	51	264% 10.6% per annum
Merchant marine (million tons)	2.3	3.3	2.9	26% 1.0% per annum
Automobiles (thousands)	45	254	227	404% 16.2% per annum
Electricity (billion kWh)	—	16	21	31%† 3.4% per annum
Steel (million tons)	5	10	6	20% 0.8% per annum
Average annual increase for the measures of industrial production				7.2%‡

Source: From data in R. C. Macridis, "France," in R. C. Macridis and R. E. Ward., eds., *Modern Political Systems: Europe,* 3rd ed., 1972, and 4th ed., 1978. Adapted by permission of Prentice-Hall, Inc., Englewood Cliffs, N.J.
*Because the time period covered by certain data overlaps the Fourth and Fifth Republics, these data are used for the computation of the percentage increase for both republics.
†Change 1925–29 to 1934–38 only.
‡Aluminum, merchant marine, automobiles, and steel only.

strong. It has allowed France to ride out periodic bursts of instability, but it has also blocked reforms that could help France adapt to social and economic change. These countervailing forces, more than any others, are essential to our understanding of French politics. They are probably also decisive for the future of the Fifth Republic.

Social and Economic Change. During the 1950s the French economy began to grow at a faster rate

than it had experienced for many years, and this growth continued during the 1960s and early 1970s. Some data for typical products are shown in Table 5.3.

The entire time spanned by the data in Table 5.3, 1909–76, can be divided into three periods, corresponding to the political regimes of the Third, Fourth, and Fifth French Republics, re-

1948–58 (during the Fourth Republic)			1958–70 (during the Fifth Republic)		1969–76 (Fifth Republic after de Gaulle)	
E	F*	G Increase, ca. 1950–57	H	I Increase, ca. 1958–69	J	K Increase, ca. 1969–76
1948–52	1955–59	100 (F–E)/E	1967–70	100 (H–F)/F	1975–76	100 (J–H)/I^H
75	218	191% 27.3% per annum	371	70% 6.4% per annum	175	33% 4.6% per annum
2.7	4.5	67% 9.6% per annum	6.0	33% 3.0% per annum	8.5	56% 8.0% per annum
286	1,283	349% 49.9% per annum	2,100	64% 5.8% per annum	3,100	48% 6.9% per annum
41	70	71% 10.1% per annum	132	89% 8.1% per annum	680	83% 11.9% per annum
9	15	67% 9.6% per annum	23	53% 4.8% per annum	27	17% 2.4% per annum
		21.3%		5.6%		6.8%

spectively; and we can then compute for each period the rough rate of annual growth for the average of five indicators of industrial growth.

The results are a little surprising. Our first period, 1909–38, falls under the regime of the Third French Republic (1875–1940), and the rate of industrial growth averages about 7 percent per year. Our second period, 1948–59, falls under the Fourth Republic (1944–58), during which General de Gaulle held political power only briefly, as president from 1944 to 1947, but during which France benefited substantially from United States economic aid under the Marshall Plan and other programs, as well as from the efforts of the French people themselves at material reconstruction. During this period the average annual rate of increase in our industrial indicators was as high as 21 percent. This period, despite its political and military difficulties, seems to have been the time of the most rapid growth of industry and of basic productive equipment. The third period, 1959–70, after General de Gaulle's return to power, appears to have returned to a slower rate of growth in our industrial indicators, roughly 6 percent per year, but these increases now occurred on a much higher basis—a basis created in large part during the preceding period. This is largely a period under the political regime of the Fifth Republic, and much of it falls under the regime of General de Gaulle, who returned to the presidency for the years 1958–69. During this time President de Gaulle received credit not only for the preservation of national unity, the end of the Algerian War, and the promotion of French independence and prestige in world affairs, but also for the economic progress and modernization that actually were largely the fruits of the economic development that had taken place under his predecessors. After de Gaulle's retirement and death, French industry grew at nearly 7 percent per year, and the Gaullists continued to claim credit for the economic prosperity and growth that had materialized under his administration.

No matter who claims credit for the economic changes, they were a visible fact in the 1960s and 1970s. Their scale and their speed were beginning to change the social structure of France at a faster pace than ever before.

Each year during the late 1960s, about 1 percent of the French work force shifted out of agriculture and into nonagricultural occupations, and in 1971–75 this shift accelerated to 2 percent per year. By 1975, persons employed in agriculture accounted for only 10 percent of registered voters. A similar shift has been under way from the countryside to the big cities. By 1975, as many as 44 percent of French voters were living in cities of over 100,000 inhabitants, including the Paris agglomeration, where 16 percent of the French people are now concentrated. Another 18 percent of the French now live in cities of between 10,000 and 100,000 inhabitants, and still another 10 percent live in small towns with populations between 2,000 and 10,000—so the French are now altogether a 73 percent urban people. The shift to the cities is continuing, perhaps at a rate of 0.6 percent per year, and small country towns and middle-sized cities are moving toward the next higher classes of population size.[12]

The increases in the share of the residents of big cities, of persons in nonagricultural occupations, and in the general level of education and exposure to mass media should tend toward increasing the share of change-oriented voters in the electorate. Some other trends, however, may work in the opposite direction. Persons in comfortable white-collar and professional occupations are not generally considered to be oriented toward social and political change. The growing share of white-collar employees and professional people in the French electorate is now 22 percent; together with the 9 percent self-employed *patrons* of nonagricultural enterprises—to whom they are linked through many social conventions, habits, and associations, as well as often through ties of family or neighborhood—they total 32 percent of the electorate, just about equal to the share of workers. In another five or ten years this white-collar and professional share is likely to be larger, easily outweighing any shrinkage that might occur during the same period among the self-employed.

Another trend is also at work to reduce the proportion of workers among the French electorate. It is the tendency to employ foreign workers in many occupations requiring heavy, boring, or ill-paid work, both in manufacturing and in the service trades. For these jobs, increasingly unpopular with French workers, foreign workers are imported from Spain, Portugal, and the Arab countries and to some extent from black Africa, so that some factories and some working-class neighborhoods are taking on a new look. There are

[12]From data in "Données sociales: Édition 1978," *Les Collections de INSEE* (Paris: Institut National de la Statistique et des Études Économiques, 1978), p. 8.

about 3 million foreigners in France, and perhaps 2 million of these may be working for wages. They are accepted as members by the labor unions, but, being foreigners, they cannot vote. In effect, this might mean that of, say, 12 million workers in France, only 10 million are defined as "French" and have the right to vote—or that about one-sixth of the real industrial work force of the country is in effect disfranchised. Yet even if they cannot vote, they and their next generation can cause trouble. Since no one at present seems to be making any major effort to let these people share in French life, this development may continue to weaken the influence of labor and of parties oriented toward promoting peaceful social change.

Other economic trends also cut in different directions. Factors that favored at least a measure of social conservatism were the doubling of real wages from 1955 to 1975 and the rapid diffusion of durable consumer goods and higher living standards. In 1974 as many as 63 percent of French householders owned automobiles, as opposed to only 14 percent a quarter century earlier. Television sets already were in 82 percent of French households, and 88 percent had refrigerators; washing machines were found in 69 percent. Many French families now may feel that they have more to lose than was the case in earlier decades. Yet, having achieved high standards of material growth, more people may become frustrated when that growth is not sustained or proves unsatisfying in terms of the quality of their lives. Both these phenomena occurred during the 1970s.

To cope with these social and economic crosscurrents, there are three elements of stability—indeed rigidity—in French politics: a tight set of elites, a powerful bureaucracy, and a constantly fragmented party system. Let us consider each in turn.

A Cohesive Ruling Class. The "directing class" (which to a large extent is the ruling class in France)—less than the top 1 percent of the population on a scale of power over the lives of others—has remained remarkably cohesive. Ex-

cluding all writers, artists, scholars, and members of the free professions from *Who's Who in France*—that is, all those persons of note who do *not* hold positions of economic, political, administrative, or military power—a team of French sociologists compared large samples of the rest, the power holders in France, for 1954, 1964, and 1974.[13] The power holders are an elite primarily by virtue of the positions they hold and not necessarily by any special talents demonstrated in competition with newcomers from other social groups, for they are themselves a tightly knit social group, closed in on itself. They are recruited from the same social setting, from among the same social class, which almost no outsiders penetrate. Consequently, the children possess the same social characteristics as their parents; in some cases they simply change their professions or their sectors.

Within this ruling group there are of course subgroups, such as the "five *great corps of the state*" (see p. 216). Similarly, the head of a great industrial enterprise may take a somewhat different view of particular problems than a less profit-oriented top civil servant in the Diplomatic Service. But all such differences are only variations on a larger theme: the underlying social unity and remarkable stability of a single, dominant set of persons at the commanding heights of French political, economic, and social life.[14]

Two cartoons sum up the situation. Whereas in earlier times three persons were playing at the poker table—a general, a frock-coated financier, and a dark-suited technocrat—now there is a single person standing before a mirror. Which of his three suits—general's uniform, banker's coat, or technical expert's suit—shall he put on next?

It follows that the French state is not simply dominated by big business, nor does it rule business as an impartial arbiter. Rather, the different

[13]Pierre Birnbaum et al., *La Classe dirigeante française* (Paris: Presses Universitaires de France, 1978). All data in this section are from this study.
[14]Ezra N. Suleiman, "Self-Image, Legitimacy and the Stability of Elites: The Case of France," *British Journal of Political Science*, vol. 7, 1977, pp. 191–215.

sectors are held together by the uninterrupted circulation of the directing personnel from one position to another, assuring the cohesion of the whole directing class; and this top class, according to the sociologists' study, has been increasing its social distance from the rest of French society.

Within this persistent basic pattern there have been some limited changes. The proportion of *patrons*—that is, owner-managers—has been declining; that of salaried managers, strongly increasing. Many of these managers, however, are sons or daughters of *patrons,* who later succeed to the ownership of the family firm; others remain managers by profession. Still other managers are former *patrons* who have become presidents or directors-general, as well as stockholders, of their enterprises after a juridical and financial merger or reorganization. A growing number of high officials and managers of public enterprises move up during later stages in their careers into high positions in the private sector, as do many of the military. The increasing demand for highly competent and technically skilled managers throughout the private sector continues to foster this mobility of top personnel from the public into the private sector. Altogether, these developments have produced an elite of decision makers who are more favorable to technological innovation, but not necessarily to social, economic, and political reform.

A Lasting Reality: The Civil Service. Death and taxes are inevitable, goes an old saying. And, since the rise of modern tax-collecting states, with the taxes come the officials to collect them and to administer their disbursement. Three figures indicate the importance of the French bureaucracy: about 40 percent of the French gross national product passes through the public sector; about 2.4 million people are employed there; and about 10,000 take part in formulating policy and directing its execution.[15]

French administration is organized, like the British, under ministries. The most important of these are the Ministry of the Interior, the Ministry of Finances, and the Ministry of Foreign Affairs. The Ministry of the Interior is in charge of the police and of all general administration throughout the country, including all departmental and local units of government. It appoints, transfers, and can remove by secret decision and at will the key official in charge of the administration of each of the ninety departments: the *prefect.* The *Corps of Prefects* forms one of the five great corps—*les grands corps*—of the French state. In 1978 a group of several hundred provincial *notables*—or prominent citizens—were asked, "Who exercises power in the province?" Almost all of them answered, "The prefect." When asked to name several power holders, their answers produced the rankings shown in Table 5.4.

The mayor—*le maire*—of any of the 36,000 French communes is elected, but then must represent not only that municipality, but also the state. The mayor's decisions regarding the local budget and local taxation must be approved by the prefect; in some other matters the prefect can order the mayor to act in certain ways. If the latter fails to obey, he or she may be suspended or dismissed by an executive order of the prefect. This *tutelage* of the central government over all municipal authorities ensures a high degree of uniformity of administration throughout France. The powers of the elected General Council of each department are much weaker; the centralized and bureaucratic chain of command prevails.[16]

The second key ministry, that of finance, has a similar centralizing function. It prepares the budget, draws up estimates, collects taxes, and to some extent controls spending. Working within it, but often reaching beyond its boundaries by its actions, is the *General Inspection of Finances,* another of the great corps of the state. It attracts many of the ablest candidates, as its officials do not merely

[16]Ibid.

[15]Macridis, "Politics of France," p. 128.

TABLE 5.4 *Who Exercises Power in the Province: Percentage of Mentions by Notables, 1978*

Prefect (appointed)	90
President of the General Council (elected)	66
Director of the chief regional or local daily newspaper	44
Mayor of the principal town or city (elected, but removable by the Minister)	28
Deputy (member of the National Assembly)	25
President of the Chamber of Commerce and Industry	23
Paymaster General	13
Senator	6
Responsible departmental functionary of a major political party	3
Responsible departmental functionary of a major labor union	3

Source: From data in *L'Express,* November 25, 1978, pp. 40–41.

inspect tax collections and expenditures; they actually take part in drawing up many kinds of legislation. Many of them eventually move on to higher office elsewhere; some are "detached" for service with other governmental agencies without losing their connection with the General Inspection.

The third key ministry is that of foreign affairs. The diplomats working under its direction form another of the great corps of the state.

Three other bureaucratic agencies are counted among the great corps, the most important of these being the *Council of State.* Since the days of Napoleon, this body, containing its own hierarchy of about two hundred high-level officials and a larger number of lower-ranking ones, has had two functions: first, to advise the head of the state and/or the government on matters of public policy

and legislation and, second, to resolve conflicts within the administration. Over time, this second task has made the Council of State a quasi-judicial body, and it has played an important part in offering citizens a recourse against arbitrary bureaucratic acts.

Another great body is the *Court of Accounts.* Its members, like judges, cannot be removed from their positions; otherwise, it functions as part of the administrative machinery, not of the judiciary. The fifth great body is the *Diplomatic Service.* And, finally, the *Supreme Administrative Court—la cour de cassation—*is sometimes considered a sixth great body. It has final power to confirm or annul the decisions of administrative agencies.

The recruitment of all these high civil servants is remarkably uniform. Most of them, perhaps 90 percent, come from the upper-middle and middle classes. Many are the children of civil servants. Their main channel of entry is through the great schools, chiefly the *École Nationale d'Administration* (see p. 199, above). Access to these schools requires stiff competitive written examinations; similar skills are indispensable for graduating with the necessary high rank in class; and middle-class children almost exclusively have the educational background for such performance. The result is a proud and competent top-level bureaucracy, open in theory, but largely closed in fact.

To a great extent this bureaucracy is permanent. Civil servants generally are secure in their jobs and careers. Ministers come and go, but civil servants remain, unless those of high rank choose the option of *pantouflage,* or the "putting on of bedroom slippers"—that is, lucrative high-level employment in the private sector. Here the permanence of the civil service shades into the remarkable persistence of the larger French managerial and ruling class. The civil service, the army, and the larger ruling elite form a heavy counterweight to the changing contest among the political parties of the *right, left,* and *center* that has been moving France this way and that during nearly two centuries.

Another Enduring Reality: A Fragmented Party System. In the United States and Britain the main constitutional arrangements are older than the parties. In France most of the parties are older than its several constitutions. The fundamental political divisions go back to the Revolution of 1789. Those French people who favored and accepted that revolution and the separation of church and state formed the left of the political spectrum; those whose sympathies lay with the monarchy and the unity of church and state formed the political right. The original terms "left" and "right" derive from the seating order of deputies in a past French legislature—a seating order that later became customary in many European parliaments. In the course of time the terms have acquired other connotations. Parties on the left tend to favor workers and the poor as well as political and social change—by radical and revolutionary methods if they are far to the left and by more moderate reforms if they are closer to the center. Parties on the right tend to favor tradition, property, and privilege as well as the interests of the well-to-do and of substantial citizens in town and countryside. Parties in the center usually seek compromises between these wings and are often paralyzed by immobilism and attacked by both sides.

In France a whole imagery has grown up around the unremitting contest between left and right. "Left is where the heart is," states a French saying; the right is seen as the side closest to the pocketbook. But although these general political tendencies seem perennial in France, issues and problems do change. New policies must be devised to cope with them and new coalitions formed to put these policies to work. In 1946, after World War II, 46 percent of all registered French voters cast their votes for parties of the left, 20 percent for parties of the center, 10 percent for parties of the right, and nearly 24 percent did not vote at all. By the second round of voting in 1978 the left had 48 percent of the vote; the old center had split, one group joining the coalition of the left (2 percent) while most of the rest merged with the

government coalition. President Giscard's center-right *Union for Democratic France (UDF),* which also included most of the former Conservative Independent candidates, won the support of 23 percent of the voters. Further to the right, but still moderate, the newly renamed Gaullist Party (RPR) had risen to collect 26 percent of the electorate. The extreme right declined to 3 percent and the nonvoters to 18 percent. Still another 1.5 percent of the votes cast was provided by scattered minor allies of the government coalition, totaling about 51 percent of the votes cast, enough to win a majority of seats in the Assembly (see Table 5.5).

For a long time the strongest group on the left was the Communist Party. Their main support comes from workers, and, to a lesser extent, from intellectuals, white-collar workers, and even some peasants. From 1920 to 1967 they were stronger than the Socialists. Nowadays they represent nearly a fifth of all eligible French voters and nearly a fourth of those who actually vote. Since 1968 the Socialists have been stronger than the Communists. They have lost much of their former following among manual workers and now get most of their support from public officials, teachers, and other white-collar groups, whose share in the work force is expanding.

More moderate than the Communists or Socialists have been a bewildering array of parties that have tried to occupy the political center. They have split, regrouped, renamed themselves, and sometimes disappeared as they have tried to steer a generally reformist course between antiparliamentary conservatives and revolutionary supporters of republicanism. The oldest of these parties (dating to 1901) are the Radical Socialists. Until recently these centrists have generally allied themselves with the left for electoral purposes and with the right for purposes of parliamentary maneuvering. A small pro-European Christian Democratic Party has taken over from a once-powerful moderate Catholic Party in recent years, while other parties and factions have developed

TABLE 5.5 *French Legislative and Presidential Voting, by Party and Candidate*

A. LEGISLATIVE VOTES BY PARTIES, 1946–78

	LEFT		CENTER			RIGHT				
Year	Comm. & Prog. (%)	Soc. & Left Soc. (%)	Rad. (%)	Reform- ists (%)	MRP* (%)	UDF "Giscardians" (%)	Gaullists (%)	Ind. & Mod. (%)	Ext. Right (%)	Others (%)
1946	21.9	13.5	11.2	—	20.3	—	—	10.4	—	0.4
1951	20.1	11.0	8.8	—	9.8	—	16.7	10.6	—	0.4
1956	20.5	11.9	10.4	—	9.0	—	3.0	12.3	10.1	0.4
1958	14.1	11.6	9.7	—	8.7	—	13.0	14.8	2.5	—
1962	14.5	8.4	5.5	—	5.8	—	21.1	9.1	0.7	—
1967	17.6	14.8	—	—	10.2	—	30.0	3.9	0.7	—
1968	15.7	16.6†	—	—	8.1	—	34.3	3.2	0.4	—
1973	19.5†	20.2	—	10.0	3.0	—	19.6	6.0	2.2	—
1978 (Round 1)	16.7	18.3	1.7	—	—	17.4	18.6	1.9	2.4	4.4
1978 (Round 2)	15.3	23.3	2.0	—	—	20.1	21.5	1.0	—	0.2
		40.6					42.6			

B. PRESIDENTIAL ELECTIONS, 1965–74

	LEFT						RIGHT			
1965 (second ballot)		Mitterand 37.4						de Gaulle 44.8		
1969 (first ballot)	16.6	18.1	3.9				33.9	2.8	—	1.8
1969 (second ballot)		Poher 27.4						Pompidou 37.2		
1974 (first ballot)		36.3		—	—	—	15.3	27.4	0.2	4.9
1974 (second ballot)		Mitterand 42.4						Giscard 43.7		

*The MRP was succeeded by other centrist groupings: *Centre démocrate* (1967); *Centre Progrès et Democratie moderne* (1968); and *Réformateurs* (1973).

†A small leftist group, the Party of Socialist Unity, followed a more radical line in 1973 and was counted, therefore, as a Communist ally in that year, despite some sectarian disputes between the two parties. Earlier, in 1968, it had been counted as a Socialist ally, and the addition of its votes and that of other Socialist splinter groups made the Socialist vote in this table appear larger than the Communist vote in that year. In 1973 and 1978 the Socialists and Communists entered the elections with a common program, but with separate candidates for the first ballot. They had agreed, however, to withdraw their candidates from the race for the second round of balloting in favor of that candidate of the left who had received the most votes in the first round; and the PSU later joined this agreement. In the 1974 presidential election, the Socialists, Communists, and Radicals entered the election with a common program.

Sources: Data for 1946–73 from R. C. Macridis, "France," in R. C. Macridis and R. E. Ward, eds., *Modern Political Systems: Europe,* 2nd ed., 1968. Also from *Le Monde,* June 17, 1969, and March 6, 1973. For Assembly elections 1978: *Keesing's Contemporary Archives,* November 24, 1978, pp. 29322–23. Data for 1974–78 from R. C. Macridis, "Politics of France," in R. C. Macridis, ed., *Modern Political Systems: Europe,* 4th ed., 1978. Adapted by permission of Prentice-Hall, Inc., Englewood Cliffs, N.J.

sources of strength at the local level if not nationally. Perhaps the most important point is that by the
late 1970s, the distinctions among all these centrist
parties at a national electoral level were tending to
become obliterated under the overarching political family of Giscard's UDF. In effect, most centrist
voters had moved to the moderate right. One new
"nonpolitical" center party, the Ecologists, received 3 percent of the votes in the first round of
voting in 1978, but lost almost all its voters to the
right and left coalitions in the decisive second
round.

To the right are those French citizens who
oppose welfare legislation and nonmilitary public
spending. Still further to the right are those who
have never fully accepted the Revolution of 1789
and the republics that followed from it. Here one
finds some of the remnants of the French nobility,
many officers' families, monarchists, and the more
tradition-minded Catholics who found the reformist center too liberal. The candidates they vote for
are often called Independents. In recent years the
Gaullist Party in coalition with the Independents
has brought many of these voters back toward the
political center and to support of the Fifth Republic, which embodies Gaullist policies. By 1978 most
of them had been absorbed into the Gaullist Party
(RPR) under Jacques Chirac or, at least, into the
progovernment majority. In addition, French individualism has produced a multitude of political
splinter groups that often disappear after one or
two elections and are usually negligible in size.
Sometimes, however, these groups have managed
to catch the political mood of the moment sufficiently to disrupt and further fragment the relationship among larger parties. They may do so
again in the future.

The interaction between change and rigidity
suggests that the dynamics of French politics are
neither simple nor likely to be found moving in
one direction. As we shall now see, political
developments in recent years confirm the idea of
crosscurrents, with the president in the middle.

RECENT DYNAMICS OF FRENCH POLITICS

Taken all together, these mutually opposing currents of social and economic change have produced something of a paradox: a country of rapid
change in economics, technology, consumption
standards, the scale of higher education, population growth, and patterns of settlement, all of
which are combined with a remarkable picture of
near immobility in politics.

In French society the middle class is strongest,
but in French politics the center seems weak. The
politically active French are on the right and left.
In the middle are the politically passive—often
about one-fifth of the electorate. As a result
French politics is often deadlocked. People often
stay out of politics until they begin to feel that
something must be done.

As in other modern countries, only more so,
French politics tends to oscillate between immobilism and emergency. When many different interest
groups or parties stop or frustrate each other, the
result is either immobility and widespread apathy
or a willingness to hand things over to a strong
leader who can mobilize the otherwise apathetic
nonvoters. Then the center becomes significant.
The strong leader, a Bonapartist or Gaullist,
sometimes can win the support of former nonvoters, together with that of the center and the
moderate right, to form a majority. That person is
then a compromise candidate and coalition builder who manages not to look like one. Such a
strategy worked for the two Napoleons and for de
Gaulle, too—for a time.

In the last half of the 1970s, the strategy of
strong and personal executive leadership also
worked for President Giscard, but in a way that
was different from the heroic Bonapartist tradition. It was symptomatic of this difference that in
1974 he referred to the presidency as "a career
rather than a divine mission" and, unlike presidents de Gaulle and Pompidou, refused to move
his family into the elegant Élysée Palace. Giscard's
leadership has been that of a skilled technocrat,
willing to try to cooperate with the legislature and
open to consultation with groups such as trade

unions, who were never before allowed access to the presidential decision-making process. In 1980, Giscard had managed to retain his presidential image as spokesperson for the national interest while skillfully maneuvering on the less elevated plain of French party politics (by uniting the various political fragments into the UDF alliance of the center and moderate right).

Ordinarily, much of French politics works through compromises among the parties, despite the reluctance of many French people to make concessions or to draw attention to them. Some need to compromise is built into the French electoral system. French elections come in two stages. On election day voters cast their *first ballot* for the candidate whom each prefers. If no candidate wins an absolute majority, a run-off election follows: voters cast a *second ballot* for the compromise candidate whom they find most acceptable among contestants.

These compromise choices determine much of the composition of the legislature. The multiplicity of parties makes it necessary to form coalitions, since often no party wins a clear majority. Usually, adherents of a party of the left vote for the candidate of some other party of the left; and there is similar mutual support among the parties of the right. Similar alliances are often formed among the center parties; and Communists vote sometimes for moderate left candidates, but the voters in the latter sector may or may not reciprocate.

Despite these deals and shifts, much of French politics had remained fairly constant in recent decades. About one-fifth of French voters usually stayed at home or spoiled their ballots. About one-third normally voted left; about half for the Communists and the other half for the more moderate left parties. Another third voted for the center and the right. Among these voters, those close to the center preferred the moderate Catholic Party; those well toward the right voted for candidates who called themselves Independents or

moderates; the extreme right has been insignificant in most postwar elections. The lion's share of votes on the moderate right—more than one-third—went in recent years to the Gaullists.

There is a *floating vote* of 10 to 20 percent of the electorate. In some years most of this vote floats left, as in 1946 and 1973, or to the moderate right, as in 1968, or it divides almost evenly, as in 1978. In other years 10 percent may go all the way to the extreme right, as in 1956; and in still other years a similar number may increase the body of abstainers, as in 1962. Table 5.5 permits us to trace such changes. They add up to a sequence of kaleidoscopic changes on the surface produced by the floating fifth that may conceal the stable political habits of four-fifths of the French voters. The stability of the many voters and the intermittent volatility of the few have marked French politics under the Third, Fourth, and Fifth Republics alike. In 1977 and 1978, despite bickering between Communists and Socialists, the floating vote went largely to the left, bringing it within 1 percent of a majority. If this alignment should be re-created, French politics may enter a new epoch.

The Political Response of the 1970s. The distribution of votes and seats for the National Assembly that emerged from the 1973 and 1978 elections closely resembled that of the previous and similar election of 1968. After that election, in 1968, about 6 percent of the French had moved temporarily to the right in a "law and order" reaction against the French students' revolt of May 1968, producing under the majority voting system of the Fifth Republic a Gaullist landslide majority of Assembly seats. By 1973 that wave of emotion had passed; Socialists and Communists had agreed on a vague anticapitalist Common Program of the left.[17] Most of the right had united behind the

---

[17]The Common Program called for extensive nationalization of French industry, higher wages and shorter hours for workers, greater welfare benefits, and a weakening of the power of the president, among other things. See *Programme commun de gouvernement du parti communiste et du parti socialiste* (Paris: Editions Sociales, 1972).

"majority" coalition led by President Pompidou and the Gaullist Party; and the result at the end of the election seemed to be a nearly complete return to the distribution of voting power in the National Assembly that had existed in 1967. In March 1978 the left again tried to coalesce to present a Common Program to the voters. In the municipal elections of 1977 its candidates had done so well that one might have expected it to win in 1978. But voting for the mayor of one's city is not the same thing as voting for those who will assume control of one's nation. As victory seemed more possible Communists and Socialists quarreled over details of the Common Program during the last six months before the election. The Communists wanted to nationalize one thousand firms, the Socialists only nine; Communists wanted a major equalizing of incomes, and the Socialists wanted to go slower. Above all, Communists demanded a guarantee that they would be given key Cabinet posts if the Socialist leader became prime minister. Just as the parties of the left found it hard to compromise among themselves, so did the parties of property find it hard to compromise with any of the leftist parties when the substantive demands of labor were raised. Instead, the governing majority appealed to the fear and caution of the voters; and it won once more.

Yet at a deeper level France may now be moving toward broader and more fundamental political changes than those that were evident on the surface in the 1970s. The large currents of social, psychological, and economic change are likely to continue, but they are not so likely to balance or cancel each other's political effects to the degree that they had done in those years. The popular vote for all leftist parties rose from 44 percent in 1967 to 46 percent in 1973 and to 49 percent in 1978. Well beyond a preference for any one party or coalition, there has been clear evidence of a widespread demand for change, for social reform, and for a more equitable distribution of incomes, career openings, access to education, opportunities for participation in decisions at one's work place and at all levels of one's community, from neighborhood to municipality, to region, and nation. The leftist coalition has stressed these demands.

The government of President Pompidou (1969–1974) responded by accepting in general terms this emphasis on change but offered the government's Gaullist coalition as a safer instrument for devising and carrying out any reforms required. The immediate response to the disturbances of May 1968 had been a series of concessions to demands for greater social and economic equality, with particularly strong rises in minimum wages for workers and farmers, increased hospital, school, and housing construction, and some reduction in the central bureaucracy's red tape. But once the emergency was past, the government did little to continue this impetus for social and economic reform. In general the Pompidou government continued the familiar policies for promoting economic growth, hopeful that a continuing rise in the tide of economic prosperity would lift all groups and still disorder. Few efforts were made to push policies for "unblocking" (as reformers put it) the economic, social, and political rigidities of French society. The tax structure remained unreformed and highly favorable to business and other better-off groups. Government control of the media was not reduced, and other administrative liberalizations remained largely paper proposals. The central bureaucracy retained its elitist recruitment patterns, and by 1973 academics were still writing books about France as "the stalled society."[18]

The 1973 elections saw Pompidou's Gaullists lose their absolute parliamentary majority, althought they retained control of the government through the support of smaller center-right parties (see Figure 5.4). The growth of the leftist parties contributed to a growing assertiveness on the part of the National Assembly. The ailing

[18]Michel Crozier, *The Stalled Society* (New York: Viking, 1973).

Pompidou and his government responded with promises of wage and pension increases, a clampdown on tax fraud, and improved working conditions for industrial labor. But the planned-for economic growth that underlay such promises did not materialize. In France, as in other countries, the years 1973–74 marked the onset of unprecedented oil price increases and an upsurge in unemployment and inflation. In 1974, for only the second time since the end of World War II, the annual growth rate of the economy averaged below 5 percent, and the annual inflation rate rose more than 5 percent (to 17 percent).[19]

These economic troubles lingered in France throughout the remainder of the 1970s and served to constrain seriously the resources available to the government for promoting reforms. Following his election in 1974, President Giscard d'Estaing was in the position of having to reconcile his promises of further liberalization and modernization in France with stringent measures to stabilize the economy. Private consumption was cut back and price controls were introduced to combat inflation, and new tax privileges for business were introduced to spur investment. Benefits were also increased for the large numbers of French unemployed, but tight controls were put on non-French "guest workers," thereby exporting some of France's unemployment problem to poorer countries.

After 1974 it became clear, however, that Giscard intended more than simply a continuation of the de Gaulle-Pompidou approach to domestic policy, which would have meant pursuing few social or economic reforms except under emergency pressures. At first Giscard relied on the Gaullist premier Chirac to help win over parliamentary support for his austerity measures. Whereas de Gaulle and Pompidou had tended to look on the legislature with some disdain, Giscard seemed to welcome the increased assertiveness of parliament as a means of relieving some of the pent-up pressures for social change. By 1976 it was

clear that the more conservative premier disagreed with the president's intentions of moving his political base of support away from the Gaullist right and more toward the center or even moderate left. Chirac resigned and was replaced by Raymond Barre, an economist whose technocratic rather than political background clearly carried forward the Fifth Republic tradition of a premiership dominated by the political will of the president.

The 1978 parliamentary election was fought by Giscard's coalition against a left that was split over the meaning of socialism as expressed in their Common Program. The program presented by Giscard's UDF contained enough conservative economic promises (cutting taxes, phasing out price controls, giving financial incentives for savings, and increasing fees for public services) to retain the support of the Gaullists. But it also gave expression to many of Giscard's desires for institutional liberalization and reductions in government regulation of the economy. It proposed, for example, giving a voice in economic planning to small businesspeople and others, strengthening the powers of municipalities vis-à-vis the administrative center, a reduction in working hours and an increase in social welfare benefits, disproportionately large pay increases for the lowest paid workers, and new taxes on large fortunes and land transfers.[20]

In the 1978 results, the government won 46 percent of the votes on the first ballot, and its main opponents, the supporters of the left, received 45 percent. On the second ballot the government coalition got 51 percent and the leftists 48 percent. Thanks to the winner-take-all system of single member districts, however, the government coalition emerged with 57 percent of the National Assembly seats (see Figure 5.4).

Both the government and the press agreed that the election had revealed a serious demand for

[19]The other year in which these two thresholds were breached was 1968.

[20]For a discussion of Giscard's own views on such matters, see his book, *La Démocratie française* (Paris: Fayard, 1976).

FIGURE 5.4 *French National Assembly: (a) 1973; (b) 1978*

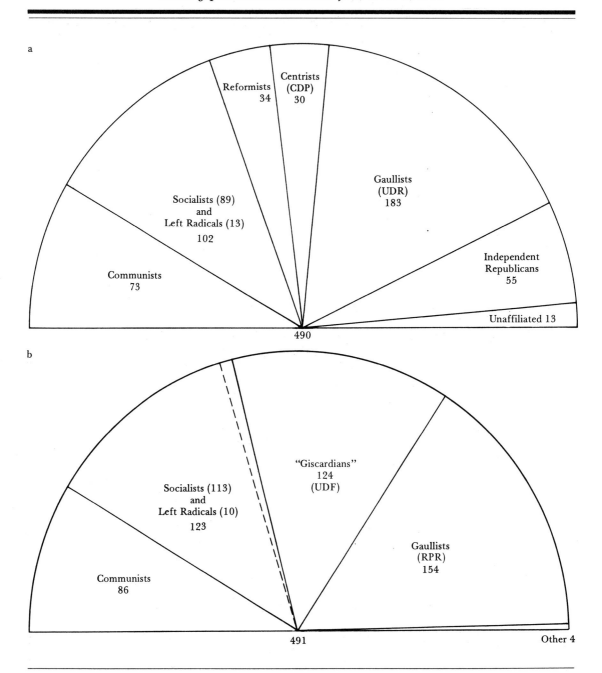

a

Reformists
34

Centrists
(CDP)
30

Socialists (89)
and
Left Radicals (13)
102

Gaullists
(UDR)
183

Communists
73

Independent
Republicans
55

Unaffiliated 13

490

b

"Giscardians"
124
(UDF)

Socialists (113)
and
Left Radicals (10)
123

Communists
86

Gaullists
(RPR)
154

491

Other 4

Source: *Keesing's Contemporary Archives*, April 23–29, 1973, p. 2584T, and November 24, 1978, p. 29323.

change and that President Giscard's promise of reforms, televised on the day before the final popular balloting, was made in response to a real popular desire. Five years earlier, on the eve of the 1973 election, President Pompidou had made a similar promise on television. The day after that election, a cartoonist drew Marianne, the symbol of France, speaking to President Pompidou. She had tied a knot into the national flag "to remind you of your promise"; if leaders should forget, the nation would remember. More people did remember in 1978, but enough voters preferred once again the old promise of moderate reforms to any more radical experiments.

To be sure government policies since 1974 have exhibited a series of pragmatic liberalizing reforms. In the educational area, for example, annual meetings between parents and teachers have been instituted, helping to reduce some of the insulating characteristics of the educational bureaucracy. In addition, greater flexibility has been introduced in the design of academic curricula. The rights of citizens against police and of prisoners against prison administrators have been given greater prominence. Birth control, abortion, and divorce policies have been liberalized, and the age for legal adulthood and voting has been lowered from twenty-one to eighteen. Government intervention in the media has become less noticeable, although the government continues to maintain its monopoly over broadcasting. The government has tried seriously to conduct a dialogue with organized labor for voluntary wage controls and a cooperative economic policy that includes taxation and restraint on top income earners. But when troubled by delays the government has also not hesitated to pre-emtorily institute price and wage controls through its immense administrative apparatus.

It is perhaps indicative of the immense rigidities in the French system that the development of parent-teacher associations, consultation with trade unions by economic policy makers, or government restraint in controlling the media should be regarded as signs of major reform. Giscard's critics emphasize that his elegantly pragmatic

reforms and promises of social justice have had little effect on basic patterns of economic distribution and social stratification. Giscardism—as it is coming to be known—has demonstrated its liberalizing intentions and instituted a more open style of government. But is that enough to accommodate the pent-up forces for change? Can such accommodation stay within the framework of the Fifth Republic's young political system? At the beginning of the 1980s the answers were far from clear. What did seem clear as France moved toward the 1981 presidential election was that the need and demand for reforms were recognized and shared in one form or another by a majority of the electorate, both on the left and in the gradually coalescing center and moderate right. These aspirations have become an important part of the stakes of French politics for the years ahead.

THE STAKES OF FRENCH POLITICS

At many times the stakes of French politics have been unusually high. At the time of the great revolution, in 1789–93, they included the freedom and property of the peasants and the middle class; the power, property, and necks of the aristocracy; the worldly power and position of the church; the entire character and structure of French society and the direction of its further evolution. In 1793–1800 the stakes included the security of middle-class property and enterprise; the claims of the poorer classes; the rise of military dictatorship; and the beginning of a policy of vast military conquest abroad.

From 1800 to 1940, conflicts about these stakes would recur: middle-class and peasant property rights against working-class claims for a more equitable distribution of income and welfare; a monarchic versus a republican form of government; a powerful church versus the separation of church and state; civilian versus military rule; absolutism or dictatorship versus constitutional government; priority for domestic improvements versus military power-politics in Europe or colonial expansion—all these were repeatedly at hazard in the political struggles and, with them more than once, the character and future of the country. France saw a kind of short-lived communist government, the Paris Commune of 1871, long before Communist governments won power in Russia or China. A modern Communist Party has been prominent in France since about 1920, winning one-quarter to one-fifth of the total vote since World War II. Should it win power at the national level, much in French life would change once more, even though the party has promised (in case of an electoral victory) to respect the rules of French multiparty democracy and to give up its share of the government if a future election should go against it. The disinclination of many French voters to trust this promise and to take any risk played a significant role in the re-election of a progovernment majority—albeit a reduced one—to the National Assembly in the 1973 and 1978 elections.

Another stake of politics from 1870 to 1945 was the fate of two major regions, Alsace and Lorraine, which had been annexed by Germany from 1871 to 1918 and again from 1940 to 1945, after having been French since the late seventeenth century or even earlier. An even larger stake during World Wars I and II and again since 1945 has been the political and economic independence of the entire country, first confronted by German attempts at conquest and occupation; and, from the late 1940s into the 1980s, against the spreading hegemony of the two superpowers of the period, the Soviet Union and the United States. Large issues of this kind have been ever present in the minds of some French people, and in intermittent crises they have aroused much larger numbers to political interest and activity.

At a less basic level the French political system today controls directly about 40 percent of the gross domestic product that passes through the public sector (including all levels of government), as well as the social security and health insurance systems and the turnover of the nationalized industries. This same public sector employs about 12 percent of the work force of the country. Indirectly, the political system controls an even larger part of the economy through its fiscal and credit policies and through its system of *indicative planning*—that is, noncompulsory plans based on careful economic forecasts and then negotiated among the government's civil service, the relevant private business firms and interest groups, the labor unions, and the regional and municipal authorities concerned. How and in what direction are all these governmental powers to be used? For growth or stagnation; inflation or deflation; price stability or full employment; greater or less social, educational, and economic inequality; more paternalistic authority or broader and more genuine participation in decision making in private industry as well as in public administration? All these elements are involved in the stakes of day-to-day politics and stimulate people to participate in them.

A NEW FRANCE?

At the end of the 1950s France had to choose what kind of country it wished to become. In following General de Gaulle, not toward what some thought he had promised—keeping Algeria French—but toward what he did in response to the will of the French people—ending the Algerian War—the French to a significant degree chose their own course. France today is no longer tied to its empire and is therefore a much more modern country than it was twenty years ago.

France still has larger shares of its population working in agriculture, living in small towns, and remaining self-employed than does Germany or Britain. But the French occupational structure is now changing more quickly. In the decade 1966–76 approximately 7 percent of the French work force has shifted from agricultural to nonagricultural pursuits, compared with shifts of only 4 percent in the German Federal Republic and 1 percent in Britain. In 1973, French agriculture comprised only 5 percent of the electorate. Even counting nonvoting teenagers and foreign laborers working on farms, agriculturists amounted to about one-ninth of the work force in 1975, and they may decline to one-twelfth in the early 1980s. If so, French politics will become very different from what it has been.

France is already in many ways a different country from what it used to be. It still has a social structure that makes unity difficult and a political culture that encourages distrust of government and withdrawal from politics. President Georges Pompidou, who in 1969 succeeded General de Gaulle, continued the policies of his predecessor, showing greater suavity of style but no major change in substance. As we have seen, the third president of the Fifth Republic, Giscard, promised more sweeping reforms of a liberal and modernizing nature. But by 1980 there were still serious questions as to how many of these promises would or could be kept.

As early as the mid-1960s, elite surveys had elicited the opinion that much of the Fifth Republic would survive General de Gaulle. The responses further indicated that the French elites wanted France to be an ally of the United States, but not a satellite.

Some of the more pessimistic French at that time forecast that, after General de Gaulle, everything in politics would be for sale. If this had turned out to be true, domestic and foreign interests with the greatest purchasing power might have picked up new political concessions. By the early 1980s they had not yet done so. Perhaps there is less for sale in the French politics of growing mass participation than both native and foreign observers suspected. French technological and industrial development, French monetary policy, and modern French big business enterprise, no less than French intellectual life and public opinion—all are likely to respond more fully to French national needs and pressures than

to any appeals from abroad, whether they come from the United States, the Soviet Union, Western Europe, or the world of multinational corporations.

What is likely to be new in French politics in the 1980s is the sustained demand for structural reforms. The French seem no less satisfied with their personal lives than people in other Western democracies, but they have yet to feel satisfied with their political system. The mid-1970s were a difficult time throughout the West, with oil price increases, inflation, unemployment, and international terrorism all raising questions about the capacities of democratic governments to govern. But as Table 5.6 shows, people's faith in their government system tended to bounce back in Britain and West Germany. It did so to a lesser extent in France.

The demands for reform in France may include a partial redistribution of incomes and perhaps of patterns of authority in many situations of daily life. France has had such waves of reforms before: in 1789–99 during and after the French Revolution; in 1934–37, when Popular Front majorities legislated social security and the five-day workweek; and in 1944–46, when social services were expanded and important industries nationalized, such as electric power, mining, and segments of the automobile and aircraft industries. Perhaps another wave of social reforms and experiments is coming again—but when, and led by whom, we cannot tell as yet.

A poll published in February 1979 offers some glimpses of the things that have remained stable in French political opinion, together with some of the changes that have occurred and that may still be continuing.[21]

What is enduring is national pride: 60 percent of the respondents define themselves as French, as opposed to defining themselves by their age (38

[21]Louis Harris, in *L'Express*, February 17, 1979, pp. 32–38. All following data in this chapter are from this survey.

TABLE 5.6 *Trends in Personal and Political Satisfaction*

	1973	1975/6	1977	1978
Percentage satisfied with own personal life				
West Germany	82	79	85	82
Britain	85	71	87	85
France	77	75	73	71
Percentage satisfied with way their democracy was working				
West Germany	44	79	78	76
Britain	44	51	62	62
France	41	42	49	49

Source: Compiled from *Euro-Baromètre*, nos. 8 and 9 (Brussels: Commission of the European Community, January and July, 1978). See Richard Rose, *Politics in England* 3rd ed. (Boston: Little, Brown, 1980), pp. 350–53.

percent), their profession (35 percent), their social class (31 percent), or their sex (24 percent). For two-thirds of all respondents one of the greatest assets of their country is the French language, "which is a language of culture and is spoken in vast regions of the world." National symbols—the national anthem, "La Marseillaise", the red, white, and blue national flag, the *tricolore;* and the Fourteenth of July, the national feast day commemorating the storming of the Bastille prison in 1789, which marked the start of the French Revolution—have kept "the same value as before" for a clear majority (56 percent); only a strong minority (39 percent) now considers them "a bit outmoded."

As for France itself, they identify it first of all with liberty (61 percent), tolerance (33 percent), and generosity (29 percent); all these are mentioned even more often by the adherents of President Giscard's party. A smaller number add equality (17 percent) and greatness (12 percent), but only 5 percent mention *mesure,* that is, a sense of proportion. As to its faults, the most conspicuous to 24 percent of the respondents is *chauvinism,*

exaggerated nationalism that downgrades other nations in order to exalt one's own. Other faults are more rarely mentioned: pretentiousness (13 percent), futility (4 percent), and imperialism (4 percent).

Among the countries of the world France is now seen as occupying "an honorable middle position" in regard to both culture (65 percent) and technology (74 percent). Only one-fifth still sees it "as one of the leading countries of the world" in its culture, and only one-eighth has a similarly high opinion of its technology. Nearly two-thirds see something else as more important. A clear majority, 54 percent, think that "superior nations" ought *not* to run the world, and nearly two-thirds (63 percent) agree with this statement: "The political power of France matters little, for what makes it strong is that it has permitted and still permits the work of great writers, scholars, and artists."

In other respects the French remain divided. Nearly one-half think that French prestige is continuing to decline (46 percent), but nearly the same proportion disagree (44 percent). Class divisions are seen as persisting. "A French worker is more similar to a worker of another country than to a French employer," say 59 percent.

Exactly 50 percent see France as invaded by "undesirable foreigners" who are not needed and should be sent back where they came from, but a strong minority—38 percent—oppose this view.

Similar divisions appear vis-à-vis international politics. Perceptions of foreign threats are scattered, the worst being seen in communism (20 percent), population growth in the Third World (19 percent), the Arabs (17 percent), multinational corporations (16 percent), regional separatism (10 percent), and "supranational Europe" (7 percent). There is somewhat more unity about who are "the friends of France," but the answer shows a surprising change. Germany is now the most popular, gaining 33 percent of all mentions and followed at some distance by the United States (22 percent) and Britain (16 percent); in earlier decades the United States and Britain led the field. Though the Communist Party had won 21 percent of the valid votes cast in March 1978, only 2 percent in the 1979 poll named the Soviet Union as a friend of France.

Underlying many of these views is a common and persistent desire to maintain the independence of their country. The atomic bomb, says a strong plurality (45 percent), should be used exclusively to defend the national territory of France; only about one-fourth would be willing to use it also to defend its allies in the event of an attack on their territories. (Here French feelings for their friends show some limits.) Every major social class sees itself as the one most strongly committed to defend French national independence, and the same applies to all major parties, but the middle class (38 percent), the working class (37 percent), the Socialist Party (31 percent), and the Gaullists (31 percent) rank highest. Least trusted as defenders of national independence are "the big bourgeoisie" (17 percent) and the Communists (18 percent).

Finally, what about "the great tasks for the future"? Highest ranking is, surprisingly enough, "to transform the understanding *(les rapports)* among persons and nations" (32 percent), followed by "aid to underdeveloped countries" (19 percent). Lower-ranking tasks are "building Europe" (12 percent), "accelerating scientific and technical progress" (10 percent), "building socialism" (9 percent), and "building the liberal society" (8 percent). Together, these six tasks should offer a wide field for the discussions and experiments in which France often has excelled.

In the past France has been the experimental laboratory of the Western world. From the thirteenth century to the intellectual and scientific ferment of the present, the French have tried out more ideas than any other people. Often they have not innovated as much in practice as in thought. But what the French now try to do both in thought and in practice may continue to be of decisive importance for the entire Western world.

KEY TERMS AND CONCEPTS

rentiers
avant-garde
esprit de finesse
Le Grand Siècle
Jacobins
First Republic
Girondists
the terror
Thermidor
Directory
eighteenth of Brumaire
First Empire
Second Republic
Second Empire
Paris Commune
Third Republic
great schools
Vichy regime
Resistance
Fourth Republic
ministrables
Common Market

economic determinism
Bonapartism
force de frappe
OAS
great corps of the state
patrons
indicative planning
abstentionism
militants
cadres
Fifth Republic
National Assembly
rule-making power
organic law
Senate
prefect
Corps of Prefects
notables
maire
tutelage
General Inspection of Finances
Council of State
Court of Accounts
Diplomatic Service
Supreme Administrative Court
École Nationale d'Administration
pantouflage
right
left
center
Gaullists
Union for Democratic France
Popular Front
first ballot
second ballot
floating vote
Common Program
tricolore
chauvinism

ADDITIONAL READINGS

Aron, R. *France: Steadfast and Changing.* Cambridge: Harvard University Press, 1960.

Brinton, C. *The Americans and the French.* Cambridge: Harvard University Press, 1968.
———. *A Decade of Revolution, 1789–1799.* New York: Random House, 1965. PB
Crozier, M. *The Bureaucratic Phenomenon.* Chicago: University of Chicago Press, 1967. PB
Ehrmann, H. W. *Politics in France.* Boston: Little, Brown, 1968. PB
———. "French Communism: Theory and Practice," in *Problems of Communism,* May-June 1978, pp. 58–64.
Grosser, A. "Nothing but Opposition." In R. Dahl, ed., *Political Opposition in Western Democracies.* New Haven: Yale University Press, 1968. PB
Hoffmann, S., ed. *In Search of France.* Cambridge: Harvard University Press, 1963. PB
MacRae, D., Jr. *Parliament, Parties and Societies in France, 1946–1958.* New York: St. Martin's, 1967.
Macridis, R. C. "France." In R. C. Macridis, ed., *Modern Political Systems: Europe.* 4th ed. Englewood Cliffs, N.J.: Prentice-Hall, 1978.
———. "Pompidou and the Communists." *Virginia Quarterly,* vol. 45, no. 4 (1969), pp. 579–94.
Métraux, R., and M. Mead. *Themes in French Culture: A Preface to a Study of French Community.* Stanford, Calif.: Hoover Institute Series D, no. 1, 1954.
Safran, W. *The French Polity.* New York: Longman, 1978. PB
Wylie, L. *Village in the Vaucluse.* Cambridge: Harvard University Press, 1974. PB

Readings in French:
Braud, P. *Le Comportement électoral en France.* Paris: Presses Universitaires de France, 1977.
Birnbaum, P., et al. *La Classe dirigeante française.* Paris: Presses Universitaires de France, 1978.
Duverger, M. *Le Cinquième République.* 4th ed. Paris: Presses Universitaires de France, 1974.
Escoube, P. *Les Grands corps de l'État.* Paris: Presses Universitaires de France, 1971.
Fauré, E. *Pour un nouveau contrat social.* Paris: Fayard, 1977.

Giscard d'Estaing, V. *Democratie française*. Paris: Fayard, 1976.

Lancelot, A. *L'Absentionnisme électoral en France*. Paris: Colin, 1968.

Laroque, A. *Les Classes sociales*. Paris: Presses Universitaires de France, 1972.

Laurens, A., and T. Pfister, *Les Nouveaux Communistes*. Paris: Stock, 1973.

Monod, J., and Ph. de Castelbajac. *L'Aménagement du territoire*. 2nd ed. Paris: Presses Universitaires de France, 1973.

Peyrefitte, A. *La Mal française*. Paris: Plon, 1976.

Stoetzel, J., and A. Girard. *Les Sondages d'opinion publique*. Paris: Presses Universitaires de France, 1973.

PB = *available in paperback*

VI

The German
Federal Republic

"To be German means to do a thing for its own sake," runs an old German saying. For good or ill, the German people often have committed themselves thoroughly to whatever they were doing at the time—to the admiration, astonishment, or horror of their neighbors. German diligence and orderliness are renowned. "In a German train," goes another saying, "not only the conductor is on duty but the passengers as well." Yet two thousand years earlier, the Roman historian Tacitus called the ancient Germans incurably undisciplined and lazy. How did a people of such great gifts go through such changes in its character?

Like the British, French, and American political systems, the various regimes by which Germany has been governed have had their roots in part in the political culture of the country. Such roots may reflect images of conflict or cooperation, hierarchy or equality, that have become embodied in the things people take for granted. These images lodge in people's minds even if they are not explicitly discussed as formal political problems.

German technology is much like that of the United States, the Soviet Union, Britain, France, and other advanced countries. But German history often has been radically different, and so has German politics. German politics cannot be understood by looking only at German institutions or day-to-day events, for all these have changed too often in this century. To discern what German politics means and how it works, we must know something of its origins and its past.

THE NATURE AND BACKGROUND OF GERMAN POLITICS

The present German Federal Republic is among the world's youngest political systems. It came into being only in 1949. But it governs three-quarters of one of the oldest peoples of Europe. In a sense the German people is even older than the English people. When the German people emerged, when the word *teutiscus,* or "German," was first used early in the ninth century, no Norman had yet come to England. Through a thousand years of history there has been a German people, but this people has lived in a united national state for less than eighty years. Today's divided Germany rings with the echoes of this past.

The Forming of the German People: Six Centuries of Expansion. German history differs radically from that of other major nations. Whereas the English, French, and Russians each spent most of their histories as subjects of a single centralized state, the Germans spent most of their past as subjects either of a vaguely defined empire or of many princes. The German people was put together in a 250-year period of consolidation between roughly 750 and 1000 A.D., which was followed by another four centuries of further expansion. But all these centuries produced no unified German state. At first, German consolidation moved southward with the expeditions of the Frankish emperors. This unification was formalized on Christmas Day, 800 A.D., when the roughneck Frankish leader Charlemagne had himself crowned emperor of the Romans by the pope. In exchange for this political service Charlemagne made his troops available to the Papacy in the triangular war in southern Italy involving the Roman Catholic church, the Greek Byzantine Empire, and Muslim power. The Franks were called in by the Papacy to decide the outcome. A monk of Ravenna, reporting the scene when the Frankish army arrived, called it incredible. The soldiers, he said, were covered with iron from head to foot—a stream of iron flowing into Italy. As the centuries advanced the stream of iron expanded northward and eastward as well as southward. Cities that today are in the middle of Germany were a thousand years ago frontier fortresses against Slavs and pagans. Later, and still more eastward, East Prussia was a province carved out by conquest.

Eventually some of the Slavic and Lithuanian non-German natives of these regions were exterminated; all survivors were subjugated and most of their descendants were assimilated. Today many of the German family names in Eastern Europe clearly show their Slavic origin. Thus, despite all legends of the purity of the so-called Aryan race, the German people is as racially mixed as any of the peoples forming the great nations of the world.

The expansion came to a stop in 1410, when for the first time a Polish army defeated the German crusaders in the Battle of Tannenberg. Earlier, a foray farther east had been stopped in 1242 by the Russians under Alexander Nevski, to the pleasure of a later generation of Soviet motion picture makers. (Both these battles were omitted or played down in German textbooks. German children, too, were taught that their nation hardly ever lost a war.) But a large part of the country south of the Baltic Sea remained German.

The First German Empire. The first German empire, which was by no means purely German, began in 800 A.D. with the crowning of Charlemagne, and was styled the *Holy Roman Empire of the German Nation.* Much of German history records how authority tried to forge one country, but reality created several. For its first forty-two years, the Holy Roman Empire, however, was not an entirely German state. It included both French-speaking and German-speaking people. Just as every German schoolchild is taught that Charlemagne was a German, every French child is taught that, of course, he was a Frenchman. According to the Dutch, both are mistaken, since obviously he was Dutch. In fact, these nationalities were not yet sharply distinguished in Charlemagne's day. In 832, some years after his death, the Synod of Tours ordered priests in the empire to preach in the "popular language." But what was considered to be the popular language was strikingly different in different regions.

In 842 the grandsons of Charlemagne divided

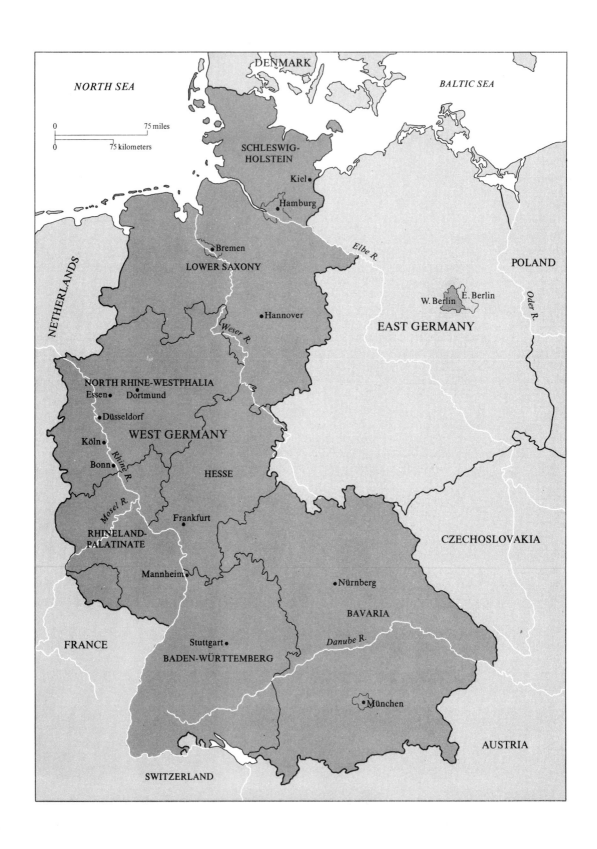

his empire. Their armies met at Strasbourg and in preference to a war swore loyalty, each to its respective new ruler. One army swore in French loyalty to the king of the West Frankish Empire, which then became France; another army swore in German to the East Frankish ruler for the part of the empire that eventually became Germany.

Though Charlemagne had failed to bring about any lasting unity between France and Germany, he did more perhaps than even his successors in unifying Germany. His main methods were authority and force. In thirty years of warfare Charlemagne subjugated the *Saxons,* tamed them, and Christianized the survivors with a sword. Many of the surviving Saxons were assimilated forcibly. A number of places in South Germany contain the word "Saxon" in their name. These at one time were settlements of deported and transplanted Saxon populations who had been put into the Frankish countryside for faster fusion with the *Franks.*

This drive prevented the rise of two nationalities, Saxon and Frankish. Instead they became one people. Early in the tenth century Henry I was the first ruler from a Saxon dynasty to become emperor of Germany. First he was king and then proceeded to have himself crowned emperor, wearing Frankish dress and ordering his Saxon noblemen to take Frankish wives.

By the end of the tenth century the Saxon emperors Otto I, II, and III had successively led their armies again and again into Italy and built up the first powerful and splendid empire, based on a combination of German military manpower and Italian money and resources. The Holy Roman Empire was rarely holy and only intermittently Roman, but it was an empire much of the time. From 1000 to 1268 it legally and symbolically claimed power and suzerainty over all of Christendom. Its emperor was the leading symbol of secular authority in the Western world. Emotionally and intellectually it was supposed to be a world government: the vision of an empire of the world in Dante's famous book on universal monarchy was its intellectual swan song. But many Germans remembered it in later ages as a German empire, and they derived from this memory an image of German world leadership and a claim to its renewal.

In fact the empire, splendid as its symbols were, was a political and organizational self-deception. It had no orderly administration. It had no means of collecting taxes and no permanent body of officials. It drew its administrators, its scant supply of literate personnel, its financial revenues, and over one-half of its military manpower from the church. More than half of the knights who rode with the emperors on the Italian expeditions held church lands and were subjects of the bishops or archbishops of the church. Since most of their money and administrative personnel came from the church, German emperors felt that controlling the church in Italy was vital. Forty times in three hundred years, German armies rode into Italy to enforce the German emperor's control over the Papacy, for to lose control of the pope meant to lose within a few years control of the German bishops. And to lose control of the bishops meant to lose money, administration, and effective power over the empire.

The Revolution of the Pope. Some thoughtful historians have argued that the popes were the first revolutionaries of Western history. According to this view, the first European revolution took place in the mind of a single man—Pope Gregory VII. In the year 1075, Gregory VII in a memo to himself, called *Dictatus Papae,* wrote that the pope and the church must never be subject to the emperor, but that the emperor ought to be subject to the pope. This stupendously bold document was the outcome of a hundred years of ferment in

---

(Left) MAP 6.1 *The German Federal Republic*

the church, but thenceforth the Papacy did everything it could to make the church free from secular domination. The hymn *Veni Creator Spiritus* (Come, Creative Spirit) became to the church what "La Marseillaise" became to the French Revolution eight hundred years later.

The Papacy made an alliance with the Italian cities. The city-states agreed to furnish the Papacy with militias, and in 1176 these militias defeated the imperial army of the Holy Roman Empire at Legnano. For the first time a noble army of armor-clad aristocrats had been beaten in pitched battle by troops of European cities. Emperor Frederick Barbarossa barely escaped with his life, and German power in Italy never fully recovered.

The wars went on. The German princes north of the Alps became more and more unwilling to supply manpower and money for an increasingly hopeless effort to subjugate Italy by German force. The church called in Norman knights, and Normans from France and southern Italy under the house of Anjou became formidable allies of the pope. The last prince of Frederick Barbarossa's dynasty to try to rule Italy and to seek to regain the title of Holy Roman Emperor (Duke Conradin of Swabia) was defeated, captured, and in 1268 beheaded in the public square at Naples with the obvious approval of the church. This church-inspired revolution of the thirteenth century was the first revolution to behead a monarch.

A GERMANY OF MANY STATES

Germany remained without a ruler until 1273 and then lived for three hundred years as a shadow empire with no emperor in effective control. For the empire it was a period of profitable anarchy, but within the smaller regions there was a good deal of order. The real units of government were a number of territorial principalities and of sovereign city-states. Perhaps one-tenth of the German people lived in well-governed and increasingly prosperous city-states. Outside the city-states the countryside remained under the rule of nobles, and the labor of the peasants made German land increasingly cultivated and fertile. Organizations of cities, such as the Hanseatic League, carried German merchants all over eastern Europe and gave them special privileges in Venice and London. Not until the sixteenth century were German merchants in London reduced to the level of English merchants in the eyes of English law.

A substantial part of Germany was under clerical domination. What is today the Rhineland was largely under the rule of the archbishops of Cologne, Trier, and Mainz; they had the effective equivalents of church-states, which they administered in their capacity as secular rulers. Medieval Germany would have been a nightmare for an adherent of a centralized modern state, but it worked for two and one-half centuries, economically as well as culturally.

The Reformation and the Religious Split. The prosperity of Germany created a middle class and increasingly self-conscious and self-confident princes who grew ever more critical of the ceaseless demands of the Roman church for more money. In the meantime Italy likewise lived under prosperous anarchy. The Italian city-states flourished, fought, and produced some of the world's outstanding treasures of art. The Papacy eventually fell into the hands of a line of fabulous bankers and art collectors, the Medici, who made up in refinements and expensiveness of taste what they might have lacked in simple piety.

The German princes also acquired the expensive tastes of Renaissance rulers, together with growing needs for money to pay for bureaucrats and mercenaries. The princes wanted to keep the silver from the German mines in their own country and spend it for their own purposes. At the same time, sincere young German monks felt disturbed by the contrast between the abnegation demanded of them and the self-indulgence they saw in Rome. They were less critical of their own princes.

Martin Luther was perhaps the outstanding

example of the profoundly conscience-driven revolutionist who relied on the German princes for protection. Very soon the princes discovered that Luther's doctrines could be highly profitable for rulers who wished to keep more money and power in their own hands while finding good, respectable theological reasons for taking over the properties of the church.

Luther's doctrines on ecclesiastical purity—the desire that the church should not be rich and arrogant, the importance of practicing Christian virtues, the value of translating the Bible so that the people themselves could read what it said, and the establishment of services in the popular language—appealed not only to the urban middle classes but also to the peasants. And when the peasants rose, their demands became a mixture of social revolution, populism, and fundamentalism. One of the peasant songs said, "Naught shall prevail but Holy Writ!" In sum, there was to be no canon law, no ecclesiastic rules; scripture was to be directly read and literally interpreted, and this would be sufficient to run everybody's lives. This is a view that still survives in some rural communities in the Bible Belt of the United States, stretching from Georgia to Kansas.

Authority Defeats the Peasants.

In Germany at that time this kind of fundamentalism meant war against the monasteries and the church. It meant plunder and violence and, in response, the ferocious repression of the peasants by the nobles. The actions of the nobles had the blessings not only of the Catholic church, but of Martin Luther, too. It was Luther who wrote in 1525 in a pamphlet addressed to the nobles and entitled *Against the Robbing and Murdering Hordes of Peasants,* "Dear Beloved Gentlemen: There is no time in which one could deserve better of heaven by killing, hanging, burning, and piercing people through than now." He urged the nobles to do this to the peasants and restore order.

It was done to the peasants with devastating thoroughness. The victory of authoritarianism over the Saxons in Charlemagne's day was now paralleled by a second victory of authoritarianism over the peasants in Luther's day. Germany began to stagnate—politically, culturally, and economically—after the victory of the nobles and princes over its peasants; and soon the princes began to win victories over the self-governing powers of many of Germany's cities.

Germany became a plurality of authoritarian princely states. The princes who ruled the seven largest had the right to elect the emperor, and they became one of the world's smallest, though most corrupt, electorates. Records show how the imperial crown of Germany was bought for cash in 1530. Charles V of Spain used the gold streaming in from the plunder of the New World and from the massacres of the natives of Mexico and Peru to bribe the German electors at the imperial diet into electing him emperor, but he had to borrow additional sums to make up the full price demanded by the electors.

Religious War, Devastation, and a Legacy of Fear.

The *Reformation* led to wars between Catholic and Protestant princes, spurred on by zealous theologians on both sides. Germany suffered. It ceased to be the source for the exercise of power over foreign countries and became a theater for power exercised from abroad. Spanish money and later Spanish armies strengthened the Counter Reformation and the Catholic princes in their war against the Protestants. In 1555 a compromise was reached in the *Religious Peace of Augsburg,* establishing the doctrine of *cuius regio eius religio* (whoever rules the land has the right to determine the religion). It was freedom for the prince, but not for his subjects. They had to accept his religion or, with luck, get out. Ever since, some German regions have remained Protestant and others Catholic; and German politics often has reflected this diversity.

The Peace of Augsburg lasted about half a century. There were disagreements within both camps whether this uneasy peace ought to last.

One of the lesser-known chapters of European history is the struggle between the doves and hawks among Protestants and Catholics alike, which ended in the defeat of the peace factions on both sides. Soon after this, the victory of the hard-liners on both sides led to an increase in political warfare throughout Europe.

The worst explosion occurred in Germany in the *Thirty Years' War* (1618–48). Foreign armies entered in the name of religion and stayed to fight for power. German princes on both sides abetted them. The war was fought without mercy. In its course, two-fifths of the German people perished. Germany, which had entered the war with 20 million inhabitants, left it with 12 million.

The trauma of Germany was lasting, leaving in its political culture a legacy of fear and distrust of foreigners. Foreign armies had made Germany the expendable battlefield for the conflicts of European power politics. But the Germans' fear and distrust of others was combined with a fear and distrust of themselves. At least half or more of the soldiers who had plundered and devastated Germany were Germans recruited in the name of the pure gospel of Protestantism or for the sake of the one and exclusive church. Either way they had been paid intermittently by their mercenary captains and had received permission to plunder and torture the population. The Thirty Years' War, thus, was as much an act of self-destruction as an act of destruction by other stronger, better-organized, and more ruthless neighboring states.

A more subtle damage preceded the war and continued after it. For a hundred years following the discovery of America, the world's trade routes had been shifting from the Mediterranean to the Atlantic seaboard. Italy and Germany—to a large extent the centers of the medieval world—were becoming the backwaters of the emerging modern age. German cities had stopped growing by the middle of the sixteenth century, and Germany was stagnating much as a river valley whose water supply is drying up. The Germans had no clear awareness of what was happening to them. They only had a vague feeling that unidentified, secret, alien forces were doing harm to them, and the fear of such anonymous threats to the German people became another theme in their political culture.

Two German Remedies: Discipline and Work. After 1648, when military and economic misfortunes had reached their peak, the surviving Germans worked their way back to security under the rule of various absolute princes. They saved themselves through discipline and diligence. The most typical political entity to emerge in this period was the principality of Brandenburg, "the sandbox of the empire," as it was called, having poor soil and few natural resources, but an incredible ability for organization, discipline, and hard work. Later it was said of Brandenburg that it had starved itself into greatness.

The key legal change was the introduction of compulsory personal service. Authoritarianism had scored a victory. The peasants not only owed services to the nobles on their fields in spring, summer, and fall, but from the seventeenth century onward they also had to work indoors under supervision, spinning, weaving, and producing useful commodities. Work became a German form of emotional therapy and eventually the basis of restored prosperity. Tireless work habits, thoroughness, and order became characteristics of the German people.

The Miracle of German Culture. Authoritarianism did not affect all aspects of German life. Despite devastation and oppression, there arose in the second half of the seventeenth century a great culture with a humanist tradition in science, poetry, and music. Hermann Hesse in his book *The Glass Bead Game* suggests that perhaps the rise of German music was one effort toward psychological and cultural healing; music put the souls of a people together again after their lives had been shattered.

The eighteenth century brought a continuation of both German traits, authoritarianism and humanism. There was absolutism under efficient cynical rulers like Frederick the Great, who wrote, "I take what I want. There will always be plenty of professors to justify what I do," and who on another occasion asserted that "prostitutes and professors can always be procured." What Frederick did not take into account was that Germany might yet produce other scholars who would do more to put the skids under monarchies than those whom he had procured to justify his exploits. The same German university culture that produced Leibniz and Goethe eventually produced Marx, Freud, and Einstein, the three men who destroyed the pillars of so many of the world's former beliefs.

Whereas German politics remained absolutist and authoritarian, German culture became increasingly liberal and humanist. The work and outlook of Lessing, Kant, Mozart, Beethoven, and Goethe shows that every one of these thinkers was a liberal. Each believed in the free development of the personality of every individual, and each thought that government ought to serve this end. Lessing and Mozart were Freemasons, and Kant and Beethoven were both self-confessed Jacobins—friends and admirers of the French Revolution—in their political sympathies and in their writings. Kant said, "I admire Rousseau. He straightened me out." But many German liberals were repelled by the eventual excesses of the French Revolution, and the silent majority of the German people remained obedient to their princes.

LIBERTY OR UNION: GERMANY'S LONG DILEMMA

In France and Britain the main struggles for popular liberties occurred within nation-states that were already unified. Likewise, "Liberty and Union—one and inseparable!" is an old slogan in American history. Germany's many states, by contrast, offered neither liberty nor union. For the German people the choice of which goal to seek first, liberty or union, was always difficult and sometimes tragic.

A Revolutionary Era. The issue was first posed by the example of the French Revolution, which found Germany politically and economically unprepared. Emerging from the turmoil of the new, revolutionary France, Napoleon's armies overran Germany easily; the vaunted Prussian armies collapsed, proving hopelessly obsolete before the French onslaught. Soon the French occupied Berlin, but under the noses of the occupying government German nationalism grew faster, and the German economy changed. In Prussia the civil service was reformed, the cities got partial self-government, and the University of Berlin was founded. In 1813 a wave of nationalism swept through Germany, inspiring the Germans to play a major role in destroying the Napoleonic armies in the military actions between 1813 and 1815.

There followed an age of utter tiredness with war and revolution. There were now over thirty German states, heirs of several hundred still smaller ones that they had swallowed. The average German man preferred to withdraw into his family and to delight in the solid comfort of his furniture. The drowsy man in stocking cap and nightshirt became the German cartoonists' symbol for the mood of their fellow citizens. It was an age of princes restored to nearly absolute rule over obedient middle-class burghers who held that to be quiet was every citizen's first duty.

Romanticism and an Unsuccessful Revolution. After 1830 the popular mood began to change. A combination of liberalism, nationalism, and *romanticism* came to the fore. The uprising of the Greeks against the sultan of Turkey attracted some German volunteers. Hand in hand with a growing interest in nationalism came an increase in romanticism. The first generation of romantics already had created the new images and concerns of romanticism: the love of the night and of the feelings for emotion, the thirst for intellectual powers, and the longing to transcend limits. Now the movement grew and broadened. Those contemporaries who thought romanticism was a movement of mere irrationality grossly underestimated its intellectual performance. Great philosophers like Hegel and Schopenhauer also belonged to that trend; as its last offshoot, so did Nietzsche with his vision of man and superman. The social critics coming out of the romantic decades—Engels, Marx, and others—were to prove intellectually and politically formidable. Most of the romantics, however, favored German union ahead of liberty or social change. Even the romantic movement was less individualistic in Germany than in France, Britain, or America. Family structure, too, may have played a role in the long history of German submissiveness to authority. In many countries families were large and extended. They included aunts and uncles and cousins, and they habituated the younger people to the authority of their elders and of the larger group. In the United States, Britain, France, the Netherlands, and Scandinavia, however, individualism and romantic love set many young people free from this authority. Mobility and travel to distant places tended to have the same effect. When industrialization and mass politics came to prevail in these countries, individualism and a spirit of criticism and pluralism were already well established in the thoughts and feelings of many individuals and showed up to some extent in all social classes. But in Germany—and even more so in Russia, China, and Japan—individualism spread only at a later date, over many more years, and among more limited sectors of the population. When industry and mass politics came to these countries, the great majority of their peoples still was used to submitting to the will of some collective and to the authority of its leaders, although by this time they might accept the new authority of a monarch, leader, party, or central committee instead of the old authority of family and elders. In Japan, China, and Russia this authoritarian and collectivist psychological heritage was perhaps still strong-

er, but among many Germans until 1945 it was strong enough to mark their political behavior.

The revolution that broke out in Germany in 1848 was the century's high point in the struggle for liberty, but it was another failure. Some cities rose, but they were small; some students, small craftsmen, and workers from the few factories of the time manned the barricades. But many of the handicraftsmen in the cities were not interested in revolution. Germany was still overwhelmingly agrarian and the lot of the peasants had been considerably improved since the days of Luther and the Thirty Years' War. When in 1848 most remnants of feudal oppression were abolished by timely reforms, most of the peasants remained conservative. Their sons in soldiers' uniforms helped suppress the 1848 revolution. In the cities the new factory owners had gotten into deep conflicts with their few factory workers and felt that revolution would make factory labor unmanageable.[1] Throughout Germany the revolution was beaten easily, and the middle class turned again to authoritarian leadership, partly to keep the working class in order and partly to maintain a strong army against foreign rivals.

Middle-class Germans sought, first, stability, and they were willing to submit to authority to get it. Second, they wanted wealth and power, and they sought union as the path to these. Only last they wanted liberty—and they sacrificed it readily whenever stability or union seemed at stake.

Throughout the nineteenth century the German middle class felt that it needed strong military protection against foreign rivals, but it never trusted its own competence to perform the great military operations. It believed that a first-class military power required aristocratic officers and generals. This is one of the sharp differences

[1]One should remember that European industry was built up in the first half of the nineteenth century by denying industrial workers the right to vote and by putting all the economic sacrifices on their first and second generations. This is quite different from modern economic development, where in most developing countries industrial labor cannot be treated in the way British, French, and German labor was treated between 1820 and 1848.

between German political culture, on the one hand, and French, British, or American, on the other.

Union from Above. In the 1850s and 1860s, Germany was transformed economically through the establishment of a railroad network and rapid acceleration of industrial growth. By the end of the 1860s, Germany was producing more steel and coal than France.

When Germany finally was unified in 1870–71, it resulted in the fourth major victory of authoritarianism in German history. Things greatly longed for by generations of Germans—unification of their country, equality before the law, and more rights for the middle classes and even for the common people—came as a gift of authority. Prussia, the most authoritarian state, and Bismarck, its Iron Chancellor and the faithful servant of its monarch, brought it about. Bismarck's ruthless moves of power politics and brilliant manipulation of alliances were all undertaken without major parliamentary or popular participation in making decisions. Most Germans gratefully accepted the results. Throughout the next four decades stability and power seemed assured. Thereafter, Germany was to become the most bellicose and unstable power in western Europe.

SEVENTY-FOUR YEARS OF UNITY

Germany was united from 1871 to 1945. During this short time—less than three generations—the country went through three forms of government and two world wars.

A Failure of Steering: The Loss of Control and Slide into World War I. The almost unlimited capacity of the Germans to trust their government made it easy for them to go wholeheartedly into World War I. In 1914, however, other people trusted their own governments no less uncritically, and

this made the coming of war more certain. Other governments on both sides shared responsibility for the war, but the German failures of realistic political decision and self-control were among the worst of the great powers.

The German people loyally supported a government and a political system that in the end proved incapable of self-steering. The German government failed to understand the danger of the world war to which its own decisions were leading. It grossly underrated the numbers, strength, and determination of the foreign enemies it was acquiring; and it failed to see the character of the war into which it was blundering and the consequences that this war would produce.

Blind leadership found blind obedience. After the German government had decided to go to war against France, it announced on August 3, 1914, that French aircraft had dropped bombs on Nuremberg. This announcement, we know now, was a lie. The commander of Nuremberg knew nothing of this alleged attack. The German press, nevertheless, published it, and the German people believed their leaders. They thought themselves attacked, and they produced 3 million poems expressing their patriotic fervor in the first nine months of the war. Never in the history of humanity was so much bad poetry produced by so many people in so short a time.

The sacrifices of the German people were vast. At the village of Langemark in Belgium, it takes a bus forty-five minutes to go past the cemetery that contains the graves of four regiments of student volunteers who were used up by the German military command in 1914 in mass infantry attacks against British machine guns. The using up of manpower continued for four years. In the end, the war was lost, the empire collapsed in revolution, and the emperor escaped to Holland where he lived in retirement—as the richest citizen of Germany. He kept his properties while the German people experimented with their first republic.

Between Revolution and Authority: The Weimar Republic. In November 1918 a revolution ended the war and created a German republic. Later its constitution was drafted by a convention in the small town of Weimar, famed for memories of the poets Goethe and Schiller and safely distant from the country's restless industrial centers. From this birthplace of its constitution it became known as the *Weimar Republic* (1919–33).

Throughout its fourteen-year existence the Weimar Republic could only rarely count on a coherent democratic majority among its people. The republic's main parties were the Social Democrats, who put democracy ahead of socialism and averaged about 20 percent of the vote; the Catholic Center Party, which represented about 13 percent; the liberal Democrats, who averaged nearly 10 percent until 1930 and then dropped to 2 percent; and, on the moderate right, the German People's Party, which averaged about 18 percent until 1928, but dropped to 3 percent by 1930. Together, these moderate parties commanded a majority of the voters until 1928. On the radical left the Communists averaged 11 percent. On the far right the conservative German Nationalists averaged another 11 percent until 1930, and the National Socialists (Nazis) held about 5 percent. From 1920 to 1930 roughly one-fifth of German voters steadily abstained from voting (see Table 6.1).

Most often the republic remained torn between the conservatism and authoritarianism of strong groups on the right and the revolutionary impatience of a minority on the extreme left. This struggle in the end strengthened the right-wing reaction.

But during the first few years left-wing uprisings were most conspicuous. Karl Liebknecht, the first member of the German Reichstag (the lower house of parliament) who had voted in 1914 against war credits (that is, in effect, against allocating money for the war), was one of a small group of radicals who from 1917 on were sympathetic to the Russian Revolution. Another was Rosa Luxemburg, one of the most brilliant women in politics of any time. They were leaders of the Spartacist League, which thought that a quick uprising in Berlin in January 1919 could win Germany for communism without going through the long and tedious process of gaining the consent and support of a majority of the German people.[2]

The uprising was quickly beaten down by troops returned from the front. A new army, the Reichswehr, was recruited largely among nationalist and military circles, and Liebknecht and Luxemburg were murdered by some of its soldiers in January 1919. A series of other radical uprisings followed—in 1919 in Bavaria, in 1920 in the Rhineland, in 1923 in Thuringia, and in 1923 at Hamburg. All were bloodily repressed. The leadership of the small German Communist Party believed that it was unimportant whether an uprising succeeded or not. Coups, combat, and uprisings were expected to have great educational value for the workers, revolutionizing them by their example. A number of left-wing leaders perished in these actions. On the whole, the *Putsch period*—the time of armed coups by small groups from 1919 to 1923—disorganized and split German labor without producing any major successes for the radicals.

Meanwhile, moderate labor and middle-class groups turned for protection to conservatives and nationalists, who became entrenched in the army. Under the new democratic constitution, social reforms were enacted, but soon the German government let the currency decline in value. German industry discovered that one could profit from inflation, and by 1923 the shock of World War I, which had expropriated the holdings of many members of the German middle class, was reinforced by another catastrophe: runaway inflation that wiped out the savings of countless others.

Many voters again supported a re-emergence of authority as a solution to Germany's problems. In 1925 they chose as president the leading representative of German militarism in World War I,

[2]Although Liebknecht and Luxemburg personally disapproved of the uprising and considered it unwise, they loyally supported the action when the majority of the organization voted for it.

Field Marshal Paul von Hindenburg. This was the fifth victory of authoritarianism. By insisting on running on a separate ticket, the Communist candidate, Ernst Thälmann, made it possible for Hindenburg to be elected rather than the moderate candidate, a Catholic politician with the surprising name of (Wilhelm) Marx. Hindenburg became president through Thälmann's insistence on not supporting the more liberal candidate. Later, in 1932, Democrats and Socialists united with conservatives for Hindenburg's re-election as a lesser evil than the election of Adolf Hitler to the presidency. They were soon to regret their success. Hindenburg appointed Hitler chancellor in January 1933. Authoritarianism triumphed a sixth time (see Table 6.2). Hitler promptly became dictator, suppressing all parties but his own. Soon he ordered Thälmann's arrest and subsequent murder. Many of the moderates also were murdered by Hitler's regime. History can be more tragic than the stage.

Government by a Death Cult: The Nazi Period. During the 1920s a small group of right-wing extremists was organized by Hitler under the name of the National Socialist German Workers' Party. Its main ideas were laid down in 1924 in Hitler's book *Mein Kampf.* This book extolled war as the be-all and end-all of politics. War, according to Hitler, was eternal and inevitable. Nations were determined by race, he said, and were destined to struggle perpetually against each other for survival like other species of animals in a world of insufficient food supplies. It was the duty of the German people to fight against all other nations and to turn itself into a *master race,* subjugating or exterminating all rivals, who, in any case, were "inferior" by definition. Jews were to be the first—but not the last—marked for extermination. For the master race the only honorable alternative to victory was death, either in combat or by suicide.

Death and its symbols were made psychologically attractive by the Nazis. Skulls and crossbones formed part of the insignia of Hitler's black-clad Elite Guard; honorable death was glorified in more than half the songs in the official Nazi songbook. Hitler tried to practice what he preached. Facing defeat at the end of World War II, he gave orders for the destruction of Germany. Many Nazi leaders ended their lives by suicide; Hitler ordered an aide to kill him and burn his body.

How could such an insane set of beliefs win the support of the German people? It happened in the four short years between 1929 and 1933 when the explosive legacies of German history and politics reached their peak under the impact of a worldwide depression.

After World War I and the great inflation, the depression of 1929 was the third of the major catastrophes within a dozen years to hit the German middle class. German political culture once again showed its unfortunate tendency of reaching toward extremes in times of crisis. As before, the more conservative people in Germany moved toward authoritarianism, while the more radical shifted toward extreme radicalism. In the United States the opposite happened: the depression was answered by a series of reform efforts, aimed at preserving not only property rights but also human rights, and at serving human needs. In England, too, Keynesian economic theory was applied, preserving both welfare spending and private enterprise. In Germany, however, rigid and outdated policies were put ahead of people. Even the Catholic Center Party advocated an extreme response to the depression: cutting public spending, lowering wages, and reducing the power of trade unions.

Hurt by the deepening depression, the masses of the middle class moved far to the right. In particular, the lower middle class flocked to Adolf Hitler's National Socialist German Workers' Party, which until 1930 had been only a minor far-right sect. From 1930 on, however, Hitler received massive financial and press support from big business groups. Some feared communism; others wanted "order" and a curb on democratic labor

TABLE 6.1 *Electoral Shares of German Parties and Groupings, 1871–1976 (by approximate percentage of all eligible voters)*

	1871	1912	Jan. 1919	June 1920	May 1924	May 1928	Sept. 1930	Nov. 1932
Citizens entitled to vote (in millions)	7.7	14.4	36.8	36.0	38.4	41.2	43.0	44.4
Valid votes cast (in millions)	3.9	12.2	30.4	28.2	29.3	30.8	35.0	35.5
1. Far Right:								
Nazis					5	2	15	26
Conservatives	12	11	8	13	19	14	10	7
2. Moderate Right:			DVP					
National Liberals (1919–33: DVP)	15	12	4	11	6	6	3	2
Subtotal Right	*27*	*23*	*12*	*24*	*30*	*22*	*28*	*35*
3. Progressives and Democrats (1928: State Party)	8	10	16	7	6	10	9	2
4. Center and Bavarian Peoples Party	10	14	16	14	13	11	12	12
5. Particularists	4	9	1	1	1	1	1	2
Subtotal Center	*22*	*33*	*33*	*22*	*20*	*22*	*22*	*16*
6. Social Democrats	2	29	32	17	15	22	20	16
Independent Social Democrats			6	13	1			
7. Communists				2	10	8	11	13
Subtotal Left	*2*	*29*	*38*	*32*	*26*	*30*	*31*	*29*
8. Nonvoters	49	15	17	22	25	26	19	20
Total	100	100	100	100		100	100	100

[1] The FDP share of valid votes cast was 5.8 percent, well above the 5 percent minimum required by the "threshold clause" of the electoral law.

[2] Includes 2 percent invalid votes.

[3] After 1969 the minimum age for voters had been lowered from 21 to 18 years.

[4] The FDP share of valid votes was 8.4 percent; thus the distance from the 5 percent threshold was enlarged. This was effected by much more use of splitting between the first and the second ballot of each voter, similar to 1961.

[5] Includes 0.7 percent invalid votes.

[6] Includes 0.8 percent invalid votes.

TABLE 6.1 *(Continued)*

Mar. 1933	Aug. 1949	Sept. 1953	Sept. 1957	Sept. 1961	Sept. 1965	June 1969	Nov. 1972	Oct. 1976
44.7	31.2	33.1	35.4	37.4	38.5	38.7	41.4[3]	42.1
39.3	24.5	28.5	31.1	31.3	32.6	33.0	37.4	37.8
39								
7								
	DP and DRP			NDP	2	4	0.5	0.3
	4	4	4	1				
1								
47	*4*	*4*	*4*	*1*	*2*	*4*	*0.5*	*0.3*
	FDP							
2	9	9	6	11	8	5[1]	7.6[4]	7.1
	CDU/CSU							
12	24	36	43	38	40	39.5	40.5	43.7
0	13	7	5	2	—	8	0.1	
14	*49*	*52*	*54*	*51*	*48*	*44.5*	*48.2*	*50.8*
16	22	25	27	31	33	36.5	41.5	38.3
11	4	2		1			0.3	0.6
27	*26*	*27*	*27*	*32*	*33*	*36.5*	*41.8*	*38.9*
12	24	17	15	16	16	15[2]	9.5[5]	10.1[6]
100		100	100	100	100	100	100.0	100.0

Sources: K. W. Deutsch, "The German Federal Republic," in R. C. Macridis, ed., *Modern Political Systems: Europe,* 4th ed., 1978. Adapted by permission of Prentice-Hall, Inc., Englewood Cliffs, N.J.; German Consulate, Boston, Mass.; for 1972.
Süddeutsche Zeitung, November 21, 1972; for 1976, International Centre for Parliamentary Documentation, *Chronicle of Parliamentary Elections* 11 (July 1, 1976–June 30, 1977).

TABLE 6.2 *Six Authoritarian Victories in German History*

1. Charlemagne subjugates the Saxons, 764–814.
2. Luther and the princes smash the Peasants' War, 1525.
3. Absolute princes rule over Germany's recovery after the Thirty Years' War, 1648–1701.
4. Prussia and Bismarck unite Germany, 1862–71.
5. German voters elect Hindenburg president, 1925.
6. Hindenburg appoints Adolf Hitler chancellor, 1933.

Similar tables of authoritarian victories could be compiled for other nations. For Britain and France, however, they would have to be interspersed with major revolutions and popular reforms. The triumphs of German authoritarianism were more frequent, bigger, and less relieved by democratic triumphs.

unions; still others expected profits from rearmament or even greater profits from war and the conquest of a new empire. The Protestant middle-class parties lost most of their supporters to the Nazis, but nine-tenths of the Catholic Center Party's voters remained faithful. The Center Party, however, decided not to collaborate any longer with liberal or socialist groups and joined forces with the right. This decision led to the voluntary dissolution of the Center Party in 1933 and was followed by a concordat between Hitler and the Vatican—which the Nazis later violated.

On the left, workers remained cool to Hitler. Both the Social Democrats and Communists kept nine-tenths of their voters. They continued to oppose the Nazis, often at the cost of their lives. The main sources of Nazi voting strength came from the middle classes, the rural population, and the newly mobilized former nonvoters. Outside the ballot box some of the military, like some business leaders, were useful to the Nazis.

The Nazi empire, according to its leaders, was to last a thousand years. It had a six-year period of arms prosperity and cheap victories over weaker or more timid opponents, followed by World War II. From 1942 to 1945 a series of military defeats brought on the complete collapse of Nazi Germany. Those upper- and middle-class groups that had supported Hitler in the belief of serving either Germany or their own group interests now discovered that the war was destroying Germany, as well as their own lives, their homes, and their children.

By the end of the war almost all major German cities were leveled. Today, guidebooks point out the few exceptions, such as Heidelberg, where most of the houses were left standing. The Nazis' projected thousand-year rule had shrunk to twelve. It left behind hundreds of thousands of tortured and murdered Germans, millions of dead German soldiers, half a million German civilian war dead, 6 million slaughtered Jews; another 60 million lives lost in World War II, and a Germany in ruins. One of the Nazis' propaganda slogans before 1942 had been, "To find Hitler's monument, look around you." It was the truest thing the propagandists ever said.

The Temporary Disappearance of a German State, 1945–49. For a time after the war there was no German government and no German political system. Germany was divided into four zones of occupation, each occupied and governed by the military forces of one of the chief Allied powers— Britain, France, the United States, and the Soviet Union. Berlin, conquered by the Soviet army in 1945 and then located deep in the Soviet zone of occupation, was similarly divided into four sectors, each under one of the four powers, with a joint Allied *Kommandatura* that was to decide common problems in the city by unanimous vote.

For a time, Germans had no share in the governing of their occupied country. Soon, however, the envisaged cooperation among the four Allies quickly dwindled and gave way to the Cold War. Each side, in gradually restoring some political life in the part of Germany it controlled, took care to establish the institutions and parties it found congenial. The Western Allies, who by 1948 had merged their zones, encouraged democratic parties, and, particularly under United States influence, encouraged private business enterprise and forbade any major nationalization of industry. In this manner, important long-term decisions about the basic structure of the German economy and political system were made, as a result of the international situation of the late 1940s. By their decisions about currency, industrial property, trade union structure, and the social welfare system, the Western Allies established in the western parts of Germany the foundations for a pluralistic and democratic political system, but also eventually for a significant degree of concentration of private wealth and economic power. The effect of these decisions later helped to make the Federal Republic somewhat more conservative and to keep the Social Democratic Party out of the national government longer than might otherwise have been the case.

The Soviet Union, in its own zone of occupation, did the opposite. It established what in effect soon became the one-party rule of a reconstituted Communist Party, even though the latter had been renamed *Socialist Unity Party of Germany (SED)* and augmented by a merger with a part of the local Social Democrats, brought about under considerable Soviet pressure. Two nonsocialist parties were also permitted a nominal existence, but without any real autonomy or power. This effective one-party system in politics was supplemented in time by Soviet-type institutions in economics, such as nationalizing of all major industrial establishments, central planning, and eventually replacing of individual or family farming by agricultural production cooperatives (LPGs). In politics, a Soviet-type dictatorship was established, dependent on the Soviet Union and leaving little or no room for free discussion or dissent.

Another Try: The German Federal Republic. Out of the ruins of World War II and the quarrels of the victorious powers there emerged by 1949 two postwar Germanys: a Communist-ruled *German Democratic Republic (GDR)*, encompassing one-quarter of the German population, in the east, and a *German Federal Republic (GFR)*, embracing three-quarters of the German people, in the west.

In some respects, the German Federal Republic represented an attempt to restore an element of continuity with the German past and particularly with the Weimar Republic. It repudiated the Hitler regime, but defined itself as the successor to its legal and moral obligations, such as the eventual paying of indemnities to victims of nazism and their families. At the same time, however, the German Federal Republic is in some ways very different from all the German political systems that preceded it.

In order to understand the changing stakes of politics in that republic, as well as the patterns of participation in its political life, it is perhaps best to reverse our usual sequence of analysis and to take a look first at its new institutions, processes, and machinery of government.

THE PROCESS AND MACHINERY OF POLITICS IN THE GERMAN FEDERAL REPUBLIC

The Federal Republic was created in 1949 out of the British, French, and American zones of occupation with major economic and political assistance from the United States. The main effort for the success of the Federal Republic has come from its own people, who worked hard and kept their heads. In the last thirty years, for the first time, Germans have reacted more often by moving toward the middle than toward the extremes. The far right and far left parties in West Germany are small. In 1976, Communist votes amounted to about 0.7 percent, down from a high of 5.7 percent in 1949. The neo-Nazi National Democratic Party (NDP) votes were about 0.3 percent, compared to a peak of 4.3 percent in 1969. Each of these percentages could probably be much increased under the right conditions, such as an economic depression, but the far right is not likely to exceed 15 percent, even under favorable circumstances, and the far left not much more than 5 percent. In 1980 a new Ecology Party polled almost 2 percent of the total vote and the remaining ten splinter parties—ranging from Neo Nazis to Communists—received 0.4 percent of the vote, (down from 0.9 percent in 1976).

A New Party System. The important news came from nearer to the middle of the political spectrum (see Table 6.1). To the right of center a new party has arisen, the *Christian Democratic Union (CDU),* with an affiliate in Bavaria, the *Christian Social Union (CSU),* which caters to local sentiment in that state, but otherwise acts most often as part of the CDU. The CDU/CSU is a successor to the Catholic Center Party, but it appeals explicitly also to Protestant voters. From the beginning of the Federal Republic it has been the chief party of the middle class in town and country, and it has received generous financial support from industry. Further, it has been the main political voice of farmers and rural laborers and of people with very high and very low incomes, the latter being mainly pensioners and dependent family members from the countryside. The CDU/CSU also attracts proportionately more votes from those over sixty, from women, and from those Catholics and Protestants who regularly attend church.

The CDU/CSU's share of the electorate increased steadily after WW II, mainly at the expense of smaller middle-class splinter groups and parties. In 1957 the CDU/CSU alliance peaked at 50 percent and since then has been fairly stable (between 45 and 48 percent of the vote in the six elections since that time). Supporters include most of the former moderate right, leaving only the extreme fringe to the NDP. On its left wing it attracts a significant contingent of votes from Catholic trade unionists and from city dwellers in the industrial Rhine-Ruhr area. Some prominent

CDU/CSU leaders, like former Chancellor Georg Kiesinger, former President Heinrich Lübke, and current Federal President Carstens, once were minor members of the Nazi Party, but the CDU/CSU commitment to constitutional and democratic government has held firm for three decades since 1949.

The only other surviving middle-class party of any importance is the *Free Democratic Party (FDP),* which attracted 10 percent of valid votes cast in 1980. Apart from its smaller size, the FDP differs from the CDU/CSU in three respects. On the issues of education and culture it is secular, if not slightly anticlerical. It favors greater separation of church and state, whereas the CDU/CSU defends public support for denominational schools and public collection of taxes for the church. It is more hostile to censorship, whereas the CDU/CSU is more willing to invoke the powers of the state in enforcing the moral views of the church. On most such issues the views of the FDP place it to the left of the CDU/CSU. Second, in foreign affairs and problems of German unification the FDP favors a more conciliatory policy toward the countries of the Soviet bloc, including East Germany. Here, too, the FDP stands to the left of the CDU/CSU. Third, in economic matters the FDP has long been to the right of the CDU/CSU. It has been more favorable to the viewpoint of employers and management, less sympathetic to wage increases and welfare spending, and more often opposed to government intervention in economic life. For this reason, the FDP has received much of its financial support from the same industrial and business interests as the CDU/CSU.

Throughout the Federal Republic the FDP has drawn votes from the free professions, civil servants, employers, and a minority of churchgoing Protestants. The party also used to attract regional support from northern Germany, some of it conservative, and from southern Germany, much of it traditionally liberal.

By the end of the 1960s some of the conservative support for the FDP was disappearing. More conservative supporters of the FDP were switching to the CDU/CSU in reaction to the party's trying to gain ground among younger and more liberal voters. This shift in its electoral base has placed the party somewhat more clearly to the left of the CDU/CSU. At the same time, the introduction of government subsidies for political parties has given the FDP a new source of income and reduced its dependence on business and industry as sources of funds. Together, these changes have made it easier for the FDP to form a coalition with the Social Democrats, and they may continue to influence FDP policies throughout the 1980s.

To the left of center stands the *Social Democratic Party (SPD),* the direct successor of the Social Democratic Party of the old empire and the Weimar Republic. In contrast to the record during the Weimar era, the SPD now receives practically all the votes of labor and of the left of center, which it no longer has to share with the Communist Party, which has been insignificant since 1949 and outlawed since 1953.[3] Throughout the 1960s and 1970s the SPD moved from its old class appeal to workers and toward a new image as a progressive party for all the people of the Federal Republic. During this period the party reduced its emphasis on nationalization and public ownership and stressed instead indirect economic policies aimed at combining economic growth, full employment, and comprehensive welfare with the flexibility of a free market. Appealing to the ambition of most Germans to own a car, one SPD poster in the 1960s showed the party's initials on an automobile license plate.

The party's new look has paid off in votes. German white-collar voters who did not identify themselves as proletarians have been quite willing to see themselves as progressives. The 1969 and 1972 elections brought the party a substantial gain in votes, placing it only a short distance behind the CDU/CSU. This opened the way to a coalition with

[3]Although the Communist Party (KPD) was declared unconstitutional, a successor party (abbreviated DKP), composed mainly of leadership from the old party, has been allowed to operate.

the FDP, which made Gustav Heinemann the first Social Democratic president since 1925 and Willy Brandt the first Social Democratic chancellor since 1930. In the elections of 1972, this coalition substantially increased its majority. It kept a slightly reduced majority in the 1976 election and improved its position again in 1980.

Together, these three parties—SPD, FDP, and CDU/CSU—have formed a new party system, which is in contrast to the many parties of the Weimar era. The two major parties, CDU/CSU and SPD, have regularly polled well over four-fifths of all votes cast. Many observers have assumed, therefore, that the Federal Republic is on its way to a two-party system and that the days of the FDP are numbered. Despite a decade of such predictions, the FDP appears alive and well. This was confirmed by the results of the 1980 general election, when the SPD vote remained at 42 percent, the CDU/CSU share fell slightly, and the FDP vote rose to 10 percent over its 7.9 percent share of the vote in 1976. Apparently, many CDU voters who could not bring themselves to vote for their party's more rightwing candidate for chancellor, Franz Josef Strauss, turned to the FDP rather than moving all the way to the SPD. Thus the FDP offers a significant alternative for those voters who are dissatisfied with the CDU/CSU but unwilling to give up a distinctive middle-class identity or to entrust their political fate completely to the Social Democrats. Being small, the FDP also can offer faster-rising public careers to younger persons of political talent, in contrast to the much less hospitable bureaucracy of the two major political parties. So long as these conditions persist, the Federal Republic's "two-and-a-half-party" system may well endure.

A New Type of Federalism. The organization of the Federal Republic is laid down in the *Basic Law.* Passed in 1949, it is a constitution in fact, though not in name. Theoretically, it is to remain valid until "a constitution comes into effect which has been freely decided upon by the German people," that is, after the hoped-for German reunification. Actually, the Basic Law is entering the fourth decade of its validity and is now considered permanent by most West Germans.

The Basic Law created a new variety of federalism. Under its provisions the federal government in Bonn has direct control of only a few matters, chiefly foreign affairs, defense, federal finances, the postal, telegraph, and telephone services, and the railroads. A second group of tasks of government belongs exclusively to the ten *Länder* (plus West Berlin), which are similar to states in the United States or provinces in Canada. The Länder directly control all matters of education, from grade schools to universities. They, and not Bonn, are responsible for most of the police power and for whatever regulations are required to ensure freedom of the press. Moreover, they own and control the radio and television media (except for one competing network established in the 1960s). The Länder also have most of the administrative machinery of the country. A third group of governmental responsibilities is given to the national government and the Länder concurrently. Here the Länder may legislate, unless federal legislation supersedes their actions. Fourth, the Länder, in addition to their own tasks, carry out all federal laws and regulations, except those few directly executed by the federal government (see Table 6.3).

The Federal Government in Operation. The most powerful office in the federal government is that of the *chancellor*. This individual appoints and dismisses, in effect, all Cabinet members; in these matters, the president is bound to follow the chancellor's proposals. In case of war or emergency the chancellor, not the president, becomes commander in chief of the armed forces. Generally, the chancellor guides public policy. Within the limits of the Basic Law he or she assigns jurisdiction among the ministries. He or she cannot be impeached and can be overthrown only if a legislative majority agrees on a successor.

Konrad Adenauer of the CDU/CSU was the first chancellor. In his long and strong administration from 1949 to 1963 he set many patterns for the office. His CDU/CSU successor, Ludwig Erhard (1963–66) was not as successful, and neither was the CDU/CSU leader Georg Kiesinger, who served as chancellor of a "great coalition" government by the two major parties, CDU/CSU and SPD (1966–69). In 1972 a new and victorious socialist-liberal coalition of SPD and FDP made Willy Brandt chancellor, with high hopes for a new policy toward East Germany in foreign affairs and reforms in domestic policies. The changes in foreign policy took place, but the internal reforms lagged. Inflation and unemployment got slightly—but disquietingly—worse, and the policy toward East Germany was criticized for having brought fewer improvements than expected. At the same time, Chancellor Brandt seemed to be losing control of some of the day-to-day operations of his administration, and one of his aides was arrested—and later convicted—as a spy for the GDR. In the resulting scandal Brandt lost support from a part of his own party, the SPD, and found it necessary to resign. His successor, Helmut Schmidt, also from the SPD, has created once again the image of a strong chancellor in effective control of his party and his administration. He has continued most of Brandt's policies at home and abroad, but has modified Brandt's emotional and socialist appeal by a deliberate stress on pragmatism, efficiency, and the capacity to get things done—an ability that many German voters like. By late 1979, polls showed the popularity of the SPD to be in the 40 percent range, and Schmidt as a chancellor had the approval of over 70 percent of the voters. The 1980 election results returned Schmidt as chancellor with little increase in his party's vote but a solid increase in the strength of his centrist coalition partner, the FDP.

The *president* is, primarily, a ceremonial head of state with a fixed five-year term of office. Unlike presidents of the Weimar regime, today's German presidents cannot claim to represent the German

TABLE 6.3 *Initiation and Execution of Laws*

Execution through:	INITIATION OF LEGISLATION BY:		
	Federation	Länder	Both concurrently
Federation	Foreign affairs, defense, federal finances		
Länder	Most other federal legislation	Education, press, communications, police	Sphere of concurrent legislation

people by direct election,[4] and their only important powers are reserved for emergencies. If the legislature has rejected the chancellor in a vote of confidence but cannot agree on a successor, the president can decide either to dissolve the legislature and call a new election or to install a minority chancellor by declaring, at the request of the federal government, a state of emergency. Another reserve power allows the president, along with the chancellor, to declare a national defense emergency—in effect a state of war—if the legislature cannot be promptly convened. Fortunately, neither of these reserve powers have as yet been needed, but in some future emergency they may prove important.

Federal legislation is carried out by a two-chamber legislature. One house, the *Bundestag,* is the main source of federal legislation. It is so much more important than the other that we might well speak of a one-and-a-half chamber system, as in Britain and France, where power has shifted to the directly elected chamber of each legislature. Vis-à-vis the executive, however, the Bundestag has less power than the House of Commons, but more than the French National Assembly. Work in the Bundestag is carried on largely in committees, and it is controlled by the parliamentary party caucuses, called *fractions.* Party discipline is tight.

The second chamber, the *Bundesrat,* or Federal Council, consists of delegates from the Länder governments. The delegation from each Land votes as a unit and follows its government's instructions. Thanks to the Bundesrat's share of legislative power, major laws and emergency laws cannot be enacted without state consent. Moreover, several states are actually urban centers with large numbers of industrial workers. This practically assures them a socialist government or else a coalition government with socialist participation. The city-states of Hamburg and Bremen are examples. Thus there is a built-in balance between Christian Democratic states like Bavaria and the Social Democratic ones. Finally, Bundesrat members are backed by the strong bureaucracies of their Länder, whose members may differ in view

[4]Presidents are indirectly elected by a special convention composed of members of the Bundestag and an equal number of members from the Länder assemblies. They can be impeached by vote of either house of the legislature and then tried before the Federal Constitutional Court for violations of federal law.

from the federal administration. This administrative expertise makes the Bundestag stronger than it appears on the surface, and it leads to passage of better laws.

In the process of making laws, nearly two-thirds of all bills are initiated by the federal government (see Figure 6.1). Most of the rest are started by the Bundestag. The Bundestag initiates roughly eight laws in a hundred. A sequence of committee reports, three readings by the Bundestag, and, when needed, joint conference committee proceedings ensure careful scrutiny of each measure.

After World War II, West Germany for the first time established a court system that is independent of the executive power of the government. The highest tribunal is the Federal Constitutional Court. It is charged with reviewing laws to determine their constitutionality, settling major disputes between the federal government and the states, and protecting individuals who complain that their human rights have been violated. Responsibility for judicial review of government actions provides German courts with more power than those in Britain or France, and, as in the United States, the courts have proven willing to use that power. In recent years the Constitutional Court has intervened decisively on matters such as abortions and workers' rights to share in management decisions. The independence of the court was demonstrated in 1973, when it decided that the government's new treaty with East Germany (see p. 256, below) was constitutional but interpreted the treaty in a way that committed the government to continue efforts at reunification of the two Germanys. Such judicial constraints on the government would have been unthinkable in imperial, Weimar, or Nazi Germany.

Political Innovation. To govern is to invent, says political theorist Carl J. Friedrich. The German Federal Republic thus far has lived up to this principle. Its political life has been characterized by at least seven political innovations new to Germany, and all of them have continued to work.

The first is the high degree of *federalism* that has given major powers to the states of the Federal Republic, together with the Bundesrat. State execution of federal laws, concurrent jurisdiction of states and the federal government, and the blend of cooperation and competition between the two bureaucracies make the West German system a new contribution to modern government.

Second, there is the *constructive vote of "no confidence."* The West German government is parliamentary in form, similar to the English; and, as in France, it may be overthrown by a vote of "no confidence." However, in an important variation, the government can overthrow a prime minister (whom the Germans call chancellor in memory of Bismarck and of the earlier empire of medieval days) only if they can agree on a new one. In other words, a government cannot be overthrown in West Germany by a negative majority. This requirement has worked and seemingly has given West Germany more stability than is enjoyed by the political systems of most other large continental countries.

The third innovation is the *threshold clause.* A party that receives less than 5 percent of the total vote in the national election gets no seat in parliament unless it obtains a very strong representation in a particular region. This helps assure that any vigorous and locally concentrated minority will be represented, but avoids giving a national platform to just any minority scattered haphazardly throughout the political system.

Fourth, there is a *two-track voting system.* The West German electoral system combines majority voting with proportional representation. One-half of the members of parliament are elected in single-member constituencies that each can carry by being personally known to the voters. The other half is elected by *party slate;* voters cast a ballot for the entire list by brand name, so to speak. Each list is drawn up by the party, often reflecting in effect the views of its national and regional bureaucracy. If the voters trust the party, they cast their ballot for the election of the whole slate of candidates. If

FIGURE 6.1 *The Passage of Ordinary Bills in the German Federal Republic*

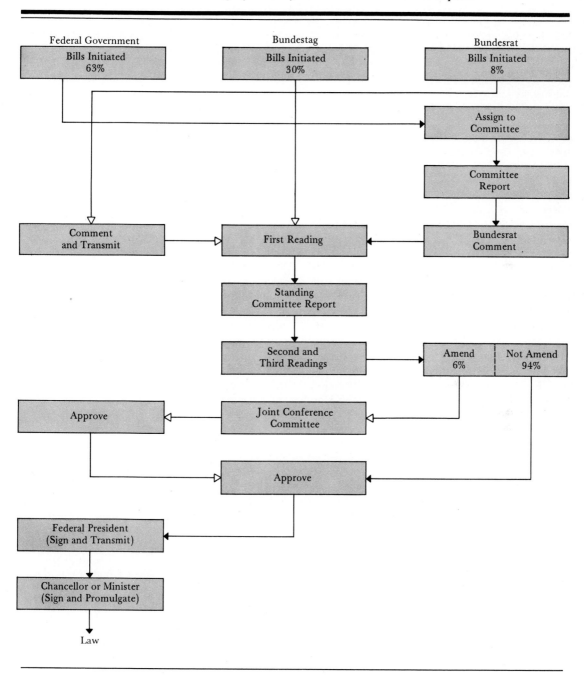

Source: K. W. Deutsch, D. Brent Smith, "The German Federal Republic," in *Modern Political Systems: Europe,* 4th ed., by Roy C. Macridis, c. 1978, p. 237. Adapted by permission of Prentice-Hall Inc., Englewood Cliffs, N.J.; and Heinz Rausch, *Bundestag und Bundesregierung* (Munich: H. C. Beck, 1976).

not, they may vote for the slate of another party, or they may refuse to vote for any slate and vote only for a single candidate. Every West German voter, therefore, has one ballot for an individual in the district and one for an entire slate of candidates chosen by the party. The result is that some reasonably obstreperous individuals can get elected by having political strength of their own, yet the parties can also maintain cohesion. In fact, parties and party bureaucracies are more powerful than individuals under this system.

Fifth, West Germany is the first country in the world that has systematically provided *public financing of competitive political parties*. This innovation has somewhat loosened the dependence of parties on their financiers. Until the 1960s the same major business organization subsidized the Christian Democrats and the so-called Free Democratic Party. As a result the two parties never voted against each other on important matters. Under the new party finance system the Free Democrats no longer have to echo the more numerous Christian Democrats. They have their own money and have used it to vote independently for the new president of West Germany, Gustav Heinemann, and to choose their coalition partners on the state and federal levels.

The sixth innovation, the civilian defense commissioner *(ombudsman),* involves the military sector, which is itself one of the stakes of German politics and which we shall discuss in detail in the following section.

The seventh innovation is the *indexing* of social security payments, maternity and disability payments, and the like *to the cost of living.* As the index of the cost of living rises, so do these payments, semiautomatically, albeit with a six-month delay.[5] This compensates the persons getting these pay-

[5]The law requires each time an enabling vote from the Bundestag to let the automatic increase come into effect. Ordinarily, it would take a bold politician to vote no on such occasions. One such increase was temporarily suspended, however, by vote of the government coalition in the Bundestag in 1978.

ments for most of the effects of inflation, and it still has permitted the German Federal Republic to have one of the lowest inflation rates among all the world's market-economy countries. Several other countries adopted this practice later, but the Federal Republic was among the first to do so.

When all is said and done, what difference can all these innovations make? What is there still to be decided by German voters and in German politics? How large and how meaningful are the stakes of the West German political process?

THE STAKES OF GERMAN POLITICS

In few other countries have the stakes of politics changed as often and as rapidly during the last half century as they have in Germany. In 1930, the stakes included success or failure in combating the depression; in 1933, the choice between democracy and dictatorship; in 1939–43, participation in an attempt at world conquest; in 1944 and early 1945, timely surrender before total destruction; in late 1945 and early 1946, a minimum of food, fuel, and shelter for survival.

Some other matters no longer were at stake in German politics. The unity or division of the country, its territory and boundaries, its economic and social order, and its basic political institutions—all these were decided by the victorious Allies. When the German Federal Republic began to function in 1949, all these decisions had already been made. Whatever German politics in 1949 and the early 1950s were to decide would have to be decided within these constraints.

The first problems that faced all political groups in the Federal Republic after 1949 were economic reconstruction and the resettlement of 10 million German refugees and expellees from Eastern Europe. Both tasks were met with remarkable success, thanks to a combination of German diligence and political stability and American aid. The next task was economic growth, and in this respect the Federal Republic, with an annual per capita growth rate of over 6 percent during the 1950s,

TABLE 6.4 *Rates of Economic Growth and Inflation in Comparative Perspective*

	Annual growth rate in GNP		Annual increase in prices (inflation)	
	1951–70	1971–78	1951–70	1971–78
West Germany	6.3%	2.6%	3.0%	5.5%
Britain	2.7	1.8	4.0	13.5
France	5.1	3.4	5.4	8.9
United States	3.6	2.8	2.7	6.7

Source: Richard Rose, *Politics in England,* 3rd ed. (Boston: Little, Brown, 1980), p. 25, as compiled from published data of the Organization for Economic Cooperation and Development.

was one of the leaders of the Western world. During the 1960s the pace slowed, but remained close to a respectable 5 percent, and the per capita income of the Federal Republic overtook that of both France and Britain. Even with its slower growth rate of 2.6 percent in 1970–78, the Federal Republic maintained its lead and increased it slightly compared to Britain (see Table 6.4).

Throughout the more than thirty years since the stabilization of the mark in 1948, West Germany has managed to combine economic growth with a remarkable degree of price stability. During the 1970s, as Table 6.4 shows, inflation rose throughout the Western nations, but even then the Federal Republic experienced one of the lowest inflation rates in the Western world. The Federal Republic has also had an excellent record in modernizing its technology and working conditions. Cooperative arrangements have been worked out between the well-organized groups of employers and unions, often to the point of sharing decisions on how the work place will be run (an arrangement called codetermination). Economic growth, fairly stable prices, and cooperative labor relations have all helped smooth the introduction of new technology and avoid disruptive strikes.

The problem of finding new markets for German industry to replace its traditional outlets in Eastern Europe, now under Communist rule, was solved by finding new markets in the United States and particularly in the European Common Market. West German governments steadfastly supported the increasing economic integration of Europe. Although this integration has remained gradual and partial and made relatively little progress in the 1960s, its importance for the Federal Republic's economy has been great.

By the end of the 1960s the Federal Republic had grown so prosperous that Chancellor Brandt's government found it advisable to revalue the national unit of currency, the mark, upward by about 10 percent—a step almost unparalleled in the Western world since 1930. In 1973 the mark was revalued upward by another 10 percent in relation to the devalued United States dollar and the currencies that remained tied to it. Another 2 percent revaluation came in the fall of 1979. From 1970 to early 1979, the mark has risen against the dollar from a value of $0.27 to $0.56. The earlier undervaluation of the mark had aided German exports. Whether the present higher valuation of the German mark would hurt exports is not yet certain.

Not surprisingly, the German postwar economic

record has been looked upon with envy by many nations. It also seems clear, however, that the 1970s saw a slowdown in growth and apparent fading of the German "economic miracle." Many Germans believe that it is necessary to sustain rapid increases in prosperity if their complex political system is not to be undercut by divisive struggles. Others, particularly in the younger generation, with little memory of hard times, object to the heavy emphasis on materialism that has accompanied Germany's economic success. Further complicating the picture is the fact that other nations that are Germany's trading partners are now more inclined to resist the exports that have traditionally driven the German economy and expect Bonn to accept more imports and offer greater financial assistance to economically weaker nations. All of this simply suggests that despite its tremendous past achievements, the economy—its pace and direction—will remain one of the vital stakes of the republic's politics.

Reunification or Détente: The Choice of an "Eastern Policy."

Other problems have proved far less manageable. German reunification has remained a widely held desire, but as a matter of practical politics it has receded to a more distant future. For over twenty years governments in the Federal Republic's capital of Bonn have refused to recognize the Communist-ruled German Democratic Republic on its eastern border, hoping that it would collapse and that its Soviet backers would withdraw. Nothing of the sort has happened. The westward flight of nearly 200,000 East Germans per year from 1949 to 1961 was reduced to a trickle by the building of a heavily guarded wall between the Communist and Western-ruled sectors of Berlin. Despite its unpopular government the GDR has had an economic growth rate similar to that of the Federal Republic, even though its per capita income and, particularly, its consumer standards have remained below those of its western neighbor. Nonetheless, by 1970 both Germanys were prosperous and growing.

By the late 1960s, both the American and West German governments seemed agreed that confrontation tactics had brought the German problem no nearer to solution and seemed willing to try new approaches through negotiations with the Soviet Union and the GDR. In 1973 the new approaches had borne fruit. The two "German states"—the GFR and GDR—had recognized each other as such, even though the GFR refused to accord the GDR all diplomatic formalities due a foreign power, because, in the GFR view, Germans could not be foreigners to each other. The GDR continued to demand full formal recognition in accordance with international law, but the substance of the quarrel had been settled in large part. A new Berlin Agreement gave the West Berliners somewhat easier access to the GDR, where many had relatives; and it also provided for easier and more elaborate guaranteed land communications between the Federal Republic and West Berlin by road and rail across the territory of the GDR. The latter had received full diplomatic recognition from France, Britain, and many other countries; United States recognition came in 1974; and the two German states applied for membership in the United Nations and were accepted there in 1973. West Germany had formally accepted that the Oder-Neisse boundary of Poland would not be changed by use of force, and the Bundestag had ratified the treaty. Chancellor Willy Brandt had received the Nobel Prize for Peace, and his coalition had won a clear-cut victory in the elections of November 1972, which gave it a larger and presumably safer majority in the Bundestag. A long-standing source of German and worldwide insecurity, the eastern frontiers of Germany, seemed to have been settled in a peaceful manner, and the same *Ostpolitik,* or "Eastern policy," was continued by Brandt's successor, Chancellor Helmut Schmidt.

A Continuing Problem: Armament and Arms Control.

Clearly, West Germany's political opinion on the eastern territories has shifted, and the approach used by chancellors Brandt and Schmidt thus far has been a success. But we do not know how it will succeed in the future in containing further and heavier rearmament or in other critical areas. The character and size of the German military sector continue to be one of the stakes of German politics. Germany was supposed to be disarmed after World War II, but the Federal Republic was rearmed to a limited degree in the 1950s, in response to American pressure more than any domestic West German demand. In 1977–78 about 3.3 percent of the West German gross national product went into defense spending. (The German Democratic Republic had comparable rearmament, in proportion to its smaller size, under the watchful eyes of the Soviet Union.)

West German armament is limited under the Pact of Paris of 1954. West Germany is barred from having or procuring nuclear weapons, chemical weapons, or bacterial weapons. Some West German politicians, such as CSU leader Franz Josef Strauss, have demanded that West Germany be given the formal right to possess any kind of weapons against any possible adversary. That is, Strauss has demanded qualitative equality with the Soviet Union and the United States. However, the West Germans have not won this right. Most of the other West German leaders do not demand it, and West German voters have not shown any interest in pushing rearmament. In 1969 the new coalition government of Chancellor Willy Brandt agreed to sign the *Non-Proliferation Treaty,* renouncing nuclear weapons, and the treaty was ratified in 1975.

The West German armies are under civilian supervision, reinforced by the sixth of the innovations mentioned earlier, this one borrowed from Sweden. This innovation consists in a civilian defense commissioner to hear and investigate complaints—an ombudsman, as the Swedes call him. In West Germany the ombudsman is a parliamentary commissioner to whom soldiers can complain directly. There is also an important office of internal leadership within the armed forces that tries to educate the soldiers to think of themselves as citizens in uniform.

Such special institutions may be needed, because the political behavior of the military posed major problems to earlier German governments. Under the Weimar Republic the military was far more nationalistic and militaristic than the majority of the voters. It acted as "a state within the state" and contributed to the overthrow of the constitutional regime. The government and major parties of the Federal Republic were concerned to prevent a repetition of these events. As late as the mid-1950s, one-tenth of West German poll respondents between the ages of fifteen and twenty-five professed open admiration for Hitler. But in another poll only 10 percent of German young men of military age said that they would consider military service as a career. These two groups are likely to overlap. The Germans who are drafted into the army for a short period constitute a cross section of public opinion. But those who volunteer to become the professional noncommissioned and commissioned officers may well be more nationalistic and more militaristic in outlook than the average German. In opinion polls in the middle and late 1960s about 33 percent of respondents agreed that "we ought to have again a single strong national party that really represents the interests of all strata of our people." Also, in elections in the 1960s, small garrison towns showered significantly more votes on the neo-Nazi party than did similar small towns where no troops were stationed. We do not know whether this will be a greater problem in the future or whether civilian democracy in the Federal Republic will somehow digest, absorb, and control it.

The Question of Social Structure. As some industrial societies become richer, questions of social, educational, and economic inequality seem to become more salient to a part of their population. Just this seems to have occurred in the German Federal Republic. Despite its prosperity, inequalities of *income* have remained high, with the top 10 percent of income receivers getting over 41 percent of the total income—a higher share than in eleven other countries for which we have data.

TABLE 6.5 *Percentage of Each Occupation Group Owning Different Types of Assets, 1973*

	Savings accounts	Accounts in home building societies	Life insur- ance	Stocks and bonds	Homes and/or land
OCCUPATIONAL GROUP					
Blue-collar workers	94	37	84	15	40
White-collar workers	96	49	81	35	37
Public employees	96	62	80	30	41
Farmers	89	47	68	14	92
Independent business- people	91	58	88	37	67
Households outside the work force	84	16	64	22	30

Source: Bundesminister für Arbeit und Sozialordnung. *Einkommens- und Vermögensverteilung,* 1977, tables 32–36, pp. 76–80.

Inequalities of *wealth* in the GFR, as almost everywhere, are much higher. In the 1960s, West Germany launched a series of programs to help spread the ownership of financial assets more widely throughout society. Not just tax relief but government-paid cash bonuses have been offered to middle- and lower-income persons who set aside money in savings accounts, home building societies, life insurance, and corporate stocks. Since that time, ownership of such wealth has become more broadly based. As Table 6.5 illustrates, the vast majority of Germans in all the major occupational groups have savings accounts and private life insurance policies (nor does the size of the typical savings nest egg differ very much among the groups). Home ownership is about equally common among blue-collar, white-collar, and public employees.

The greatest inequalities dividing the German social structure are not these assets associated with middle-class (burgerliche) life but those associated with capitalist wealth, or what Germans term "productive assets." Productive assets include factories, commercial transportation facilities, machinery, and ownership shares in these things. As Table 6.6 shows, the distribution of productive wealth is even more unequal than the distribution of all wealth. There is some evidence that the share owned by the richest 1 or 2 percent of Germans has declined somewhat in recent years, but the redistribution has been mainly to the next-richest groups. The latest data (for 1973) indicate that the richest 20 percent own 78 percent of all wealth and 86 percent of productive assets in West Germany.

The government of the GFR has a good deal of leverage to reduce this relatively high degree of inequality and to bring it down to the level found

TABLE 6.6 *Distribution of Households and Ownership of Wealth, 1973*

	Percent of all German households	Share of total net wealth	Share of productive assets*
OCCUPATIONAL GROUP			
Blue-collar workers	28	16	0.5
White-collar workers	20	15	2.6
Public employees	6	4	1.6
Farmers	3	9	5.8
Independent businesspeople	7	35	87.8
Households outside the work force	35	21	1.7

*Includes ownership of common stocks and bonds

Source: Calculated from H. Mierheim and L. Wicke, "Die Vermögenskonzentration in der Bundesrepublik," *Wirtschaftsdienst,* December 1974, pp. 604–8.

in Scandinavia or Britain, if enough of the influential political groups and actors should so desire. In 1977 the total income of the public sector in West Germany accounted for 56 percent of national income, and public sector employment amounted to 10 percent of the work force.[6] Here again, the potential stakes of politics are high.

A final stake of politics may be what is sometimes called the "quality of life." In West Germany this problem has become linked in part with the conflict between generations. These are troubles that the Federal Republic shares with other West-

[6]*Germany, June 1978: O.E.C.D. Economic Surveys* (Paris: Organization for Economic Cooperation and Development, 1978); and Statistisches Bundesamt, Wiesbaden, *Statistisches Jahrbuch für Bundesrepublik Deutschland, 1978.* (Stuttgart: Kohlhammer Verlag, 1978).

ern countries, but in its own case have become particularly acute. Impoverished by the war, a generation of Germans concentrated their thoughts and efforts on restoring material prosperity and later on increasing it. Now a generation of young Germans is in revolt against what seems to be an excessive preoccupation with material gain. In their eyes the moral authority of their elders is more suspect than in any other country: what did their parents do during the years of Hitler's crimes? German student protest has been more vehement than elsewhere, and poll results suggest that nearly two-thirds of young Germans between the ages of fifteen and twenty-one sympathize with these protests. Whatever the cause of this unrest, it can hardly have been excessively permissive education. Most German families are still authoritarian, and few German parents ever become followers of Dr. Spock.

Rising German discontent—of the young as well

as of some of their elders—has extended to the political parties and to the machinery of government. The late 1960s saw the growth of a new political movement, the *Extra-Parliamentary Opposition (APO),* which included many writers and other intellectuals and was highly critical of all three major parties. Before the 1969 and 1972 elections, however, prominent writers like Günter Grass campaigned to swing the votes of the discontented behind the candidates of the SPD, and they succeeded to a large extent. In the 1976 election the practice continued.

From Discontent to Terrorism. In the 1970s acute discontent declined among the many, but became extreme among a few. Small numbers of people, mostly in their twenties and early thirties, found normal professions and politics unpromising or unattractive and resorted to conspiracy and *terrorism.* Their language and ideology were borrowed from the anarchist and Marxist far left, but their actions reminded many people of the right-wing student assassins of the early 1920s who had killed such statesmen of the Weimar Republic as the Catholic leader Matthias Erzberger and the Liberal Walter Rathenau.

This time, terrorism began with attacks on banks and department stores to get money for the terrorist organization. Those who conducted these raids, in the name of a vague "proletarian revolution" did not hesitate to kill real workers— salespeople, bank clerks, and drivers—who got in their way. Some were soon caught and sentenced to long prison terms, but others, remaining at large, then tried to kidnap hostages to force the release of these prisoners. In 1977 they killed a prominent hostage, Hans Martin Schleyer, president of the German Employers Association and a former SS member, when the Schmidt government refused a bargain of this kind. Another victim, banker Jürgen Ponte, was killed in the same year when he resisted his kidnappers, one of whom was his own goddaughter.

The German terrorists had allies in small groups in other countries and also ties with Palestinian terrorist groups. Through the latter they arranged in October 1977 the kidnapping of a large German tourist plane with its crew and passengers: 106 men, women, and children. The lives of these people, they announced, were to be bartered for the freedom of some prominent convicted terrorists, imprisoned in the maximum security prison at Stammheim in Baden-Würtemberg in southern Germany. The plane was flown first to Baghdad, where one pilot was killed for having tried to escape at the airport, and then continued to Mogadishu in Somalia, while the German government negotiated with the terrorists.

But the Schmidt government did not surrender. With Somalia's permission a hand-picked troop of German border guards stormed the plane at night, dazzled the kidnappers with a strong source of light, and killed or wounded all of them before they could harm the hostages. When the surviving crew and all the passengers returned to Germany, millions watched their rousing welcome on television, and Chancellor Schmidt's popularity rose higher than ever. Many people felt that if the German government had given in to the terrorists' demands, the people of the Federal Republic might have been at the beginning of a new journey into fear—a journey toward government by the gun—as taken by an earlier generation of Germans in the 1930s and early 1940s.

But with the triumph at Mogadishu there came a tragedy at Stammheim. It was announced that three well-known terrorists imprisoned there had committed suicide on learning of the final failure of the airplane hijacking. Some underground groups, claiming that the three had been murdered by the West German authorities, threatened revenge through further attacks on West German passenger flights. In fact, no major attacks of this kind occurred. Among young and old, students, workers, and intellectuals, opinion swung decisively against the terrorists, and thus far it has remained overwhelmingly opposed to them. A careful investigation, in which international experts participated, produced overwhelming evidence that the three prisoners had indeed committed suicide, coordinated by radio sets and carried out with weapons smuggled into their cells with the connivance of prison guards who had been intimidated by threats against their families. Also revealed was a remarkable laxity in the actual conduct of the prison, which had contributed to the tragic outcome.

The three dead were buried by their families and friends in a major cemetery near Stuttgart in a public ceremony attended by more than a thousand people and carried on television. The CDU mayor of Stuttgart, Manfred Rommel (son of a World War II general whom Hitler had forced to commit suicide), had given his permission. Over two thousand years earlier the Greek poet Aeschylus, in his play *Antigone,* had told the Athenians that every dead person has the right to a decent burial—even an enemy of the state. At Stuttgart in 1977, although many would have liked to see the public funeral forbidden, Aeschylus's view prevailed.

What had the terrorists imagined they were doing? As they became more expert in plotting ambushes and handling guns and explosives, they became more primitive in their political ideas. Some naive souls saw themselves as urban guerrillas whose bold and violent deeds would add courage to the long-seething anger of the rural and urban poor, in West Germany just as in the poorest Latin American republic, and would thus spark the long-awaited revolution of the masses. Even in poor countries this theory of the triggering of *excitatory terror* most often has remained a dream. In the prosperous, orderly and welfare-oriented German Federal Republic it was political madness.

Other terrorists professed a more complex theory. True, they admitted, German workers, peasants, and the general run of the people had no desire for revolution now. But the rulers and leaders, together with the upper and middle classes, could be provoked by terrorism so that they would overreact and install an overtly fascist dictatorship. Such a fascist regime, they reasoned, would soon stumble into some catastrophe and become so unpopular that then a left-wing revolution would follow—on the rebound.

This theory of *provocative terror* was dubious in its morality. It proposed to manipulate millions of people like billiard balls or chess pawns, to use terror and killings to move them this way and that without their own knowledge. It was no less dubious in its realism. The last installation of a right-wing dictatorship in Germany—Hitler's in 1933—had led not to a revolution, but only to vast destruction and suffering. The overwhelming majority of people in the Federal Republic would have nothing to do with all these theories.

Most of the terrorists believed and acted as they did out of despair. They despaired of being effective in democratic politics, of ever making a worthwhile contribution in a regular profession or career, of ever getting a real share in the intellectual, cultural, and political leadership of their country and of their own generation. Despairing of the efficacy of persuasion, they turned to the gun and to any theory that seemed to justify its use.

Each young person who turns to terrorism is a loss to democracy, perhaps most often a loss from despair. Is such despair inevitable, even for a gifted few? Whether the political system of the Federal Republic will manage to draw such persons and such forces of discontent into new programs of constructive change remains a major question for the 1980s. Clearly, this decade will continue to test the republic's capacity for political creativity and innovation in the realm of civic and political participation.

PARTICIPATION IN POLITICS

During most of the national elections in the Weimar Republic, from 1920 through 1932, between one-fifth and one-fourth of the eligible voters did not bother to cast their votes. Only at times of major excitement, in early 1919 and 1933, did voting participation rise to 83 add 88 percent, respectively, most of the increase going to the left in the first year and to the far right in the second. In neither case did the moderate parties of the center benefit much from the newly mobilized voters, and these voters, in turn, soon reverted to apathy after 1919 and to the posture of obedient followers after 1933.

Changes in Voting Behavior. In the Bonn republic, voting behavior has been very different. Only in the first general elections in August 1949 did 21.5 percent of the eligible voters stay at home. Already in 1953, however, voting participation had risen to 86 percent, and from then on it increased steadily, to a peak of 91 percent in 1972, 1976 and 1980. The victory of the Brandt-Scheel socialist-liberal coalition in that year was endorsed by the highest voter participation in any free general election in German history, whereas this same election reduced the share of the votes cast for the extremist parties on the far right, such as the NDP, and on the far left, such as the Communists, to insignificance. In the 1976 election, participation remained high at nearly 90 percent; the socialist-liberal coalition was confirmed in office and the share of votes for extremist parties on the right and left was further reduced (see Table 6.1). The same results occurred in the 1980 general election.

Increases in participation went hand in hand with changes in attitude. Women in Germany for a long time had been far less concerned with politics than men and, when they did vote at all, had voted more often on the conservative side. In the Federal Republic, women's votes thus had been a major asset to the CDU/CSU ticket until the late 1960s. By 1972, however, this attitude had changed: for the first time in that year the SPD received the same proportion of votes among women as it did among the general electorate. In particular, it appeared that younger women, those under thirty or thirty-five, had departed from the voting habits of their older sisters. In 1976 this trend continued,

and the shares of the two major parties in the women's vote remained similarly close.

The lowering of the voting age to eighteen years has worked in the same direction. The young voters have thus far resisted the temptation to withdraw into extremism, perfectionism, or indifference, and have cast their votes where they counted, in the choice between the major parties nearer to the political center and thus, in the decision between the two major trends of policy that the two contending sides—the socialist-liberal coalition and the CDU/CSU—represented.

Other Channels of Political Participation. The changes in voting habits at the federal level have clear implications for the Land and municipal elections, which come at different times in each Land, and they may well enhance the importance of the activities of the political parties and their members, who now have to respond to the newly enhanced political interests and concerns of these new strata of voters.

The SPD has about 1 million party members, roughly 1 for every 16 votes; and their membership dues furnish about half of the party's income. In the CDU/CSU local party members are less important. There are only 730,000 of them, about 1 for every 44 votes; and their dues account for only one-quarter of the CDU/CSU income. This situation is similar to that prevailing in the FDP, whose 75,000 members—about 1 for every 27 voters—pay dues that yield about one-fifth of its income. Correspondingly, nationwide interest groups—such as the trade unions, consumers' cooperatives and municipal enterprises for the SPD, and private financial, industrial, business, and farming interests for the CDU/CSU and FDP—are important sources of support for all parties, but the dependence of these last two parties on interest group support and financing is markedly greater. All parties, however, have become less dependent on interest group support under the new Party Finance Law, which provides them with public subsidies in proportion with their share in the electoral vote (see p. 254).

Neo-Nazi youth groups, more or less clandestine, were estimated in 1979 to have between 1,000 and 2,000 members—enough to desecrate some cemeteries, but not enough to count in politics.

Some age groups are more likely than others to use the parties as channels of participation. Persons of fifty years or older constitute 47 percent of the membership of the CDU/CSU and 50 percent or more of the members of the SPD. In the latter party, about 24 percent of the members are under the age of thirty-four. Recent and current recruitment efforts of the SPD may modify this picture. Of new party members who entered since 1967, five out of ten are under thirty; and there has been a 30 percent increase in the under-thirty age group during a ten-year period.

In addition, each major party has a youth organization affiliated with it as a source of current support and future membership, talent, and potential leadership. The SPD's Young Socialists (*Jungsozialisten* or, abbreviated, *Jusos*) number almost 300,000. The CDU/CSU's *Junge Union* is somewhat smaller with about 214,000 members; and the youth group of the FDP is smaller still. All major youth groups tend to outgrow the status of passive echoes of the views of their elders. They attempt to formulate policy proposals more in line with the views of their members; and these policies tend to be more change-oriented and radical and less concerned with considerations of cost, feasibility, and support or opposition from existing interests. The result is recurrent clashes between each youth organization and the leadership of its adult party, which usually tends to win out in such disputes, for each youth organization depends on its party not only for financial support, but also for political influence, career opportunities for active members, and a general link to political reality. Each party, in turn, must make some compromises with its unruly youth organization if it is not to handicap its own political future.

An increasing role in the political push-and-pull within each party is played by its local organization at the municipal, constituency, and Land levels. It is at the constituency level that many nominations for the Bundestag are decided, even though, in the absence of any American-style primaries, only about 3 percent of the party members participate directly in the nominating process. Though national party headquarters have the power to put candidates of their choice in safe places on their lists of candidates—from which lists one-half of the Bundestag is elected (see p. 254—the provision of 248 relatively small constituencies for the other half of all Bundestag mandates has shifted political power to some extent downward from the national party leadership to the constituency level, where younger or more reform-minded party members sometimes have a better chance to make their views prevail.

Old Interest Groups in the New Party System. Under the political system of the Federal Republic most of the old interest groups have survived. Only the large landowners have lost the power they enjoyed in the days of Bismarck and in the Weimar era. Most of the large estates were in East Germany and were expropriated by the Communists. Those landowners who escaped to the German Federal Republic had to make new lives for themselves in business, the armed forces, or the civil service.

Business interests in the Federal Republic have proved far more durable. Factories and enterprises were rebuilt after World War II, often with Marshall Plan aid. By the mid-1950s the Federation of German Industries (BDI) and similar organizations were again powers in the politics of the Federal Republic. Farm groups, too, soon became well organized and influential again, but their electoral weight has been gradually reduced by the steady migration from the country into the towns. The civil service continued to function and soon was serving the Federal Republic as routinely as many of its members had served the Hitler regime. Over 160,000 civil servants discharged by the Allies after the fall of the Nazis, most often because of Nazi ties, were back on their jobs by late 1953. Nearly all civil servants and public employees, regardless of their politics, are members of strong professional organizations that press effectively for higher salaries, security, and other interests.

German labor is also strongly organized. In the Weimar Republic labor was divided among Catholic, Nationalist, and more or less Social Democratic trade unions. In the Federal Republic, all wage earners' labor groups have merged into the German Confederation of Trade Unions (DGB), which, with 7.8 million members, includes about 34 percent of all wage and salary earners. The DGB is a unitary organization; there are no important unions outside it. It is organized by industries, not crafts, and it makes use of a highly legalized system of industrial relations to a much greater extent than is the case in most other Western industrial countries. The DGB is also the republic's largest organization of white-collar employees and civil servants, exceeding by a moderate margin its competition, the specialized organizations for white-collar employees, civil service workers, and the Christian Trade Union Federation. Taken all together, unions organize about 43 percent of the labor force.

Four major interest groups remain: the military, the mass media, the churches, and the universities. The military is less powerful than under either the empire or even the Weimar Republic. Although the armed forces have nearly 500,000 members, their leaders have thus far stayed out of German politics. The mass media have been more liberal for the most part than the average German. Radio and television are for the most part publicly owned, but control of them is largely decentralized among the states. A powerful and somewhat nationalistic newspaper chain has sprung up under the leadership of Axel Springer, but other newspapers and magazines remain diversified and vigorous. The Protestant and Catholic churches continue to exercise political influence, sometimes through direct pronouncements but more often through lay organizations responsible to their leadership. The universities have expanded greatly, but are now so poorly organized to look after their interests that their traditional self-government is in danger of being ground down between state control from above and student protest from below.

THE GERMAN PERFORMANCE

Almost an entire generation has passed since the Nazi tyranny. Its total collapse and defeat marked the time when German political development had brought itself to the point of self-destruction. After that fateful break in continuity it had been foreign, not German, decisions that set the framework for the start of reconstruction and the emergence of two new German states. As time has passed, each state has repaired the physical damages of the war and outgrown the economic levels of the prewar period. Never in their history have the German people been as prosperous as they are now, and never have they turned in a more impressive peacetime economic performance.

At the same time, they have outgrown much of the emotional and ideological heritage of the Nazi past. Anti-Semitism, militarism, dreams of dictatorship and renewed conquests survive on the fringes of the political system, but they have been decisively weakened at its heart. In 1979 the television movie entitled *Holocaust,* dramatizing the fate of Jewish victims of Nazi mass murder, was watched by 16 to 18 million German viewers. Their overwhelmingly positive response to its anti-Nazi message confirmed once more how much Germany has changed. It would take a very unusual combination of political and economic circumstances to revive German fascism once more as a formidable danger. The very sensitivity and vigilance of many Germans, as well as of Germany's neighbors, against any revival of Nazi-type ideas or actions make such a revival more unlikely.

These economic and political successes have given rise to new problems, some of them involving unfinished business from the past. The German Democratic Republic now has to try to make a

Soviet-style bureaucratic socialism work at an economic and technological level as high as or higher than that of the Soviet Union itself. But the GDR, like the Soviet Union, will have to do this in the face of continuing difficulties created by the practices of dictatorship and tightly enforced ideological conformity, which do not accord well with the rising educational, technological, and intellectual levels of its own population.

In the Federal Republic the institutions of pluralistic democracy have made it easier to manage the problems of a more educated and potentially more politically active population and of higher levels of prosperity. But many structural problems have remained under the prosperous surface. Great concentration of wealth and economic power, a high degree of social and economic inequality, the continuing partial self-closure of some professional groups, such as the West German judiciary, the high ranks of the civil service, and perhaps the military—all will continue to pose potentially serious problems in the 1980s.

The mass recruitment of cheap foreign labor from underdeveloped countries to fill the lowest-paying and least desirable jobs in the West German occupational structure will pose a growing set of problems. In 1979 there were 1.9 million migrant workers (called "guest workers" in German) residing in the republic, plus 2.1 members of their families (including 1 million children). These workers may join unions and vote in elections for factory councils, but they cannot vote on any level of government—local, state, or national. If one-tenth or more of West German labor is legally defined as "foreign," automatically disfranchised, and relegated to inferior jobs that are not competitive with those staffed by German labor, social divisiveness can only increase. Moreover, what will happen to the social time bomb represented by the 1 million children of these officially second-class German residents? Part of the problem might be solved by a law similar to the British Nationality Act of 1947, which gave Irish citizens the right to vote in British elections after working only six months in the United Kingdom. But this would deal with only a small part of the problem of integrating cheap labor into the larger framework of comfortable German prosperity. Thus far neither the SPD nor any other major party or labor union seems to have given the problem much consideration.

Like other pluralistic democracies, the German Federal Republic offers only relatively poor political opportunities to groups that have little power or are poorly organized, no matter how urgent their needs and concerns may appear to their members. Such groups then must choose between accepting the rules of the game (and perhaps being disregarded or underrepresented for a long time) or else using more unconventional and drastic means, including confrontation tactics, occupations, disruptions, and even force in order to compel attention, raise the self-confidence of their own constituents, and wrest concessions from other interest groups and from the public authorities.

If these tactics succeed, however, they may generate among those who use them the expertation that more pressure will produce more benefits. The leaders of the formerly underrepresented group now may be tempted to overreach themselves and to provoke massive hostile reactions not only from other groups and the government, but also from general public opinion, including many of their own former sympathizers and potential allies.

This has been one of the problems of the minority of radical critics—mainly students and other young people—in the Federal Republic. Their use of attention-getting overstatements sometimes has escalated to the casual or even deliberate employment of untruths and slander against individuals who disagree with them; confrontation tactics have grown into deliberate disruption and the use of force. Such efforts to produce better universities or a better society in the name of some high-sounding ideology, but by means of force and fraud, raise once again the issue of the relationship of means and ends and of the feedback effects from the former on the latter.

It is an issue that has arisen more than once in Germany during the last two generations, and young Germans may have to meet it yet again.

A Problem of Means and Ends: The Decree Concerning Radicals.

For a time it seemed as if the second strategy of the terrorists—the provocation strategy (see p. 261, above)—might have at least partial success. Opinion was indeed aroused against them, within the ruling socialist-liberal coalition as well as in the conservative opposition party, the CDU/CSU. From 1974 onward, the latter, following the usual strategy of conservative opposition parties in such situations, accused the government of weakness and clamored for stronger repressive and preventive action. All radicals on the left side of the political spectrum, they argued, ought to be suspected as potential terrorist "sympathizers" who collectively formed a kind of social and cultural background out of which the actual terrorists arose and from which they drew moral and practical support. Critical writers, such as Heinrich Böll, a Catholic and Nobel Prize winner, were then accused of having prepared the ground for bomb throwers and murderers. By late 1977 this new public mood of intolerance seemed to be reaching ominous proportions.

In the meantime, the federal government, still under the chancellorship of Willy Brandt in 1974, produced the *Decree Concerning Radicals,* as it became known in public discussion, which ordered the investigation of all public officials or applicants for employment as officials if they could be suspected, for any reason, of lacking loyalty to "the fundamental libertarian-democratic order" of the Federal Republic. By 1979 more than 500,000 persons had been subjected to investigation and hearings under this decree. Fewer than 500—or less than 1 in 2,500—were denied government employment on grounds of insufficient loyalty to the constitution;[7] no one knows if any of these were actually terrorists. Rather, a primary school

teacher and a railroad engineer were denied employment for being overt members of one or another Communist or radical organization. The investigations had labored like a mountain, it might seem, and produced a few mice.

But people are not mice. More than one-half million people had been presumed guilty and made to bear the burden of having to prove their innocence, often at considerable cost in time, money, human relations, and peace of mind. This practice contrasted with the principle that one is innocent unless proved guilty, which is normal in Anglo-American—and ordinarily also in West German—law.

The threat of being denied employment in any job as an official was serious in the Federal Republic, where the public sector of the economy is large and many more job holders are classified as officials *(Beamte)* than is the case in many other Western countries. In many fields—from grade school teaching to telephone, telegraph, and railroad work—practically no jobs exist outside the public sector. Denial of employment as a public official in such situations was equivalent to effectively prohibiting the rejected candidates from exercising the vocation or profession for which they often had spent years preparing themselves. Even for innocent persons the fear of such an outcome was not to be taken lightly. The West German investigations were more sweeping and, for a time, less controlled by legal safeguards than the security programs for "sensitive" defense-related jobs in the United States, except perhaps at the time of Senator Joseph McCarthy in the early 1950s.

From 1974 to early 1979 the federal political police—the "Service for Protection of the Constitution" *(Verfassungsschutz)*—was routinely asked for any derogatory information, evaluated or unevaluated, in its files about any person under investigation. Police organizations in Germany, as in the United States, keep in their files all kinds of tips, hearsay, rumor, gossip, and accusations made out of spite, although these are not evidence

[7]For comparison, there were 745,000 applicants rejected in 1976 and 1977 because of insufficient openings or a lack of qualifications.

admissible in court. In the West German investigations of the 1970s, however, they were permitted, and it was left to persons under investigation to disprove them if they could.

Moreover, certain details and standards of these investigations sometimes seemed to be made of rubber, stretchable in various directions. Of one registered member of the neo-Nazi NDP the authorities said that it did not necessarily follow that he agreed with the antidemocratic statements in the platform of his party. Members of far-left parties or organizations rarely, if ever, benefited from such leniency. The federal decree was carried out by the Länder under the German form of federalism (see pp. 249–50, above), and its execution varied widely with the political climate from Land to Land, more temperate under socialist-liberal administrations, as in Bremen or Hessen, and more zealous in conservative states, such as Bavaria.

On the whole, these investigations caught no terrorists, intimidated some radicals and dissidents and many more people closer to the middle of the political spectrum, and alienated and radicalized a not inconsiderable minority among the young. Demonstrations resounded in the streets and at universities against the *Berufsverbot,* or the "ban on exercising one's profession," which was the critics' name for what government spokespeople called the *Radikalenerlass,* or the Decree Concerning Radicals. Some critics did not mention that similar bans on public or professional employment for dissenters were common practice in the neighboring Communist-ruled German Democratic Republic. Others did mention it and found it one more reason to consider the practice distasteful.

Ultimately, cooler heads prevailed. Even among the earlier supporters of the decree, many turned away from it as doing more harm than good to democratic government. In early 1979 the federal policy was modified. Routine requests for information from the Service for the Protection of the Constitution were abolished, and the rights of persons under investigation were greatly strengthened and their appeals to the courts facilitated. Much would still depend on how the new policy would be implemented by the various states, but it seemed clear that the German Federal Republic in 1979 was far from turning into the right-wing dictatorship that some of the terrorists had hoped to bring about.

Another Experiment in Means and Ends. All politics is an experiment in means and ends, but in Germany that experiment often has been more stressful and more tragic than in many other countries. Some of the most serious problems of Western civilization at high levels of industrialization and technology have occurred in Germany. In the 1920s Germany was the most educated country in continental Europe; it had the biggest university system and an illustrious intellectual tradition. Yet it fell into the most murderous barbarism under the Nazis. Universities can be, as they have been in Germany, centers of humanity and enlightenment, but they can become centers of brutality and barbarism. As late as 1950 the three most pro-Nazi sections of the West German population were the peasants, the long-term veterans of World War II, and the Ph.D.'s. The new generation of West German students is different in its political aims from its parents' generation. Though it often professes left-of-center views, it has sometimes resorted to violent means. One hopes that it can remain different in the methods that it considers acceptable.

Swiss playwright Friedrich Dürrenmatt wrote these words, spoken by a survivor of a Nazi concentration camp: "One tells us today one should forget these things, particularly in Germany, and that other countries, too, have had their cruelties and atrocities. I refuse to forget them because I am a human being. As a human being I refuse to distinguish between good peoples and bad peoples and to distinguish between virtuous and wicked nations. But I must distinguish between good persons and bad persons, and I must distinguish between those who inflict pain and those who suffer it. I refuse to make a distinction among any of those who like to torture people. They all have the same eyes."

What Dürrenmatt wrote in Switzerland is now being widely read in Germany. With luck it will be remembered—in Germany and in other countries.

KEY TERMS AND CONCEPTS

Holy Roman Empire of the German Nation
Saxons
Franks
Dictatus Papae
Reformation
Religious Peace of Augsburg
cuius regio eius religio
Thirty Years' War
romanticism
union from above
Weimar Republic
Putsch period
master race
Socialist Unity Party (SED)
German Democratic Republic (GDR)
German Federal Republic (GFR)
Christian Democratic Union/Christian Social
   Union (CDU/CSU)
Free Democratic Party (FDP)
Social Democratic Party (SPD)
Basic Law
Länder
chancellor
president
Bundestag
fractions
Bundesrat
federalism
constructive vote of "no confidence"
threshold clause

two-track voting system
party slate
public financing of political parties
ombudsman
indexing to the cost of living
codetermination
Ostpolitik
Non-Proliferation Treaty
Extra-Parliamentary Opposition (APO)
terrorism
excitatory terror
provocative terror
Jungsozialisten
Junge Union
Decree Concerning Radicals

ADDITIONAL READINGS

Böll, H. *Billards at Half-Past Nine.* New York: Avon, 1975. PB
———. *Group Portrait with Lady.* New York: Avon, 1974. PB
Brzezinski, Z. *Alternative to Partition: For a Broader Conception of America's Role in Europe.* New York: McGraw-Hill, 1965. PB
Dahrendorf, R. *Society and Democracy in Germany.* Garden City, N.Y.: Doubleday, 1969. PB
Deutsch, K. W. "The German Federal Republic." In R. C. Macridis, ed., *Modern Political Systems: Europe.* 4th ed. Englewood Cliffs, N.J.: Prentice-Hall, 1978.
Dürrenmatt, F. *The Physicists.* New York: Samuel French, 1963.
———. *The Visit: A Tragicomedy.* New York: Grove, 1962.
Edinger, L. J. *Politics in West Germany.* 2d ed. Boston: Little, Brown, 1977.
Goldman, G. "The German Political System." In S. H. Beer and A. Ulam, eds., *Patterns of Government.* New York: Random House, 1973. PB
Grass, G. *Dog Years.* Greenwich, Conn.: Fawcett World Library, 1969. PB

————. *From the Diary of a Snail.* New York: Harcourt Brace Jovanovich, 1973.

————. *The Tin Drum.* New York: Random House, 1971. PB

Grosser, A. *Germany in Our Time: A Political History of the Postwar Years.* New York: Praeger, 1971. PB

Hesse, H. *Steppenwolf.* New York: Modern Library, 1963. PB

Hitler, A. *Mein Kampf.* Translated by R. Manheim. Boston: Houghton Mifflin, 1943. PB

Montgomery, J. D. *Forced to Be Free.* Chicago: University of Chicago Press, 1957.

Weber, M. *The Protestant Ethic and the Spirit of Capitalism.* New York: Scribner's, 1930. PB

PB = *available in paperback*

VII

Japan

EDWIN O. REISCHAUER

The Japanese see themselves and are often seen by others as a unique people. Certainly, they have had an extremely distinctive history, developing from an isolated tribal society into a leading industrialized nation, outdistanced in economic production only by the world's two larger super-powers, the United States and the Soviet Union. Over time and particularly during the past century and a half, Japan has changed more rapidly and more significantly than most other countries. It stands out today among the major industrialized democracies as the only one with a non-Western cultural background and, therefore, with probably the most distinctive patterns of organization and operation.

During the process of change the Japanese have often developed close parallels to the attitudes, institutions, and procedures of other nations. They consciously imitated the Chinese political system in ancient times, unconsciously paralleled medieval European feudalism in a later period, and then adopted modern Western political mod-

els in recent years. But at the same time, certain distinctive Japanese traits have shown a remarkable degree of persistence, giving a special quality to Japanese institutions that were basically like those of other countries. These points of similarity and dissimilarity make of Japanese politics and government a particularly interesting area for comparative study.

THE ARENA OF POLITICS

Most countries have established their identities and borders only over a long time and with difficulty. In the case of Japan, however, geography made this easy, for the Japanese islands form a clearly defined geographic unit. The example of Japan's great neighbor, China, which consolidated itself into a centralized state at an early date, also encouraged Japan to see itself as a united nation. It is no accident that the three existing countries of the world that first emerged in essentially their present geographic shape and with their present people and language were China in the third century B.C. and then its two neighbors, Korea and Japan, in the sixth and seventh centuries A.D.

The basic problem facing the Japanese has been not their own identity or unity, but rather their relationship or lack of it with the rest of the world. During most of their history they have lived in comparative isolation from other lands, experiencing only sporadic periods of intense interaction with foreign peoples. Today, however, their heavy industrialization and their large population of 115 million people, living on a narrow geographic base that is poor in most natural resources, force them to rely for their very existence on a vast interchange of goods with virtually all parts of the world. No other large country is more dependent economically on the outside world or more vulnerable to the vagaries of international trade. In this sense, the Japanese are now the world's most global people, facing multiple and complex problems of international relations for which their traditional isolation has ill prepared them.

The Ethnic Unit. Throughout its history Japan has been characterized by a relatively high degree of *cultural homogeneity*—that is, a high degree of linguistic and cultural similarity among the people throughout the country. As early as the seventh century, the Japanese, who then occupied the western two-thirds of the island chain, seem to have been relatively homogeneous for that period in history. And over the years the culturally distinct and more primitive people of the northern third of the islands were pushed back or absorbed. Their remnants, the Ainu of the northern island of Hokkaido, now number only a few thousand and are on the verge of total absorption. They constitute, thus, more of a cultural curiosity than a political problem.

The Japanese islands are strung out over a long distance and are broken up into many small pockets by rugged mountainous terrain. Throughout most of Japanese history the country was not well unified politically, but was divided into many relatively autonomous feudal domains. It is not surprising, therefore, that dialect differences existed in the Japanese language and the local customs sometimes differed sharply. But the distinction between the Japanese and all their neighbors was much greater. This was true even of the Koreans, who come closest to the Japanese in language and in early culture. From the seventh century on, Japan was always seen as a political and cultural unit, sharply distinguished from its neighbors.

The differences among the Japanese in dialects and customs, moreover, are no more pronounced than those among the Germans, who inhabit a much more consolidated piece of terrain. The contrast of the Japanese with the peoples of the British Isles is marked. Even though the British Isles are much less mountainous than Japan and spread out over only 600 miles (in contrast to 1,200 miles of the main islands of Japan, or 2,000 miles if Okinawa in the south is included), their inhabitants still remain divided into two language groups, four national traditions, and two religions. Although it has almost twice the population of the British Isles, Japan has no comparable divisions of language or national tradition, and the multiple religions of Japan—native Shinto; the many sects of Buddhism, a religion derived from India by way of China and Korea; and, more recently, Christianity—have been the source of political discord only for brief spells in the now distant past.

Up until the seventh century there was a flow of people from the Korean peninsula into Japan, but since then there has been almost no infusion of outside blood. The only significant foreign minority in Japan today consists of about 600,000 Koreans, who are the residue of a large number of forced laborers brought to Japan from its Korean colony during World War II. Though in large part culturally assimilated, they are discriminated against by the Japanese and, in resentment, form a troublesome political minority, quarreling among themselves and with the Japanese government over relations with the two mutually hostile regimes in Korea. Somewhat less than half as many Chinese, largely from Japan's former colony of Taiwan, form a smaller and less contentious minority, whereas other foreigners are so few and usually so physically distinct as to be considered complete outsiders only temporarily residing in Japan.

Another minority group is larger and provides a source of even greater problems than the Koreans, but it is not physically distinct or culturally very different. It consists of the descendants of the semioutcasts of feudal times, once largely known as *eta,* but now normally called *burakumin,* meaning "people of [special] hamlets." The *burakumin* are ethnically indistinguishable from other Japanese and have enjoyed legal equality since 1871, but they remain subject to strong social prejudice and discrimination. Living largely in the western half of Japan, they often constitute an explosive element in local politics there.

The strongly centralized political and educational systems of the past century, the tight network of modern communications, and the spread of the mass media, such as television, have in recent generations made the Japanese very much more homogeneous than they ever were before. Probably no other country of comparable size and population has achieved as high a degree of homogeneity as contemporary Japan.

Relations with the Outside World. Japan's geographic isolation has made problems of foreign relations a secondary concern at most times in the past. One early period of important foreign contacts was the seventh to the ninth centuries, when the government embarked on an ambitious effort to adopt the centralized political institutions and most of the higher culture of China, which at that time was probably the most advanced nation in the world. Between 607 and 838 a series of large formal embassies was dispatched to China, serving as a major vehicle for obtaining the necessary knowledge from the continent.

Then followed several centuries of virtually no contact with the outside world, broken finally in 1274 and 1281 by two massive, though unsuccessful, invasions by the Mongols, who had recently overrun China and most of the known world as far west as the Middle East and Russia. These were the only foreign onslaughts the Japanese were ever to experience before World War II. Japan was saved from the Mongols less by its few doughty warriors than by adverse weather conditions. The *kamikaze,* or "divine wind," a fortuitously timed typhoon, strengthened the Japanese in their belief that their land was unique and divine.

At about this time Japanese warrior-traders began to sail abroad, taking by the sword what they could not obtain by trade. These piratical adventurers gradually extended their sphere from Korea to the coasts of China and then to Southeast Asia. This period of activity abroad culminated in 1592 and 1597 in two great Japanese invasions of Korea. These were the only military expeditions dispatched abroad by the Japanese government between the seventh and the late nineteenth centuries. Thus, Japan had for more than a thousand years a record of almost uninterrupted peace with the outside world—a record that few other peoples can match.

In the meantime, Europeans had reached Japan in the middle of the sixteenth century, bringing with them Christianity and firearms. Both proved popular in Japan, but the government came to view Christianity as involving dangerous foreign loyalties that threatened the stability of the native feudal system, which had only recently been consolidated at the national level. Therefore, it stamped out the new religion, abandoning in the process a lucrative trade with the outside world and plunging Japan into almost complete isolation. A small Chinese merchant community and an

(Right) MAP 7.1 *Japan*

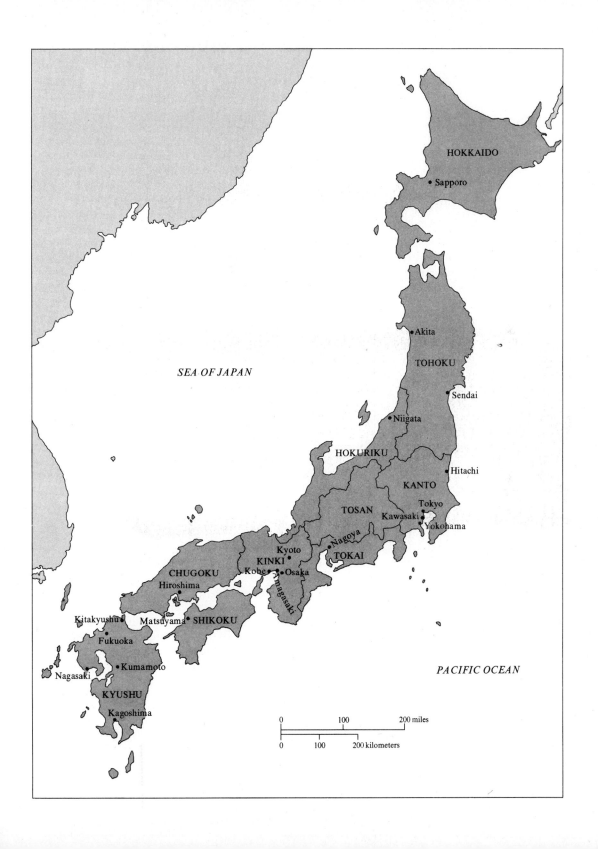

HOKKAIDO

• Sapporo

SEA OF JAPAN

•Akita

TOHOKU

•Sendai

•Niigata

HOKURIKU

•Hitachi

KANTO

TOSAN

Tokyo

Kawasaki•

•Yokohama

•Nagoya

Kyoto

KINKI

TOKAI

CHUGOKU

Kobe•

•Osaka

Hiroshima•

Amagasaki

Kitakyushu•

Matsuyama•

SHIKOKU

•Fukuoka

Nagasaki•

•Kumamoto

KYUSHU

•Kagoshima

PACIFIC OCEAN

0   100   200 miles

0   100   200 kilometers

outpost of Dutch traders in the western port of Nagasaki were Japan's only important contacts with the outside world between 1638 and 1853.

In isolation Japan enjoyed prolonged peace and a rich cultural flowering. It developed great cities, a complex central government, and an advanced money economy, but it fell technologically behind the West. By the mid-nineteenth century it faced an Occident that was now well into the Industrial Revolution and incomparably stronger than the European powers that the Japanese had driven away in the seventeenth century. From this point on, Japan's foreign relations, which had hitherto been relatively unimportant, became the dominant force in shaping the destiny of the nation.

The superior military and economic technology of the West threatened to reduce the Japanese to the colonial or semicolonial bondage already forced by Europe on most non-Western lands. The few Japanese scholars who had been studying Western science through Dutch books had received little encouragement, but now they realized that they must catch up in technology and win security from the West and political equality with it. This effort necessitated a thorough restructuring of their political and social institutions, but in the end the Japanese proved successful, becoming by the early twentieth century one of the major modern industrial and military powers and standing on a footing of legal equality with the West.

In the process, Japan had fought and won wars with China in 1894–95 and Russia in 1904–5. Through these conflicts it had obtained the beginnings of an empire—like those of the West—in Taiwan, Korea, and South Manchuria. Modern industry had also made Japan dependent on the resources and markets of foreign areas. Starting as a reliance on foreign cotton, wool, and minerals, such as iron ore, this dependence grew in time to include energy resources, such as oil and coal, most mineral resources, and even food.

In the aftermath of World War I the Japanese faced a choice: they could seek economic security through a further expansion of empire or instead they could rely on a peaceful world system of open trade, accepting the dictum of the United States and the European powers that the age of empire—or, rather, the age of acquiring new empires—was now at an end. Initially, the Japanese accepted the second option, but the economic stagnation of the 1920s and the Great Depression that followed convinced some of them that they had been duped by the Western powers, which already had won their empires. The result was a return to imperial expansion in the *Manchurian Incident* of 1931 and the China War of 1937. Rising nationalism, however, had indeed brought an end to the age of overseas empires. Japan bogged down in the quagmire of Chinese nationalism and, in attempting to escape from it, fell into the catastrophe of World War II.

Japan emerged from this war in 1945 as a thoroughly destroyed nation, shorn of empire and controlled by a nominally Allied, but largely American, army of *occupation* under General Douglas MacArthur. Its future, particularly its economic viability, seemed dubious, and it was subjected by the American occupation to a sweeping series of political, social, and economic reforms. However, the Japanese political and social systems were reinvigorated by these reforms and sprang back to life. And the nation, permitted by the Americans to enter freely into world trade again, began a rapid industrial recovery and new growth that soon came to be called an economic miracle. By the late 1960s Japan had become the third largest economic unit in the world, and in the course of the 1970s it became evident that this was one of the most stable and successful of all the modern industrial democracies.

This stable and affluent new Japan, however, remains completely dependent on the outside world. More than 90 percent of the energy that it consumes comes from abroad—most of it in the form of oil from the Persian Gulf. Almost all the natural resources used in industry must be imported, and much of its food comes from the United States, Canada, and Australia. To pay for all these imports, it must export its manufactures to all areas of the globe, particularly to the lands of the West, which are best able to purchase the advanced products of modern industry that Japan turns out in great abundance. Japan thus relies entirely on the maintenance of a huge worldwide trade. Its vital lines of supply extend far beyond any military defense that Japan itself could conceivably provide. Its worldwide trade can be preserved only by world peace and an open world trading system. There could be no sharper contrast than that between contemporary Japan's complete dependence on world trade and the state of isolated self-sufficiency in which its people lived only 150 years ago.

THE DEVELOPMENT OF POLITICAL INSTITUTIONS

The political system of Japan has varied greatly over its millennium and a half of existence, but certain elements and characteristics have persisted to become part of Japan's modern political and social system. It is these features inherited from the past that account for much of Japan's extraordinary success in modern times and the distinctive way in which its society and political system operate in comparison with those of other modern industrial democracies.

The Heritage of Early Japan. The earliest Japanese political system of which we know much was that of the fifth and sixth centuries. It was characterized by a number of hereditary clanlike units, known as *uji;* they had a considerable degree of autonomy under the largely religious authority of a so-called imperial clan, from which the modern Japanese emperors are descended. Controls were loose, but legitimate political authority was seen as deriving from the emperors, who have been accepted as the fountainhead of legitimacy ever since. Usually their role has been more as symbol or puppet than as actual ruler, but they have served as a powerful reminder of the identity and unity of the Japanese nation.

The *uji* system was one of hereditary authority. The role of heredity in the transmission of power, privilege, and wealth remained paramount in all succeeding political systems until comparatively recent times, and even today some vestiges of it remain. The Japanese have also always had a strong sense of *hierarchy,* or rank. Even today, in a basically very egalitarian society, positions are carefully graded by age, length of service, education, and the like. Leadership in almost all fields, however, is now determined not by birth, but by education, success in various types of qualifying examinations, and performance on the job.

It was the *uji* system that the Japanese tried to make over between the seventh and ninth centuries into a centralized bureaucratic state on the Chinese model. Eventually the effort foundered, as the taxable public lands disappeared into privately held, tax-free estates and the central organs of government atrophied for lack of financial support and functions. But a considerable residue lingered on after this period, influencing the rest of Japanese history.

The concept of Japan as a unified state had been greatly strengthened. A capital city, the modern Kyoto, had been created; it remained the recognized national capital until 1868. The position of the emperor as temporal ruler of a centralized state as well as religious leader had been strengthened in theory, if not in practice. The concept of rule by a civil bureaucracy based on educational attainment had become familiar, even though it was not maintained. The Japanese had also imbibed a number of ideas from the Confucian tradition of China: that the state was supreme in society, that good government was an exercise in moral leadership more than a matter of military power, that education was important for the training of superior leaders, and that government service was the highest goal of the superior man.

Though many of the Chinese concepts and institutions seem to have been lost sight of in the feudal age that followed, some of them later re-emerged to help shape the modern Japanese state. So also did a lesson from the early attempt to borrow from China. In the nineteenth century the Japanese were already well aware that many useful things could be learned from abroad and thus were gaining a head start over other non-Western societies, most of which came to this realization only in the twentieth century.

The Feudal Heritage. The Chinese-style centralized bureaucratic state of the seventh to ninth centuries gradually dissolved into a feudal system, which went through a series of phases that historians now see as the only close parallels to Western feudalism anywhere outside Europe. In the first phase, local warrior bands formed in the provinces to protect the private estates, which the weakened central government could no longer defend. Clashes between contending bands of warriors grew until the late twelfth century, when the captain of one such band won effective control over the whole nation, including the imperial court. Taking the title of generalissimo, or *shōgun,* he and his successors ruled Japan with reasonable effectiveness through their hereditary military retainers, or *samurai,* scattered throughout the private estates of the nation as stewards, or managers.

This first feudal regime was overthrown in the fourteenth century and was succeeded by a new feudal system, in which a hereditary line of *shōgun* attempted with less success to control the country through a number of territorial lords, who came to be known as *daimyō.* During the almost incessant warfare of this period, particularly from the late fifteenth century to the end of the sixteenth, political conditions in Japan most closely resembled those of high and late feudalism in Europe.

In the late sixteenth century three successive conquerors succeeded in reuniting Japan and restoring order. The third managed to perpetuate

from 1600 to 1867 the rule of his *Tokugawa* family from its castle headquarters in what is now the city of Tokyo. The Tokugawa *shōgun* ruled about a quarter of the land directly, but left the remainder divided into 265 or more semiautonomous feudal domains, each of which had its own *daimyō* lord and his *samurai* retainers.

The heritage of more than seven centuries of feudal rule has had a profound influence on modern Japan. Its strong military traditions made its people clearly aware of Western military superiority in the nineteenth century and encouraged them to build up their own capabilities, until Japan became one of the great powers of modern times. The Spartan self-discipline of the feudal warriors gave to the modern Japanese their superb sense of self-discipline, which has made them capable of prodigious feats in many fields. The strong bonds of loyalty demanded by a feudal system were susceptible to being developed into a fanatical sense of loyalty to the emperor as the symbol of the state or, more generally, to the Japanese nation as a whole.

Five other less predictable results of the feudal experience also proved equally or even more important to modern Japan. First, throughout the feudal age, but particularly in the Tokugawa period, the *shōgun* and *daimyō* were often mere figureheads, like the emperors, and effective leadership was exercised by councils of their retainers. So the Japanese became accustomed to look not to personal or charismatic leaders, but to group leadership. During the Tokugawa period, in fact, they developed a sort of bureaucratic form of rule, even though the make-up of the bureaucracy was basically determined by hereditary class.

Second, the Tokugawa period was a time of complete order and stability. With the establishment of national isolation in 1638, Japan settled into a prolonged period of peace that was not broken until 1863, after its doors had been forced open again by the Western powers. This was a long-lasting experience of peace and stability that no other large nation has known in modern times. The Japanese became accustomed to orderly processes of law and an administration that was not arbitrary, but instead was based on precedent and known regulations. They came to take for granted the existence of law and order. All this undoubtedly helped them to pass through the great wrenching changes of modern times with a minimum of domestic disorder.

Third, the Tokugawa system, though outwardly characterized by feudal division and autonomy, was in actuality quite centrally controlled. One of the chief means of achieving this centralization was the system of *alternate attendance* of the *daimyō* at the *shōgun*'s capital: all *daimyō* had to leave their wives and heirs as hostages at the *shōgun*'s capital, and they personally had to spend alternate years in residence there and in their own domains. The costs of maintaining large residences at the capital and of moving with their great retinues each year, back and forth between the capital and their domains, forced all the *daimyō* to produce cash exports to the rest of Japan to pay for these expenses. This situation made all of Japan into a single great market and greatly developed the economy. The congregation of much of the political leadership at the capital also helped to unify the nation intellectually. A measure of the relative advancement of the economy, as well as of education in Japan, is the estimate that by the middle of the nineteenth century some 45 percent of men and 15 percent of women were literate—figures not far below the more advanced lands of the West at that time.

Complete domestic peace and order, an established and predictable system of rule, and a nationwide unified economy combined to permit the merchant and later the peasant classes to engage in long-range entrepreneurial activities, a fourth outcome of the feudal experience. Such entrepreneurial habits and skills proved extremely valuable to the Japanese when in the nineteenth century they were forced to open up to world trade and had to compete economically with the technologically more advanced lands of the Occident.

Finally, under feudalism the Japanese acquired habits of group identity and skills in group cooperation that have served them well in modern times. Under the Tokugawa the two most important groupings were the feudal domains for the ruling *samurai* class and the autonomous peasant villages for the bulk of the population. Most *samurai* were gathered into the capital towns of their domains, leaving the villagers free to run their own affairs, as long as they maintained order and paid their taxes. Neither the domain nor the autonomous village has survived into the modern era, but the Japanese have transferred the attitudes and skills developed in them to more modern groupings, such as the local community or the work unit of factories and business organizations. This sense of belonging to and working through a group, in contrast to the Western emphasis on the individual as the basic unit, has perhaps helped the Japanese to pass through the great social and political upheavals of modern times and the traumatic transformation from a rural agrarian people to an urban industrial society with less sense of alienation and disorder than most Western peoples.

The Creation of a Modern State. The nineteenth-century Japanese had a sophisticated and advanced civilization, inferior to the West only in technology, and they inherited from the past many attitudes and skills that would prove useful in modern times. Their feudal political and social structure, however, was not sufficiently flexible or centralized to meet the challenge posed by the West. Within a few years of the opening of Japan by an American naval expedition in 1853–54, the Japanese were thrown into a frenzied effort to find effective means to fend off Western economic and military dominance.

Groups of iconoclastic younger *samurai* from some of the greater domains of western Japan, particularly Satsuma and Choshu, banded together around the ancient symbolic figure of the emperor, overthrew the Tokugawa regime in 1868, and installed themselves as a new "imperial" government at the old Tokugawa capital, now renamed Tokyo. This epoch-making revolution is usually called the *Meiji Restoration,* named for the reign period of the new boy emperor, which lasted from 1868 until 1912, and for the theory that imperial rule was being restored.

The new leaders saw that the old feudal disunity of autonomous domains and hereditary classes would have to be replaced by a new political and social unity. By 1871 they had abolished the domains and by 1876 had stripped away all hereditary powers and privileges from the *samurai* class, which constituted 6 or 7 percent of the population. Most of the new leaders, of course, emerged from the *samurai* class, which hitherto had monopolized all leadership, but the bulk of the *samurai,* unable to accommodate themselves to the new conditions, sank into anonymity as mere commoners.

The new leaders saw themselves as returning to the imperial rule of early times, but they did so only in the pretense that the emperor was ruling and in the restoration of old names for some of the new institutions. In actuality, they established a sort of rule by council, much like the system of Tokugawa times, and then in a piecemeal and pragmatic fashion they introduced Western institutions that were seen as helping to produce a strong nation that could withstand the West.

They developed a modern navy and a modern army to replace the Tokugawa class army. For the navy they quite naturally chose the British model; for the army, first the French and then the German models. They created a modern monetary and tax system, and after an experiment with the decentralized American banking system they adopted a centralized banking system based on that of Belgium. For local government they followed the centralized French model with some Prussian overtones. For the judicial system and the civil service they used German models, which they adapted and perfected for their own needs. Modern ministries were created one at a time, and eventually in 1885 the ministers at the top were grouped together into a modern type of cabinet under a prime minister. In reality the new Cabinet

was simply the old council of former *samurai* leaders organized together under a new name.

In education the new leaders followed the trends of the time in Europe, but in some ways forged ahead in creating a more uniform system than any Western nation then had. They early decreed elementary education for all children, girls as well as boys, and eventually by 1907 did get all of them into schools. At the intermediate level they created various technical schools, in order to produce men of more advanced skills, and a more strictly academic track leading to the state universities, which were to produce the leadership for the nation. Since all these schools were wide open to talent, the new educational system began rapidly to erase the class lines of feudal times.

The Development of Constitutional Government. The new Japanese leaders, noting that the most advanced nations of the West had constitutions and parliaments, saw elements of modern power in these institutions. They also were aware that within the large former *samurai* class were many persons who were restive at their loss of a share in political leadership and that among the other classes there were rising men who also hungered for a share in power. For these two reasons and because of their own eagerness to end the period of experimentation and to return to an established permanent system, like that of the Tokugawa, they decided to have the emperor grant a constitution that would define an unchanging, new system of government, including a popular national assembly. The final decision on this was made in 1881, and the constitution, usually called in English the *Meiji Constitution,* was promulgated in 1889.

According to the Meiji Constitution, the emperor was not only sovereign, but actually "sacred and inviolable." In theory all power emanated from him, but in reality he could do nothing without the advice and consent of his ministers and the laws passed by the new assembly. The leaders who created the constitution obviously assumed that they themselves would make the decisions for the emperor, as other councils had done for titular leaders in Japan for close to a millennium, but they failed to specify this in the constitution. They probably just took it for granted and may have assumed that their own group, by now known as the *genrō,* or "elder statesmen," would be self-perpetuating. If so, they were quite wrong. They also failed to realize the extent to which the Japan that they had set in rapid motion would inevitably continue to change. They had urgently begun to industrialize Japan in order to protect it from foreign manufactures and to give it the economic foundations needed for military strength. Now the rapid spread of industrialization and universal education were creating a new Japan and a new Japanese people that could not easily be contained within the centralized pattern of rule they had devised.

The *genrō,* after experimenting for a decade with elected assemblies in local governments, created through the constitution a popular national assembly, called the *Diet.* This body was carefully limited in its electorate and powers. It consisted of a House of Peers, modeled on the British House of Lords, and a House of Representatives, elected only by the higher taxpayers. Together the two houses had the power to pass on taxes, budgets, and other legislation. The *genrō* thought of the Diet as a safe way to share a modicum of power with others, to permit a safety valve for the expression of discontent, and to build up the sort of popular support for the government that the countries of Europe seemed to derive through their parliaments.

In practice, however, the Diet proved a great disappointment to the leaders. From the start the House of Representatives proved hostile to the Cabinet, which they correctly saw as being dominated by men from Satsuma and Choshu, the two former feudal domains that had taken the lead in the Meiji Restoration. The leaders also found that they had given away more power to the Diet than they had intended. Their German advisers had assured them that they could keep control of the national purse strings by a provision in the consti-

tution permitting the use of the previous year's budget if the Diet failed to vote a new one. In actuality, the previous year's budget was never enough at this time of rapid economic growth and could suffice for an extra year only with great difficulty. Constrained by fear of the Westerners' contempt if Japan failed in its borrowed Occidental institutions and worried that this in turn would result in the refusal of the West to accept Japan as a legal equal, the leaders did not take the otherwise simple course of revising the constitution that they had themselves drawn up. Instead they resigned themselves to living with it.

As a result, the period between 1889 and the 1920s was one of constant struggle between the Diet and the Cabinet and of rapid parliamentary evolution, comparable to the historic growth of the British Parliament. The Diet, taking advantage of its control over the budget, steadily increased its powers. Parties like those in the West appeared, winning their way into the Cabinet and steadily increasing their membership in it. Finally in 1918 it was decided that the prime ministership itself should be given to the head of the leading parliamentary party, and Japan embarked on more than a decade of largely party Cabinets. The electorate also had been steadily increased, and in 1925 all adult males were given the vote. Meanwhile many of the liberal tendencies then current in the West had begun to spread throughout Japan, too.

The original *genrō* eventually died off, the last in 1924, leaving only one later member to represent, with greatly diminished strength, their old role as the spokesmen for a theoretically all-powerful emperor. This situation revealed another major flaw in the 1889 constitution. The *genrō* had themselves created the modern Japanese military as well as the civil government, and they originally were in full control of both, but their bureaucratic and parliamentary successors did not have comparable powers over the military, which claimed to be answerable only to the emperor. When a sharp division occurred on foreign policy over the advisability of depending on open world trade or returning to empire building through military conquest, this lack of central control permitted the army to act on its own in the Manchurian Incident in 1931 and the China War in 1937. Such military activism was strongly backed by many young officers who were inspired by concepts derived from Japanese warrior traditions, as well as by ideas derived from European fascism. These young zealots did not shrink from assassination to further their policies. Wartime conditions and the early successes in this return to imperial aggrandizement made it possible for the military to infiltrate and gradually win dominance over the civil government, until by 1941, at the outbreak of war with the United States, the Cabinet and civil government were little more than adjuncts to the military.

Both the rapid evolution toward a British type of parliamentary government during the first four decades after 1889 and the sudden shift to military control of the government in the 1930s occurred as perfectly legal and constitutional developments. Both were made possible because of the ambiguity and vagueness of the Meiji Constitution regarding the key point of who in fact was to exercise the vast theoretical powers of the emperor.

Reform and a New Start. The American military occupation of Japan at the end of World War II might have seemed a poor way to sponsor healthy political growth and an almost certain way to inspire a violent nationalistic reaction. Instead, the sweeping reforms carried out by the occupation helped clear the ground for a sturdy flowering of the parliamentary form of government that the Japanese had themselves been developing up through the 1920s, and despite much resentment at the temporary American dominance over the nation, the foreign-led reforms produced no major nationalistic or reactionary response.

The chief reason for this surprising outcome was that both the mass of the Japanese people and the American planners wished to see Japan develop in the same direction. The war had proved that

Japan could not find economic security in empire, but must rely on peace and an open trading world. Revolted by the carnage and suffering of war and convinced that only world peace would give them a chance of survival, the Japanese turned abruptly from being the fierce warrior nation of recent years and became instead the world's most ardent and sincere pacifists. Disgusted with the follies and the heavy-handed indoctrination of their military leaders, they wanted no more dictators, but rather a return either to the parliamentary rule of the 1920s or, as the more radical envisioned, some more utopian socialist regime.

The American occupation forces arrived well prepared with plans worked out in Washington during the war. These were designed to help make Japan a more peaceful and democratic land, just as the Japanese themselves wished. The plans wisely called not for the introduction of American forms of democracy, but for the strengthening of the British parliamentary system, with which the Japanese were already familiar. They also advocated supplementary social and economic reforms to create a stronger base for a democratic form of government. The reforms were carried out with great dramatic flair by General MacArthur in his position as *Supreme Commander for the Allied Powers (SCAP)*. MacArthur actually exceeded his instructions when in February 1946 he had his staff draft a new constitution for Japan. After some small emendations and formal acceptance by the Japanese government, this replaced the Meiji Constitution in May 1947.

The new constitution, though, basically following the lines of Washington planning, corresponded to the hopes of most Japanese. It relegated the emperor in theory, as well as in practice, to a purely symbolic role and made the Diet the supreme "organ of state power." The House of Representatives, which remained unchanged, now was given the power to elect the prime minister from among its members, and the House of Peers was supplanted by a purely elected *House of Councilors*. Local governments were given more autonomy, and all their chief officials were made elective. The constitution guaranteed a detailed list of human rights, and the courts were assigned the duty of seeing that laws and government rulings did not infringe on them. Women were given the vote, and family control over adult members of the family was eliminated. Perhaps most surprising of all, Article IX of the constitution renounced forever the right to make war and maintain military forces. The Japanese ever since have enthusiastically called this document the *Peace Constitution.*

In addition to the constitution, many other reforms were carried out. The great financial, trading, and industrial combines, which were known as the *zaibatsu* and had grown up under prewar policies of fostering rapid economic development, were entirely dissolved, though their great component corporations, which had once been slated for breakup, were subsequently allowed to continue in existence. Labor unions were encouraged and soon embraced over 7 million members. All military officers and most higher civil officials were purged from positions of public responsibility. A sweeping land reform was carried out, outlawing absentee ownership of agricultural land, limiting the size of individual holdings (in most cases to a maximum of about ten acres), and transferring through virtual confiscation most of the 45 percent of the land worked by tenant farmers to the hands of these former tenants.

In education, compulsory schooling was extended to nine years, efforts were made to eliminate indoctrination and encourage independent thinking, and the various tracks of education were unified in the American manner into a single track that would make all students eligible for the next higher level. With Japan's subsequent rise to economic affluence, the Japanese may by now have become the world's best-educated people. More than 90 percent of its young people go through the extremely rigorous twelve years of education leading to graduation from senior high school— probably the world's record—and close to 40

percent go on for some higher education, a figure exceeded only in the United States.

The occupation reforms were concentrated largely in the early years. Between 1947 and 1949 the American authorities, distressed by the failure of Japan to recover economically and worried by the growing Cold War with the Soviet Union elsewhere in the world, began to put more emphasis on economic recovery and to slow down reform programs, which had already for the most part been completed. The Japanese have called this change of emphasis the *"reverse course."* Actually, little in the reform program was reversed, except for the abandonment of the plan to break up large corporations, a relaxation of the purge measures, the outlawing of strikes by public employees, the creation of a paramilitary police reserve, and a shift from friendly tolerance of Communists to open harassment.

After the end of the occupation in 1952 the conservative Japanese government then in power continued the "reverse course" somewhat further, despite the vehement opposition of the parties of the left. It dropped the purge measures completely, reconsolidated in part the control of the central government over the police and education, and changed the police reserve into the small, but more clearly military, *Self-Defense Forces (SDF).* At the time of the peace treaty it also entered into the *Mutual Security Treaty* with the United States, which gave Japan protection, but left American bases and troops in the country. All this happened in the 1950s, and thereafter the "reverse course" went no further. Although the conservatives had hoped to amend the constitution by eliminating the no-war clause and restoring theoretical sovereignty to the emperor, they eventually had to give up these plans as politically unfeasible.

Animosities and suspicions derived from the prewar and wartime experience between left and right, however, dominated Japanese politics for two or more decades after the war. The leftists, generally known as the *progressives,* feared that the conservatives wished to turn the clock back to the prewar system of the 1930s. They also felt that the security treaty, far from giving Japan security, might embroil it in war. The conservatives feared that the progressives were aiming at making Japan a communist country. Mutual fear made both sides battle desperately over what would have otherwise seemed to be small and relatively innocuous differences of opinion or organization. Large public demonstrations and confrontations in the halls of government were the order of the day.

In time these fears and animosities began to ease. The postwar economic miracle made the Japanese for the first time in their history a relatively affluent people. The economic pie had grown enormously and was divided more equally than in most other countries. A recent study shows that among the industrialized democracies Japan, next to Sweden and Australia, has the least discrepancy of income between the richest and the poorest members of society. The security treaty with the United States and the existence of American bases and the Japanese Self-Defense Forces have not embroiled Japan in foreign wars or lessened the prevailing pacifist mood. Much of the old style of political confrontation developed in the 1950s lingers on, but the parties of left and right and still more the voters who support them have drawn closer together, and the new concerns—about foreign trade and the domestic clash between economic growth and the quality of life—engender less sharp divisions in politics.

The progressives throughout have strongly supported the reforms of the occupation, while decrying the alliance with the United States. The conservatives throughout have championed a close alliance with the United States, while regretting what they felt had been the excesses of the occupation reforms. Gradually, however, both sides have coalesced in firm support of the existing political system embodied in the 1947 constitution. Few constitutions in the world have more complete or enthusiastic popular support.

The Japanese today enjoy an extraordinarily stable and fully accepted political system. It is basically defined in the 1947 constitution and its supporting legislation. They are based largely on the parliamentary evolution that took place in Japan between 1889 and the 1920s, which in turn was an outgrowth of the efforts to modernize the Japanese government between 1868 and the promulgation of the Meiji Constitution. Finally, this modernized Japanese government incorporated some of the political attitudes, habits, and skills that the Japanese had developed over the preceding millennium and a half. Thus, there is a long and significant history lying behind Japan's present political system. This gives us all the more reason to believe that it will remain relatively solid and stable in the future.

THE MACHINERY AND PROCESSES OF GOVERNMENT

The Diet. At the center of Japanese politics is the Diet (see Figure 7.1). Floating vaguely above it is the symbolic figure of the emperor, and the bureaucracy and local government operate partly in subordination to it, partly in tandem with it. But the Diet is supreme—by constitutional definition "the highest organ of state power" and "the sole law-making organ."

The transference of sovereignty in the 1947 constitution from the emperor to the Japanese people was a shattering blow for some old-fashioned, conservative Japanese. In the Meiji Constitution the emperor had been described not only as the holder of all sovereignty, but as a "sacred and inviolable" figure, deriving his authority from his "lineal succession unbroken for ages eternal." According to the new constitution he is now no more than "the symbol of the State and of the unity of the people." The Japanese as a whole and the imperial family, too, have adjusted to the change with little or no regret. The new definition has simply brought theory into line with what had been in fact age-old practice.

The emperor himself was never a contender for

FIGURE 7.1 *Government Structure of Japan*

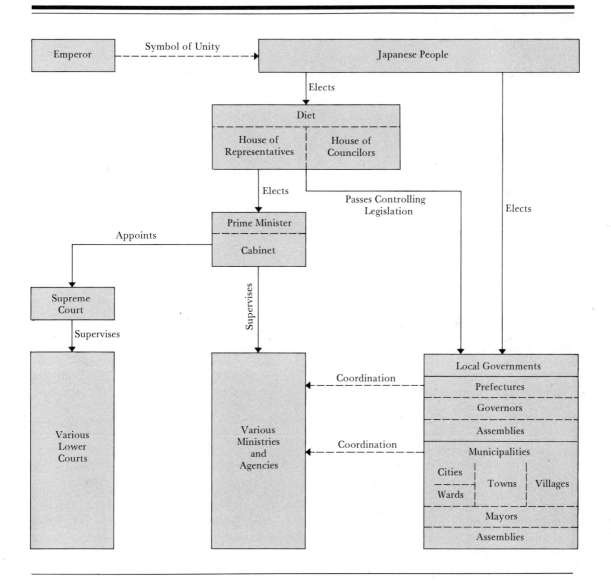

power with the Diet, and all those organs that were, because of their claim to speak in his name, have been eliminated. The *genrō* have long since ceased to exist: the sole remaining member died in 1940. Other august bodies that were beyond Diet control, such as the Privy Council, have been abolished. The military, which was the branch of state that had successfully challenged and largely destroyed parliamentary power in the 1930s, exists only in attenuated form. The Self-Defense Forces, which now substitute for the old army and navy, are relatively small, having a strength of only about 250,000 persons and a budget that absorbs less than 1 percent of Japan's gross national product. (Comparable figures are 3 to 5 percent in most Western European countries, around 6 percent in the United States, and between 10 and 20 percent in the Soviet Union and several highly militarized nations.) The SDF by law are under strict civilian control, enjoy only the lukewarm toleration of most Japanese, and carefully eschew any sign of exercising political influence. A measure of their political insignificance is that although the conservative party in power has long wished to raise the Defense Agency, which supervises the SDF, to the status of a Defense Ministry, this move has never seemed worth the risk of the determined political opposition that it would face.

The Diet is not only the sole source of law in Japan, but it also has the right to choose the prime minister. Theoretically, both houses of the Diet jointly select this official from among their memberships, but since the will of the lower house prevails in case of disagreement between them, it is the House of Representatives that in fact elects the prime minister, so far always from its own membership. The prime minister selects the rest of the Cabinet, but since this individual is elected by the Diet, which can elect a new prime minister at any time, he or she in no sense has independent powers comparable to those of an American president. In fact, the prime minister and Cabinet are merely a sort of executive committee operating on behalf of the Diet.

Both Diet houses are elected, but by differently constituted electorates and for different terms, as is the case of the American Congress. Half of the 252-member House of Councilors is elected every three years for a six-year term. Of the total, 100 are elected from the nation at large; this means that a mere 2 percent of the vote can elect 1 councilor among the 50 who win in each election. The remaining 152 are elected from each of Japan's forty-seven prefectures, which correspond to our states. The smallest prefecture elects 1 each time, and the most populous elects 4. This difference in the number of councilors per prefecture, ranging from 2 to 8, is far less than their differences in population. The most populous is at a 5-to-1 disadvantage compared to the least populous, but this is much less than the 75-to-1 discrepancy in the most extreme case in the American Senate.

The representatives of the lower house are elected for a four-year term according to a system established in 1925 and called the *middle-size electoral district system*. Between three and five representatives are elected from each electoral district, but each voter can cast only one ballot for one specific candidate, not a party. It is a unique system among the major legislatures of the world and, as we shall see, has a profound influence on the conduct of electoral politics in Japan. Like the electoral system for the upper house, it produces a certain degree of proportional representation, because minority groups can win some seats. Thus, 20 percent of the vote cast for a candidate in a five-seat district ensures his or her election. The system also produces more stable results than occur in other nations. In the Anglo-American one-seat, winner-take-all system a shift of a small percentage of the votes in a large number of electoral districts can bring a change of landslide proportions. In the Japanese system a similar shift would produce only a small change, reducing, for example, a majority party's representation in a five-seat district merely from three to two.

The size of the House of Representatives, set in 1925 at 466, continued into the postwar period, but then was slowly increased to allow for the return in 1972 of Okinawa as Japan's forty-seventh prefecture and to compensate slightly for the great demographic changes that were taking place as people left the countryside and swarmed into the larger cities, which were given a few additional seats. In 1976 the size of the lower house was set at 511, elected from 130 districts. This still leaves discrepancies of as great as 4-to-1 voters per representative. Court rulings have pointed out that this is a sort of political discrimination not permitted by the constitution, but, unlike the American courts in their "one man one vote" rulings, the Japanese courts left it up to the Diet to take the necessary corrective action, which it has shown little inclination to do.

The House of Representatives only rarely lives out its full four-year term. In the British manner it can pass a vote of "no confidence" against the Cabinet, forcing the prime minister either to resign or to dissolve the lower house. In fact, this has occurred only twice, in 1948 and 1953, but what does happen frequently is that the prime minister voluntarily dissolves the lower house at some time short of its full four years, forcing a new general election; this, in turn, necessitates a new selection of a prime minister by the Diet. The reason for dissolving the lower house usually is to take advantage of a situation that appears more propitious for the prime minister's party than the end of the full four-year term may prove to be.

Both houses elect their own officers and have their own rules and precedents of procedure. Each is divided into sixteen committees, corresponding for the most part to the ministerial subdivisions of the government, and these are divided into various subcommittees. The system was modeled on that of the United States, but in fact operates quite differently. Whereas the American congressional committees serve as major organs for the investigating of problems and the drafting of legislation, these functions are mostly performed elsewhere in the Japanese system. The Japanese Diet committees do pass on all legislation before it goes to a

full, or plenary, session of the house, and sometimes they amend the draft laws. But primarily these committees serve as a first arena for public partisan debate, in which the oppostition parties can question, or interpellate, the government ministers and their assistants who are sponsoring the proposed legislation. The objective is more to embarrass the party in power or delay the legislative process rather than to shape legislation, though sometimes emendations do result. The large budget committee of fifty members is the chief arena for this process of *interpellation*. The whole procedure bears more resemblance to British parliamentary processes than to American.

The lower house has superior powers over the upper. Not only does it elect the prime minister, but it can override the upper house with a two-thirds vote. Since the party composition of the two houses has always been about the same and the party in power has never had a two-thirds majority, this situation has never in fact arisen. On certain types of legislation the House of Representatives can take action without the concurrence of the House of Councilors. The budget passed by the lower house, to which it must be presented first, goes into effect if the upper house fails to take concurrent action within thirty days. This same provision applies to the ratification of treaties. Amendments to the constitution, however, require positive action by two-thirds of the members of both houses and then a majority vote in a national referendum. Not surprisingly, there have been no amendments, just as the Meiji Constitution was never amended during its fifty-eight-year existence.

The Bureaucracy. The executive branch of government is headed by the prime minister and the Cabinet that he or she chooses. The Cabinet is made up of the ministers of the twelve regular ministries and the heads of a few agencies, who are appointed Cabinet members as ministers without portfolio. The ministries are regarded as having varying degrees of importance. The Finance Ministry, which has chief responsibility for the budget, unquestionably ranks at the top, and the Ministry of Foreign Affairs has always been important, whereas the *Ministry of International Trade and Industry (MITI)*, has loomed very large since the war because of its key role in the spectacular economic development of the nation. The agencies are administrative units that rank slightly below the ministries, but will be lumped together with them hereafter, for convenience. Among those agencies that normally carry Cabinet membership for their directors are the Defense, Environment, Economic Planning, and Science and Technology agencies. The chief Cabinet secretary and the head of the prime minister's office, which gathers under it a miscellany of administrative functions in much the same way as the executive office in Washington does, are also Cabinet members.

The ministers (including the agency directors) are virtually all politicians, drawn from the membership of the ruling party in the Diet. So also are the one or two parliamentary vice ministers (or vice directors) for each ministry (or agency). Their function of liaison between the bureaucracy and the Diet is largely nominal, and they exist primarily to create more high-sounding titles to be passed around among the politicians. Even the ministers (and directors) hold their posts normally for only a year or two and thus have little chance to learn about their respective ministries or to establish firm control over them.

The actual operation of the bureaucracy takes place quite apart from these politicians nominally at its top. Starting with the adoption in 1885 of a perfected form of the German civil service system, the Japanese have built up an extremely efficient, dedicated, honest, and highly professional bureaucracy. The original concept was that all graduates of the government universities would qualify for membership, but from the start more judges were needed than the universities could supply, so special examinations were held for these positions. Soon it was discovered that too many university graduates were being turned out to be accommodated in the other posts. As a result, examinations

came to be required for all positions. In 1900 the top bureaucratic posts were sealed off from all those who had not passed the examinations, thus protecting the Japanese bureaucracy from what they felt to be the corrupting influence of the political spoils system practiced in the United States. By the 1920s the whole system had taken on its contemporary shape. Candidates, qualified by graduation from either government or private universities, took examinations for admission into the various ministries or other bureaucratic branches of government, and a select few were chosen each year for a career of service in that particular branch of government.

Because of the traditional Japanese emphasis on government service, the cream of the Japanese educational system has tended to go into the bureaucracy, making it a very elite corps with high prestige, as is the case in many of the democracies of Western Europe, though not in the United States. The bulk of the high bureaucrats have traditionally come from Tokyo University, and this is still the case, at least for the older members. This situation probably results not so much from the fact that Tokyo University professors devised the examinations, as from the fact that a large percentage of the ablest students from all over Japan (or at least those most skilled in taking examinations) gain admission into this most prestigious of Japanese universities by passing its stiff entrance examinations.

Once accepted into the government, the new bureaucrat has career-long security and is promoted more or less routinely by seniority. The most capable at each age level are given the most important and interesting jobs open to that level and thus are groomed for the top jobs, which only a few will hold. Eventually one member of each age cohort is selected for the top bureaucratic job of *administrative vice minister* (or vice director). This is the person who really runs the ministry (or agency). His or her peers, usually still in their early fifties, must then retire. To supplement their retirement pay, they usually must seek post-retirement employment, commonly as advisers in industry or in various governmental supervisory agencies. Promotion up and out is relatively rapid, bringing individuals of two or more decades of professional experience—but still in the prime of their vigor—to the top bureaucratic posts. This often provides a marked contrast to the American system with regard to both age and professionalism.

The bureaucracy, including that of local government entities, extends far beyond the higher civil service described above. It includes large numbers of secretaries, clerks, specialists, and local officials; all workers for the national railway system and certain government monopolies, like tobacco; all police officers; and teachers in all government schools, from the elementary grades through the university. All these varied functionaries and specialists achieve their posts through a diversity of educational qualifications and sometimes special examinations, but they are to be distinguished from the higher civil service.

The prestige, professionalism, and relative independence of this higher civil service gives it a comparatively large role in government. Each ministry, comprised of a stable and self-confident group of professionals, tends to have its own policies on matters that concern it. These are worked out by negotiation and compromise between the various component units and factional groupings within the ministry. Naturally, nothing can be achieved unless the politicians of the Diet are willing to pass the necessary legislation, and the bureaucrats must, therefore, trim their sails to parliamentary winds, but they still feel free to differ with the prime minister and Cabinet in a way that few American bureaucrats would dare.

The bulk of the drafting of all legislation, usually after extensive consultations and negotiations, is done by the bureaucracy, not by the legislators, as is the American tradition. Most laws are usually framed in general terms, leaving room for interpretation by the bureaucracy when putting them into effect. While the courts watch carefully to see that individual rights guaranteed in the constitution are not transgressed, they do not take the lead in making rulings to implement legislation or the constitution, as they sometimes do in the United States. There are also fewer outside regulatory bodies deciding how laws should be implemented; and, as a result, the bureaucracy is allowed greater scope in making decisions on implementation. Thus, from the original deciding on policy, through the drafting of legislation, to the implementing of it, the Japanese bureaucracy plays a larger role than its American counterpart.

Standing close to the bureaucracy, but in a sense remaining distinct from it, are certain other bodies. A relatively autonomous Board of Audit keeps a careful eye on all financial matters, and the National Personnel Authority sees to the honest and fair functioning of the bureaucracy itself. The court system, which since its inception in the Meiji period has prided itself on its independence from the rest of government and on its strict adherence to legal principles, is nonetheless constituted along much the same lines as the rest of the bureaucracy.

The members of the Supreme Court are selected by the Cabinet, but must be confirmed by popular vote at the next general election and every ten years thereafter. This confirmation by popular vote sounds enlightened, but has proved meaningless so far, because the justices are not sufficiently well known to the public. The Supreme Court is vested with the rule-making authority for all lesser courts and thus supervises the whole system. However, persons qualify for the judiciary in much the same way that they do for the higher civil service. A few hundred are selected each year by rigorous examinations from among university graduates and then are put through a two-year training program conducted by the Japanese Legal Training and Research Institute. On the completion of this course, successful candidates then choose between careers as judges, public prosecutors, or lawyers.

After experimenting somewhat with the Anglo-Saxon jury system, the Japanese decided it was too erratic and opted instead for a system in which the decisions as well as the sentences are determined by the judge. Trials are conducted according to the continental European system of having the judge direct the inquiry, rather than by the adversary system conducted between lawyers, as in the American tradition. On the whole, the Japanese judicial system operates with honesty, fairness, and reasonable efficiency.

Local Government. Japan is divided into forty-seven *prefectures,* which are analogous to American states but have much less autonomy. Curiously, there is no single word for "prefecture" in Japanese, the forty-seven being divided into one *to* ("metropolis"), one *dō* ("circuit"), two *fu* ("urban prefectures"), and forty-three *ken* ("ordinary prefectures"). In population the prefectures average over 2 million each, but there are great discrepancies among them, and most are closer to Rhode Island or Massachusetts in geographic size than the larger American states. Each prefecture is completely divided into municipal units known as cities, towns, or villages, depending on the size of their populations. The nine largest cities are subdivided into administrative wards, which are much larger than American city wards, but smaller than the boroughs of New York. Tokyo itself is unusual in having no city government, but the twenty-three wards that constituted the prewar city of Tokyo have the status of "special cities," though with less autonomy from the prefectural government (Tokyo metropolis) than other municipalities.

Before World War II all these local units had popularly elected assemblies with very restricted powers. The assemblies selected the mayors, who had to be approved by the national administration. The linchpin in the whole system of local government was the prefectural governor, who was a bureaucrat appointed by the Home Ministry of the central government, and most of the work of local administrations was simply to carry out the tasks assigned to them by Tokyo.

A major political objective of the American occupation was to increase *local autonomy,* which was seen by the Americans as a key ingredient of democracy. The postwar constitution decrees that the chief executive officer of all local public entities, meaning both the governors and the mayors, must be popularly elected. Greatly increased powers of taxation and other authority for local affairs were given to the various types of assemblies and chief executives. The strong control over local government by the prewar Home Ministry was sharply curtailed, and its duties were broken up to some extent. The new Police Agency, for example, took over control of police matters. The remaining functions of the Home Ministry were assigned to a greatly weakened administrative authority, at first known as the Autonomy Agency, but later upgraded to become the *Autonomy Ministry.*

The American efforts to create strong local self-government fell far short of the goal. Japan is simply too small a country geographically and the people too accustomed to centralized government to adapt themselves easily to the American concepts of local government derived from a very different geographic situation and historical tradition. In addition, the local tax base proved inadequate for much autonomy of action, and local governments have remained heavily dependent on financial support from the national government.

After the end of the occupation some of the powers given to the local administrations were actually restored to the central government, despite the strong opposition of the political left. A police system divided into independent municipal units and prefectural rural police had proved inefficient and too costly. In 1954 it was reconsolidated into a prefectural police system under close national supervision. A largely decentralized educational system under elected municipal and prefectural boards of education also did not win general popular confidence. In 1956 a compromise system was adopted, in which locally appointed boards of education replaced the elected ones and were placed under careful Ministry of Education guidance. Local administrations also slipped back into the old position of devoting most of their energies to nationally determined and funded programs; governors and mayors came to spend much of their time in Tokyo, lobbying for local interests with the central government; and bureaucrats of the central government ministries were dispatched for lengthy periods of service in the local governments in order to gain practical experience in their respective fields and to strengthen the links between central and local governments.

Local administrations, thus, are far from being as independent as those of the United States, but they do have considerably more autonomy than similar bodies in a still more centralized democracy, like France, which originally was Japan's major model for modern local government. Local elective politics for governors, mayors, and ward, municipal, and prefectural assemblies is extremely lively, giving a strong foundation for national electoral politics. Local government bureaucracies sometimes enjoy equal or better financial treatment than the national bureaucracy and are rising in relative prestige. One reason for this is the increasing importance of local government, as problems of pollution, urban crowding, social services, and the environment, all of which have a strong local component, have in recent years begun to loom large on the national political docket. Actions on these problems taken by local governments have often led the way toward later action on a national scale, showing the influence and significance that local government is capable of achieving.

POLITICAL PARTICIPATION AND THE PARTY SYSTEM

However perfect the machinery of government may be, the true test of a country's political system is its efficiency in actual operation. Three things

are required of it. First, it must be effective in making necessary political decisions and maintaining order. Second, it should allow the people as a whole to feel a sense of participation and, at least in a democracy, actually participate in a meaningful way in the decision-making process. Finally, it must be able to steer itself by means of a successful feedback system that allows it to respond to external stimuli resulting from new or changing conditions.

The premodern Tokugawa government of Japan met the first criterion of making decisions and maintaining order, but had little sense of popular participation, except for the limited *samurai* class, and in its later years proved notably weak in responding to a changing environment. The various intermediate regimes between the Meiji Restoration and World War II continued to meet the first criterion, but handled the other two with only varying degrees of success. Japanese politics today, however, seem to measure up quite well in all three respects.

Popular Participation and Electoral Politics. In ancient and feudal Japan a vast gulf existed between the rulers and the ruled. This was epitomized by the phrase *"kanson-minpi"*: "the officials honored, the people despised." Today, despite the relatively high prestige of the higher civil service, bureaucrats are seen not as a superior class nor as distant imperial officers, but as public servants, and they are held to extremely exacting standards of honesty and hard work. Elected politicians, who are a modern phenomenon and were never very highly regarded, are looked on with as much contempt as respect, as is common in most modern democracies. In any case, no one has any doubt that they are the representatives, not the rulers, of the people.

The shift in attitude toward those in authority is particularly marked in the case of the police, who not long ago were greatly feared as well as respected. The postwar police have gone out of their way to change this image. They act with restraint and without arrogance. Established in small local "police boxes," where two or more are always on duty or are out on patrol of their area on foot, they take pains to establish themselves as trusted members of the local community. The intimacy and mutual respect between the residents of the community and their local police produce close cooperation. As a result, Japan has one of the lowest crime rates among major industrial nations, and the statistics are tending to fall rather than rise. In addition, almost no crimes go unsolved, which is hardly the situation in the United States.

However important attitudes may be, the key to popular participation in a democracy is a meaningful electoral system. Although completely unknown in traditional Japan, elections have been held for local assemblies since 1879 and for the national Diet since 1890 and are now a thoroughly familiar and central element of the political system. All persons above the age of twenty have the right to vote for all those who have the power to make both local and national political decisions. These are the members of the prefectural, municipal, and ward assemblies, the mayors of municipalities, the governors of prefectures, and the members of the two houses of the Diet, which in turn selects the prime minister.

The Japanese take their duties as voters very seriously. Like the voters in most other advanced democracies, many of them are cynical about the results of electoral politics and are critical of politicians. The bulk of the voters, in fact, disdain to associate themselves with any particular party, insisting on their status as political independents. Still, when it comes time to vote, they pour out in large numbers. For national elections, their voting rates are likely to be 75 percent or more of those eligible, in contrast to the rates of 55 percent or less that are common in the United States. They also show discrimination in the elections they respond to. More vote in elections for the more powerful lower house of the Diet than for the less important upper house. Voting rates run highest in the less urbanized areas, and the highest ratios of all are found in local assembly or mayoral elections in less urbanized areas, where the candi-

dates are more likely to be personally known and the issues more directly felt. This situation contrasts with that in the United States, particularly in urban areas, where elections for national office commonly draw many more voters than elections for the welter of local elective positions.

Voting in Japan started with local elections, first in rural areas and then in the cities, and the early restricted electorates, made up of those who paid the highest taxes, were largely well-to-do farmers who paid the land tax, the major direct tax of that time. Gradually the tax restrictions were lowered, but it was not until 1925 that the bulk of male urban dwellers got the vote, and their first chance to exercise it came in 1928, just before the Manchurian Incident began to swing Japan from parliamentary leadership to military dictatorship. As a result, early electoral politics in Japan had largely rural roots, and urban Japanese voters became a significant electoral force only after the war.

Strongly personalized tendencies have always been combined with the rural roots of Japanese electoral politics. In any small community the known personal qualities of a candidate are likely to loom larger than the party label under which he or she may stand. This is particularly the case in Japan, where personal relationships have always been strongly emphasized. Between 1890 and 1925 several different electoral systems were used in national elections, but candidates always ran as individuals rather than as members of a party slate.

Since 1925 the middle-size electoral district system has further emphasized the importance of the individual. Since three to five persons are elected from each district, a candidate from a major party is usually forced to run against one or more other candidates from his or her own party; and these fellow party members are in a sense the most important competition, because they are likely to appeal to the same type of voter. It is necessary, therefore, for each candidate to establish his or her own image and own electoral machine. Somewhat the same situation exists in prefectural, municipal, or ward assembly elections, in which the same multiseat electoral district system exists or, in the case of smaller units, all candidates run at large against all the rest.

Because of the necessity of running as individuals, virtually all candidates in local elections originally ran as independents on their own personal reputations and contacts. Today there is still a large preponderance of such independents in smaller municipalities, even though most of them are actually supporters of the conservative party in power. Over time, however, there has been a growing tendency for politicians at the national and prefectural levels and in the more heavily urbanized communities to adopt party labels. This is because adequate personal contacts are difficult to maintain in the larger units or under the less intimate conditions of modern urban life. A party label helps to establish the candidate's political stand and image. As a result, there have been virtually no true independents in the Diet for some time, though some pseudoindependents do win seats at each election for special reasons. Independents have also become almost equally rare in prefectural and large urban assemblies and exist in large numbers only in the assemblies of small cities, towns, and villages.

Governors and mayors form something of a special case. Since only one person can be elected to each post, a candidate normally faces no competition from other members of the party, so it might seem natural to use the party label. But this is not needed for party members and is felt to run the risk of driving away some otherwise prospective supporters. In some cases, also, the support of other parties is necessary to win election. This is particularly true of the various opposition parties, which are all too small to elect a candidate on their own strength and must rely on a coalition of parties. As a consequence, governors and mayors frequently are nominal independents, though normally it is well known which party or parties were behind their election. Once elected, they tend to have considerable political longevity, since their relatively weak powers save them from the frequent dilemma their American counterparts face in an electorate that simultaneously demands more services and less taxation. Governors and mayors in their fourth or fifth consecutive four-year terms are not at all uncommon.

In any of the multiseat electoral systems existing in Japan each candidate must secure an adequate share of his or her party's vote in the district. Traditionally, this was done by building up a strong base in one part of the electoral district. The traditional Japanese village, now downgraded to the status of an unofficial hamlet incorporated into an expanded administrative village, town, or even city, was always a tightly knit social group. The villagers from the start realized that they would have more political clout—that is, they would be more likely to elect a candidate to represent their interests—if they agreed to vote in unison for one person. Some ambitious, locally strong candidate would put together an adequate number of such voting blocs to win election to the municipal assembly; a series of such groups would be put together for a seat in the prefectural assembly; and a grouping of these larger units would combine for a Diet seat. A local base of this sort, called a *jiban,* usually constituted a geographically contiguous area within the electoral district that could be counted on to deliver the bulk of its vote to a local figure of prominence. A strong *jiban* of this sort—an "iron" *jiban,* as it was called—might persist for a long time, being passed from a politician to his or her political heir, who might well be a son by birth or adoption or perhaps a nephew.

In the highly urbanized Japan of today such localized or "vertical" *jiban* are hard to maintain. There is not sufficient community solidarity in an urban environment, and even in the countryside a large percentage of farm dwellers actually commute to nearby towns and factories to work. Other connections and loyalties have superseded the old village solidarity, and the bloc system of voting has therefore seriously eroded.

To adjust to this change, politicians have developed what is called the "horizontal" *jiban:* a base spread more evenly throughout the whole electoral district. The key organ of this sort of *jiban* is the *kōenkai,* or personal "support society." Because of the strict limitations set by Japanese electoral laws, which keep electoral campaigning to specified short periods, sharply restrict activities, and set very modest budgets, the *kōenkai* cannot admit to being the election organizations that they in fact are. Instead, they pose as cultural and educational societies that maintain a year-round program of enlightening activities, such as informative lectures by the prospective candidate, supporters from within the district, and political friends from national or prefectural politics. The *kōenkai* aim in particular at specific voting blocs within the district, usually having special divisions for women, young people, farmers, workers, and the like.

The above description applies particularly to the politicians of the conservative party in power, which is the continuation of the major prewar parties and is deeply entrenched in rural Japan. It applies less or not at all to the politicians of the smaller opposition parties, who rely to a greater extent on the voters in cities, where the old vertical *jiban* is quite impossible to establish and even the *kōenkai* system is difficult to maintain. These politicians usually depend on groupings like labor unions for their support or on the appeal of their respective ideologies, made clear by the party labels they must use. As Japanese society steadily becomes more urbanized and depersonalized, the old personal type of politics will no doubt decline still further, and politics by party organization and ideology is likely to become even more the rule.

Parties. Although independents still linger on in local politics, the Japanese parties have a long history (see Figure 7.2). By the 1870s and 1880s two party lines began to form around two former members of the oligarchic ruling group who, breaking with the others, demanded a larger political role for former *samurai* and others ex-

cluded from meaningful participation in the political system. It was in part to meet these demands that a Diet was created through the Meiji Constitution, and it was people from these political lines who dominated the Diet from its inception in 1890 and successfully battled the Cabinet for a larger share in power. The older of the two lines originally called itself the Jiyūtō, which literally means "freedom party," but has been more tactfully translated as the Liberal Party. In 1900, parts of it merged with elements in the bureaucracy to form the Seiyūkai, which can be translated as "the association of political friends." The Seiyūkai was the dominant party most of the time until the 1930s. The other political line had a more checkered career and changed names frequently. In 1927 it eventually settled on the name of Minseitō, which means "people's government party."

The military forced all the parties to disband in 1940 and join a loose organization called the Imperial Rule Assistance Association, but with Japan's defeat in 1945 the old parties sprang back to life at once, the Seiyūkai under its early name of Liberal Party and the Minseitō alternating between the names of Progressive Party and Democratic Party. These two revived prewar parties dominated postwar politics, and when they saw the rising opposition vote of the left as a dangerous challenge, they merged in 1955 to form the *Liberal Democratic Party (LDP),* which has been in power in the national government ever since.

Partly as a result of the Russian Revolution of 1917 and the liberal ideas that swept Europe after World War I, various leftist intellectual stirrings took place in Japan in the 1920s and penetrated the labor movement. A small Communist Party was founded in 1922, but it was soon suppressed and its leaders either imprisoned or driven into exile. A socialistic Farmer-Labor Party was formed in 1925, and from it was spawned a variety of short-lived parties, which usually divided into two or three mutually contentious lines. Eventually in

FIGURE 7.2 *Political Parties of Japan*

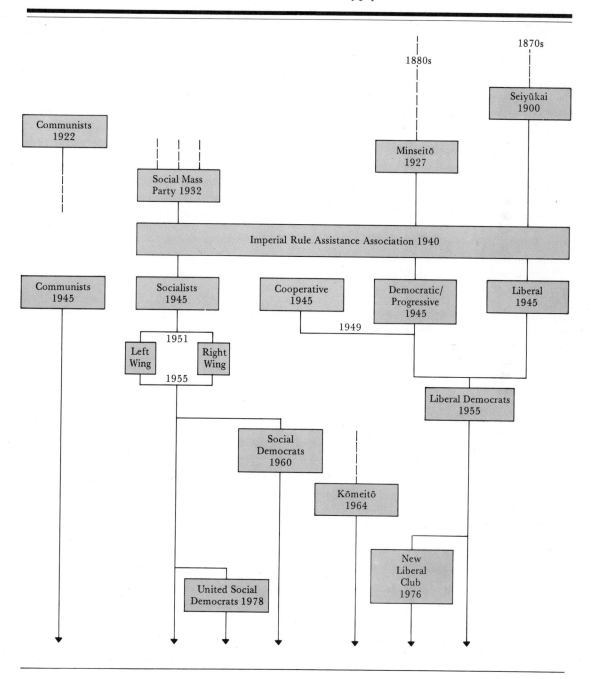

1932 the more moderate elements of the socialist movement formed the Social Mass Party; it won a small, but rapidly rising, vote until it, too, was absorbed in 1940 into the Imperial Rule Assistance Association.

After the surrender in 1945 the parties of the left also came back to life. Emerging from prison or returning from exile in the Soviet Union or China, the communists re-established their now legal *Communist Party (JCP)*, and the Social Mass Party was resurrected under the forthright name of the *Socialist Party (JSP)*. The divisions of the 1920s still persisted among the Socialists, however. Between 1951 and 1955 the party split into left and right wings, and in January 1960 the more moderate elements of the former right wing broke off again, this time permanently, to form the *Democratic Socialist Party (DSP)*.

The disturbed conditions after the war also gave birth to a welter of new parties, but none had much significance except the Cooperative Party, which merged into the Democrats in 1949 and, thus, into the LDP in 1955. The only postwar party of lasting importance is the *Kōmeitō* (sometimes called the Clean Government Party), which gradually came into being between 1955 and 1964, when it adopted its present name. It is unusual in having started as the political wing of a religious organization called the *Sōka Gakkai*, which is an offshoot of Buddhism.

More recently, other parties have split off from the older ones, but their long-range influence is doubtful. In 1976 a few younger LDP Diet members left their party to form the *New Liberal Club*, which with new recruits did very well in the election for the lower house in December 1976, but was less successful in the upper-house election in July 1977 and won only four seats in the lower-house election of October 1979. In 1978 an even smaller group of moderate Socialists left their party to form a United Social Democratic Party but won only two seats in the 1979 election.

Party Support. The LDP, as the inheritor of the two traditional party lines that go back all the way to the 1870s and 1880s, is strong in rural Japan. It is known as the party of the farmers, but this fact is of declining significance. Even though rural Japan has a disproportionately high share of Diet representation, farmers themselves have shrunk from about half of the population at the end of World War II to less than 15 percent today, and many of these people are also engaged in nonagricultural jobs. The LDP is also known as the party of big business, called the *zaikai*, or "the financial world." This is because the LDP is the most conservative and probusiness party in Japan, providing spectacularly successful economic leadership, and because most of its economic support comes from big business, which is permitted to make contributions to political parties in the same way as labor unions.

The LDP, however, cannot depend on big business or even the farmers for the bulk of its voting strength. This must come from those members of the general public who see it as the party best able to direct the nation's affairs. The greatest strength of the LDP has always been the pragmatism and lack of dogmatism of its politicians. They are ready to accept a large government role in business or a drift toward a welfare state, as long as the measures taken appear popular and practical. In fact, the dilemma and frustration of the opposition parties have resulted from the LDP's readiness to co-opt their most popular and workable policies, while projecting the image of being the only party with the practical experience that will enable them to carry these policies out effectively.

The Socialist Party relies heavily on organized labor for financial support, votes, and leadership. In particular, it depends on *Sōhyō*, the largest of the labor federations, which has more than 4.5 million members. The Sōhyō unions are largely made up of government and white-collar workers, such as teachers and petty functionaries in the national and local governments, who tend to constitute the radical wing of the labor movement, since the best way they have to achieve their goals is to exert direct influence on the government.

The Democratic Socialists depend to a large extent on *Dōmei,* a labor federation of slightly over 2 million members, largely from blue-collar unions in private industry. These form the more moderate wing of the labor movement, concentrating on bargaining over wages and working conditions with their private employers and on avoiding disruptive strikes for fear of hurting the competitive position of their respective companies, with which they usually have lifetime employment.

The Kōmeitō draws its support largely from members of the Sōka Gakkai. These tend to be lower-income city dwellers who, lacking affiliation with large companies or other prestigious bodies, have joined the religion as a means of finding a group with which to identify. As an opposition party, Kōmeitō takes a generally leftist stance against the LDP, but its membership is actually rather conservative, coming on the whole from the less educated, more old-fashioned, and more traditional sectors of urban society.

The Communists rely for their support on certain labor unions and the small, but determined, band of communist believers. Since they are tightly and efficiently organized, they also attract many of the floating voters of the larger metropolitan areas, who, though not necessarily attracted by Communist policies, use the party to register a protest vote against what they feel are the unsatisfactory conditions of contemporary urban life. Some of the urban floating vote also goes to Kōmeitō, since it, too, is seen as a well-organized, effective party.

The conservatives, united since 1955 as the LDP, have dominated politics throughout the postwar period. The only partial break in their rule was during a period from May 1947 to October 1948, when there were two Socialist-Democratic-Cooperative coalition Cabinets, one led by a moderate Socialist called Katayama. The long dominance of the LDP has made the other parties very bitter and induced them to assume the stance of a permanent uncooperative opposition. Some people have described Japanese politics not as a two-party system, but as a "party-and-a-half" system. The Marxist background of most of the opposition parties has widened the division between them and the LDP, and memories of prewar and wartime oppression of the left have contributed to a deep suspicion and hostility toward the party in power. Thus, a serious cleavage has existed in postwar Japanese politics between the conservative camp of the ruling LDP and the so-called progressive camp of the opposition. This confrontation was particularly marked in the years immediately after the end of the American occupation and began to fade only in the early 1970s.

During the postwar period the LDP vote and number of seats in the Diet have both slowly eroded. The conservative parties won their highest proportion of the popular vote in 1952 with 66 percent, but thereafter the LDP vote slowly declined, until by 1967 it was 49 percent and in 1976 only 46 percent, even including the New Liberal Club defectors. With the aid of some independents and the division of the opposition into a number of parties, the LDP has maintained a bare majority in the two houses of the Diet, but not enough in recent years to be in full command of all Diet committees. This slow shift in votes away from the conservatives appears to have been largely the result of demographic changes: an increase in the number of urban residents, a movement of the labor force from agriculture to manufacturing and service industries, rising educational standards, and generational changes, all of which have favored the progressives over the conservatives.

The Socialist Party was once expected to succeed the LDP as the majority party, but it has gradually faded as other opposition parties came on the scene. It reached its high point in popular votes at 33 percent in 1958, but in 1979 was down to less than 20 percent. The Communists and Kōmeitō each get around 10 percent of the vote; the DSP, somewhat less.

The decline of the LDP vote seems to have slowed down or stopped of late, and it appears possible that the party may maintain its slim margin for some time into the future. If it does not, many people have assumed that a coalition of the progressive parties would take over, but this is most unlikely. There are deep historical fissures between the Communists and the Socialists, within the JSP itself, and between these parties of the left and Kōmeitō and the DSP in the center. Meanwhile the issues that once divided the conservatives and progressives have faded to a large extent, and the voters for all of the parties have tended to drift toward the center on most issues, dragging their parties with them. If the LDP can no longer rule alone, it seems probable that at first an informal and then possibly a formal coalition will be worked out with the parties of the center. It is also possible that eventually a reshuffling of parties might take place to produce a large new ruling party that is nearer the center of the political spectrum and consists of the Kōmeitō, the DSP, the bulk of the LDP, and probably some moderate elements from the JSP.

In any case, ever since the 1976 and 1977 elections for the lower and upper houses, a sort of informal coalition has existed between the LDP and the center parties, which separately lend the LDP support from time to time on controversial issues. The LDP, moreover, is careful to make as much of its legislation as possible acceptable to the other opposition parties. Thus, whatever the trend in votes may be over the next few years, there seems little reason to believe that the balance of political opinion or power in Japan will shift radically either to the left or to the right.

Party Organization. Most Japanese consider themselves political independents, not tied to parties—an attitude that is becoming increasingly common in the United States, too. But many Japanese do get involved in party politics, and most vote with fair consistency for one party or another. The contrast between small formal party membership and wide party support is particularly marked in the case of the LDP.

The core of the LDP consists of the party members who are elected to the two houses of the

Diet (see Figure 7.3). They constitute the bulk of the delegates to the party convention, which is held on average every two years and elects the party president and the other party officers. These include at times a vice president, if there happens to be a suitable candidate, but the second most important party post is that of *secretary general,* the person who oversees the running of the party while the president is running the Cabinet and government. Other important party positions are the chairs of the party's *Executive Council* and the Policy Affairs Research Committee. The party president is always elected prime minister by the LDP majority in the lower house, and this official and other party leaders choose the Cabinet ministers and the various party committees that supervise the operations of both the government and the party.

This preponderance of control of the party by the LDP members of the Diet and the prevalence of independents at the lowest grassroots levels have given rise to a picture of the LDP as an inverted pyramid or a "ghost party," for it has a clear head, but only shadowy feet. This, however, is not a correct representation of the situation. Beneath the core of Diet members are the local groups of LDP politicians, who are would-be or elected assembly members, mayors, or governors in prefectural and municipal governments, and below them, the many *kōenkai* of politicians in national and local politics. Through the latter, very large numbers of people become directly involved in LDP politics.

In the autumn of 1978, moreover, a new primary system for the selection of the party president was introduced in order to get more grassroots participation. Party members who had paid their dues or made other financial contributions voted by prefectures for candidates for the party presidency, and the final selection was then made by the party Diet members between the two candidates with the highest votes. More than 1.3 million votes were cast, and, in this case at least, the popular vote proved decisive in determining a change in December 1978 in the presidency and prime ministership from Fukuda to Ōhira.

This primary vote amounted to only 5 percent of the vote that the LDP can count on in national elections, but frantic efforts in early 1980 to increase the party's registered members in preparation for the second primary to be held in December of that year gave promise of larger votes in the future. The unexpected results of the first primary and the resentments raised by it also probably help account for the refusal of Fukuda's backers to vote for the reelection of Ōhira as prime minister following the disappointing showing of the LDP in the lower house elections of October 1979. This was the first time that the party had not unified behind a single candidate for prime minister, indicating a new divisiveness within the party, produced at least in part by the more public rivalry of the new primary system.

One surprising feature of Japanese politics and

FIGURE 7.3 *Decision-Making Organs of the Japanese Government and the Liberal Democratic Party*

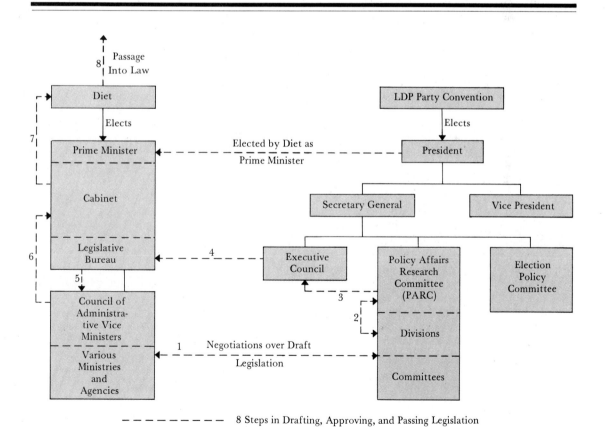

TABLE 7.1 *Hypothetical Results of Unbalanced and Balanced LDP Voting*

Parties	UNBALANCED LDP VOTE		BALANCED LDP VOTE	
	Vote	Results	Vote	Results
LDP	110,000	Elected	80,000	Elected
LDP	52,000		68,000	Elected
LDP	48,000		62,000	Elected
DSP	53,000	Elected	53,000	
Komeito	58,000	Elected	58,000	
JSP	70,000	Elected	70,000	Elected
JCP	60,000	Elected	60,000	Elected

especially of the LDP is that even though most successful members of the Diet get elected on the basis of their own individual images and personal electoral machines, they adhere to a system of strict party discipline, almost always voting in unison, once they are congregated together in the Diet. In the United States, where candidates have strong local roots and are elected in large part on their own personal strength (as in Japan), there is little semblance of party discipline in Congress, and each member votes according to his or her own conscience or interests. On the other hand, in countries that have strong party discipline, candidates are usually elected not because of personal strength, but because of the party they represent, and frequently they have only weak ties with their constituencies. The Japanese ability to combine strong personal electoral politics with strict party discipline at the parliamentary level is unusual and offers a measure of their skill in group organization.

A particularly difficult problem for the LDP is the selection of candidates to run for the lower house of the Diet. In the middle-sized three-to-five-seat districts, if too many LDP candidates run or the vote is distributed too unevenly between them, the LDP may win fewer seats than its number of votes would entitle it to. Table 7.1 presents a hypothetical example, showing how this might work in a five-seat district in which one of the LDP candidates is extremely popular and runs away with too large a proportion of the votes. Similarly, if the LDP runs too many candidates, there can be the same sort of disastrous results, as Table 7.2 illustrates.

It is obviously imperative to spread out the votes between the party candidates and to avoid running too many, but this is not easy to accomplish. There is no primary system to select candidates, and there are many ambitious local LDP politicians who are eager to run for the Diet and have been building up their local support with this objective in mind. The way in which this problem is solved is through the party's Election Policy Committee, which has the duty of deciding on the number of candidates and the specific individuals in each electoral district. Sometimes disappointed would-be nominees, confident of their electoral strength and unwilling to accept the committee's decision, will defy it by running as nominal independents. If they succeed, replacing in all probability one of the party's regular candidates, they will almost always rejoin the party at once.

One feature of the LDP is that virtually all of its Diet members are divided into *factions*. These are informal clubs led by prominent politicians, who

TABLE 7.2 *Hypothetical Results of Voting for Four and Three LDP Candidates*

Parties	FOUR LDP CANDIDATES		THREE LDP CANDIDATES	
	Vote	Results	Vote	Results
LDP	60,000	Elected	76,000	Elected
LDP	52,000		68,000	Elected
LDP	50,000		66,000	Elected
LDP	48,000			
DSP	53,000	Elected	53,000	
Komeito	58,000	Elected	58,000	
JSP	70,000	Elected	70,000	Elected
JCP	60,000	Elected	60,000	Elected

usually are striving for the party presidency and prime ministership. The factions are almost universally condemned as being disruptive of party unity, but their very persistence shows that they do have a function. They usually do not represent ideological differences and thus are in no sense miniparties, as they are sometimes called. Although the leaders do vary in their political stances, the members of their factions normally spread over the whole range of political opinion in the party.

The factions actually serve many functions. Of course, they are useful to the leaders as a base for their efforts to exert influence in the party and eventually to achieve the party presidency. For the members, too, the factions are of help in a variety of ways. A factional alignment may have aided a Diet member originally in getting the nomination of the party. It is likely to be a source of extra campaign funds beyond those provided by the party, and the ability to raise political funds is, therefore, a prime requisite for a successful faction leader. In the Diet the faction's meetings serve as a sort of seminar for the new members and a device by which members of the party leadership keep in touch with rank-and-file sentiment. So the factions are useful in helping the party reach a consensus that can serve as the basis for a unified vote in the Diet. The factions also help their members attain the coveted positions of committee chairs, parliamentary vice ministers, and eventually Cabinet members.

To be at all effective, a faction must have at least ten or twenty members in the two houses of the Diet; but if it grows much beyond eighty or ninety members, it is likely to become unwieldy and run the risk of division. Since the factions are so important in the operation of the LDP at the Diet level, it is necessary that there be a certain factional balance in Cabinet appointments, in other government and party posts, and particularly in key bodies such as the Executive Council, the Policy Affairs Research Committee, and the Election Policy Committee.

Many of the leaders of LDP factions in recent years have been members of the Diet who originally served in the bureaucracy. In fact, the Japanese government has been led by prime ministers of such background during the better part of the post–World War II era. The list of former bureaucrats who became prime minister is impressive: Shidehara (1945–46), Ashida (1948), Yoshida (1946–47, 1948–54), Kishi (1957–60), Ikeda (1960–64), Satō (1964–72), Fukuda (1976–78), and

Ōhira (1978–80). Bureaucrat-politicians have predominated because the bureaucracy has traditionally drawn a high percentage of the most talented citizens, and when it became evident at the end of the war that the Diet was the center of power, quite a few of them shifted from the bureaucracy to electoral politics and then achieved the highest post because of their native ability and deep knowledge of the working of government. It is doubtful, however, that the bureaucratic leadership of the LDP will continue far into the future. Two of the recent prime ministers, Miki (1972–74) and Tanaka (1974–76), did not have this background, and increasing numbers of the LDP Diet leaders are emerging from lifetime careers in local and national politics.

Most of the other parties have organizations more or less comparable to that of the LDP, except that they do not have the problem of dividing up government positions, since they are not in power, and, with the exception of the Socialists, they are all too small to have major factional divisions or to face the problem of running more than one candidate in a lower-house electoral district. In the case of the JSP, its drastic loss of lower-house seats from 140 to 90 between 1967 and 1969 was directly caused by its overoptimistically running too many candidates in 1969.

The Communists and the Kōmeitō are the most tightly organized of the parties and have proportionately larger official memberships than the others. Both have a clear-cut and strong leadership. The Kōmeitō is financially supported primarily by the Sōka Gakkai and the Communist Party primarily by its newspaper, *Akahata* ("Red Flag"), which has a daily circulation of several hundred thousand and a Sunday circulation of close to 2.5 million.

The JSP and DSP depend heavily both for funds and for votes on the Sōhyō and Dōmei labor federations, respectively. Representatives of the JSP's prefectural and local organizations, in which Sōhyō often plays a major role, make up the bulk of the membership at the party's conventions, where the party chairperson and other top officials are selected. Since Sōhyō and the other local

activists tend toward the left, the results of these conventions often show a leftward drift; but since the JSP must also appeal to more moderate voters to elect its candidates, at times of national elections the party often swings back toward the center. Ever since the war the JSP has been plagued by factionalism, which, being based on ideological differences, is very disruptive in a way that the LDP factions are not. Always lying beneath the surface and sometimes breaking to the top, a rather sharp cleavage between left and right exists within the Socialist Party, and at times a rather clear center group can be identified as well.

THE SELF-STEERING SYSTEM

The Decision-Making Process. The Japanese traditionally have preferred consensus, whenever possible, rather than simple majority decisions. They show this tendency throughout their society, including big business, where decisions are usually arrived at after lengthy consultation up and down the chain of command and not simply by a few top executives. The same applies to government and the whole political process.

The central core of decision-making organs in politics consists of the bureaucracy and the Diet—more specifically, the party in power. The bureaucracy, of course, is divided into a number of ministries and agencies, each with its own area of authority, which it jealously guards, and its own policies, hammered out between its many functional divisions and internal groups with differing opinions. The LDP is similarly divided into various factions and occasional policy groupings that transcend factional lines. Between these two bodies and their various elements, it is no simple task to work out draft legislation that will receive majority Diet support and thus become law.

One key organ in achieving this result is the *Policy Affairs Research Committee (PARC)* of the LDP (see Figure 7.3). It has seventeen divisions, which correspond to the major divisions of the bureaucracy, and beneath these some fifty-five committees (as of 1978) that work on issues of interest to specific political pressure groups. Individual LDP Diet members belong to two of the divisions of PARC, but can attend any of the committees they wish, thus having a say at this lowest level of national decision making on any legislation in which they have an interest. The various ministries and agencies come up with draft legislation, but only after intensive intraministry consultations and, when appropriate, interministry negotiations and also with an eye to prevailing opinions in the Diet and among the public. Similarly, the committees and divisions of PARC, reflecting the interests of LDP Diet members, and their readings of their constituents' desires, produce their own suggestions for legislation. After careful negotiations between the bureaucratic and PARC groups concerned, draft legislation is produced, which then goes through a long process of scrutiny and emendation.

Draft laws must first win approval of PARC as a whole and then the party's Executive Council, both of which are factionally balanced groups. Then they are passed to the Legislative Bureau under the Cabinet, which clears them through the Council of Administrative Vice Ministers, the group in day-to-day control of the various branches of the bureaucracy, to be sure that there are no bureaucratic problems remaining. The draft legislation is then ready for adoption by the Cabinet and presentation to the Diet, where, after all this careful work, it is assured of LDP support and, therefore, probable passage.

Such broad LDP and bureaucratic consensus, however, cannot always be achieved by this process. In such cases it is usually up to the leaders of the LDP to make the decisions. Here the faction system has its value, because the leaders, in close touch with the members of their respective factions, can judge what sort of compromise can win general approval. Sometimes the leaders meet informally as faction heads to make these decisions, but at other times they may get together more formally as the occupants of the top party

posts. Occasionally a prime minister has to make the decision alone, despite the risk that members of the party may subsequently repudiate this decision and unseat him.

Throughout this interplay between the LDP and the bureaucracy in drawing up draft legislation, both sides are mindful of public opinion and the attitudes of the opposition parties. Unpopular laws may lose votes in the next election, and legislation that the opposition parties disapprove of bitterly will require a lot of time for passage through the Diet. In fact, the chief tactic that the opposition employs in the Diet is attempting to delay action both in the committees and at the plenary sessions. Though time is strictly allotted for the debate of each issue, the opposition hopes that through interpellation they can trick an LDP minister into some unwise remark that can, for example, be interpreted as denigrating democracy, human rights, or popular sovereignty. They then can blow this remark up into a new issue that must be debated, using up valuable Diet time in the process.

Earlier, in the 1950s and most notably during the great Mutual Security Treaty debate of the spring of 1960, the opposition also used cruder methods, such as keeping the speaker bottled up in his office by force, disrupting sessions by fisticuffs, boycotting sessions, and demanding innumerable procedural votes and then dragging these out as long as possible. The LDP would respond to these delaying tactics by "ramming through" legislation, as it was called, through trickery or force. For example, the key vote in the 1960 debate was taken by suddenly calling a session and taking a voice vote before the opposition realized what was happening.

Such undignified parliamentary procedures are now rare, but the ability of the opposition parties to delay and sometimes block legislation by uncooperative tactics remains strong. In large part, this is because of the traditional preference of the Japanese for consensus decisions. They tend to sympathize with the minority and feel it should have its full say and, if possible, a share in the decision. The Japanese are quick to condemn what they call "the tyranny of the majority," though none would prefer "the tyranny of the minority." The net result is that only a few truly controversial bills can be passed in any one session of the Diet. This makes it necessary for the LDP to make the maximum number of its draft laws noncontroversial and to limit the controversial elements of the others as much as it can. As a result, the opposition parties have a much larger role in the decision-making process than is usually realized. In recent years, as the representation of the LDP in the Diet has gradually shrunk to virtual equality with the opposition parties, the influence of the latter has naturally grown, producing an increase in consultations with them during the drafting process and more emendations of draft laws at their instigation during Diet debate.

Pressure Groups. Japanese voters, of course, exercise ultimate control over the political decision-making process through their election of members of the Diet and, at a lower level, the members of the local governments, but the public also exercises its influence more directly. Throughout Japanese society there are special interest or *pressure groups* that seek to influence political decisions that concern them.

One particularly powerful and well organized group has exerted such great influence that it has drawn special attention. In fact, some observers have felt that it should be regarded as part of the inner decision-making core of the Japanese political system. This is big business, or the *zaikai*. It is closely integrated through a number of bodies, the chief of which is the Keidanren, the Association of Economic Organizations. Big business naturally had a major role in Japan's amazing postwar industrial expansion. During the 1950s and 1960s, when rapid economic growth was the central Japanese concern, it played a very influential part in establishing economic policies, together with the LDP politicians and the bureaucrats, and in putting these into effect in cooperation with the bureaucracy. This situation has given rise to

descriptions of Japanese politics as being in the hands of a triumvirate made up of the LDP, the bureaucracy, and the *zaikai*. The residence of most of the members of all three groups in Tokyo, the graduation of many of them from Tokyo University, a certain degree of intermarriage between them, and the movement of some bureaucrats after retirement into business positions or politics all tended to confirm this picture.

This triumvirate model, however, is basically misleading. It never applied to most policy fields, but only to matters of industrial economic growth—the area of interest to the *zaikai*. It has also proved much less correct even in this area during the 1970s than before. As rapid economic growth produced serious problems of pollution and overcrowding in the cities, the interests of LDP politicians and of bureaucrats began to diverge from those of big business executives. Sensitive to the demands of the public, the politicians and bureaucrats became concerned with pollution controls, the quality of life, social security, and other matters that conflicted with economic growth. The *zaikai*, of course, remains as certainly one of the most influential pressure groups, but it is now and has always been merely one among many.

Pressure groups are found in almost all realms of Japanese life. Through their huge cooperatives the farmers exert a great deal of political influence and with the aid of the LDP, which depends on their vote, have managed to get a system of agricultural price supports that has given rural Japan a full share in the affluence that industry has brought the country. The labor federations and their component unions are also large and powerful pressure groups, though they normally stand in an adversary relationship with the LDP and seek to achieve their ends through the opposition parties. Smaller groups such as doctors, dentists, and other professional people have more restricted, but still effective, pressure groups, as do other bodies of citizens that center around interests other than strictly economic ones.

Pressure groups get their voices heard in a variety of ways. Most ministries and other bureaucratic agencies have several *shingikai,* or advisory boards, made up of experts or concerned individuals from among the public who are expected to give advice on legislation or serve as sounding boards for legislative proposals. More important, the various pressure groups establish direct contacts with the branches of the bureaucracy and the committees in PARC that are concerned with the problems of interest to them. In addition, they naturally work on individual Diet members and enlist them as the champions of their respective causes. When they feel the LDP will not aid them, they work through the opposition parties and their Diet members.

Pressure groups also attempt to affect political decisions directly through popular *demonstrations.* During the turbulent early postwar years, marches and other demonstrations in the streets were to be seen everywhere, and the word *demo,* a short form of the English "demonstration," became one of the most frequently used words in the Japanese vocabulary. At times of political excitement, as during the security treaty debate in 1960, demonstrations brought out several hundred thousand people into the streets of Tokyo and became quite unruly. Even today pressure groups of all types are prone to stage street marches, usually in very orderly fashion, or to call at government offices and vociferously present their demands.

Violence as a means of exerting political pressure, however, has usually proved counterproductive. In the early postwar years, occasional acts of violence by the extreme left tended to drive away voters, and similar acts of violence by the extreme right have always met universal condemnation. When the student radical movements in the late 1960s became increasingly violent, they also lost all popular support and in a sense placed themselves outside of the meaningful Japanese political spectrum.

Often direct popular pressures are exerted by larger bodies transcending the usual special interest groups. In the early postoccupation years such movements, called *citizens' movements (shimin undō),*

were commonly sponsored by the opposition parties and supported particular political causes. These movements frequently concentrated on showing opposition to the presence of American bases and military personnel in Japan. They would call attention to unpleasant incidents involving the American military, and they also helped build anti-American feelings through demonstrations against nuclear weapons, particularly on August 6, the anniversary of the dropping of the atomic bomb on Hiroshima.

In more recent years such citizens' movements have been replaced for the most part by what are called *local residents' movements (jūmin undō).* These are concerned largely with local matters, such as pollution, crowding, factory and road construction, nuclear power plants, and other such problems of modern urban life, and they normally try to avoid involvement in party politics. These local residents' movements have been quite successful in drawing the attention of local governments and, eventually, the attention of the national government as well.

The Mass Media. An outstanding feature of Japanese politics is the extremely large role of the mass media, especially newspapers, since the Japanese are avid readers and consumers of news in all forms. There are two national television networks and four or five commercial ones covering Japan. Weekly and monthly magazines number in the hundreds and are available everywhere. Newspapers, however, loom largest as purveyors of news and shapers of public opinion. There are three national dailies with upwards of 5 million in circulation, two others only slightly smaller, four regional newspapers of around 1 million each, and many smaller publications. Almost without exception, all these papers maintain high standards of detailed and accurate reporting on both national and international news. The Japanese are probably better served by the press in terms of news reporting than any other major nation, and collectively the newspapers exert an influence on public opinion and through it on politics that is possibly unmatched elsewhere in the world.

Most of the newspapers pride themselves on being politically neutral. They sit in judgment on politics, as it were, and through their huge circulations help determine the public response. Much of Japanese politics, especially what goes on under public scrutiny in the Diet, is determined by fears or hopes regarding the way it will be reported by the press and, thus, will affect popular attitudes and future votes. Newspapers are still influenced by their formative years, when they saw themselves as critics of an all-powerful government. This makes them tend to be especially critical of any group in political power. On the whole, this is a salutary situation, though at times criticism of the government has been carried to extremes, unduly arousing political passions.

One unusual aspect of the Japanese mass media is the so-called *press club*. A press club is a group of reporters from the various papers, wire services, magazines, and networks that concentrates on one particular branch of government, political party, or leading politician. Press clubs develop a special privileged relationship with their specific institution or person, which results in a far more detailed knowledge of what is going on politically than most journalists in other countries can obtain. At the same time, the press clubs also develop a sort of symbiotic relationship with their subject. The latter provides them with news, but they in turn serve as mouthpieces for their subject's views. This situation induces the members of the press clubs to hang back from investigative reporting or exposés that would damage this relationship and result in cutting off their source of information. So the press club system has its weaknesses as well as its strengths.

On the whole, however, the Japanese mass media and especially the newspapers provide the public with more copious and more accurate news than do the mass media of other countries, and they play a more important role as critics of government and shapers of public opinion. Together with the vigorous direct participation in politics of pressure groups and local residents'

movements, they provide Japanese politics with ample feedback, which combines with the whole electoral process to produce a successful self-steering system.

THE STAKES OF POLITICS

If one looks back over the vast political, economic, and social changes the Japanese have been through during the past 150 years, one can see that much is at stake in the way the political process works in Japan. This is no unchanging society, but one that has been in almost constant ferment for the last four or five generations. Only in recent years have there been signs that some stability has been reached for the first time since the middle of the nineteenth century, when pressures from the outside world set Japan off in rapid motion.

The Political System. Between 1853 and the end of World War II the key question was how Japan was to be governed, and for several years after the war this question still remained uppermost in Japanese minds. Both the Japanese people and the American occupation authorities were determined that the virtual dictatorship of the military during the war years should be ended, but there was a wide divergence of opinion between those Japanese who felt that only a slight modification of the parliamentary system of the 1920s would be adequate and those who wanted to see a fully communist or socialist system in which the proletariat clearly ruled.

People divided into conservative and progressive camps. The very terminology showed the degree of hostility and suspicion that lay between them. The progressives feared that the conservatives were trying to turn the clocks back to the militarism and suppression of individual freedoms of the prewar system. The conservatives felt the progressives to be impractical zealots who would wreck Japan economically and sacrifice its national character.

In this atmosphere almost any policy dispute might blow up to crisis proportions. Such was the case in the somewhat theoretical disagreement over whether the emperor or the people possessed sovereignty and the rather technical problem of the degree to which the central government should exercise control over the police and education. The recentralization of some police controls during the 1950s was seen as a step toward the re-creation of a police state and was met with frenzied opposition. The appointment, rather than election, of school boards and the institution of teacher rating systems and courses on ethics were seen as preparations for the use of education to indoctrinate the people, as before the war. The political powers of organized labor were also matters of bitter contention. The use of the general strike was outlawed as running the risk of chaos and revolution, and the right of government workers to strike was also denied. One of the most fiercely contested issues was whether Japan, in view of Article IX of the constitution, had the right to maintain the Self-Defense Forces.

As the postwar system gradually stabilized and people became accustomed to it, many of these issues either disappeared or dwindled in significance. But some still remain very much alive. A running battle continues between the Japan Teachers Union and the Ministry of Education over a wide variety of matters concerning the organization of schools and the textbooks and other contents of education. The right of government workers to strike is hotly maintained by their unions and the parties that back them, and strikes of this sort do in fact occur. Most of the opposition parties continue to disapprove officially of the Self-Defense Forces, though public opinion has gradually swung to their support at their present, very modest levels of strength, and the issue, therefore, is no longer a major one.

On the whole, the Japanese people seem content with the basic nature of their postwar political system as well as the social and economic systems that lie behind it. Opinion polls reveal that 90 percent of them consider themselves to be middle class; in fact, 60 percent describe themselves as the middle of the middle class. They like their egalitarian system in which good education is fully available to everyone and produces an educational meritocracy that runs the nation. They constantly complain, however, of the pressures of educational competition and the "examination hell" that this system imposes on their children. Few would want or can even imagine any political setup other than their present electoral and parliamentary system. Except for tiny fringes at the extreme left and right, there is complete support for and great pride in the Peace Constitution and a strong determination not to change it in any way, however slight, for fear of opening the door to more significant changes.

This does not mean that there is not disenchantment with the way in which the political system sometimes operates. The supporters of the opposition parties feel that there is something unfair about a situation in which their parties seem destined to remain out of power. Throughout society there is a feeling that politics is dirty and politicians corrupt. Too much in politics seems to depend on the lavish use of money, and clearly politicians are breaking the spirit—if not the letter—of the law in their free use of money and large-scale electoral campaigns disguised as educational and cultural activities. Occasionally the whole nation is rocked by a scandal, when some particularly large or blatant use of money in elections or other political dealings comes to light or is suspected to exist. Complex bureaucracies often seem insensitive to personal and local needs, although there is little reason to think that bureaucrats are dishonest or corrupt, in contrast to conditions in many countries. Thus, there is a large pot of political issues that is constantly boiling away, raising incessant political controversies, but in recent years none of these issues has really concerned the basic make-up of the Japanese political system. In fact, the Japanese political system at present seems to be one of the most stable and secure in the whole world.

Foreign Relations. Ever since 1853, Japan's relationship with the outside world has been the chief force behind the rapid change in political, economic, and social conditions, and so, quite naturally, foreign relations have frequently been the major area of political controversy. This was true in the great transformation of 1868 and during the tremendous convulsions surrounding World War II and is still the case today. Since the war, divisions over foreign policy have been more basic and persistent than controversies over the political system itself.

The conservatives, though irritated by their having to accept aspects of the American reforms and by MacArthur's having drafted their postwar constitution, have felt throughout that a close relationship with the United States was necessary for both economic and security reasons. The progressives have feared that this association would endanger Japan by embroiling it in the Cold War and in what they felt was the inevitably aggressive and imperialistic foreign policy of the world's largest capitalist country. They have also felt that this association with "American imperialism" would strengthen domestic "monopoly capitalism," thus precluding Japan from the possibility of building a socialist system. The progressives preferred a policy for Japan of unarmed neutrality or, in the case of the extreme left, of open alignment with the Communist powers.

Since the American bases and military personnel in Japan and the Mutual Security Treaty offered tangible targets of attack, and since the natural distaste for the presence of foreign forces on Japanese soil easily stirred nationalistic feelings, the opposition forces found these issues the easiest to exploit in their battles with the conservatives. As a result, the alignment with the United States was at the heart of the controversy between the left and right in Japan throughout the 1950s and 1960s. Every opposition party condemned the security treaty and advocated the withdrawal of American troops from Japan, though with varying

degrees of vehemence and with different timetables in mind. Public opinion surveys also showed a preponderance of sentiment for this side. The conservative government, however, held staunchly to the American alignment as absolutely necessary for Japan.

Beneath this violent conflict over relations with the United States, however, there existed a broad, but largely unconscious, consensus over foreign policy. Even the conservatives wished to limit Japan's involvement in international controversies as far as possible and concentrate instead on establishing friendly relations with all countries, Communist and non-Communist alike, and on developing Japanese trade with all parts of the world in this way. Japan was extremely successful in this policy. It made reparations settlements with its neighbors in Southeast Asia, which laid the groundwork for later great export markets in these countries. It became a major trading partner for both the Soviet Union and China—in fact, China's largest trading partner. At the same time, of course, the bulk of its trade remained with the Western nations and the countries economically associated with them.

Japan's policy of maintaining a low profile in world politics and concentrating on the development of its own trade had widespread support at home, but brought it some criticism from abroad. The United States complained at times of Japan's lukewarm cooperation and the "free ride" it was taking at the expense of American defense efforts. De Gaulle once contemptuously called the Japanese prime minister a "transistor salesman." Later, when the Japanese economy had grown powerful, the Japanese were accused of being merely "economic animals." The developing nations, especially those of Southeast Asia, became bitter about Japan's failure to provide them with more aid, whereas the industrial nations of the West, including the United States, became incensed over the imbalance of trade in Japan's favor and the flood of Japanese industrial goods that threatened parts of their own economies. Still, Japan's postwar foreign policy did prove eminently successful in removing that nation from the line of fire in most international controversies, allowing it to keep its own military expenditures to a minimum, and laying the basis for its extraordinary growth to economic affluence and its present position as the third largest economic power in the world.

Even the one area of formerly bitter debate in Japan, foreign policy, has shrunk in importance in recent years. There are many reasons why this has happened, but perhaps the most fundamental has been the rift between the Soviet Union and China, which became progressively more evident and irreversible after 1960. Fearful and resentful of each other, these two important neighbors of Japan began to seek better relations with both the United States and Japan and to give tacit approval to the Japanese-American military alliance, thus undermining the arguments of the opposition parties.

Clearly, the intimate connection with the United States had not led to the dire results formerly predicted by the left. The Cold War faded, and a détente developed in American relations with both the Soviet Union and China. Nixon's visit to China in 1972 made the Japanese feel free to go a step beyond the United States in establishing full diplomatic relations with China more than six years before the United States did so and to sign a full peace treaty with China in 1978. The United States also promised in 1969 to give back political control over Okinawa, Japan's forty-seventh prefecture, and did return the islands in 1972, before Japanese resentments over this lost province reached the boiling point. Meanwhile the American military presence in Japan was gradually declining in size and visibility. The Vietnam War, which had revolted most Japanese and given credence to assertions that the United States was an inevitably imperialistic nation, also died away gradually in the early 1970s.

For all these reasons, the problem of the American alliance slowly faded as a political issue in Japan. The public came to accept it, not with enthusiasm, but as a matter of course. Some of the opposition parties formally shifted to a less hostile stand on the security treaty, and none saw fit to make it a major issue in the elections for the lower and upper houses in 1976 and later. In its place, foreign economic relations arose as the major foreign problems, but on these, unlike the issue of the American connection, no clear-cut political divisions between left and right have emerged.

Economic and Social Issues. Since the opposition parties in Japan stem largely from Marxist origins, one might assume that fundamental economic issues would lie at the heart of political controversy in Japan, but this has not been the case. In the early years after the war some labor unions attempted to get control of industry, and some Communist and Socialist adherents appeared committed to trying to establish a socialist economy, but these conditions did not last long. At first the problems of mere economic survival overshadowed everything else, and, in any case, control by the American occupation precluded the possibility of a serious experiment with a socialist economy. Later, the land reform program and economic recovery through private industry guided by government planning proved so successful that, unlike the situation in many other countries, little push developed in Japan for government ownership of industry or the collectivization of agriculture.

Almost all Japanese felt that the first task was to restore the economy and help it to grow as quickly as possible. Here was another area of very broad consensus, and it was difficult to fault the general strategy of the government once economic recovery began to pick up speed after 1950. Even the parties of the left gradually settled into tacit acceptance of the existing economic system and came to concentrate on attempting to correct its imperfections rather than on overturning it. They tried to do this through advocating a more equitable division of the economic rewards of the system, strengthening competition through supporting fair trade legislation, and championing small business against big business. In other words, the parties of the left seemed more intent on making the free enterprise system work well than on creating a truly socialist alternative.

Unlike the sharply drawn battle lines over foreign policy that existed in the early postwar years, political contests over economic and social matters have usually seemed more like myriad small skirmishes in a guerrilla war. Although accepting the conservative policy of concentrating on expanding the economic pie as a whole, the opposition parties fought constantly for a more equal division of its slices. Approving in general of the postwar political and social system, the progressives nevertheless found countless issues on which to attack the government's disregard of the needs or rights of some particular group. The opposition parties saw themselves in particular as the defenders of the many human rights guaranteed by the constitution. These, of course, are so sweeping as to raise many difficult problems of interpretation and implementation. There is plenty of room for disagreement, and political conflict of this sort continues unabated.

The conservatives themselves, however, have become increasingly committed to full support of constitutional rights, and during most of the 1950s and 1960s economic growth was so rapid that the individual slices of the economic pie automatically grew at a very satisfactory rate. In time, Japanese personal incomes in monetary terms rose to the levels of Western Europe and the United States and were more equitably divided between rich and poor in Japan than in most Western lands. Thus, no fundamental clash ever developed over the basic economic issues, though extraordinarily high prices in Japan, because of the scarcity of space and resources, made the Japanese in fact less affluent than the monetary figures would suggest.

The late 1960s and the 1970s, however, saw the emergence of a new set of economic and social problems. Rapid economic growth in Japan's limited terrain was beginning to cause serious overcrowding and pollution, especially in metropolitan areas, and a dangerous degradation of the natural environment. Housing was scarce and terribly crowded in cities. Many people were

forced to commute long distances to work each day—often between one and two hours each way. Urban streets were glutted with traffic, and commuter train lines and subways, though numerous and excellent, were crowded beyond capacity. Air and water pollution became serious hazards to health and produced in some cases spectacularly injurious ailments, such as the famous Minamata disease from mercury poisoning, which was caused by eating contaminated fish. Continued rapid economic growth that worsened these conditions was seen as lowering the quality of life rather than enhancing it.

The Japanese have developed a concept broader than pollution, which they called *kōgai,* or "public nuisance." *Kōgai* includes not just the ordinary types of air and water pollution, but also "sound pollution" from airports, highways, and railways, undue crowding of every sort, and even the obstruction of the individual's access to sunshine, which figures importantly in Japan in wintertime heating and in year-round drying of laundry. The Japanese have also proved very sensitive to the dangers of nuclear radiation, and constant battles rage over the locating of nuclear power plants, which are important for an energy-poor country.

Long concentration on economic growth at the expense of other matters also produced social foundations woefully inadequate for the ponderous economic machine that they now bear. Public services, such as sewage systems, lagged far behind those of other modern industrial societies, as did the social security system. This latter weakness was all the more serious because of a changing age structure in the Japanese population. Birth control, which had swept Japan since the war, had made the two-child family typical and had brought population growth down to about 1 percent per year, with zero growth being a predictable result before long. Simultaneously, life expectancy in Japan had risen rapidly, until it surpassed that of Sweden as the highest in the world. All this meant a rapidly aging population and a new problem of caring for the aged, since crowded urban living conditions were ruling out the traditional method of accommodating the elderly as live-in grandparents.

Japan in the 1970s thus faced a whole new series of economic and social issues, such as pollution controls, compensation for those injured by pollution, limitations on factory and road construction that were seen as undesirable by the local community, increased retirement and social security benefits, and free medical care, especially for the aged. As we have already noted, many of these issues were brought to public attention largely by local citizens' movements and local governments, which in the metropolitan areas were commonly in the hands of the progressive parties by the late 1960s. The courts also played a key role in several landmark decisions in the early 1970s, which established that polluters must pay for the damage they cause.

These various issues could well have produced a new fundamental split between the opposition parties, representing the urban population, and the LDP, representing the interests of big business and rural people, who were less concerned by *kōgai* issues. Both the LDP and the bureaucracy, however, proved sensitive to these problems—the LDP, no doubt, because of the votes that were at stake. They co-opted the issues at the national level and together with the opposition parties began working vigorously on their solution. Japan quickly established and enforced stringent limitations on the emission of pollutants and the first system in the world for making those who produced pollution compensate those who suffered from it. Social security, retirement benefits, and free medical care, especially for the elderly, have also been rapidly expanded in recent years.

The oil crisis growing out of the Arab-Israeli War in the autumn of 1973 and the resultant quadrupling of oil prices was a particularly severe shock to Japan, which depends for close to three-quarters of its total energy resources on imported oil, most of it from the Persian Gulf. The growth of the economy in real terms tumbled in a single year from 11 percent to less than zero and then recovered to only around 6 percent. No major country suffered a worse economic blow, and it is a measure of Japan's stability that it withstood it without any serious political or social tremors. In fact, in some ways the oil shock was a blessing in disguise, since it came just at a time when the country was considering a shift from high growth policies to a greater emphasis on social services and the quality of life. The enforced economic slowdown made this shift more natural and less controversial. The complete lack of panic in Japan and easy accommodation to the second oil shock of rising prices and shortages in 1978–80 show that resources-poor Japan has prepared itself better to deal with such energy problems than have the United States and some other industrial countries. Still, the second oil shock brought Japanese balance of payments from large surplusses into deficits and slowed economic growth once again almost to a halt. Entering the eighties, Japan had reason to view its future energy prospects with deep gravity.

Myriad specific problems remain, however. Most of the decisions will require tradeoffs between conflicting interests and must be made through budgetary decisions that involve controversies among the various branches of the bureaucracy and also among the many different pressure groups. As in most advanced democratic countries, budgetary changes tend to be slow, complex, and sharply contested. Here lies a vast area of continuing political controversy, but there is no broad chasm in Japanese politics over these problems, nor do they threaten the basic stability of the political system.

UNRESOLVED PROBLEMS

Japanese government and society present on the whole a picture of great efficiency and stability that is hard to match elsewhere. The country does, of course, face a great number of problems, but the Japanese appear to be quite capable of handling them in a satisfactory manner. They need to do a great deal to improve the social underpinnings of their tremendously efficient economy. High land prices, intolerable crowding, and countless other urban problems pose vast difficulties. But there is no reason to fear that the Japanese will not tackle these with reasonable effectiveness within the severe constraints imposed on them by geography. Viewed in purely domestic terms, few countries seem to be in as sound shape as Japan. But when one looks abroad, the situation is by no means as reassuring.

The country is extremely vulnerable to unfavorable external conditions. It must have a huge flow of trade in and out of the islands simply to live. For this commerce there must be general world peace and a strong international trading system, both of which depend less on the Japanese themselves than on the actions of other nations. Japan could not conceivably protect by military means the foreign sources of food, energy, and raw materials on which it depends, the markets that must pay for these imports, or even the life lines of its world trade. To try to develop military power of a sort that could defend even a small proportion of these vital economic interests would probably do much more harm than good, for this would frighten Japan's trading partners, making them more hostile, and it would put a heavy burden on the Japanese economy and an intolerable strain on internal political consensus.

Japan cannot even defend itself in a nuclear age. The people, quite wisely, are determined not to build a nuclear force themselves. In part, this is because of their unique experience with nuclear weapons. On August 6, 1945, when the Japanese government was known to be trying to find a way to surrender, a single American atomic bomb wiped out the whole city of Hiroshima. Whether or not this bombing was justified in order to convince die-hard Japanese militarists that the war was indeed lost, there was certainly no justification for the dropping three days later of a second bomb, which destroyed the city of Nagasaki.

Japanese attitudes, however, are not based merely on their historical memories. Japan is so small and crowded that it could not survive a first attack by nuclear weapons. To have any security, it must rely through the security treaty on the American nuclear umbrella—a position the people have slowly and reluctantly come to accept—and beyond that on the maintenance of world peace by those who possess nuclear weapons. How best Japan itself can contribute to the maintenance of this world peace is a question that the Japanese have not yet answered fully, but it will undoubtedly be a problem of growing importance to them in the future.

The maintenance of a healthy and growing world trading system is a matter of equal concern, because without it the whole world will no doubt stagnate and Japan will eventually be plunged into catastrophe. This is a problem that presses more immediately on Japan, because economically it is the third largest superpower and because its rate of economic growth—more rapid than that of the other great industrial nations—and its somewhat distinctive economic organization have made it appear, at least to others, as creating major disturbances in the world economic system. Japan's large balance-of-trade surplus, especially with the United States, and its inundation of foreign markets with advanced industrial goods, such as motorcycles, electronic equipment, automobiles, and steel, have raised great anxieties abroad, again particularly in the United States.

For some years now, such economic problems have recurrently risen to crisis proportions, and each crisis has become progressively more severe as the Japanese economy grew in relative size. The result normally has been strong political repercussions, including demands for retaliatory protectionist trade policies. If this cyclical pattern is allowed to continue and grow worse, the outcome may well be just such restrictionist measures. These in turn could easily set off a trade war and a downward spiral of international trade, ultimately leading to disastrous results for everyone. The stagnant world trade of the 1920s and the economic collapse at the end of that decade, which led eventually to worldwide tragedy, are sobering reminders of the dangers of such a course.

These economic problems that revolve around Japan are the product of Japanese successes more than failures. They derive in part from a very efficient economic system in which mutual trust and close coordination between government and business permit a smooth transformation from inefficient, declining industries to strong, growing ones. They are also based on some fundamental Japanese characteristics: a strong work ethic, possibly the highest educational levels in the world, deeply entrenched habits of saving and reinvesting, and superb skills at organization and cooperation. The Japanese economy has undoubtedly become one of the most efficient in the whole world.

Another reason for the recurrent frictions between Japan and its trading partners is that the Japanese economy is geared somewhat differently from those of the other advanced industrialized nations. Japanese business executives are less concerned with the profits that their companies make than with their size, growth, and market share. Their own salaries are less affected by profits than in the West, and they derive more of their rewards in psychological terms from the importance of their posts. In other words, they are more like bureaucrats. In addition, they finance their businesses through bank loans at fixed interest rates more often than through equity capital. They also regard their employees as being permanent members of the company who should never be fired, if that is at all possible. For all these reasons they are less concerned with quarterly profits (which in the West are the way to attract capital) and are more interested in the maintenance of or increase in rates of production.

All this gives the Japanese entrepreneur a much longer time horizon in planning for expansion and also strong incentives not to cut down on production, even during periods of recession. As a result, when a recession brings reduced production in the West in order to maintain profits, the Japanese economy, despite a slackening of domestic demand, tries to continue at full blast, channeling an even greater proportion of its product abroad and thus compounding the problems there. In the past, times of crisis in international trade have usually been ameliorated by Japan's eventually adopting so-called *voluntary controls* on certain exports, but only after political damage had been done and anxieties and ill will had been raised on both sides.

The second oil crises of 1978–80 and the slow down of world economic growth that accompanied it brought these problems again to crises proportions. Although the record deficit of American trade with Japan of more than $12 billion in 1978 was appreciably reduced in 1979, American cries for restrictions on imports from Japan, especially in automobiles, continued to mount in 1980, while Japan remained desperately dependent on an excess of imports to the United States to help pay for its necessary and increasingly costly energy imports. Once again voluntary controls by the Japanese, or open restrictionist policies by the United States, or possibly a combination of the two, seemed probable. In the long run, a system would seem necessary to restrict recurrent economic crises of this sort between Japan and its major trading partners, particularly the United States, before they come to the political boiling point.

Trade with the other industrialized nations, thus, is an area of many extremely difficult problems that demand immediate attention. But so also is the field of economic relations with the so-called developing nations. Here are to be found some of the greatest problems for the future of the whole world. The developing nations and particularly Japan's neighbors in Southeast Asia feel, with considerable bitterness, that Japan has been stingy in its aid to them and often unfair in its economic dealings. These relations with the developing world demand far greater attention by the Japanese people and more decisive action, not only for the sake of the developing nations themselves, but equally for the future of Japan and the stability of the world.

Unfortunately, the Japanese do not seem as well prepared to work on their problems of foreign economic relations as on domestic problems. Their long isolation and sense of being unique and separate from the outside world may make them somewhat insensitive to the viewpoints of others. Their language—which is sharply different from those of all the countries of importance to them, with the single exception of Korea—stands as a massive barrier to easy communication with others. A century and a quarter of scrambling madly to catch up to a technologically more advanced Occident and the realization of their present complete dependence on world trade make them feel that they must have a thick economic cushion and that other countries should realize this. Indeed, the terms of trade in the future are sure to turn against them in a world of limited agricultural land and natural resources, of which they themselves possess so little.

So the Japanese will continue to face a multitude of domestic problems that require constant political attention and some much more crucial and difficult decisions on foreign policy. Obviously, they will have to maintain an efficient system for making policy decisions. They also will need strong, farseeing leadership. In particular, they will have to develop and display a level of diplomacy and leadership in world affairs that has been notably lacking in the past.

KEY TERMS AND CONCEPTS

cultural homogeneity
burakumin
Manchurian Incident
occupation
uji
hierarchy
shōgun
samurai
daimyō
Tokugawa
alternate attendance
Meiji Restoration
Meiji Constitution
genrō
Diet
Supreme Commander for the Allied Powers (SCAP)
House of Councilors
Peace Constitution
zaibatsu
"reverse course"
Self-Defense Forces (SDF)
Mutual Security Treaty
progressives
middle-size electoral district system
interpellation
Ministry of International Trade and Industry (MITI)
administrative vice minister
prefectures
local autonomy
Autonomy Ministry
jiban
kōenkai
Liberal Democratic Party (LDP)
Communist Party (JCP)
Socialist Party (JSP)
Democratic Socialist Party (DSP)
Kōmeitō
Sōka Gakkai
New Liberal Club
Sōhyō
Dōmei
secretary general
Executive Council
factions
Policy Affairs Research Committee (PARC)
pressure groups
zaikai
demonstrations
citizens' movements
local residents' movements
press clubs
kōgai
voluntary controls

ADDITIONAL READINGS

Austin, L., ed. *Japan: The Paradox of Progress.* New Haven: Yale University Press, 1976.

Baerwald, H. *Japan's Parliament.* New York: Cambridge University Press, 1974.

Burks, A. W. *The Government of Japan.* New York: Crowell, 1972. PB

Campbell, J. *Contemporary Japanese Budget Policies.* Berkeley and Los Angeles: University of California Press, 1977.

Curtis, G. *Election Campaigning Japanese Style.* New York: Columbia University Press, 1971.

Destler et al. *Managing an Alliance: The Politics of U.S.-Japan Relations.* Washington, D.C.: Brookings Institution, 1976. PB

Emmerson, J. K. *Arms, Yen and Power: The Japanese Dilemma.* New York: Dunellen, 1971.

Fukui, H. *Party in Power: The Japanese Liberal-Democrats and Policy Making.* Berkeley and Los Angeles: University of California Press, 1970.

Ike, N. *Japanese Politics: Patron Client Democracy.* New York: Knopf, 1972. PB

———. *A Theory of Japanese Democracy.* Boulder, Colorado: Westview Press, 1978.

Kawai, K. *Japan's American Interlude.* Chicago: University of Chicago Press, 1960.

Langdon, F. *Politics in Japan.* Boston: Little, Brown, 1967. PB

McNelly, T. *Politics and Government in Japan.* Boston: Houghton Mifflin, 1972. PB

Maruyama, M. *Thought and Behaviour in Modern Japanese Politics.* London and New York: Oxford University Press, 1969. PB

Packard, G. *Protest in Tokyo: The Security Treaty Crisis of 1960.* Princeton, N.J.: Princeton University Press, 1966.

Passin, Herbert, ed. *A Season of Voting: The Japanese Elections of 1976 and 1977.* Washington, D.C.: American Enterprise Institute for Public Policy Research, 1979. PB

Patrick, H., and H. Rosovsky, eds. *Asia's New Giant: How the Japanese Economy Works.* Washington, D.C.: Brookings Institution, 1976. PB

Pempel, T. J., ed. *Policymaking in Contemporary Japan.* Ithaca, N.Y.: Cornell University Press, 1977.

Reischauer, E. O. *Japan: The Story of a Nation.* New York: Knopf, 1974. PB

———. *The Japanese.* Cambridge: Harvard University Press, 1977. PB

Richardson, B. *The Political Culture of Japan.* Berkeley and Los Angeles: University of California Press, 1974.

Scalapino, R., ed. *The Foreign Policy of Modern Japan.* Berkeley and Los Angeles: University of California Press, 1977. PB

Steiner, K. *Local Government in Japan.* Palo Alto, Calif.: Stanford University Press, 1965.

Stockwin, J. A. A. *Japan: Divided Politics in a Growth Economy.* New York: Norton, 1975.

Thayer, N. *How the Conservatives Rule Japan.* Princeton: Princeton University Press, 1968.

Tsuneishi, W. M. *Japanese Political Style.* New York: Harper & Row, 1966. PB

Tsurutani, T. *Political Change in Japan.* New York: McKay, 1977.

Vogel, E. *Japan as No. 1: Lessons for America.* Cambridge: Harvard University Press, 1979. PB

Vogel, E., ed. *Modern Japanese Organization and Decision-Making.* Berkeley and Los Angeles: University of California Press, 1975. PB

Ward, R. E. *Japan's Political System.* Englewood Cliffs, N.J.: Prentice-Hall, 1978. PB

———, ed. *Political Development in Modern Japan.* Princeton, N.J.: Princeton University Press, 1978.

Watanuki, J. *Politics in Postwar Japanese Society.* Tokyo: Tokyo University Press, 1977.

PB = *available in paperback*

PART II

CHINA AND THE THIRD WORLD

VIII

The Chinese People's Republic

ROY HOFHEINZ, JR.

China presents the greatest challenge to any comparative analysis of politics and government. The sheer weight of its population makes China the largest of the world's nations. It is estimated at nearly one billion[1]—more than all of Europe and almost a quarter of all humankind. One of China's provinces, Szechwan in the rich upper valley of the Yangtze River, is roughly the size of Britain, France, or Germany. China is more than a nation among nations: it is at one time a continent, a state, and an idea.

THE NATURE AND BACKGROUND OF CHINESE POLITICS: A CONTINUITY OF IMAGE AND ARENA

The political idea of China is older than the idea of a unified Europe. Other ancient kingdoms—such

as those of Egypt, Persia, Rome, and India—spawned at the beginning of the Iron Age and disappeared within a few centuries; but the Chinese successfully maintained their centralized government through many periods of disorder for more than two millennia. Though the structure of the government, its relationship to the population, and to some extent its informing ideology have changed from dynasty to dynasty, the concept of China as an indivisible political-cultural unit remains far more alive than the often expressed idea of a reunified Europe.

As vast as China's size have been its sufferings since the mid-nineteenth century. Two gigantic cataclysms, the Taiping Rebellion (1850–64) and the Anti-Japanese War and Civil War (1937–49), were perhaps the most murderous conflicts in human history. Each of these wars snuffed out the lives of more people than are living today in such small states as Holland, Nigeria, or Vietnam. Whereas the Russian, French, and American revolutions built up over a period of years to culminate in a brief period of violence that was soon terminated by a return to normalcy, the Chinese

[1]U.S. Department of Commerce, Bureau of the Census, Foreign Demographic Analysis Division, "China: Estimated and Projected Population and Vital Rates" (May 1979).

chaos—in the form of banditry, "warlordism," social degeneration, and administrative disintegration—lasted for decades. It is for good reason that the Chinese Communists speak not of a Chinese "revolution," but of several phases of China's "revolutionary civil wars," which ended only with the establishment of the People's Republic of China on October 1, 1949. The startling recurrence of civil disorders during the Great Proletarian Cultural Revolution of 1966–67, though only the tiniest of ripples in comparison with the great tidal waves of the past, reminds us of the history of China's recent political turmoil.

In addition to the size, longevity, and recent instability of China's political system, analysts must face a frustrating "inscrutability gap" in dealing with this vast nation. The distance between Chinese culture and language and our own has led many to assume incorrectly that the "wily Orientals" are somehow unfathomable—that they "always do things upside down," in the words of missionary W. Dyer Ball. The obvious differences between East and West make it easy to jump to misleading conclusions about the Chinese, based often on wrong or oversimplified views of our own Western political system. This heritage of ignorance and error is easily strengthened by very real gaps in our knowledge about China, caused in part by China's recent disorder, which make collection of data difficult, and in part by the lack of a tradition of making information public in China. It is fair to say that we know far less of China, in those realms of knowledge useful to political analysis, than we do of any other of the world's major nations. This inscrutability should not lead us to think that politics is absent from the Chinese scene or that the government in China fails to perform functions similar to those of governments in America, Europe, or the Soviet Union.

"Traditional" and "Modern" Politics. In recent years, with the emergence into the world political system of so many new nations, it has become fashionable to speak of the difference between "traditional" and "modern" political systems. *Modern* (or *developed*) *systems* have elections, parlia-

ments, codified laws, political parties, rationalized public administrations, and centralized, integrated national governments. Their citizens are politically conscious, believe in their ability to affect their fates through political action, and are capable of being mobilized for politically relevant action on short notice. By contrast, *traditional systems* lack these elements of modern politics. Monarchs are absolute; governors are patrimonial; officials are privately corrupt; the populace is sharply stratified between literate city dwellers and illiterate peasants; and citizens are considered mere subjects. Certainly there is a great deal of truth and usefulness to these two opposed ideal types of political systems.[2] But just as modern British parliamentary democracy depends in large degree on the deference to royal authority and the system of social class that we know to be traditional in England, the elements of tradition in non-Western countries such as China may play a critical role in shaping modern institutions.

China is no exception to this pattern of the *"modernity of tradition."* Indeed, for many centuries after the "discovery" of China (ca. 1272) by the Italian explorer Marco Polo (1254?–1324?), the Chinese were considered to be more advanced and progressive in political matters than the Europeans. As late as the middle of the nineteenth century, when the renowned British reformer Sir Charles Trevelyan was searching for a model on which to reform the British civil service, he turned to China, which since the eighth century had possessed a system of official *entrance examinations* by which entrants to the career of mandarin were recruited. (The *mandarins* were the bureaucratic administrators of the empire.) Europeans could not fail to marvel at the prolonged unity of the Chinese state, at the extensive network of official

[2]The father of much political development theory of this type is the German sociologist Max Weber.

(*Right*) MAP 8.1 *The Chinese People's Republic*

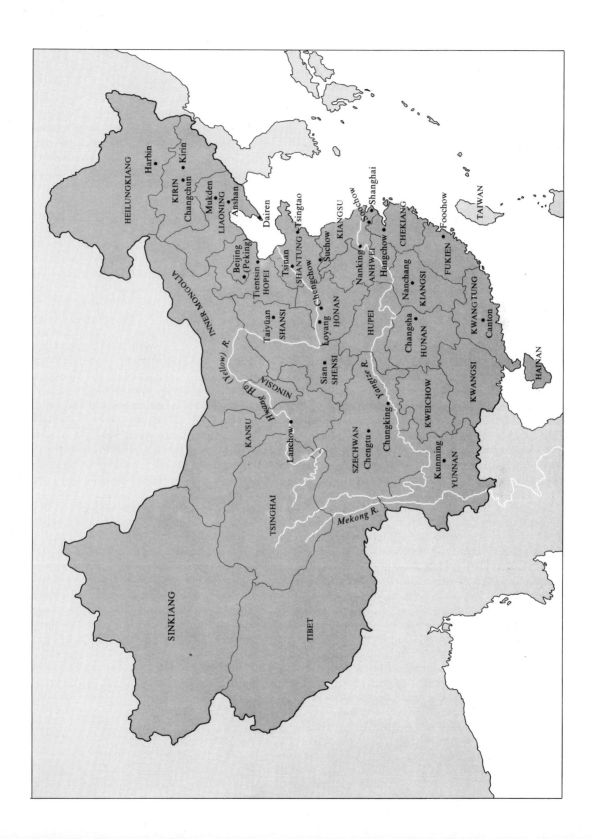

bureaucracy, at the relative openness of competition for public office, which contrasted so sharply with eighteenth-century European practice. In our own day we can still look back to traditional China for examples of attitudes and practices that seem modern to us. The implicit faith in the value of education, the distrust of hereditary privilege, the belief that officials should be aware of the moral and environmental impact of their decisions—all these were part of the broad tradition of Confucian statecraft.

The long heritage of Chinese statecraft did not, however, originate with *Confucius* (551–479 B.C.). Indeed, the founder of Confucianism taught that he was merely rediscovering and extending the "way" *(tao)* of emperors of ancient times whose lineage myths supposedly extended forty-five thousand years into the past. Likewise, the tradition that bears his name includes many philosophical and practical elements unfamiliar or alien to Confucius, a moralist and itinerant adviser to the kings of a divided China. Whereas Confucius stressed the importance of proper ethical and social behavior according to one's station in life, his follower *Mencius* (373–288 B.C.) made emperors responsible for the well-being of their subjects and gave those subjects the implicit right to overthrow their ruler when he failed to provide for their livelihood. In turn, other ancient Chinese political theorists offered alternatives to the Confucian-Mencian notions of social and political order. The *Legalist (fa-chia) school* of the third century B.C. emphasized the importance of law and administrative fiat in assuring order; and the *Taoist philosophers* doubted that any political system could function without the existence of innate, natural, unconscious harmonies among people.

The variety of Chinese political thought is as great as that in the West, and so, too, is the complexity of Chinese political practice during the historical era. But in several important respects there is a continuity in the Chinese political tradition that dates from shortly after the unification of China in 221 B.C. by the great First Emperor of the Ch'in dynasty, Shih-huang-ti.

Three important elements define this core of the Chinese political tradition.

First, there is the consciousness of the inseparability of political and social, economic, or moral matters. At the heart of Confucius's concept of proper behavior is the notion of *social relationships (lun),* which are all pictured as forming a coherent single unit. Thus the relationship between ruler and subject is analogous to that between neighbor and neighbor, brother and brother, husband and wife, and especially parent and child. Rulers are most effective when they rule not by brute power, but by the example of their propriety in preserving relationships. The ideal emperor is the most perfectly filial son: a great Manchu emperor, Ch'ien-lung, honored his "sacred mother" with innumerable poems, elaborate palaces, and extravagant tours of China's scenic southern wonders, but never once visited the scene of fourteen disastrous Yangtze floods.[3] Far from discrediting him, Ch'ien-lung's piety toward his ancestor gave him leverage over those bureaucrats who were in charge of flood control and other matters. He consciously used his exemplary behavior in human relationships as proof of his legitimacy as ruler of the Chinese state.

In accordance with this notion of the unity of all human relationships, the Chinese tradition assumed the *unity of public and private realms.* It made no distinction between them, and thus in principle it permitted the government to intervene at will in all matters, somewhat similar to the overlapping powers of church and secular government in medieval Europe. A vast portion of the codified laws of the Chinese state pertained not to public concerns, but to what we would regard today as private matters: the regulation of behavior toward parents or of proper clothing and coiffure: the Manchu dynasty (1644–1911), for example, ruled that all subjects would shave their foreheads and

[3]Harold L. Kahn, *Monarchy in the Emperor's Eyes: Image and Reality in the Ch'ien-Lung Reign* (Cambridge: Harvard University Press, 1971).

wear their hair long and plaited into a queue. Likewise, the judicial system itself functioned in civil matters less as a system of adversary proceedings than as one of role-patterned mediation. The best judges were those who understood the importance not of principle, but of compromise. In criminal cases punishments fell often as much on the innocent as on the guilty, as judges strove to teach all subjects to handle their conflicts without resort to the law.

Whereas the imperceptible merging of private and public matters appears to grant great powers to the emperors and officialdom, in fact the absolute despotism of Chinese rulers often conflicted directly with the needs of society. If the emperor was the parent of society, he had to provide for society's basic needs. His failures, as measured by the extent of hunger or disorder in the realm, diminished his virtue in the eyes of his subjects. Chinese political philosophy, from the time of Mencius onward, provided an escape valve for revolutionary sentiment: the theory that emperors enjoy their *divine mandate (t'ien-ming)* as long as they continue to rule a peaceful and well-fed realm. Unlike Western absolute despots, Chinese emperors were not protected from the turmoils of their society by an airtight theory. Loyalty to the state was compatible with resisting—and overthrowing—grossly unsuccessful emperors. The permanence of the Chinese state, thus, included cycle after cycle of dynastic rise and fall. When modern visitors to China remark on the extent of government interference in private lives, on the pervasiveness of organization in China, on the lack of dividing lines between politics and everything else, they are inadvertently describing the constant features of the Chinese political structure over the ages.

Officialism and Officials: The Scholar-Bureaucrats. The second enduring characteristic of the Chinese tradition was *officialism.* The legalist school, which stood behind the reforms of the First Emperor, insisted that he reward his loyal followers not by giving them land, as had been the practice, but by assuring them territories to rule in

his name. Thus, the Chinese state from its earliest times embodied restraints against the development of feudalism that helped erode and dissolve the Roman Empire. By turning potential feudatories into the salaried minions of a central government, the Ch'in emperor established the world's longest-lasting permanent bureaucracy.

To be sure, the Confucian bureaucrat was a far cry from Max Weber's idealized "legal-rational" officeholder. The weakness of administrative law subjected him to the arbitrary whim of emperors. (The Ch'ien-lung type of emperor with a flip of his vermilion-colored brush could condemn hundreds of lifelong public servants to death because they had made mistakes in penmanship.) The ideal of all-round moral and ethical perfection for the scholar-bureaucrat limited his ability to master specialized subjects. Confucian stress on personal relationships, and on sincerity of character rather than performance, made corruption and personal indulgence the rule rather than the exception. But, for all these faults, the Chinese bureaucracy was a remarkably long-lived and effective political machine.

Its effectiveness depended on a combination of several characteristics. Access into the civil service was rigorously controlled by a system of examinations established as early as the Sui dynasty (589–618 A.D.). While these examinations in later years tended to stress artistic and classical literary skills more than statecraft, they assured at least a minimum of education and literacy among the official class. Officialdom was divided into an extensive territorial hierarchy that reached down to the county *(hsien)* level, as well as into specialized ministries in the imperial capital. Rigorous "rules of avoidance" prevented officials from being assigned to their own home districts in order to limit the temptations of corruption; their meager salaries ($300 or so by the nineteenth century) could be supplemented by "honesty encouragement" fees that were hundreds of times larger in amount.

Imperial attacks on officialdom (in this, as in other matters, Chairman Mao Tse-tung was able to draw on a long tradition) were balanced against a long tradition of remonstrance and censorial criticism, which on occasion might reach as high as the imperial person himself. Chinese officials, in essence, represented not just the bureaucracy, but the entire elite of literate society, which considered itself an independent body of scholarly custodians of public ethics. This tradition—with its polarity between a professionalized, expert staff of clerks and a critical, ambitious, and somewhat independent pool of aspiring moral engineers—finds strong reflections in China's present-day handling of its official cadre class.

Practicality and Humanism. The third characteristic of the Chinese tradition is what we might call *humanism*. A society that stresses social relationships naturally avoids uncompromising absolutes. The transcendental religions of the Middle East and of South Asia, which encourage the denial of self and the realities of this world, are not found in the Chinese scene. Even when they employ supernatural concepts, as in the case of Taoism or Maitreyan Buddhism, Chinese religions are profoundly immanent and practical—on the human (and not the divine) scale.

In contrast with the absolute Christian concept of love, the Confucian ideal of *jen,* or benevolence, emphasizes the relativism of affection. The Chinese tradition of humanism assumes that human beings naturally care more for those with whom they are in *socially determined* contact. This tradition differs sharply from Western "individualism"—an expression that, when translated into Chinese, sounds overly personalistic and selfish. Although the orthodox tradition of Confucianism frowns on private coalitions of interest—since groups such as secret societies, merchant guilds, or religious sects may potentially threaten the bureaucratic state and the social order—the heterodox tradition of humanism positively encourages such coalitions. Indeed, for many modern Chinese it is the "little tradition" of humanism, as exemplified in the popular novels of bandit kingdoms or socio-religious bands, that demonstrates the powerful traditional Chinese drive to human solidarity. This characteristic of the folk culture, which in China is more democratic, egalitarian, and iconoclastic than the more forbidding orthodoxy of Confucianism, lies behind many of the striking features of modern Chinese politics.

THE DIMENSIONS OF A REVOLUTION

Of course, the present is not just a reflection of the past. There has been a revolution in China far more profound than any of the previous dynastic changes. Lost is the purity of the Chinese concept of a world order with Peking at its center. Though Lin Piao, Mao's erstwhile successor-designate, spoke in 1965 of Peking as the center of the "world revolution," the People's Republic has since joined the United Nations. No longer is the Chinese state content with less than 2 percent of the national product or staffed by fewer than thirty thousand cadres. Chinese subjects, though perhaps no more able to chart their own course than before, are not any more the illiterate "stupid people" despised by their gentry protectors. The "People's Middle Kingdom," to use John Fairbank's phrase, is a vastly different political system from that of the ancient empire. What are the dimensions of the political change that produced the present government of China?

The Impact of the West. To a considerable degree the political history of modern China can be described as a response to the West. Whereas other nations studied in this volume developed their national political systems without the direct interference of foreign powers, China's modern history is one of constant challenge by the European and American states. Despite the fierce independence of the Chinese and the strength of their political tradition, modern China still owes much to the outside world for its present system of government, as well as for the changes that brought it about.

The Western nations came to China unannounced and largely unwelcome. Appearing in the Pacific at about the same time as the discovery of America, European traders seeking spices and tea were soon followed by European navies protecting trade, by colonists seeking new homes, and by missionaries seeking converts to the European religions and way of life. Many Asian nations succumbed to the tides of European empire building—the Spice Islands to Holland, India and Burma to England, Indochina to France. But China's enormous size, its distance from the European centers, and its domestic political cohesiveness combined with the naturally balancing rivalries of the great powers to prevent a takeover by any one Western nation.

Instead, the Chinese follow their famed nationalist leader Sun Yat-sen (1888–1925) in calling China a "semicolony" during the nineteenth century. China was not a full colony even though tiny Western detachments could destroy Chinese armed forces at will. Each of a number of small, but humiliating, defeats brought new concessions from the increasingly inept Chinese ruling dynasty—itself a dynasty of foreign rulers from inner Asia. The Opium War of 1840–42, while forcing the Chinese government to accept the importation of debilitating narcotics, established also the right of foreigners to claim permanent enclaves on Chinese soil. The present British colony of Hong Kong is, along with the Portuguese colony of Macao across the bay from it, the last vestige of the enclave system of the nineteenth century. The Anglo-Chinese War of 1860 extracted from the Chinese the right to declare major trading centers, even along the inland rivers, to be official "treaty ports"; this was sanctified by what the Chinese have since termed the "unequal treaties" signed by the old dynasty and the West. Within these new enclaves Westerners were subject to laws and to court systems different from those of ordinary Chinese. The Boxer Rebellion of 1900, the result of an ill-conceived Chinese imper-

ial attempt to side with an antiforeign politico-religious movement known as the Boxers (from their practice of the Chinese martial arts), demonstrated the incapacity of the traditional, unreformed government to resist determined Western military power and brought a new wave of foreign investment in mining and railroad concessions throughout the Chinese subcontinent.

Yet, through all these humiliations the Chinese continued to grope for adequate responses to Western incursion. Early resistance came from upright mandarins who resented, among other things, the "barbarian" habit of opium smoking. Then military commanders sought to reform China's war-making capacity by importing new technology. By the 1860s a new school of "self-strengthening" *(tzu-ch'iang)* had arisen to urge that China's social fabric would have to be toughened (along traditional lines, to be sure) to meet the Western challenge. By 1898 those who urged reform from within were able to gain a brief moment of power in Peking and to force through important changes in the domestic constitution, changes that, when later put into effect, would restrain rampant official corruption, refocus priorities on military resistance, increase the pool of Western knowledge, and restrain the selfish and ineffectual imperial monarchy that had ruled since 1644. The *Revolution of 1911,* which overthrew the Manchu dynasty and declared China a republic, marked the end of a century of domestic turmoil over the way to respond to the Western challenge.

Much of the Chinese political scene of the early twentieth century derived from the clash between the potent old tradition and the new styles of Western power. The new republic, having open political parties, elections, and national and provincial legislatures, very quickly succumbed to older forms of rule; by 1916 the nominal president, Yuan Shi-kai, attempted unsuccessfully to restore the monarchical system with himself as emperor. A new breed of rulers, Western in their command of military force and their ruthless pursuit of power in their territories, but Eastern in their strong belief in personal loyalty and stern moralism, sprang up to rule in province after province as central power continued to erode. These "warlords" *(chün fa)* benefited from an unprecedented militarization of Chinese society, which increased the number of men in arms nearly a hundredfold between 1900 and the 1940s. The Japanese invasion of China after 1937 thus marked the last in a century-long series of foreign intrusions. And the two Chinese forces who combated them, the Nationalists and the Communists, likewise were the modern descendants of the official, scholarly, intellectual, and mass antiforeign movements that had convulsed China for almost two centuries.

Western Ideas in Chinese Garb. Perhaps the most obvious dimension of China's modern revolution is the introduction of political concepts and practices from the West. The very longevity and apparent permanence of the traditional state encouraged a resistance to European ideas and attitudes more powerful than that encountered by the European intrusion of capital and armed forces into China in the nineteenth century. Unlike Japan, Thailand, Turkey, and many other non-Western countries, the Chinese resisted Western notions to the extent of hampering China's ability to defend itself or even to maintain domestic order. After first rejecting all European influence as uncivilized and barbarian, the Chinese in turn attempted to limit contacts with Westerners, while privately employing Europeans and Americans as advisers to the government. But the growth of trade, especially in the treaty ports of the China coast after the Opium War of 1840–42, and the expansion of missionary activities after their legalization in 1858 made contact between the West and ordinary Chinese subjects inevitable. Western ideas such as national sovereignty and constitutionalism followed in the footsteps of the missionaries, traders, and arms sellers.

What made China's response to these ideas unique was the way in which the Chinese channeled them into their view of the nation's needs. Popular participation in government, for example,

became a slogan during and after the abortive Reform Movement of 1898, but not because of any widespread clamor of popular interests for the vote. Rather, the proponents of constitutions argued that only through collective action that involved and changed the people could China strengthen its military might and repel such potential aggressors as the Japanese. Likewise, only after the victory of the Russian Communists in 1917, which demonstrated the power of Marxist ideas to build the state and resist external aggression, did Chinese intellectuals turn to the serious study of socialism. Political parties and parliaments, tried several times in the decade after the Revolution of 1911, proved uniformly impotent to solve the basic problem of China in the twentieth century: the construction of a national government that would be rich and strong enough to control domestic disorder and resist external pressures.

The history of the *May Fourth Movement of 1919* illustrates the fate of transplanted Western ideas in twentieth-century China. That movement originated among a new generation of students, who were the first to emerge since the abolition of the traditional examination system in 1905 and who felt that China's national interests were being betrayed by a government that continued to deal with expansive Japanese imperialism. This new generation thought of itself as modern and called itself variously the "new culture movement" or the "new tide" or "new youth." It demanded many changes from traditional Chinese practice: abandoning the classical style of writing for the popular language, encouraging freedom from familial and other social restraints on the younger generation, relaxing restrictions on political organization and protest. But although European and American heroes such as Bertrand Russell or John Dewey were models at the start of the movement, and although "democracy and science" were the main themes of one phase of the cultural and literary outpouring after 1917, by the early 1920s these heroes and themes had become discredited; they were no more capable than parliaments and parties of solving China's problem as the Chinese perceived it.

Marxism-Leninism, Chinese Style. Nor was the answer Marxism-Leninism. Many still regard the growth of the Chinese Communist Party after its formation in 1921 by a splinter group from the May Fourth Movement as further evidence of the Westernization of Chinese politics. But in fact it took the success of Lenin's revolution to make Chinese aware of the great European Marxist tradition. The founders of the Chinese Communist Party (CCP), Ch'en Tu-hsiu and Li Ta-chao, knew nothing of socialism until that time, but were quickly converted when they saw how rapidly Lenin had turned Russia from an invaded and disordered land into an independent and outspoken nation. The history of the CCP after 1921 showed how readily the Chinese would discard essential elements of Leninism in order to further their goal of unifying and building a new China. Western ideas were indeed important in China's transformation, but less as models for Chinese behavior than as symptoms of a deeper drive to regenerate China's proud national existence.

The earliest Chinese Communists proved far too faithful to the *Soviet model of Leninism.* Lenin had taught them that in the "semicolonial" areas of the world, like China, Communist parties had to ally themselves first with the representatives of the bourgeois class of their own nation. The Chinese proletariat, after all, numbered less than one-half of 1 percent of the Chinese population. After Lenin's death Stalin interpreted the "national bourgeoisie" in China to mean the *Kuomintang*— the party of Sun Yat-sen, which in late 1922, after a decade of resistance to the post-1911 parliamentary system, had finally gained a foothold in the southern province of Kwangtung. The Communists dutifully contributed their full energies to building the Kuomintang, only to find after Sun's death that they were constructing their own nemesis. By 1927 the powerful Nationalist army of the Kuomintang, now led by Chiang Kai-shek,

backed by landowners, middle class, and business interests, and fortified by Soviet advice and arms, had turned on the Communists and crushed their hopeful mass organizations in a bloody massacre that shaped the survivors' outlook for decades.

Out of this debacle rose the party of Mao Tse-tung. Mao, a young Hunanese intellectual who had studied in Peking University during the May Fourth period, helped found the *Chinese Communist Party* in 1921, served dutifully as a Kuomintang bureaucrat in Canton, and in late 1926 deeply imbibed the local peasants' enthusiasm for the "National Revolution" in his home province of Hunan. Voicing the attitudes of the Communist wing of the Kuomintang toward the collective potential of the *peasantry,* Mao declared in his famous *Report on the Peasant Movement in Hunan* that "the peasantry represents 70 per cent of the power of the revolution"—a view that brought him into conflict with the more orthodox Leninist Ch'en Tu-hsiu. During the disastrous months of August and September 1927, Mao led a series of hapless uprisings against Kuomintang power in Hunan and retreated with the remnants of his "worker-peasant Red Army" into the mountain fastness of southeastern Hunan. From this tiny force grew the powerful People's Liberation Army, which twenty years later would sweep back into Hunan on its way to victory.

In those two decades Mao developed both a strategy and a body of practice for the Chinese revolution that peculiarly suited Chinese conditions. He demanded and got independence of his troops from the interference of Moscow and the urban-based Chinese Communist Central Committee. He resisted the demands of his superiors to waste his forces in futile attacks on the cities, outlining instead a strategy of building base areas in the remote mountains and in the broad countryside. After he gained full power over the Party during his army's heroic *Long March* (1934–35), which took them through thousands of miles of the interior, he moderated in his village work Moscow's hard-line "class struggle" doctrines, which had lost the party considerable support. During the Anti-Japanese War of 1937–45, (the Chinese name for World War II), Mao developed a delicate balancing strategy of a *united front* with all anti-Japanese elements (including Chiang's Kuomintang) that permitted him to expand his party manyfold. Each of these tactical and strategic innovations strained his relations with his superiors in Moscow, but admirably suited his overarching goal of revolutionary victory.

Chinese Communism during these revolutionary years developed a distinctive style of political interaction with the Chinese population. Mao's troops contrasted sharply with those of the warlords and the Nationalist central government at Nanking and later wartime Chungking: they were disciplined, mostly literate, and above all politically conscious. Red Army practice emphasized inner-party democracy and forthrightness. Military goals yielded to political. The masses—most often the peasants—deserved considerate treatment in regard to their property, their families, and their customs and beliefs, because they were needed to support the Communist army in the countryside. Soldiers and their political officers had to be all-round, independent fighters capable of long periods of separation from central Communist authority.

Many of these practices reached maturity during 1936–40, the period when the Party Politburo resided in the remote northwestern town of Yenan. In many ways *the Yenan experience*—characterized by its comradely small-town warmth, its fierce sense of national purpose, its new discovery of unsuspected support among broad segments of the peasant population in northern China—represents today a golden age of the Chinese Communist past. Most Chinese Communist leaders today retain much of the antiurban, anti-intellectual, antibureaucratic, and, above all, strongly nationalistic outlook they acquired during their revolutionary struggles. With these memories and this outlook the Chinese Communists at the end of the civil war in 1949 found themselves the rulers of the largest and oldest country and people in the world.

The Causes of the Chinese Revolution. China's revolution, which produced the People's Republic of China in October 1949, was at least as enormous an event as any of the great European revolutions—the English of the seventeenth century, the French of the eighteenth, the Russian of the early twentieth. It took longer to occur—nearly a century of violence preceded it—and spilled more blood than any other revolution. Yet the causes of this event are often obscured behind arguments for one side or the other in the civil wars of China in the first half of this century or behind more abstract arguments about the nature of the good society. Some will single out the misbehavior of foreigners on Chinese soil, or the exploitation of the common peasantry by an irresponsible landlord class, or the rise of new ideas of democracy or egalitarianism, as the major cause of the Chinese revolution. We may all agree that Western "imperialism" had its bad aspects or that warlords did not treat their common subjects generously, but still fail to understand the rise of the Communist Party to power.

The Chinese Communist Party differed enormously from the Soviet Communist Party of Lenin in its history, its personnel, and especially in its sources of support. Lenin's party was a conspiratorial offshoot of intellectual socialists trained in the European political tradition. Lenin came to power in October 1917 almost by accident: his "party" of a few thousand members proved more adept at parliamentary politics and more ruthless about seizing dictatorial powers than any other force in St. Petersburg. Insofar as any real mass support for Lenin's coup of 1917 was required, it came largely from organized urban workers, as well as from war-weary soldiers and sailors, while the rural masses of Russia remained silent either from ignorance or from deliberate abstention. While the ravages of World War I and the incompetence of the czarist government gave Lenin's party the chance it needed, the leadership of the Russian Revolution fell to him in part by chance, as well as by dint of the hard work and organization that had prepared his followers to seize that chance when it came. Only after November 1917 did the peasants' desire to seize the land (and the soldiers' eagerness to end the war against the superior German artillery) add that large mass support that the regime of Lenin's party needed in order to survive.

By contrast, the Chinese party, which sought for thirty years to build a Leninist party and to follow the footsteps of their Russian comrades, took a different course entirely. Since China had no real proletariat, except in a few large cities that governments or warlords could easily control, the Chinese Communists had to turn quite early to building a rural organization. China in the early twentieth century had no national center such as Moscow, so that power could not simply be seized at the capital and extended over the rest of the country, as in Russia. Finally, the disorders that overwhelmed the Manchu dynasty in 1911 were far more extensive than the problems of the czar, who until his fall in 1917 still commanded a nationwide bureaucracy and a national army. Communists in China were forced to overthrow not just a national state apparatus, but hundreds of local power holders and petty militarists.

The Chinese Communist Party, which began as a small but independent subset of the Nationalist Party and grew from perhaps fifty thousand in 1927 to a giant army of millions by 1949, conquered China as an army, not as a purely political force. To be sure, much of the credit for the idea of a Communist "party-army" must be given to Soviet advisers to the Chinese in the 1920s; but after 1927, Mao Tse-tung built his Red Army into a formidable military-political weapon.

The Red Army (called the People's Liberation Army after 1945) built its bases largely among the peasantry and often in easily defensible, remote regions of the vast Chinese countryside. It was not until the late 1940s that the Communists began to translate their real military power into nationwide administrative control. But this fact should not obscure the reality of Communist skills in the Chinese political arena. The Red Army under Mao Tse-tung showed an uncanny ability to voice the desires of a large number of ordinary Chinese. Mao's party openly declared war on Japan long before the Nationalist leader, Chiang Kai-shek, dared to do so. The Red Army, though often relying on doctrinaire theories and heavy-handed methods, still convinced the populace that it supported the desire of many villagers to be free from the multiple squeezes of usury, rack-rents and uncontrolled violence. The Communist Party by World War II had indisputably won over to its side the independent and antiestablishment voices of the new Chinese intellectual elite. When liberation came in 1949, there was no question that the vast majority of Chinese welcomed the chance to build their nation in peace. The Communist Party's skill in enlisting and utilizing popular aspirations in the game of politics was probably the most important cause of the Chinese Revolution of 1949.

THE STAKES OF CHINESE POLITICS: THE FUTURE CHARACTER OF CHINESE SOCIETY

As in the Soviet Union, so in today's post-revolutionary China do the stakes of politics include not merely some allocations of desired values, but the structure and development of the entire society and of much of its culture. Further, the attempted redesign of human society in China, as in Russia, also involved attempts to establish a new image of the human personality, of relations among the sexes and the generations, and of life in the family, village, and place of work. At stake also was the economic infrastructure of railroads, roads, and ports; the social infrastructure of schools, hospitals, and laboratories; and the future organization, equipment, and performance of factories and farms. The Chinese Revolution by 1949, like the Russian Revolution by 1917, was becoming a huge attempt to remake an entire society by means of politics; and for a time almost everything in China, as earlier in Russia, became political.

The First Decade of Communist Rule: Efforts to Apply the Soviet Model.

Certainly the Communists had been only a small part of the Chinese political system of the first half of this century. The population of the China that they won over in October 1949 was much larger than their membership, though by that date the CCP already numbered about 4.5 million members and was about the same size as the Communist Party of the Soviet Union.

Also, some elements of modernization had come into being before the Communists came to power. For nearly forty years the central government of China, under constantly changing leadership, had groped falteringly for formulas to build a new China. At least seven constitutions had come and gone since 1907. A large and moderately successful central bureaucracy had come into being under Chiang Kai-shek's national government in the 1930s. The Kuomintang, while remaining a party supported primarily by the well-to-do classes of the cities and some landowners in the countryside, had expanded its membership to become an extensive political organization, resembling in many of its features the European Fascist parties of that era. Above all, the Chinese people in the republican era, despite the extent of the chaos that surrounded them, had begun to create the basis for a modern economy in the cities and the rudiments of a nationwide communications system that would be helpful in integrating the nation after 1949.

China's revolution of 1949 resembled the Russian events of 1917 only because China, too, was a poor, non-Western country ravaged by war and famine. The differences were striking: China's political traditions were rich and highly developed, its Communist party far more mature and experienced in ruling, its social fabric far more torn by a century of disorder than even that of wartime

Russia. And yet, despite these differences, in the decade after 1949 the Chinese Communist government exerted every effort to engineer a society and government that closely resembled the Soviet Union's. "We must lean to one side," said Chairman Mao Tse-tung in a famous speech in 1949, in order to build a "new democratic dictatorship" on the Soviet model.

Already in this first decade there were signs that the Chinese would not be fully satisfied with a mere carbon copy of Soviet government and politics—the Stalinist variety. *Mao's theory of "democratic dictatorship"* expanded Lenin's, including the massive peasantry of China (some 85 percent of the population) as partners in rule. But Russian quickly replaced English as the major foreign language taught in Chinese schools, and translations from the Russian represented a significant proportion of the output of Chinese presses in the first decade after 1949.

The new institutions built to replace Nationalist organizations closely resembled the Russian models: the Communist Party dominated an extensive state apparatus of pyramidal shape; a modicum of regional autonomy was encouraged for regions where China's minority populations lived; the educational establishment was centralized in a group of institutes located largely in Peking; the new and vastly expanded press system, in which the *People's Daily (Jen-min Jih-pao)* was the central organ, even imitated the formats and style of *Pravda* and *Izvestia*. The Constitution of the People's Republic of China, promulgated in September 1954, and the Rules of the Communist Party of China, drawn up in 1956, codified many of these Soviet-style structures. The Russian model for the 1950s encouraged the Chinese to centralize their bureaucracy, mechanize their agriculture, concentrate on heavy industrial production, and build watertight divisions among specialized ministries and organizations.

While Russia was moving in the mid-1950s toward limited political de-Stalinization—though retaining Stalin's stress on the primacy of heavy industry—the Chinese departed more fundamentally from Stalinism, even though they continued to speak more favorably of him as a political leader of the Soviet Union. Already by 1955 the Chinese had decided to abandon the Stalinist pattern of preceding rural collectivization with the mechanization of agriculture. Mao Tse-tung startled the Russians by announcing first in 1955 that China would soon be totally collectivized (a point that the Soviet Union has still not reached) and then in 1958 that Chinese agriculture was rapidly approaching the stage of communism—in which all property would be owned by the state acting through local territorial units called *communes*. The Chinese argued that these units, with around twenty thousand people in each, would replace not only the favored Russian collective farm *(kolkhoz),* but the organs of local government as well. Despite an angry Khrushchev's warning that the Russians had tried such experiments in the 1920s and failed, the Chinese by late 1958 had grouped virtually their entire rural and urban population into these new units, which promised to hasten the arrival of communism by caring for infants and the elderly, by shouldering the main burden of military training, and by providing for each member according to his or her needs and the commune's ability to pay. Although very shortly thereafter the Maoist leaders had to back off from their rasher claims, because of material lacks and bureaucratic failures, still the people's commune (though now around seven thousand members in size) remains China's basic local unit of political and economic power.

The Chinese likewise developed to a far higher art than the Soviets the technique of the campaign *(yun-tung)* as a device for drumming up support for party policy. "Rectification campaigns" *(cheng-feng yun-tung),* aimed at bringing party members and cadres (a more common term in China than in Russia) into line, took place virtually every year. In one of these, the Hundred Flowers Campaign of 1956, Mao Tse-tung seemed almost to encourage active criticism of Communist Party members by students, writers, and professors. In military policy

China after 1957 de-emphasized the Soviet-style development of massive conventional forces in favor of guerrilla-like local militia training, which paid off in increased local discipline and productiveness.

All these phenomena suggested that Chinese leaders would not remain satisfied by merely imitating Soviet practices and institutions. Indeed, the open break in diplomatic and party relations with Moscow, which followed bitter public denunciations in 1960, climaxed a period of increasing dissatisfaction in Peking with playing second fiddle to the heirs of Stalin in Russia. The favorable atmosphere for Russian borrowing lasted even more briefly than the half-century of receptiveness to American and European ideas and practices that had preceded it.

Yet the fact that the Chinese explicitly reject the more corrupt and "revisionist" elements of Soviet practice—bureaucratism, hedonism, "great-nation chauvinism," and so on—should not blind us to the parallels between Chinese and Russian nation building after their respective revolutions.

Reintegrating a National Arena of Politics. First, the Chinese, like Lenin, had to reintegrate a ravaged society. In China this task of national unification was initially more difficult, whereas in Russia the cultural and economic dominance of the two main cities of Moscow and Leningrad made imposition of control over the provinces relatively easy. Chinese politics had been polycentric for decades, as each province's tens of millions of people had been governed solely by their resident warlord, or *tuchün.* The proclamation of the People's Republic in Peking began the process of building central political structures in China. Real power remained in the hands of *military administrative committees* in the six major regions of China until the formation in 1954 of the State Council under Premier Chou En-lai. Yet existence of the People's Liberation Army, nearly five million strong, made these regional committees (which corresponded to the garrison regions of each) relatively easy to coordinate. It was the political military—virtually the entire Central Committee of the CCP in 1949 had combat experience in the revolution—who cemented together the new government and kept order during the difficult period of transition. Civilian governments, staffed by former army commissars, party leaders, and a smaller number of non-Communist former Kuomintang bureaucrats, assumed power in the provinces only after this period of tutelage. From 1949 to the present the Communist government has preserved essentially the same regional structure, sometimes allowing it formal representation as a level of state authority (1949–54), sometimes relying on the party regional bureaus (1954–66), and sometimes preserving only the twelve great military regions (after 1966). But regional and provincial variety, in some years greater than in others, has flourished since 1949 only with the tolerance of central officials, who now command far more power over their regional subordinates than ever before.

Within two years of 1949 the income passing from the provinces to Peking through the budget, to pick an example, had multiplied by a factor of ten. Railway construction in the first decade more than doubled the track mileage linking Peking with the provinces and roughly quadrupled the amount of interprovincial trade. Central policy discouraged the use of nonstandard Chinese dialects in party and government meetings and supported extensive teaching of the Peking dialect. The system of *autonomous regions* for minority nationalities, such as the Uighurs in Sinkiang, the Mongols in Inner Mongolia, and the various Thai populations in southwestern Yunnan, did not permit the formation of separate Communist parties for each nationality (as in the Russian case). A number of rectification campaigns during the 1950s were aimed at rooting out "localism" among party cadres and ensuring the absolute authority of the central line. When the Cultural Revolution broke out in 1966, it was virtually certain that China would not fall apart again into groupings by warlord or region, simply because earlier integration efforts had been so exhaustive.

The Development of Political Participation. The second task of the early years was participation building. The Communists' victory came largely as a result of their success in involving China's rural population in their cause. The first decade after 1949 saw a participation explosion in China on an unprecedented scale. Certainly, the Russian Communists discovered quite early the advantage of mass mobilization for their political goals. But the transformation of Chinese mass attitudes to government after 1949 was by all accounts more striking because the vast majority of Chinese had been so systematically excluded from the political process until that date.

"Participation" is not the word that the Chinese use to describe their process of involving the masses. They prefer time-honored Leninist phrases like "democratic centralism" or the "mass line." But the essence of their practice closely resembles what political scientists call participation in other nations. The *mass line* involves three major elements, each of which binds the ordinary citizen more closely to the new political structures that the CCP created after 1949.

First is the *awareness* of government and policy. Whereas ordinary Chinese in pre-Liberation China (as the old society is often called today) either knew nothing of their government or feigned ignorance in the hope of avoiding taxes and other complications, the Communists demanded that every citizen understand how the government affected him or her. Under the pressure of Communist cadres and organizers, public matters came to occupy a larger portion of the consciousness of the ordinary worker or farmer.

Second, there was much wider *sharing* in the output of government. The citizen of the new system, at least in the early stages of the post-1949 transformation, benefited from the ploughing under of the old order. Carrying out land reform in the countryside, remolding urban businesses and factories, and reforming the legal structure to favor the working classes gave millions of Chinese a sense of real participation in the process of reconstruction and economic growth during the 1950s and that sense of participation through sharing is still widely perceived in China today.

Finally, after sharing came *joining*. The new government explicitly demanded that, in return for the real interests gained from the revolution, the citizenry be willing to participate actively in the new society. Private associations such as clans, religious societies, and business corporations came under sharp attack in the first few years and by 1956 had been virtually eliminated from China. In their place, cadres built myriad *public associations:* women's associations, professional societies, labor unions bearing the official seal of approval, and

especially the Communist Youth League and the Chinese Communist Party. Some data are shown in Figure 8.1.

As a result, the weekly schedule of ordinary people soon filled with innumerable public meetings to discuss public problems and to learn the government's policies. Participation in this last sense carried with it an obligation of civic responsibility that was not uniformly welcomed. But there was no denying that by the end of the 1950s the Chinese Communists had generated participation on a vast scale and that the effect of this new-found sense of belonging to a new nation was irreversible.

FIGURE 8.1 *Growth of Participation in China since 1949*

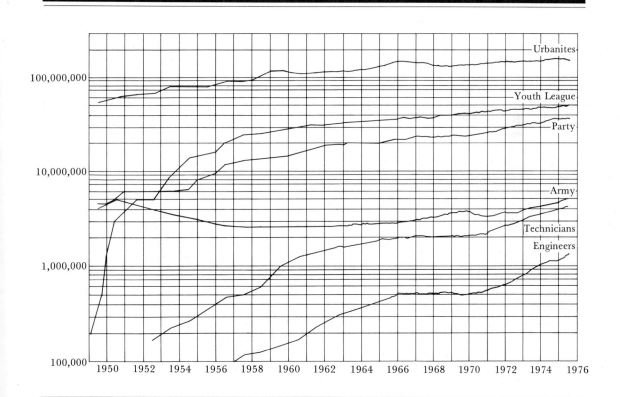

Institution Building: A New Machinery of Politics.
The third task of the first decade was institution
building. Though there was no lack of institutions
in premodern and transitional China, the Communist government came to power determined to
undermine and destroy what it regarded as the
corrupt and evil political organs of the oppressive and exploiting ruling classes. The extensive
government, armies, and parties of the pre-
Communist era fell almost at one blow in 1949–50
and were replaced by the Communists' own version—which in many instances closely resembled
the old institution, but with new personnel.

The new central, provincial, and local government built after 1949 very often included a
number (though always a small minority) of officials held over from the Kuomintang government,
individuals who had successfully remolded themselves to fit the revolutionary image. Some of these
people, like several of the ministers in Chou
En-lai's new State Council of 1954, had shifted
their allegiance to the Communists at a key point
in the last days of the struggle for power. In other
cases, non-Communist politicians were kept on to
indicate the new government's tolerance of non-
party "democratic personages" in the government
during the transition period.

But the lion's share of official positions fell to
new people, those whose loyalty to the new system
was unquestioned. Staffing these positions required a massive recruitment campaign that
swelled the ranks of the Youth League and the
Party in the 1950s. By 1958 the CCP, with 17
million members, had become the largest organized political elite in the world.

The Chinese Communist Party of the 1950s was
closely modeled in structure on the Communist
Party of the Soviet Union under Stalin. The 1956
Party Rules provided for a Politburo; a Central
Committee with a Secretariat and several Departments; and provincial, district, and local
party committees outside Peking. Elections to
higher-level party committees followed the same
democratic-centralist pattern of nomination from
below and confirmation from above. In theory and
in the rules, the Party stood apart from the even

larger body of state employees and state government organizations, though the Party was intended to be the guiding and policy-making force in
government at all levels, as in the Soviet Union.
But what was striking about Chinese Communist
institutional structures after 1949 was their rapid
growth and their flexibility within the letter of the
rules.

After 1958, however, many of the new institutions, including the Communist Party, were to be
tested severely once more by major strains and
pressures for another round of revolutionary
restructuring.

FROM "GREAT LEAP FORWARD" TO "GREAT PROLETARIAN CULTURAL REVOLUTION"—THE MAOIST DECADE

One of the great paradoxes of modern politics is
that those groups who most prominently claim to
represent impersonal forces of history or society so
often evolve into the personal followings of single,
powerful leaders. This process, which Michael
Walzer has so admirably described in his book
about the Puritan revolution in seventeenth-
century England (see p. 154, above) is justified
in the Leninist tradition by the theory of the
dictatorship of the proletariat. Since, in Lenin's
view, the working class of any nation may be
misled by faulty leadership or selfish economic
interest into betraying the true cause of revolution,
it must be represented by a core or vanguard of
professionals who see farther and clearer than
others. In the Russian case this status of near-
sainthood was always reserved for the Party, not
for the leader himself, despite the worship of
Lenin after his death. Even as he systematically
decimated the ranks of top leaders to heighten his
personal power, Stalin never implied that the idea
of the vanguard party ought to be challenged. Mao
Tse-tung, the leader of the Chinese Communist
Party from 1935 until 1976, came perilously close

to undermining the idea of a vanguard Communist Party organization in the decade between 1958 and 1968.

There were five elements to Mao's programs during this decade, each of which could be traced back to his own personal revolutionary experience before 1949 and to his distrust of Soviet imports into China. First, his so-called *Great Leap Forward* of 1958, while it promised all-round rapid advances in China's First Five-Year Plan, in fact reoriented Chinese economic policy away from urban industrial growth to a stress on rural industry and agriculture. Decentralization of power to local party committees in the provinces, reliance on large-scale labor-intensive rural projects, and creation of huge politico-economic units called *People's Communes*, having thousands of members—all these added up to an extensive *ruralization* of China's development plan.

Second, beginning with the Great Leap, Mao increasingly stressed the importance not of material wealth, but of will, strength of character, and especially political loyalty in building the new socialist China—a *voluntarism* that dated back to guerrilla days when an iron will was the best weapon of the Red Army soldier.

Third, *antibureaucratism* became a major theme of government propaganda, especially after the overenthusiastic (and economically disastrous) exertions of the Great Leap came under criticism from lower-level party authorities who had to carry them out.

Fourth, Mao increasingly turned to the People's Liberation Army as the model for the *remilitarization* of a China that had become too complacent, he thought, after revolutionary victory.

Finally, Mao turned his energies against the growing signs of disaffection with his policies among the intellectual class, which, a decade earlier, had been his strong supporter. The *proletarianization of culture*—by which he meant the purging of corrupt "bourgeois" works of art as well as the silencing of vocal critics of his politics (who were accused of "taking the capitalist road")—became the slogan that launched China's great purge of 1966–67, known as the *Great Proletarian Cultural Revolution*.

All five of these Maoist policies of the 1960s placed great strain on the new institutions of Party and state that had been so carefully built up during the 1950s. They would have been impossible to impose on China without the enormous prestige enjoyed by the Party's great leader. We need not believe that "the great helmsman," Chairman Mao, actually swam fifteen kilometers in sixty-five minutes in the turbid Yangtze in his seventy-third year, as the Chinese press reported,[4] in order to recognize that his personal influence was, for a time, more potent than that of his party.

But bureaucracies die hard, and the Chinese are as adept as any people at protecting the entrenched interest of officialdom. The Cultural Revolution was hailed as a massive onslaught against the inequities and privilege of the cadres of party and government. Yet the signs are clear that it merely substituted one group of cadres for another and, indeed, that virtually all the discredited "capitalist roaders in authority" have made striking comebacks since 1967.

The impact of the Maoist decade was greater in the less tangible fields of style and rhetoric than in major structural change. In the 1970s the rebuilt Chinese Communist Party was less preoccupied with formal rules of promotion and demotion, had fewer desk-bound officials, and extended farther into the countryside than a generation earlier. Education, ever the esteemed path to mobility in China, became more open to people from less privileged backgrounds (around two-thirds of high school pupils in the 1960s still came from cadre or "free professional" backgrounds); and certainly intellectuals, and especially writers and artists, tread more warily within earshot of authority. And yet, despite Maoism, the process of

[4]*China Quarterly,* no. 28 (October–December 1966), pp. 149–52.

governing China continues to require an enormous amount of paperwork, communications skills in high degree, and dedicated professional civil servants.

NEW DEPARTURES IN OLD PATTERNS: CHINA AFTER MAO

Chairman Mao's death in September 1976 brought to a close a remarkable reign. But like the passing of Stalin in 1953, it opened the floodgates of rapid change as Chinese leaders adjusted to new priorities. To ease the transition, Mao's successors pushed forward a much younger man, fiftyish Hua Kuo-feng, to take on his ceremonial roles, indicating the need for youth in government. Considerable real power remained, however, in the hands of an old guard of revolutionaries of Mao's generation, many of whom felt a need to moderate the stridency of late Maoist policy. Beginning scarcely a month after Mao's death, the successors, led by Teng Hsiao-p'ing, turned against Mao's closest personal aides, including his widow, and launched a new program of rapid modernization.

Many aspects of this drive seemed new and striking to observers accustomed to Maoist China. Economic rationality, including the emphasis on planning as far ahead as the twenty-first century, came to be stressed instead of revolutionary fervor. High standards of training and performance seemed to be preferred over political purity and proper worker-peasant-class origin. Teng Hsiao-p'ing's slogan of "Seek the truth from the facts" supplanted Mao Tse-tung's cry of "Rebellion is justified." And, most surprising of all, China began to open its doors to students and experts and to establish extensive commercial ties with the capitalist world, even choosing to end a three-decade-old diplomatic separation from the United States by mutual recognition on January 1, 1979.

Yet the new departures suggested echoes of the past and confirmed underlying patterns in the governance of China. The state Constitution of 1978, for example, drew heavily on the Constitution of 1956, which Teng Hsiao-p'ing had helped to shape. New economic plans, with their heavy stress on science and technology and on military preparedness, seemed to be extensions of the planning efforts of the 1950s. The careful preservation of the image of Mao, concurrent with a rejection of his policies, resembled the delicate de-Stalinization of Russia, about which the Chinese had been deeply concerned. The new stress on democracy did not move far beyond the essentially centralized notions of rule that had dominated the political systems of Communist parties in power since Lenin. Even the turn to the West and to the United States was justified as a tactical move necessary to deal with the "main enemy"—this time the Soviet Union on China's north. The events of the 1970s show how difficult it is for a nation, especially one so large and so deeply steeped in tradition as China, to break away from old paths. This recent sluggishness makes all the more remarkable China's about-face of 1949 and suggests that true revolutions are by nature short-lived political phenomena.

SOME RESULTS—AND SOME UNRESOLVED PROBLEMS

The performance of governments must be judged in the light of the problems that governments face. On this test, the first three decades of Chinese Communist rule must be counted as a great success.

Three Areas of Accomplishment. First, government succeeded in stopping a century or more of disorder and civil warfare and imposed peace on a weary population. By 1951 all China, except the offshore island province of Taiwan, rested easily in the control of new rulers committed to rooting out disruptive elements.

Second, the self-destructive tendencies of inflation, excessive urbanization, and overpopulation that have plagued other Asian societies in this century had to be curbed. By 1960, China had reduced the net reproduction rate to around 2 percent, had eliminated currency instability, and had actually reversed the flow of population into the cities by using the tactic of compulsory rustication *(hsia-fang)*.

Finally, the national economy had to be not only revived, but actually transformed to meet the requirements of an ever growing population and the desires of a nation-building elite. The Chinese government, deciding after 1960 on a strategy of "agriculture as the root, and industry as the main branch," has presided over growth in these two sectors ranging from 2 to 7 percent per year, with an average of perhaps 5 percent.[5] In contrast to the situation thirty years ago, the Chinese economy is now no longer dependent on foreign loans, imports, and advice. "With one's own strength alone can one be victorious" is a classic Chinese expression that has now become a standard and ubiquitous slogan.

Some Continuing Economic Problems. The post-Mao Chinese government has decided on a dramatic scheme of modernization of the economy. In the economic sphere China remains, in Mao Tse-tung's words, "poor and blank." Farm families in model villages still earn less than ten dollars a month in cash income. Productivity in farms and factories is still far below that of non-Communist Chinese economies such as those smaller and more manageable ones of Hong Kong and Taiwan, where market forces, rather than state plans, determine business decisions, and where the international economy with its technology and buying power still has an important impact. Despite tremendous efforts to bring modernization to China's vast countryside, villagers are still far less

literate, less well educated, and less well fed and clothed than are urban dwellers.

In the industrial sphere, despite three decades of effort, China has yet to join the modern world. Nearly two decades of political vacillation have left the managerial elite uncertain about the future, the working population relatively unskilled, and the industrial plant outmoded. Ambitious plans call for importing capital goods worth almost as much as the national debt of the United States by the year 2000, but China's exports are too few at present to finance even a more modest program. The younger generation of workers, deprived of consumer goods for years, now seeks higher wages at the same time as rural dwellers are being promised a better living standard. The top-heavy Chinese political system is still unprepared for the clamor caused by rising expectations, even if the target of 8–10 percent annual industrial growth can be achieved.

Education continues to be a major problem for the Chinese system. The Soviet-style elitist educational structure of universities and research institutes gave way in the 1960s to a great expansion in mass education, including high quotas for relatively unprepared, but politically reliable, rural youth. The turmoil of the "Gang of Four" period of the early 1970s created an extended hiatus in higher education and research that ended only after Mao's death. Striking plans to send tens of thousands of Chinese abroad to fill the resulting generation gap have been cut back for want of foreign exchange to pay for them and in hopes of satisfying political critics who fear excessive foreign influence.

Recurring Political Strains: Generations, Regions, and Civil-Military Relations. The death of Mao Tse-tung has left serious tensions in the Chinese system. In his last years Mao used his great personal esteem to undermine the authority of the Communist Party bureaucracy. Yet the very officials who replaced him are unable to abandon

[5]National Foreign Assessment Center (CIA), *China: A Statistical Compendium* (Washington, D.C.: July 1979), p. 3, "China Indicators of Aggregate Performance."

easily the symbol of Mao as the great helmsman of the Chinese revolution without undermining their own legitimacy. Hua Kuo-feng attempted to imitate Mao's style, even his haircut, to gain acceptance as the successor. China thus faces a classical problem described by Max Weber: how to "routinize the charisma" of a lost leader.

In part the problem is generational. The present members of the Politburo have an average age of over seventy and share the common experience of guerrilla warfare, one that does not help them to deal with critical economic, educational, and international tasks. This generation finds it hard to understand the demands of the younger, technocratic group that is managing China's modernization. Younger people, for their part, remember little of the days when personal sacrifice for the revolution was a necessity. Many expect to be given substantial responsibility while still junior. Mao Tse-tung's reliance on young Red Guards for support in 1966 has not been forgotten.

In part the problem is regional, since few of the current top leadership came from China's most industrialized regions, such as Shanghai and Liaoning. In a developing nation such as China, regions develop differently, and less advanced provinces such as Szechwan or Honan have a strong stake in a political system that redistributes the benefits of growth. It may be no accident that such provinces have been well represented in the Politburo. China remains divided by many dialects (though the written Chinese language is common to all) and by many nationalities—most of these in China's sensitive border regions. Regional unity in China is now, as it always has been, a matter of high political priority.

Another tension in the political system is that between civilian and military rule. This dichotomy is an element of the classical tradition that stressed rule by the word (wen, or "written culture") over the weapon (wu, or "military force"). Yet behind the changes in political vocabulary, style, and leadership in China since liberation has stood the inexorable power of the People's Liberation Army,

now the unchallenged masters of domestic security. The army stood behind the authority of Chairman Mao through the tumultuous Cultural Revolution despite blows to its own integrity, and the army swung behind Hua Kuo-feng at the critical moment of Mao's death.

The experimental army intervention in politics in the late 1960s left a legacy that would be familiar in other developing countries: professional military members, with their natural concern for discipline and order, may be natural leaders in times of crisis when these virtues are essential. But they cannot, while remaining military members, sustain the workings of a complex political system. Fewer than 3 million soldiers cannot make governing decisions for nearly half as many villages and retain their organized fighting strength. The Communist Party, grown to 36 million by 1979, can provide the personnel and the day-to-day presence to do that job. At the same time, China's leaders may feel they continue to need the stamina and the imputed objectivity of the loyal military to overcome the tendencies toward sloth and selfishness that they abhor. Military strength will be particularly needed around China's periphery and in the provinces, where local diversity demands firm control of peace keeping forces.

It might be worth remembering, however, that thus far in all Communist-ruled countries civilian party rule has remained predominant, in contrast to many less developed countries in the non-Communist world, where military dictatorships have been common. If the Chinese People's Republic should at some future time fall under military rule, this would not be a new thing in China's long history, but it would be a new departure in the shorter history of the Communist world, where dictatorships have been essentially party-based and civilian.

Developing a Role for China in World Politics. The final residual problem for China is its position in world affairs. To be sure, China is not yet a "superpower" (to use Chou En-lai's derogatory term for the United States and the Soviet Union), nor is it likely to become one in the near future.

China has a smaller land army than that of the United States and virtually no air force or navy, except for coast defense vessels and conventional submarines. While Chinese weapons experts have developed and tested fission and fusion bombs (more than a dozen tests since the first in 1964) and are on their way to deploying short- and medium-range delivery systems, the Chinese industrial plant cannot sustain full-scale conventional war in the way that the Soviet Union, Japan, or the United States might. China's problem is not so much to build up strength for offensive warfare, but rather to act on the world stage in order to minimize the likelihood of being isolated and attacked by potential enemies. China's strategy of playing one potential enemy against another coincides with Mao Tse-tung's tactical approach to guerrilla warfare as much as it does with classical Chinese strategic concepts. A million Russian troops on China's northern border, stationed there since the Sino-Soviet split broke into brief open warfare in mid-1969, symbolize the need to develop a flexible, multifaceted diplomacy. The recent turn toward a reconciliation with the United States after a quarter century of hostility suggests that the Chinese have learned much about the world since challenging the United Nations in the Korean War (1950–54). Perhaps the United States, too, has learned something of China's real intentions and capacities.

At the same time, the task of fitting China into the world system of nations will not be easy, even though China itself poses little real military, economic, or political threat to the other large nations. The province of Taiwan, occupied by ethnic Chinese of several dialects and ruled by Mao Tse-tung's ancient ally-turned-rival, Chiang Kai-shek, remains an international issue despite Chinese and American attempts to defuse it. President Carter's recognition of the government of the People's Republic of China as the legitimate government of China has left Taiwan without diplomatic status, but it remains a nation-sized political unit, being 16 million strong and wielding considerable influence in the world economy. In addition, there is British-ruled, Chinese-run Hong Kong; and in Singapore and throughout Southeast Asia reside 20 million ethnic Chinese who possess great economic power. The world's third largest economy, that of Japan, vastly overshadows the still essentially rural nation of China and will continue affecting the nations on the rim of Asia. The legacy of China's break with Soviet communism, having such deep geopolitical, ideological, and cultural roots, may last many years. It is doubtful that newly reforged bonds with America, which historically has been sympathetic to China's causes, will work miracles in the arduous job of bringing a quarter of humankind into a peaceful world arena.

KEY TERMS AND CONCEPTS

modern (or developed) political systems
traditional political systems
"modernity of tradition"
entrance examinations
mandarins
Confucius
Mencius
legalist school
Taoist philosophers
social relationships as model
unity of public and private realms
divine mandate of the emperor
officialism
humanism
Revolution of 1911
May Fourth Movement of 1919
Leninism (Soviet model)
Kuomintang
Chinese Communist Party (CCP)
Mao's view of peasantry
Long March of 1934–35
united-front strategy
the Yenan experience
Mao's theory of "democratic dictatorship"
communes

military administrative committees
autonomous regions
mass line
public associations
Great Leap Forward of 1958–59
people's communes
ruralization
voluntarism
antibureaucratism
remilitarization
proletarianization of culture
Great Proletarian Cultural Revolution of 1966–67

ADDITIONAL READINGS

Barnett, A. D., ed. *Chinese Communist Politics in Action.* Seattle: University of Washington Press, 1969. PB

Bennett, G., and R. Montaperto. *Red Guard: The Autobiography of Dai Hsiao-ai.* Garden City, N.Y.: Doubleday, 1971. PB

Karnow, S. *Mao and China: From Revolution to Revolution.* New York: Viking Press, 1972.

Lewis, J. W., ed. *Party Leadership and Revolutionary Power in Communist China.* London: Cambridge University Press, 1970.

Orleans, L. *Every Fifth Child: The Population of China.* Stanford, Calif.: Stanford University Press, 1972.

Scalapino, R. *Elites in the People's Republic of China.* Seattle: University of Washington Press, 1972. PB

Schram, S. *Mao Tse-tung: A Political Biography.* Baltimore: Penguin Books, 1968. PB
———. *The Political Thought of Mao Tse-tung.* Rev. ed. New York: Praeger, 1969. PB

Schurmann, F. *Ideology and Organization in Communist China.* 2nd ed. Berkeley and Los Angeles: University of California Press, 1968. PB

Schwartz, B. I. *Communism and China: Ideology in Flux.* Cambridge: Harvard University Press, 1968. PB

Smedley, A. *The Great Road.* New York: Monthly Review Press, 1956. PB

Snow, E. *Red Star over China.* Rev. ed. New York: Grove Press, 1968. PB

Solomon, R. *Mao's Revolution and Chinese Political Culture.* Berkeley and Los Angeles: University of California Press, 1971. PB

Terrill, R. *Eight Hundred Million: The Real China.* New York: Dell, 1972. PB

U.S. Congress, Joint Economic Committee. *Chinese Economy Post-Mao.* Washington, D.C.: U.S. Government Printing Office, 1978.

PB = *available in paperback*

IX

The World of the Emerging States

In the world of today, most states are young. Of the 153 present-day states for which data have been collected, less than one-sixth are older than the American Revolution. More than one-half came into existence only after 1925; more than one-fourth became independent only after 1959. Except for the 21 nation-states that were already sovereign in 1775, all the remaining 132 states have emerged at some time during the last two hundred years. (Figure 9.1 summarizes the record.)[1]

Accordingly, *emerging states* can be defined as countries that have only relatively recently acquired a status of formal political *sovereignty;* a significant amount of the modern political and administrative *machinery and institutions;* and some relatively widespread popular habits of mutual communication, compliance, and loyalty vis-à-vis their government and a significant portion of their compatriots. But the emerging states also have many other things in common, beginning with their departure from what their populations and societies were like before they began to move at a faster pace toward modernity.

We examine emerging states because they are becoming increasingly important for the world in which we will live. We also study them because we can learn about processes of change there that shed light on aspects of historical change in the countries studied earlier in this book. Thus, much of the material in this chapter will discuss *universal* processes of change that, with important exceptions and variations, of course, matter for the study of the politics of all countries.

The next two chapters will look more closely at seven less developed countries: India, Nigeria, Egypt, Iran, Cuba, Mexico, and Brazil. The last section of this chapter will introduce a brief comparative overview of some political aspects of

[1] See data in C. L. Taylor and M. C. Hudson, *World Handbook of Political and Social Indicators,* 2nd ed. (New Haven: Yale University Press, 1972), pp. 26–29, table 2.1

FIGURE 9.1 *Emerging Modern States, 1776–1978*

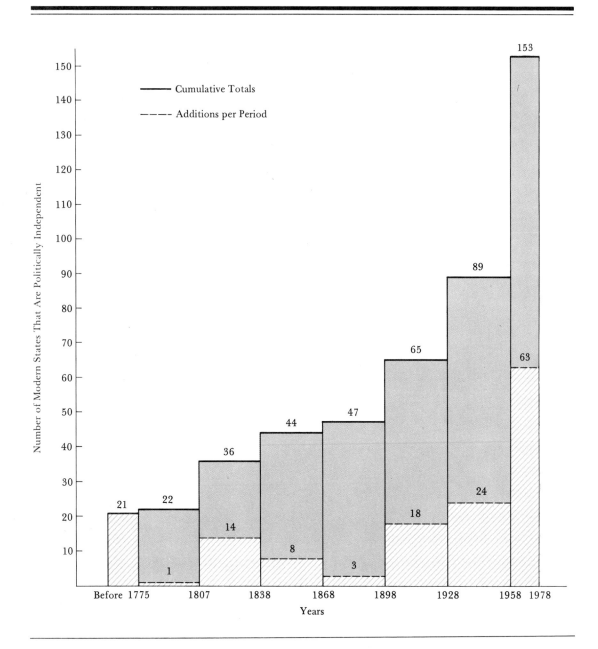

Sources: 1775–1973: C. L. Taylor and M. C. Hudson, *World Handbook of Political and Social Indicators,* 2nd ed. (New Haven: Yale University Press, 1972), pp. 26–29. 1973–78: John Paxton, ed., *Statesman's Yearbook 1978–1979* (London: Macmillan & Co., 1978), pp. viii–xii, 10–11.

these seven countries. You may wish to return to this section after you have read the next two chapters.

THE STARTING POINT: TRADITIONAL SOCIETIES

There has been a good deal of recent research and writing on traditional societies, some of it being of high quality; and yet in the world of the 1970s there are hardly any countries left that could be called entirely traditional. What we now call a *traditional society* is in fact most often a construct— that is, an image put together from many elements found scattered among different real-life countries. Few countries, if any, now correspond to this full-fledged *ideal type* that is supposed to have all these traits together and none that would not fit in with them.

Until recently, only such countries as Chad, Ethiopia, Malawi, Nepal, Burundi, and Rwanda were reasonably close to this picture, even though Ethiopia has now been shaken by a "Marxist" revolution. The number of countries of this type was larger even twenty years ago and still larger fifty or a hundred years ago. At some time in the past every country went through a stage when its life was governed largely by tradition; and substantial elements of a traditional society can still be found in over a hundred countries in the present-day world.

What, then, is this traditional society, and what are its major elements and features that still survive in so many places? To answer these questions, we shall first consider what the different wholly or partly traditional societies tend to have in common, so that we can perceive them as belonging to one type; and then we shall examine some of the very important major differences among them and their influence on the different patterns of politics, society, and culture that succeeded each traditional society.

What Traditional Societies Have in Common. No country has broken away entirely from some of the traditions that have prevailed in the past. For example, religious beliefs are strong traditional components of countries such as the United States, Britain, the Federal Republic of Germany, and France, and they are still quite important to their peoples today. Ethnicity remains a long-lasting feature of the collective and individual lives of peoples in such different countries as the United States and the Soviet Union. Certain core family values dealing with affection and respect still survive in most of the countries we study. Love for country, or patriotism, is also often a durable traditional trait. As we shall see, some elements of tradition have faded away in many places, however, and that is a crucial theme in this chapter. The discussion of "transitions" away from tradition is thus necessarily relative. We can call attention to the relative decline in a "package" or a syndrome of traditional traits even though some elements of tradition certainly persist and become intermingled with new elements that emerge in what we will call modern societies.

In addition, as the brief listing above of some traditional traits that tend to persist suggests, many of us may cherish some aspects of these and other traditions. Similarly, many regret the "transitions" away from a fuller and tighter package of traditions. Some of the major political struggles the world has known—including most recently the revolution that broke out in Iran in the late 1970s—are fought over the "proper" balance between tradition and change. You might think about how your own values affect your evaluation of the relative balance between tradition and modernity.

Because traditions persist and combine with new, modern elements, and because philosophical perspectives within traditional and modern world views may differ greatly, the term *transition* must be used with great caution. Transition suggests a move away from certain aspects of traditional society, as it will be described below. It also suggests the appearance of certain traits shared in common—higher income, greater literacy and exposure to mass media, nonagricultural employment, and so forth. We do not, however, imply that all modern societies, and even less their political systems, are identical. Transitions there are, indeed, but the final outcome is open-ended and variable. The discussions of countries that have changed so much, and that are described earlier in this book, should already indicate to you that there are many paths to the modern world, where new differences may be as great and as significant as those inherited from the past.

The first characteristic of a traditional society—there were only about a dozen left in 1976—is its poverty: a per capita income of $120 or less at 1976 prices. *Early transitional societies,* which are partly traditional and of which there are about fifty-six, are also poor, but somewhat less so; per capita incomes range from $120 to about $800 in 1976 terms. India, Egypt, and Nigeria belong in this category. *Advanced transitional societies* have higher per capita incomes, ranging from $800 in 1976 (Cuba, Mexico, and Brazil) to about $3,000 (Portugal, Iran, and Greece). In 1976 there were about twenty-five countries in this category; and each of these had preserved some lesser, but still substantial, elements and aspects of the traditional society within its system. The next richer category, the *industrialized societies,* includes about seventeen countries with 1976 per capita incomes ranging from $3,000 to $5,000; representative nations are Italy, Finland, Czechoslovakia, and the Soviet Union. In these countries fewer elements of the traditional society have survived the process of industrialization.

Finally, there are about eleven very highly developed countries, whose 1976 per capita incomes exceeded $5,000, such as Australia, the United States, Sweden, and Switzerland. In these countries, industrialization is largely completed: new industries are more likely to replace older ones than to take the place of preindustrial pursuits, such as traditional handicrafts or agriculture. In these countries, also, there is a rapid growth of service industries, of professional and white-collar employment, of secondary and higher education, of computer technology and automation, and generally of information-processing occupations and industries. Some observers have called such societies *postindustrial;* perhaps a more positive description would be to call them countries entering the *information revolution*—the next great wave of change after the classic industrial revolution that these countries have already more or less completed. In the countries in this last group, the balance has shifted the most from tradition to modernity.

A schematic overview of these five groups, with their income ranges and the countries that belong to each, is presented in Table 9.1.

The typical traditional society is not only poor; it is predominantly rural. In most countries of this type relatively few people live in cities of any size, and very few—usually less than 10 percent—live in cities of more than 100,000 inhabitants. The overwhelming majority of the work force, 80 or 85 percent, is engaged in agricultural or pastoral occupations. The nonagricultural occupations are weak and static in number, often segmented into specialties, disinclined to free communication across professional or status boundaries, and inhospitable to any large or rapid change or innovation. What communication there is remains largely within the conventional channels of family, locality, ritual, occupational specialty, and social class. There is little geographic or social mobility. Most people stay where they are—in their locality, their station in society, their culture and subculture, their old memories, and their old ways of thinking, feeling, and acting.

Both birth rates and death rates used to be high and tended to remain so; many people passed through their short lives quickly. There often still is much interest in tombs, charnel houses, cemeteries, funerals, and other commemorative ceremonies for the dead. Population then used to grow very slowly or not at all, for the many deaths—from disease, malnutrition, neglect of effective health care and infant care, infections in childbirth or after accidents—all mounted up to balance the high rate of births.

But even in traditional societies, parents did not like traditional death rates among their children. With the coming of modern medicine and public health, death rates were pushed down, although birth rates remained high. Thus, population often doubled within a generation, requiring twice as much food and making many traditional practices untenable. In this way many traditional societies began to disrupt themselves.

Rates of change and social learning remained low. Arts, crafts, methods of technology, styles of art, rituals of religion, and doctrines of science or philosophy changed but slowly, if at all. Where there was large change, it often occurred over the period of about one century, as in the spread of maize in the seventeenth and eighteenth centuries in Turkey and Italy, the spread of potatoes in much of northern Europe, the spread of maize and millet in eighteenth-century China, or the spread of manioc—the plant from which tapioca is prepared—through much of precolonial Africa. Where large changes proceeded more quickly, they usually remained limited to a sector of life, as in the acceptance of a new religious ritual or a sectarian doctrine, or in a change of dynasty, or in the conquest of a region. Even today, many of these changes have remained on the surface of society. Daily life for most people continues as before.

In a static or slow-changing social and natural environment, experience is the most valuable form of knowledge and conservatism the safest strategy of action. Habits and prejudices, once acquired, have a good chance of proving useful as well as convenient. Memories, habits, traditions, and long-established institutions are likely to become part of the local community and family patterns and the personality structures of many individuals living in such a society.

Together, these patterns interlock and reinforce one another, preserving what all traditional societies have in common: an established way of life with its adaptation to local conditions and its ignorance of more distant facts; its depth of traditions and its narrowness of choices; its apparent mood of stability and security, and its real anxieties and fears, high rates of death, hunger, and disease; its persistence through centuries and its pervasive resistance to all major change.

What counts is not the age of a tradition, but its power over the lives of people and its resistance to change, once it has become established. Traditions can be established very quickly, for they are the result of combinations of memories and patterns of behavior that need not depend for their effectiveness on the speed or slowness with which they were put together. Sparta, Islam, such sects as the Sikhs of India or the Hutterites and some other groups in the United States—all go back to a certain act or brief period of foundation; but, once founded, they proved remarkably persistent and often came soon to conform to the pattern of smaller or larger traditional societies. Other traditional societies go back to a brief and lively period of immigration or of transition to a new type of agriculture; yet after the change has been adopted, a traditional society may emerge and last for a long time.

Such a traditional society is rarely found today in anything like its pure form. But if traditional societies are being infected by elements of change, many countries are shot through with elements of conservatism and tradition in many sectors and aspects of their lives. Here we find the conservative peasants and other rural voters; the traditional-minded artisans; the groups of devout believers in a supposedly unchanging religion and its hallowed ritual; the local folk distrustful of strangers and things new; and those who feel that what was good enough in the past will remain equally good for them in the future.

Given the proposition of sociologist Talcott Parsons, that every social system needs to maintain its own patterns and needs certain persons and institutions to perform this function of *pattern maintenance*, we can see readily that some traditional elements will survive and often contribute to this pattern-maintaining function in all countries.

TABLE 9.1 *Traditional, Transitional, Industrialized, and High-Information Societies, ca. 1975*

A. STRUCTURE	1 GNP per cap. ca. 1976	2 % Econ. growth p.a. per cap. 1970–76	3 % Work force in agric. ca. 1975	4 % Urban (100,000) ca. 1975	5 Pop. growth ca. 1970–76	6 Pop. total (million) ca. 1976	7 For. trade (imp. & exp.) as % of GNP ca. 1975	8 Concentration of export receiving countries (index) ca. 1975	9 Concentration of commodities exported (index) ca. 1975
TRADITIONAL SOCIETIES									
Ethiopia	100	0.2	84	5.3	2.6	29	21	10	20
Malawi	130	3.2	89	4.2	2.9	5	59	18	24
EARLY TRANSITIONAL SOCIETIES									
India	140	0.5	69	9.8	2.1	620	12	11	6
Pakistan	180	1.1	59	16.2	3.0	71	28	10	21
Egypt	280	3.1	54	33.9	2.3	38	54	17	20
Ghana	370	0.7	58	14.4	2.9	10	27	12	38
China	370	4.3	68	—	1.7	836	—	—	—
Nigeria	400	5.4	62	11.3	2.6	77	55	14	88
Bolivia	510	3.4	55	22.7	2.7	6	49	12	—
ADVANCED TRANSITIONAL SOCIETIES									
Cuba[a]	840	-0.5	31	31.3	1.7	9	101	—	75
Chile	1050	-2.3	24	48.9	1.8	10	32	9	56
Mexico	1060	1.7	45	32.9	3.5	62	15	71	5
Brazil	1300	7.4	46	38.9	2.8	110	20	10	11
Argentina	1580	1.8	16	55.5	1.3	26	18	7	17
Yugoslavia	1750	5.8	50	12.6	0.9	21	36	11	6
Iran	1660	13.3	46	43	2.9	33	55	12	94
INDUSTRIALIZED SOCIETIES									
Soviet Union	2800	3.1	26	35.7	0.9	257	11	7	16
Poland	2880	5.3	39	19.7	0.9	34	26	—	11
Italy	3220	2.0	19	28.7	0.8	56	47	10	9
United Kingdom	4180	1.7	3	62.6	0.1	56	46	6	10
Saudi Arabia	4420	9.5	66	25.6	3.0	9	102	9	100
HIGH-INFORMATION SOCIETIES (POSTINDUSTRIAL)									
Japan	5090	3.9	20	57.8	1.3	113	23	10	17
France	6730	3.3	14	44.5	0.7	53	34	9	9
West Germany	7510	2.0	7	34.5	0.2	62	40	6	12
United States	7880	1.7	4	71.8	0.8	215	14	11	10
Canada	7930	3.5	8	54.9	1.3	23	42	63	8
Sweden	9030	2.1	8	27.5	0.3	8	53	8	11
Switzerland	9160	0.5	8	30.4	-0.2	6	50	7	13

TABLE 9.1 (cont'd)

B. COMMUNICATION	10 % Adult literacy ca. 1970	11 Higher education enrolment per 100,000 ca. 1975	12 Newspaper circulation per 1,000 ca. 1975	13 Radios per 1,000 ca. 1975	14 TV per 1,000 ca. 1975	15 Telephones per 1,000 ca. 1975	16 Physicians per 100,000 ca. 1975	17 Infant deaths per 1,000 live births ca. 1975	18 Inequality index: sectoral (Gini) ca. 1970	19 Central govt. expend. as § of GNP 1975	20 Defense expend. as % of GNP 1975	21 Milit. partic. per 1,000 work age pop. ca. 1975
TRADITIONAL SOCIETIES												
Ethiopia	6	23	2	6	1	2	1	84	—	13	3.8	3.4
Malawi	22	23	2	21	0	4	2	151	47	13	0.7	1.9
EARLY TRANSITIONAL SOCIETIES												
India	33	559	16	22	0	3	24	122	48	9	3.3	5.0
Pakistan	15	163	—	27	2	3	25	124	33	11	6.3	14.1
Egypt	44	1212	21	132	16	13	21	101	43	25	11.7	19.0
Ghana	30	92	51	82	3	6	10	156	—	12	1.6	4.1
China	—	—	—	16	1	—	—	—	—	—	11.01	8.4
Nigeria	15	52	9	23	2	2	7	—	—	13	4.6	8.2
Bolivia	63	921	35	282	0	9	48	77	—	13	2.7	6.8
ADVANCED TRANSITIONAL SOCIETIES												
Cuba[a]	85	872	5	155	63	30	86	27	—	—	6.1	22.7
Chile	88	1460	—	144	73	43	43	56	51	13	4.3	18.1
Mexico	74	879	113	278	82	49	53	48	58	11	0.9	3.2
Brazil	66	993	39	60	97	31	44	—	57	10	2.2	7.6
Argentina	93	2351	154	379	177	79	212	59	44	10	2.3	9.9
Yugoslavia	84	1853	89	166	131	61	117	40	35	—	4.5	19.3
Iran	37	405	24	229	51	24	39	139	50	17	8.6	24.0
INDUSTRIALIZED SOCIETIES												
Soviet Union	100	1903	397	390	216	67	288	28	—	—	—	27.7
Poland	98	1701	248	174	180	76	172	25	26	—	—	19.2
Italy	94	1775	113	218	215	264	198	21	—	14	2.8	14.1
United Kingdom	99	1247	388	626	317	376	134	16	34	22	5.0	9.8
Saudi Arabia	2	295	11	11	14	18	40	—	—	12	5.8	20.2
HIGH-INFORMATION SOCIETIES (POSTINDUSTRIAL)												
Japan	98	2024	526	546	234	410	114	10	39	11	0.9	3.2
France	99	1963	214	316	268	261	147	10	52	15	4.0	17.4
West Germany	99	1355	312	323	307	318	195	20	39	21	3.6	12.6
United States	99	5228	287	1416	566	697	158	16	42	19	6.0	15.5
Canada	99	3588	235	742	412	576	172	15	33	20	2.0	5.2
Sweden	100	1962	572	380	348	654	156	8	39	25	3.2	14.1
Switzerland	99	990	402	296	267	599	176	12	—	13	1.9	5.8

[a]These data have been included for Cuba for the sake of facilitating comparison, but other evidence suggests that Cuba had positive rates of real economic growth per capita in the first half of the 1970s (along with much poorer performance in the 1960s and in the late 1970s). In addition, literacy rates, defense expenditures as a percent of gross product, and military participation per population are all somewhat higher. See Jorge I. Domínguez, *Cuba: Order and Revolution* (Cambridge: Harvard University Press, 1978).

Source: Except as otherwise noted data are from C.L. Taylor, *World Handbook of Political and Social Indicators*, 3rd ed. (New Haven: Yale University Press, forthcoming); cols. 1, 2, 3, and 6 are from World Bank, *World Atlas* (Washington, D.C.: World Bank 1978); and col. 18 is from S. Jain, *Size Distribution of Income* (Washington, D.C.: World Bank, 1979).

Those persons and institutions that maintain cultural patterns and transmit them to the next generation—the women, the family, and the educational system in many countries—will tend to preserve and transmit elements of an older traditional culture and society.

The content of this traditional culture and social system, however, may differ very much from one country to another. It is only when they are viewed from a great distance—both intellectual and emotional—that all traditional societies may look alike. In reality the differences among them are often profound, and these can have major effects on the probable speed and character of their eventual development.

Some Major Differences Among Traditional Societies. Traditional societies differ profoundly in their labor productivity, in their technologies and economies, in their capacity to produce concentrations of wealth at least in some localities or sectors, and in the level of their intellectual and artistic culture.

Some traditional societies derive their livelihood mainly from gathering, hunting, or fishing, such as the Eskimos or various Indian tribes in South America. Other traditional societies live mainly on livestock raising and related pastoral activities, such as many nomadic Bedouin tribes or the Mongolian herdspeople in both Outer (Soviet) and Inner (Chinese) Mongolia. More often, even very poor traditional societies practice some primitive forms of agriculture, nomadic or sedentary, yielding just enough food to permit survival on a basis of more or less equal poverty.

Where agriculture is steadier and more efficient, its surplus product—beyond the subsistence needs of the producer—is large enough to support other occupations, and most often entire social classes, such as warriors and landlords, scribes, priests, builders and artists, rulers, tax collectors and administrators, artisans, merchants, and moneylenders. Where the soil is fertile and well watered by rains or irrigation, the climate favorable, and the crop-plants relatively high yielding,

traditional societies have developed into elaborate class systems and states, religious establishments and doctrines, monuments of art and architecture, warlike aristocracies, monarchies and armies, often expanding into empires holding sway over neighboring poorer regions and populations. When other processes of change set in (discussed in the next section), the commercialization of agriculture may contribute to further far-reaching changes. Examples of prosperous but still traditional societies are, broadly speaking, the cultures of ancient Egypt and Iran; of the rice and grain fields of India and China; and of the grain fields of medieval Europe. Temples and cathedrals, palaces and monuments, aqueducts and roads, large enterprises of conquest and great works of art—all testify to what a traditional society can do under such favorable circumstances. But it is well to remember that these glories most often involved directly less than 5 or 10 percent of the population and that the great mass of the people went on living and dying in the same poverty-stricken and unchanging monotony, generation after generation. Today, most of the traditional empires are gone.

The division of labor already existent within the traditional society and culture may make a major difference to the subsequent development of the country. Are the people, both men and women, habituated to sustained and diligent labor, as in most of the cultures of South, Southeast, and East Asia? Or is agriculture still a primitive affair, left largely to women, while men are habituated to spending much of their time on hunting, fishing, cattle raising, participating in local and tribal politics, and perhaps perpetrating raids, cattle thefts, and petty warfare—as well as on gossiping, smoking, and indulging in plain idleness? Clearly, men already used to doing steady and dependable work are more likely to adjust well to industrial employment and big-city life. On the other hand, those more accustomed to relying on the labor of their womenfolk, while themselves remaining idle between bouts of hunting, politicking, or fighting, would be more likely to become paupers, drunks, or criminals in modern urban and industrial society. The first type of culture requires relatively little learning for the shift from the steady work of advanced traditional wheat or rice culture to the steady work needed by industry; the second type of culture may require a much greater effort of social learning and psychic readjustment for a similar transition to modernity.

A related difference is the presence or absence of highly developed handicraft skills, and perhaps of home industries, in the traditional society. Chinese, Japanese, and Hindu craftsmen were renowned for their patience and skill in many different trades and crafts. Competence in the production of high-quality textiles, metals, and carvings in ivory, wood, or stone offers potential resources of skill and habits of care and accuracy for the later growth of industry. Let us remember the marvelous steel swords of medieval Japan, the famed Damascene steel of early medieval Syria, and the wood carvings and icons of the village craftspeople of medieval and early modern Russia.

Related to this is the extent to which a traditional culture already has taught the population some of the merchant's skills and virtues: the ability to read, write, and calculate numbers accurately; to save, to learn, and generally to work for distant goals; and to develop a high degree of accuracy and dependability in dealing with money, time, and contractual obligations. Among the Japanese and the Chinese and among such trading castes or peoples as the Parsees, the Jains, and the Marwaris of India, the Scots in seventeenth- and eighteenth-century Britain, the Ibo people in Nigeria, and the Jews in medieval eastern Europe—in the cultures and traditions of each of these groups was a merchant strain that prepared them for a faster and more successful transition to modernity, albeit sometimes at the cost of making them unpopular with their less successful neighbors. Other traditional cultures may teach people a different set of skills, less well suited to success in industrial, commercial, bureaucratic, or scientific occupations: the warriors' preference for the virtues of

the sword over those of the book and the pen; their contempt for the merchants' thrift and care; their alternation between the austerity of warfare or the hunt and the wealth expended on days of feasting or victory; their delight in physical prowess and their disdain for paperwork, study, and examinations; their reliance on intuitive judgment and their distrust of explicit rules and reasoned explanations; and their respect for past deeds and heroic ancestors and their relative lack of interest in any changes in the future.

Accordingly, members of some soldierly or religiously oriented cultures, such as the Muslim or the Spanish Catholic, have at times difficulties in the transition to modernization. Muslims in colonial India and Nigeria often did less well in British civil service examinations than did their Hindu or Ibo competitors. In high schools in Hawaii, according to some reports, the children of Filipino workers often have done less well than their fellow students of Chinese or Japanese ancestry who were recruited from the same occupational groups and social strata.

Something similar may even apply to entire countries. Bruce Russett and his collaborators found that Muslim countries, and also Catholic countries, appeared to perform less well on a number of indicators of social and economic development and of political modernization than the average of all countries of the world. Historians similarly record that most Spanish-speaking or Muslim Arab countries have been deficient in many aspects of social and economic development during the last four hundred years.[2]

[2]Countries with a higher percentage of Muslims tend to have higher rates of birth, natural population growth, and infant death than prevails elsewhere in the world. They had more of their work force occupied in agriculture, spent a larger share of their incomes on defense, and had smaller shares of urban population and urban growth. They were marked by lower levels of literacy, public school enrollment, and higher education. They also had less industry, shorter life expectancy of the population, fewer physicians and hospital beds, and

More subtle differences among traditional societies exist in regard to many values and attitudes that are apt to be crucial for the success or failure of rapid social, political, and economic modernization. Some nations and cultures put stress on *achievement motivation;* that is, they treat heroism, great deeds, victory in contest and feats of skill, gains in wealth, or the production of substantial or outstanding works of art, architecture, or economic construction as things to be admired and desired. Similarly, societies differ in their evaluation of manual labor and also of steady and persistent work, of reliability and truth, of accuracy and accountability. European craftspeople were traditionally proud of working with their hands, whereas high-caste Hindus were taught by the traditions of their caste system to disdain and avoid manual work. Some traditional societies teach people to

value the future and to work for distant goals; others teach them to live for the past or the present, to persist in playing age-old social roles, or else to snatch every brief moment of happiness as soon as they can. Some traditions teach trust and cooperation, whereas others may teach mistrust and the expectation and practice of betrayal and deceit, often outside the circle of one's family, but sometimes even within it.

Related to these differences are the different levels of desire for and competence in the organization and conduct of autonomous small groups holding real powers of decision over at least some activities or aspects of life that truly matter to the people concerned. And related to these, in turn, is the desire for self-government on the local, regional, or national level, as in the case of the self-governing cities of much of medieval western Europe, and later of the American colonies and the United States, and of the self-governing town councils—the *cabildos*—found in parts of Latin America. Other forms of self-government may develop on the basis of craft or occupation (as in the medieval European guilds) or for groups of religious believers (as in the congregations of certain Protestant denominations in seventeenth-century Britain). Once developed within the framework of a still wholly or largely traditional society, such skills, habits, and institutions of *group solidarity and self-government* may then be available for the faster and more thorough social and political growth of the country in which they exist.

Other conditions that developed within the traditional society may also greatly influence the effects of the cultural values, attitudes, and institutions just mentioned. Geographic proximity to large markets tends to favor the more rapid emancipation of the peasantry. Peasants learn quickly to use money and to adapt at least some of their produce to the market; landlords discover that if the peasants are left free to do this, they will earn more money, of which the landlord then can get a share in the form of rent. Under such conditions individual freedom, economic rationality, and political self-government have a relatively good chance to develop quickly.

---

fewer mass media, but they also had slightly lower levels of income inequality.

Countries with a higher percentage of Roman Catholics, compared with all countries, tended to have higher levels of income inequality and to keep it even after taxes. They also showed greater inequality in landholdings, and a larger proportion of their wage and salary earners was unemployed. But they were less agricultural in income and employment; their per capita incomes tended to be higher, and so were their levels of literacy, higher education, school enrollment at the primary and secondary levels, and mass media saturation—such as by radio, newspapers, television, and motion pictures. Their rates of birth, population growth, and economic growth did not differ significantly from those of the rest of the world, but relative to their population they had fewer marriages and more physicians and hospital beds and, nonetheless, higher rates of death and infant death.

This does not necessarily mean, of course, that Islam or Catholicism caused these conditions, which may have existed in some of these lands before their present religions were adopted and which are often shaped by other factors. Rather, this simply points to the fact that countries where Muslims and Roman Catholics live disproportionately—such as the seven nations studied in the next two chapters—have these characteristics.

For data, see B. M. Russett et al, *World Handbook of Political and Social Indicators* (New Haven: Yale University Press, 1964), pp. 286–87.

Being located a great distance from the nearest major market tends to have the opposite effect. Peasants then will depend on intermediaries to buy, transport, and market their products; and these intermediaries are likely to find it less troublesome to deal with a few landlords than with many peasants. Once landlords form a coalition against the peasants, they are likely to profit and grow stronger and to exploit the peasants more. Serfdom, peonage, chattel slavery, and half-forced contract labor have developed under such conditions, and the introduction of worldwide markets and shipping services has sometimes made these conditions even worse. Cases in point include the spread and tightening of serfdom in sixteenth- and seventeenth-century Prussia, Poland, and Russia; the growth of slave labor between 1810 and 1860 in the cotton kingdom of the South of the United States; and the growth and partial persistence of the plantation system in colonial Latin America, Indonesia, Malaysia, and Indochina.

Even within these traditional or semitraditional societies of unfree labor there are differences. Chattel slavery tends to weaken or destroy family ties and solidarity, since individuals can be sold away at any time. Peonage (laborers bound in servitude because of unpaid debts) may at least respect family ties, but it usually ignores or suppresses the formal or informal solidarity and self-government of villages. Only serfdom (laborers bound to the soil and subject to the will of the local lord), though it denies freedom to the individual, tends to leave both families and village communities intact. In this latter case, therefore, the eventual shift to economic development, the process of social and political modernization, and the emancipation of the people by their own efforts should tend to be relatively easier and quicker.

Another critical set of conditions inherited from the traditional society is the extent of *ethnic, linguistic, cultural, and religious diversity or uniformity* and, hence, the ease or difficulty of communication and cooperation among different elements of the population. Pakistan and China have similar low per capita incomes, but China had inherited from its long premodern past a much higher degree of cultural and linguistic unity. In 1971, Pakistan had broken in two: a new state, Bangladesh, of over 80 million population who were almost entirely Bengali-speaking; and a much diminished rump state, still called Pakistan, but in fact limited to the former West Pakistan. The over 70 million inhabitants of Pakistan belong to several different ethnic language groups that have remained separated from one another, despite their common Muslim religion, by continuing difficulties in the way of broad social communication, cooperation, and civic solidarity. From the 1960s to the 1970s, China passed through its Great Proletarian Cultural Revolution and then through a period of attempted economic modernization, emerging stronger and apparently more united than before. It is natural for the Chinese Communist government to claim credit for this success. It is likewise natural for the dictatorial military government of Zia ul-Haq that ruled Pakistan in 1980 to be blamed for the country's continuing difficulties. But, in fact, the Chinese rulers may well have been helped—and the Pakistani generals hindered—by the different ethnic and linguistic traditions of the two countries.

THE IMPACT OF MODERNITY

Whatever the heritage of a country from its traditional past and whatever the extent to which elements—or even major patterns—from its past have survived intact, sooner or later every society and culture in today's world is likely to be challenged and changed by the impact of modernization. This impact is likely to be uneven. It will interfere with some sectors and practices of the traditional society much more than with others. It may destroy or transform some, bring others into being, and leave still others largely undisturbed.

The sources of modernity, likewise, are not spread uniformly over the country or throughout the society. They are concentrated in particular localities, groups, practices, and institutions, which thus play a key role in the modernizing process.

Domestic Sources of Modernization. An underlying source of *modernization* consists in some increase in the productivity of labor—more ample crops, more abundant livestock, a greater catch of fish, a special material to be gathered or hunted (such as amber or ivory), or a special product of handicraft (such as textiles or metal goods)—that now can become objects of trade. Such trade may be local, from one village to another or from several villages to a nearby marketplace; or else it may be long-distance trade, moving some local product to a distant market, either directly or through a chain of intermediaries. The more trade increases in volume, the larger the number and diversity of persons and localities involved in it; and the greater the efficiency of transport that permits the involvement of relative strangers, the more likely it is that people eventually will find it convenient to trade for money rather than to exchange goods or services in kind. Growing productivity and transport thus tend to produce growing trade; growing trade tends to produce an increasing *monetization* of economic life; and money and monetization are powerful solvents of past habits and traditions.

At the same time, increasing productivity also permits an increase in the division of labor. Even the poor peasants in a village in India often produce enough food to support some village artisans, such as a blacksmith or a barber, who serve their needs. Or such artisans may serve several villages, visiting each in turn. Other artisans, such as weavers, may live in a village and spend some or all of their time producing goods to sell in nearby markets or to traders for sale in more distant ones. In this manner there arises, in the midst of a rural and agricultural society, a small, but growing, nonagricultural population, a population gaining its livelihood mainly from nonagricultural work.

As the number of people in nonagricultural occupations grows, some of them will move closer to a marketplace where their services and products are more in demand and, hence, can be exchanged or sold on more favorable terms. This concentration of nonagricultural occupations in combination with a market constitutes one major element in the economic and social character of a city.

A *marketplace,* in turn, usually requires a location at a crossroads, a ford, a bridge, the head of a caravan trail, or some similar *node of transportation,* where travelers and merchants stop to rest, take on supplies, perhaps also change their means of transport, and repackage their loads and goods. But a *market* as an economic institution is primarily a place or region within which the decisions of many buyers and sellers are closely interdependent, so that when one seller charges more, prospective customers can quickly survey whatever alternative offers are available to them, and when one seller raises or lowers the price, all others can quickly learn about it and decide whether or not to follow suit. In this sense a market is made primarily not by geography, but by transport and communication. The markets for wheat and oil are worldwide and have been so for many decades, thanks to cables and power-driven ships. Other markets may be confined to a few villages and a small market town that serves them or, as sometimes happens, exploits them.

But a market also has some political requirements. It requires a high probability of peace and security for merchants and customers and their money and goods. It also needs some law, or rather, a high probability that contract obligations will be fulfilled and debts will be paid. Within many countries, merchants and market towns are, therefore, among the first to press for stronger local government that can assure a high degree of local "law and order." They are also likely to support the development of a strong central government that will ensure safety on the highways and waterways between the different cities and that will credibly promise to enforce contract obligations throughout the country.[3]

Some political and economic centers of this sort may arise in premodern times and only later become centers for the spread of industry and the eventual transformation of their countries. Cairo in Egypt, Teheran in Iran, Moscow in the Soviet Union, Warsaw in Poland, Mexico City in Mexico, and Peking and Nanking in China are centers of this kind.

Wherever they keep growing on a sufficiently large scale, markets and money thus tend to mobilize people from their old habits and their local isolation. They promote a trend toward stronger and more effective government and, more often than not, toward political and administrative centralization as well. But the same mobilizing and modernizing process also promotes the rise of local and regional centers and activities; and these, in turn, generate demands for local and regional political autonomy and political power. In this manner the spread of money and the rise of markets will tend to foster both the growth of central governments, eager to monopolize power, and the rise of local and minority movements increasingly determined to resist them. Far from being a smooth pathway toward ever larger and more perfect integration, the road of economic and political modernization more often leads to growing political conflicts. Political stability may be threatened if existing or new institutions fail to adapt to these changes. Governments may thus be overthrown.

Cities also are gateways to modernity in another sense. Within their shelter there arise new occupa-

tions and new social classes, and these, in many countries, tend to organize themselves eventually for the pursuit of political power. In medieval Europe growing numbers of urban merchants and artisans were followed by the rise of guilds and often by the entry of these guilds and their members into political activity. Under more modern conditions factories, rather than artisans, and large corporations, rather than small merchants, have been the main carriers of economic modernization. But these larger firms, too, have tended to pursue their interests also in the field of active politics; and their workers and clerical employees have tended to form or join labor unions and to support labor-oriented parties and, thus, to enter deeply into politics of such different countries as Finland, Brazil, Cuba, India, and Japan. The spread of money and markets, the growth of cities and industry, and the increase of artisans, workers, and white-collar employees have to some degree transformed society and politics in every part of the world: first in northwestern Europe and the United States; later in central, Mediterranean, and eastern Europe and in Latin America; still later in China and India; and most recently in the Arab world and in black Africa.

External Bridgeheads of Modernity. In many countries, as in much of Western Europe, this process of modernization has grown autonomously. It was initiated mainly from domestic centers, and it has been sustained and enhanced mainly by domestic personnel and resources. In other countries, such as the Soviet Union and Japan, minor or transitory foreign centers, organizations, and individuals supplied some of the initiative, but the main developments were soon taken over and carried further by native and internal elements. In still other countries the main economic and financial activities have remained much longer concentrated in foreign hands, as in much of black Africa and Latin America; or at least the main commercial, industrial, and banking firms have remained foreign-owned and foreign-controlled, directly or

[3]To be sure, markets and money also function on the level of the international system, where there is no central world government to protect property and enforce laws and contract obligations. Such world trade and finance, however, function often less reliably, and they operate only with greater difficulties, risks, and costs. Private international trading and financial interests often are found among the supporters of a stronger system of international law and of agreements among governments that would make international transactions more stable and predictable and international contracts more enforceable.

indirectly, even though the large majority of low-level and middle-level personnel eventually came to be recruited from native—and much cheaper—labor. This latter pattern is still characteristic of much of Latin America, Asia, parts of Africa, and to a lesser degree even of parts of southern Europe.

Bridgehead Cities. In many cases, money, modern commerce, banking, transport, and industry all tend to be concentrated in a few foreign or foreign-dominated economic centers. These are usually located at the geographic periphery of the developing countries, usually at a port city, often of relatively recent origin. Examples are Bombay and Calcutta in India; Shanghai and Canton in China; Hong Kong, just off the Chinese coast; Singapore at the tip of the Malaysian peninsula; Buenos Aires in Argentina; Bahia, and later Rio de Janeiro in Brazil; Havana in Cuba; Oran in Algeria; Accra in Ghana; Lagos in Nigeria; Zanzibar and Dar es Salaam in Tanzania; and there are many more.

In other cases a foreign-dominated city may be established deeper inland, first as an administrative and military center, perhaps later becoming a commercial, financial, and industrial one as well. Such has been the role of Santiago in Chile, Lima in Peru, Delhi in India, Nairobi in Kenya, Salisbury in Zimbabwe (formerly Rhodesia), and Lusaka in Zambia.

Direct Foreign Rule. Often the impact of foreign-dominated geographic bridgeheads of modernity is supplemented or surpassed by that of direct foreign conquest and administration, followed by a substantial inflow of foreign settlers, as in Mexico, Brazil, Cuba, and elsewhere in Latin America; in the Republic of South Africa; in Kenya and Zimbabwe; in Algeria, Tunisia, and Madagascar. Such direct intrusion of foreign rule and foreign settlers tends to accelerate some aspects of the modernization process, such as the inflow of foreign capital, skills, and innovation. However, it often destroys, or makes difficult, a capacity for persisting local self-government by natives, and it tends to slow down other aspects of the same process, such as the development of skilled middle-level and higher-level native personnel in government, finance, industry, and large-scale commerce. It may also slow down the process of local capital formation and investment if foreign businesspeople and settlers get most of the higher salaries and profits and remit much of them back to their home countries. In Brazil and Mexico formal colonial empires lasted until the early nineteenth century and in Cuba until 1902.

Indirect Rule. Methods of indirect rule tend to be slower in spreading technical innovations and economic, political, cultural, and social change. But a capacity for local self-government persists far more effectively, even under colonial rule, than under direct rule and foreign settlement. Direct rule spreads change faster; indirect rule helps to retain the old order. Under this system a foreign power would leave a native sultan, rajah, sheikh, or tribal chieftain, usually with his entourage, in charge of the province, district, or tribe that traditionally had been under his authority, on condition that he henceforth would maintain a type of "law and order" and a general state of affairs favorable to the operations of foreign business interests, and sometimes to foreign settlers, and perhaps also to the strategic interests of the "protecting power"—with the latter often taking charge of all foreign political trade relations, major military matters, and, often, taxation and public finance. In exchange for his collaboration, the native ruler could henceforth count on the military and police support of the foreign power, not only against neighboring tribes or rulers, but also—and sometimes primarily—against his own subjects. In the past native chieftains could be deposed more or less freely by the members of the tribe whenever they became sufficiently unpopular. But they now became virtually irremovable, thanks to the backing of the seemingly invincible machine guns, cannon, and airplanes of the foreign power.

Usually these arrangements were extended to the priests or teachers of the locally established religion, who were protected against critics, heretics, or major religious rivals and who were aided, directly or indirectly, in their suppression. (Christian missionaries most often made so few converts that the power of the established religion and of its priests, teachers, or, among animist tribes, its witch doctors was not seriously threatened.) Similarly, indirect rule would protect the power and privileges of local landowners, high castes of priests or warriors, rich merchants or moneylenders, and the like. By this method, the foreign power not only avoided provoking popular resistance by upsetting native traditions and culture, but it actually changed the relationships of political power within the native community by making an alliance with its most powerful elements and giving them a vested interest in collaboration.

Past examples of indirect rule include the British rule of important parts of India through maharajahs and similar local rulers such as those of Travancore, Baroda, Hyderabad, and Kashmir until independence in 1947. Other examples are afforded by British rule through local and tribal chiefs in Ghana; through emirs and other rulers in northern Nigeria; through sheikhs of small, but oil-rich, sultanates or tribal territories in the Arab peninsula, such as Kuwait, Qatar, and Oman; and British backing for larger monarchies, such as Egypt, Jordan, and Saudi Arabia. The British and the Russians played similar roles as indirect rulers in Iran at least until the 1924 coup (discussed in the next chapter).

Though indirect rule slows down some aspects of modernization and perpetuates some old forms of oppression, injustice, and neglect, it still preserves a larger pool of native leadership talent. It offers more opportunities than does direct rule for the training and employment of new skilled native personnel; and it preserves a larger, deeper, and more varied stock of native cultural memories and symbols. At the same time, it avoids some of the worst effects of foreign conquests: the expulsion, in one form or another, of many natives from their land holdings—tribal, familial, or individual—and their replacement by white settlers who then tend to become bitter-end fighters against native equality and emancipation. The bloodshed that accompanied the eventual winning of independence of Kenya, Algeria, and Madagascar—all countries that then had many white settlers—contrasts with the relatively bloodless transition to independence of such countries as Morocco and Egypt, which earlier had been under indirect rule, and of Ghana, Nigeria, Senegal, and the Ivory Coast, all of which had few, if any, white settlers.

But formal political independence does not end the process of social and political modernization. In some cases, rather, it marks the beginning; in others, the gathering of speed and strength. How can we gauge the speed and strength of this process, and how can we estimate its probable outcome?

SOCIAL MOBILIZATION VERSUS CULTURAL ASSIMILATION: A RACE FOR THE DESTINY OF COUNTRIES

Developing countries—and let us recall that in some sense all countries today are developing—are being transformed by three broad types of social and economic processes: (1) processes of *growth,* which increase the number of persons or of their material possessions without changing immediately the structure of the society and the proportions among its elements; (2) processes of social *mobilization;* and (3) processes of *assimilation.* The interplay among these three types of processes of social and economic change goes far toward setting the choices of politics and the conditions under which political decisions must be made. Each type of process, therefore, deserves closer examination.

Processes of Growth. In most countries in the world the population increases at a rate of about 2 percent per year, and this is also the approximate mean and median growth rate for all 153 countries for which we have data. If growth should continue at this rate, the population of the world, and of each country, should double in about thirty-five years.

In many of the less highly developed countries, population growth is higher. While the crude birth rate for a country near the median, such as Brazil, is still a nearly traditional 38 per thousand, the death rate in that country already has been brought down to a nearly modern 9 per thousand, leaving a net population increase of as much as 29 per thousand. At this rate, typical of many countries at this stage of *demographic transition,* there will be twice as many Brazilians within about twenty-four years (not counting any future immigrants). Large developing countries such as India and Egypt are in the same situation. The general problem of the demographic transition, as many demographers see it, is illustrated in Figure 9.2. Literacy rates are used in the figure and below as a central measuring device for levels of development (the concept of literacy is discussed in a later section).

As the curves of the birth and death rates scissor apart because of an early fall in the death rate at a relatively early stage of development (represented, perhaps, by a 20 percent literacy level), the rate of population growth—which is roughly proportional to the distance between them—rises steeply and then often remains high, at 3 percent and more, until a much higher level of development. There, however, perhaps in the neighborhood of 80 percent literacy, birth rates in most countries start dropping sharply. (Venezuela offers a conspicuous exception, as shown in Figure 9.2). At high levels of development—with 90 percent literacy or more—birth rates then tend to be as low as 2 percent or less, and the rate of population growth goes down again to 1 percent or even 0.5 percent or less.

If a country had to start nearly from scratch, such as Upper Volta in Africa, and if it behaved as the average of countries in the recent past, it might require about seventy or eighty years to get to the 80 percent literacy level; it would spend about fifty years in the period of high population growth at 3 percent per year or more; and it should settle down at the end of this half century with 80 percent literacy or better—and presumably with other corresponding indicators of development—but with a population that is four times larger.

Fortunately, most countries do not have quite so far to go. India is today over a third literate (the figure was 28 percent around 1965); China and Cuba have virtually universal literacy; and the world average in 1975 was 73 percent for 140 countries. For much of humankind in the emerging states, therefore, the transition period of high population growth is likely to be over early in the next century. The populations of these countries may well double during this period, but thereafter their growth should slow down.

World population has grown in recent decades at about 2 percent per year; per capita income at about 3 percent; aggregate income, again as a world average, at about 5 percent; and world consumption of energy also at 5 percent. There has also been an annual increase of about 7 percent in many kinds of traffic and communications and in demands for a wide variety of services from all kinds of public and private agencies.[4]

The larger number of people makes society more complicated, leading to more and different kinds of interactions and conflicts. More people require more housing, streets, water, and utilities; more energy and fuels; more food, metals, and materials. Providing all these over the next thirty years will be almost impossible without many rearrangements in economic, social, and political practices and institutions. The growth in our sheer weight of numbers will work as a poorly directed, but powerful, engine for change.

[4]For data on telephone traffic, air travel, and other service loads, see Manfred Kochen and Karl W. Deutsch, "Toward a Rational Theory of Decentralization: Some Implications of a Mathematical Approach," *American Political Science Review* 63 (September 1969), 734–49, and especially p. 748 n. 16.

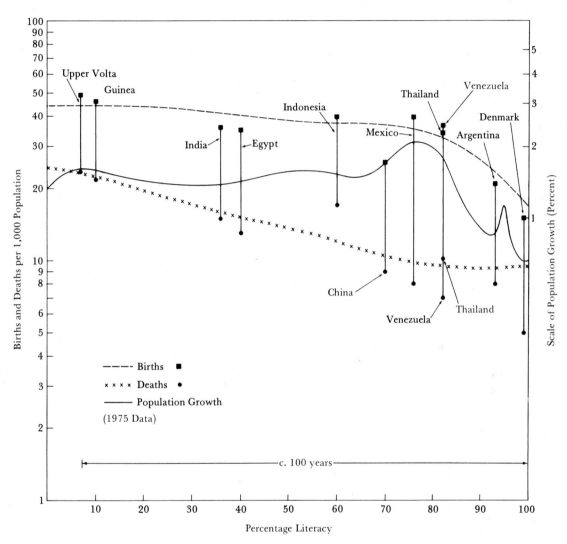

Note 1: The composite curve indicates the general process. Birth and death rates of particular countries are scattered around it, as shown.
Note 2: Other indicators of development will give substantially the same result as literacy does.
Note 3: The time scale of 100 years is based on the estimated annual shift into literacy of 1 percent of the population, and corresponding speeds of modernization in other respects. At slower rates of modernization, the demographic transition might take longer, and the resulting population increase would be higher.

Sources: For birth and death rates and percentage population growth: *World Development Report, 1978* (Washington: World Book, 1978), table 15, pp. 104–5. For percentage literacy: Ruth Leger Sivard, *World Military and Social Expenditures, 1978* (Leesburg, Va.: WMSE Publications, 1978), pp. 24–28.

Pressures from Migration. In certain sectors the impact of demographic growth will be reinforced, or even overshadowed, by the *impact of migration.* About 0.15 percent long-term foreign immigrants per year were reported in the early 1960s for such countries as the United States, Britain, France, and West Germany; about 0.1 percent for Brazil; but between 1.2 and 1.8 percent for Australia, Canada, and Venezuela. By the late 1960s the proportions had risen slightly to 0.2 percent for the United States and France and to 0.4 percent for the United Kingdom.[5] Short-term migrants and foreign "guest workers" greatly exceed these percentages in many countries; and the figures for *internal migration,* from villages to towns and cities, from towns to large cities, and from city to city, do so still more. The houses, wells, streets, and sewers—such as they may be—left behind by migrants from a town or district losing population become largely useless, whereas in the fast-growing regions and areas where the migrants congregate, a mounting demand is generated for new housing, utilities, and infrastructure installations such as hospitals and schools. Often the demand is not met. Guest workers in Western Europe are often poorly housed; the housing for inhabitants of the shantytowns on the fringes of many big cities in Latin America, Asia, and Africa is worse; and the potential for newer kinds of political activities and the needs for newer and more urban services are apt to increase.

On an average for the world about 0.4 percent of the population has been moving each year into cities of more than 100,000 inhabitants. In many countries the figures are higher; this entire movement is very hard to stop. But the process of development not only mobilizes some people's bodies for migration. It also mobilizes larger numbers for changes of occupation, even though not all of them may change their residence; and it mobilizes still larger numbers for new forms of

communications and for new dimensions of imagination and thought.

Changes of Occupation. Every year, on the average about 0.6 percent of the work force in the developing countries leaves its employment in agriculture and shifts to nonagricultural pursuits. A smaller, but substantial, number—perhaps 0.4 percent per year—moves from self-employment or family-type work into wage-earning or salaried positions; but only about 0.2 percent per year move into employment in industry. By now, almost one-half of humankind—47 percent in 1977—has ceased to work in agriculture.[6] This vast change in the occupational structure of most countries will continue to be a major and unceasing force for political and social change for the next half century or more.

Changes in Communication. Modern life is penetrating most regions of the world with ever new demonstrations of human powers and possibilities. Every airplane overhead demonstrates that people can fly. Every truck, jeep, or station wagon passing on the road or through a village demonstrates a new scale of speed and power. Every advertising poster, every shop window, every mail-order catalog, and every market with factory-made goods demonstrates the possibility of new riches. Every hospital, pharmacy, or patent medicine sales outlet demonstrates that diseases, far from being ordained by fate, might be cured by human effort—which governments might have to organize. And every bit of money, every coin that people touch, and every purchase or sale for money that they learn to make introduces them to a world of possible rationality and calculation and to the possibility of having to deal, seriously and continuously, with a succession of relative strangers. Such demonstration effects reach each year an addition-

[5]Russett et al., *World Handbook I,* p. 233; *United Nations Demographic Yearbook, 1970* (United Nations, 1971), pp. 754–55.

[6]*FAO Production Yearbook, 1977,* vol. 31 (Food and Agriculture Organization, United Nations, 1978), pp. 61–62.

al fraction of the population of many developing countries, pushing back the realm of subsistence economy, barter, and work within the family.

The *impact of mass media* works in the same direction. About 2 percent of the population of many countries enter the radio audience each year; about 0.5 percent of families per year are newly reached by newspapers and periodicals; 0.7 percent of families start watching television. (This is again an average figure; in richer countries television has been spreading faster.) Still others are reached first by motion pictures. The new film industries of India, Japan, the Arab world, Mexico, Brazil, Cuba, and China are adding to the mass impact of the older ones of the United States, Western Europe, and the Soviet Union.

Still more important in its depth of impact is the spread of literacy, which now proceeds at an average rate of about 2 percent per year. This is the proportion of the population over age fifteen that is being added each year to the proportion already literate. Most of this rapid rise in literacy is occurring in the Far East and the Near East; in southern Asia, Latin America, and Africa current changes are slower.[7] On this basis we may then say that for many countries the shift from 5 to 10 percent literacy (the level of Ethiopia, Upper Volta, or Guinea) to about 95 percent (the level of Italy and China) can be accomplished within two or three generations, as indicated on the time scale in Figure 9.2.

The mobilization into literacy is a more fundamental change, since it opens so many different sources of stimulation and information to people, and since it tends to support and enhance autonomous thought and activity more than mere passive participation in the mass media audience could do. What is most important for the political effects of the mass media on political development is not so much how they compete with one another, but rather how they supplement and reinforce one

another in mobilizing the imagination and aspirations of a growing number of individuals.

This ability to imagine oneself at different places and in different social roles is—as the social scientist Daniel Lerner has pointed out—a major internal aspect of social mobilization.[8] It takes place within the mind of each individual, but it also can occur within the small worlds of many families and groups. To imagine oneself a sailor or a cowpuncher, a monarch or a revolutionary, a factory worker or a business executive, a detective or a criminal, a colonel or a spy—all this one learns from books, films, plays on the stage or in the streets, newspapers, radio, and television. But once a person has learned it, his or her intellectual and emotional worlds—and the world of perceived political possibilities and choices—will never be the same.

The Interlocking Processes of Social Mobilization: A Composite Picture. The various components of *social mobilization* tend to grow at different speeds. Yet, with only rare exceptions, they all operate in the same direction. They are clearly correlated with each other. If one indicator—such as per capita income—grows, then other indicators—such as literacy or the proportion of radios or physicians to the population—will also grow. It seems legitimate, therefore, to look at most of them as different indicators of one and the same underlying process, whose components tend to reinforce each other. Increased literacy will increase the expectable audience of newspapers, and the availability of newspapers and periodicals will increase the motivation to become literate. A news story in the press may stimulate curiosity to find out what happened next and to find out more quickly from the radio; and a short news item on the radio may stimulate interest to read more about it in the papers. Demonstration and mass

[7]From data in Ruth Legar Sivard, *World Military and Social Expenditures, 1974* and *1978* (Leesburg, Va.: WMSE Publications, 1974 and 1978).

[8]See Daniel Lerner, *The Passing of Traditional Society* (New York: Free Press, 1956).

media effects stimulate the desire for money to buy some of the new things seen or shown; and money buys more opportunities to watch or listen to such demonstrations and such media.

Countries that are still almost entirely traditional have, of course, only slow *rates of mobilization,* as indicated by the spread of literacy and similar indicators. Very highly developed countries, on the other hand, usually have not many people left to learn to read, so their indicators also will be low. It is mainly in the range between 10 and 90 percent of literacy, or of other indicators, that rates of social mobilization will be fast.

The scheme in Figure 9.3 illustrates this point. It should be noted that the growth of industrial employment in the 1970s has slowed down in many countries, adding the strains of greater unemployment or underemployment to those of the mobilizing process.

Social mobilization makes people more available for change. It does so by inducing them or teaching them to change their residence, their occupations, their communications, their associates, and their outlook and imagination. It gives rise to new needs, new aspirations, new demands and capabilities. But all these new patterns of behavior may disunite a population or unite it. They can make people more similar or more different. They may produce cooperation or strife, integration or secession. To learn to judge the probable outcome in each case, we must now turn our attention to the problem of assimilation.

Assimilation: The Concept and the Process. Assimilation is a special case of social learning. It is the learning of habits of behavior that are so similar to the habits of another person, or a group, that the behavior of the *assimilated* person cannot be distinguished readily or reliably from that of the person or group to whom he or she has become assimilated. Assimilation is, therefore, a matter of degree. People's behavior may be more or less similar, more or less easily distinguishable by themselves or by outside observers. Nonetheless, there is a

FIGURE 9.3 *How the Speed of Further Social Mobilization Changes with the Levels Already Attained: A Schematic Presentation*

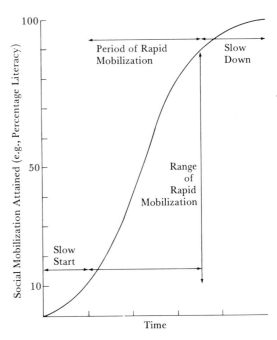

Note: The changing slope of the curve represents the changing speeds of further mobilization.

critical threshold in assimilation to a group, a culture, or a people. This threshold is marked by the *ability to pass* as a member of the group. In somewhat more technical terms, an assimilated member of a long-established group has passed this threshold if anyone's judgments about the membership of this person will have the same distribution of errors as would be found in such judgments about any other member of the group.

The same reasoning applies to the degree of assimilation among two or more groups. A group is assimilated to another if its members can no longer be distinguished effectively from their counterparts in the other group.

Dimensions of Assimilation. Assimilation can occur in regard to many different aspects of behavior. Eight among these are outstanding for their political significance: assimilation of (1) language; (2) culture; (3) ethnicity with its social associations, organizational memberships, and family connections; (4) aspirations; (5) capabilities; (6) attainments; (7) civic compliance; and (8) political loyalties.

Any two or more of these aspects of behavior, or even all of them, of course, may coincide in some particular case and work in the same direction. To the extent that they do so, they will tend to reinforce one another and form an interlocking structure that may be stronger than the sum of its components. Anyone who has learned English as it is spoken habitually in the United States, perhaps even without an accent; who has become steeped in childhood memories, education, and culture common in the United States; who has entered deeply into the old-stock community in terms of personal friendships, social associations, ties of intermarriage, and family connections in the United States; who has learned to have aspirations and values, such as those of mobility, equality, success, and wealth characteristic of many people in the United States; who has developed the capabilities needed and valued in United States culture, such as competence, efficiency, capacity for hard work, skill, energy, persistence, initiative, a talent both for self-direction and for cooperation with others, together with a reasonably discriminating capacity for showing trust and being trusted; who has attained the characteristic level of rewards of U.S. culture in terms of health, wealth, knowledge, and respect; who obeys laws in the manner most other U.S. citizens do; and who will actively support U.S. interests and institutions to the same degree as other citizens do—such a person will indeed have become a U.S. citizen in every significant way.

Similar checklists for these eight dimensions of assimilation could be made for the assimilation to British, French, German, Soviet, or Chinese Communist culture.

Assimilation and Marginality. In many actual cases, however, assimilation may not proceed equally in all dimensions. Individuals may learn the vocabulary and grammar of a language, but retain a distinctive accent; they may acquire U.S. work habits, but remain ignorant of much of the rest of the culture; or they may come to share aspirations of wealth and status, but fall short of the standards of skill, competence, initiative, efficiency, and self-direction in sustained hard work that prevail in the United States. Still others may be fully assimilated in terms of both aspirations and capabilities, but may continue to avoid and discourage intermarriage outside their smaller ethnic or religious group, and they may tend to keep their closest friendships and major social ties within its confines.

Wherever assimilation in one or more of these dimensions is absent, or where the degree of assimilation in two or more of these dimensions differs substantially, there we are likely to find groups that have remained *marginal* in the community toward which their uneven and incomplete steps of assimilation had been directed.

Assimilation and Acceptance. Success in some dimensions of assimilation, moreover, does not depend only on the efforts of groups or persons making them. In regard to language, culture, and capabilities, the existing speech habits and culture patterns may ease their task or make it much more difficult. Entry into an ethnic community through intermarriage, family connections, friendship ties, and social associations depends on the *social acceptance* of the would-be assimilant by the members of the group. Even more critically, and sometimes tragically, the assimilation of attainments even by highly skilled and hard-working outsiders or by members of minority groups may depend critically on the absence of *discrimination,* explicit or implied.

Members of the established in-group or the favored ethnic or social group would have to be willing to accept the work and other contributions of the would-be assimilants on equal terms, and these terms themselves would have to avoid any concealed form of actual discrimination.[9]

The outcome of the process of assimilation, and the different forms and degrees of merging or marginality that it is likely to produce in various cases, will thus depend on the interplay of assimilation in all eight dimensions and also on the interplay of efforts at assimilation and acceptance within some of them. Often this interplay tends to have a major effect on the motives for making continued efforts at assimilation (or else for abandoning them) and for learning or unlearning assimilated habits.

Motives for Assimilation or Disassimilation. Why should people try to unlearn old habits and endeavor to learn new ones? And even if they made no conscious efforts of this kind, why should they learn these new habits, anyway?

We have said that assimilation is a form of social learning. Like all learning, it requires a drive—a need or imbalance—that will tend to move the person, group, or learning system away from its present state and toward some "preferable" or "goal" state in which this actor's inner drive or disequilibrium will be reduced. People who are assimilating do so, first of all, because in their unassimilated state they lack something that they need. This missing something may be physical or emotional security, as in the case of refugees; or economic or social opportunity, as in the case of many economically motivated immigrants; or better chances in employment, career, or business, which are available to the speakers of the favored language and members of the favored ethnic

group; or the greater richness of knowledge, beauty, and prestige that a more highly developed language and culture may offer. Others may be moved by the desire to belong to a stable and well-identified group and to be accepted by it; this motive has been measured by the psychologist Daniel McClelland under the name of *need for affiliation.* Or there may be a combination of several needs, deficiencies, or hungers that drive persons or groups to forsake a part of their earlier identity and to enter the pathway of assimilation.

Another element of social mobilization may be even more crucial. It is the presence or absence of *rewards for assimilation* and the terms and conditions under which they are available. If relatively moderate efforts at and small increments in some dimensions of assimilation are positively and readily rewarded materially and emotionally, these rewards will tend to reinforce the behavior and elicit further efforts at learning. If there continue to be no such rewards, or if they are forthcoming only after discouragingly long delays and under difficult conditions, most people are likely to reduce or give up further efforts at assimilation, and they may even unlearn some or much of the assimilated habits already acquired.

In such cases the process may reverse, for there may also be *rewards* available from *differentiation and secession:* from setting up one's own distinctive group, from striving for its independence from the dominant language, nationality, or country, or even from striving for its predominance. If the ruling nationality fails to reward assimilation, and if it lets its language and culture become associated with repeated experiences of frustration and oppression, while the different language and culture of a submerged group remain attractive and rewarding to them and their fellows, then the members may unlearn some of their assimilated ways, and their children may do so even more. They all may then prefer to strengthen the distinctiveness, language, cultural cohesion, and political solidarity of their own, still-disadvantaged group

[9]Examples are, "On this program all fashion models and television announcers, black or white, must have thin lips and long straight hair"; or "Any employee, man or woman, will be discharged in case of pregnancy"; or "Each candidate for this scholarship must prove that he or she has only American-born grandparents."

and to struggle for its independence and power in the future.

Experience has shown that attempts by the government to penalize such behavior are likely to make matters worse, often tending to produce more resentment than genuine compliance and loyalty. In this manner some Algerian *évolués*—Arabs who are assimilated to French language and culture—of the 1930s, such as Ferhat Abbas, were disappointed by continuing French privilege and unresponsiveness and eventually turned into leaders of the Arab-oriented Algerian independence movement in the 1950s.

Similarly, the partial assimilation of many Jews in the Soviet Union to the Russian language and to Soviet culture and political loyalty during the 1920s and early 1930s was reinforced for a time by the granting of equal rights, by the successes of economic modernization, and by the threat of Hitler's Germany. The process was eventually reversed for at least some of them, however, by Stalin's persecutions and later by the continued frustration of the rising aspirations and self-confidence of many Soviet Jews who found top positions more often barred to them, as they saw it, than to their non-Jewish competitors. Perhaps also the rising attractiveness of the new state of Israel, between its victorious war against Egypt in 1967 and the indecisive Egyptian attack of 1973, was a contributing factor. Since other Soviet Jews have continued to identify themselves culturally, politically, and emotionally with the Soviet Union, the social learning processes of assimilation and disassimilation seem to have divided what was earlier a relatively more homogenous community of Soviet Jews.

In each specific case the outcome of the learning process of assimilation will depend on the interplay of specific conditions and processes along the various major dimensions that were surveyed above. In order to enable each of us to study any such case more thoroughly by ourselves, it will be helpful to take a closer look at least at some of the balances or imbalances among the rates of change in these different dimensions.

The Imbalance Between Social Mobilization and Assimilation. Most is known about the assimilation of language groups. They are more easily identified; the language spoken habitually or customarily in their homes can be ascertained. With the spread of systems of military conscription and public education, the language that soldiers or schoolchildren actually speak and understand acquires obvious public importance.

Linguistic assimilation of larger settled populations to any other language proceeds very slowly. The average rate of their shift to the favored or predominant language is only about 0.15 percent per year ± 0.25: that is, between 0.4 percent per year under the most favorable conditions and -0.1 per year under the least favorable ones.[10] In the latter case, therefore, linguistic assimilation will be reversed, and people will actually shift away from the language of the favored group and back into the language of the disfavored one, albeit slowly.

Even at best, then, the average speed of linguistic assimilation is less than one-half of that of the shift into literacy, which now is about 2 percent per year, and under more normal circumstances it will be only about one-sixth of the latter. In any case it will be much less than the rate of entry into the radio audience or into the circle of users of money. It is much slower, in short, than many of the processes of social mobilization; the latter, therefore, will tend to produce in many multilingual countries growing numbers of socially mobilized, but linguistically unassimilated, people, displaying potential for linguistic and political conflict.

Something similar will hold for the spread of radio, newspapers, and other mass media into the countryside. Of every five or six rural people mobilized into the mass media audience, only one will be likely to learn the predominant language.

[10]K. W. Deutsch, *Tides Among Nations* (New York: Free Press, 1977), pp. 304–6.

The other four or five will furnish a ready-made public for a new literature and mass culture in the formerly submerged popular language or languages and an array of new writers, reporters, editors, and publishers in those newly risen idioms. The spread of school enrollment and literacy tends to have similar effects, since most of the new reading and schooling has to be for the unassimilated population and their children; it has to be done in their native language, by teachers who know it well and are recruited, ever more often, from this native group itself. The teachers, like the editors and writers, soon tend to become available as the intellectuals and potential spokespeople and leaders of the formerly submerged nationality groups, often in a struggle against their privileged neighbors.

Similar imbalances exist among other dimensions of assimilation. The assimilation of aspirations spreads almost as fast as the results of demonstration effects and membership in mass media audiences, but the assimilation of capabilities is likely to proceed much more slowly. Aspirations in developing countries or among emerging peoples tend to grow much faster than the peoples' capabilities to attain them. This has some striking implications. A schematic example is shown in Figure 9.4.

If the spread of modern aspirations throughout the population of some country (or the members of some ethnic group) should take about 40 years, then the corresponding period for assimilation of capabilities by the entire population will be 120 years. During this period many members of the population will experience a real gap between aspirations and capabilities, and their numbers will grow quickly. Already, after the first 10 years one-sixth of the population, and after 20 years one-third of the people, will have greater aspirations than capabilities. From the thirtieth to the sixtieth year a majority of them will feel the gap; in the fortieth year the maximum number, two-

thirds of the population, will be reached. These are not good prospects for political stability.[11]

The Payoff: Attainments. Aspirations and capabilities produce attainments in different values. Even a brief look at the data suggests that some processes of attainment might take a long time. The gap between average black and white earnings in the United States in 1977 was about 100:57; if some past rates of change should continue, it may be closed within about fifty or sixty years. But the gap between the wealth of the highly developed countries and the poverty of much of the emerging world would take, even at best, more than one hundred years to close, if an international action to that end were begun today—one large enough to redistribute each year about 4 or 5 percent of world income—and if it did so in the most effective manner. This is unlikely to happen just now—although it may come to pass within the lifetime of today's students—and under current practices the huge income gaps among rich and poor nations seem likely to persist for centuries.

The large gaps in levels of health, life expectancy, and educational attainment are closing somewhat more quickly among nations, and they have become smaller within many of them. But within the United States the smaller gap of about 8 percent between white and black life expectancies and the gap between white and black years of completed education—about 4 percent in 1977, or fourteen years, as opposed to thirteen and one-half—seem to have changed but little in the last ten

[11]Slower rates of assimilation of aspirations and capabilities would make matters worse, as long as the 3:1 ratio between the two rates remained (and which is reflected in Figure 9.4 for purposes of illustration). Cutting all speeds in half, 1.25 percent per year for the spread of aspirations and 0.42 percent for that of capabilities, would merely double the length of the whole process, including the duration of the period of very large gaps between the population with new aspirations and the much smaller one that would have new capabilities as well. A more than 50 percent gap would then persist not for thirty, but for sixty years.

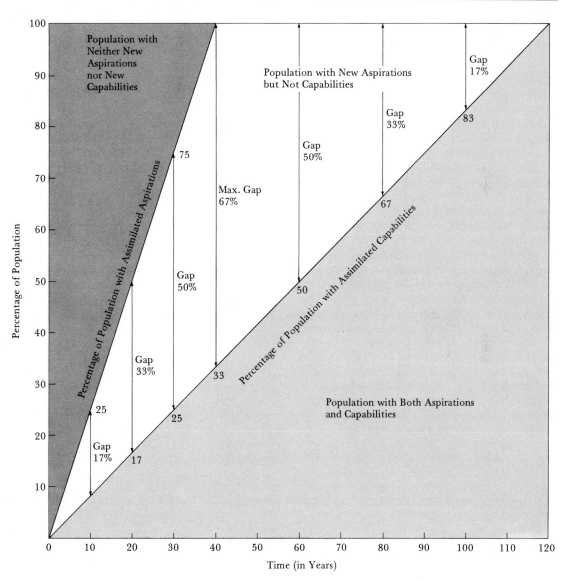

FIGURE 9.4 *A Quick Learning of Aspirations Versus Slower Learning of Capabilities: A Schematic Presentation*

Assumptions: Rate of assimilation: of aspirations, 2.5 percent per annum; of capabilities, 0.83 percent per annum. Both are estimates for illustrative purposes.

Note: If the speeds of both assimilation rates were cut in half, all time periods would double but the vertical dimensions of the diagram would remain unchanged. The maximum gap would still be 67 percent, but it would be reached in 80 years, not 40, and a gap of 33 percent or more would persist not for 90 years but for 180.

years; and these percentage figures ignore any differences in the quality of the health care and schooling actually available to blacks and whites. Yet the achievement of such material attainments might well be reached within the next thirty to fifty years, should a serious political effort in that direction be resumed. Internationally, too, levels of health might be brought fairly close together, at Western levels or higher ones, within the next half century. Differences in educational levels among states might be reduced considerably within the next one or two centuries. The linguistic diversity of the world, however, including notably the emerging states, seems likely to remain large for at least two hundred years, and most probably longer, if present rates of linguistic assimilation should continue.

Finally, rates of intermarriage among blacks and whites in the United States were so low up to the 1950s and early 1960s that it was calculated by Michael Leiserson that assimilation in regard to intermarriage in the United States—that is, making interracial marriages about as frequent as could be expected from a model of random pairing—would take more than nine hundred years to reach. To be sure, rates of intermarriage can change strikingly, from less than 3 percent to more than 30 percent within about thirty years, as they did among some Jewish groups in the United States between the 1920s and the 1950s. In the world at large, however, most of the 950 million Chinese, the 630 million Indians, and the over 300 million black Africans south of the Sahara are overwhelmingly likely to marry within their own respective racial groups. Even though smaller subgroups, such as some African tribes, may come to experience much higher rates of intermarriage with other tribes in their countries, the large racial divisions of humankind—Far Eastern, southern Asian, and black African in particular—are likely to persist for another five hundred or one thousand years or still longer.

The major languages and races of the world will not be wiped out any time soon by assimilation. It is unrealistic to expect them to merge quickly.

What can be done is to help to improve relations among them and to improve the position of the diverse individuals, lovers, friends, and families within each language group or race, providing them with full opportunities to reach out for human ties beyond their boundaries.

AN OVERVIEW OF POLITICS IN THE EMERGING COUNTRIES

We have traced at some length several characteristics of the emerging countries: their incomplete transition from tradition to modernity; their partial dependence on the particular content of the traditional cultural, social, and economic heritage; and the race among the several processes of fundamental change, particularly that between the processes of social mobilization and linguistic, cultural, and political assimilation, which does so much to set the conditions for the political development of each country.

Now we shall turn to the basic political issues and decisions in the emerging countries. We cannot treat these countries here in the manner of the states that have been discussed earlier in this book in relative detail. The emerging states are too numerous and too diversified for that. But a brief look at a few major issues may aid the reader in analyzing one or another of these emerging states on his or her own. Additional information on seven such countries is presented in the next two chapters.

The first issue in almost every such country has been *independence,* usually from some colonial power, sometimes also from indirect forms of foreign hegemony and military, political, and financial control. There is great variation, however, in the timing and process of the achievement of independence among the seven less developed countries under study. Brazil and Mexico achieved their independence by the third decade of the nineteenth century, making them just a bit younger than the United States as sovereign states. At the opposite end of the spectrum lies Nigeria, the most recently independent state we will examine. These states' ways to independence are also quite different. For example, Brazil, Mexico, Nigeria, and India can all point to a single date of formal independence. Cuban independence, however, points to two dates: in 1902, virtual independence was achieved, but under a formal U.S. protectorate that lasted until 1934. Egyptian independence was recovered gradually during the twentieth century. And Iran never formally lost its independence, even though, in fact, it had been subjugated by foreign powers that limited its exercise of sovereign rights. These were also regained gradually during the twentieth century. Yet another difference is the degree of violence needed to achieve independence. Mexico and Cuba witnessed bloody wars of independence. Nigerian independence required virtually no violence, and Brazil's very little. Moderate amounts of violence were required in Iran, less in Egypt, and primarily nonviolent civil disobedience was used in India.

A closely related second issue is the continuity of regime types and freedom from external conquest after independence has been achieved. None of these seven states was conquered by a foreign power after independence was achieved in the twentieth century (although Egypt voluntarily submerged its independence—while keeping its pre-eminence—into the United Arab Republic with Syria from 1958 to 1961). Mexico was invaded, however, and almost conquered, by foreign (especially French) troops in the 1860s seeking to establish an empire under Archduke Maximilian of Austria. Mexico also lost vast territories to the United States in the 1840s through war, and it was invaded by U.S. troops as recently as the second decade of the twentieth century. Mexico was also marked by major changes in regime: it was twice an independent empire in the nineteenth century (briefly in the 1820s and again in the 1860s), although it has been a republic since the 1860s. Brazil, too, was an independent empire until 1889, when it became a republic. Egypt was an indepen-

dent monarchy until 1952, and Iran was one until 1979, when both became republics. Perhaps the most dramatic changes, however, occurred as a result of major revolutions that brought new regimes to power in Mexico during the second decade of the twentieth century, in Cuba in 1959, and in Iran in 1979.

The arena of politics has been further affected by the fact that all but Nigeria (which suffered a major civil war) have experienced international wars. Mexico's have already been mentioned. Brazil went to war primarily in the nineteenth century; in the twentieth century, its only participation in international war was a modest but not insignificant contribution to the Allied effort in World War II. Egypt has fought four major wars against Israel since the 1940s (in 1956 it also faced France and the United Kingdom) and another war in Yemen in the early 1960s. India has fought Pakistan three times since their independence, China once, and it conquered Portuguese territories on the Indian subcontinent by force. Cuba has sent troops in the 1970s to fight major wars in Angola and in the Horn of Africa, and it has been involved in a host of other, smaller military conflicts. Iran's major international confrontations occurred earlier in connection with its efforts to maintain its independence. But in recent years it has occupied some islands in the Persian Gulf by force, and it went to war with Iraq in 1980 over the delimitation of boundaries and general regional influence.

The third general issue is *stability:* how to preserve the property, interests, and positions of the dominant elements within the national territory or in the national society. These dominant elements and institutions may be landowners, bankers, merchants, or manufacturers, native or foreign (in which case the stability and independence issues may be in conflict). Or they may be the leaders, party members, and officials of a Communist regime, with their state-owned industries, collective institutions, and vivid desire to keep their regime, its institutions, and development plans from being overthrown.

None of the seven less developed countries has today the same type of political order it had when it became independent, uninterrupted by coups or unconstitutional alterations of the political system. India, however, approximates that kind of stability the most. Only once, and briefly, in the mid-1970s, when Prime Minister Indira Gandhi proclaimed an "emergency" and proceeded to rule arbitrarily, was the Indian constitutional order broken. But even then, Mrs. Gandhi held elections and the opposition won. In addition, India's political economy has also shown considerable continuity. There is an important role for both private and public enterprises under the guidance of national plans.

The next closest approximation of that kind of stability is provided by Nigeria and Brazil. Their political economy has altered only very gradually over time. There has always been an important role for private (including foreign) business, but the role of state enterprises, and of government regulation, has increased in both nations over time. Both countries, however, have witnessed several military coups that have broken the constitutional order (and earlier Brazil also witnessed a shift from an empire to a republic), and Nigeria fought a civil war.

Next in order of stability come Egypt and Mexico. Each witnessed a major shift of political order in the twentieth century—Mexico through a bloody and prolonged revolution, and Egypt through a military coup that overthrew the monarchy. In each case, major confrontations followed with foreign governments; the property of a number of foreign firms was expropriated. The state assumed rather quickly a much larger, and at times sudden, role in the economy than in the past. Since each of the major events became somewhat consolidated, the new order has proved more stable than in the past—much more so, however, in Mexico than in Egypt.

Finally, there are Iran and Cuba. Iran had endured forced abdications and assassinations of its monarchs repeatedly during its modern history; Cuba had witnessed several coups since independence. What sets them apart is that each experienced a major revolution that has already changed, in the case of Cuba, and that promises to change, in the case of Iran, major features of social, economic, and political life well beyond the changes experienced in the other countries under discussion. These, too, have had major fights with foreign governments and foreign corporations and have redefined the nature of the country's political economy drastically. Unlike Egypt and Mexico, however, Cuba and Iran have yet to go through an orderly postrevolutionary political succession, that is, a peaceful transfer of power from Castro and Khomeini to their successors (it is likely that, because of the latter's advanced age, Iran will face this question sooner).

The fourth issue is *development* itself—the change from poverty to prosperity, illiteracy to widespread education, an obsolete technology to a modern one, inefficiency to competence, high death rates to low ones, national impotence to national power. The emphasis on this or that element in the mixture may vary, but the basic thrust remains the same, and it goes far in determining what politics is all about.

There are great variations in development strategy, which will be detailed in subsequent chapters. However, it may be useful here to point to some key common elements. Except for Cuba, where the private sector is limited to a minority of agricultural production and to relatively insignificant petty services, the six other less developed countries allocate an important role to the private sector. Again, except for Cuba, all permit, in addition, the operations of foreign firms within their national territories (although the situation in Iran is unsettled as of this writing). But all restrict to some important degree the economic sectors into which foreign businesses may enter, and they regulate the conditions of their operations as well as their relations with the national government, national business, and labor. Moreover, state enterprises have become influential in the politics, economics, and social life of the nations. They are particularly important in such sectors as petroleum, mining, public utilities, and steel, even though there are variations from country to country. In none of them is development left simply to the interplay of private economic and social forces; in all of them the state has assumed considerable responsibility for the direction, shaping, and often the implementation of the development process.

The Stakes of Politics. In many developing countries the stakes of politics are at times almost all-encompassing. They include the independence of the country, or its continuation in colonial status, or its relapse into a colonial position or into some disguised form of dependence—military, political, or economic—in what is now sometimes called a pattern of *neocolonialism*.

At stake in some critical periods may also be the social order of the country. Is it to be Communist or anti-Communist (and, hence, probably capitalist in its economic orientation)? Or is it to be a search for a "third force," a form of African socialism, or an Indian or Asian variety thereof? Which class or classes are to rule or to have the most influence? Which regions and which ethnic groups are to have the best opportunities for getting influence and favors in politics, economics, and social life?

The entire character of the national culture—as well as the national language—may be at stake in domestic affairs. So may be the country's relationship to the great international alliance systems in its military and foreign policy and, hence, its probable sources and amounts of foreign economic aid.

We have already seen that the stakes of politics have been very high in the seven less developed countries. One, Cuba, shifted toward communism. All the others have witnessed major political struggles during their independent histories that have profoundly affected the internal distribution of resources. Ethnic and regional struggles have thus far had their greatest effect on the stakes of

politics in Nigeria, where one of the country's largest ethnolinguistic communities—the Ibos, disproportionately concentrated in the country's southeast—attempted unsuccessfully to secede in the late 1960s to form the independent state of Biafra. They were prevented from doing so only because they lost a brutal civil war. India has been the second country most affected in its contemporary history by ethnic and linguistic conflict. Although there has been no secession and no civil war over these issues, the states of India underwent massive reorganization in the 1950s (with more gradual changes since then) to respond to ethnic, linguistic, and regional pressures. Many state policies are strongly affected by India's great diversity.

Whereas India and Nigeria are comprised of a large number of languages, religions, cultures, and customs, Egypt and Iran are marked by the pre-eminence of a single group but with the persistence of some diversity that is still relevant for politics. In Egypt, for example, although Sunni Muslims predominate, Coptic Christians are an important religious minority, and there are also substantial regional variations. Iranian Shi'ites predominate overwhelmingly in Iran, but there are several important ethnic or religious minorities, some of whom took up arms against the majority after the 1979 revolution, especially Arabs and Kurds.

Cuba, Mexico, and Brazil stand in contrast to these other states. Apart from a relatively small foreign community, Spanish is the only language spoken in Cuba. But for a small number of Indians, Portuguese is the only language spoken in Brazil (again excepting a small foreign community). Spanish is overwhelmingly preponderant in Mexico, but about a million of its citizens speak no Spanish—only the ancient Indian languages—and another 1 or 2 million speak both Spanish and one or more Indian languages. Both Cuba and Brazil have a large black minority; Mexico's population includes a large proportion of people who are still culturally Indian, even if they may have forgotten, or never learned, the language of their ancestors.

An important political contrast between the three Latin American countries and the other four less developed countries has been the absence of overt, politicized ethnic conflict. Mexico has not had a political party or movement based on race, language, or color since the revolution in the 1910s. Cuba's last black political party was crushed violently at about that same time. Brazil, too, has been free of ethnic party politics, although it has a small black civil rights political movement in the early 1980s, and it had a small black political party that was suppressed in the 1930s. Ethnicity matters informally in the social structure, in the distribution of wealth, status, power, and education of the three Latin American countries, but, surprisingly perhaps, it has not served as the basis for the kind of political organization and conflict evident in other countries.

Mexico and Cuba (though not Brazil) approximate other countries more on the question of religion as a subject for political conflict. Mexico, overwhelmingly Roman Catholic, witnessed a civil war between church and state in the late 1920s, and several times before then, over the powers and privileges of the church. Predominantly but only nominally Roman Catholic, Cuba witnessed a major political conflict between church and state in the 1960s that sharply curtailed the former's role in Cuban society, whose scars still remain today.

One set of major stakes is likely to recur. It is the issue of civilian or military government, of *constitutionalism or authoritarian dictatorship*. When the military take power in an emerging country, they often do so in the name of stability—that is, in the defense of property and the present highly unequal distribution of social and economic opportunities and status. Military governments that promote even modest social and political reforms are relatively rare. There are, however, some exceptions: Kemal Atatürk's regime in the Turkey of the 1920s; the military or semimilitary regimes of Mexican revolution, from General Venustiano Carranza in 1917 to Lázaro Cárdenas in the 1930s; the military regime that ruled Peru from 1968 to 1980; and the Argentine regime of General Juan

Perón and its offshoot, the Peronista Party that won an Argentine election of 1973, but has been kept out of power by the current military dictatorship headed by General Videla. All these military governments were involved in reforms and efforts at limited social change that were not trivial.[12] Whether these developments will prove significant enough to change in the future the predominantly conservative role of the military in the emerging nations remains to be seen.

There is considerable variation in the propensity for military intervention in politics in the seven countries, as well as in the form it takes. Independent India has never had a military coup, although the armed forces acquiesced in Prime Minister Gandhi's declaration of an "emergency" in 1975. Mexico has had no unconstitutional transfer of power since the election of Lázaro Cárdenas in 1934. At the other end of the spectrum, independent Nigeria has been governed mostly by the military, and Brazil has had only military officers serving as the country's president since 1964 (although civilians have prominent roles in other positions in the government). In between these extremes, the armed forces have never ruled Iran directly, but they were essential to the monarchy's survival until the 1979 revolution. In Cuba, although the revolutionary military officers that won in 1959 have been important in many posts, and military means have at times been used in the conduct of social and economic policy, the armed forces as such do not rule, and have never ruled directly since Cuba became independent, but they

[12]The temporary participation of Chilean army leaders in President Salvador Allende's Marxist-oriented government in the winter of 1972–73 and the orderly return to a fully civilian cabinet in the spring of 1973 seemed for a time to point in the same direction. In September 1973, however, a right-wing group of military, naval, and air force generals overthrew the government; forced the few loyalist army leaders, such as General Carlos Prats Gonzalez, out of office and into exile; and established a dictatorship.

have been essential factors of power. They were the agents of several coups before the revolution. In Egypt, apart from the coups of the early 1950s, the military have largely served as an instrument of the presidency without ruling directly themselves.

In general, wherever there is a strong party (as in Mexico, and eventually in revolutionary Cuba) or a strong party system (as in India), or a strong political leader (as in Cuba, Egypt since the rise of Nasser, and Iran under the shahs and Khomeini), military coups, or direct rule by the armed forces, are much less frequent. In their absence—as in Brazil, Nigeria, Egypt before Nasser, or Cuba before Castro—military intervention in politics is far more frequent.

The Participants in Politics. Whether reform-oriented or conservative, most military governments tend to restrict political participation, often very sharply. Military leaders are most often elitists. By instinct and training they tend to think in terms of *chain of command*—in which orders and rewards flow from the top down, and only reports are expected to flow up—and not in terms of popular participation.

Nonetheless, the politics of the emerging countries has been marked generally by a large increase in popular participation. Among the population aged twenty years and older, perhaps 2 percent per year shifted from nonvoting to voting in major elections between the late 1950s and the mid-1960s, reaching an average value of 72 percent for the latter period in these countries that held elections. Certainly in many countries such an act of voting was more a public affirmation of support for the government than a genuine choice, but even this symbolic participation did suggest that the views and acts of ordinary men and women counted for something.

Mass participation in developing countries, even in one-party regimes, also means experience in a relatively wide range of organizations, such as a political party, trade unions, farmers' and women's organizations, youth groups and students' organizations (even though they are often state-sponsored), consumers' or producers' cooperatives, and many more. From participating in these a significant part of the population learns the basic skills of political activity: to speak publicly, to work in a committee, to conduct a meeting, to propose a motion, to take a vote, and to perform other participatory functions.

This gradually increasing pool of politically experienced personnel is likely eventually to confront any authoritarian or military regime in their country, and the shifting balance between politically mobilized and traditionally inert groups may in time increase the chances of the civilians and the partisans of high participation to prevail.

Elite participation in many developing countries has some peculiarities. First, elites tend to be small, in line with the modest level of general wealth and of secondary and higher education. Second, they are often divided between pronationalist and proforeign interests and factions. Third, many of them are bilingual and bicultural, as one part of the personality is connected with the native language and culture and the other with some foreign language, literature, and sector of civilization. Thus, in an age of rising nationalism it is a part of the elite that is becoming marginal in its own country.

The peasants may be behind the urban groups in their rates of social mobilization and political participation, but the spread of money and other aspects of social mobilization tends to remind many peasants of the pressure of their rents and taxes, as exacted by landlords and governments. Even more, it may remind them of the importance of the question of land ownership and land reform. In time, and in the absence of reforms, peasants may begin to develop radical movements, particularly if conscription has taught some of them military skills.

If demands for change from the city and the countryside should become synchronized, in the name of nationalism, communism, or a combination of the two, then the combined movement may well carry the day or, at least, force the overburdened government to call in foreign aid, which may or may not be forthcoming.

Perhaps the governments most successful in meeting these problems without falling under major foreign influence or native military rule have been those that have undertaken major land reforms and other changes, either with the help of a democratic coalition, as did India, or with the early help of a foreign occupying power, as did Japan in the late 1940s, or else with the aid—and at the cost—of a major revolution, as did China in 1949.

An interesting feature of political participation in the seven countries under study is that political parties matter to some degree in all of them, in marked contrast to what would be the case in a traditional society where parties (as opposed to mere elite factions) might not exist. Cuba stands at one end of the spectrum. Only the Communist Party is legal. It is a selective party: not all those who wish to join can do so because one must be chosen to be a member. The Communist Party is Cuba's leading political institution, which supervises and directs the work of mass organizations, such as labor unions, peasant organizations, or the women's federation, as well as of the government bureaucracy.

The party systems of Iran before the 1979 revolution and those of Egypt have shared some similarities. In both instances, there has been a large government-sponsored political party and, at times, all other parties have been illegal. When opposition parties have been allowed to participate in elections, they have typically been given only a small share of the announced vote. None of these parties, however, compares with the rigor, selectivity, discipline, and coherence of the Cuban Communist Party, nor with the latter's links to other organizations in society. The party system in Iran since 1979 has not yet fully crystallized for comment.

Mexico, too, has had a party in power without interruption since it was founded in 1929. However, small opposition parties have always been allowed (although some of them have been banned at times) and have competed in elections where they are reported to have won a small share of the votes. The large dominant party in Mexico has strong links to labor unions, peasant federations, and other such groups that are directly affiliated with it. It is a much stronger party than has existed in Iran or Egypt, and it is bigger but not so strong as Cuba's.

At the other end of the spectrum, India has had an effective multiparty system for most years since independence. Parties compete openly for the support of the voters. The Congress Party has ordinarily received a plurality of the votes and a majority of the seats in Parliament. As the next chapter will show, that pattern was interrupted temporarily in the late 1970s but seemed to reappear as the 1980s began.

Nigeria and Brazil are entering the 1980s with some interesting similarities. In both, military rulers have tried to reshape politics to permit wider, more open competition among political parties while seeking to prevent some of the sharper disputes and polarizations that prevailed in both countries the last time a full-fledged multiparty system was working in the early 1960s. Nigeria's military has already turned power over to civilians. Although there are some changes from the early 1960s, continuities are especially strong, as we will see, suggesting that the military's experiment with reshaping a party system might not succeed in the long run. Brazil still has a military president, under whom a wider range of political party activities are permitted. But here, too, the similarities with the party system before the 1964 military coup are already striking, although some changes have occurred.

The Arena and Images of Politics. Only a few of the emerging states' boundaries have been determined by internal forces and processes. More often they have inherited the territories as drawn for administrative or political convenience by foreign colonial rulers, as in the cases of India, Egypt, Brazil, and Nigeria. Others have as their core some territory of a premodern state or kingdom (China, Thailand, Iran, Ethiopia) or are the residues of international wars, as in Mexico. The territory and identity of some emerging countries have been the result of a major revolution, counterrevolution, or civil war (Bangladesh, North and South Korea, Vietnam, Uruguay). Some, like Cuba, were luckier, because island boundaries are defined more easily.

Despite their varied origins the territories of the emerging states most often make some *geographic sense*. Colonial powers often found it convenient to run their boundaries through more or less unpopulated territories, such as mountains, deserts, or jungles, and even the native wars and revolutions often stopped at these natural barriers. Other pieces of land, however, remained long in dispute between two or more nations. Moreover, some governments took to ransacking the archives in search of documents that could be used to develop a claim on a certain long-lost piece of territory or to discover an "unredeemed" group of fellow ethnics or compatriots, unfortunately now still under foreign yoke. China has raised such territorial claims or semiclaims, based on old maps, against several of its neighbors, including India. The great majority of African states have decided—probably wisely—not to press territorial disputes and claims against one another. The disputes between Algeria and Morocco over the former Spanish Sahara and between Ethiopia and Somalia over pasture lands and its people are two exceptions.

The territory of the state has for many developing countries a symbolic function as starting point for the hoped-for development of loyalties to the nation. As in seventeenth- and eighteenth-century Europe, so now in the emerging world, it is *patriotism*—the solidarity of all those living in a country—that precedes ethnic nationalism, the solidarity of those belonging to an ethnic group. In many emerging countries, such as Nigeria, India, and even Brazil, there is no one ethnic group comprising all or most inhabitants. Loyalty in such countries has grown, if at all, around a territory, perhaps a heritage of history, and probably a way of life attractive and rewarding enough to encourage the learning of common loyalties.

Ideologies alone will not suffice. A proclaimed commitment to Islam did not preserve the unity of Pakistan. Communist Serbs and Communist Croats have quarreled repeatedly in Yugoslavia. More fundamental political theories seem to have emerged only in a few places. Certainly the ideas of Mao Tse-tung in China, of Mahatma Gandhi and Jawaharlal Nehru in India, of Fidel Castro and Che Guevara in Cuba, and of the Ayatollah Khomeini in Iran deserve some serious attention, regardless of how much one might disagree with them. But a richer flow of political theories from the emerging countries may yet come.

EMERGING POLITICAL SYSTEMS: THEIR STEERING, MACHINERY, AND PROCESSES

Many emerging nations had to make their start with the mere rudiments of a modern political system, as was the case for Mexico and Brazil in the 1820s. Most of them inherited a foreign-directed civil service from their immediate colonial past. In the case of traditionally independent countries, such as China, Thailand, Ethiopia, Turkey, and Iran, there were elements of a premodern, or even partly modernized, administrative staff. Such countries, as well as the former colonies, had some soldiers and police officers, and some schools, teachers, and public health officials. Much of this top- and middle-level personnel was foreign, but there were some middle-level and many lower-level native clerks, who often had good talents and training.

The first task of most governments of the emerging countries after 1945 was to keep operating. This meant recruiting some new nationalistic native personnel and retaining the services of irreplaceable foreign experts. And this in turn meant getting money to pay these soldiers, police officers, and bureaucrats and continuing to get such money for some time.

Some of this money came from abroad, most often from one or the other of the competing superpowers, the United States and the Soviet Union. Sometimes both sides paid. Between 1946 and 1975, India got about $9 billion from the United States, or about $15.00 per capita over thirty years (about $0.50 per head per year). And during 1954–76 it also got over $2 billion from the Soviet Union, or over $4.00 per capita. This brought its total take to $11 billion, an average of less than $0.75 per Indian per year. Egypt got over $1.3 billion from the Soviet Union and nearly as much from the United States, yielding a total of about $3.00 per Egyptian per year. Iran, Afghanistan, Greece, Turkey, and Tunisia also got substantial amounts from both sides; but the American aid was much larger to Greece, Turkey, and Tunisia than the Soviet contribution. Other countries had only one large benefactor: Cuba, between 1961 and 1980, has received several billion dollars from the Soviet Union, the world's leading per capita recipient of Soviet aid. Massive American aid, but no Soviet aid, has been going to Jordan, Israel, Liberia, and, in lesser but substantial amounts, to Brazil. Brazil and Mexico also began to borrow heavily from international private banks in the 1970s and thereafter.

Other short-term tasks were to collect taxes and to maintain essential government services. As these matters were dealt with successfully, national independence could at least begin to take on meaning.

Other tasks have to be started soon, but involve middle-term policy commitments of about five to fifteen years. Here we find the perennial problem of encouraging domestic capital formation and the inflow and investment of foreign capital—in countries (unlike Cuba) where foreign investment is welcomed—while trying to discourage capital flight or withdrawals. Another middle-term task is

to win popular support and eventually to consolidate it into firm habits, loyalties, and institutions.

The long-term tasks (fifteen to twenty-five years) of the government are, then, to deal with some of the basic structural problems of development. *Quantitative modernization* can be measured simply by noting by how much the national performance has improved according to any one or a few indicators, considering each indicator in isolation from all others. *Qualitative modernization* can be judged, on the contrary, by noting the relationships and balances—or imbalances—among the different sectors, elements, and dimensions of development.

Here the government must develop an effective policy for dealing with the center-periphery problem, since central regions and populations tend to be more favored, prosperous, and quick to develop, leaving the peripheral districts and their population more and more behind. Related to this is the problem of what Gunnar Myrdal has called the *backwash effect,* that is, the draining away of mobile capital, skilled personnel, and money from the peripheral and poorer districts and the concentrating of these mobile factors of production in the central or otherwise already advanced regions. This process is the opposite of the *spread effect,* so confidently predicted by the classical economists; they felt that wealth would spread out gradually from any area of early concentration until the entire country had been made more or less uniformly prosperous.

Other long-term and structural problems are related to those just named. As population grows, as migration from the countryside proceeds, and as people move out of agriculture into urban and industrial employment, all these changes require large amounts of capital—to construct the housing, the social infrastructure, and the factories and work places to house and employ these migrants. Wherever capital formation and investment fall short of these needs, there will appear a population for whom there are no machines, work places, housing, and other facilities available.

Another long-term problem is likewise related to capital formation. It takes capital to build a factory or bridge where an engineer can be employed or to build and equip a laboratory where a scientist can work. Lacking such capital, a society will force its intellectual talent into the capital-extensive occupations, such as law and journalism.

Several of the countries we will examine in the next two chapters have already adopted policies to address some of these problems. India was the first among them to devise redistributional policies shortly after independence in 1947 to benefit the poorer regions of the country. Cuba has probably gone furthest in this direction, however, since Castro came to power in 1959. Although its capital city, Havana, looks run down, many impressive programs have been implemented to improve the lot of the rural areas. Nigeria had to learn the hard way the political lesson that redistributional, ethnocultural, and regional problems cannot be ignored. The Nigerian civil war in the late 1960s posed many of these issues in their crudest and most violent forms; subsequent governments have been much more conscious of the need to address these matters. Mexico and Brazil, too, have designed policies to aid the less modernized regions of the country, but, as we shall see, inequalities remain quite serious.

Other features are, of course, relevant to a study of the machinery of government, only some of which can be mentioned in this overview. All seven countries have had strong chief executives and much weaker, and at times nonexistent, national legislatures. For example, there was no national legislature during the first decade and a half of revolutionary rule in Cuba (1959–76); laws were simply issued by the Council of Ministers. National legislatures have been suspended at times, invoking emergency powers in extraordinary circumstances, in Nasser's Egypt, Brazil in the late 1960s and 1970s, and in Iran and Nigeria. At those times, the executives made all the laws, too.

Only India and Mexico have had parliamentary institutions without interruption for several decades. However, the authority of India's Parliament was effectively gutted during the 1975–77 "emergency." Mexico's national legislature (the Congress) has been controlled overwhelmingly by the official government party, even though it began to show somewhat greater independence in the late 1970s.

As the 1980s opened, however, all seven countries had elected national legislatures. The Indian Parliament remained, by far, the most significant of all of them, but trends toward greater authority and decision-making power for national legislatures were evident in Brazil, Cuba, Mexico, Egypt, and Nigeria. The situation in Iran remained very cloudy, but it seemed possible that the national legislature would eventually have greater authority than under the monarchy. In the early 1980s, the chief executive's party had overwhelming control of the national legislature in Cuba (where there is no legal opposition at all) and in Mexico and Egypt (where opposition parties are very weak). There is somewhat greater but still quite limited competition in the Brazilian Congress and, because of the Congress Party's overwhelming electoral victory in the openly competitive 1980 elections, in the Indian Parliament as well. Only Nigeria had a rather fluid parliamentary balance of power.

With regard to chief executives, the picture has altered considerably over time. All the monarchies and empires are gone from the seven countries under study, and all but India have political systems where the president is both the formal head of state and the effective head of the government. In India the president is the formal head of state but has few real powers; the prime minister is the head of the government with the real ability to govern. Iran appears to be faced by conflicting forces: parliamentary dominance or presidentialism. The Shi'ite clergy still remains a formidable check.

An alternative way to consider chief executives is to look at the real conditions of their tenure. Three principal types can be identified. The first is the fixed-term, renewable chief executive. This prevails in India, where the prime minister serves for a definite number of years, after which there is an openly competitive election. At the other end of the spectrum, there is the "open-ended" tenure system. Chief executives may be nominally elected for a fixed term but, in fact, those elections are not openly competitive. They are essentially formalities that continue to ratify the supreme leader's rule. That is the case of Fidel Castro in Cuba, of Nasser and Sadat in Egypt, of the several military presidents Nigeria had in the 1960s and 1970s, and of the shahs in Iran until 1979, whose terms of office were literally open. Although political succession can be, and has been, handled readily and effectively in India, it has not been confronted at all in Cuba, where Fidel Castro is entering his third decade as chief executive. In Egypt, the peaceful political transition from Nasser to Sadat was accomplished only upon the former's death. In Nigeria under military rule, and in Iran under the shahs, political succession occurred essentially through military coups, assassinations or forced abdications. The "open-ended" tenure system may at times give the appearance of political stability, but, at best, it postpones the crucial question of executive succession to a later time and, at worst, is an invitation to coups and revolutions.

A third procedure is more readily found in Latin American countries such as Mexico and Brazil. It is the fixed-term, nonrenewable chief executive. Presidents serve for a definite number of years, after which they must turn over power to a successor. Mexico has had this method in effect since the 1930s without interruption, and it is one of the keys to its impressive political stability. Along with other factors, this method helps to prevent dictatorships. It assures ambitious politicians that they will have their turn. It opens up possibilities for innovation and change on a regular schedule. For countries that are thus far unable or unwilling to have openly competitive politics, which has prevailed in Western Europe, North America, Japan, and India, the fixed-term, nonrenewable presidency may be quite appealing. Brazil has shown, since the mid-1960s, an interesting adaptation: its military presidents have rotated on

a fixed schedule, too. Other countries, especially in Latin America, have been adopting this method in recent years.

All such problems can only be indicated here. Some emerging states have been facing them for many years. How have they performed?

THE PERFORMANCE OF
THE EMERGING STATES

The emerging states are so different that it seems hard, if not impossible, to arrive at any kind of common judgment about all of them. Yet, two facts may be noted as a first indication. First, with rare exceptions,[13] most emerging states have done well enough as sovereign nations since 1947 to remain in existence. Second, more states have emerged into independence—and with less bloodshed, relative to the numbers of states and people involved—since 1947 than during any other thirty-year period in history.

On the whole, most of the new states have promoted health care, reduced general death rates and child mortality, and spread mass education—at all levels—faster and further than did the colonial administrations that preceded many of them.

Finally, many of these emerging states have made at least a beginning in self-government. They have carried it forward, to some extent, at the level of the nation, the locality, and the smaller voluntary groups and organizations.

Fifty years ago, many seasoned observers would have called impossible what many of these new states in fact have done already. Their record to date is mixed, uneven, contradictory. But, withal,

[13]Zanzibar, independent in 1963, was absorbed into Tanzania in 1964; Syria and Egypt submerged their independence—under Nasser's leadership—between 1958 and 1961.

it is the story of one of humankind's great beginnings.

KEY TERMS AND CONCEPTS

emerging states
traditional societies
ideal type
early transitional societies
advanced transitional societies
industrialized societies
postindustrial societies
information revolution
pattern maintenance
achievement motivation
bases for group solidarity and self-government
ethnic, linguistic, cultural, and religious
   conditions
process of modernization
monetization
marketplace
node of transportation
market
bridgeheads of modernity
direct foreign rule vs. indirect foreign rule
processes of growth
demographic transition
impact of migration
internal migration
impact of mass media
interlocking process of social mobilization
rates of mobilization
concept and process of assimilation
dimensions of assimilation
marginality
assimilation and acceptance
motives for assimilation
need for affiliation
rewards for assimilation
differentiation and secession
linguistic assimilation
independence, stability, and development
constitutionalism vs. authoritarian dictatorship
chain of command

mass participation
elite participation
geographic origins of states
patriotism
quantitative modernization
qualitative modernization
backwash vs. spread effect
nonrenewable, fixed-term chief executive

ADDITIONAL READINGS

Apter, D. *The Politics of Modernization.* Chicago: University of Chicago Press, 1965. PB

Black, C. E. *The Dynamics of Modernization.* New York: Harper, 1967. PB

Deutsch, K. W. *Nationalism and Its Alternatives.* New York: Knopf, 1969.

———. *Nationalism and Social Communication.* Rev. ed. Cambridge: MIT Press, 1966. PB

Emerson, R. *From Empire to Nation.* Boston: Beacon Press, 1962. PB

Fanon, F. *The Wretched of the Earth.* New York: Grove Press, 1965. PB

Foltz, W. J. *From French West Africa to the Mali Federation.* New Haven: Yale Univeristy Press, 1965.

Galtung, J. "A Structural Theory of Imperialism." *Journal of Peace Research,* July 1971.

Hartz, L., et al. *The Founding of New Societies.* New York: Harcourt, 1969, PB

Hudson, M. C. *The Precarious Republic.* New York: Random House, 1968.

Huntington, S. P. *Political Order in Changing Societies.* New Haven: Yale University Press, 1968. PB

Johnson, C. *Revolutionary Change.* Boston: Little, Brown, 1964. PB

Kohn, H. *The Idea of Nationalism.* New York: Macmillan, 1944. PB

McAlister, J. T. *The Vietnamese and Their Revolution.* New York: Harper & Row, 1970.

Merritt, R. L., and S. Rokkan. *Comparing Nations.* New Haven: Yale University Press, 1966. PB

Perham, M. *The Colonial Reckoning.* London and Westport, Conn.: Greenwood Press, 1976.

Pye, L. *Aspects of Political Development.* Boston: Little, Brown, 1966. PB

Race, J. *War Comes to Long An.* Berkeley and Los Angeles: University of California Press, 1971. PB

Regmi, M. C. *A Study in Nepali Economic History 1768–1846.* New Delhi: Manjusri Publishing House, 1971.

Russett, B. M., et al. *World Handbook of Political and Social Indicators.* New Haven: Yale University Press, 1964.

Safran, N. *Israel: The Embattled Ally.* Cambridge: Harvard University Press, 1978.

Stephens. H. *The Political Transformation of Tanganyika, 1920–67.* New York: Praeger, 1968.

Taylor, C. L., and M. C. Hudson. *World Handbook of Political and Social Indicators.* 2nd ed. New Haven: Yale University Press, 1972.

PB = *available in paperback*

X

Poor to Almost Rich:
India, Nigeria, Egypt, Iran

What we can say about developing countries in general will rarely be true about one country in particular. They are too different. Even a brief look at a few emerging countries gives an impression of their diversity. The people of each country have endured different experiences, faced different conditions, and chosen different actions by which to make their fates.

For these brief sketches, seven countries have been chosen. Two are located in Africa: Nigeria and Egypt. Two others belong to Asia: India and Iran. Three are in Latin America (and will be dealt with in the following chapter): Brazil, Mexico, and Cuba. The last of these, Cuba, belongs to a different social and economic system. The development of these countries varies widely. Their per capita GNPs in the mid-1970s ranged from $140 in India to $1,660 in oil-rich Iran. Their urban populations ranged from 9.8 percent of the total population in India to 43 percent in Iran. Similar contrasts hold for their accomplishments in education and health. Literacy ranged from 15 percent in Nigeria to 74 percent in Mexico and at least 85 percent in Cuba. Life expectancy at birth varied from a short forty-one years in Nigeria to sixty-three and seventy years, respectively, in Mexico and Cuba.

Behind these statistical signposts are memories of ancestral peoples and nations: the ancient cultures of Egypt, India, and Iran; the old culture of Nigeria-Benin; the Indian and Spanish heritage of Mexico; the colonial history of Cuba; and the mingled colonial and pioneering history of Brazil. Throughout their histories, these countries have made political choices that have either reinforced their social and economic fates or else changed them. We begin with those countries that have the furthest to go in their economic development, as indicated by their per capita GNP.

INDIA

India is the poorest of the countries discussed in this chapter. In 1976, its per capita GNP was only $140, only 9.8 percent of its population lived in

377

cities, and only 31 percent of its work force was in occupations outside agriculture, forestry, and fishing. But 33 percent of its 1970 population was literate, compared with only 17 percent in 1951. Life expectancy at birth in 1976 was fifty-three years, an improvement by a dozen years since the 1950s, and by about twenty-one years since the last decade of British rule. How did so much improvement become possible in so vast and poor a country? To seek an answer, we must first look at India's history and at her human, cultural, and political resources.

One of India's assets is its sheer size. After China, India is the largest of the world's developing countries. In 1978, its population was 656 million; in 1981, it is likely to be close to 700 million. Geographically, it covers most of a subcontinent. It is the home of one of the oldest continuous cultural traditions of humankind, covering about 3,500 years, from the Bronze Age to the nuclear age. Politically, it has been both independent and almost unified only three times: once in about 250 B.C. under King Ashoka, who ruled two-thirds of the subcontinent, a second time under Aurangzeb in 1707, and since 1947, after the secession of Pakistan.

A Grid of Transportation Routes. India's transportation routes have lasted longer than its changing political regimes. They have provided a means of national communication that has held India together over the centuries. The routes form a diamond standing on its southern tip at Cape Comorin, where the Arabian Sea and the Bay of Bengal meet, with a blunt northern tip in the western Himalayas and the valley of Kashmir. The long Indian coast of the Arabian Sea forms the southwest side of the diamond, and the coast of the Bay of Bengal forms the southeast one, with coastal shipping along each of these. The northwest side of the grid is marked by the Indus River, which flows from the western Himalayas southwestward to form with its tributaries the fertile "five-stream land," the *Punjab,* and then continues to the sea. The diamond is completed by the valley of the huge Ganges River, which flows eastward along the Himalayas and then southward into the Bay of Bengal near Calcutta.

Most major Indian cities lie either at or near the seacoasts, such as Surat, Bombay, Madras, and Calcutta, or on the big rivers and their tributaries. India's capital, Delhi, lies at the junction of two such tributaries of the Ganges River on the landbridge where the distance between the river systems of the Indus and Ganges is smallest. Away from the coasts and the waterways, communications are poor, most soils not fertile, and populations thinly settled. There are the high plains of the Deccan, high mountains and large tracts of jungle. In the Deccan there are some old principalities, such as Hyderabad and Mysore, and some considerable cities of more recent importance, such as Nagpur and Bangalore.

Ancient Conquest from the North: The Heritage of Caste. Far beyond the major cities and transportation routes, Indian culture has penetrated deeply almost everywhere on the subcontinent. Polished stone tools were used in India before 3000 B.C. and the Bronze Age began there well before it did in China. A decisive change came with the gradual conquest of India between 2000 and 1200 B.C. by the *Aryans,* light-skinned invaders from the north who spoke Indo-European languages. They pushed back, subjected, and in part absorbed the darker-skinned Dravidian-speaking inhabitants.

By 1200 B.C., a common language, *Sanskrit,* had emerged in northern India, with an oral literature of religion and law. The modern languages of northern India, such as *Hindi* (spoken by about 35 percent of the population), Urdu, Bengali, Marathi, and Gujarati, are descended from Sanskrit and are still mutually intelligible. But in the south, the old *Dravidian languages,* quite different from the Indo-European ones, have continued in such modern forms as Telugu, Kannada, and Malayalam.

Laws and religion were written down in Sanskrit in about 1000 B.C. in the *Vedas,* of which the Rigveda was the most important. They embodied the code of a patriarchal agricultural society, dominated by the conquerors. Between 800 and 550 B.C., the Aryans expanded their conquests eastward to Bihar, and the Vedic rules of caste were elaborated and made more stringent.

The caste system, sanctioned by Hindu tradition, has its special strength in the villages. There are a few thousand castes, or *jati,* in local communities in India. Castes are endogamous social units; that is, their members are expected to marry only among themselves. Each caste is linked to the traditional occupation of its members. The caste system defines the social status of all members of a particular area. Castes are distinguished by costume and dietary habits, speech, manners, and style of life. The caste system is based on the expectation that most people will abide by its rules, under penalty of punishment by elders or by the "higher" castes. The local castes have classically been divided according to the framework of the estate, or *varna,* system. Four estates were delineated and continue to exist today. Topmost were the priests, or *brahmans,* as the guardians of knowledge, writing, and religion. Second ranked the noble warriors, or *kshatriyas;* third were the mercantile classes, or *vaisyas;* and fourth were the *sudras,* people who worked in agriculture and in crafts. Beyond the *varna* system are the outcasts, or *untouchables,* polluted by their life's work and thus clearly found at the bottom of this traditional social structure. Taboos of ritual, cleanliness, and food continue to distinguish the castes within the estate system and between it and the untouchables. The untouchables were charged with the most undesirable and infection-prone occupations, such as tanning, sweeping, cleaning, and removing carrion and excrement. Eventually, it was taught that even the shadow of an untouchable would defile the food of an upper-caste Hindu.

The caste system has lasted so long because it linked conquest, language, and, originally, physical appearance with the social division of labor. A somewhat similar division of labor among priests, warriors, and peasants persisted in medieval and early modern Europe for a thousand years. Moreover, castes and subcastes offered social niches in which newly conquered or converted tribes could be integrated and even their tribal cults and deities could be accommodated. In this manner, Hindu culture united its believers not in a uniform nationality and creed, but rather in a vast mosaic that preserved and even sharpened their differences.

To believing Hindus, caste was unchangeable. No one could escape from the caste of birth, except by losing it and becoming an outcast to be shunned by all. Fate was to be borne in patience, not to be mastered by action. At best, peace of mind could be reached through contemplation. A doctrine of reincarnation developed, according to which everyone would be reborn in a higher or lower caste, or even in animal form, depending on the merits or demerits they accumulated in their current life. Efforts to escape one's caste counted as demerits, to be punished by rebirth at lower stations in one's lives to come. This doctrine was gradually supplemented by child marriages, polygamy, and the burning of widows. The latter practice was ended by the British government in the nineteenth century.

These doctrines and practices reinforced one another. They did not destroy the profound spiritual elements of Hinduism as a religion, but they often distorted it into a system of social stability without parallel in history. For three thousand years, kings and kingdoms came and went but the caste system remained.

Alternatives to Caste. Castes did not remain without resistance. About 500 B.C., the Jain sect and, shortly thereafter, Buddhism arose, offering alternatives to the harsh caste rule of the brahmans. Both religions survived as minorities in India. (Buddhism, in various forms, eventually spread to Sri Lanka, Burma, Tibet, China, and Japan, where its influence has endured.) Almost two thousand years later, the Muslim conquerors offered a creed

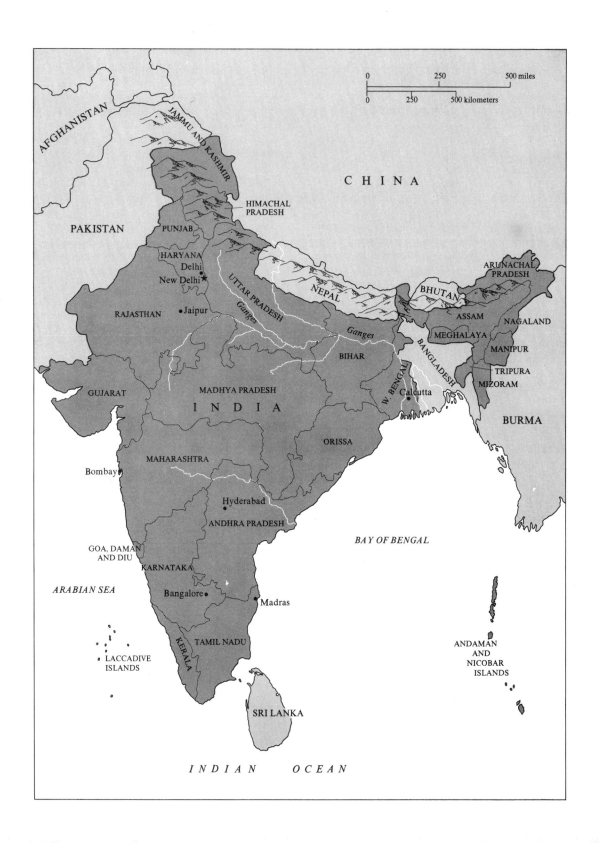

that promised the brotherhood of all believers. In East Bengal and elsewhere in India, some low-caste Hindus accepted the promise and converted to Islam. Later, some Muslim rulers of small Indian principalities converted to Hinduism, perhaps hoping to ensure high-caste status for themselves and their descendants.

Other Hindus turned against both caste and Muslim pressure. In the Punjab, a fifteenth-century religious order, the *Sikhs,* turned into a thoroughly militarized sect in the seventeenth century and, eventually, also became a people. The order had started out both proclaiming monotheism and Muslim-Hindu fellowship and opposing priestly rule and caste restrictions. In time, it became a formidable anti-Muslim military force, as well as a thriving community whose bearded and turbaned men have remained a conspicuous part of India's military and economic life.

All these religious groups have persisted, and so have other sects. Jains, Marwari Hindus, and Parsees (an offshoot of the old Persian Zoroastrian religion) all are prominent in business and finance. Sikhs, Raijput Hindus, and the Gurkhas from Nepal, once classed by the British as "martial races," still have their share in the armed services.

Across these divisions, modern industry has created masses of both industrial workers with their labor unions and employers and business-people with their class interests. There are large and small landowners, farmers, and peasants, and they all press for the political representation of their interests. Language, ethnicity, religion, caste, class occupations, and geography thus make India's politics rich and complex.

Through the years, India most of the time was made up of small monarchies and principalities, often under native rulers. Sometimes, some re-

(Left) MAP 10.1 *India*

gions were ruled by Muslim conquerors, such as the Moghul emperors who united parts of India from the sixteenth through the eighteenth century without being able to prevent the step-by-step conquest of India by foreign powers.

A New Conquest by the West. In 1498, the Portuguese sailor Vasco da Gama opened a sea route from Europe to India. In 1660, after establishing earlier footholds at Surat and Madras, the English set up a fortified trading post where the city of Bombay is today. In 1690, they founded Calcutta.

They organized these areas not as a foreign state but as a commercial corporation, the English *East India Company,* which was chartered in 1600 and continued to be backed by British naval and military power. In addition to its monopoly of trade with Britain, the company came to exercise political and military powers in India, whereas other European powers, mainly the Portuguese, Dutch, and French, eventually were defeated and expelled or confined to small enclaves.

In the eighteenth century, able officials of the company, such as Robert Clive and later Warren Hastings, intervened in the wars between local Indian rulers. Those siding with the English eventually won, but the company gained most of the power. Clive and Hastings conquered large and populous territories for the company, such as Bengal, and enriched themselves greatly in the process. Despite famines among the native population, pickings were easy for the conquerors. "I was astonished," Hastings later said, "at my own moderation."

Individuals took little in comparison to what the company collected. In the territories that it controlled directly, taxes were levied on the peasantry through local landowners, called Zamindars, who also functioned as tax collectors. This arrangement left deep traces in India's social structure. British people functioned increasingly as magistrates and judges. After 1793, Indians were excluded from all higher posts. In other regions, the company ruled indirectly through agreements with local rulers, who put themselves under British protection. They and their subjects then paid for this protection in one form or another.

Directly and indirectly, vast amounts of wealth were transferred to Britain during the eighteenth and nineteenth centuries. British rule brought an end to local wars and, from the second half of the nineteenth century onward, important improvements in transportation, public health, and education. Whether India would have done better or worse under its native rulers is a matter British and Indian scholars still dispute.

The British conquest continued between 1785 and 1819. Much of south India and the lands of the Marathas around Bombay were conquered, and the rulers of Hyderabad and Rajputana put their large territories under British protection. In the 1840s and 1850s, most of the rest of northern India, including Sindh, the Punjab, and Delhi, were occupied. This occupation substantially completed the British conquest of India.

After controlling foreign trade and taxes on land, the British entered India's internal market. British rule kept it open to the products of British industry. As the Industrial Revolution progressed, cheap British machine-made goods wiped out some of the handicraft industries in India. Industry in Manchester was prospering, but, as one British governor reported in 1834, "the bones of the Indian weavers are bleaching in the plains of the Deccan."

For more than two centuries, the company had been both a large business enterprise and a big government. By the late 1850s, the combination became untenable. In 1857, a vast uprising shattered the company's rule throughout much of the subcontinent. It started among the company's Muslim mercenaries but spread quickly to the general population, with Hindus joining in. In many places, British people and their families were massacred or became victims of atrocities. Eventually British regular troops suppressed the uprising. They tied rebel leaders to the mouths of British cannons, which tore them to pieces. The British called the uprising *"The Great Mutiny."*

Indian schoolchildren were long taught that it was a war of liberation. Although it was defeated, there are now monuments to it in Indian cities.

The events of 1857 fundamentally changed the political system of India. The British government replaced the company as the political and administrative power. Educational reforms were started and universities founded, construction of a railroad network was begun, a civil service was organized. Thomas Babington Macaulay wrote in the 1830s in his famous *Minute on Educational Reform in India* that the subcontinent would be transformed within one hundred years. As it turned out, he was right.

The lower ranks of government administration became filled with native clerks. Hindus competed best in the examinations for these civil service posts. Muslims for a time were distrusted by the British who remembered the mutiny of 1857. The railroad system eventually proved too small for the country's needs, but in the meantime it transformed the subcontinent. Famines became rarer as food supplies could be moved, but 5 million lives were lost in 1876–78 in a famine in Deccan, and another 2 million died in widespread famines from 1896 to 1900. Even so, the population grew, and the towns and cities grew faster. By the mid-1880s, British-ruled India was a different country from what it had been in the days of the East India Company.

A New India Begins. As India changed, more Indians began to think of national unity and independence. In 1885, the *Indian National Congress* was founded, uniting Muslims and Hindus in their demands for more Indian self-government. Bal G. Tilak, Gopal K. Gokhale, and later *Mohandas K. Gandhi* became major political leaders. Muslims came to demand a larger share of public jobs and other opportunities and to fear their minority status in a Hindu-dominated self-governing India. The British administration now welcomed Muslim aspirations, and in 1906 the

All-India Muslim League was founded, and *Mohammed Ali Jinnah* became a prominent Muslim leader.

Gandhi's and Jawaharlal Nehru's Congress Party tried to keep Hindus and Muslims together. Indian self-government was to be secular: religion and the state were to be kept separate. At all times, some Muslim leaders held prominent offices in the Congress, side by side with Hindus, but other Muslims feared that majority rule would give power and privilege to Hindus. As the British conceded increased self-rule to India during the first half of the twentieth century, they insisted on separate electoral rolls (registers of voters) for Muslims and Hindus, with separate shares of the elective offices assigned to each. The Muslim League welcomed this. Congress and other critics saw it as deliberate support of religious separatism, in accordance with the ancient tactic of "divide and rule." Still others considered it adaptation to political reality.

When India became independent in 1947, the regions with Muslim majorities, except Kashmir, formed the new state of *Pakistan,* first as a self-governing British dominion with Mohammed Ali Jinnah as its governor-general. Jinnah died in 1948, and Pakistan became an Islamic republic in 1950. In 1971, it broke up into two states: Bangladesh to the east of India and today's Pakistan to the west, each with more than 70 million inhabitants, still including some Hindu minorities. Today, more Muslims are living as a minority in India than in either of these Muslim states—more than 11 percent of India's population, or perhaps 77 million people.

Partition (or separation) in 1947 had a high cost in blood. An estimated 1 million lives were lost in riots and massacres, sometimes carried out with the connivance of the police on both sides of the new border. Debtors killed creditors, peasants attacked landlords, workers rioted against employers, wherever the new cleavage of nationality was added to the old "communal" one of religion. There had been smaller communal riots in the past, and if the size of the catastrophe of 1947 had been foreseen and safeguarded against, many lives could have been saved. No adequate protection of minorities was offered on either side of the border. Leaders of the Congress had denied the danger, preferring to believe in the unity of India. Muslim leaders had been preoccupied with setting up their new country. The British government, withdrawing its troops and leaving the unprotected minorities behind, may have considered their responsibility ended; some British officials, relieved to be rid of a thankless job, may have felt that such riots would merely confirm their belief in India's incapacity for self-government.

Despite the lives lost, and the millions of refugees exchanged between India and Pakistan, this pessimism proved unwarranted. India, Pakistan, and Bangladesh all are functioning as states today. However, the Pakistan-Bangladesh partition in 1971 claimed many lives, *communalism* remains a political problem, and bloody communal riots between Hindus and Muslims in India continue to occur.

Newly independent India also had fresh solutions to some of these old problems. Notwithstanding its extraordinary diversity, India has maintained its unity and territorial integrity since independence. The national government has adopted policies that have maintained this coherence. India's federal structure has provided for some decentralization of decision making, so that state governments can meet the concerns of their own people. More important was the reorganization of the federal states in the 1950s along linguistic lines. State boundaries within India were redrawn to include within each state communities that spoke the same language. Many problems remain, but this has helped to limit many linguistic disputes; it met the demands of the major linguistic communities for home rule; and it gave new content and meaning to the federal system. In addition, autonomous tribal states were established in the north and east of the country. As political conflicts, linguistic or otherwise, have arisen within the states, the government of India has sometimes responded by creating yet other states. The central government's language policy has also been fairly flexible. Regional languages predominate within the linguistic states, where they serve an official role. At the national level, there is a commitment to an expanded role for the Hindi language, but English is still used in part because non-Hindi speakers have pressed to retain it as an official language, too.

The government of India has been controlled by the Congress Party since independence, except for a brief period between 1977 and 1980. The Congress Party, and consequently the government of India, has derived special electoral support from many of the country's minorities, such as the Muslims, the untouchables (renamed *harijans*, or children of God, by Gandhi), the scheduled tribes (tribes with officially recognized status), and the Christians. The Congress Party's commitment to a secular state has reassured the religious minorities. In addition to the tribal states already mentioned, the government of India has reserved some parliamentary constituencies to ensure the political representation of the untouchables. Just as important, the central government has allocated many of its economic, educational, public health, and other resources to redress regional imbalances and to assist the poor. India's unity amidst diversity has not occurred by chance, but by the pursuit of difficult but workable policies that have already succeeded for the many decades since independence.

The Vast Stakes of Indian Politics. Perhaps more is at stake in the politics of India than in those of most other countries. India is the largest noncommunist country in the world, but in two states, Kerala and West Bengal, Communist parties have participated in coalitions that formed state governments. India, almost unique among the world's large emerging nations, has been under a democratic and constitutional government since independence, but this, too, has come under strain. The problems of caste in political, social, and economic life, of persistent poverty, of occasional famine such as that in the Ganges Plain in 1967, and of population growth demand political action.

The life and death of millions affect and are affected by politics in India. Public health and life expectancy, famines and epidemics or their avoidance, depend on public policy. Many issues press for political decisions: economic development; its orientation toward industry or agriculture; the interests of Indian and foreign corporations, of Indian big business, small business, labor unions, and the unemployed, of landowners, big farmers, small peasants, and the landless rural poor, of the highly educated, the merely literate, and the illiterate majority. And so do many matters of family and personal life, or custom and culture, press for political decisions—matters that in other countries are settled and stable: which caste rules to reject and which ones to obey; with whom to eat or not to eat; what dowry to pay to the husband of one's daughter; how to arrange a marriage between children; how many children to have; to accept sterilization, practice contraception, or let marriage and nature take their course. Politics in India has thus acquired greater intensity and personal relevance than is found in the politics of many other countries.

Political Participation. By the mid-nineteenth century, British conquests had enlarged the domain of direct and indirect British rule, and population growth worked in the same direction. Modernization, particularly from the 1850s onward, enlarged the scope of government. Decade after decade, more decisions had to be made concerning more people than ever before. The growing administrative burden in India, together with rising wages and living standards in Britain, made British clerks more expensive and required hiring ever larger numbers of Indian clerical employees. In this manner, Indians increasingly participated in the administrative process.

It also became prudent to ask at least some Indians more formally for their opinion and advice. Under the rule of the East India Company, the governor-general of India created in 1853 an appointed legislative council to advise him. After the Government of India Act of 1858, the governor-general became a viceroy, British administration replaced that of the company, the viceroy's administration was enlarged in 1861, and similar councils on the provincial level were added in 1862. The appointees serving on these bodies included a small share of Indians, picked by the British from among the more cooperative members of the Indian elites. In the early 1880s, Lord Ripon, a liberal viceroy, introduced local self-government. But a further reform that would have permitted Indian judges in outlying areas to try Europeans was defeated by the fierce opposition of British residents. In the early 1890s, the legislative councils were further enlarged and their powers increased. Henceforth, their "nonofficial" European and Indian members were to be nominated by local bodies, so that these members were tacitly elected. By the Morley-Minto Act of 1909, the legislative councils were again greatly enlarged and given increased power. Several provincial councils now had elected majorities, but Hindu and Muslim voters had separate electoral rolls, and the more substantial class of citizens was restricted from voting.

Further reforms came in 1918 after the presentation of the Montague-Chelmsford report to Parliament, with the announced aim of developing self-governing institutions in India, but the report was denounced as unsatisfactory by many Indian leaders. Despite these protests, its recommendations were enacted through the Government of India Act of 1919. Henceforth 70 percent of the council members were to be elected. However, according to a principle of dyarchy (double rule), important matters (such as defense, police, and finance) were "reserved" for the provincial governor and the appointed British members of the executive council; the less important (such as education, health, and agriculture) were to be "transferred" to the Indian members. The right to vote, however, was still limited by property qualifications. In 1932, the franchise was extended to members of the *"depressed classes"*—the untouchables—who already had begun to organize politically. They became important allies of Gandhi and of the Indian National Congress. Today their leaders play a significant part in Indian politics, and there are special quotas reserved for *harijan* students at Indian universities.

In 1935, another Government of India Act—sometimes called in Britain the India Bill—gave wider autonomy to the provincial legislatures but reserved emergency powers for the governors (who remained British). A two-chamber central legislature at Delhi was created, consisting of a "council of state" with 34 elected and 26 appointed members and a "legislative assembly" of 40 appointed members and 105 members elected by the provincial assemblies. Defense, foreign affairs, and certain financial powers remained under the governor-general and hence in British hands. Under these provisions, Britain in 1939 took India into World War II without real Indian consent. Until its independence in 1947, India had no universal and equal suffrage or full control over its military and financial affairs.

The story of the gradual increase of self-government in India is also a story of Indian political pressure and opposition. Through occasional riots and sustained peaceful political organization, through economic and political strikes and large campaigns of nonviolent civil disobedience, millions of Indians learned to act in politics and to struggle for their rights. A generation of Indian political leaders, including Mahatma Gandhi and *Jawaharlal Nehru,* became graduates of British jails. They symbolized readiness for self-sacrifice to their people.

In the end, increasing self-government and political opposition may have worked together. The slow extension of Indian self-government by the British rulers gave India three generations of political experience within a constitutional order. Motilal Nehru was an important political leader in the 1920s, demanding dominion status for India, similar to the very large degree of self-government already then enjoyed by Canada and Australia. His son, Jawaharlal Nehru, was the prime minister of independent India from 1947 to 1964. Nehru's daughter, Indira Gandhi (for whom, in the early 1930s, when she was still a teenager, he had written in jail a long version of world history[1]), was prime minister from 1966 to 1977, and was again elected to that post in 1980. At the same time, it was through their own growing efforts, organization, struggle, and readiness to sacrifice that Indians developed the self-confidence and the moral and political capabilities for sustained self-government and independence with constitutional democracy.

During much of the three-generation period, 1885–1977, the National Congress was India's major political party. Outside of today's Pakistan and Bangladesh, it was also the chief vehicle of effective political participation. As already noted, the Congress Party long derived much support from India's minorities, such as the Muslims, Christians, the scheduled tribes, and the untouchables. The party also had been strong throughout the years in Hindu-speaking northern India, especially among professionals, urban dwellers, and landless workers. This large party represented for many the symbols of Indian independence. Committed to a secular state and economic development, the Congress Party also developed an effective network of political party machines in many of the regions and states of India. Nonetheless, the party never received an electoral majority since independence even though it received enough parliamentary seats to govern the country. The key to this parliamentary success can be found in the party system and the election rules. For many years there had not been a single large opposition party fighting against the Congress Party; instead, there had been several small parties that disliked each other as much as they disliked the Congress Party. They fragmented the opposition vote at election time. India used a single-member plurality election system, also known as winner-take-all. The candidate of the Congress Party in an election

district did not need to win a majority, only a plurality of the votes, whenever two or more opposition candidates entered the competition in that district.

India has handled well the political succession from prime minister to prime minister. Jawaharlal Nehru was replaced by Lal Bahadur Shastri (1964–1966), and he in turn by *Indira Gandhi*. When she lost the 1977 elections, she turned power over for the first time in India's independent history to the opposition *Janata Party* and its prime minister, *Morarji Desai*. Desai was unable to maintain the unity of the Janata Party; after two short-lived governments headed by the fragments of this party, Mrs. Gandhi's Congress Party returned to power in the elections held early in 1980. However, the story of party politics in India is more complex than this line of succession at the top.

Although Mrs. Gandhi had been supported for the position of prime minister in 1966 by many of the old state party bosses of the Congress Party, she soon asserted her independence, leading to a major split in the party in the late 1960s, after the party had registered its worst performance so far in the 1967 elections. Mrs. Gandhi's Congress Party, however, won the 1971 elections, increasing its parliamentary representation from 228 to 352 seats. But deteriorating internal economic and political conditions led her to proclaim "emergency" rule in 1975. In particular, a court had ruled her 1971 election invalid because of fraud. For the first time since independence, an Indian government retreated drastically from liberal democratic principles. Mrs. Gandhi suspended many civil rights, jailed leaders of the political opposition, and imposed stringent economic controls. The court case against Mrs. Gandhi was set aside, of course. Confident that she had brought a new sense of order and economic growth to India, including an increase in food production, Mrs. Gandhi surprised many by calling elections in mid-1977. Leaders of several opposition parties,

---

[1]J. Nehru, *Glimpses of World History* (London: Longmans Green, 1935).

believing that this was a crucial moment in Indian history, put aside their previous differences to form the *Janata Party*.

The Janata Party included the *Jan Sangh,* which had been a party of Hindu nationalists, and the *Lok Dal,* which had been a peasant party based in northern India. It also drew in old and new fragments of the Congress Party. Morarji Desai, an 84-year-old conservative economist who eventually became the Janata Party's prime minister, brought the support of many former Congress Party bosses who still had much local power. And the *harijans,* led by Jagjivan Ram, broke with the Congress Party for the first time and joined Janata, in part because the forced sterilization program imposed by Mrs. Gandhi's government affected untouchables the most. The former Socialist Party also became a part of Janata. The Janata Party was difficult enough to put together, but the combination of votes that it received was even more astonishing. Suffering under forced sterilization policies and slum clearance programs, Muslims broke with the Congress Party to vote for Janata, notwithstanding the Jan Sangh component of the latter. The tribes followed suit. Mrs. Gandhi was routed throughout northern India, where the Congress Party had historically been strong, and was left with only 35 percent of the vote and 153 parliamentary seats.

Prime Minister Desai's Janata Party government lifted the emergency, released political prisoners, restored civil rights, cancelled the forced sterilization policy, but found it increasingly difficult to agree on other aspects of a government program. After a number of prominent figures resigned from the government and began to reconstitute their pre-existing parties and factions, Desai lost his parliamentary majority and, under the constitution, was forced to resign. When other caretaker prime ministers were unable to sustain parliamentary majorities, elections had to be called. Mrs. Gandhi returned to power with 42.5 percent of the vote, but again facing a fragmented opposition, her Congress Party amassed a huge majority of 350 seats in parliament in the January 1980 elections. She regained the support of northern

India and of the religious, tribal, and *harijan* minorities. Mrs. Gandhi's slogan was "Elect a government that works." She may have learned to be more respectful of India's political traditions than she had been earlier in the 1970s, but the country's politics in the 1980s is likely to feature a good deal more centralized rule than had been the historical norm.

Some Stable Images of Indian Politics. To the relatively stable limits of current Indian politics we must also add some images in Indian political thought. The first of these is the vastness and unity of India and the depth of the attachment of many people to it. India is seen as the great mother. The cry *"Jai Hind!"* ("Long live India!") still appeals to millions.

A second image comes from outside India, but has become part of the national tradition. It is the British idea of government by discussion, of playing by parliamentary rules, of respect for individuals and civil rights. Members of the Indian elite for two generations learned civilized politics at British schools like Eton and Harrow and at the universities of Cambridge and Oxford, where their families sent them to be educated. The image is still alive for many of India's leaders today, even though it is becoming more remote for the new generation of Indian politicians, some of whom come from nonelite strata.

A third image stems from the unique Indian tradition created, or at least developed by, Mohandas K. Gandhi, who was called *Mahatma* ("great soul") even in his lifetime. It reaches back to the old Indian religious tradition of the holy man who lives in poverty but enjoys general respect and has great moral influence. Gandhi also drew on Thoreau's ideas of civil disobedience and Tolstoy's ideas of pacifism and nonviolence. As Gandhi developed his political philosophy, nonviolence became more powerful, both as a moral philosophy and a political strategy. Large campaigns of *ahimsa* (nonviolence) and *satya-graha* (truth force) forced Britain to concessions and at the same time

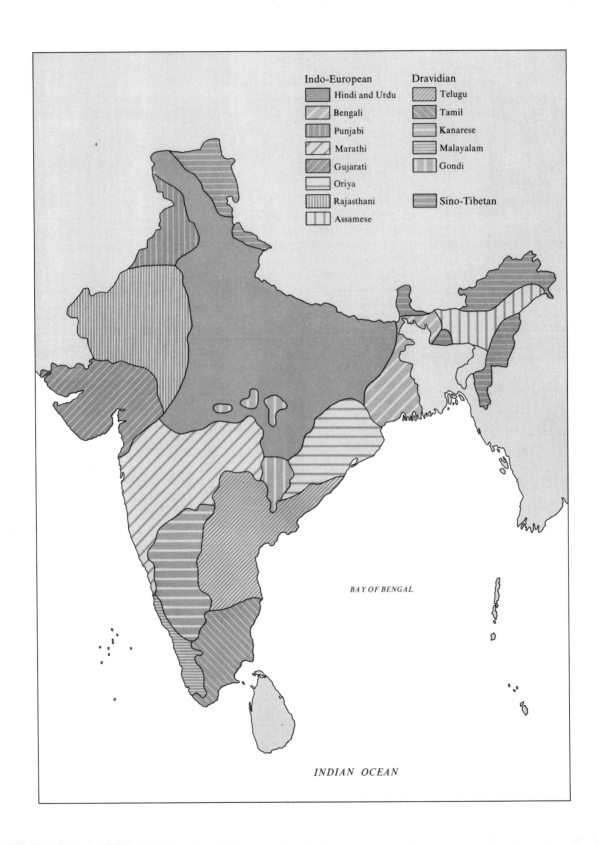

Indo-European	Dravidian
Hindi and Urdu	Telugu
Bengali	Tamil
Punjabi	Kanarese
Marathi	Malayalam
Gujarati	Gondi
Oriya	
Rajasthani	Sino-Tibetan
Assamese	

BAY OF BENGAL

INDIAN OCEAN

reduced the intensity of conflicts among various groups of Indians themselves.

To this day, success in Indian politics requires a moral basis. A would-be leader must be something of a wise and holy person to win one of the highest offices. A woman must have, or seem to have, a similar stature through the example of her own life and family background. By contrast, the politics of Machiavelli with its single-minded pursuit of power, even by force and fraud, has little charm for most Indians. Their intellectuals know that amoral ruthlessness was proclaimed by the Indian writer Kautilya in a handbook for rulers, *Artha-sastra,* more than a thousand years earlier—and that it had not worked very well. Gandhi, Nehru, Lal Bahadur Shastri, Indira Gandhi, Morarji Desai, and the Socialist opposition leader, Jayaprakash Narayan, have all clung to this anti-Machiavellian position of personal moral leadership in addition to their interest in power. For many years to come, probably every successor of these leaders will find it advisable to do the same.

The Arena of Indian Politics. Indian traditions thus far have tended to work against any further disintegration or secession because of geography or language. India with its present borders is still widely perceived as a unit. China's occupation in 1962 of an almost empty strip of territory near the disputed and poorly marked border of Tibet aroused a remarkable amount of popular indignation.

Territorial unity has been supported by federalism and by respect for regional languages. In the 1920s, Mahatma Gandhi induced the Congress Party to delimit its regional organizations according to language and no longer according to either traditional or British-imposed administrative divi-

---

(Left) MAP 10.2 *The Regional Languages of India*

---

sions. After independence in 1947, several states in the federation of India still cut across language boundaries, but, as discussed earlier, their borders had been redrawn to conform to the language of their populations. The British terms *dialect* and *vernacular* have been replaced officially by the term *regional language.* Most university education at the undergraduate level since the 1970s has been offered in these regional languages—even though it takes fourteen of them to reach 90 percent of India's population.

In its scope, India's government is more comprehensive than those of many other developing countries. It has accepted responsibility for guiding family planning, much of the economy, mass education, public health, agricultural development, and a host of other matters. It has many governmental organizations and institutions at the levels of village, district, city, state and federation. The performance of these institutions and the political experience they have made possible may have held Indian politics together.

Self-Steering in Politics. Within its large territory, how does the Indian government find out what has to be done? Perhaps the most important channel between the population and the government is the political parties. In second place are perhaps the labor unions and, third, the press. After many years of rule since 1947, the Congress Party became more rigid and less responsive in the 1970s. Other political parties, actions by labor unions, and criticism by the press all became more persuasive. As noted, these combined pressures split the Congress Party and defeated it in the elections of 1977.

In addition to political parties, labor unions, and the press, a private opinion-research organization conducts political surveys of limited reliability. There are also many excellent government surveys of such matters as economic life, popular habits of spending, investment and consumption, health and social patterns. These are carried out by the Indian Statistical Institute and other public agencies. They are repeated periodically and their results stored, to be used to help steer the Indian political system in the future.

The government has many other channels to the people. A direct channel functions through legislation and the administrative machinery. Another works through the state-owned radio and television system, and a third through the political parties currently represented in the government and supporting its policies. Finally, the government also has some influence on the press. It can create news that the latter must report, and it can often induce the press to back its policies.

The Process and Machinery of Government. According to one school of thought, India belongs to the "*soft states*" of the world; that is, the decisions of its government have only a small chance of being carried out. Inefficiency, black markets, the poverty of many clerks and officials, the resulting petty corruption in private and public life, and the large-scale corruption at higher levels of society and politics all contribute to this result. The inertia of age-old customs and beliefs together with the rigidity of a large bureaucracy often immobilize the system.

Another view sees Indian government as surprisingly effective in running things from day to day, in carrying out large reforms, and in guiding the country through major stresses and changes.

The truth most likely rests somewhere in between. There are many small frustrations, often related to poverty. Stamps sometimes are stolen from letters that were supposed to be posted. Official permits sometimes take a long time to obtain and only money speeds them up. But the country on the whole has grown and improved in income, nourishment, health, and education—more than a really soft state could have accomplished.

One key to India's success is the civil service. Introduced by the British in the nineteenth century, it offered at least some opportunities to a small number of gifted Indians. Their access to its higher ranks was small indeed, but not too small to permit the development of an Indian administrative elite and tradition, oriented toward British standards. Since independence, a large civil service has been built, staffed almost entirely by Indians and maintaining the morale and the standards of this tradition.

An important aspect of the spreading scope of government has been a commitment to planning. A national Planning Commission has now formulated several five-year development plans for India since its independence (the first was begun in 1951). Planning has required a detailed analysis of India's resources, constraints, and opportunities, as well as assessments of costs and benefits. The impetus for planning began with a concern for the effective use of economics, but it has had to operate in a political environment. Thus, the allocation of resources through these national plans has been accomplished in spite of the diversity of the country. The National Development Council and the Finance Commission play special roles in the regional distribution of resources.

The Indian government's commitment to a "mixed economy" has also affected the institutions of government. In a mixed economy, privately owned businesses operate alongside publicly owned or state enterprises. State enterprises are particularly active in India in sectors that require large capital investments. Although India has welcomed private direct foreign investment in some areas of its economy, it has also closely regulated the terms of entry and the conditions of such firms' operations. Foreign businesses are excluded from some economic sectors where only Indian enterprises operate.

At the top of the machinery of government is the prime minister. To be prime minister, a political leader must command a majority in the *Lok Sabha,* or lower house of parliament. The president of India, who is formally head of state, has only limited powers in fact, many of which are essentially ceremonial or diplomatic. Although the president formally nominates the prime minister before parliament, he or she must nominate the head of the Lok Sabha majority; the latter is the effective head of the government. Prime ministers serve for the duration of their parliamentary majority. Because those majorities had been rather large and durable under the governments of the Congress Party, prime ministers did not have to fear defeat between elections. Indeed, Prime Minister Nehru served from independence until his death in 1964, and Prime Minister Shastri also died in office in 1966. Indira Gandhi lost power in 1977 because she was defeated in an election, not because her power had waned between elections. For the first time, in mid-1979, a government fell because the prime minister lost his parliamentary majority because party discipline broke, eventually forcing the 1980 election with the return of Mrs. Gandhi and the Congress Party to power. Prime ministers are assisted by the cabinet, or Council of Ministers, whose members are selected by the prime minister for their political influence as well as for their abilities.

The upper house of parliament, called the *Rajya Sabha,* is primarily composed of representatives of the states of India who are elected by state legislative assemblies for staggered terms of six years (one-third stand for election every two years). In addition, about a dozen of its members are directly appointed by the president for their special expertise. Members of the Lok Sabha, in contrast, are directly elected by the people in districts with seats allocated according to population. Universal adult suffrage has prevailed, and India has characteristically had a majority of the electorate voting in national elections.

The Lok Sabha is by far the more powerful of the two parliamentary chambers. Although the Rajya Sabha has the right to be informed, only the Lok Sabha has the right to censure, and hence to defeat, the government. To become prime minister one needs only a majority of the Lok Sabha. The Rajya Sabha has only a suspensive veto over legislation dealing with taxes and government expenditures. If such a bill is approved by the Lok Sabha but defeated by the Rajya Sabha, the former need only approve it again by a simple majority for the bill to become law. Similarly, the president has only a suspensive veto. He can request that a bill that parliament has approved be reconsidered, but if the parliament approves the bill again by a simple majority, it becomes law regardless of the president's wishes. In most matters, and for most years, however, both parliamentary chambers have been controlled by the Congress Party. Minor differences between the two chambers have been resolved in conference committees. Duplication, rather than conflict, has often marked intraparliamentary politics.

The Performance of the Indian Political System. No other country on earth is at once so poor, so large, and yet so democratic in the rights it grants to its citizens. Independent India by 1981 has been a constitutional country for nearly one-third of a century, without real interruption. Even during Indira Gandhi's "state of emergency," people retained the right to organize politically and to defeat in an honest election that state of emergency and the government that imposed it.

India in 1980 had more than ten times as many university students as it had during its days under British rule. Literacy has doubled and there are four times as many children in school. The gain of almost a decade in average life expectancy speaks for itself.

A recent street scene in Bombay can be taken as a symbol of India. A heavy cart with wooden disks for wheels drawn by a tired buffalo was overtaken by two buses, one on each side, and these were marked "Indian Atomic Energy Commission." India's past is weighty, but its future is open.

NIGERIA

Nigeria's cultural heritage is an old one from several ancient kingdoms. Modern Nigeria, however, is the child of a short history. For several years prior to 1900, a coastal region near Lagos was administered by a private corporation under British protection. Direct British colonial administration of this region commenced in 1900, and by 1914 the territories of present-day Nigeria were united under it.

A major reason for this territorial merger seems to have been convenience of river transportation. The great river Niger forms a pattern like the letter Y and links three major regions that differ in their peoples, languages, cultures, and in some cases geographic conditions. The coastal regions of the southeast and southwest are hot, moist rain forests, suitable for agriculture. The north is drier, with extended grasslands suitable for cattle raising and horseback riding, and crossed by extended caravan trails. The main peoples are the *Yoruba* in the southwest, which includes Lagos, the *Ibo* in the southeast, and the *Hausa* and *Fulani* in the far north. Each people has a different language developed from a combination of local dialects. Both Yorubas and Ibos still practice the traditional religions of their cultures, but a preponderance of Nigerians are Christian or Muslim, in almost equal numbers.

The north is Muslim, with elements of Arab cultural influence. Its main languages are Hausa and Fulani. Its society and politics are still characterized by aristocratic feudal traditions, supported by a traditional governing class. This society contrasts with the more urban and decentralized political culture of the Yorubas and even more with the egalitarian, commercial, and competitive traditions of the Ibos. A multitude of smaller groups, languages, and religions supplements these three major groups and seems likely to persist.

Growth Toward Independence. The Yorubas of the southwest and the Ibos of the southeast relatively quickly took to Western education, commerce, social mobility, and eventually to labor unions, political parties, and aspirations for independence from Britain. The north for a long time tended to remain proud, traditional, illiterate, socially conservative, and more or less content with British

rule. Not surprisingly, British colonial administrators, both military and civilian, felt comfortable with northern nobles who rode horseback and played polo and uncomfortable with the argumentative lawyers and politicians from the steamy coastal regions.

From 1914 to the 1950s, Nigeria's population grew, and so did its cities and towns and the nonagricultural occupations within them. The use of money increased, as did literacy, mails, and the mass media audience. During World War II, local industries multiplied. More soldiers and officers were trained, and some went overseas to aid the British war effort. After 1945, there was an increase in labor unions, newspapers, and political agitation, demanding more self-government and the eventual end of foreign rule.

By the later 1950s, Britain was ready to concede legal independence to Nigeria and to replace colonial rule by the more indirect means of economic and political influence. But Britain wanted the country to stay together and expected the conservative north to exert its influence throughout the country as well as encourage the confidence of foreign investors. The federal constitution of Nigeria deliberately favored the north at independence. It assigned to the north a larger number of peoples, so as to give it a majority of the population, electorate, legislature, and armed forces of the new federation that was formally established in 1960.

Within a few years, regional rivalries and political instability threatened the existence of the federation. The effective head of government was a northerner, Prime Minister *Abubakar Tafawa Balewa.* Southerners counted on the advantages of their own peoples in education and commercial and technical skills to eventually shift the social, economic, and political leadership to them. Particularly for the Ibos, these expectations soon seemed to come true. Their businesses prospered. Their young men came out on top in the competition for better jobs in the railroad

MAP 10.3 *Nigeria*

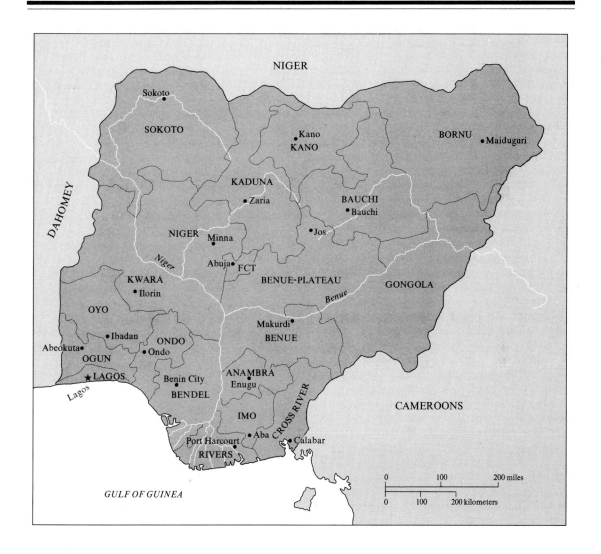

NIGER

Sokoto

SOKOTO

Kano
KANO

BORNU • Maiduguri

DAHOMEY

KADUNA

• Zaria

BAUCHI
• Bauchi

NIGER Minna

• Jos

Niger

Abuja• FCT

BENUE-PLATEAU

GONGOLA

KWARA
• Ilorin

Benue

OYO

Makurdi•

• Ibadan

ONDO
• Ondo

BENUE

Abeokuta•

OGUN

★LAGOS

Benin City
•

ANAMBRA
• Enugu

Lagos

BENDEL

CAMEROONS

IMO

CROSS RIVER

• Aba

Port Harcourt
•

• Calabar

RIVERS

GULF OF GUINEA

0   100   200 miles

0   100   200 kilometers

and telegraph services, in much of public administration throughout the country, and even in the military services.

In the early 1960s, Nigeria was profoundly affected by the politics of ethnicity and region. Three major political parties emerged, each in control of a region. The Northern People's Congress (NPC) controlled the northern region and 45.5 percent of the seats in the federal House of Representatives on independence day. The National Convention of Nigerian Citizens (NCNC) controlled the eastern region; it joined the NPC to form the first national government under an NPC leader, Prime Minister Balewa. The Action Group (AG), the third major party, controlled the government of the western region. Of course, the Hausa and Fulani led in the NPC, the Ibos in the NCNC, and the Yorubas in the AG. Politics was further complicated by diversity within regions. In each of the three areas there were cultural and linguistic minorities that were often allied with outside groups to oppose the majority within the region. The political order gradually began to fragment in response to the many levels of competition.

Corresponding to ethnicity, region, and parties, three major political leaders emerged. Chief *Obafemi Awolowo*, a Yoruba and AG leader, emerged as the prime minister of the western region. *Nnamdi Azikiwe* (called "Zik") emerged as the pre-eminent Ibo leader in the eastern region; when his NCNC aligned with the NPC to form a government, Azikiwe became Nigeria's first governor-general and eventually its first president (then a largely ceremonial post). The third major leader was a Fulani traditional aristocratic ruler in the north, Alhaji Ahmadu Bello, the *Sardauna of Sokoto,* who led the NPC with the support of Muslim landowners, traditional emirs, and local rulers. Thus, modern competitive party politics did *not* displace Nigeria's traditional political environment but was grafted onto it. The politics of lords and languages, rulers and regions, persisted and became manifest through the new parties.

In January 1966, a coup instigated by a group of

predominantly Ibo officers overthrew Prime Minister Balewa's northern-dominated government. A military government under Major General Johnson Aguiyi-Ironsi, an Ibo, was established. In July, however, anti-Ibo violence started in the north and culminated in another military coup that reestablished a northern government, this time under General *Yakubu Gowon*. During these events, thousands of Ibos were massacred in the north, and thousands of propertyless survivors fled back to the Ibo lands in the southeast.

Ibo opinion now turned in favor of secession. This trend was reinforced by the recent discovery of substantial oil deposits in the Ibo-dominated eastern region. These promised considerable economic benefits, either for all Nigeria under its military government or else for an independent Ibo state, should it succeed in keeping the oil fields for itself. But if the oil discoveries promised an economic reward for Ibo secession, they also promised a reward to the Nigerian government for preventing secession.

The result was a civil war that lasted thirty months, from May 1967 until January 1970. The Ibos declared the independence of their region, called it *Biafra,* and established a government headed by *Odumegwu Ojukwu*. They asked for foreign aid, both military and humanitarian, while hinting that they might express their gratitude in economic concessions to helpful foreign firms and countries. The Nigerian government blockaded Biafra, causing much starvation, and eventually conquered the entire region. During the civil war, Biafra received some aid from France, Portugal (then still under a conservative and procolonialist dictatorship), and South Africa, as well as from scattered firms and groups in other countries. Nigeria, however, retained the diplomatic recognition and actual support of Britain, the United States, the Soviet Union, and most other countries, and with it access to vital military and economic supplies. In the end, about a million people had perished in the civil war, but the unity of Nigeria was preserved.

Before the civil war, Nigeria's army had numbered about 20,000. At its end, it had grown tenfold, to about 250,000. Since then it has decreased in size, but its political influence has persisted. All Nigerian governments remained under military control until 1979.

Government leaders continued to change. In July 1975, General Gowon was deposed while out of the country at a conference of the Organization of African Unity (OAU) at Kampala, Uganda. His place was taken by Brigadier General Murtala Rufai Muhammed. Less than a year later, Muhammed was assassinated and Lieutenant General *Olusegun Obasanjo* became the head of government.

Party Politics in the 1980s. Nigeria at the start of the 1980s has a population of 80 million. The old three regions, north, southeast, and southwest, have been replaced by nineteen states, in the hope of reducing the likelihood of conflicts among large regions. After suppressing the attempt at secession, the Nigerian military government embarked on a policy of reconciliation, permitting the return from abroad of many Ibo refugees, including some political leaders.

The Nigerian military government embarked on a program to transfer power back to civilians, but only after some institutional safeguards had been put in place to avoid the pitfalls of earlier history. These included several unique constitutional innovations, such as requiring ethnic balance in the internal governance of political parties. The principle of reflecting "the federal character of Nigeria" is applied to the composition of a wide range of institutions. It is too soon to tell whether these safeguards will work, but the record so far is both encouraging and worrisome. On October 1, 1979, the military transferred power to an elected civilian president. To avoid the extreme competition among ethnic groups between and within regions, the number of states was increased. Interstate conflict, it was hoped, would have a less ethnic character and, at the same time, the smaller ethnic groups could have their own states. These

two objectives were obviously somewhat contradictory.

The new constitution abandoned the reliance on a prime minister and parliamentary government based on the British model and, instead, adopted a federal presidential system somewhat like that of the United States. To prevent parliamentary coalitions from threatening government stability, the cabinet could not be overthrown by the new National Assembly because it responded to the president's policies. To be elected president, a political leader had to receive at least one-quarter of the votes in two-thirds of the states, in order to guarantee a modicum of support throughout the country, rather than the pre-1966 extreme ethnic-regional fragmentation. Cabinet ministers must be appointed from all nineteen states. To further decentralize decision making the capital was moved from the large coastal city of Lagos to the center of the country, in Abuja. The military rulers who had led the country, including General Obasanjo, left the government in 1979 and returned to civilian life.

Some problems soon arose. When the military government announced the call for elections, two of the five presidential candidates were the now elderly Awolowo and Azikiwe. In the north, however, two major events had some impact. The Sardauna of Sokoto was killed in the 1966 coup, and the reorganization of the states divided the formerly huge northern region so that politicians other than Hausa-Fulani aristocrats could emerge in the new smaller states in the country's northern area. In fact, two did. One was Alhaji Waziri Ibrahim, not a Hausa-Fulani, who founded the Great Nigeria People's Party (GNPP). He was a very rich man who had made his fortune in the arms business during the civil war. The other was Alhaji Aminu Kano, who had been active in Nigerian politics since the preindependence period. His People's Redemption Party (PRP) had opposed the Hausa-Fulani aristocracy from its base in the northern city of Kano. Nevertheless, the pre-eminent politician to emerge in the north was a Muslim Fulani from Sokoto in the northwest, Alhaji Shehu Shagari.

When the votes were counted, the persistence of ethnic identities became all the more evident. Awolowo's Unity Party of Nigeria (UPN) won all four Yoruba-dominated states with over 80 percent of the vote in those areas. Azikiwe won both Ibo-dominated states at the head of the Nigerian People's Party (NPP) ticket. Shagari's National Party of Nigeria (NPN), however, won not only five states in the north but also two states in the southeast that the Ibos did not dominate, and was elected president. Moreover, the NPP won one state in the north. The PRP won only in Kano and the GNPP won two northeastern states. All parties made efforts to "balance the ticket" by including candidates of the major ethnic groups on their slate. A crucial question was how the Ibos would be reintegrated after the civil war experience. All vice-presidential candidates (except for Azikiwe's) were Ibos, and Azikiwe's participation in the election also helped to reintegrate the Ibo population.

Another sign of continuity with the pre-1966 First Republic, but which nevertheless had great value, was the establishment of an alliance between the NPN and the NPP, between Sokoto and the Ibo regions. The NPP entered Shagari's cabinet and obtained a reaffirmation of the constitutional pledge that Nigeria would be a secular state where all religions could flourish. This coalition also provided the government with substantial majorities in both the federal Senate and House of Representatives, though not in most of the state legislatures, where more local patterns of power prevailed. The elected state governors were also a mixed group of party adherents.

In short, some changes appear to have occurred in Nigeria that may make the country more stable. But at the level of political identities and loyalties, the military interlude between 1966 and 1979 was unable fundamentally to alter political patterns. Ethnicity remained the principal factor in Nigerian politics. (The various party platforms showed very similar ideological content—differences emphasized *who* one was and supported rather than *what* might be done differently.) Even some of the same leaders arose from the same historical areas, emphasizing very similar political alliance patterns.

There were other uncertainties in the electoral process. As evidence of their integrity—corruption was a major issue in Nigerian politics—all candidates were required to publish their income tax returns for the preceding three years. Only Awolowo did so in complete form, and Azikiwe only in part.[2] More seriously, the election raised cries of fraud. After investigation by the powerful and independent Federal Election Commission, only twenty-five elections were declared void and held again under supervision. A further problem was that Shagari did not win the required minimum of one-quarter of the votes in 13 states (two-thirds of all states). The constitution provided that, in such a case, an electoral college composed of all federal and state legislators would choose between the top two candidates. The Election Commission ruled, however, that Shagari had received one-fifth of the vote in the state of Kano, and that $12\frac{2}{3}$ of the states were equal for these purposes to 13 states. An outraged Awolowo appealed to the Supreme Court, which supported the commission's ruling, and Awolowo accepted the decision. The departing military leaders modified the constitution to abolish the electoral college and replace it with a run-off election, should it be necessary in the future.

The machinery of government was characterized by a strong presidency, occupied by the 55-year-old Shagari. The National Assembly was the elected federal legislative body, divided into a 95-member Senate and a 449-member House of Representatives. Each state had an elected governor and an elected state House of Assembly. The 1979 elections were held in five separate rounds to allow the voters to focus on each level of government on its own merits—a marathon of competi-

---

[2]*Der Tagesspiegel*, Berlin (West), June 24, 1979, p. 31, with reference to the *Nigerian Herald*.

tive elections. All citizens over age eighteen were eligible to vote (women had been denied the franchise in the Muslim-dominated northern region before 1966). However, given the lack of electoral habits, turnout was only 35 percent in the presidential election (a higher figure than in the other elections). The Supreme Court acquired an important role in easing the transition to civilian rule and also serves as another key component in the system. The greatest imponderable, of course, is whether all of this will work, and whether the armed forces will truly stay out of politics. They plainly keep a watchful eye on the transition, and especially on the behavior of political organizations and the mass media.

The Stakes of Politics. With an average per capita GNP just above $400 in the mid-1970s and with only a small fraction of Nigeria's population literate, urban, and employed in nonagricultural occupations, much of the population is still uninvolved in politics. But still unbeknown to them, politics matters, as we have seen.

Oil is a key to Nigeria's future. The oil fields have been developed and their output has grown. They have already paid for much of the cost of the civil war. They can yield about 3 million barrels of oil per day and furnish 14 percent of the oil exports to the United States, contributing substantially to the financial stability and relative prosperity of the country—which still has remained poor.

The reality is a bit more complicated. Changes in the world price of petroleum in the late 1970s led to fluctuations in Nigerian oil output that amounted to almost one-third of total production. This made planning all the more difficult. The oil revenue has stimulated a serious inflation in the urban areas that, along with slow industrial growth and problems in agriculture, present serious economic problems. But oil is also facilitating an economic growth rate well in excess of a high (2.6 percent) population growth rate. Ill-timed development expenditures in relation to rapidly changing oil prices also caused difficulties.

Although the military government welcomes private direct foreign investment, it also adopted a series of regulations increasingly characteristic of legislation in many emerging states. These directives required that foreign firms hire increasing proportions of Nigerian citizens for all posts and that they divest of a part of their equity by selling shares to Nigerian partners. (The Nigerian subsidiary of British Petroleum was nationalized in 1979 as a limited response to British dealings with South Africa, of which Nigeria disapproved.) President Shagari has declared his intention to stimulate foreign investment without retreating from the established rules.

Another fundamental question will be the disbursement of federal revenues to the states, so that the oil wealth will assist in reducing regional imbalances. This is clearly a serious matter for relations among the states as well as between them and the federal government. Because the oil fields are concentrated in the southeast—the scene of the Biafran secession attempt of the late 1960s—the matter is unusually delicate. Federal policies also affect more generally the distribution of income, investments, and career opportunities for peoples and groups from the various linguistic and ethnic regions.

Nigerian foreign policy has been officially "nonaligned" in the conflict between the United States and the Soviet Union. But Nigeria has been very active in African international relations, especially since the defeat of the Biafran secession and the increase in oil prices. General Obasanjo played an important role in bringing international pressure to bear on the white minority regime in Rhodesia, eventually working well with the United States and others to achieve a transition to an independent, new state of Zimbabwe. Nigeria has served as a mediator in the civil war in Chad and has deployed troops into Chad as a peace-keeping force with the consent of the contending parties there. Nigeria also gave early support to the radical nationalist party and government in Angola. It has taken direct boycott action against South Africa and has, at times, indirectly boycotted South Africa's trading partners. Nigeria has sought to mediate in

POOR TO ALMOST RICH: INDIA, NIGERIA, EGYPT, IRAN

other major disputes in Africa and has warned against major-power intervention—from East or West—in African affairs.

Despite its problems, Nigerians rightly look on their country as the largest state in black Africa and as the only one with the potential of becoming a middle-sized power within the next ten or twenty years.

Nigeria's political system is still weakly integrated. Civic loyalty and skills, communication channels between government and governed, administrative accountability and efficiency, are still incompletely developed. Even so, Nigeria's performance since the Biafran war deserves respect. Since that time, there has been relatively little bloodshed or repression, measured by the size of the country and the standards of many other developing nations. Economic gains have been matched by gains in education, symbolized by universities in Lagos and Ibadan. With skill and luck, it may remain the world's fourth largest country ruled by civilians elected in competitive elections. Starting from a heritage of poverty and severe interregional cleavages in colonial days, Nigeria has done better than many observers expected.

EGYPT

Egypt is a very poor country. Its per capita GNP in 1976 was $280, ranking well below Nigeria's for the same year. Average gross domestic product per capita during 1965–75 grew in real terms only by 0.8 percent per year, and not much of that reached the poorer strata of the population. Yet Egypt ranks much higher on other indicators of development. Its 1976 population was 34 percent urban; 46 percent of its work force was in nonagricultural occupations; and 44 percent of its population over ten years old was literate. Average life expectancy in 1975 was fifty-two years, a gain of seven years since 1960.

For most practical purposes, Egypt is the Nile Valley—a thin strip of highly fertile land running north from the border of the Sudan to the Nile delta at the shore of the Mediterranean Sea. This is where the important cities are, as well as almost the entire population. The rest of the country is mostly desert.

Organized government has existed in the Nile Valley for more than four thousand years. Yet its political system seems poorly developed: there is no strong tradition of mass competitive politics nor of efficient government. It has left a legacy of obedience and political passivity among many people.

The First Three Thousand Years. Government in ancient Egypt meant water. Kings and their officials directed the construction and maintenance of the extensive dams that were indispensable for irrigation. Priests alone could predict the day when spring would come and the flood waters of the Nile, fed by the melting snow from far-off mountains, would cover the fields with water and fertilizing mud. Together, kings, officials, and priests formed an irrigation bureaucracy that people did not dare to disobey for many centuries.

A Succession of Conquerors. Later conquerors—Assyrians, Babylonians, Greeks, Romans, and Byzantines—found an easy prey in the rich country and its obedient people. Capital cities changed often, both under native and foreign dynasties. So long as taxes were collected, it mattered little in what city the rulers chose to spend them by setting up their court there. After 332 B.C., when Alexander the Great conquered Egypt and founded the city of Alexandria, first Greek and later Roman gods replaced the old Egyptian ones. For a time, Alexandria led the ancient world in commerce and learning. Greek and Roman laws governed Egyptian life. Egypt served as a granary for imperial Rome, and from the fourth century A.D. on, the country became Christian in religion and Byzantine in administration.

Greek and Roman influence decreased with the Muslim conquest after A.D. 639. The conquerors spoke Arabic. In 712, they founded the city El-Kahira, "the victorious," today's Cairo. More Arabs moved into the country and merged with the local population. By about 950, more than one-half of the inhabitants of Egypt spoke Arabic. By about 1350, this proportion had risen to about 90 percent. The mass of the people had become Muslim and Arabic, and it remains so today, although Coptic Christians remain an important religious minority.

New regimes evolved—Seljuks, Mamluks, and Turks. But now they, too, belonged to the world of Islam. Twice the court of the sultans of Egypt became a brilliant center of Muslim culture: once in about A.D. 1000 under the Fatimid dynasty and again about two centuries later under Sultan Saladin. Early in the sixteenth century, Portuguese fleets cut off Egypt's trade through the Red Sea with India. For awhile, an impoverished Egypt fell under the direct administration of the *Ottoman Empire* under a governor, later called viceroy. The Mamluks remained noble landowners; the peasants, the *fellaheen,* continued to work for whomever was in power.

After more than a thousand years of Islam, European influences broke into Egypt. In 1798, General Napoleon Bonaparte of the French republic landed with an army and defeated the Mamluk cavalry in the Battle of the Pyramids. "Forty centuries are looking upon you," he exhorted his soldiers. He conquered the country, only to find his sea lanes to France cut by the British navy. He had to evacuate his army and return the country to the Ottoman Empire in 1801.

But the country was no longer quite the same. French and English trade and influence remained and grew. Its sultan, now a Turkish viceroy (called a *khedive*), had more money and could borrow still more. From 1805 to 1848, a strong viceroy, *Mehemet Ali,* of Albanian extraction, began to modernize the country. In the 1820s and 1830s, he raised a strong army and offered to help the Turkish sultan reconquer Greece. The scheme was

stopped by the threat of French and British intervention, but it was the first time in centuries that anyone had tried to project Egyptian military power beyond its borders.

Mehemet Ali's successors, particularly his grandson Ismail (1863–79), focused their attention on administrative reforms, roads, railroads, and new dams, financed largely by foreign loans, albeit with high costs in usurious interest and discount rates. Inefficiency and corruption continued among the domestic elite of landowners and bureaucrats. When Civil War in the United States pushed up the price of cotton, long-staple cotton planting was introduced in Egypt with British aid. When cotton prices fell again after the Civil War was over, England wanted Egypt to continue as an additional source of cotton for the British textile industry. More loans to Egypt were forthcoming, but at ever stiffer terms. French business interests pushed the old project of a *Suez Canal* toward realization. The canal opened in 1869, putting Egypt once more on the main trade route to India and the Far East. The French Suez Canal Company, however, ran out of money in 1875, after France had been weakened by its defeat in the Franco-Prussian War of 1870–71. In 1877, the British government bought up the khedive's share and became the company's largest shareholder. Now Britain was the chief creditor of Egypt, and Egypt was becoming unable to pay.

Expansion, Militarization, and Indebtedness. In the meantime, Egypt expanded its political and military power in Africa. Between 1865 and 1879, it occupied the Red Sea coast; completed the conquest of the Sudan begun in the 1820s; and waged an inconclusive war with Ethiopia. All this activity pushed Egypt more deeply into debt and financial dependence on foreign powers. But just as economic developments strengthened Egypt's middle class, so the military actions produced new strata of Egyptian officers, soldiers, and bureaucrats. They resented Egypt's dependence and became increasingly ready to respond to appeals for a new Egyptian nationalism.

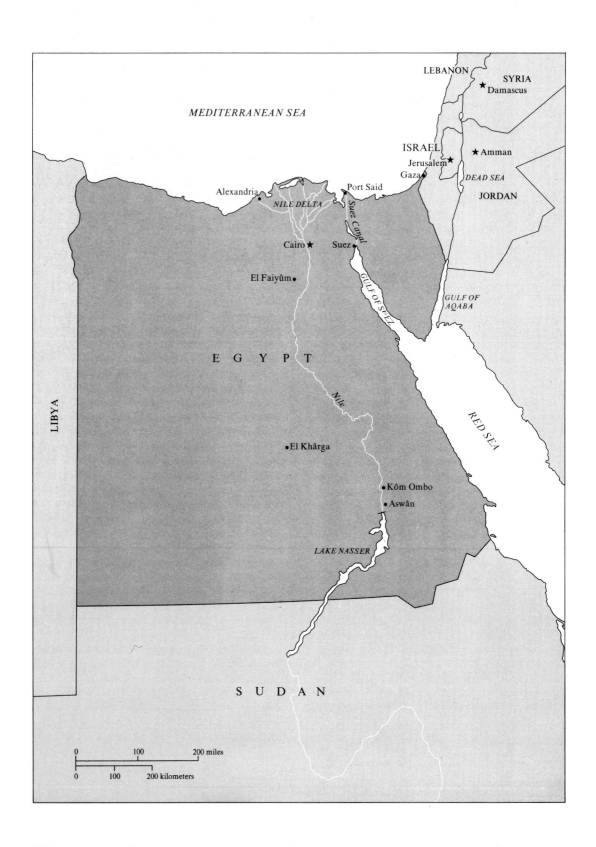

MEDITERRANEAN SEA

LEBANON

SYRIA
★ Damascus

ISRAEL
Jerusalem ★ ★ Amman
Gaza ●

DEAD SEA

JORDAN

Alexandria ●
NILE DELTA

Port Said ●

Suez Canal

Cairo ★   Suez ●

El Faiyûm ●

GULF OF SUEZ

GULF OF
AQABA

E G Y P T

LIBYA

Nile

RED SEA

● El Khârga

● Kôm Ombo
● Aswân

LAKE NASSER

S U D A N

| 0 | 100 | 200 miles |

| 0 | 100 | 200 kilometers |

In 1876, a British and a French controller were appointed in charge of Egypt's finances, leading to a brief Anglo-French condominium in the interest of the creditors. Two years later, an Englishman was made minister of finance and a Frenchman minister of public works. When that foreign-dominated government fell after a demonstration of army officers in 1879, perhaps encouraged by the viceroy, Ismail, the Turkish sultan deposed Ismail under pressure by the European powers. Ismail was replaced by his more pliable son, Tewfik. In 1880, a new Law of Liquidation (of Egypt's debts) provided that all surplus should go toward repaying the debts, regardless of the country's other needs.

Early Nationalism and British Occupation. In 1881, the Egyptian officers forced the appointment of a nationalist, Mahmud Sami, as war minister and, in early 1882, the appointment of a nationalist ministry. The nationalists were led by Ahmed Arabi, called "*Arabi Pasha.*" They were inspired by the famous progressive Muslim teacher *Jamal-el-Din el-Afghani,* who since 1871 had preached resistance to the Europeans and the necessary adoption of European political methods for defense.

Britain and France intervened. In May 1882, their warships appeared before Alexandria, ostensibly in support of the khedive against his nationalist government. An Anglo-French ultimatum forced the resignation of the government, but the khedive soon had to call them back into office. In June, riots in Alexandria killed some fifty Europeans. According to some, the khedive instigated the riots to force European intervention in his favor. Within weeks, the British navy bombarded Alexandria, landed troops, and occupied Cairo. Arabi surrendered and was eventually banished to Ceylon. Egypt remained under British occupation from 1882 until 1946.

(Left) MAP 10.4 *Egypt*

British Rule Becomes Indirect. The legal forms changed. Egypt remained nominally subject to the sultan of Turkey until 1914, when it was declared a British *protectorate.* Khedive Abbas Hilmi was deposed, replaced by his uncle Hussein Kamil, with the title of sultan; and by Sultan Ahmed *Fuad* after Kamil's death in 1917. In 1922, Britain unilaterally terminated the protectorate. Egypt was declared independent; Fuad took the title of king. In 1924, a relatively liberal constitution was promulgated. It was suspended in 1928, replaced by a less democratic one in 1930, but restored in 1935. In 1937, Egypt became a member of the League of Nations. In fact, British power remained dominant, but gradually Egypt's own government became somewhat stronger.

A Second Wave of Nationalism. During the same decades popular nationalism mounted. A nationalist party, *Wafd,* was formed under the leadership of Saad Zaghlul at the conclusion of World War I to present the demands of Egyptian nationalists to the Paris peace conference. It became Egypt's major political party until it was abolished after the 1952 revolution. When in 1919 the British deported Saad Zaghlul and other nationalist leaders, a national insurrection followed. British troops put it down. Zaghlul returned in 1921, was deported again in the same year, returned once more in 1923, and became prime minister in early 1924. Large anti-British riots continued in 1922, 1924, 1930, 1933, and 1935. But as elections and some press freedom were permitted, the nationalists turned to the polls. They won a string of victories in the elections of 1923, 1925, 1929, 1933, and 1936, were eclipsed by internal dissensions and government pressure in 1938 and 1945, but again won an overwhelming majority in 1950. Mass nationalism had come to stay. All that might change were its leaders and channels of expression.

British power was eroding. Twice, in 1924 and 1928, a British ultimatum forced major concessions on the Egyptian government, followed by the resignation of its prime minister. King Fuad accepted British advice to suspend constitutional liberties and used Britain as an ally to preserve his power within the country. After his death in 1936, he was succeeded by his sixteen-year-old son, *Faruk*. In his reign, Egypt moved to the threshold of real independence and modernity.

In 1936, a treaty between Egypt and the United Kingdom obligated Britain to withdraw all troops from the country, except for ten thousand men in the Suez Canal zone. The same treaty established a twenty-year alliance between Egypt and Britain.

In 1937, a British military mission arrived to advise the Egyptian government on building a modern army. Soon, the first officer training courses were begun and, in 1938, universal military training was instituted. All this preparation took place in the face of the mounting threat of World War II. When the war came in 1939, however, the Egyptian government did not enter it, although it severed diplomatic and economic relations with Germany. The Egyptian army, many of whose junior officers were militant anti-British nationalists, did not fight, even when German and Italian armies moved toward Cairo in 1940 and 1942. Britain, on the contrary, did fight on Egyptian soil, controlling its territory, ports, and resources. British troops drove from El Ala-mein in October 1942, meeting in the spring of 1943 with the American army in Tunisia, and ending the German and Italian military presence in North Africa. The Egyptian government finally declared war on the Axis in February 1945 and thus formally qualified as a member of the United Nations. In the same year, the League of Arab States was established, with headquarters in Cairo.

The Egyptian army, in alliance with troops from other Arab states, all of which regarded Zionism as a manifestation of Western imperialistic penetration of the Middle East, invaded Israel in 1948. It was defeated in that war, occupying only the Gaza Strip of 150 square miles and several hundred thousand Palestinian Arabs and refugees.

The Egyptian Revolution: Nasserism. Younger officers returning from the war blamed the monarch, the politicians, and the old elites for the weakness of their country and conspired to bring about a change. In 1952, King Faruk was overthrown. Soon his property was placed in state custody, the titles *bey* and *pasha* were abolished, and all political parties, including the Wafd, were dissolved, to be replaced in early 1953 by a single *Liberation Rally*. A major step was a far-reaching land reform that led to the expropriation of large landholdings. In June 1953, Egypt was proclaimed a republic, with *General Mohammed Naguib* as its president and prime minister. In 1954, Naguib was ousted by Lieutenant-Colonel *Gamal Abdel Nasser,* who became prime minister and, in 1956, president.

Nasser tried to legitimate his rule through the promotion of an activist state at home and abroad. Nationalist in his relations with the United States and Europe, Pan-Arabist and anti-Israel in the Middle East, and economically interventionist at home, he led Egypt through tumultuous times. Populist in domestic politics, Nasser first tried to get aid from the United States. He was rebuffed by U.S. Secretary of State John Foster Dulles, who refused U.S. aid for arms and a projected high dam at Aswan. That dam was completed with Soviet aid. Egypt embarked on a formally neutralist but actually somewhat pro-Soviet course in foreign policy that lasted for eighteen years.

In 1956, Nasser nationalized the Suez Canal in retaliation for refusals by the United States and the United Kingdom, and the World Bank to finance the building of the Nile river dam. In the ensuing dispute over his decision, Britain, France, and Israel initiated a war against Egypt. The Egyptian troops in the Sinai were defeated by the Israelis, but the main strength of the Egyptian army held out in Egypt proper. British and French landings won no decisive successes. The opposition of the United Nations, the Soviet Union, the United States, a large part of the Commonwealth and the British Labour Party, and much of British public opinion soon brought the war to an end. Nasser was left more or less a victor.

In domestic affairs, Nasser developed a policy of Arab socialism, under which he strove to drive out major foreign business firms, to nationalize banks, various industries, and services, but to leave room for small and middle-sized Egyptian businesses, artisans, and farmers. This policy led to slow economic growth, much bureaucratic regulation, recurrent difficulties with currencies and credits, and an almost constant tug of war within the government party between adherents of the public and the private sectors. There was some success, however, in reorganizing the agricultural sector through the land reform, the organization of cooperatives, and the improvement of village living standards.

In foreign affairs, Nasser aimed at national greatness. He stressed *Pan-Arabism* and strove to continue Egypt's role as a leader of the Arab world by virtue of its central geographic location, its large population, and long tradition as an Islamic religious center and focal point of Arabic culture. Pan-Arabism required accepting the independence of the Sudan, something earlier Egyptian governments had opposed. This policy still left Egypt free to promote its influence, by radio broadcasts and in other ways, among the populations in Africa south of the Sahara. At the same time, Egypt under Nasser became the major adversary of Israel, encouraging Arab guerrilla attacks on Israel from neighboring countries. Other Arab states, particularly Syria, followed the same policy. But in the 1950s and 1960s, Egypt's size and power supplied the main strength of the Arab coalition that refused to recognize Israel's existence.

In 1958, Syria and Egypt joined to form the United Arab Republic (UAR), with which Yemen became associated. Nasser was president of the UAR, but the governments, armies, and administrations of Syria and Egypt remained separate. When efforts were made to merge them, it soon appeared that the Egyptians, five times more numerous than the Syrians, would hold most top jobs in the proposed joint army and administration. Efforts to nationalize Syrian industries within the UAR offered similar prospects. In 1961, the Syrian army revolted and restored Syria's independence. In the same year, Nasser dissolved Egypt's association with Yemen, denouncing the rule of the country's traditional monarch and religious leader as reactionary. Civil war in Yemen followed. From 1962 to 1967, Nasser sent forty thousand Egyptian troops to that country to support the pro-Nasser republican faction there, with indifferent success.

The Six Day War. Nasser tried to keep his role as leader of the Arab opposition to Israel's existence. He ordered threatening troop movements, encouraged increased guerrilla activity, and closed the Strait of Tiran from the Red Sea to the Israeli port of Elath. In June 1967, Israel responded by a "pre-emptive" attack on Egypt, Syria, and Jordan, defeating all three within six days. Egypt lost the Gaza Strip and the entire Sinai peninsula to Israeli occupation, as well as the much-needed revenues from the Suez Canal, which became the border between the Egyptian and Israeli military positions and was closed to traffic.

By late 1967, Nasser's Pan-Arabism had failed, and his domestic policies had not done much better. Armaments and war had depleted Egypt's resources. Western currencies and credits were scarce or unavailable. Egyptian entrepreneurs wanted more freedom; workers demanded more power for their unions. Economic growth was disappointing. Many people leaving agriculture and moving to the cities found little housing and no jobs. And the army resented the memory of its defeat by Israel in 1967. Nevertheless, despite the great dissatisfaction with Nasser's regime, he succeeded in making Egypt into an influential regional power and a voice heeded in the Third World. He also instilled a feeling of pride in many Egyptians, whereas before the revolution the country was considered the preserve of the royal family. When Nasser died in 1970, the country was ready for a change.

A New Course: Anwar el-Sadat. The change came step by step after Nasser's vice-president and associate, Anwar Sadat, succeeded to his office. Sadat tightened his grip on the government party and the government-controlled mass media, arresting some cabinet members in 1971 on charges of conspiracy. He played down Nasser's Arab socialism and made some economic concessions to business interests and the middle class. He strengthened the army and built up its modern equipment, largely with Soviet aid. Then, when he had accumulated a stock of Soviet arms, he dramatically reversed a major part of Egypt's foreign policy. In 1972, he ordered all Soviet advisers, military and civilian, to leave the country and soon began to work to improve relations with the United States and the other Western powers.

The October War of 1973. At the same time, Sadat stepped up war preparations against Israel. On October 6, 1973, the Egyptian army struck. It crossed the Suez Canal quickly and broke through the Israeli defense lines there—something Israeli experts had considered impossible. Egypt's attack was synchronized with an attack by Syria, and during the first few hours it seemed a triumph for the Arab cause. Within a very few days, however, the Israeli army and air force, despite heavy losses in men and materiel, stopped the Egyptian and Syrian tanks, drove a salient across the canal into the Egyptian mainland, and threatened to cut off an Egyptian force of 20,000 men. When the United Nations, supported by the United States and the Soviet Union, imposed a cease-fire, Egypt claimed victory. The Israelis claimed that they would have won a victory within a few more days, but no one could have known how a protracted war would have ended. When the war did end, Israel had lost 2,500 young men out of her small population of less than 3 million, and Egypt and Syria had lost larger numbers out of a joint population that was about fifteen times larger. Serious, too, were the economic costs, both for Israel and its larger but poorer adversaries. In

blood and treasure, both sides had become poorer. Until well into the 1980s, any further round of warfare seemed likely to produce nothing more than another such stalemate.

In November 1977, Sadat again reversed Egyptian policy. In a dramatic gesture, he flew to Jerusalem to visit Israeli Prime Minister Menachem Begin, to address the Israeli parliament, or Knesset, and to start serious negotiations for a peace treaty between Egypt and Israel that would end thirty years of conflict between the two countries. The move, preceded by two agreements whereby Israel had turned over small areas of the Sinai to Egypt, had been prepared on both sides with the aid of the United States. In exchange, Egypt expected to gain the return of the Sinai peninsula and the Gaza Strip, occupied by Israel since the 1967 war; a lightening of the burdens of repeated wars and war preparations; an increase in Western private investment; and substantial economic and military aid from the United States.

The negotiations on the draft treaty were mainly completed in late 1978 at *Camp David* in the United States, with the personal participation of President Carter. Ratification by both countries followed. In 1979, Prime Minister Begin visited Egypt and was cheered by friendly crowds. In November 1979, a substantial part of the Sinai peninsula was returned to Egypt and Egypt and Israel exchanged ambassadors. Eventually, Palestinian Arabs on the west bank of the Jordan River, occupied by Israel since the 1967 war even though it had belonged to Jordan, were to be given a degree of self-government. But the Israeli and Egyptian positions on this matter remain apart.

In the meantime, Sadat was bitterly criticized in the Arab world for having broken its solidarity and having recognized Israel. The *Arab League* suspended Egypt and removed its headquarters from Cairo to Tunis—a move Egypt refused to recognize. Most Arab governments broke diplomatic relations with Egypt; Saudi Arabia and other oil-rich states cut off their subsidies. The United States and other Western countries have replaced these sources of income only in part. Sadat's support within Egypt came to be challenged more often. If Egyptian nationalism should become more Egyptian than pro-Arab, Sadat might succeed. If Nasser's Pan-Arabism should prevail, Sadat's difficulties might well increase.

The High Stakes of Egyptian Politics. The stakes of Egyptian politics have always been high indeed. Egypt fought a war against Israel every decade since their effective independence. It intervened in a long war in Yemen and tried to absorb Syria. In the early 1980s, at risk were war or peace with Israel; greater militarization of the country or more civilian development; more or less land and equipment for most peasants and their children; deepening poverty or new industrial growth and investment; nonalignment in foreign policy or membership in either the Western or the Eastern bloc.

In time, even the basic social order of the country would be decided by the outcome of its politics. Would private enterprise dominate and, with it, petty traders, partisans, and peasants? Or would a strong national ruling class of big and middling bankers, businesspeople, and landowners emerge victorious, strengthened by kinship ties to high-level bureaucrats and military officers? Would it become a market economy dominated by multinational corporations? Or would Egypt once more move toward a more collective and centrally planned social and economic system? And would whatever future pattern that might emerge still be considered Arab socialism? Would social and economic inequality decline or would most peasants still stay impoverished? In all these respects, the fate of the Egyptian people still hangs in the balance at the beginning of the 1980s, almost thirty years after the officers' revolution of 1952.

The Narrowness of Political Participation. The revolution of 1952 made the politics of modern Egypt, but it was made by a few officers, not by the mass of the people. Although 44 percent literate, the Egyptian people have little choice among political parties, no truly autonomous organizations, no substantial power of political decision making. They can say yes to governmental policies and candidates, cheer them in the streets, vote for small opposition parties, or keep silent. When labor unions in the few industrial plants demand higher wages or more rights and are suppressed, when students are arrested or newspapers censored, the rest of the country hardly stirs.

Religion offers an indirect outlet for expression. Muslim theologians, worshipers at mosques, teachers and students at religious universities such as Al Azhar in Cairo, inevitably form groups to discuss ideas, although most often traditional or fundamentalist ones. The "*Muslim Brotherhood*" (Ikhwan) could have become a political spearhead for such trends and has been held responsible for some acts of terrorism. Currently, it is suppressed. The underground strength it may have kept is hard to measure.

All political parties had been abolished in 1953 to promote unity and to facilitate control. But an organization called the National Liberation Rally, also founded in 1953, began to serve as if it were a political party building support for the new government and helping government control. Dissolved and renamed through various stages, it came to be called the *Arab Socialist Union (ASU)* after 1962. Other political parties remained illegal. Members had to be selected by the ASU; not everyone could join who wished to do so. The ASU sought to establish organizations to support the government throughout the country, with special attention to the control of labor union politics. Under President Sadat, the ASU at first continued to play an important role of political mobilization and control but only after Sadat took charge of the organization and dismissed and replaced many of the leaders not to his liking. Membership in the ASU had grown to several million people. As an organization, however, it was never very independent of the president of the republic. Its period of greatest autonomy may have been the late 1960s; President Sadat, in contrast, soon curtailed some of the ASU's leadership leverage, while at the same time he sought to open up some new avenues for political expression and participation within the ASU and in the larger society.

In late 1976 President Sadat authorized the establishment of groups within the ASU that represented the main ideological tendencies—from the political left to the right—within the ranks. That was the beginning of the end for the old ASU. After a number of further changes, the ASU was at last officially abolished in 1978. However, how real the charges have been is not yet clear. A new government party was launched immediately, now called the *National Democratic Party (NDP)*. Virtually all of the ASU's former members in the *People's Assembly*—Egypt's national legislature—joined it, so that the NDP is fairly similar to the ASU, and its political tasks are also quite comparable.

The main change under President Sadat, however, has been the legalization of some small opposition parties. The *Liberal Socialist Party* emerged as one of the ASU groups in 1976 and has come to stand on its own. It advocates a greater role for private enterprise in the Egyptian economy. The Socialist Labor Party, organized after the ASU's formal abolition, criticizes the regime from the political left, underscoring a call for policies to reduce inequalities of wealth in different regions. Existing legislation on political parties, however, still prevents the emergence of parties that can truly challenge the government. Three important political forces remain illegal. One is the *Egyptian Communist Party* (as well as several other Communist parties of varying persuasions). It is noteworthy that the Communists were outlawed as a political party by Nasser, not withstanding his good relations with the Soviet Union. A second major clandestine force is the Wafd Party that had been the principal political vehicle before the 1952 revolution, which can draw support from certain rural areas and urban upper-class people. The third major illegal political movement is the Muslim Brotherhood, outlawed in 1954, which still seeks to make Egypt more faithful to its Islamic heritage, reversing

many of Nasser's and Sadat's policies. It is, however, virtually impossible to assess the real political influence of any of these forces.

There have been a number of elections and plebiscites since the 1952 change of government. However, because political competition had been so restricted, the meaning of these elections was clouded. They served primarily to underscore support for the regime. For example, Nasser was reelected in 1965 in a presidential plebiscite to his last six-year term by the reported approval of 99.9 percent of the voters. Similarly, even in the somewhat more open elections held in October 1976 for the People's Assembly, the opposition parties garnered only 14 of 350 seats. The remainder were either formally affiliated with one of the wings of the ASU or were pro-Sadat independent legislators. In the June 1979 elections, Sadat's NDP won 330 of the contested seats.

More generally, Sadat's claim to legitimate rule differs from Nasser's. Sadat has attempted to make peace with Israel and seeks support within Egypt with the promise of no more wars. He has consequently retreated from the Pan-Arabist ideal in fact, although not quite so much rhetorically. His deteriorating relations with the Soviet Union and the improvement of relations with the United States and Europe have also facilitated the rise of commerce with the Western countries as well as increases in direct foreign investment and loans from them. The mild political openings also are consistent with these changes. Peace, prosperity, and competitive politics may be far more a goal than a reality in the Egypt of the early 1980s; but already these issues certainly present a quite different internal constellation of political forces and suggest the possibility of a different future.

An Uncertain Arena. Just what are Egypt's boundaries at the start of the 1980s?

Southward: The Sudan. Even in 1850 B.C., Nubia, including part of the Sudan, was part of the

Egyptian empire, and it remained so for centuries. Many Egyptians, from the 1820s on, considered the Sudan to be part of their country or at least part of its legitimate sphere of expansion. They had expected the Anglo-Egyptian condominium over the Sudan to be replaced by Egyptian dominance in one form or another. By the mid-1950s, these prospects had become remote. The Sudan had its own government, army, and administrative state machinery. This Sudanese state was dominated by the Arab-speaking and Muslim population of Khartoum and the north, but only grudgingly obeyed by many of the black inhabitants of the south, who spoke African tribal languages and professed either animist religions or Christianity. Neither northerners nor southerners showed any inclination to accept Egyptian rule.

Westward: Libya. To the west, the former Italian colonies of Tripoli and Cyremaica became the Arab state of Libya. From the sixteenth to the nineteenth century, both Egypt and Libya were closely united under the Ottoman Empire, until Egypt's occupation by the British in 1882 and Libya's conquest by Italy in 1911. Libya's population in 1952 found itself in a sovereign pro-Western monarchy under King Idris I.

In 1969, Idris was overthrown by an officers' revolution led by 27-year-old Colonel Muammar el-Qaddafi, who became the new head of state. A stridently nationalistic and leftist republic was established, with only about 2.5 million inhabitants but a remarkable degree of oil-based wealth, and with Arab unity and hostility to Israel as major elements in its foreign policy. In the name of Arab unity, Libya signed an agreement in 1971 to form a three-nation federation of Arab republics, but nothing came of the project. Since then, Libya has alternated between offers of unity with Egypt, sometimes going as far as offering to merge the two countries, and angry accusations and threats against Sadat's government for its allegedly insufficient zeal in pressing the Arab cause against Israel. Egyptian responses thus far have been cautious or negative, despite the lure of Libya's oil riches for Egypt's large but poor economy and the presence of many Egyptian workers in Libya. Whether Libya will remain forever separate from Egypt, or go to war with it, no one can say.

Eastward: The Sinai, Palestine, and Israel. The sparsely inhabited Sinai peninsula has been a part of Egypt since ancient times. Before 1800 B.C., a pharaoh reorganized Egyptian mining operations there.

Palestine's links to Egypt are almost as old. The country was conquered by Egypt in about 1470 B.C. and held more or less effectively until about 1100 B.C. Later, both Palestine and Egypt were conquered by the Arabs and Islam, ruled for some centuries by the caliphs of the empire of Islam, and belonged to the Ottoman Empire. From 1918 to 1946, both countries in effect were under British control, in one form or another. In the war of 1948 against Israel, Egypt acquired the Gaza Strip with some Palestinian refugees but lost it again to Israeli occupation in the war of 1967.

For Arab solidarity, Egypt would be obliged to support the claims of the Palestinian Arabs against Israel. Nasser did so with vigor and at great cost; Sadat has continued to do so, albeit more moderately and without thus far making full peace with Israel dependent on the satisfaction of these claims. From the viewpoint of pan-Arab nationalism, Egypt should continue to seek mergers with other Arab states, not only with Libya and the Sudan, but also with Syria, the Yemens, Jordan, Lebanon, and eventually even with Saudi Arabia and Iraq. Finally, from the viewpoint of Islamic solidarity, as propagated by the Muslim Brotherhood, Egypt should champion the cause of Islam against Israel and against the Christian minority in Lebanon.

None of these viewpoints is currently prevailing over all others in Egypt, nor would a policy based on any one of them be likely to succeed. They mean that the arena of Egyptian politics is not sharply delineated. In particular, to the east and north, the boundary between Egyptian domestic politics and the politics of the Palestinian Arabs,

Syria, Jordan, and Lebanon is less sharply and solidly drawn than in most modern states. Any Egyptian government could be strengthened by success in these areas, any major failure there could threaten its stability.

The Changing Images of Egypt. One answer to the question "What is Egypt?" depends on the answer to another question: "Who are the Egyptians?" Are they mainly the descendants of the people of the ancient empire and the pyramids, towering over the centuries long before Islam? Or are the ties of the Arabic language stronger than those of ancestry and of the land in the Nile Valley? Or is the religion of Islam in its *Sunni* form the strongest source of identity for most Egyptians? Finally, how many people see themselves as members of a class, whether peasants in the country or workers in the few industrial districts of the cities. How many take seriously the visions of a new social order, Arab or otherwise?

At present, Egypt's leaders try to appeal to all these images. Nasser stressed the images of Pan-Arabism and socialism; Sadat balanced these themes somewhat with appeals to Egyptian interest. Which image or combination of images will prevail in the future politics of Egypt still seems an open question.

Political System and Administration. Channels of communication from the government to the people appear strong, through radio and, to a lesser extent, the press. Feedback channels from the people to the government seem weak. The one-party system, government control of the media, the strong military and police, the weakness of labor unions, students, and intellectuals, and the absence of autonomous peasant organizations not only usually keep the people quiet, they keep the government ill informed about the people's feelings. The government is, thus, consequently unprepared for outbursts of discontent, such as occurred in 1977 when the government sought to increase the price of basic foodstuffs.

If President Sadat has been able thus far to steer his country through a zigzagging path of policy changes, it has been in part because government broadcasts have been loud, political participation small, and political apathy great. But these are dwindling assets—if indeed they are assets at all. Industrial, social, and economic modernization will erode them.

Egypt's underdevelopment is lessening. One area showing signs of improvement is the administration. Despite such high-sounding titles as *pasha, bey,* and *effendi,* the foreign image of Egyptian administrators for well over a century has been one of lassitude, laziness, inefficiency, and corruption. *Baksheesh,* the Arab word for a gratuity or bribe needed to get anything done, long has been notorious. But the old titles are gone, and contemporary Egyptian administration has proved more effective than some foreigners had anticipated.

When Egypt took over the Suez Canal in 1956, many foreign observers predicted that it would fail to maintain the canal and that Egyptian pilots would be incapable of guiding the larger ships through it. Egyptians proved competent in coping with all these tasks. Similarly, in the October War of 1973, the organization and discipline of the Egyptian army and its logistic support proved to be more effective than most foreigners had expected. More than once, Egypt's administration has passed severe tests of performance.

Although political succession at first passed easily to Sadat upon Nasser's death, in fact a major government crisis occurred soon thereafter in 1971. Sadat prevailed, but several key political figures were either dismissed or resigned, including Vice President *Ali Sabri,* People's Assembly Speaker Muhammad Labib Shuqayr, ASU Secretary-General Muhsin abu al Nur, and War Minister General Muhammad Fawzi. This shakeup clearly permitted a recentralization of political power in President Sadat's hands, preventing more open challenges to his rule, because the leaders of contending power centers were imprisoned. Presidential control is, indeed, the central feature of the machinery of the Egyptian government.

According to the constitution of 1971, the president is nominated by the People's Assembly and elected by referendum for a six-year term. Only Sadat has been president under it; in 1980 the constitution was amended to make him president for life. The People's Assembly is elected for five-year terms; ten additional members may be appointed by the president. Ten of the seats are also reserved for *Coptic Christians;* the president has used his powers of appointment to fill this quota when fewer than ten Coptic Christians are elected. The president retains, however, most powers of decision making. He can rule by decree between Assembly sessions and, during them, he has the overwhelming support of most legislators, who are politically in his debt.

One of the internal political effects of the many wars Egypt has fought in recent decades has been to centralize political power at the center, in the president's hands, at the expense of local and regional government, parliament, and the courts. If wars indeed become less likely, Egypt's political future could witness a decline in this extraordinary centralization of existing power.

The Performance of the Egyptian Political System. Since the revolution of 1952, nutrition, health, and life expectancy have significantly improved. Banks and industries, government agencies, and the military function tolerably well under Egyptian personnel and management. And President Sadat's government has been able, thus far, to move away from recurrent warfare to a search for peace that in the fall of 1980 appeared serious and sincere. As in many other developing countries, the outcome of all these policies is still open—but there is room for hope.

IRAN

Iran is the richest of the developing countries sketched in this chapter. In 1975, its per capita income of $1660 put it ahead of Argentina. But its low levels of literacy, industrialization, and access to higher education, its high infant mortality rate, and its high index of economic inequality suggest how incomplete and uneven its economic and social development has been.

To study Iran is to examine religion and the state, dictatorship and revolution. Tensions between religion and the state have been recurring for many centuries. In our century, Iran has had three revolutions: an incomplete middle-class one in 1905, an authoritarian "revolution from above" by the two Pahlavi shahs from 1925 to 1978, and the revolution of 1979 that is not yet completed.

At the start of the 1980s, we cannot study Iran the way we can study most other countries. Ordinarily, a nation changes so slowly that we can study its structures as if they were standing still, and its processes as if they were highly repetitive. We can sketch maps of its political system. But for contemporary Iran, we need not maps but a film—a film that reaches far back into the past where changes came from and suggests where some of them may be going.

This section will say little, therefore, about Iran's current administration, laws, and institutions, since they may change significantly within a year or two. But it will deal with Iran's history and the recurring conflicts that once more broke into the open in 1979.

An Ancient Culture of Contrasts and Refinement. Iran (until 1935 called Persia by foreigners) is one of the oldest civilizations in the world. It is one of the world's first regions where agriculture was developed and refined. A Bronze Age culture existed there before 2000 B.C. The ancient Indo-Europeans or Aryans settled in Iran before 1500 B.C.; some of them went on to invade India. The cultivation of peaches and the use of houses were known in Iran before they became known to the Greeks. Persian cooking is considered one of the great cooking traditions of the world. Sophistication and refinement, imagination and curiosity, have been described as continuous elements in Iranian culture.

Throughout its history, except during the last sixty years, the borders of Iran have been fluid. At various times, Armenia, Azerbaijan, and parts of today's Iraq have belonged to it, as have Afghanistan, Khiva, and Bukhara. Many movements and leaders have come from these lands, but the regions around Shiraz, Isfahan, Qum, and Teheran always have been its core.

The country is variegated, even in its central regions. There are plains and towering mountains, deserts and fertile, gardenlike valleys. Much of the country depends on irrigation, and the peasants in these areas have depended on the landowning nobles who controlled the distribution of the water. No single river, like the Nile in Egypt, provided a permanent basis for a central government and perpetual obedience to it. Mountain peoples and tribes in the plains have always been ready to resist governmental authority if it became too onerous. The interplay of all these elements has led to strangely mixed events. In some periods of their history, Iranians have obeyed absolute rulers; but more than once, revolutionary movements have shaken the country.

A History of Grandeur and Catastrophes. Political systems in Iran have been discontinuous. One period of imperial glory lasted a little over two hundred years. It began in about 550 B.C., when Cyrus the Great conquered the Iranian kingdom of Media, subdued Lydia and Babylonia, and founded the Persian Empire, which stretched from the Indus River to the Mediterranean and from the Caucasus mountains to the Indian Ocean. His son, Cambyses, conquered Egypt. His successors, Darius I and Xerxes, tried to conquer Greece but failed. Yet the Greeks were so impressed by the size of the empire and its capabilities that their victories seemed to them won against overwhelming odds. At that time, the empire was centralized, divided into twenty provinces, each under a royal governor, or *satrap*. The king himself had four residences, at Persepolis, Susa,

Ecbatana, and Babylon. Good roads, with stations for royal messengers, permitted regular communications within the empire. The king could raise vast armies and amass and spend large treasures. The rulers professed the *Zoroastrian religion*, according to which a supreme god of light fights against a supreme god of darkness and evil. Conquered tribes and people were left free to worship their own deities. Belief in the devil and religious tolerance thus may have ancient Iranian precedents.

Decline set in after 450 B.C., with struggles for the throne, assassinations, and civil war. Within three years, between 334 and 331 B.C., the ruler of Macedonia, Alexander the Great, aided by troops from nearly all the Greek cities, conquered the entire empire. After Alexander's death, it was divided among his generals and a period of partial Greek cultural dominance began. About a century later, the Parthians expanded their rule into Iran. They were splendid horsemen and archers who spoke a language akin to Old Persian. By 138 B.C., their empire covered most of present-day Iran and beyond. Beating off Roman efforts at conquest, their rule lasted more than three hundred years, but, it seems, with few cultural accomplishments.

A second period of Iranian greatness followed, between A.D. 226 and 651, under the *Sassanian dynasty.* Son of a vassal-king of the Parthian Empire in Fars-Persia proper, Ardashir I defeated the last Parthian ruler and conquered several neighboring regions. He created a strong centralized state, supported by the priesthood (called *Magi*) of the Zoroastrian religion. The privileges of the Magi greatly developed. Under his successors, the empire expanded and fought Rome to a stand-off. By A.D. 380, the empire had reached a peak of its power.

Recurrent Tensions Between Religion and State. During this period and in the ups and downs that followed, religion and the state were sometimes in alliance. Already in about A.D. 275, the new sect of

MAP 10.5 *Iran*

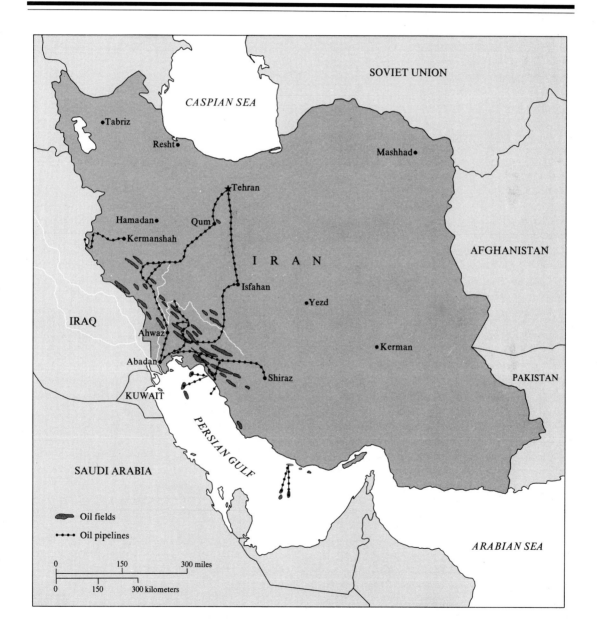

Manicheanism was outlawed and its founder, Mani, executed. Christians were sometimes tolerated but more often persecuted; the power of the Magi was occasionally curbed. A communistic sect following the doctrines of Mazdak was supported by a king, Kobad, whom the nobles then deposed. When Kobad returned to power in 501, he turned against Mazdak. The Mazdakites were massacred in 523.

A new peak of Iranian power and royal spendor occurred between 531 and 628 under kings Anushirwan the Just (Chosroes I) and Khusru Parviz (Chosroes II). It was ended by the murder of Khusru by his own troops, followed by struggles and assassinations, and succeeded by the Muslim conquest of the country between 639 and 651. Persia became part of the empire of the Arab *caliphs,* who ruled most often from Damascus and later from Baghdad.

Social revolts sometimes led by religious chiefs—Magi or Muslim—kept recurring in Persia and in the caliphate: the Zindigs in Khorasan and western Persia after 775; the Khurramites, led by the Magian Babek, from Azerbaijan after 813 until Babek's defeat and execution in 838; the slave uprising of the Zanj rebellion (869–883); and the revolt of the Carmathians (891–906), who temporarily took Mecca. All these revolts of the poor were defeated but they may have left memories rather different from those of the more obedient people of Egypt.

On a higher social level, a Persian cultural revival began under Arab rule. With the caliphs now ruling from newly founded Baghdad (around 762), Persian culture and refinement soon permeated the court and the lifestyle of the elite, even though Arabic remained the predominant language there. In the tenth century, Persian was revived as a literary language, particularly in the eastern Persian province of Khorasan at the court of the local Saffarid dynasty and their successors, the Samanids and Ghaznawids. Eventually, these rulers extended their power over modern Persia. At the court of the greatest of them, Mahmud the

Idol-Breaker, the great Persian poet Firdausi flourished about the year 1000, at the same time as the physician and philosopher Ibn Sīna, whom the West called Avicenna. At that time, Islam and Persian culture spread to parts of northern India.

There followed conquests by Seldjuk Turk and Mongol rulers. For a time, Persian intellectual life flourished again in the days of the ruler Malik Shah (1073–1092) and the mathematician and poet Omar Khayyam. Underground, below the surface of changing rulers of the Near East, from Persia to Syria, the traditions of dissident sects and rebel movements lived on as secret societies. In 1090, a formidable sect was founded at the mountain stronghold of Alamut in northern Persia. They relied on secrecy and political murders and they used hashish (a stronger variety of marijuana). Accordingly, they were called "hashish eaters," *hash-shāhshīn* in Arabic, from which the word *assassin* in several European languages derives. Western crusaders and Near Eastern rulers fell to their daggers, until the grandson of Jenghis Khan, Hulagu, exterminated the sect in 1256.

A century of provincial rulers, called *Il-Khans,* under the Mongols followed. Then *Timur,* the vizier (minister) of such a ruler, overthrew his master and embarked on a vast career of conquest. He conquered Persia, Baghdad, Mesopotamia, all the lands between Moscow and the Great Wall of China, invaded India, and sacked Delhi, inflicting numerous cruelties. His son, Shah Rukh, ruled in splendor over eastern Persia and parts of central Asia for nearly half a century (1405–1447). Once again conquest followed, this time by the Turkomans, and there were further dynastic conflicts. But then came a bigger change.

In a spectacular turn of events in 1500, Iran got a national ruler and a national dynasty, the first in many centuries. This striking change depended on a rearrangement between the two contending forces—religion and state—that so often had been in conflict throughout Iranian history.

Shi'ism: A Dissident Tradition in Islam. The faith preached by the Prophet Muhammad after A.D. 622 had been revolutionary in many ways. Its sign had been the curved sword and later, by the Turks, identified with the crescent. Where it conquered, it swept away the wealth of the Byzantine church and the tax collectors of the Byzantine state. Muslims usually were armed and free from taxes; only non-Muslims had to pay them for tolerance and protection. Islam had no highly organized church to accumulate land and wealth. Its law, the *Koran,* protected the property of artisans, merchants, peasants, and landholders, but forbade lending at interest. It commanded simple living without alcohol or luxuries, made almsgiving a duty, and proclaimed the brotherhood of all believers. The doctrine soon became more accommodating to the interests of the powerful and rich, and at times more tolerant of luxury and ostentatious display. But time and again, as in Christianity, some sect would raise the old demands for a return to Muslim virtue, simplicity, and justice.

Islam had to have a single military leader, the caliph, against the world of infidels. The caliph had to be a legitimate successor of the Prophet, a requirement that became the formal point of division between Islam and its main sects.

After the death of the Prophet Muhammad, each of the first four "orthodox" caliphs attained the office of head of the Muslim state, commander-in-chief of the armies, and supreme judge either through election or by appointment by the predecessor, or by some combination of both. Once in office, each caliph was still bound by the Koran, the traditional sayings of the Prophet *(hadith),* as well as by custom and public opinion. The second caliph, Omar, under whose reign Persia had been conquered, was murdered by a Persian slave. The third caliph, Othman of the Omayyad family of Mecca, was resented by the Hashimite family of Mekka, accused of nepotism, and murdered at Medina.

Eventually, Ali, cousin and son-in-law of the Prophet Muhammad, was elected caliph. Like the Prophet himself, Ali was of the Hashimite family,

and some partisans of the Omayyads accused him of complicity in Othman's murder. The Omayyad governor of Syria, Muawiya, rose against him. After an inconclusive battle, the two claimants submitted to arbitration, which in 658 gave the caliphate to Muawiya. Ali refused to accept the decision, which might have reflected the majority view of Arab notables. He insisted on his claim, based on his belonging to the house of the Prophet and hence on divine rights. Among his own army, however, twelve thousand of the most radical, called Kharijites, rose against him, claiming that by submitting to arbitration he had already betrayed their cause. They wanted to submit to no caliph, but only to the "Lord alone." Ali dispersed them, had many of the Kharijites killed, and was murdered three years later (661) by a Kharijite. Muawiya became caliph and moved the seat of government to Damascus, where his successors ruled as the Omayyad dynasty of caliphs until 750.

Ali's older son submitted to Muawiya and was allowed to live in comfort at Medina. Eight years later he was poisoned. According to Persian tradition, this was done on Muawiya's orders. In 680, Ali's younger son, Husayn, was invited by the Arabs of Kufa in Iraq to assert his hereditary title to the caliphate. Betrayed by the Kufans, he was slain in the battle of Kerbela. The power of the Omayyads was safe for a time, but Ali, Hasan, and Husayn became more powerful as martyrs than they had ever been in life.

Their adherents did not give up. Called *Shi'ites* (partisans), they became the chief religious opposition party in Islam. To this day, perhaps 85 percent of the world's Muslims adhere to the orthodox tradition of Islam, the *sunna,* and are called *Sunnites.* Their faith accepts the outcomes of ancient Arab politics, the decisions of the caliphs, and the age-old influence of the elites of the Arab and Turkish world. Sunnis form the vast majority of Muslims in the Arabian peninsula, Egypt, North Africa, and almost all Muslim countries— but not in Persia. There, and in southern Iraq, Shi'ism, the religion of the underdogs in those ancient sectarian struggles, has lived on.

Shi'ites believe that only the descendants of Ali are the divinely appointed hereditary successors to the caliphate. They believe that this supreme authority consists less in the secular power of the caliph over government and armies and more in the caliph's role as *imām* (spiritual leader) of the faithful. The main branch of the Shi'ites counts twelve such *imāms,* ending with Muhammad al-Muntazar ("the unexpected one"), who in 878 as a boy vanished in a mosque in Iraq. Since then, according to Shi'ite tradition, he has lived on as the twelfth, or "the hidden *imām*," among the people, to appear on the last day as the *Mahdi* ("the divinely guided one") to bring an era of universal Islamic prosperity and peace. Until then, governments are only provisionally legitimate and kings are akin to usurpers. At best, a monarch may be called a "shadow of the *imām*" by the Shi'ite priests, if they approve of him and his actions. But they may choose to give this approval or to withhold it.

For more than eight hundred years after the deaths of Ali and Husayn, the Shi'ite religion lived on as a heresy. It was disclaimed by the Sunni governments of all Muslim countries, at best tolerated, but often persecuted and driven underground. In these centuries, the Shi'ites developed their doctrine of *dissimulation:* it is lawful for Shi'ites to deny their faith and to profess outwardly any other religion that may protect them from persecution. "Even the recording angel withdraws," goes a saying, "when two Shi'ites meet."

With the martyrs Ali and Husayn, Shi'ism extolled the losers in a power struggle. Its adherents often kept an emotional distance from the strong, the successful, the rich—and from the Arab rulers and elites, particularly the Omayyad caliphs. This made Shi'ism particularly appealing to the people of Iran, where Shi'ite uprisings repeatedly occurred. According to a Persian tradition, Husayn married the daughter of the last Sassanid king, Yezdigird, so that Husayn's descendants are legitimized both as heirs of the Persian kings and as descendants of the Prophet. It was in eastern Iran, in the province of Khorasan, that the black banner of the Abbasid claimants to the caliphate was

raised. It was under the Abbasid caliphs at Baghdad that Persian culture rose again to prominence. But Shi'ism itself had to survive as best it could, remote from government.

It did so by developing a stronger organization of its clergy than the majority branch of Islam, the Sunnis, had. Islam has no ordained priests, supernaturally different from mere lay people, as many Christian denominations have. Its clergy differ from lay people only by their learning. But among Shi'ites to this day, these preachers and teachers of religion, called *mullahs*—their number estimated today at somewhere under twenty thousand—are highly respected and strongly organized. A *mullah* who studies the religious law or theology may become a *mujtahid,* if accepted by the established *mujtahids.* A *mujtahid* has the right to give individual views on religious problems (which under Islam can include almost everything in law, politics, economics, and society). *Mujtahids* are expected to give views within the Shi'ite tradition. As Sunnis, they would be much less free to decide, since under that faith both tradition and the law give less leeway and are seen as fixed. Even under the shahs, the *mujtahids* have had much prestige and influence among the populace. At the start of the 1980s, Iran had perhaps one thousand *mujtahids.* A few of the *mujtahids* may rise through further study and exemplary conduct to the rank of *ayatollah.* In 1979, Iran had about twenty *ayatollahs,* of whom only four held the supreme title of *ayatollah al-ozma.* In late 1979, one of these was murdered. Another, Ayatollah Khoi, is the most highly respected of the four, but he is ninety-four years old, lives at Karbala in Iraq, and thus far has kept out of politics. This leaves only two topranking *ayatollahs,* Ruhollah Khomeini and *Shariat Madari.* The latter is the spiritual leader of the Turkic-speaking Shi'ites of Azerbaijan, and a potential rival to the influence of Ayatollah Khomeini in that region and perhaps elsewhere in Iran. Throughout the centuries, this organizational and emotional power of Shi'ism has been reinforced through pilgrimages to the sacred Shi'ite cities of Mashhad, Ardebil, and Qum. The last of these has been called "the Rome of the Shi'ites." In 1500, Shi'ism became the state religion of Persia.

The Shi'ite Monarchy, 1500–1924. Ismail, the leader of a war band, began to establish his power in Persia about the year 1500. His ancestry was mixed, chiefly Turkoman and Greek. On his father's side, he was descended from a line of chiefs of a small monastic military state at the town of Ardabil in Azerbaijan. One of their ancestors had been a shaykh Safi, from whom the Safavids derived their name Safi and his heirs also claimed descent from Caliph Ali. The dervish order that was the backbone of the state of Ardabil was fanatically devoted to Shi'ism. Ismail's father reorganized these dervishes, many recruited from Turkoman tribes in the region, into a powerful military organization, known as "red-heads" from the color of their headdresses. But it was Ismail who assembled a band of followers, defeated rival tribes, and conquered Tabriz, where he had himself proclaimed shah. He made Shi'ism the state religion and conquered all of Persia. At that time and even today, the bonds of religion were stronger than the links of language. To be a Shi'ite was to be a Persian, even though people in Azerbaijan might speak a Turkic language and the people in Khuzistan, near today's Iraq, might speak Arabic. The new state did not turn these populations into Persian speakers, but with the help of Shi'ism it assimilated them into Persian culture. (The last decades of our century will test just how deep this assimilation has been.)

Even so, the new state was the first truly Persian one in many centuries. It was Persian in the religion, culture, geography, and language of most inhabitants. Yet it had its ups and downs. After Ismail's rule followed years of war against Uzbegs and Turks and quarrels about the successions with executions and assassinations. But under Shah Abbas the Great (1587–1629), another period of splendor and prosperity followed, not only in economic and military matters but also in cultural affairs. Then came decline, rivalries for the throne, and wholesale executions once more.

In 1711, Afghanistan seceded, defeated the Persian troops, and became an independent state. In the 1720s, the Afghans took Isfahan and an Afghan ruler, Mahmud, became shah. Russia and Turkey made an agreement for the dismemberment of Persia. But a Safavid prince, Tahmasp, called for national resistance and was aided by a powerful tribal chief, Nadir Kuli of Khorasan. By 1730, the Afghans were defeated and expelled. Tahmasp became shah, but Nadir soon deposed him and in 1736 became shah himself.

Nadir Shah was the last spectacular military conqueror to rule Iran. He led a Persian army to the conquest and sack of Delhi, the capital of the Moghul Empire in India, with vast massacre and immense booty. But, returned to Iran, the conqueror became miserly in guarding his loot. He turned against Shi'ism. His attempts to stamp it out provoked growing unrest, and in 1747 Nadir, "hated by all," was assassinated by one of his own tribespeople.

Eventually, the *Qajarite dynasty* came to power in 1794 and held it until 1925. Throughout the nineteenth century, absolutism and traditionalism predominated. Reforms were slow and few, and the royal finances were troubled. Foreign influences, particularly British and Russian, penetrated and eventually divided the country into spheres of influence. Yet foreign penetration was not deep. The people and the national culture and economy slowly became consolidated. There were no bloody succession struggles within the royal family, nor any other powerful claimants to the throne. Succession became orderly, by inheritance. Persia's border with Turkey was to be demarcated, according to a treaty concluded in 1823 and confirmed in 1847; in the northwest, after a war with Russia in 1828, the boundary became the Aras River. The Persia-Afghanistan border was defined in 1872.

In 1878, a *Persian Cossack brigade* was organized under Russian officers. Russian influence grew rapidly from the 1880s on. British and Russian financiers competed at the court. In 1890, the government granted a concession for tobacco production and export, which aroused so much religious and popular opposition that the concession had to be canceled. Six years later, Shah Nasir-ud-Din was assassinated after forty-eight years of rule.

Under his successor, Muzaffar-ud-Din, the Qajar monarchy was engulfed by revolution. A major oil field was found in 1908. The *Anglo-Persian Oil Company*, forerunner of today's British Petroleum (BP), was founded in 1909. Otherwise, however, Persian finances were getting worse. In 1900 and 1902, Russia, through a bank it controlled, granted large loans to the shah. These loans were to replace past and future British loans and were to be secured by part of Persia's customs. In addition, Russia got a road concession and a new Persian tariff favoring it over Britain. In 1903, Persian customs were put under the control of a foreigner, M. Naus, a national of Belgium.

Popular opposition to the absolute monarchy had been growing since at least 1890. Religious leaders and the commercial classes objected to taxes, corruption, government inefficiency, and the privileges of foreigners. Since the shah was leaning toward Russia, British influence also was brought to bear against him.

The *Persian revolution* began in December 1905. In July 1906, twelve thousand revolutionaries, including merchants and religious leaders, took refuge on the grounds of the British legation in Tehran, and a group of the *mujtahids* left for Qum. The shah had to yield to popular pressure. He dismissed his chief minister, unpopular for corruption and favoring foreigners, and agreed to call a national assembly, or *majlis*. In the words of the shah's decree, it was to be "an assembly of delegates elected by the Princes, the Mujtahids, the Qajar family, the nobles and notables, the Landowners, the merchants and the guilds . . . formed . . . by election of the classes above mentioned."[3]

The *majlis* met in October and produced a liberal monarchical constitution. The shah signed it but died a few days later.

His son, Mohammed Ali Shah, tried to circumvent the constitution and bring back the old order. He appointed a reactionary minister, Atabegi-Azam, who was assassinated in August 1907. In December, the shah tried a coup d'état, which provoked a popular uprising in several regions. The shah had to yield but tried again in 1908. With the help of the Russian legation and the Russian-officered Persian Cossack brigade, the shah closed the *majlis* and had many liberal leaders killed. He controlled Tehran but the people of Tabriz in the north rose against him. A deadlock followed until, in March 1909, Russian troops occupied Tabriz for the shah and brutally suppressed the rebels. In June, a leader of the southern and pro-British *Bakhtiar tribe* marched on Tehran to defend the constitutional regime, took the city in July, and deposed the shah in favor of his twelve-year-old son, Sultan Ahmad Shah, who ruled as a figurehead until 1925.

In reality, power in Iran had been divided between csarist Russia and Britain. In 1907, the two countries agreed to a compromise on Persia as part of Russia's joining Britain and France in the Triple Entente, preparing for the possibility of war against Germany that came in 1914. Britain was to remain in southern Persia where the oil was; the northern half of the country was to be a Russian sphere; and a central belt was available for concessions granted to either side. The agreement also reaffirmed the formal independence and integrity of Persia.

From 1909 to 1914, Russian influence prevailed in the north and in the center. In 1914, Persia declared its neutrality in World War I but could not enforce it. On occasion, Turkish and Russian troops fought each other on Persian soil. In 1915, with Russia in difficulties in its war against Germany and Austria, German influence grew in Tehran. Allegedly, to counter this influence, the Russians

---

[3]Cited in Sir Percy Sykes, *A History of Persia,* vol. 2 (London: Macmillan & Co., 1915), p. 509.

invaded northern Persia in November, and in early 1916 Sir Percy Sykes organized the *South Persia Rifles* and later in the year marched northeast to Isfahan, which the Russians were already occupying, and then to Shiraz in the south of Persia. The foreign contest for Persia seemed at a peak.

In March 1917, the Turks withdrew from Persia after their defeat by British and Indian troops at Baghdad; in November, following the Bolshevik revolution, the Russians began to withdraw. Only the British stayed, sent troops into northern Persia, and organized a flotilla into the Caspian Sea. In 1919, an *Anglo-Persian agreement* was drawn up to seal the British ascendancy. Under it, Persia's independence and integrity were formally reconfirmed, but in fact its government would have remained largely dependent on Britain.

The *majlis* refused to convene to ratify this agreement. In May 1920, the Bolsheviks, victorious in Russia's civil war, sent their Caspian fleet to take the Persian cities of Enzeli and Resht, to occupy most of the province of Gilan on the shore of the Caspian, and to set up there the short-lived *Soviet Republic of Gilan* (1920–21). The Persian Cossack brigade under its anti-Bolshevik Russian officers fought them with some initial success but then was driven back in defeat. The British tried to reorganize it, but in 1921 British forces began to withdraw from Persia in response to British troubles elsewhere and a war-weary domestic attitude. Persia's chance for greater independence had come. One officer took it.

The Monarch as Dictator: Pahlavi Rule. *Reza Khan*, an officer in the Persian Cossack brigade, engineered the dismissal of the Russian officers, took up negotiations with the writer and reformer Zia ud-Din, and marched with three thousand Cossacks on Tehran for a coup d'état. On February 21, 1921, he set up a new government with Zia ud-Din as prime minister and himself as minister of war, commander-in-chief, and the real holder of power. The new government at once dropped the unratified treaty with Britain. Five days later, it

concluded a treaty with the Soviet government. The latter, hoping to destroy the British ascendancy, agreed to evacuate the country; cancel all debts, concessions, and special privileges; and turn over all Russian property in Persia without compensation. In October the Soviet Republic of Gilan was ended and the province brought back under the authority of Tehran. A treaty of peace and friendship with Turkey linked Persia to the revolutionary nationalist regime of Mustafa Kemal in that country. Reza Khan's regime was on the way to consolidation.

Reza followed up on his first successes. From 1922 on, an American economic expert named Dr. Arthur C. Millspaugh was given wide powers to reorganize Persia's finances. In 1923, Reza took over as premier and Ahmad Shah Qajar left for Europe, never to return. Agitation in the following year for a republic on the Turkish model was opposed by the Shi'ite leaders and Reza. Also in 1924, Reza's government subdued the Bakhtiari chiefs, not far from the oil fields that had made the chiefs almost independent with the aid of the Anglo-Persian Oil Company and the British government. Most of Persia was now under government control.

In 1925, Reza was voted dictatorial powers, and later in the year he had himself proclaimed shah. He took the pre-Islamic name Pahlavi from Sassanian times and ruled as *Reza Shah Pahlavi* until 1941. Under his rule, Iran went through a drastic face-lifting operation. Modernization was announced for many sectors of life, was promoted seriously in some, and succeeded in a few. Since the Shi'ite leaders opposed many reforms, the shah turned against them and gave his regime a secular cast. He promoted pre-Islamic memories and symbols as a base for a new nationalism and as a counterweight to Shi'ite influence. Women were encouraged to discard the veil and, among the small urban upper middle classes, many did so. In 1935, foreigners were ordered to call Persia by its native name, Iran. A new judicial system was introduced in 1928, modeled on the French and greatly reducing the jurisdiction and the power of the *mujtahids'* religious courts.

There were also some material successes. A *trans-Iranian railroad* from the Caspian to the Persian Gulf was begun in 1927 and completed in 1939. The lines of the Indo-European Telegraph Company within the country were taken over by the government. The oil concession to d'Arcy and his successor, the Anglo-Persian Oil Company, was canceled and replaced in 1933 by a new concession more favorable to Persia. And there were various plans for improvements in the countryside, in health and education, and in the lifestyle of a small elite.

For Iran as a whole, most of these reforms remained cosmetic. The life of the peasants, then still a majority of the people, changed hardly at all. The life of small artisans in the towns and cities and of the small merchants in the bazaars did not change much more. Neither did corruption, or the power of money and connections in administration, or the application of the law change. The industrial working class remained small, even including those working in the oil fields, who remained in poverty.

Foreign Occupation and a Precarious Constitutional Interlude.
During World War II, Iran's independence once more was temporarily submerged. After Nazi Germany attacked the Soviet Union in June 1941, Iranian neutrality (on which Reza Shah insisted) would have blocked one of Russia's last supply lines from Britain and the United States. In August, British and Soviet forces entered Iran and established a regime that would cooperate with them. Reza Shah abdicated and was replaced by his son, *Mohammed Reza Pahlavi,* who for a time governed under a constitution. Under the new shah, Iran declared war on Germany in 1943, but British troops continued to hold the south of the country and Soviet troops the north, including Tehran. When the Allied leaders, Franklin D. Roosevelt, Winston Churchill, and Joseph Stalin, met at Tehran in 1943, Stalin was host.

In 1945, after the surrender of Germany, the government of Iran requested Britain, the United States, and the Soviet Union to withdraw their forces from the country. Withdrawal was promised by these powers for March 1946, but in November 1945 the Communist-led *Tudeh* ("masses") *Party* organized an uprising in Azerbaijan and then set up a Soviet-style regime there. Armed government intervention was prevented by the continued presence of Soviet troops, but pressure from the United States, Britain, and the United Nations brought a change. Iran and Russia agreed on the withdrawal of all Russian troops (completed by May 1946) as well as on reforms in Azerbaijan and the setting up of a Soviet-Iranian oil company for northern Iran. In June, government troops reoccupied Azerbaijan without serious resistance.

As the image of preponderant U.S. power emerged in the first postwar years, and as the United States replaced Britain as the leading Western power in the Near and Middle East, the shah moved to a pro-U.S. orientation. An agreement with the United States provided for a U.S. military mission and purchases of American military equipment. The new *majlis,* elected with a progovernment majority, canceled the Soviet oil agreement. In 1949, the Tudeh Party was banned; the constitution was revised to give the shah the power to dissolve parliament; a seven-year plan of economic development was announced, to be directed by U.S. specialists; and a new agreement with the Anglo-Iranian Oil Company was drawn up, so as to give the government a somewhat larger share of the profits. A prosperous royal dictatorship seemed just ahead.

A Brief Swing to the Left: The Mossadegh Regime.
The next political developments occurred in the opposite direction. From mid-1951 on, the United States was engaged in the Korean War. In April 1951, the *majlis* made the leader of the non-Communist leftist *National Front, Mohammed Mossadegh,* prime minister. His government promptly

nationalized the oil industry. Britain and the British management of the Anglo-Iranian Oil Company resisted nationalization by all means short of war. They involved the International Court of Justice, withdrew all British technicans from the oil fields, and eventually organized a worldwide boycott of Iranian oil. Arab monarchies increased their oil output, partly replacing Iran's share. From the United States, President Truman in July 1951 sent a personal message to Iran to urge a compromise. In early 1952, U.S. military aid to Iran was suspended for almost four months. Mossadegh resigned in July. A pro-Western premier replaced him for five days but was overthrown in bloody rioting. Mossadegh returned to power, and parliament voted him dictatorial powers. In October, he broke diplomatic relations with Britain, but could not overcome the economic pressure of the international oil boycott.

By the spring of 1953, Stalin had died in the U.S.S.R. and his successors were busy with domestic politics. The Korean War was winding down. In the United States, President Eisenhower had come into office; on June 26, the Korean armistice was signed. On June 29, President Eisenhower informed Mossadegh that no further aid would be granted until the oil dispute with Britain was settled. On August 16, Mohammed Reza Shah tried to dismiss Mossadegh and then fled to Iraq, which then still had a pro-British government, and then to Rome. Three days later, Mossadegh was overthrown by a coup backed by the Tehran police and some military officers, led by General Fazollah Zahedi, the shah's earlier choice for premier. Various employees of the U.S. Central Intelligence Agency (CIA) later claimed credit for having engineered the coup and its success.

After three more days, on August 22, the shah was back in Tehran. Two weeks later, the United States made a grant of $45 million to Iran. Mossadegh had been arrested and later was tried and jailed. Soon diplomatic relations with Britain were restored, negotiations for a new oil agreement started, and parliament dissolved. In early 1954, police and troops suppressed antigovernment demonstrations, and the government announced a great electoral victory. A new oil agreement was concluded with a consortium of major United States, British, and continental oil companies, with a substantial increase in Iran's share of the profits.

The Shah in Full Power. Mohammed Reza Shah was now firmly established. For the next quarter century, he controlled parliament and the entire state. Iran as a whole grew richer, and the shah and his family got richer even faster. Some wealth fostered new industries, some of them state-owned. Several profitable state enterprises were later sold to the private sector. Often they ended up as the personal property of the shah, his family, or his favorites. Iran eventually became a member of the *Organization of Petroleum Exporting Countries (OPEC)*. After 1973, the country, and even more so the shah, grew richer still when the world price of oil grew many times what it had been.

Some of the wealth was spent on extravagant display. An elegant city of tents was built in 1971 for the 2,500-year anniversary of King Cyrus near the ruins of Persepolis, the symbol of ancient Iran. Thousands of members of the international elite were entertained there in elaborate festivites. With his personal wealth the shah purchased a 25-percent share in the West German steel firm of Friedrich Krupp and Company.

Another large part of the new wealth was spent on the armed forces, armaments, and the police. Iran was to become a naval power in the Gulf of Persia. Destroyers and other war vessels were ordered from abroad. Claims were raised for various territories in the Persian Gulf, such as oil-rich Bahrain and several small islands. The shah and his government kept recalling the greatness of the empire of King Cyrus in 550 B.C. and its territorial extensiveness. Should it not be Iran's destiny to rise again to similar greatness? In any case, the army was well equipped with tanks and the strong air force with modern fighter planes.

The United States encouraged some of this spending on armaments. Iran was considered a major U.S. ally in the Middle East. And if Iran spent a part of its oil wealth on costly American weapons, wouldn't this help the U.S. balance of payments and the international value of the dollar? From 1972 to 1978, the United States sold Iran about $14 billion worth of military goods. In the end, it was the shah who made the decisions, but his allies did little to dissuade him.

Other expenditures went to the police. There was a local police, a national gendarmerie, and a dreaded secret political police, known as *SAVAK*. U.S. advice on efficient technical police work was sought and sometimes accepted, but it was merged with long-standing practices of cruelty and torture. The result was a long succession of atrocities and the popular hatreds they provoked.

These issues highlight some of the problems faced by the monarchy. The shah himself was not a charismatic or popular political leader. He was not an effective or dramatic public speaker. His physical appearance was conventional. He tried, instead, to build an aura of mystery and majesty around the monarchy, since it was more difficult to do so around himself. The pomp and power of monarchical Iran was displayed ostentatiously and frequently—in palaces, court rituals, and gala celebrations—in order to build some legitimacy and popular support. When that failed, the state's military might was turned to repression. Repression, however, undermined the claim to lawful rule in the long run, and the ostentation itself was often distinctly un-Islamic. The magnificent celebrations at Persepolis, for example, were held amid monuments to pre-Islamic religion (Zoroastrianism). The feasts were a symbolic affront to Islam: liquor flowed, women danced, Western fashions replaced the veil, and pork was not excluded from the banquets. The splendor of the pre-Islamic past might have served as one claim to monarchical legitimacy, but plainly at the risk of alienating the real Islamic allegiances of most Iranians.

The Pahlavi dynasty, however, had another claim to legitimacy: modernization. Accelerating in the early 1960s, it was officially called the *"White Revolution."* There was an important (though limited) land reform program and a serious (though insufficient) effort to reduce illiteracy. There was special attention to industrial growth and to the adaptation of Western technology. The size of the Iranian middle class doubled from the mid-1950s to the mid-1970s, when it comprised about one-fifth of the population. To achieve this modernization program, there were over forty thousand U.S. business managers, technicians, scientific experts, military advisers, and diplomats and their dependents in Iran by 1978. There was at least a comparable number of Iranians in the United States, most of them students. But a majority of Iranians still remained poor, and their lives benefited insufficiently from these changes.

Much political participation remained, in fact, a threat to the regime. The shah experimented with a number of party systems, but these were somewhat artificial and served primarily to control people. The government's Iran Novin Party lasted from 1963 to 1975, when it was replaced by the National Resurgence Party, which collapsed in the upheavals that began in 1978. Generally, twentieth-century Iran has been characterized by factions or personal followings rather than by the more structured and less personal political parties found in other countries studied in this book. Popular leaders created and maintained their own organizations; thus, it was difficult for a party to continue after the death of the founding leader. Leader-focused politics was one of the country's weaknesses, just as it had been Mossadegh's weakness in the early 1950s. Iran in the 1980s will also have to overcome such dependence on particular leaders. Iran's religious tradition, which stresses the personal eminence of *ayatollahs,* reinforces this personalized pattern of politics.

There were, of course, more spectacular manifestations of political discontent. Since the last shah came to power in 1941, he endured many attacks on the monarchy until he was overthrown in 1979. He survived at least two assassination attempts in 1949 and in 1965. Two of his prime ministers were assassinated. And he had ordered his troops to fire on masses of people in 1952, in 1963, and finally and unsuccessfully in 1978.

Other limited forms of political participation were elections and referenda. Referenda or plebiscites have been used repeatedly in contemporary Iranian history as one mechanism to shore up the regime, but often without allowing the opposition adequate opportunity to express its point of view. Mossadegh sponsored a referendum to legitimize his break with the shah's policies, as Khomeini would do almost two decades later. The shah himself sponsored a referendum in 1963 to ratify his "White Revolution." Elections to parliament, or *majlis,* provided another limited avenue of participation. Because the shah did not welcome much overt political opposition, his adversaries were weakly represented in these institutions. Moreover, riding the crest of rising oil prices and the splendor of the Persepolis monarchical celebrations, the shah increasingly shut off even the very modest opposition that had been represented in the *majlis.* All political parties other than the official National Resurgence Party were banned in 1975, so that Iran legally became a one-party system. The *majlis* elected that year was the first in three decades to have no formal opposition members. The shah was further cut off from public pressures by the fact that he appointed half of the members of the Senate in the bicameral legislature. Elections to the *majlis,* however defective, had served, since 1906, certain important politically legitimating purposes of special appeal to Iranian intellectuals and other middle-class professionals. The effort to scuttle the *majlis'* role through these political changes seriously weakened one of the possible pillars of a regime that was already crumbling, without the shah's knowing it.

In 1975, Iran's per capita income was more than six times as high as that of Egypt; but inequality in Iran was substantially higher, Iran's rates of literacy and higher education were lower, and its rate of infant mortality exceeded that of Egypt by more than one-third.

The shah's political system was destroying itself. The growing number of workers—larger in 1979 than it had been in the days of Mossadegh—were angered by the suppression of effective labor unions and labor parties, and by the inflationary rise in the cost of living. Peasants remained poor. Bazaar merchants and artisans felt harassed by government regulations and the often corrupt way in which these were administered. The professional and upper middle classes, too, had grown frustrated by censorship, a police regime, and an inefficient authoritarian bureaucracy—and so did many of the clerks and bureaucrats themselves. Since the shah claimed the power to decide everything, he was blamed by everyone for all results.

In addition, the shah continued his father's course of head-on collision with religion. He opposed the Shi'ite community, whose priests had a long tradition of judging critically the legitimacy of a shah. Now many of them became his enemies. Of the three major challenges to the shah's rule, two—in the early 1960s and the late 1970s—had crucial religious origins (the first was Mossadegh's). The religious leaders inspired urban riots in the early 1960s that led the shah to order the armed forces to shoot the rioters. That was followed by the "White Revolution" program and the forced exile of one of the country's leading *ayatollahs,* Ruhollah Khomeini. Ayatollah Khomeini proceeded to oppose the regime vigorously as an exile until the shah fell in 1979. But the shah also fought against other religious leaders. In 1977, one of Iran's most respected theologians, Ayatollah Taleqani, was sentenced to ten years in prison. More generally, there were three major sources of dispute between the shah and the religious establishment.

The first was the most explosive politically. The *mujtahids* were not only men of religious learning but also, generally speaking, men of great integrity. They had served as unofficial social welfare agents, receiving charitable contributions and disbursing them to the poor with little corruption. They were the guardians of social justice and morality. As such, they were in stark contrast to the public perception of the Iranian government, which was characterized by widespread corruption and insensitivity to individuals and to Islam. The shah's splendor conflicted with the simplicity of the *mujtahids*. As support for a moral rejuvenation of Iran spread, the *mujtahids* stood well politically and morally to challenge the Pahlavi monarchy.

The second issue was more narrowly clerical. The Pahlavi shahs had challenged the religious establishment, taking away many of its rights and privileges. Religious presses were shut down and religious gatherings were broken up by security forces. Leading *mujtahids* and *ayatollahs* were harassed, imprisoned, and some were executed. The clergy clearly felt deeply threatened by government policies.

The third issue was perhaps the most problematical. Some of the results of the "White Revolution" brought about social changes that challenged some important religious interests. In particular, the land reform took away some Islamic landholdings to redistribute to others. The push in favor of women's rights at times clearly broke with more traditional interpretations of proper Islamic behavior for women. The shah was also rather tolerant of Jews, Christians, Sunni Muslims, and Bahai religious minorities, all of which at times displeased some of the stricter Shi'ite religious leaders. In addition, among many of the newly mobilized ex-villagers, who in recent decades had moved into the poorer quarters of rapidly growing cities and oil fields, religion had retained its hold. Indeed, in the bewildering new environment in which they now found themselves, these ex-villagers thirsted for clear, simple, and undoubted authority. Many of them offered a potential following for a movement of religious fundamentalism. Such a movement did develop and it too turned against the shah.

While the storm gathered, the shah's public relations personnel denied it, and he may have done so himself. Foreign powers joined in the chorus of admiration for the shah. Britain and the United States saw him as an ally and supported him accordingly. European businesses saw him and his country as good credit risks and customers. The Soviet Union in the mid-1960s signed a trade agreement, bought Iranian natural gas, and undertook construction of a steel mill near Isfahan. The shah was elaborately welcomed on visits to the Soviet Union and other Soviet bloc states and was given honorary degrees by some of their universities, just as he received similar honors from some major universities in the United States.

Critics in Iran were silenced by SAVAK or driven into exile. Iranian students abroad were watched by police agents sent to keep them under control. The CIA had promised the shah in the 1960s not to have any contacts with the opposition, and it seems that they kept their word; the opposition may have seemed unimportant to them anyway. It all seemed safe—and then the roof fell in.

Of Mohammed Reza Shah's five predecessors since the beginning of revolutionary agitation in 1890, four had been overthrown, assassinated, or exiled. He was next.

The Revolution of 1979. Some of the cracks in the structure had been growing for more than a decade. In the 1960s and 1970s, agitation against the shah had been increasing among Iranian students abroad. Some religious leaders had been living in exile, such as the Ayatollah Ruhollah Khomeini in Iraq and then in Paris. And a small but growing body of critical technical experts, including some economists and engineers, had found employment abroad or were living there on private incomes.

In 1978, opposition became visible in Iran, and it came from all sides. Agitation, strikes, riots all increased. Police arrests and cases of SAVAK torture multiplied; troops fired into crowds. It has been estimated that government repression in 1978 and 1979 killed several thousand people. Funerals of the victims sometimes turned into demonstrations. Popular antagonism was reaching a critical point. Suppressing it by the shah's forces became difficult.

In 1979, unrest reached its peak. Bazaar merchants and artisans shut their shops. Workers at the oil refinery at Abadan went on strike, and so did the employees at the Iranian central bank. Students walked out of their classes. Bankers, business managers, professional men, and their emancipated wives and daughters turned against the shah, with many of these women wearing the veil again. The Communists from the Tudeh Party, long outlawed but living underground, turned against him, even though the press and radio of the Soviet Union for a long time avoided any criticism of the monarch. *Mullahs* and *mujtahids* preached against the shah, and the words of the Ayatollah Khomeini from Paris, condemning the shah, were spread through the land.

Most of SAVAK stayed reliable. But the common soldiers were the sons, brothers, and cousins of the peasants, artisans, and laborers from whose families they had been recruited. They, too, were Shi'ites, and the voice of religious leaders, speaking from the sacred city of Qum, meant more to them than that of the shah journeying abroad or recalling the pagan glories of Persepolis. Even officers remembered their ties to the middle classes from among whom many had come. When air force officers still seemed likely to obey the shah's orders to act against the rebels, their mechanics immobilized their planes. Later, on many younger officers and cadets, like the mechanics, joined the revolution.

The shah first tried to order repression. When this failed, he appointed a former enemy, opposition leader *Shahpur Bakhtiar,* as prime minister. The shah then went abroad but avoided formal abdication. Before he left, his orders had escalated the bloodshed and the consequent hatred. When President Carter permitted him to come to the United States for medical treatment, Iranian hatred also became focused on the United States.

The Bakhtiar government was soon swept away by Khomeini's revolution. Khomeini appointed Mehdi Bazargan as prime minister, pending the approval of a new constitution and elections. The new government demanded extradition of the shah, to put him on trial for what were now seen as his crimes. Some religious leaders pronounced that anyone who murdered the shah would act justly and please God—a sentiment in line with Iran's long history of pious assassinations. The Ayatollah Khomeini shared this view. When it was reported that the shah had cancer (the eventual cause of his death, in Cairo, in 1980), the unforgiving old priest was reported as saying he hoped that was the case. In early November, students occupied the United States embassy in Tehran and held its personnel as hostages in defiance of diplomatic immunity for the professed purpose of forcing the United States to return the shah to Iran for trial and also to repatriate the wealth of the shah that in their view had been acquired illegally.

The Ayatollah Khomeini endorsed the action of the students and their refusal to negotiate until the shah was returned. President Carter, in turn, backed by U.S. public opinion, refused to negotiate about anything else until all the hostages were released. A ruling by the International Court at The Hague and a unanimous vote by the United Nations Security Council confirmed the illegality of Iran's holding diplomats and embassy personnel as hostages and demanded their unconditional release, but the council further urged patience and caution on all parties so as to avoid war. As the hostages remained captive, the United States broke diplomatic relations and imposed economic sanctions on Iran. While women and blacks were released within weeks, about fifty hostages were still being held a year later—despite U.S. diplomatic efforts, economic sanctions, and a military rescue effort that failed.

The Iranian revolution of 1979 throws doubt on the assumption that modern weapons make uprisings hopeless and governments irresistible. Weapons systems are also human systems. Tanks and airplanes need people to operate them and still more people to maintain them and to furnish them with fuel, spare parts, and other supplies. When enough people of different backgrounds all become hostile to government and are able to coordinate their efforts, the government will fall despite its arms. This is what happened to the shah's regime. It was the most heavily armed among the Muslim states, but inside its armor it was dying. The Pahlavi dictatorship fell because it had become incompatible with Iran's present social structure, religion, and past history. What will take its place?

The Current Political System. Most of what can be written now about Iran may change quickly in the early 1980s. Revolutions bring rapid changes, and Iran's revolution is not finished. But real revolutions also cannot quite be reversed, and the Iranian revolution of 1979 seems genuine enough. Which of the changes it has brought so far are likely to endure?

The Higher Stakes of Politics. Between 1954 and 1978 few important things, if any, could be decided by politics outside the royal palace. Major matters seemed to be fixed: the power of the monarch; the powerlessness of religion and most interest groups; the obedience of the army and police; the subordination of peasants, workers, clerks, and intellectuals; the wealth of landowners and the few big business firms, many of them foreign.

Now almost everything is at stake. Banks and large industries have been nationalized; they may stay so or they may be returned to private ownership. Some peasants are holding their own land; others are tenants. One kind of land reform could make more peasants into competing property owners; another could push them into cooperatives or collectivization. The economy could be developed or left to stagnate, linked more closely to the world market or isolated from it. The country as a whole might move more toward a free market system or toward central planning. Politically, it might move toward combining dictatorship or democracy with either of these economic patterns. Or it might seek some combination of a few big industries, particularly oil and petrochemicals, with an economy of small peasants, artisans,

and merchants. At least in the short run, oil production declined drastically in 1979–80, inducing an economic recession.

Much of Iranian culture is at stake, too. Now that the religious leaders have much power, they must make decisions about economics, politics, the law, education, and daily life, and they will increasingly be seen as responsible for them. At the moment, one eighty-year-old leader, the Ayatollah Khomeini, has the chief voice, but different leaders will favor different policies in time.

Already the revolution has wiped out many of Reza Shah's legal reforms and returned a great deal of judicial power to the *mujtahids*. Which way will their decisions go, year after year? Once the Shi'ite community of priests has moved from the sidelines to the center of decision making—even if only for a time—that community of priests will never be the same again.

Also at stake are health, education, and the rights of women. Emancipated women are few. They supported the revolution, but now they may be forced back to the household and to wearing the veil in accordance with Muslim tradition. Already the segregation of the sexes has been imposed on all schools. Will education and health care be oriented toward science and modernity or toward tradition and religion? And will lay persons or priests run these activities?

In its foreign policy, will Iran move toward cooperation with the Soviet bloc, will it restore the weakened links with the West, or will it try for a more or less genuine nonalignment? What level of armaments will Iran choose, and where will they come from? Will it go to war with Iraq again, as it did during the last months of 1980, and perhaps also fight against other Arab states?

In politics, will the secular parties dwindle or will they survive and grow stronger? Which ones will gain—the liberal pro-Western groups, such as that of former Prime Minister Bakhtiar who won office early in the revolution but then went into exile? Or the Communists of the Tudeh Party, which has returned to a legal existence, no one knows for how long. Or will it be the partisans of the shah, secular in culture, technocrats in economics, conservatives in matters of politics and social services? Will the pragmatic proponents of an Islamic Republic prevail over the Islamic fundamentalists? Or will Iran become an ever-tightening religious dictatorship? Each of these outcomes still seems possible.

The Increase in Political Participation. Genuine revolutions bring new masses of people into political activity. Dispatches speak of demonstrations by hundreds of thousands of people, and of meetings of up to a million. Even if these reports were exaggerated, they show that participation has changed.

Most of this increased participation has occurred in the large cities with more than 100,000 population. These cities contained almost half the people of Iran in 1978 (43 percent in 1975). There, almost all strata seem to have become active participants—students, industrial workers, professional people, clerks, artisans, and bazaar merchants. But less activity has been reported from the villages and the agricultural sector, which in 1975 employed 46 percent of the work force.

Some of the new participation has occurred within institutional channels. A new constitution more closely following Islamic precepts, was approved in 1979 by referendum. The monarchy was abolished; a republic was established. Presidential elections were held in 1980. Political parties, as had been the case in Iran before, developed primarily around personalities of great public appeal. A pragmatic economist who was also deeply devout and Khomeini's long-time advisor, *Abolhassan Bani-Sadr,* was elected president. However, Bani-Sadr's real powers were effectively limited by the persistent political role of Ayatollah Khomeini, who continued to make all the truly important decisions and left less important administrative matters to Bani-Sadr's government. The government was also constrained by its international dispute over the hostages in the U.S. embassy. The constitution also called for a new parliament. A fundamentalist Islamic party defeated Bani-Sadr's adherents in the 1980 parliamentary elections, and went on to capture a majority of the seats in the *majlis.* They imposed their own people as prime minister and as cabinet members on Bani-Sadr. The war with Iraq, however, reconcentrated authority in the presidency—as commander-in-chief—at least temporarily. The balance of power between executive and legislature in the 1980s remains unsettled.

Political support appears to vary the most by region. In the constitutional plebiscite in 1979, Tehran and central Iran backed Khomeini in approving the constitution, whereas voters in Azerbaijan overwhelmingly boycotted the polls. A result of the plebiscite was to make Khomeini the *faghih*—the supreme religious leader with powers to depose the government and to decide on matters of war and peace. A constitutional theocratic dictatorship had been established.

The Threatened Arena of Politics. In the revolution of 1979 and its consequences, Iran's borders have become fluid again.

The Kurdish minority in western Iran is demanding autonomy; some of them are demanding secession from Iran and a sovereign Kurdish state. The *Kurds* are settled astride the mountainous borders between Iraq, Turkey, and Iran. Their nationalism has brought them into conflict with all three governments, though usually not at the same time. When Iran and pro-Soviet Iraq quarreled, the shah supported the Kurds against Iraq and so sometimes did the United States. Currently, the Kurds have risen in some cities against Ayatollah Khomeini's Islamic republic, perhaps with some covert aid from Iraq, or the West, or both, despite their differences.

The Iranian army, though weakened by the revolution, has occupied some of Iran's Kurdish districts. So have Khomeini's *revolutionary guards.* Since most Kurds are Sunnis, Iran's Shi'ite-led revolution has little appeal to them and the conflict has become bitter. Several hundred people in Iranian Kurdistan have been executed, mostly by the revolutionary guards, but nearly always by the order of special courts. Whether Iran will keep its Kurdish regions or whether they will secede and establish a new state, only the future will show.

Another minority region is *Khuzistan* in southwest Iran. Its population is Arabic speaking but in large part professes the Shi'ite faith. Khuzistan contains the main oil fields of Iran. Since the triumph of the revolution at Tehran, some pipelines and refineries have been sabotaged. The Tehran government blames these incidents on counterrevolutionaries and foreign agents, but some Western observers have been inclined to see in them signs of an awakening Arab nationalism there.

It was over this area that a major war broke out between Iraq and Iran in September 1980. Iraq wanted to overturn an agreement it had accepted in 1975, whereby the boundary between the two countries was the middle of the Shatt-al-Arab river, through which vast quantitites of oil are shipped. Before 1975, Iraq had exclusive sovereignty over the river; in 1980, Iraq sought to return to the pre-1975 boundary. Moreover, Iraq was led by a secular regime, although its leaders were drawn primarily from Iraq's Sunni community (even though most Iraqis were Shi'ites). The Iraqi leadership felt thus deeply threatened by the Iranian revolution; Ayatollah Khomeini had called for a Shi'ite revolution in Iraq, too. Tehran, Baghdad (Iraq's capital), and many other cities were bombed. Oil wells and other facilities were destroyed. Fighting was bitter. Oil production and exports from both countries plummeted for months. Each country's oil wealth and territorial integrity was at stake. The future was uncertain.

A third minority area, in the long run perhaps the most important, is that inhabited by the 5 million *Azerbaijanis* who speak a Turkic language. They live in the north around the city of Tabriz and extending up to the border of the Soviet Union's *Republic of Azerbaijan*. Smaller groups of them, often economically prosperous, live in many major cities of Iran. They are Shi'ites but have been jealous of their distinctiveness and desirous of autonomy. Their religious leader, Ayatollah Shariat Madari, has been the main top-ranking cleric to challenge Ayatollah Khomeini's authority. In December 1979 aroused adherents of Madari and the secular *Khalq Party* occupied the Tabriz broadcasting station and held it for bargaining during negotiations with the central government.

As for the shah's hopes for Iranian expansion to include Bahrain and perhaps Kuwait and some other territories on the Gulf of Persia, they are currently suspended, but they might be revived at some future time.

Which Revolutionary Image for Iran? The Pahlavi shahs and their followers tried to establish an image of a powerful, modern Iran: rich, well armed, and continuing the heritage of the pre-Islamic empire of the ancient Persian kings. The small Westernized elite wanted their country to develop toward a modern Western-style constitutional regime, open to moderate foreign investment favoring domestic private enterprise. The Communists presumably wanted to make Iran a Soviet-style "people's republic."

By 1979, a different image emerged. Iran was declared an Islamic republic based on the authority of the Koran and ruled by its Shi'ite clergy. In such a state, according to Shi'ite tradition, it should be the religious leaders who set the goals and limits for the policies, watch over their execution, and correct any deviation from the course that the clergy has been setting. On this issue many *ayatollahs* are agreed. They supported the revolution and Khomeini's leadership.

But momentum carried events further. Most people find it easier to look to a person as a leader, and partly as a model for imitation, than to interpret and follow any more abstract political program or theological doctrine. In times of great change, when people find that many of their old habits no longer apply and that they must find and learn new ones, they look for a personal leader rather than for a party platform or a book. In such situations, they seek a leader with *charisma*—a personal grace that makes someone seem naturally prominent and admirable in the follower's eyes. Mohammed Reza Pahlavi was not charismatic.

In the summer and fall of 1979, Khomeini became such a leader. His ascendancy over the people is without parallel in the last seventy years of Persian history. Mehdi Bazargan, the prime minister appointed by Khomeini, said in an interview in Tehran: ". . . his relationship with the masses is in fact very special in that he and they think in the same way and speak the same language—a nod and they understand each other."[4]

This image of the charismatic leader can be found in the transition phases of many revolutions in other times and countries. In Iran, however, a special element has become linked to it, no one knows for how long, but with great potential power while it lasts. This is the Shi'ite doctrine of the *imām*.

On October 26, 1979, it was reported from Tehran that, according to the state radio, millions took part in a "march of solidarity with *Imām* Khomeini." The mass rallies had been called by the clergy to denounce the government of Premier Bazargan and to call for a far-reaching purge. According to the press report, the crowd at Tehran shouted "Khomeini the idol smasher is the Imām of our people."[5]

This is the most exalted role available in all Iranian history and culture. Can Khomeini take it seriously? The hidden *imām* was believed to be so pure that his body cast no shadow, but Khomeini's body does. The hidden, or twelfth, *imām* is to come back as a savior; calling Khomeini the *imām* implies

[4]"Bazargan Calls Khomeini Primitive—But a Genius," *International Herald Tribune* (October 31, 1979), p. 1. The interview was described as "recent."
[5]"Islamic Clergy Denounces Premier, Calls for Purge," United Press International, in *International Herald Tribune* (October 27–28, 1979), p. 1.

vast expectations. Although Khomeini himself has not made any explicit claim to this most exalted role, he has not objected to Iranian radio and television frequently using the title *imām* for him in such a way as to imply and hint at just such mounting expectations. Can he live up to these expectations or must he sooner or later disappoint his followers? Is this vast overstatement of the capacities of an individual—any individual—a prelude to his fall?

Perhaps there is no turning back for Khomeini and for some of the clergy who pushed his image to such extremes. But revolutions have a way of continuing beyond their charismatic stage. If they are not crushed, some of the great changes that they brought will remain, and people will turn to the less dramatic but no less important task of making them work in day-to-day practice.

One problem emerges from the Shi'ite approach to religious leadership. Since the disappearance of the twelfth *imām*, the Shi'ite community has come to depend on the "charisma of the office" of the religious establishment rather than on the "charisma of the individuals" who occupy those positions. To the extent that Khomeini seeks to break with that pattern, then he may be claiming an unprecedented political as well as religious authority for which there may not be enough warrant among the faithful.

Until these problems are sorted out, the machinery of government in Iran will remain somewhat crippled. Charismatic political authority has some radically simplifying political effects: power flows to the charismatic leader. The risks of great error for the sake of symbolic triumphs are, of course, magnified. And yet, after Khomeini's passing, there may be once again greater political differentiation in Iranian politics. A new executive branch, headed by Iran's president, may reacquire political authority, checked and supervised by a revitalized *majlis*. The religious establishment is likely to play a much more important role than it had under the monarchy, especially through its interpretations of Islamic law in ways that will affect government policy.

So far, the Iranian revolution has produced two

channels of political communication and power, each backed by different social groups and interests. Much will depend on which of these two sets prevails.

Two Competing Systems of Political Communication and Power. The Iranian revolution gave rise to an alternative network of communication and decision making that competed with the official bureaucracy of the state that had developed under the shah. Its basis was the old network of mosques and *mullahs,* of preaching and pilgrimages. But in the 1970s, this old network carried new political messages. They carried complaints from the mass of people to the *mullahs* and *ayatollahs,* and they carried their appeal and instructions to the masses. Through this feedback process, clergy and people learned to respond to each other on matters of burning interest to both of them: the oppressive regime of the shah and what to do about it.

Then came groups of lay people forming an association with the mosques and the clergy. They passed on the messages of the Ayatollah Khomeini from his Paris exile to the Iranian people. Here were then recruited some of the people who later staffed the revolutionary committees, the revolutionaries that were to parallel the old authorities at the local district and provincial level, and the revolutionary militia that would eventually parallel and replace much of the shah's police and regular army.

Other elements, too, in time joined these parallel structures. Leftist groups, some trade unionists, and others did so, but the preponderant influence and power has remained with the religious and populist elements that accept Khomeini's leadership.

Compared to these new channels and structures (Khomeini and the clergy, the revolutionary councils and committees, and the revolutionary courts), the older authorities (the secular government, the professional military officers, and the regular courts of justice) retained only a shadow of their former power. Without Khomeini's backing, they could not count on the obedience of the civilians and soldiers. Prime Minister Mehdi Bazargan complained in 1979 about this situation, and about "the deplorable state in which the army, police and security forces find themselves, all of them indispensable bodies for establishing law and order. Since the people consider them a . . . threat left over from the imperial regime, we have not succeeded in putting them in shape."[6]

The dual structure of power and political communication in Iran is not likely to last. The clergy and the revolutionary authorities either will permeate and take over the government and army, or else they will be replaced by them. And there are attacks by outright counterrevolutionaries, as well as by extremists of the left. Thus far, several close associates of Khomeini have been assassinated, and more may follow. The future character of Iranian politics is yet to be decided.

The Performance of Iran. The "White Revolution" of the Pahlavi shahs brought the country some modernity, mainly in the oil industry, some other industrial sectors, and some big cities. It made Iran one of the richest of the developing countries, with a per capita income of $1660 in 1975 and $2180 in 1977. It awed its smaller neighbors by large armaments and dazzled the world by lavish displays and well-financed public relations. It built some highways and railroads, and it encouraged the growth of a small industrial working class. A Westernized section of the professional, upper, and middle classes sent their sons abroad to study at Western universities. Their wives and daughters began to demand new rights for women that went beyond the narrow limits granted them by Muslim tradition.

But the shahs who reformed Iran's technology did not reform its society in any depth. Iran's Gini index of inequality (see Table 9.1) remained at 50 percent in 1975, among the highest of the countries for which we have such data. Even with its oil wealth, Iran's per capita income was still low

[6]Interview, *International Herald Tribune* (October 31, 1979), p. 5.

enough that this inequality was bringing real suffering to those at the short end of it. The infant death rate in the first year after birth in 1975 was 139 per thousand, substantially worse than the rates for Pakistan, India, Egypt, and Ethiopia. Life expectancy in Iran averaged fifty years, no better than that for India, a vastly poorer country. Of its adults in 1970, 63 percent were illiterate. No other large or middle-sized country shows such contrasts between wealth and backwardness. To preserve these contrasts, repression has been used often.

Positive results of the revolutionary regime that came to power in 1979 have been slow in coming. Iran is now less dependent on any foreign country, more fully in possession of its industries, utilities, and mineral resources. But the output of all these was much lower as the 1980s opened than it had been under the shah. Machinery is in danger of going unrepaired; there is less security in streets and homes; some revolutionary tribunals are no less arbitrary and unpredictable than SAVAK used to be. A new Islamic view of what may be printed has led to a censorship in some ways as narrow-minded as the one that existed under the shah. The women in many places have to struggle against being pushed back into seclusion and having to wear the veil. The costs of the revolution are here for all to see, but so far not many achievements promised by the revolution have taken shape. The coming years may yet bring some of the achievements hoped for, or they may bring bloodier conflicts and catastrophes either within Iran or through other wars with Iraq or other countries. For good or ill, the country's future is open and hopeful, but at the same time full of risk and danger for itself and the peace of the world.

KEY TERMS AND CONCEPTS

India:
Punjab
Aryans
Sanskrit
Hindi
Dravidian languages
Vedas
varna
brahmans
kshatriyas
vaisyas
sudras
untouchables
Sikhs
East India Company
"The Great Mutiny" of 1857
Indian National Congress
Mohandas K. Gandhi (Mahatma Gandhi)
All-India Muslim League
Mohammed Ali Jinnah
Pakistan
Bangladesh
communalism
depressed classes
jati
Lok Sabha
Rajya Sabha
Lok Dal Party
Jawaharlal Nehru
Indira Gandhi
Janata Party
Morarji Desai
Jan Sangh Party
Mahatma
nonviolence
"truth force"
"vernacular" vs. "regional language"
"soft states"
civil service
state of emergency

Nigeria:
Yoruba
Ibo
Hausa
Fulani
Nnamdi Azikiwe

Abubakar Tafawa Balewa
Yakubu Gowon
Biafra
Odumegwu Ojukwu
Obafemi Awolowo
Alhaji Shehu Shagari
Northern People's Congress
Sardauna of Sokoto
Olusegun Obasanjo
Nigerian People's Party

Egypt:
fellaheen
Ottoman Empire
Mehemet Ali
khedive
Suez Canal
Arabi Pasha
Jamal-el-Din el-Afghani
protectorate
Wafd
King Fuad
King Faruk
Mohammed Naguib
Liberation Rally
Gamal Abdel Nasser
Nasserism
Suez War, 1956
Arab Socialist Union (ASU)
National Democratic Party (NDP)
Egyptian Communist Party
Liberal Socialist Party
People's Assembly
Ali Sabri
Coptic Christians
Arab socialism
Pan-Arabism
United Arab Republic (UAR)
Six Day War, 1967
Anwar el-Sadat
October War, 1973
Camp David agreements, 1978
Arab League
Muslim Brotherhood

the Sudan
Sunni
pasha
bey
effendi
baksheesh

Iran:
Achamenian dynasty, 550–331 B.C.
satrap
Zoroastrian religion
Sassanian dynasty
Magi
Caliphs
Assassins *(hash-shāhshīn)*
Il-Khans
Timur
Shi'ism
Islam
Koran *(Q'uran)*
Ali
Omayyad dynasty
Husayn
sunna
Sunnites, Sunnis
imām
Mahdi
doctrine of dissimulation
tallebe
mullah
mujtahid
ayatollah
ayatollah al-ozma
Ayatollah Ruhollah Khomeini
majlis
"White Revolution"
National Resurgence Party
Abolhassan Bani-Sadr
charisma
Shahpur Bakhtiar
Ayatollah Shariat Madari
Qajarite dynasty, 1794–1925
Persian Cossack brigade, 1878

Anglo-Persian Oil Company
Persian revolution, 1905
Bakhtiar tribe
British-Russian agreement, 1907
South Persia Rifles, 1916
Anglo-Persian agreement, 1919
Soviet Republic of Gilan, 1921
Reza Khan
Reza Shah Pahlavi
Pahlavi dynasty, 1925–79
trans-Iranian railroad, 1927–39
British-Soviet occupation, 1941
Mohammed Reza Shah Pahlavi, 1943–79
Tudeh Party
National Front
Mohammed Mossadegh
International oil boycott, 1952–53
CIA-assisted coup, 1953
Organization of Petroleum Exporting Countries (OPEC), 1973
SAVAK
Kurds
Khuzistan
Iranian Revolution, 1979
revolutionary guards
Azerbaijan, Azerbaijanis (in Iran)
Azerbaijan, Republic of, in Soviet Union
Khalq Party
constitution of 1979
faghih
Qum, holy city of
Shah Abbas the Great, 1587–1629
Nadir Shah, 1736–47

ADDITIONAL READINGS

India:

Appadorai, A., ed. *Documents on Political Thought in Modern India.* Vol. 1. New York: Oxford University Press, 1974.

Bhagwati, J. and T. N. Srinivasan. *Foreign Trade Regimes and Economic Development: India.* New York: Columbia University Press, 1976.

Bose, N. *The Structure of Hindu Society.* Columbia, Mo.: South Asia Books, 1976.

Brecher, M. *Succession in India: A Study in Decision-Making.* London: Oxford University Press, 1966.

Bueno de Mesquita, B. *Strategy, Risk and Personality in Coalition Politics: The Case of India.* Cambridge: Cambridge University Press, 1975.

Chatterji, S. K. *Indo-Aryan & Hindi.* Rev. and enl. 2d ed. Calcutta: Firma K. L. Mukhopadhyay, 1960.

————. *Languages and Literatures of Modern India.* Calcutta: Bengal Publishers, 1963.

Cohen, S. P. and R. L. Park. *India: Emergent Power?* New York: Crane-Russak, 1978. PB

Desai, A. R. *Recent Trends in Indian Nationalism,* 2d ed. New York: International Publications Service, 1974.

Eldersveld, S. and A. Bashiruddin. *Citizens and Politics: Mass Political Behavior in India.* Chicago: University of Chicago Press, 1978.

Erickson, E. H. *Gandhi's Truth: On the Origins of Militant Non-Violence.* New York: Norton, 1970. PB

Frankel, F. R. *India's Green Revolution: Political Costs of Economic Growth.* Princeton. N.J.: Princeton University Press, 1971.

Gandhi, M. K. *An Autobiography: The Story of My Experiments with Truth.* Boston: Beacon Press, 1957.

————. *Collected Works.* 70 vols. Delhi: Ministry of Information and Broadcasting, 1958.

————. *The Essential Gandhi: An Anthology Edited by Louis Fischer.* New York: Random House, 1962.

————. *The Gandhi Reader.* Edited by Homer Jack. Bloomington: Indiana University Press, 1956.

————. *Thoughts on National Language.* Ahmedabad: Navajivan Publishing House, 1956.

Harrison, S. *India: The Most Dangerous Decades.* Princeton, N.J.: Princeton University Press, 1960.

Karve, I. *Kinship Organization in India.* 3d ed. New York: Asia Publishing House, 1965.

Kothari, R. *State and Nation Building: A Third World Perspective*. Columbia, Mo.: South Asia Books, 1976.

———, ed. *Caste in Indian Politics*. Atlantic Highlands, N.J.: Humanities Press, 1970.

Lamb, B. *India: A World in Transition*. New York: Praeger, 1975. PB

Maddison, A. *Class Structure and Economic Growth: India and Pakistan Since the Moghuls*. New York: Norton, 1972.

Mehta, V. *The New India*. New York: Penguin, 1978. PB

Mukherjee, R. K. *Social Indicators*. Columbia, Mo.: South Asia Books, 1975.

Narain, I. *Election Studies in India*. Columbia, Mo.: South Asia Books, 1978.

Nayar, B. *Minority Politics in the Punjab*. Princeton, N.J.: Princeton University Press, 1966.

———. *National Communication and Language Policy in India*. New York: Praeger, 1969.

Nehru, J. *Selected Works*. 11 vols. Columbia, Mo.: South Asia Books, 1972–78.

———. *The Unity of India*. London: Drummond, 1941.

———. *An Autobiography*. London: Bodley Head, 1953.

———. *Glimpses of World History*. New York: John Day, 1942.

———. *The First Sixty Years*. Condensed ed. 2 vols. Edited by D. Norman. London: Bodley Head, 1965.

Singh, T. *Poverty and Social Change: With a Reappraisal*. 2d ed. Westport, Conn.: Greenwood Press, 1975.

Singh, Y. *Social Stratification and Change in India*. Columbia, Mo.: South Asia Books, 1978.

Srinivas, M. N., et al *Dimensions of Social Change in India*. Columbia, Mo.: South Asia Books, 1978.

Subrahamanayam, K. *Self-Reliance and National Resilience*. Columbia, Mo.: South Asia Books, 1975.

Veit, L. A. *India's Second Revolution: The Dimension of Development*. New York: McGraw-Hill, 1976.

Weiner, M. *Politics of Scarcity: Public Pressure and Political Response in India*. Chicago: University of Chicago Press, 1962.

———, ed. *Electoral Politics in the Indian States: Party Systems and Cleavages*. Vol. 4. Columbia, Mo.: South Asia Books, 1976.

Nigeria:

Coleman, J. S. *Nigeria: Background to Nationalism*. Berkeley: University of California Press, 1971.

Luckhman, R. *Nigerian Military: A Sociological Analysis of Authority and Revolt, 1960–67*. New York: Cambridge University Press, 1971. PB

Melson, R. and H. Wolfe, eds. *Nigeria: Modernization and the Problems of Communalism*. Lansing: Michigan State University Press, 1971.

Ostheimer, J. M. *Nigerian Politics*. New York: Harper & Row, 1973. PB

Peace, A. J. *Choice, Class and Conflict: A Study of Southern Nigerian Factory Workers*. Atlantic Highlands, N.J.: Humanities Press, 1979. PB

Shatz, S. P. *Nigerian Capitalism*. Berkeley: University of California Press, 1978.

Sklar, R. *Nigerian Political Parties: A Study of the Political Parties of the First Republic*. New York: NOK Publishers, 1980. PB

Wayas, J. *Nigeria's Leadership Role in Africa*. Atlantic Highlands, N.J.: Humanities Press, 1979.

Egypt:

Baker, R. W. *Egypt's Uncertain Revolution Under Nasser and Sadat*. Cambridge: Harvard University Press, 1978.

Berger, M. *Bureaucracy and Society in Modern Egypt*. Princeton, N.J.: Princeton University Press, 1957.

Binder, L. *In a Moment of Enthusiasm: Political Power and the Second Stratum in Egypt*. Chicago: University of Chicago Press, 1978.

Bowie, R. *Suez 1956*. New York: Oxford University Press, 1974. PB

Hussein, M. *Class Conflict in Egypt, 1945–1970*. New York: Monthly Review Press, 1973.

Mabro, R. *The Egyptian Economy, 1952–1972*. New York: Oxford University Press, 1974.

———. *The Industrialization of Egypt, 1939–73*. New York: Oxford University Press, 1976.

O'Brien, P. *Revolution in Egypt's Economic System: From Private Enterprise to Socialism, 1952–65.* New York: Oxford University Press, 1966.

Richmond, J. *Egypt in Modern Times.* New York: Columbia University Press, 1969, 1977.

Safran, N. *Egypt in Search of Political Community: An Analysis of the Intellectual and Political Evolution of Egypt, 1804–1952.* Cambridge: Harvard University Press, 1961.

Vatikiotis, P. J. *Nasser and His Generation.* New York: St. Martin's, 1978.

Waterbury, J. *Egypt: Burdens of the Past, Options for the Future.* Bloomington: Indiana University Press, 1978.

Iran:

Ahmad, Eqbal, et al. "The Explosion in the Moslem World: A Round Table on Islam." In *The New York Times* (December 11, 1979), pp. A16–17.

Amuzegar, J. *Iran: An Economic Profile.* Washington, D.C.: Middle East Institute, 1977.

Brockelmann, C. *History of the Islamic Peoples.* New York: Putnam, 1960. PB

Frye, R. N. *Persia.* Rev. ed. London: Allen and Unwin, 1968.

Ghirshman, R. *Iran.* New York: Penguin, 1978. PB

Graham, R. *Iran.* New York: St. Martin's, 1979. PB

Halliday, F. *Iran: Dictatorship and Development.* New York: Penguin, 1979. PB

Sykes, P. M. *A History of Persia,* 2 vols. London: Macmillan & Co., 1915, and in Iran/Persia Series, New York: Gordon Press, 1976.

Wilber, D. *Iran: Past and Present,* 8th ed. Princeton: N.J.: Princeton University Press, 1976. PB

PB = *available in paperback*

XI

The Political Development of Cuba, Mexico, and Brazil: Three Latin American Cases

VAN R. WHITING, JR.

The countries of Latin America occupy a special position between the older, highly developed nations and the newly independent nations that are often among the least developed of countries. Despite rising incomes, inequalities continue in the countries of the region. In some of them, the rich live in luxury and the poor live at near-starvation levels of poverty; in all, poverty and underdevelopment distinguish them in absolute wealth, in human welfare, and in standards of constitutional freedom from the industrial countries of Europe and North America. Foreign powers have heavily influenced their history, boundaries, traditions, and economies. The predominant languages and cultures of these countries are Western, derived from Spain and Portugal; the pre-existing Indian civilizations were largely absorbed or wiped out in many cases.

Most of the Latin American nations won their independence in the nineteenth century, often by successful revolutions, long before many Asian and African nations became independent. Since independence, their elites and their economies have been influenced by Britain, France, and the United States, as well as by the former colonial powers, Spain and Portugal. Western science, technology, literature, and mass immigration have been available to them, although these resources have not by themselves been sufficient to produce development. In short, the countries of Latin America represent a combination of developed and Third World conditions and traditions, with Indian, Latin-Iberian, northern European, American, and in some cases African elements intermingling and combining into new patterns. The political development of the countries of the region reflects this diversity and uniqueness.

The three countries chosen for this chapter—Cuba, Mexico, and Brazil—are richer than most other countries in Asia, Africa, and Latin America, and their politics has been more stable for the last fifteen years or more. They are countries of different sizes and traditions. One country (Mexico) has a strong Indian heritage, and the two others have been influenced by African traditions. Cuba largely depends on a one-crop economy based on sugar, Brazil on a broadly diversified economy, and Mexico on its considerable natural riches, including oil. All are closely tied to the United States by geography, strategy, and past or present economic links. They include one egalitarian, Communist-ruled dictatorship, one growth-oriented, anticommunist military regime, and one nationalist regime dominated by a single party. All three countries now are striving for economic development and real national independence.

CUBA: THE SOCIALIST "PEARL OF THE ANTILLES"

The Republic of Cuba is a nation of islands. As the largest of the Antilles chain, the *"pearl of the Antilles"* is located in the Caribbean just south of Florida. The rich soil and warm climate have long been conducive to growing tobacco and sugar cane, thus providing a base for the Cuban economy and a dependence on foreign markets that even socialism has not been able to escape. Agricultural *monoculture* (dependence on one crop) is only the most constant aspect of Cuba's dependence, leading to another: the political dependence on foreign powers. Despite a strong tradition of national pride, Cuba was subject to the Spanish Crown until the uprising of 1895 and the Spanish-Cuban-American War of 1898. After Cuba's formal independence, the United States first ruled, then indirectly dominated the island. Since the revolution of 1959, Cuba has been beholden to the Soviet Union. The first socialist nation in the Western Hemisphere, Cuba has, since 1975, assumed a more active role in the world—especially by sending troops to Africa. The small nation has captured the attention of the world in recent years.

History Prior to the Revolution. Cuba was discovered by Christopher Columbus on his maiden voyage in 1492. The Spanish quickly vanquished the few primitive Indians on the island, and by 1539 established Cuba as a minor colony of Spain. The Spanish *conquistadores* (conquerors) put most of their energies into searching for gold in the richer Indian empires in Mexico and Peru; for a time Cuba was neglected. For most of the sixteenth and seventeenth centuries and into the eighteenth, Cuba was an underpopulated and relatively unimportant Spanish colony, devoted to tobacco farming and cattle raising. Havana was a meeting place for ships and sailors. But in the late eighteenth century, plantation agriculture, sugar production, and the importation of African slaves all began to expand. In the 76 years that followed the brief British occupation of Havana in 1763, more than six times as many slaves (some five thousand per year) were imported to Cuba than in the preceding 250 years. In that time, the number of whites declined from a majority to a minority of the island population.[1] The independence of most of Spanish America in the early 1800s left Cuba, with its new importance as a major sugar producer, as Spain's richest colony. Finding trade outlets with the United States, the planter elite, observing slave revolts in nearby Haiti, remained politically loyal to Spain. Their loyalty earned Cuba the sobriquet, *"la isla siempre fiel"*—the ever-faithful isle.

Though the British had ended their slave trade in 1807, the existence of slavery elsewhere (especially in the United States) meant that the Cubans could get slaves without trouble. By about 1840, nearly 80 percent of the Cuban work force was slave labor. Forty years later, by 1880, slavery was in decline. Changes in the technology of the sugar industry, the end of slavery elsewhere, and the immigration of whites, Chinese, and Indians from Mexico's Yucatán peninsula had reduced the number of slaves to less than one-quarter of Cuba's total work force.

Even in the ever-faithful isle there were those

[1]Franklin W. Knight, *Slave Society in Cuba During the Nineteenth Century* (Madison: University of Wisconsin Press, 1970), pp. 10, 22.

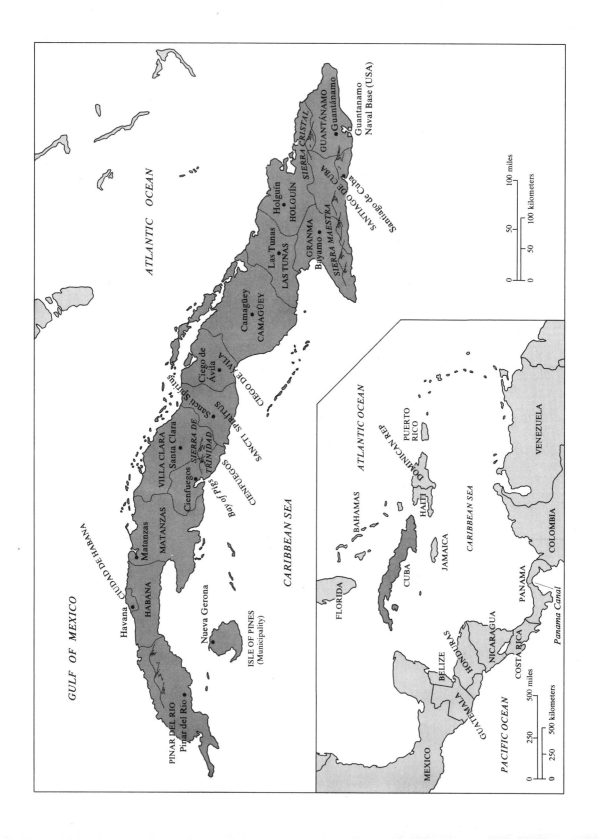

who sought independence from Spain. Bloody though unsuccessful struggles for independence were fought in the Ten Years' War from 1868 to 1878 and in the "little war" of 1879; together they took over 200,000 lives. Trade between Cuba and the United States nevertheless increased. Cubans resented the mother country's control more and more, and in 1895 the independence struggle broke out again. With the intellectual inspiration of the patriot José Martí and the fighting skill of soldiers such as Máximo Gómez, Calixto García, and Antonio Maceo (all experienced in the Ten Years' War), three more years of war ensued. Martí himself was killed in the first weeks of fighting.

The United States, which before their Civil War had tried to purchase Cuba from Spain, intervened in 1898 after the U.S.S. *Maine* was sunk in Havana harbor. The result was the misnamed Spanish-American War.[2] In a quick victory over Spain, the United States acquired Puerto Rico and the Philippines and dominated Cuba. From 1898 to 1902, the United States ruled Cuba with military governors. To the constitution of 1901 was added an amendment by Senator O. H. Platt of Connecticut (the *Platt Amendment*) by which Cuba limited its ability to make foreign treaties or to contract foreign loans; the United States was granted a naval station (still existing at Guantánamo) and the right to intervene to protect "life, property, and individual liberty." In effect, Cuba was a U.S. protectorate.

When in 1906 the first president of Cuba, Tomás Estrada Palma, called on the United States to protect his re-elected government from rebel opposition, President Theodore Roosevelt agreed to send troops to govern Cuba. He then appointed Charles Magoon governor of Cuba for three years. U.S. troops were in Cuba again in 1917 to prop up President Mario García Menocal at the time of the United States' entry into the First World War; this time they stayed five years. The fifth Cuban president after independence, Gerardo Machado (ruling from 1925 to 1933), used dictatorship and repression to counter unrest caused by the fall of sugar prices and to enrich himself and his family. Gradually a broadly based revolt forced him to resign in 1933. After Sumner Welles, U.S. ambassador to Cuba, failed to install a new president there, the United States pulled back from its imperial policy, abrogating the Platt Amendment in 1934. (Notably, there was a surplus of sugar in the U.S. market that year.) The United States would no longer try to dictate who should rule Cuba—or so they said.

Sergeant *Fulgencio Batista* took advantage of the 1933 revolt against Machado and dominated politics in Cuba for the next eleven years. With the backing of the army, Batista was the power behind the president until 1940, and himself president from 1940 to 1944. During his presidency, he supervised the modernization of much of the country's roads and public works. But after two terms out of office (during the civilian but often corrupt administrations of Ramón Grau San Martín, 1944–1948, and Carlos Prío Socarrás, 1948–1952), Batista came back to power through a coup, this time as a dictator. As such, he ruled for another six and a half years, directly or through a shadow president.

The United States, no longer imposing direct rule on Cuba, lobbied there for its business interests and generally supported a strong central government.[3] U.S. foreign direct investment grew

---

[2]The war is properly named the Spanish-Cuban-American War, since Spain and Cuba had already been at war for three years before the United States got involved. See Philip S. Foner, *The Spanish-Cuban-American War and the Birth of American Imperialism* (New York: Monthly Review Press, 1972).

[3]For a comparison of U.S. imperialism up to 1933 and "hegemony" from 1933 to 1958, see Jorge I. Domínguez, *Cuba, Order and Revolution* (Cambridge: Harvard University Press, 1978), chapters 2 and 3.

(Left) MAP 11.1 *Cuba*

in importance in mining, manufacturing, and tourism. The economies of Cuba and the United States were tied closely together.

The most recent period in Cuba's history is overshadowed by Fidel Castro. Even during his days as a law student, Castro was active in student and party politics. After the coup of March 1952, which returned Batista to power, a band of about 170 young rebels, convinced that only insurrection would throw off Batista's oppressive rule, attacked the army barracks at Moncada on July 26, 1953. (This attack later provided the name for the revolutionary *26th of July Movement*.) Many of the rebels were killed; Castro was captured and put on trial. An edited version of his defense speech at the closed trial has become famous under the title, "History Will Absolve Me!"

Released from jail in a general amnesty in 1955, Castro went to Mexico to organize and train for armed resistance. Returning to Cuba on the yacht *Granma*, arriving on December 2, 1956, the small band led by Fidel Castro (and including the Argentinian Ernesto "Che" Guevara) began a guerrilla war in the Sierra Maestra mountains with the quiet support of the peasantry. The gradual disillusionment with Batista among the middle class and the army, as well as among peasants, students, and workers helped speed the success of the movement. Within two years and one month, the movement triumphed and Batista fled. Castro took power on January 1, 1959.

Fidel Castro was probably not a communist or a socialist when he came to power. However, he had a radical vision of land reform and the restructuring of society, and soon his policies brought him into conflict with the United States. Besides proceeding with an extensive land reform that hurt large American landowners, Cuba expropriated numerous North American industrial enterprises, mining firms, oil companies, hotels, and utilities. Matters moved toward a collision. Possible compensation agreements worked out by U.S. Ambassador Phillip W. Bonsal were turned down by Washington. Cuba continued to attack the United States verbally, most noticeably in Castro's speech before the United Nations in September 1960. In the United States, Castro was attacked as a Communist and his government opposed long before he declared, "I am a Marxist-Leninist." During their last year in office, President Dwight Eisenhower and Vice President Richard Nixon considered various plans of action against Cuba and approved the one that was later followed. Less than four months after John F. Kennedy took office, in April 1961, the Central Intelligence Agency (CIA) sponsored an abortive invasion by about 1,200 Cuban exiles at the *Bay of Pigs*. The invaders were killed or captured; 2,500 CIA agents within Cuba as well as tens of thousands of other opponents of the regime were imprisoned, although many were held only briefly.[4] This victory helped Fidel Castro consolidate his position.

On December 2, 1961 (the anniversary of the landing of the *Granma*), Castro announced his commitment to Marxism-Leninism. In January 1962, Cuba's membership in the Organization of American States (OAS) was suspended. Then, in October of that year, U.S. intelligence detected the construction of nuclear missile sites in Cuba and the presence of Soviet-built nuclear missiles. The *Cuban Missile Crisis* involved a face-off between the United States and the Soviet Union over Cuba. By firm but careful diplomacy and the imposition of a naval blockade of the island, the United States succeeded in getting the Soviet Union to remove the missiles and to agree not to place offensive weapons in Cuba in the future. (This brief *blockade*, which physically impeded entrance or exit from Cuba, should be distinguished from the long-lasting *trade embargo*, which forbids the direct sale of goods to Cuba by U.S. firms.) As its part of the agreement, the United States undertook not to support any further invasions of Cuba. So far, both the United States and the Soviet Union have kept their word. If there had been any doubt before, it was clear after the Bay of Pigs and the

---

[4]Hugh Thomas, *The Cuban Revolution* (New York: Harper & Row, 1977), pp. 581, 587.

Cuban Missile Crisis that Cuba was a revolutionary socialist country and that the island enjoyed the economic and military support of the Soviet Union.

The Stakes of Politics in Cuba. The revolution has changed the stakes of politics in Cuba. Politics still affects in important ways the welfare of the Cuban people, their participation in government, and the position of Cuba in the international sphere. Under a socialist dictatorship, these factors have taken on new meanings.

The revolutionary regime has brought changes in the ownership of land and other productive facilities, and in the distribution of wealth and property. These changes mean that most Cubans are assured basic standards of food, clothing, health, and education. Shantytowns have also been eliminated. These accomplishments of the last two decades are considerable, both by historical Cuban standards and by comparison with other Latin American countries.

Cuba has encountered difficulties in providing more than basic necessities for its people. Two questions significantly affect the welfare of most individuals: economic growth (or lack of growth) and the allocation of material goods and services. As long as the economy does not grow, there is little chance for improving the material well-being of the people. Though Cuban factory workers may have enough food and may have roughly the same living space or access to recreational facilities as a writer or schoolteacher or government official, the limited overall growth of the economy restricts variety in their material possessions and improvement in their standard of living. Many people have only one pair of shoes. Housing shortages continue, since fewer housing units have been built than the population has needed. For many years the houses of Havana went without basic maintenance. Scare resources have been used elsewhere in the economy.

Recent state policies have made more goods available to some but not to others. Since about 1970, material incentives have rewarded those who work more or more productively, according to the socialist principle, "From each according to his abilities, to each according to his needs." Cuba has clearly not arrived at communism, that is, an economy of abundance in which all would receive according to need. As long as Cuba is a *society of scarcity,* the tension between incentives for growth and distribution for equity will not easily be resolved.

Other policies may also affect the distribution of goods in the society. The policy of rapprochement with the *"Cuban community abroad"* adopted in late 1978 introduces unequal access to material goods that conflicts with the egalitarian goals of the revolution. Cubans living in the United States may bring gifts to their relatives in Cuba, or buy gifts for them with dollars in special stores.

At stake in socialist Cuba is also the amount and kind of popular participation in the government. New forms of popular participation have been accepted since a new socialist constitution was adopted in 1976. Decision-making power, however, remains with those who agree with the basic policies of the government. In a regime based on the controlled mobilization of the people, tension will continue to surround participation in formulating policy as well as in discussing and carrying out policies already formed.

Finally, the military and diplomatic position of Cuba in the world is a major issue for Cuban politics. The advantages of continued dependence on the Soviet Union may decrease if Soviet aid decreases and as payments on past aid come due. Similarly, access to advanced technology and a large nearby market makes relations with the United States an issue that will recur in Cuba's foreign affairs. The role of Cuba in the Third World is an issue that not only involves the prestige of the nation; when Cuban troops fight in Africa— troop estimates at times reached a total of about 35,000—the lives of Cuban soldiers are the most graphic stakes of politics.

Participants in Politics. Cuba is a mobilized social-ist society. Participation in the political system involves the majority of the population, since most people come into contact with a mass political organization at their school, at their work place, or in their community. Of course, not all these members are activists. Another organization groups together the activists in Cuba: the Commu-nist Party.

Mass organizations in Cuba exist for workers, peasants, youth, and women; there are also neigh-borhood organizations in which all are encour-aged to participate. Workers as well as peasants participate in mobilized mass organizations, which are effective at educating Cubans about new policies and goals of the revolutionary govern-ment. New ideas may filter upward from the mass discussions, though the revolutionary leadership decides which suggestions to accept. The Cuban Labor Confederation (CTC) brings workers to assemblies to consider major new laws or propo-sals; there are also smaller meetings at the factory level for local issues. Anywhere from 60 to 90 percent of the members attend the assemblies, and government proposals are typically approved by overwhelming majorities. Since most participants support proposed policies, only the negative votes are counted. It thus becomes significant if 1, 2 or 3 percent of the voters disapprove a proposal. In the late 1970s, the Cuban government admitted that the impact of these assemblies on decisions at the factory or the government level was often limited.

Major policy proposals are discussed by nearly everyone, not just workers. Such discussions have been held for the 1971 law on vagrancy (to combat excessive absenteeism); the 1975 family code (in-cluding rules on marriage, the family, and parent-hood); and the 1979 penal code. But the most massive discussions were about the 1976 constitu-tion. In those discussions, perhaps 6 million peo-ple participated (often on several occasions) in a country whose total population was just under ten million. In the first discussion in 1975, 88.5 percent of the participants approved the draft constitution without any changes; about 10 per-cent supported amendments proposed by 16,000 participants around the country; less than 2 per-cent opposed it altogether. In the 1976 referen-dum of the proposed new constitution, 98 percent of all registered voters participated; 97.7 percent of them approved.[5] Under the terms of the constitution, Cuba remains a one-party "dictator-ship of the proletariat," and any organized opposi-tion is illegal.

Although Cuban citizens may react to govern-ment or party initiatives, they have little influence on the formulation of policy. But participatory activities (such as discussing laws in assemblies or voting for representatives to organizations and to the new Assemblies of Peoples' Power) provide information to the Cuban people, increase the likelihood of their commitment to the govern-ment, and gather suggestions from many people.

In the countryside, the National Association of Small Peasants (ANAP) has changed from a lobby-ing group for farmers in the early 1960s to an organization for controlled mass participation in the 1970s. It is now easier for information about government decisions to reach the peasants, but more difficult for their input to carry weight in policy making. Some changes are made in re-sponse to peasants' wishes: for example, peasants on small private farms (still allowed in Cuba) can join private cooperatives instead of state farms and can sell some of their produce privately.[6]

Perhaps the best-known and certainly the largest of Cuba's mass organizations are the *Committees for the Defense of the Revolution (CDRs)*. Founded in 1960, the CDRs were a security apparatus, organ-ized in every community to observe and denounce counterrevolutionary activity. At the time of the Bay of Pigs invasion, the CDRs complemented the work of the armed forces at Playa Girón (the beach

---

[5]Domínguez, *Cuba* pp. 299–302. Unless otherwise noted, data in this section and the following on the Communist Party are from this source.

[6]Most tobacco, one-quarter to one-half of various fruits and vegetables, and 18 percent of sugar cane were produced privately in 1975. Domínguez, *Cuba*, p. 452.

bordering the Bay of Pigs) and made possible the mass detention of suspected subversives. Since 1960, the membership of the CDRs has increased from less than 1 million to almost 5 million, and their functions have become more mundane. Denunciations now are more likely to focus on the parents of school truants or on apprehending common criminals. Effective mass public health campaigns, literacy and education drives, neighborhood improvement, and voluntary labor projects and political vigilance are all functions of the CDRs. In 1980, however, the CDRs sponsored meetings to denounce those neighbors leaving the country. Violence at times broke out; the meetings were controversial within the government as well as among government opponents.

Women are gaining importance in national politics. Although women still hold only a small percentage of elected offices, the Cuban revolution has explicitly recognized the equality and importance of women. A steadily increasing proportion of women are integrated into the paid work force (28 percent in 1975), but that is probably due to the general modernization of the economy and the society (a process taking place in capitalist as well as socialist societies). The Federation of Cuban Women (FMC) brings together women who work for pay and those who do not; its membership has gone from a scant 17,000 in 1961 to over 2 million in 1975—approximately 80 percent of the adult female population. In addition to education, training, and health care services, the FMC organizes volunteer labor in the sugar harvest and elsewhere. Perhaps most important for the working mothers, it operates approximately seven hundred day-care centers.

Like workers and peasants, both male and female, children also participate in mass organizations. Nearly 99 percent of Cuban schoolchildren belong to the Pioneers. Like the other mass organizations (and like the Boy Scouts elsewhere), the Pioneers help socialize the children to patriotism and loyalty. Educational functions and recrea-

tional incentives, such as organized vacations, also encourage participation. Similar organizations exist at the high school level. In addition, all young people spend three years of compulsory service in the army, in the Army of Working Youth (which engages more in civilian than in military work), or in other government-approved tasks.

Cuba is a highly integrated society by American standards. A country with a history of slavery, Cuba has a white majority with a large black and mulatto minority. As before, there are still few blacks at the highest levels of government. However, all services and institutions are open to blacks and whites alike. Black and white children play together on the beaches near Havana, and black couples honeymoon at the luxurious Havana Riviera Hotel, which had been beyond their reach in earlier days. Since blacks were more likely to be poor before the revolution, they have benefited more than most from redistributive policies of the regime.

Participation is difficult if not impossible for dissidents in Cuba's centralized and mobilized system, and economic upward mobility is limited for individuals. For those dissatisfied with life in Cuba for economic or political reasons, emigration remains a preferred option. For many years emigration was strictly controlled in Cuba, but following the opening that began in 1977, the leadership authorized exit visas for more people than other countries were willing to accept as immigrants. Prospective migrants became extremely frustrated, since those who declared their desire to leave were ostracized at work and in their neighborhoods, and may have lost their jobs.

Their frustration led to the dramatic invasions of the Peruvian and United States embassies, and the massive migration of more than 125,000 Cubans to the United States in 1980, via a flotilla of small ships and boats from Florida. (Those who went to Peru strongly expressed their preference for coming to the United States.) The operators of the boats were Cuban Americans seeking to bring back their relatives. The Cuban government offered them a roughly "two-for-one" deal, by which the boats were required to carry two government-designated migrants for each relative. In this way Cuba exported not only those who had invaded the Peruvian embassy but also a large number of other discontented Cubans, reportedly including some common criminals. Unlike the waves of migrants in the 1960s, the 1980 emigrants were not primarily professionals, technicians, and intellectuals; most were simply seeking a better life. Faced with economic problems, Cuba used the outlet of migration to avoid the potential political opposition posed by those discontented with the revolution.

The Communist Party of Cuba. Before the revolution, Cuba's Communist Party (PSP) was quite independent of the eventually more important 26th of July Movement. In the first years of the revolution, the old Communist Party united with the 26th of July Movement and the Revolutionary Directorate of university students into the Integrated Revolutionary Organization (ORI). Then the old Communist leader, Aníbal Escalante, was sent off in 1962 to Prague, Czechoslovakia, for "sectarianism" in what came to be called the first "Escalante affair." ORI evolved into the United Party of the Socialist Revolution (PURS) in 1963, and into the new Communist Party of Cuba (PCC) in 1965. In 1967, Escalante, having returned from Eastern Europe, tried again to influence the party and was arrested, tried, and imprisoned as the leader of a pro-Soviet "microfaction." After years in prison, he was released sometime before his death in the mid-1970s.

Though the party was weak through the 1960s, it has grown to become the leading political organization of the country. By about 1975 there were over 200,000 party members in Cuba (up from about 15,000 in 1962 and 100,000 in 1970). There are over one hundred members of the Central Committee; the direction of the party is in the hands of the small Secretariat and Political Bureau.

Politics in Cuba is highly centralized. The Communist Party is still both small and hierarchical. Authority in the mass organizations is centralized at the national level. Although few leaders of mass organizations at the local level are party members, the party can and does exercise authority over promotion criteria and leadership selection in the mass organizations. Although the party is young, having held its First Party Congress only in 1975, it is the most powerful ruling group in Cuba.

Images of Politics. Fidel Castro is the leader of the Cuban revolution; since the days in the Sierra Maestra, he has been the principal revolutionary actor and Cuba's premier public speaker. One of the most vivid political experiences for many Cubans is to gather in the Plaza of the Revolution with hundreds of thousands or even a million fellow citizens to hear a speech by their president—an experience that happens with considerable frequency. Fidel Castro is a charismatic leader. With his beard and green army fatigues, he himself symbolizes the revolution.

Anti-imperialism is a recurring theme in Cuban politics. The image of Cuba as a small but valiant David facing the giant Goliath ninety miles to the north is implicitly evoked in references to the relations between Cuba and the United States. The defeat of U.S.-supported forces at the Bay of Pigs validated this image. The external threat to the nation posed by "Yankee imperialism" provides a galvanizing external force that facilitates nationalist celebrations of Cuba's strength and autonomy. It also demands increased sacrifice. The Soviet Union, never having challenged the Cubans by force, is also more distant and therefore less threatening. Given Cuba's location, it is unlikely that the Soviet Union would be able to dominate Cuba against the wishes of its leaders. Therefore, imperialism rather than socialist dependence provides the politically more vivid image of a foreign threat.

The Cuban revolution is young by world standards. In the 1960s, the image of the new man and the new woman were held up to Cubans as images of the new society they were trying to build. Cuba was seen as being on the forefront of history, perhaps the first nation to cross the bridge from socialism to communism. That period of radical idealism, relying on the commitment of the people to moral rather than material incentives and on spontaneity and enthusiasm rather than on discipline and organization, ended with the failure of the year-long push to harvest 10 million tons of sugar in 1970. Although the harvest was large, it did not reach the goal, and the disruptions in the rest of the economy were massive. Since that year, the government has emphasized institutionalization of the revolution. Institutions like the party, popular assemblies, and the courts have been strengthened. There has been a return to material incentives in an effort to increase production and productivity. And yet, for many who remember participating in the revolution and defending the island against foreign attack, the Cuban revolution is still youthful. Many are still hopeful and willing to sacrifice in a way that citizens in more mature socialist countries are not.

Finally, Cuba aspires to a position of leadership in the Third World. In the 1960s, under the influence of *Che Guevara,* Cuba exported the revolution. In addition to ideological support, it provided arms and money to Communist parties and insurrectionist movements throughout Latin America. This support ended, however, with the death of Che and his small group of Cuban followers in the jungles of Bolivia in 1967, following upon their failure to win effective peasant support in that region and their defeat by a U.S.-aided antiguerrilla campaign. Cuba has also supported independence movements and struggles for national self-determination. Rather than Cuban volunteers acting as individuals, the Cuban state now gives official support and military assistance at the invitation of foreign governments. The Cubans consider this international solidarity to be "paying their debt to humanity." They are returning the fraternal support they received when they were vulnerable and under attack and are also gaining much political influence in the world thereby.

In the 1970s, Cuba turned to Africa. It is easier for the Cubans to be seen as leaders by elites in the poorer countries of Africa than in the relatively more developed countries of Latin America. For their part, some Cubans see themselves returning to help liberate the lands of their ancestors.

Cuba has sought international leadership, not only by military and economic aid to Angola, Ethiopia, and other African nations, but also, in 1979, as a leader of the *Nonaligned Movement.* Cuba hosted the sixth summit meeting of the Nonaligned Movement in Havana in September 1979. At that time, Castro tried to move the group toward a position hostile to the United States and more positive to the Soviet Union, but with little success. Most major nations in the movement preferred to continue the tradition set by Marshal Tito of Yugoslavia, as well as by India, of maintaining independence from both major powers. Although Cuba will hold the chair of the movement for three years after 1979, it is unlikely to have a major impact on the policies of the leading nonaligned countries.

For many people, Cuba's image is darkened by the lack of individual freedom, particularly for intellectuals. Cuba's most effective leadership is by example, a revolutionary regime with relatively high levels of social welfare and equity at home. It is these achievements in satisfying basic needs—by building on what had already been achieved before the revolution—rather than Cuba's alliance with the socialist bloc, that make Cuba an attractive model for some in the Third World.

The Political Arena. Since Cuba is an island, the territorial definition of its political arena is straightforward. Yet the recurring dependence on the great powers leaves several open questions about Cuba's sovereignty over Cuban territory. At the time of the Bay of Pigs invasion, Cuban exiles, with the support of the CIA, attempted to overthrow the Cuban government from the outside.[7] The United States has confirmed that CIA agents

[7]The exile force had been based in Guatemala and Nicaragua.

have made continued attempts on the life of Fidel Castro. Although these failed, the threat of direct foreign intervention has helped strengthen the nationalism and unity of Cuba.

A large community of Cubans live in the United States, which further extends the arena of politics. From 1960 to 1974, nearly 600,000 Cubans left the island. Nearly one-third left in the first three years; most of these were property owners, government officials, or professionals who came to the United States.[8] For years some Cuban expatriates acted as a threat to the survival of the Cuban revolution. In addition to invasion attempts, bombings, and other acts of terrorism, some Cuban Americans lobbied against normalizing relations. However, by 1979 many Cubans in the United States were no longer seeking to overthrow the Cuban government; the latter then changed its policy on the Cuban community abroad, making it possible for large numbers of expatriates to visit their relatives in Cuba for the first time since their departure. Approximately 100,000 Cubans returned to visit the island in 1979. The maneuver of bringing Cubans in the United States into the political arena has been partially successful: in June 1979, a committee of Cuban Americans presented ten thousand signatures to the U.S. government requesting normalized relations with Cuba.[9]

The most blatant illustration of the divided political arena is the *U.S. naval base at Guantánamo.* Claimed by the government of Cuba and retained by the United States as a perpetuation of early treaty rights, the base reminds Cubans that they do not control all the territory of the island. The mock landing of marines on the beaches of Guantánamo as a show of U.S. force in October 1979, after the announcement that Soviet combat troops

were in Cuba, was an angry demonstration of U.S. ability to intervene militarily in Cuba if necessary to confront the Soviet Union—an ability that was never in doubt.

Besides the base at Guantánamo, questions of sovereignty have arisen with regard to Cuba's airspace. This has been an area of conflict at times when the United States has conducted surveillance overflights of the island, a practice that President Carter suspended in 1977 but renewed in the fall of 1979. The Soviet Union uses Cuba as a communications intelligence base for its own purposes, but with the permission of the Cubans.

In the summer and fall of 1979, there was a conflict when the United States announced the presence in Cuba of a Soviet military unit of about three thousand soldiers. Both the U.S.S.R. and Cuba said the troops had been there for many years and the United States later admitted that the troops had probably been in Cuba "at least" since 1975. In fact, ground troops were not excluded from Cuba by the U.S.-Soviet understandings dating from the missile crisis.

Not all issues involving the political arena have resulted in conflict between the United States and Cuba. Both the treatment of hijackers who fly to Cuba and the definition of maritime boundaries and fishing rights in territorial waters shared by Cuba and the United States have been negotiated amicably.

The Cuban Political System. The political system of Cuba is composed of three parallel structures: the Cuban Communist Party; the apparatus of the state, including all the ministries and functional divisions within the state; and the structures of "popular power" *(poder popular),* that is, the elected organs authorized in the 1976 constitution. The party provides the leadership and the direction necessary for managing politics and the economy. Its top organ is the Political Bureau and its leader and Secretary-General is Fidel Castro. It is the transmission belt for decisions made at the top; it

[8]Domínguez, *Cuba,* p. 140.

[9]The Cuban community in the United States has become deeply divided. Many Cubans continue to visit their homeland from the United States. However, extremists who oppose any contact with Cuba while Fidel Castro is in power have killed, or attempted to kill, some of the exile leaders who favor these new contacts.

provides the cadres (party activists) with the correct interpretation of current government policy. The ministries and special committees are set up along functional lines to carry out the day-to-day business of the government. The Council of Ministers brings together, under the direction of its president, Fidel Castro, all the heads of the various ministries: foreign affairs, foreign trade, public health, education, sugar industry, and so on. The Council of State, on the other hand, is an organ of the National Assembly, which carries out the legislative functions of the assembly during the greater part of the year when the assembly is not in session. As its president, Castro is also head of state.

What is most striking about the Political Bureau of the party, the Council of Ministers, and the Council of State is that many of the members overlap, holding positions in several or all. Three individuals stand out from the rest: Fidel Castro, his brother Raúl Castro, and Carlos Rafael Rodríguez. Fifteen other leaders make up a small group—an interlocking directorate—occupying the major posts in the Cuban political system. These eighteen people hold several important decision-making positions and constitute the highest political elite of the country. Most of these leaders, like Fidel and Raúl Castro, were active fighters with the rebel army in the 1950s. Direct participation in the revolution is still a major legitimating factor for the political elite.

The Communist Party is an effective mechanism for steering government in the desired political direction. Although the voters and the agencies supposedly have autonomy at the local level, it is nonetheless the party that indicates the direction for policy and action.

Although the political steering mechanism operating through the party is strong, the mechanisms for feedback from the people are relatively weak. Some feedback is obtained from the suggestions put forward in the mass organizations. Unlike more open systems, newspapers and other mass media are a relatively poor source of feedback to the government since they are tightly controlled. Although specific complaints about poor goods

and services are aired in the press, nothing critical of the regime's major policies can be included on television, on the radio, or in books and pamphlets with mass circulation.

The principal unsolved problem of the political system is succession. Rule by Fidel and Raúl Castro (Fidel's formally designated successor) has provided continuity over time, but there is neither experience nor a proven mechanism for converting to a new leadership should something happen to the top two leaders. By now, however, Cuba seems sufficiently consolidated to cope with any such successor problem. Under a successor, some of Castro's policies might change, but the basic character of the regime seems likely to endure. In the meantime, the great concentration of power in the hands of one man and the small group surrounding him means that decisions can be made easily within that group. Controversies can be resolved by the president and changes in direction can be made relatively rapidly. However, much of the learning that takes place in the system occurs inside the head of Fidel Castro. The consultative mechanisms of the mass organizations and research undertaken by government organs provide some input from the people as to their likes and dislikes. But the strictly controlled press and the limitation on political expression mean that the political leaders are unlikely to hear significantly divergent views.

The State Machinery. For the first decade after the Cuban revolution, there was almost no separation of functions in the state. Executive discretion was almost unlimited, and though much was made of frequent conversations and discussions by Castro with broad groups of the population, the government was in fact run by a handful of men. The same executive group legislated new laws and took responsibility for their implementation. Justice was dispensed through a varied and changing court system, which for a time gave prominence to the so-called popular tribunals made up of lay rather than professional judges. The country functioned practically without a constitution and the number of law students in the universities dropped to almost nothing.

By 1970, after the failure of the drive for a 10-million-ton sugar harvest, a period of institutionalization that continued through the seventies began to formalize and differentiate the powers of government. The Communist Party, with closer links to the enlarged mass organizations, became a vital and functioning socialist party organization, responsible for the formulation and general direction of policy. Under the *constitution of 1976,* and following two years of experiments in the province of Matanzas, popular assemblies were organized and elected at the municipal, provincial, and national levels. No opposition parties were allowed to operate in these elections; and only municipal assembly delegates were elected directly by the people. These assemblies and the Council of State, operating at the national level during the recess of the National Assembly, discuss and legislate laws and regulations. These laws are always based on the general direction set by the party, but include the suggestions and proposals of party working committees, of the Council of Ministers, the Council of State, and of various other organizations with the capacity to propose new legislation.

As part of institutionalization, law once again became an important area to study. Lawyers are trained to work as prosecutors in the renovated court system, to work as defense counsel in collective law offices around the country, and to work as legal counsel in the expanding offices of state enterprise. The law school of the University of Havana now trains some five hundred lawyers per year. Regular channels for the protest of abuses or the discussion of specific problems have been established, so that appeals to Castro or letters to the editor of national journals, though they persist, are less necessary than they once were. As the socialist regime in Cuba has become more stable and institutionalization proceeds, the political machinery becomes more differentiated and a separation of powers, though still modest, has begun to emerge.

Still, faced with economic and political problems, many government officials—including a third of the Council of Ministers—were dismissed in 1980. The attorney general and the ministers of Interior and of Justice were dismissed in part because they were judged to have fought crime insufficiently. The role of lay judges has been reduced. Institutionalization has not necessarily implied decentralization. This may portend some modification in the 1980s of the trends of the 1970s.

Performance of the Political System. The Cuban revolution has done well for most of the people that supported it. Especially for the poorest members of the society, the redistributive measures and the socialization of the economy have resulted in dramatic increases in living standards. Although overall income (per capita GNP) was relatively low, about $800 in 1975, most people had the necessities of life. Literacy was almost universal, probably the highest of any country in Latin America. Other indicators shown in Table 9.1 likewise ranked Cuba as an advanced transitional society. Also impressive is the improvement in such indicators as infant mortality, which was at twenty-seven per thousand in 1975 and has continued to drop, thus approaching the levels of health found in advanced industrial societies. Indeed, the free provision of education and health care and the subsidized provision of other services have meant that the mass of the Cuban population live much more comfortably than do citizens of other countries with a similar per capita GNP.

Still, the mobilized and equitable socialist system has not increased the overall levels of production. Growth has been negligible for many years, resulting in stagnating welfare increases. Housing shortages are pronounced. Public transportation performs poorly, and the limited number of new private cars is reserved for elites. Improvements have tended to go to more qualified and skilled technical sectors of the population and to members of the bureaucracy. But as socialism has leveled the society, this equality has left some intellectuals and bureaucrats dissatisfied. Their services are needed, especially given the massive emigration of professionals after the revolution, so distribution of goods and services through bureaucratic channels, particularly through the work place, has been unequal. This same system has meant that more subtle pressures for conformity can now be brought into play. Whereas once dissidents might be detained or imprisoned, there are now economic disincentives to dissidence.

The performing arts, such as dance, theater, and cinema, have flowered in Cuba. More than in most developing countries, the graphic arts have also been highly developed. Yet the intellectual freedom of artists, writers, teachers, and university professors is constrained in Cuba. "Subversive" art is not tolerated. Nevertheless, Cuba seems to be more open in this respect than many other socialist countries.

In the international sphere, Cuba is looking for a position as leader of the Third World, while maintaining its allegiance to the Soviet Union. There is also a strong interest in resuming economic relations with the United States, to take advantage of natural trading economies offered by geography and to gain access to U.S. technology. Both the United States and Cuba are interested in eventually returning to normal diplomatic relations. Steps in this direction were taken in the mid-1970s, leading to the establishment of diplomatic interest sections (in the Czech embassy in Washington and in the Swiss embassy in Havana), but further moves have been chilled by the United States because of the presence of Cuban troops in Africa, the 1979 flap over Soviet troops in Cuba, and the 1980 conflict over emigration.

In the long run, improved ties and normalized relations are likely. Cuba already has diplomatic relations with 117 countries, and consular relations with 2 others. The United States, for its part, has found the way to normal relations with China, the Soviet Union, and other socialist countries. More than four hundred U.S. firms have held talks with the Cubans in Havana, and many of them conduct business through their overseas subsidiaries. Educational, cultural, and artistic ties have increased. Ironically, however, these moves have partially eased the pressures for rapid normalization of diplomatic relations.

A number of outstanding problems remain to be solved. The Cuban-American community remains divided on the advisability of renewed relations with Cuba under Castro, and an active minority is violently opposed. Many in the United States are concerned about remaining political prisoners in Cuba, although most were released in 1979. The compensation for property of U.S. firms expropriated after the revolution remains a more difficult problem, but one that the two governments could solve with good faith. Most intractable are the problems in the international sphere. Cuba refuses to tie its foreign policy in Africa or elsewhere to U.S. wishes, and the United States has been unwilling to negotiate its naval base in Guantánamo or to drop the embargo. These circumstances mean that although there will be increasing visits by Cuban Americans, by scholars and students, and by other American tourists to Cuba, and increased trade with the overseas subsidiaries of U.S. companies, the full normalization of diplomatic relations between the United States and Cuba, though likely in the long run, was, at the beginning of the 1980s, still a distant goal.

MEXICO: CONTRASTS OF WEALTH AND POVERTY ON THE U.S. BORDER

"Mexico is the country of inequality," said the German traveler and scientist Alexander von Humboldt in the eighteenth century. From the time before Columbus when the *México* (or *Azteca*) people dominated the Indians of the central valley; to the Spanish colonial period when fabulous silver wealth made white men rich while Indians starved; to the rule of the dictator Porfirio

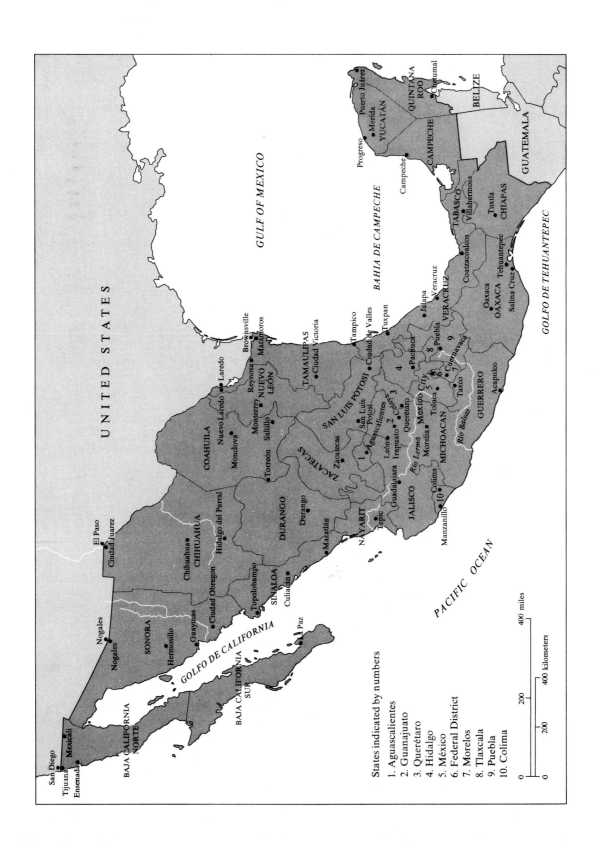

UNITED STATES

GULF OF MEXICO

BAHIA DE CAMPECHE

GOLFO DE TEHUANTEPEC

PACIFIC OCEAN

GOLFO DE CALIFORNIA

San Diego
Tijuana
Ensenada
Mexicali

BAJA CALIFORNIA NORTE

Nogales
Nogales

SONORA
Hermosillo
Guaymas

El Paso
Ciudad Juarez

Chihuahua
CHIHUAHUA
Ciudad Obregon
Hidalgo del Parral
Topolobampo
SINALOA
Culiacán
Mazatlán

BAJA CALIFORNIA SUR
La Paz

DURANGO
Durango

COAHUILA
Monclova
Torreón
Saltillo
Monterrey
NUEVO LEÓN

Nuevo Laredo
Laredo

Reynosa
Matamoros
Brownsville

TAMAULIPAS
Ciudad Victoria

ZACATECAS
Zacatecas

SAN LUIS POTOSÍ
San Luis Potosí
Ciudad de Valles
Tampico
Tuxpan

NAYARIT
Tepic

JALISCO
Guadalajara

1
Aguascalientes
2
León
Irapuato
3
Querétaro
Río Lerma
Colima
COLIMA
Manzanillo
10

Pachuca
4
Río Balsas
Morelia
MICHOACÁN
Toluca
Mexico City
5
6
Cuernavaca
7
Taxco
GUERRERO
Acapulco

8
9
Puebla
Cuautla

Jalapa
Veracruz
VERACRUZ
Oaxaca
OAXACA

Coatzacoalcos
Tehuantepec
Salina Cruz

TABASCO
Villahermosa
Tuxtla
CHIAPAS

Campeche
CAMPECHE
Progreso
Mérida
YUCATÁN
QUINTANA ROO
Puerto Juarez
Chetumal
BELIZE
GUATEMALA

States indicated by numbers
1. Aguascalientes
2. Guanajuato
3. Querétaro
4. Hidalgo
5. México
6. Federal District
7. Morelos
8. Tlaxcala
9. Puebla
10. Colima

400 miles

400 kilometers

0   200

0   200

Díaz at the end of the nineteenth century; to the oil-rich days of the present; the distribution of wealth and income in Mexico has been one of the most unequal in the world.[10] Nor is the contrast of wealth and poverty confined within the national boundaries. The northern border of Mexico, stretching from Tijuana and San Diego on the Pacific Ocean through Matamoros and Brownsville near the Caribbean, separates a proud and struggling Mexican people from one of the wealthiest and most powerful nations on earth—the United States.

A Tradition of Three Cultures. Mexico is heir to an Indian empire and Spanish colony fused in a *mestizo* nation. (Mestizos are people of mixed Indian and Spanish blood.)

Before the conquest of New Spain, Mexico was one of the two great centers of Indian civilization in the New World. (Peru, with its Inca masters, was the other.) In the fifteenth century, the Aztec people had consolidated its rule over various subjects, from west of the capital Tenochtitlán, where Mexico City now stands, east to the Caribbean coast at Veracruz. All the nations paid tribute to their masters, who used a common language, *Nahuatl,* to communicate with the dominated peoples.

When Hernán Cortés landed near Veracruz in 1519, the technology of his army (including horses, crossbows, and artillery), his lust for gold, and the dissatisfaction of the subject peoples enabled him to conquer the Méxica tribe in only two years. The linguistic skills of Malinche, the Indian mistress of Cortés, aided greatly in the conquest,

giving rise to the derogatory term *malinchista,* referring to those Mexicans who prefer things foreign.

The Spaniards imposed their language, their religion, and their economic interests on the Indians. Hispanic culture, colonialism, and Catholicism were all new to the Indians and disastrous for their old civilization. Scholars have suggested that in the first century or so after the conquest (from 1519 to 1650), at least six-sevenths of the Indian population of Central America was decimated by new diseases and other hardships brought by their new masters.[11] Those who survived were ruled by administrators appointed by the Spanish Crown, but their daily contact was more likely to be with the priests and friars who baptized literally millions of Indians, bringing them elements of the Catholic faith and of Spanish culture.

With their former shrines and temples everywhere destroyed and replaced by Spanish churches, the Indians adopted the saints and symbols of the new religion as their own, often creating unique forms of folk Catholicism that mixed old beliefs with the new forms of religious expression. The Spanish language, however, was only partially adopted. Indeed, although the friars were charged by the Crown with both converting Indians and teaching them Hispanic language and culture, they often converted the Indians either in Nahuatl or in their native tongues.

Indians became Catholics of sorts and learned

[10]See column 18 of Table 9.1. The 0.58 Gini index of inequality given there shows Mexico as the most unequal of the countries considered.

[11]Eric Wolf, *Sons of the Shaking Earth: The People of Mexico and Guatemala—Their Land, History and Culture* (Chicago: The University of Chicago Press, 1959), p. 195. Other scholars give more drastic estimates: "Within less than a century the population of central Mexico shrank from approximately twenty-five million to under two million; the tropical coasts became the disease-ridden wastes that they have remained until recent decades" (Woodrow Borah and Sherburne F. Cook, "Why Population Estimates are Important in the Interpretation of Mexican History," in *Latin America: A Historical Reader,* ed. Lewis Hanke [Boston: Little, Brown, 1974], p. 119).

(Left) MAP 11.2 *Mexico*

enough Spanish to labor on the extensive land-holdings *(haciendas)* of the Spanish elite or in the gold and silver mines, which provided Spain with the greatest wealth to come out of the New World. Not only did the Indians in Mexico have to give their labor under conditions of peonage (near servitude), but they also paid an individual tribute (tax) for being Indians. By the end of the eighteenth century fully two-thirds of Spain's revenues came from Mexico.[12] But formal colonialism was not to last.

A Stormy Independence: Defining the Nation-State Arena. The first revolts for independence from Spain, led by the parish priests Miguel Hidalgo and José María Morelos, were violently repressed and ended in failure. But as Spain lost power in Europe and turned liberal, more conservative *creoles*[13] in Mexico established an independent Mexican monarchy on September 16, 1821. Two years later a republic was declared. Slavery was abolished, though it had never been very important in Mexico. The conditions of the Indians were scarcely improved; they lived on under their village chiefs, known to the Indians as *caciques,* and increasingly under the control of the landowners. The creoles fought among themselves for political control of the country, and U.S. and British investors replaced the Spanish as bankers and mine owners. Local landowners and former army officers, now also called *caciques* (bosses), built up local bases of power. But at the national level there was no unity. Two issues divided the country: whether there would be a strong central government or decentralized regional rule (federalism), and whether or not the new state would control the church.

During the generations of uncertainty that followed independence, the arena of politics in Mexico changed dramatically. Settlers from the United States moved to Texas, and although the Mexican Generalísimo Antonio López de Santa Anna fought several battles to keep Texas, badly defeating the U.S. settlers at the Alamo in 1836, the territory eventually separated from Mexico and became an independent republic. In 1845, Texas was admitted to the Union by the United States. Mexico went to war, again under the leadership of Santa Anna. But the U.S. army that invaded through Veracruz eventually took Mexico City, despite the resistance of the Mexican "boy heroes," young cadets still honored today for dying rather than surrendering to the foreign army. These events have left very different images of heroes and villains in the collective memories of the two countries. Youngsters in the United States learn to "Remember the Alamo!" whereas Mexicans honor the boy soldiers who died opposing the invading army.

In the conqueror's settlement in 1848, Mexico lost what is today California, Arizona, and New Mexico, amounting, with Texas, to half its prewar territory. The United States expanded to the Pacific, increasing its own size by two-thirds.[14] The new border ran through an unpopulated wasteland to meet the Rio Grande, which flowed down past Texas to the Gulf of Mexico.

By the 1850s, the outer boundaries of Mexico had largely been fixed, but sovereignty had not yet been attained, either domestically or internationally. Since independence, various Indian groups had revolted, seeking autonomy and a return to the traditional patterns of their village life. These included both the Yaqui tribe in what is now northern Mexico and the independent Maya on the Yucatán Peninsula. It had taken the Spanish a generation to conquer the Maya in the sixteenth century. In 1847, the Maya revolted again in the so-called Caste War of the Yucatán. Although such

---

[12]John Lynch, *The Spanish-American Revolutions, 1808–1826* (New York: W. W. Norton, 1973), p. 303.
[13]Creoles were Spaniards born in the New World, in contrast to the mestizos, who were of mixed Spanish and Indian heritage.

[14]Robert H. Ferrell, *American Diplomacy* (New York: W. W. Norton, 1959), p. 106.

revolts were contained, this regional and local diversity still exists in the loyalty of many Mexicans to their region and section: their *patria chica,* or "little homeland." In a country of few recent immigrants from other lands, these ties resemble the ties immigrant groups elsewhere may feel to the habits and traditions of the "the old country."

International status as a sovereign state was slow in coming. Besides the war and territorial losses to the United States, Mexico also had to contend with attempts at domination by the French. The French had briefly occupied Veracruz in 1838 in the so-called Pastry War, touched off by a French baker's claim for damages suffered in a previous civil disturbance. In 1861, while the United States was involved in its own Civil War, Spain, France, and Great Britain jointly landed troops in Veracruz, partly in an effort to enforce debt collection on the shaky government led by President Benito Juárez, a Zapotec Indian from Oaxaca. The French, without the British or Spanish, decided to march on Mexico City, which they occupied in 1863. Under the tutelage of Napoleon III and with the support of the pope, Mexico was ruled as an empire by foreign monarchs, Maximilian of Hapsburg (Austria) and his wife Carlota, until 1867. With the Civil War in the United States over and with war threatening France in Europe, Napoleon was unwilling to invade Mexico again. Juárez was able to depose and execute Maximilian; Carlota was exiled and later went mad. There was no popular support in Mexico for the foreigners.

The defeat of this empire by Juárez and the republican general Porfirio Díaz helped pull the nation together. Reforms limiting the economic power of the Church and instituting the federalist republic first outlined in the liberal constitution of 1857 were finally implemented. Yet the country had lost half its territory and had become impoverished by the nearly constant wars since 1810.

Economic Modernization and Authoritarian Rule: The Porfiriato.

Five years after Juárez died in 1872, Porfirio Díaz came to power by force of arms, though with considerable popular support. He remained as president from 1877 (except for one term, 1880–84) until the Mexican revolution deposed him in 1911. His presidency is called the *Porfiriato.* As Europe increasingly embraced free trade, Mexico under Díaz entered a period of economic modernization. With the help of British banks and British and U.S. investment companies, and with the ideological underpinnings of positivism, extensive railroad lines were built and gold, silver, copper, and lead mining expanded. Especially in the northern city of Monterrey, the manufacture of steel, textiles, beer, and other products proceeded apace. Roads were built, telephones introduced, and ports expanded. Foreign trade doubled and doubled again. After the turn of the century, oil became an increasingly rich line of production.

The price of this growth was repression. With the help of the rural police *(rurales),* Díaz controlled with force the unrest that accompanied the intrusion of modernizing capitalism into the traditional countryside. The liberal reforms that broke up large Church landholdings were also used to force the sale of community property *(ejidos)* in the villages. Through these reforms and by concessions to private interests and speculators, the formerly public lands concentrated in the hands of large private landholders during the *Porfiriato* amounted to over one-quarter of the total area of the republic. Over three-quarters of the population lived in the countryside, and over half of these residents were tied to the large haciendas. Concentration of land and wealth was great.

The Mexican Revolution.

The Mexican revolution, which began in 1910, ranks with the later Russian and Chinese revolutions as one of the major political upheavals of this century. It was costly and bloody. Haciendas and railroads were captured, recaptured, and often burned; many peasant soldiers lost their lives in the battles and skirmishes. The first rebel, Francisco I. Madero, took as his slogan in 1910: *"Effective Suffrage, No Re-Election."* This motto is still a key to understanding the Mexican political system and has increasingly become an ideal for other governments in Latin America.

Díaz fell, and Madero became president during 1911–12. The peasant leader Emiliano Zapata challenged Madero, demanding the restoration of the village *ejido* lands to the peasants. After a military coup by General Victoriano Huerta in 1913 led to Madero's assassination, the military failed to repress a constitutionalist revolt led by Venustiano Carranza in 1914. Then Carranza and one of his generals, Álvaro Obregón, joined forces against Zapata in the south and Pancho Villa in the north in 1915–16. Sufficient order was established to write the constitution of 1917, which laid the bases for extensive land reform, for the protection and encouragement (and control) of the labor movement, and for some limitation of foreign ownership of land, water, and minerals.

The revolution had its share of international as well as domestic conflict. By the time the United States entered World War I, President Wilson had twice authorized the invasion of Mexican territory. U.S. troops occupied Veracruz in 1914 in response to a supposed affront to the dignity of the United States, and troops under Pershing advanced into northern Mexico in retaliation for Pancho Villa's border raids.

Madero, Zapata, and Carranza had all been killed by 1920, but the foundations for stability had been laid. During the 1920s, under the official or unofficial guidance of Plutarco Elías Calles, Mexico was able to lessen the factionalism of the military leaders of the revolution, survive a three-year rebellion of reaction inspired by the Roman Catholic Church (the *Cristero* revolt), and begin to incorporate workers and peasants into national political participation through the foundation in 1929 of the National Revolutionary Party, the forerunner of the dominant party of today.

The consolidation of the revolution was completed by the powerful and popular president Lázaro Cárdenas, who held office from 1934 to 1940. Under his leadership, the Mexican system took on the institutional form it has maintained, with some modifications, since those years.

Cárdenas is still remembered as the greatest of Mexico's presidents since the revolution. As the worldwide depression resulted in economic hardship and unemployment in Mexico, Cárdenas responded in a way that won him the affection of the people and the approval of many historians. He confronted the manipulations of Calles and established the precedent of an independent president whose great power is limited by relinquishing the position to a successor after six years. The principle of "no re-election" was instituionalized in fact as well as in form. The extensive distribution of land to the peasantry, applying the promises of the 1917 constitution, incorporated the rural dwellers *(campesinos)* into national political life and helped establish the legitimacy of the regime. Though land on the *ejidos* formally belongs to the nation and is held in trust by the entire *ejido* community, most of the peasants prefer to work on individual parcels. The efforts begun by Lázaro Cárdenas to collectivize the operation as well as the ownership of the *ejidos* never succeeded.

The commitment of Cárdenas to the Mexican system is revealed by the fact that he kept the rural peasants organized in the National Peasant Confederation (CNC), and separate from the urban workers, who had joined together in the Federation of Mexican Labor (CTM), headed by the leftist Vicente Lombardo Toledano. Thus neither became an autonomous political force. Rather, each became one of the mainstays of the national party, the Party of the Mexican Revolution, as it was renamed in 1938. This party was in turn re-formed and renamed the *Institutional Revolutionary party (PRI)* in 1946.

The Oil Expropriation. Lázaro Cárdenas is best remembered for his nationalization of the oil industry. Though raw materials have now been reclaimed from foreign companies by many governments around the world, in 1938 such a step was highly unusual. However, Article 27 of the Mexican constitution of 1917 had laid the groundwork by establishing that natural resources belong to the nation. In the early 1920s, when Mexico was the world's third largest producer of petroleum, the United States and Mexico had clashed over oil. U.S. oil interests influencing the administration of Warren G. Harding (later implicated in the Teapot Dome scandal) were able to prevent for three years the U.S. recognition of the government of Álvaro Obregón (president of Mexico from 1920 to 1924). Obregón finally agreed in writing that Article 27 of the constitution would not be applied retroactively to oil companies that had drilled their wells before 1917. The United States then recognized the government of Mexico in 1923.

Nevertheless, two years later U.S. Secretary of State Frank B. Kellogg put Mexico "on trial before the world" for not giving sufficient protection to U.S. nationals. President Calles finally reached agreement in 1927 when Calvin Coolidge sent Dwight Morrow to Mexico as the new ambassador. Calles extended the concessions of the oil companies beyond the earlier fifty-year limit, and the United States recognized the sovereignty and jurisdiction of the Mexican government to resolve any future disputes with American companies.

This precedent was important when a new conflict arose in the 1930s. A labor conflict resulted in a wage settlement imposed on the oil companies by an arbitration board and upheld on appeal by the Mexican Supreme Court. When the companies ignored the court order and thus challenged the sovereignty of Mexican law, Cárdenas nationalized the foreign oil companies. Britain broke off diplomatic relations, but with the earlier U.S. recognition of Mexico's sovereignty, with President Franklin D. Roosevelt's noninterventionist "good neighbor policy," and with the threat of Hitler in Europe urging hemispheric unity, the United States agreed to accept the nationalization if a compensation agreement could be negotiated.

Sinclair Oil settled with Cárdenas in 1940 for $8.5 million. The joint U.S.-Mexico settlement commission finally reached agreement in November 1941 (after Cárdenas had left office). The other U.S. companies received $24 million (plus 3 percent interest from 1938). The last payment was made on schedule in 1947; no longer did anyone contest that the oil belonged to Mexico.[15]

The Stakes of Politics in Mexico. In modern Mexico, the stakes of politics are less likely than in the past to be a matter of life or death, but the stakes are still high. The sovereignty and independence of the country have been assured, and most of the residents of the country feel themselves part of the nation and proud of their revolutionary heritage, though that pride is often tempered by a skepticism about results and a cynicism about the meaning of the revolution today. The political system, legitimized by the revolution and resting on a strong president, has proved remarkably stable, especially when compared to other developing countries.

The true issue in Mexico is development: the political problem of providing the conditions for economic growth while making the benefits from that growth available to all the people rather than to just the elite and the middle class. The population, which reached 70 million in 1980, has been growing since 1960 at an average of 3.5 percent per year, one of the highest rates of population growth in the world (even though that rate is finally beginning to slow). High population growth of 3 percent or more means that the entire economy—all goods and services, including food production, transportation, schools, health facilities, housing construction—must grow at least by 3 percent per year just to maintain a constant level of development. Any improvements require either much higher growth rates or policies distributing the goods and services in a more equitable way. The rapid growth of the population in recent

[15]The British companies did not reach any agreement until 1947, when they settled for $130 million. See Lorenzo Meyer, *Mexico and the United States in the Oil Controversy (1917–1942)*, trans. M. Vasconcellos (Austin: University of Texas Press, 1977). See also Howard F. Cline, *The United States and Mexico* (Cambridge: Harvard University Press, 1967), pp. 248–49.

years has made a *"population pyramid"* that is very wide at the base: there are many more young people than middle-aged or older people. Thus, with about half the population under fifteen years of age, there is a special strain in two crucial areas: education and jobs. These challenges must be met for the stable civilian rule, which has so distinguished Mexico, to survive.

The Participants in Politics. Not everyone participates equally in politics in Mexico. Mexico is ruled by a political and economic elite. The middle classes receive some benefits and have varying degrees of access to this elite. The same is true, though to a lesser extent, for organized workers and peasants. There is a large group of rural workers and urban poor who are not organized, have no access to the elite, and receive few if any benefits.

The political elite in Mexico has been called the "revolutionary family" or the "revolutionary coalition." Originally composed of those who actually participated in the revolution, it now includes those who occupy the political offices, such as the president, the president's cabinet, and staff; directors of state-owned industries and banks; state governors; officials of the major party (PRI); and ambassadors, senators, and deputies. These people are likely to have a similar upper- or middle-class background and to have received their education at the national university, often in law or another professional specialization. The economic elite is made up of the owners and executives of large firms in banking, insurance, manufacturing, and agriculture. More likely to have been trained in expensive private schools and universities than members of the political elite, these individuals are able to influence politics through the organizations that represent their industries and that have officially sanctioned consultative status with the government. They also influence politics through intermediary groups such as lawyers or ex-politicians and directly through personal contact with the political elite at political and social functions.

Members of the middle class, who may be small business owners or administrative workers in business or government, have little influence on decisions, but can often obtain a job, gain a benefit, or cut through red tape thanks to a friend or relative (or the friend of a friend, or the relative of a relative) who is in a position to help them out. The middle classes, like the elite, can often afford to pay bribes (the *mordida,* or "bite") when necessary or convenient.

Workers or peasants may occasionally have access to that kind of influence, but they are more likely to have to rely on their representative organizations, the leaders of which can influence political decisions and distribute benefits. A majority of unionized workers still belong to the government-controlled CTM, although independent unionism has increased recently as workers attempt to achieve better representation. Similarly, many peasants are still organized within the CNC. Together with a "popular" confederation of owners of small businesses and white-collar workers, the CTM and the CNC form the base of support for the official party, and the basis for government control of workers and peasants.

The landless, unorganized rural workers and the recent migrants to the city who are unemployed or have only occasional work have almost no chance of influencing politics. They may benefit from one government program or another, from time to time, or they rarely may organize for a brief time with their neighbors to request the provision of a supply of water or the closing of a open sewer. These unemployed and underemployed workers and peasants constitute at least a third of the population. Monolingual Indians, now only about 2 percent of the population, also figure among the politically weak.

Images of Mexico. The Mexican revolution is still a powerful symbol of the nation. As with other nations that have undergone such a societal upheaval, the revolution at once represents the high ideals that men and women died for, and the fearful specter of a conflict that pitted citizen against citizen. Today, as the last living participants in the war become octogenarians, the rhetoric of Mexico as a revolutionary nation is more vivid than the reality. Land reform, the great aspiration of the revolution, has come to a halt in the absence of new expropriations of the illegally large landholdings, the *neolatifundia*. The official labor organizations are more efficient at enforcing wage guidelines than at obtaining new benefits for the workers. The oil expropriation, with its base in the constitution, is still remembered on the national Day of Economic Independence. But the benefits of oil wealth are yet to reach the people.

Despite these realities that tarnish the image of the revolution, Mexicans remain committed to the nation. Though few Mexicans expect results from the political system, they remain loyal to the symbols of the nation—especially against any challenge from the outside.[16] In dealing with the United States, the Mexican president expects Mexico to be treated with all the respect due any important nation, and in this he has the full support of his people. Now that Mexico has petroleum in exportable quantities again, the United States is beginning to pay more attention to Mexico. Unfortunately, this misses the point: Mexico wants to be treated as an equal for itself, not for its oil.

The image of Mexico at home may be that of a society with a revolutionary heritage and, bilaterally, one of equality, but regarding other developing countries Mexico's self-image is one of leadership. President Luis Echeverría Álvarez (1970–76) was a spokesman for the New International Economic Order and sponsored the Charter of Economic Rights and Duties of States before the United Nations. President José López Portillo similarly hoped to establish Mexican leadership in the energy field when he visited the United

Nations in 1979 to propose a world energy order under U.N. auspices. Recently Mexico has also become more active in Central America and the Caribbean.

The Arena with a Permeable Border. Mexico's territory is probably safe today from direct foreign threats. Furthermore, Mexico practices what it preaches: a staunch defender of nonaggression and nonintervention, Mexico has no designs or claims on the territory of other nations.

The long border between Mexico and the United States means that the line between Mexican and U.S. political arenas is sometimes blurred. Many of the twin border cities have grown up together, moving from village to town to city with an international border between the two parts. These twin cities share commerce and industry (merchants accept both dollars and pesos); they also share common problems such as crime control, waste disposal, and pollution.

The United States has become more willing to negotiate on some issues. Mexico claimed an area that had been relocated in the United States by a shift of the Rio Grande River. Called "El Chamizal," it was returned by the United States in the 1960s after a half century of dispute. Further agreements were signed to prevent such disputes in the future. And in 1973 the United States agreed to Mexico's demand that it decrease the saline content of Colorado River water that runs from the United States into Mexico.

With such a long and busy frontier, the movement of people is difficult if not impossible to control. Unemployment, and especially underemployment, are high in Mexico, and U.S. employers are eager to get low-paid, hard-working, and nonunionized workers. Thus there is a steady flow of illegal migrants (also called "undocumented workers") from Mexico to the United States. The same conditions have encouraged the establishment of border industries—U.S.-owned plants on the Mexican side of the border to assemble textiles or electronic equipment. These plants employ

[16]This contrast is revealed in interviews conducted in the 1960s by Gabriel A. Almond and Sidney Verba, *The Civic Culture* (Boston: Little, Brown, 1965), p. 203, as well as in more recent surveys.

unskilled Mexican workers, usually young women, who work for less than one-quarter the minimum wage in the United States. More than four hundred firms have set up shop as part of the Border Industrialization Program, in which the Mexican government suspends restrictions on foreign ownership and on exports and imports that apply to foreign firms located elsewhere in Mexico. The six major border towns have grown from a combined population of less than one-half million in 1950 to over 2.5 million in 1979. Trade, investment, migration, border towns—all these make the U.S.-Mexican border a unique and difficult region. In that zone, the United States and Mexico have a small part of their political arenas in common.

The Process of Politics. Mexico has a presidential system, and the country's major political event is the election of the president every six years. Because one party dominates the system, however, this election does not have the same significance as presidential elections in countries with truly competitive parties. The candidate of the official party, the PRI, has always won, ever since the party was founded; in 1976, José López Portillo obtained 94.4 percent of the vote. Significant also in this situation is the level of participation. In the 1976 presidential election, 69 percent of eligible voters actually went to the polls; in the congressional elections of 1979, where turnout is usually lower, that proportion fell below the 50 percent mark. For about fifty years, the PRI candidate for president has been selected from among cabinet ministers; usually the candidate is a man who has served as a state governor or senator prior to joining the cabinet. Although opinions from the worker, peasant, and "popular" sectors of the party are solicited, and surely from the private sector as well, the outgoing president effectively names his successor.

Three parties of the right and center-right for years have competed weakly with the PRI for the presidency, for seats in the congress, and for state governorships. Of these conservative parties, the National Action Party (PAN) is strongest, with a firm electoral base in the north of Mexico. It was the only opposition power that has elected members of the Chamber of Deputies, town mayors, and assembly members for many years.

With the 1977 political reform, three new parties of the left were given official recognition, among them the Mexican Communist Party (PCM), a moderate party of eurocommunist persuasion which has its quite limited base in urban areas, especially Mexico City. According to the reform, one-quarter of the seats in the Chamber of Deputies are reserved for opposition parties.[17] In this way, though the relative power of the PRI will be diluted, the system as a whole should be strengthened. The Senate, however, is still completely in PRI hands.

This co-optation of the opposition into the system, as with past and present co-optation into the PRI, is used to supplement the selective repression of opposition by the police and the army. The army massacre of at least fifty student demonstrators in 1968 and the wounding of some five hundred others in the Plaza of Three Cultures is only the most striking use of force in recent times.[18] Peasant leaders frequently disappear forever when they violate the rules of the game. There were some guerrilla groups active both in the country and in the city in the early 1970s, such as the sectarian Communist League of the 23rd of September, but although crimes are sometimes still attributed to them, most of them were killed or captured by the end of the decade.

The Machinery of Administration. The political process in Mexico has been effective at co-opting and controlling the organized political energies of the people. The traditions of the Mexican revolu-

[17]One opposition party on the left, the Socialist Workers' Party (PST), did not participate in the reform. Its leader, Heberto Castillo, is a well-known columnist for a major Mexican weekly newsmagazine, *Proceso.*
[18]Judith Adler Hellman, *Mexico in Crisis* (New York: Holmes and Meier, 1978), p. 142. These are the most conservative casualty figures. Other sources estimate that 200 to 400 students were killed in the 1968 massacre.

tion, moreover, have absorbed the loyalties of most Mexicans. The presidency in Mexico is strong compared to other political institutions. In contrast, the actual administration of politics is neither as efficient nor as effective as one might expect from such a centralized system. Mexico is a soft state, even though the *scope* of state actions and the *domain* of state concerns are both large.

Although concentrating decision-making power in the president makes the adoption of policy relatively easy compared to other systems in which the legislature has a more significant role and in which the courts exercise more real control, the same concentration often impedes effective implementation of adopted policies. Members of the bureaucracy charged with implementing and administering announced policies hesitate to act firmly if they have any doubts about the desires or intentions of either the president or their bureaucratic superiors. Everyone looks upward before acting. Thus the president's speech of today is taken as an indication of whether or not to implement the policy of yesterday.

Elites representing economic interests or competition from other parts of the bureaucracy can also impede effective implementation. Since these elites have access to those with political power at higher levels, lower- and middle-level bureaucrats are unlikely to implement a policy that would negatively affect a powerful friend of their superiors. The courts, although not as strong as in the United States, can be used to restrain and slow down government actions. Exceptions are also made for one's own friends and relatives, and not a few in the bureaucracy make new friends easily, for the right amount of cash.

This ineffectiveness in implementation is complicated by the inefficiency in hiring and promotion. Since one's position depends on loyalty to one's superior rather than to an agency or its mission, a change of administrator often means that an entire team or *equipo* will change as well. Good superiors will take "their people" with them

to the new job. Both the old office and the new office are robbed of continuity in day-to-day operations. It is a good system for making friends and contacts who may later help with a favor or a job; it provides cohesive groups of politically loyal workers, but it is not a very good system for accomplishing the business of government.

Some recent changes may help to improve administration. There is now a national school for public administration. More use is now being made of the resources of academic institutions such as El Colegio de México (a research and teaching institute that offers graduate degrees and sponsors research, increasingly on government projects). As an aid to more effective administration in foreign affairs, several centers for the study of the United States have finally been established, at the Center for Economic Research and Training (CIDE), a government-supported institute in Mexico City; at El Colegio de México; and at the National University, among others.

System Performance and Problems. The Mexican political system has well served the interests of the economic elites, and it has maintained the significant benefits of peace and political stability. Many middle-class Mexicans (not in the middle but rather in the upper one-third of the population) have also benefited. Increasing networks of roads and highways as well as the expansion of mass communications have brought more and more of the population into contact with the modern world. Literacy has continued to increase, if slowly, reaching approximately 82 percent in 1978. Economically, the policies of "import-substitution industrialization" that favored large national and foreign firms have led to a positive rate of economic growth in both total and per capita terms. Gross domestic product per capita has averaged 2.3 percent growth per year since 1960.

These positive aspects of the Mexican system have had their costs. There is not only growth but also inequality; overall, many people's welfare has improved, but the results have been very uneven. The very processes of modernization have led to an increased migration to the cities, especially to Mexico City, now a megalopolis of at least 13 million (the world's second largest metropolitan area after New York) with a growth rate of 5 percent per year. Infant mortality has declined drastically during this century, but it increased somewhat in the 1970s. Although the average calories per capita potentially available in the country have increased, the shortage of food for the most needy groups has meant considerable malnutrition. Likewise, the growth in overall GNP has not succeeded in improving the income distribution; indeed, the share of income of the bottom fifth of the population declined from 1950 to 1977.[19] The growth of manufacturing industries has led to a balance of payments deficit because of the importation of intermediate and capital goods, and the dependence on foreign loans to finance growth has made Mexico, with Brazil, one of the leading debtor nations in the world. Mexico's oil resources, however, may be sufficient to cover future debt payments.

In its relations with the United States, Mexico has continued to be dependent in spite of the discovery of large quantities of oil and natural gas that promise to make Mexico a major energy producer. As Table 9.1 shows, nearly three-quarters (71 percent) of Mexico's trade is concentrated with one partner, the United States. The United States also provides a major labor market for millions of Mexicans. When the U.S. government vetoed a gas agreement reached by Mexico with some U.S. firms, Mexico began to switch its domestic industry to gas and will only sell the surplus. Before President López Portillo met President Carter in Washington in the fall of 1979, a gas agreement was signed for the small residual

amounts, at prices much higher than those that were vetoed the year before.

Internationally, oil will increase Mexico's bargaining power and will make it less likely that the *"colossus of the north"* will simply ignore its southern neighbor as it so often has done in the past. Indeed, the United States is likely to encourage Mexico to export as much oil and gas as possible, but resist receiving Mexican migrants, manufactured exports, and food products. Energy, migration, and trade will continue to be major bilateral problems between the United States and Mexico.

Domestically, the income from oil will buy some time. But it will also raise the expectations of those who travel the new roads to the oil fields. If oil contributes to growth but not equity, if Mexico continues to be a country of great inequality, as it was in the days of great silver wealth, then the half-century-old stability of the Mexican system may be shaken.

Several outcomes are possible. The changes in the rules for political participation resulting in the legalization of new parties may result in a more pluralistic, multiparty system with legitimate channels for real participation by greater numbers of people. However, these reforms are more likely to consolidate the existing system than to transform it.

On the other hand, the tensions produced by growth without improved income distribution may result in popular unrest and a consequent increase in repression on the part of the armed forces. Protest will be especially likely if inflation erodes the gains of the middle class and of unionized workers. But stability and inequality have long coexisted in Mexico. The army lost influence after the 1920s and 1930s in terms of budgets and official positions held by military officers. Mexico's military budget is one of the world's lowest relative to its GNP. However, their budget has been increased in recent years as has their autonomy. If the young officers trained at the new Colegio Militar in the south of Mexico City should decide that they are more qualified to maintain internal order than the civilian political leaders provided for under the constitution, Mexico could see

---

[19]Inter-American Development Bank, *Economic and Social Progress in Latin America, 1978* (Washington, D.C.: Inter-American Development Bank, 1978), p. 322; and Enrique Hernández Laos and Jorge Córdova Chávez, "Estructura de la distribución del ingreso en México," *Comercio exterior* (Mexico) 29, no. 5 (May 1979), pp. 505–20.

military intervention or increased military participation in decision making. With the tensions produced by Mexico's new oil wealth, it is unlikely that the present system will be able to continue without further structural and institutional changes.

BRAZIL: THE "LAND OF THE FUTURE" UNDER MILITARY RULE

Brazil is a large country by any standard, and its rapid rate of growth in recent years led some to hold Brazil as a model of development for poor countries. Brazil ranks fifth in the world in area; it occupies half of the continent of South America, includes a broad range of climates, and is larger than the continental United States excluding Alaska. In population Brazil ranks sixth in the world, with over 115 million people, and growing at 2.8 percent per year. In total gross domestic product (GDP) Brazil ranks ninth among the countries of the world. A diagram of the intersection of the world's most populous countries and the world's richest countries would show that although Brazil is not one of the five major "superpowers," it is approaching that "big power" intersection. Yet, because of the uneven pattern of growth and the concentration of wealth, Brazil is still an underdeveloped country, ranking only forty-third (in 1976) in national production per capita.

The rapid growth and capital accumulation that have taken place in Brazil have been termed "the Brazilian miracle." The country's GDP grew at a rate much higher than the Latin American average in the 1960s and 1970s. From 1968 to 1974 Brazil grew at just over 10 percent annually, one of the highest rates in the world, though its growth was slower both before and after that period. The absolute level of production achieved by the country from colonial days until 1967 was doubled in less than ten years. This growth was a success story for only some Brazilians, however; much of Brazil was left behind. The modern steel and glass architecture in the new inland capital of Brasília and the huge agro-industrial projects in the Amazon basin contrast sharply with both poverty and malnutrition in the northeast of Brazil and squalor in the *favelas* (shantytowns) of Rio de Janeiro and São Paulo.

Early History of Brazil. Brazil was discovered in 1500 by the Portuguese explorer Pedro Cabral, who was looking for India. Yet strangely enough, through an agreement with Spain, it belonged to Portugal even before the South American continent was discovered. In that agreement, the "Tordesillas Line" was drawn 370 leagues west of the Cape Verde Islands, with Portugal owning anything discovered east of that division. Brazil was further explored by Amerigo Vespucci in 1501–02 during his second voyage to the New World. At that time, perhaps a million Indians, broken into small and dispersed tribes, were scattered throughout the huge territory. In the early years, Brazil's chief export was brazilwood, though later gold and diamonds were discovered, and sugar, cotton, and coffee became primary export commodities.

Other colonial powers did not concede the huge colony to Portugal without a struggle. Portugal had to fight with the Dutch and the French as well as the English to establish clear dominion over the territory. The French established missions along the Amazon River in the seventeenth century and the British attacked coastal towns. The Dutch, with their Dutch West Indies Company, were perhaps the most aggressive contenders. It was not until 1654 that the Portuguese defeated them, signing a peace treaty in 1661.

Slavery was introduced early into Brazil and raiding parties from São Paulo explored the interior of the colony in search of slaves. Black slaves from Africa, eventually numbering in the millions, were also imported. Sugar plantations using slave labor predominated on the vast landholdings in the seventeenth and eighteenth centuries; sugar dominated the economy.

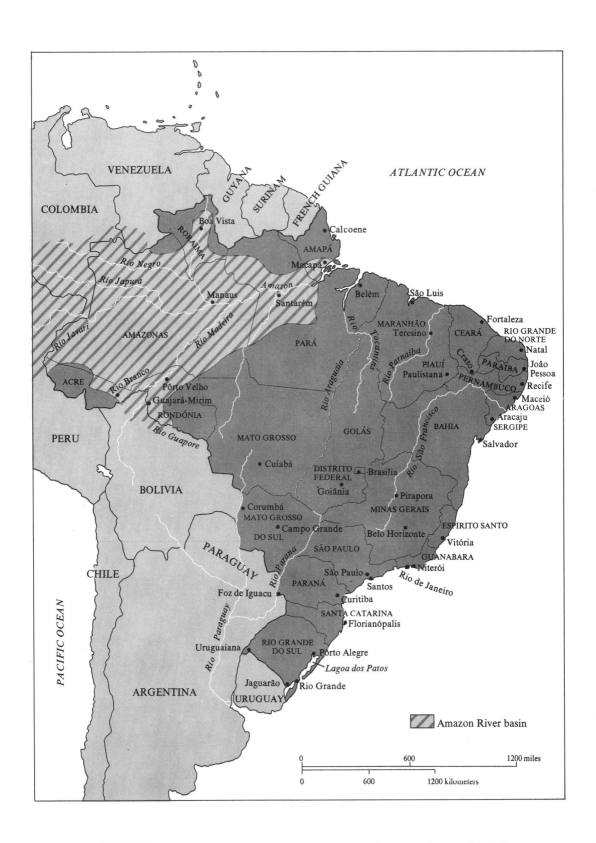

VENEZUELA

COLOMBIA

GUYANA

SURINAM

FRENCH GUIANA

ATLANTIC OCEAN

RORAIMA

Boa Vista

Calcoene

AMAPÁ

Macapá

Rio Negro

Rio Japura

Amazon

Belém

São Luis

Manaus

Santarém

MARANHÃO

Teresino

Fortaleza

CEARÁ

RIO GRANDE
DO NORTE

Natal

Rio Iavari

AMAZONAS

PARÁ

Rio Madeira

Rio Araguaia

Rio Tocantins

Rio Parnaíba

PIAUÍ

Paulistana

Crato

PARAIBA

João
Pessoa

PERNAMBUCO

Recife

Rio Branco

ACRE

Pôrto Velho

Guajará-Mirim

RONDÔNIA

Rio Guapore

MATO GROSSO

GOIÁS

Rio São Francisco

BAHIA

Maceió
ARAGOAS

Aracaju
SERGIPE

Salvador

PERU

Cuiabá

DISTRITO
FEDERAL

Brasilia

Goiânia

Pirapora

MINAS GERAIS

ESPIRITO SANTO

BOLIVIA

Corumbá

MATO GROSSO
DO SUL

Campo Grande

Belo Horizonte

Vitória

GUANABARA

Niterói

PARAGUAY

Rio Parana

SÃO PAULO

São Paulo

Santos

Rio de Janeiro

CHILE

PACIFIC OCEAN

Foz de Iguacu

PARANÁ

Curitiba

SANTA CATARINA

Florianópalis

Rio Paraguay

Uruguaiana

RIO GRANDE
DO SUL

Pôrto Alegre

Lagoa dos Patos

ARGENTINA

Jaguarão

Rio Grande

URUGUAY

Amazon River basin

0   600   1200 miles

0   600   1200 kilometers

Both the Portuguese and the Africans who came to Brazil were for the most part single men. The absence of immigrant women ensured that the Brazilian population was from the beginning a thorough mixture of races. Early in the twentieth century the sociologist Gilberto Freyre popularized the importance of the mixture of three races—Indian, European, and African—in his book, *The Masters and the Slaves*. These men of mixed blood were the principal adventurers *(bandeirantes)* who pushed the Brazilian frontier westward, especially after 1650.

The most unique aspect of Brazilian history is its constitution as a monarchy. It was the only colony in the Americas to successfully preserve the institution of monarchy after separating from the mother country, in contrast to monarchical failures in Mexico and Haiti. With the colonial reforms of the Portuguese minister Pombal after 1750 and in spite of several unsuccessful revolutionary attempts, including one by the nationalist Tiradentes (Joaquim José da Silva Xavier—"the toothpuller") in 1789, Brazil remained close to the parent country. When Napoleon set out to invade Portugal in 1809, Prince João (John) fled to Brazil with British assistance and established the Portuguese monarchy at Rio de Janeiro.

By that time, Brazil had a population of approximately 3 million, already larger than that of Portugal. In the new monarchy, Prince João issued decrees encouraging trade, banking, agriculture, and industry. He also encouraged the expansion of Brazil north to French Guyana and south toward Rio de la Plata. At a time when Spanish America was shaken by wars of independence, Brazil was ruled by a foreign monarch. No violent break with the past marked Brazil's birth as a nation.

In 1822, Prince João returned to Portugal and left the government of Brazil in the hands of his son, Dom Pedro. The Portuguese *cortes* attempted to control Brazil once again from the mother country, but in 1822 Dom Pedro, with the support of the Brazilians, issued a declaration called the *Grito de Ypiranga* (Cry of Ypiranga), proclaiming the independence of Brazil. Dom Pedro became the constitutional emperor of the new monarchy, reigning as Pedro the First. For a number of years, politics in Brazil was unsettled, with provincial revolts and warfare between Brazil and Argentina (resulting in 1828 in the independence of Uruguay). In 1840, Pedro's fourteen-year-old son came to power as Pedro II. Throughout his rule, until 1889, Brazil continued to develop rapidly. Railroads were built, coffee production grew in importance as well as sugar production, and commercial rubber production was introduced in the Amazon. Britain replaced Portugal in the nineteenth century as the major sea power and as Brazil's principal trading partner. Brazilian coffee and other exports paid for British manufactures imported to Brazil.

Brazil expanded to the west and the southwest, joining in a Triple Alliance with her old enemies Argentina and Uruguay in a successful five-year war against Paraguay from 1865 to 1870. Given its size, perhaps the most amazing thing about Brazil is that it was able to remain unified as a single country. Unlike the Spanish-American countries, Brazil was concerned not with loss of territory or foreign domination, but with expansion and the consolidation of its own rule. The experience as a monarchy during most of the nineteenth century also established a long traditon of powerful executive rule handling many of the functions of government.

Between 1870 and 1890, while coffee production for export grew, the abolition of slavery proceeded by stages. Since slavery could no longer provide enough workers for the coffee plantations, it was hoped that free labor would meet the demand for workers. In 1871, all children born to slaves were declared free. In 1885, slaves attained

---

(Left) MAP 11.3 *Brazil*

their freedom at the age of sixty-five. Finally in 1888, the so-called Golden Law abolished slavery for good. Though agriculture, mining, industry, and trade continued to expand rapidly, the dependence on coffee and rubber markets abroad led to economic instability and frequent overproduction.

During the same period, republicanism began to grow and the Republican Party was formed in 1870. By 1889, the army overthrew the emperor and declared a republic. Political inexperience and economic pressures initially led to frequent turnover among the presidents of the new republic, with the changeover often at the instigation of the army. Nevertheless, some reforms were adopted. Church and state were separated at least nominally, and in 1891 a constitution was adopted. The rebellious province of Rio Grande do Sul, having rebelled in 189l, revolted for the second time in 1893–95. But the government of the republic was able to keep the nation together, in spite of regional competition and political rivalries. Brazil learned to manipulate world coffee markets to increase the international prices paid for its coffee. Economic growth continued, and with the disruption of world trade by World War I, Brazil began to develop a domestic industry based on a strategy of import substitution.

In 1930 Getúlio Vargas, then governor of Rio Grande do Sul, led a swift and successful revolution and came to power. With the populist support of workers and with urban interests opposed to the landed oligarchy, Vargas was able to control a somewhat populist state in Brazil from 1930 to 1945. In 1934, a new constitution increased the centralization of the government and reduced regional conflicts. Vargas was elected president under the constitution.

In 1937, Vargas proclaimed a new constitution giving himself dictatorial powers over the organization of the society and the economy. Labeling this new regime the *Estado Novo* (New State), Vargas instituted an elitist and paternalistic government that set the pattern for Brazilian politics in the modern period. Participation by workers and peasants was permitted but carefully controlled by the state. The Estado Novo was based on the support of the military, the collaboration of business, the legitimacy of the Catholic Church, and the control of the people.

During the thirties, both the Communist Party and the Fascist middle-class movement (the *integralistas*) grew in power. Although Brazilian politics had some elements in common with European totalitarian regimes, Brazil entered World War II on the side of the Allies. Brazil, in fact, was the only Latin American country to send ground troops to Europe. The close coordination of the United States and Brazilian militaries and the intense group experience of the officers in the Brazilian Expeditionary Force (FEB) were formative elements in the attitudes of the military men who would later take power in 1964.

In 1945, Vargas was forced to resign and War Minister and General Eurico Dutra was elected president, as head of the Social Democratic Party, one of the two parties founded by Vargas (the other being the Labor Party). Yet another constitution was drawn up, and when elections were held in 1950, Getúlio Vargas was once again elected, this time on a platform of populist and democratic social reforms. Four years later, in August 1954, Vargas was pressured to resign. Instead, defeated and threatened by the armed forces, he took his own life. Since his death, he has become a national hero; the main thoroughfare in Rio de Janeiro bears his name.

A period of constitutional democracy prevailed in the 1950s and early 1960s, in which many parties contended in reasonably honest elections, but under military tutelage and occasional intervention. In 1955, Juscelino Kubitschek won the presidency with João Goulart as his vice president. They took office in 1956 and ruled for five years. The capital of the country was moved in 1960 to the new city of Brasília in the interior of the country. The next president, Jânio da Silva Quadros, came to power in 1961 but resigned after less than seven months, saying that he could not accomplish the reforms necessary for the country. João Goulart, also vice president to Quadros, succeeded to the presidency. But the Brazilian military opposed him and forced him and the Congress to accept a drastic weakening of the presidency as a condition of Goulart's succession to office. Nevertheless, from 1962 to 1964, there was the beginning of a distribution of federal lands to the peasantry, greater responsiveness to workers' demands, and some limited nationalization of basic industries and expropriation of private landholdings, with compensation. But inflation ran rampant, and the Brazilian military (as well as many United States officials) feared an even greater shift to the left. In April 1964, Goulart left the country, the presidency was declared vacant, and the military took power.

The military, under General Castelo Branco, immediately repressed the left, and especially the Communists. In 1965, Castelo Branco assumed dictatorial powers as the head of the military government. In a series of "Institutional Acts," the military, with the support of the United States, segments of the Church, and the owners of land and property, moved to institutionalize their rule. Under the constitution of 1967 and especially the Fifth Institutional Act of 1968, the military gave the president extensive powers to declare a state of siege, to remove officials from office, and to suspend the Congress and political freedoms.

The Stakes of Politics in Brazil. Just as Brazil is a big country, the stakes of its politics loom large as well. The political process in the coming years will determine who rules, what kind of development will take place, who will benefit from that development, and what growth will mean for the country. Because of Brazil's importance in the region, and increasingly in the world, these stakes matter not only to Brazilians but to neighbors and international allies as well.

The first question raised by politics in Brazil is whether the military government that has ruled since 1964 will continue in power, and, if so, how much civilian participation in running the country will increase. Unlike the traditional pattern of military intervention in Latin America, the military in Brazil has stayed in power for nearly two decades, and a regular rotation in the presidency has evolved. Only generals have served as president, but they do so only for a fixed number of years, and re-election is forbidden. A carefully controlled party system has been developed to legitimate the military government. For most of their rule, the military has effectively controlled workers, peasants, students, and even the private sector. It will be important to see whether the limited liberalization of the late 1970s will result in greater real participation in government or, rather, merely an improved stability for the military regime. During this liberalization, the Fifth Institutional Act was repealed. Parties were reorganized and given greater freedom, as was the Congress. Labor strikes were allowed and most censorship of the print media was lifted.

Although Brazil continues to depend on international capital and the international system for its development, there is no disputing the fact that it has developed. At stake in the future is the kind of development and its direction: whether development will be capital-intensive, benefiting large corporations owned by multinationals, large private firms, and state enterprises competing in world markets and benefiting from cheap labor in Brazil, or whether development will include the poor and unemployed marginal people left out at present.

Who controls the economy may depend on the power of the state, and particularly of state-owned enterprises, relative to the power of national, private capital—sometimes called the "national bourgeoisie"—and of transnational corporations, often from the United States.[20] At stake for the mass of the population is whether they will participate in (and benefit from) the growth of the

[20]Peter Evans has studied who controls the economy and how in *Dependent Development: The Alliance of Multinational, State, and Local Capital in Brazil* (Princeton, N.J.: Princeton University Press, 1979).

economy that has so distinguished Brazil from its Third World neighbors. Evidence is clear that the present pattern of economic growth is increasing inequality.

Political decisions will influence the national and international implications of economic growth and development for Brazil. Will Brazil become less dependent on foreign capital, foreign markets, and foreign firms or will it increase its dependence on these external factors? Significant regional disparities exist between the industrialized cities and regions in the south, the large, barely explored tracts of jungle in the Amazon, and the rural poverty in the northeast. Will these contrasts be exacerbated or improved with development?

Finally, how will the present developmental model and the present political system affect Brazil's future role in the world? Will Brazil become a world power? Will the development of nuclear energy be confined to peaceful purposes or will Brazil try to join the superpowers armed with nuclear weapons? Will Brazil expand its influence in South America? Will it become involved in the politics of Portuguese-speaking Africa? Or will it turn inward and find its challenges in developing its own people and resources, building on that strength to become a self-confident and powerful nation?

The Participants in Brazilian Politics. Who participates in politics in Brazil? We can start the list with those who rule the country—the military and the technocrats who support them—followed by those who run the ever-growing number of state-owned enterprises. (Some call these state managers the "state bourgeoisie.") We should also consider industrialists and large landowners as well as workers, peasants, and the urban poor. The Roman Catholic Church is also a political force that cannot be overlooked in today's Brazil.

The military clearly holds the controlling positions in government. Since 1964, they have had responsibility for the political direction of the country, as opposed to their earlier pattern of merely handling the transitions between alternating civilian governments. By the 1960s, the Brazilian military had accepted many aspects of U.S. military training, particularly the importance of maintaining internal security—that is, security from threats to public order orginating inside the nation rather than coming from a foreign country. The logical consequence of this new mission, as Alfred Stepan has argued, was a new professionalism that led to the military's remaining in power rather than alternating with civilian rule.[21] A generation of military officers, who shared fighting experience in Europe during World War II and had close ties to the United States military, studied together at the Higher War College and forged a new military ideology that distinguished the 1964 coup from earlier military coups in Brazilian history. Once in power, the military ended the old political parties, created their own, and relied on technocrats, rather than on party politicians, to accomplish the business of government.

The military has agreed that economic growth is a primary goal of the regime. Thus, the managers of large enterprises, be they multinational, national, or state-owned, stand to benefit from military rule. Even though businesspeople, too, are organized in state-promoted, corporate representative bodies, their influence is much greater than that of workers or peasants. Both large landowners and industrial elites are able to organize separate pressure groups outside the formal state-authorized groups and are thus able to exercise a leverage that is not allowed workers and peasants.

The workers and peasants are restricted to the organizations set up by the state in their name; they have been repressed if they attempt to go outside those organizations. The workers, organ-

[21]These arguments are elaborated in Alfred Stepan, "The New Professionalism of Internal Warfare and Military Role Expansion," in Alfred Stepan (ed.), *Authoritarian Brazil: Origins, Policies, and Future* (New Haven: Yale University Press, 1973). pp. 47–65. See also his more complete study, *The Military in Politics: Changing Patterns in Brazil* (Princeton, N.J.: Princeton University Press, 1971).

ized in official unions, or *sindicatos,* are controlled by leaders screened by both the government and the police. Collective bargaining and the right to strike—two tools fundamental to the defense of labor interests—have been severely limited in Brazil. (Labor union rights widened, however, in the so-called democratic opening that began in 1979.) Similarly, peasants are greatly constrained in what they can do to lobby for their interests.

The Church in Brazil is historically linked to the government with an intimacy unusual in Latin America. The state allows it to perform certain roles in society, such as education, which the state subsidizes. As an institution, the Church has been primarily a conservative force, legitimating the social order. The Church has sought and has accepted military protection for its institutional interests. But the Church also emerged as the major independent critic of military rule in the 1960s and 1970s. It has provided refuge against the worst abuses of military repression and protected some of its victims. But its ability to protest has been limited; preservation and strengthening of the Church as an institution remains a major goal of the Church hierarchy. In the late 1970s the Church lost some institutional support. Divorce was legalized by an act of Congress, initiated by President Ernesto Geisel (a Lutheran), despite the complaints of Catholic bishops. Still, Brazil is one of the largest Catholic countries in the world, and when the Pope visited Brazil in 1980, the popular response demonstrated the strength of the Church there.

Political parties in Brazil have been very different from other parties we know. The military in power had the support of a party formed by conservative civilian politicians, known as Arena (Aliança Renovadora Nacional). There was also an officially authorized opposition party, Movimento Democratico Brasileiro (MDB). According to one Brazilian, one party said "yes" to the government, while the other said "yes, sir." By the late 1970s, however, the MDB had become associated with some degree of genuine opposition, and further party reforms were begun in late 1979.

Despite these changes, the structure of representation is such that in the 1978 election, out of twenty-three Senate seats open to direct election, the opposition MDB was awarded only eight, even though it won 46.8 percent of the vote, because electoral districts overrepresent rural areas, where the government is strong. Arena, on the other hand, received 34.7 percent of the vote, yet received fifteen seats, plus twenty-one out of twenty-two seats in the Senate that are allocated by an electoral college rather than by direct vote. Thus, with 35 percent of the direct vote in 1978, the party in power, Arena, received 80 percent of the Senate seats.

Images of Brazil. Brazil has long seen itself as an important and aggressive world actor. This was strikingly demonstrated in June 1926, when the country withdrew from the League of Nations after failing to obtain a seat on the Permanent Council. When the United States refused to sell nuclear technology in the 1970s, Brazil achieved an agreement with West Germany. Brazil maintains a large army with military expenditures reaching approximately 9.4 percent of the federal budget. Brazil's military expenditures as a percent of GNP are lower than those for the United States, European or Asian countries, but high by Latin American standards. The large size of the Brazilian GNP makes the absolute level of military expenditure significant. Brazil has begun the direct manufacture of conventional arms and military supplies, and increasingly sells military equipment abroad.

Brazil asserts that it is an integrated society, though the reality is quite different. The image that most Brazilians, black and white, hold of their country is of a nonprejudiced society. Unlike the situation in the United States, there is not a sharp boundary between black and white in Brazil. Yet there is, in fact, a great deal of racial inequality in access to education, jobs, income, and status. Most whites believe that they have no prejudice and that any dark-skinned Brazilians in a lower economic or social position are there because of some personal, rather than social, handicap. Many blacks also accept that view, so that they may underestimate their own real potential. But even these blacks hope for greater opportunities for their children. They tend to support a more open society and increased pluralization of the political system. More recently, some Brazilian blacks have begun to champion Afro-Brazilian culture, paralleling the "black power" movement in the United States.

Politically, the most common image of Brazil held by social scientists is that of a corporatist state. Though it may sound like it, *corporatism* does not refer to modern corporations. Rather, it refers to the organization of society along functional lines, that is, by industries or occupations, with employers and employees organized separately within each. The corporatist sees society as a unit, with workers, peasants, the Church, businesspeople, and students organized as functional parts, much as legs, arms, head, and heart function in a human body. This all-encompassing, holistic, and nonconflicting vision of society is an alternative to individualistic, liberal ideology as well as to Marxist ideology based on class conflict. Whereas the liberal and the Marxist see the state as acting in response to interest groups or dominant classes, the corporatist, in principle, subordinates interest groups as well as class-based organizations to the state.

In this unifying view, then, the state has considerable autonomy in dealing with private groups and classes in the society. More than that, the state actually establishes and controls the organizations through which functional groups may participate. Thus, the state controls and authorizes labor unions, peasant federations, and workers' associations. Likewise, the state has a special relationship with the Roman Catholic Church, within whose traditions the corporatist ideal was developed. Given both the paternalistic authority found in Brazilian society since it was a colony, and the strong influence of the Catholic Church, the

corporatist image for a time seemed realistic to many Brazilians. In practice, corporatist notions in Brazil have tended to discourage major reforms and to limit the pursuit of separate interests, particularly by disadvantaged groups and classes. Corporatist controls are still strong for labor and peasants, but much less so for business.

Another image of politics in Brazil was coined by the Argentinian scholar, Guillermo O'Donnell: the "bureaucratic-authoritarian" state. When there are high levels of popular mobilization, combined with import-substitution industrialization (the replacement of imports with locally manufactured goods), a structural economic crisis follows. That crisis encourages the replacement of civilian political authority with military, technical, and bureaucratic authority. This bureaucratic-authoritarian regime often engages in political repression while seeking enormous growth.

In 1964, several factors combined to precipitate a military coup in Brazil: a rapid rise in popular political participation in the 1950s and early 1960s; the threat of large-scale land reform, which implied weakening economic and political power among the landed elites; an increase in class-based organizations; and violent political activity, which threatened the military's monopoly on force. Perhaps a structural crisis of the economy stimulated political change, but it was political participation and class conflict that determined the rate and timing of the change. Once the military broke the previous pattern of civilian rule and mass political participation, the state took control of popular organizations. The technocratic elites (sometimes called a "technocracy")—those whose jobs depend on technical expertise rather than patronage or political skill—exercise much power.

These four images of Brazil all represent aspects of current Brazilian reality. Brazil is a powerful nation aspiring to be a major actor in the world. It has succeeded in bringing together citizens of different racial and ethnic backgrounds, although problems remain. The state is organized along corporatist lines; that is, it directs and controls organizations for different functional groups in society. Its character can be described as bureaucratic-authoritarian: A repressive, controlled authoritarian regime is governed by a bureaucratic, technocratic group of rulers, rather than by a single, charismatic leader or a democratic plurality.

Brazil: The Arena of Politics. The enormous size of Brazil has already been pointed out: 8.5 million square kilometers and a population estimated to grow to 200 million by the year 2000. In contrast to many developing countries, there have been no successful challenges to Brazilian sovereignty. Rather, Brazil responded to such challenges in the eighteenth and nineteenth centuries by expanding. Such has been the force of Brazilian expansion that some countries worry about being overwhelmed by their giant neighbor, but Brazil has not gone to war since the 1870s. Brazil directly borders every country in South America except Chile and Ecuador. As Brazil's regional trade and investment expands, especially with Paraguay, Uruguay, and Bolivia, some critics suggest that Brazil is becoming a "subimperialist" power. It is clear that Brazil is likely to become involved in any regional disputes that may occur. For example, Brazil has an interest in a Bolivian outlet to the sea, since Brazil could indirectly benefit. The recent development of the world's largest hydroelectric plant on the Paraná River led to a long dispute with Argentina, settled only in 1979, over the use of river waters. As a regional power, Brazil may increase or decrease conflict.

The internal frontier poses immediate problems for Brazil. First, the government must incorporate the Indians of the interior into national life without killing them all. Second, it must meet the sheer physical challenge of conquering and cultivating for human use the enormous potential of the Amazon basin. There is a serious danger that this type of industrial development will disrupt the fragile ecology of the Amazon, which is still only partially understood. Whether this area is developed by nationals, by the state, or by foreigners will influence the future political arena. Daniel Ludwig, one of the richest men in the United States, has begun to operate a million-acre farm for growing selected hardwoods in the Amazon region. Likewise, foreign mining firms have been allowed to exploit and develop untapped mineral resources.[22] This reliance on, or partnership with, foreign capital and technology is sure to speed the development of resources, but if control of those resources passes outside the country, the political arena will be narrowed.

The Process of Politics and the State Machinery in Brazil. As described in the section on participation in Brazilian politics, the political system in Brazil is tightly controlled from the top by military leaders. There have been strict controls on the press and on the opposition, although some were relaxed in the late 1970s. Even so, discussion is allowed only within clear limits. A government council supervises all radio and television broadcasting. The partial opening has provided the military with improved feedback on sources of popular discontent and possible sources of opposition without allowing that opposition any increase in real power or participation in political decision making. Thus, the military remains the group that steers the country. The rest of society follows its lead.

Brazilian society, led by the military, is very efficient at accomplishing some tasks, particularly the organization and direction needed for rapid economic growth. It is growth that provides the only legitimacy for the regime in power. Opposition to the regime is controlled and, when necessary, repressed.

Although there is no pretense that the president of Brazil is popularly elected, the military has succeeded in finding a formula for regular succession to the presidency. The first four military presidents were officially elected by the Congress.

[22]See H. O'Reilly Steinberg, "Development and Conservation," in Karl W. Deutsch, ed., *Ecosocial Systems and Ecopolitics* (Paris: UNESCO, 1977), pp. 337–358.

The first president, General Humberto Castelo Branco, was replaced in 1967 by Marshal Artur da Costa e Silva. When he was taken ill, Congress selected General Emílio Garrastazú Médici, who ruled until General Ernesto Geisel took office in 1974 for a five-year term. According to the procedure in effect at present, the presidential candidate chosen by the military is ratified by an "electoral college" of municipal councilors for a six-year term. The first president selected under these rules was General João Baptista Figueiredo, who took office in March of 1979. Presidents cannot immediately succeed themselves in office.

The Senate and the Chamber of Deputies were directly elected (by literate voters over the age of eighteen) until 1977, when one-third of the Senate were selected by the electoral college. The allocation of seats for deputies is by total population, not number of voters. Rural areas with large populations but few voters usually favor the government candidates. Because of restrictions, about 40 percent of the adult population is ineligible to vote. The military has devised a system acceptable to its own members. But by manipulation of electoral rules, and restrictions on political parties, the press, radio, and television, the degree of real competition in Brazilian politics is limited.

However, tensions are building. The image of the military as capable of accomplishing any economic feat is made questionable by a rising inflation rate, and corruption and scandals within the military likewise tarnish their technocratic image. Competition from state-owned enterprises run by the military has weakened the support of private businesspeople for military rule. The Catholic Church, in response to the repression of the people, has organized grassroots movements under the leadership of several bishops, including Dom Helder Câmara. The unions, in spite of controls by the government, have re-emerged as significant pressure groups, with a number of strikes in 1978 and 1979, particularly in the crucial automobile industry.

In 1979, in a much discussed *abertura* (democrat-

ic opening), several political leaders from the days before the 1964 coup were allowed to return to the country, most notably Leonel Brizola and Miguel Arraes, both former leaders of the opposition parties. Although it is unlikely that the Communist Party will be allowed to function openly, the labor parties may be allowed to function. But as the 1978 election shows, even if this opening absorbs organizational energy and provides a safety valve for some discontent, it is still open to question whether it will result in truly open competition among political parties in Brazil.

Performance of the Political System. The inequality of Brazilian society shows both in the high figures of the Gini index of inequality (see Table 9.1) and, even more dramatically, in the figures of infant mortality, which reflect the welfare of the poorer segments of society. The figures indicate that ninety to one hundred infants per thousand live births die in their first year. The contrasts and the similarities between Brazil and Cuba are striking. In Brazil, the military has taken power and encouraged high rates of economic growth and some reconcentration of wealth, while poverty for large groups of the population has remained widespread. In Cuba, with a centrally planned economy, the state has mobilized to gain support for the regime through policies of distribution rather than policies of growth. Cuban society, then, is much more equal than Brazilian society, and health and welfare standards are higher, but Brazil has been able to grow much more rapidly than Cuba. Dissidents have been repressed, with violence at times, in both countries.

The Brazilian regime has done best in mobilizing the society for high rates of economic growth. It has attracted foreign investment through transnational corporations and has enabled the country to qualify for large foreign loans. With a 1978 foreign debt of $42 billion, Brazil is the developing country with the highest level of absolute foreign indebtedness. Its success in maintaining political tranquillity depends on a high level of economic growth. At the very high levels of growth that Brazil has been able to achieve, some "trickle-down" improves the standard of living for much of the population, even if their relative share of total income has declined. Were this growth to slow or to halt and the well-being of workers, middle-class employees, and the urban poor to deteriorate, the stability of the regime would be called into question. The military might return to more repression.

Brazil has been quite successful in achieving national unity, but it remains to be seen whether the alliance of national, state, and foreign capital will be successful in such ambitious projects as developing the Amazon region. There is also some doubt whether this alliance can hold together if national business presses, as it increasingly has, for a greater share of the gains. It also remains to be seen whether Brazil will assume a position of more active leadership in Latin America or in Africa based on its economic successes. There are indications that the Brazilian government will continue to resist complete dependence on the United States and will try to diversify its trading partners and political allies. But the huge foreign debt requires both more capital from abroad and more access to foreign markets. Payments on the foreign debt in 1978 were equivalent to two-thirds of Brazil's export earnings. It seems likely that Brazil will continue to pursue a high-growth strategy, seeking to ally state capital with national and foreign firms. However, Brazil's poor will probably continue to suffer and will only benefit when some of the new wealth happens to trickle down their way.

The Hopes for "Decompression." During the second half of the 1970s, an increasing number of Brazilians, including some thoughtful members of the military, sought ways to bring about a "decompression" of the Brazilian political system. By this they meant a relaxation of repression and political controls, and more freedom for political parties, the press, and various interest groups, including labor unions. How to achieve this without precipi-

tating civil strife and frightening away the foreign capital required for the success of the "Brazilian model of development" remains a problem. But Brazil has, in fact, "decompressed" in these years. Labor unions have increasingly exercised their right to strike, led by the automobile workers in São Paulo, in spite of the removal from office of some of the more militant labor leaders by the government. Other steps toward liberalization have been taken under presidents Ernesto Geisel and João Baptista Figueiredo, as noted earlier in this chapter. Under the 1979 amnesty, even the communist Luís Carlos Prestes was allowed to return from exile in Moscow. The political *abertura* will probably be limited and controlled. But popular pressure, and the electoral strength of the opposition, argue for further decompression. The examples of peaceful exits from dictatorships in Portugal, Spain, and Greece may encourage Brazil's military rulers to risk continued steps in that direction.

KEY TERMS AND CONCEPTS

Cuba:
Pearl of the Antilles
sugar monoculture
conquistadores
the ever-faithful isle
"Spanish-Cuban-American War"
Platt Amendment
Fulgencio Batista
26th of July Movement
yacht *Granma*
Bay of Pigs invasion
Cuban Missile Crisis
the United States blockade
trade embargo
society of scarcity
Cuban troops in Africa
Committees for the Defense of the Revolution (CDRs)
Communist Party of Cuba

Ernesto (Che) Guevara
Nonaligned Movement
Cuban community abroad
U.S. naval base at Guantánamo Bay
Fidel Castro and Raúl Castro
the socialist constitution of 1976
institutionalization of the revolution
"History Will Absolve Me"

Mexico:
Aztecs (México Indians)
Nahuatl language
ejido
colonialism
haciendas
mestizo
creole
liberal reforms of Benito Juárez
colossus of the north
"Effective Suffrage, No Re-Election"
PRI (Institutional Revolutionary Party)
Lázaro Cárdenas
land reform
1938 oil expropriation
PEMEX (*Petróleos Mexicanos*)
population pyramid
mordida
peonage
Cristero revolt
Mexican American War of 1848
Luis Echeverría Álvarez (1970–76)
José López Portillo (1976–82)

Brazil:
regional power
the Brazilian monarchy
bandeirantes
corporatism
dependent development
Estado Novo
sindicatos
bureaucratic-authoritarianism
national, transnational, and state-owned firms
Arena and MDB (national political parties)
technocrats, technocracy
infant mortality
"trickle-down"

Brazilian model of development
capital accumulation; growth versus equity
import-substitution industrialization
decompression
abertura

ADDITIONAL READINGS

Cuba:
Bonachea, R. E. and N. P. Valdés, eds. *Cuba in Revolution*, New York: Doubleday, 1972, PB

Castro, F. *Fidel Castro Speaks*. Edited by M. Kenner and J. Petras. New York: Grove Press, 1970. PB

Domínguez, J. I. *Cuba: Order and Revolution*. Cambridge: Harvard University Press, 1978.

Fagen, R. *The Transformation of Political Culture in Cuba*. Stanford, Calif.: Stanford University Press, 1969. PB

González, E. *Cuba Under Castro: The Limits of Charisma*. Boston: Houghton Mifflin, 1974. PB

Goodsell, J. N., ed. *Fidel Castro's Personal Revolution in Cuba: 1959–1973*. New York: Knopf, 1975. PB

Knight, F. W. *Slave Society in Cuba during the Nineteenth Century*. Madison: University of Wisconsin Press, 1970. PB

Mesa-Lago, C. *Cuba in the 1970s: Pragmatism and Institutionalization*. Albuquerque: University of New Mexico Press, 1974. PB

O'Connor, J. *The Origins of Socialism in Cuba*. Ithaca, N.Y.: Cornell University Press, 1970.

Thomas, H. *The Cuban Revolution*. New York: Harper & Row, 1977. PB

Zeitlin, M. *Revolutionary Politics and the Cuban Working Class*. New York: Harper & Row, 1970. PB

Mexico:
Almond, G. A. and S. Verba. *The Civic Culture: Political Attitudes and Democracy in Five Nations*. Boston: Little, Brown, 1965. PB

Baird, P. and E. McCaughan. *Beyond the Border: Mexico and the U.S. Today*. New York: North American Congress on Latin America, 1979. PB

Bazant, J. *A Concise History of Mexico from Hidalgo to Cárdenas, 1805–1940*. New York: Cambridge University Press, 1977. PB

Brandenburg, F. R. *The Making of Modern Mexico*. Englewood Cliffs, N.J.: Prentice-Hall, 1964.

Brenner, A. and B. Leighton. *The Wind that Swept Mexico*. New York: Harper & Row, 1943.

Cline, H. F. *The United States and Mexico*. Rev. ed. Cambridge: Harvard University Press, 1967.

Cosío Villegas, D., et al. *A Compact History of Mexico*. Trans. M. M. Urquidi. Mexico: El Colegio de México, 1974. PB

Domínguez, J. I. *Insurrection or Loyalty: The Breakdown of the Spanish American Empire*. Cambridge: Harvard University Press, 1980.

Eckstein, S. *The Poverty of Revolution: The State and the Urban Poor in Mexico*. Princeton, N.J.: Princeton University Press, 1977.

González Casanova, P. *Democracy in Mexico*. Trans. D. Salti. New York: Oxford University Press, 1970. PB

Grindle, M. S. *Bureaucrats, Politicians, and Peasants in Mexico: A Case Study in Public Policy*. Berkeley: University of California Press, 1977.

Hansen, R. D. *The Politics of Mexican Development*. Baltimore: Johns Hopkins University Press, 1971, 1974. PB

Hellman, J. A. *Mexico in Crisis*. New York: Holmes and Meier, 1978.

Herring, H. *A History of Latin America from the Beginnings to the Present,* 3d ed. New York: Knopf, 1968.

Lewis, O. *Five Families: Mexican Case Studies in the Culture of Poverty*. New York: Basic Books, 1959. PB

Lynch, J. *The Spanish American Revolutions, 1808–1826*. New York: Norton, 1973. PB

Meyer, L. *Mexico and the United States in the Oil Controversy, 1917–1942*. Trans. M. Vasconcellos. Austin: University of Texas Press, 1977.

Meyer, M. C. and W. L. Sherman, *The Course of Mexican History*. New York: Oxford University Press, 1979. PB

Padgett, L. V. *The Mexican Political System*, 2d ed. Boston: Houghton Mifflin, 1976. PB

Reyna, J. L. and R. S. Weinert, eds. *Authoritarianism in Mexico*. Philadelphia: ISHI, 1977. PB

Smith, P. H. *Labyrinths of Power—Political Recruitment in Twentieth Century Mexico*. Princeton, N.J.: Princeton University Press, 1979. PB

Stevens, E. P. *Protest and Response in Mexico*. Cambridge: MIT Press, 1974.

Wolf, E. *Sons of the Shaking Earth: The People of Mexico and Guatemala, Their Land, History, and Culture*. Chicago: University of Chicago Press, 1959. PB

Womack, J. *Zapata and the Mexican Revolution*. New York: Vintage Books, 1968. PB

Brazil:

Black, J. K. *United States Penetration of Brazil*. Philadelphia: University of Pennsylvania Press, 1977.

Burns, E. B. *A History of Brazil*. New York: Columbia University Press, 1970. PB

Davis, S. H. *Victims of the Miracle: Development and the Indians of Brazil*. New York: Cambridge University Press, 1977. PB

Della Cava, R. "Catholicism and Society in Twentieth-Century Brazil." *Latin American Research Review*, 9, No. 1 (1976), 7–50.

Erickson, K. P. *The Brazilian Corporative State and Working-Class Politics*. Berkeley: University of California Press, 1977.

———. "Brazil: Corporatism in Theory and Practice." In *Latin American Politics and Development,* edited by H. J. Wiarda and H. F. Kline. Boston: Houghton Mifflin, 1979, 144–181.

Evans, P. *Dependent Development: The Alliance of Multinational, State, and Local Capital in Brazil*. Princeton: Princeton University Press, 1979. PB

Haring, C. H. *Empire in Brazil: A New World Experiment with Monarchy*. Cambridge: Harvard University Press, 1958. PB

Jaquaribe, H. *Economic and Political Development: A Theoretical Approach and a Brazilian Case Study*. Cambridge: Harvard University Press, 1968.

Leff, N. H. *Economic Policy-Making and Development in Brazil, 1947–1964*. New York: Wiley, 1968.

Malloy, J. M. *The Politics of Social Security in Brazil.* Pittsburgh: University of Pittsburgh Press, 1979.

Mendonca de Barros, J. R. and D. H. Graham. "The Brazilian Economic Miracle Revisited: Private and Public Sector Initiative in a Market Economy." *Latin American Research Review* 13, No. 2 (1978), 5–37.

Mericle, K. S. "Corporatist Control of the Working Class: Authoritarian Brazil Since 1964." In *Authoritarianism and Corporatism in Latin America,* edited by J. M. Malloy. Pittsburgh: University of Pittsburgh Press, 1977. PB

Robock, S. H. *Brazil: A Study in Development Progress.* Lexington, Mass.: D. C. Heath, 1975.

Roett, R., ed. *Brazil in the Seventies.* Washington, D.C.: American Enterprise Institute for Public Policy Research, 1976.

Schmitter, P. C. *Interest Conflict and Political Change in Brazil.* Stanford: Stanford University Press, 1971.

Schneider, R. M. *Brazil: Foreign Policy of a Future World Power.* Boulder, Colo.: Westview Press, 1976.

——. *The Political System of Brazil: Emergence of a "Modernizing" Authoritarian Regime.* (New York: Columbia University Press, 1971).

Skidmore, T. E. *Politics in Brazil, 1930–1964: An Experiment in Democracy.* New York: Oxford University Press, 1967. PB

Stepan, A. C., ed. *Authoritarian Brazil: Origins, Policies, and Future.* New Haven: Yale University Press, 1973. PB

——. *The Military in Politics: Changing Patterns in Brazil.* Princeton, N.J.: Princeton University Press, 1971. PB

PB = *available in paperback*

INDEX

473

ABCDEFGHIJ-D-821